The Ministers Manual for 1996

By the same editor

Best Sermons 1
Best Sermons 2
Best Sermons 3
Best Sermons 4
Best Sermons 5
Best Sermons 6
Best Sermons 7
Biblical Preaching: An Expositor's Treasury
God's Inescapable Nearness (coauthor with Eduard
  Schweizer)
A Guide to Biblical Preaching
Learning to Speak Effectively
Minister's Worship Manual (coeditor with Ernest A.
  Payne and Stephen F. Winward)
Preaching
Surprised by God
The Twentieth Century Pulpit, Volumes I and II

SEVENTY-FIRST ANNUAL ISSUE

THE MINISTERS MANUAL

1996 EDITION

Edited by

JAMES W. COX

HarperSanFrancisco
A Division of HarperCollinsPublishers

Editors of THE MINISTERS MANUAL

G. B. F. Hallock, D.D., 1926–1958
M. K. W. Heicher, Ph.D., 1943–1968
Charles L. Wallis, M.A., M.Div., 1969–1983
James W. Cox, M.Div., Ph.D.

Translations of the Bible referred to and quoted from in this book may be indicated by their standard abbreviations, such as NRSV (New Revised Standard Version) and NIV (New International Version). In addition, some contributors have made their own translations and others have used a mixed text.

Other acknowledgments begin on page 333.

THE MINISTERS MANUAL FOR 1996.
Copyright © 1995 by James W. Cox. All rights reserved. Printed in the United States of America. For information, address HarperCollins Publishers, 10 East 53rd Street, New York, NY 10022.

FIRST EDITION

Library of Congress Catalog Card Number
25–21658
ISSN 0738–5323
ISBN 0–06–061622–9 (cloth: alk. paper)

95 96 97 98 99 HAD 10 9   8 7 6 5 4 3 2 1

CONTENTS

PREFACE

Most listeners to sermons like to hear messages that are illustrated. A common complaint is this: "Our preacher has good ideas for us but doesn't use enough illustrations." One would think that in view of Jesus' way of preaching and teaching, all of us who share the biblical Word would take a cue from Jesus and often illuminate our ideas with stories and images—and even with various kinds of explanatory redundancies.

The primary goal of *The Ministers Manual* is to present the generalizations, not the particulars of sermonic material. One must have something to say: one cannot illustrate *nothing*. However, this *Manual* does suggest illustrations of various types that may illuminate, extend, and impress the main ideas of the sermon. These illustrations are therefore not in all cases *stories*. Most of the sermons in this volume are followed by illustrations. The exceptions are Sections VIII, IX, and X, although illustrations are often embodied in these sections. Also, there is a section called "A Little Treasury of Sermon Illustrations." Preachers should find the indexes in the back of the book specifically useful for finding illustrations.

Please note that *The Ministers Manual* once again bases a number of the lectionary messages in Section II on the Old Testament or Epistle lesson rather than on the Gospel lesson.

I have again attempted to bring together some of the finest homiletical ma-terials from excellent preachers of the past and present times. It is hoped that what is presented here will stimulate thought; provide inspirations and ideas for sermons; and highlight examples of noteworthy sermonic structure, illustration, and style.

Many individuals have contributed to this volume. From their reading and from their pulpit ministry they share with you their discoveries and their own thoughts and creations as well. I continue to be grateful for the secretarial support provided by the Southern Baptist Theological Seminary, and I wish to thank preachers and publishers for permission to quote from their material. Clara McCartt and Lee R. McGlone over many years have made special contributions, and to them I again offer my hearty thanks. I am most grateful also to Laura Allen, Loren Johnson, Brenda Wessner, and Bev Tillman, word-processing operators who typed the manuscript, and to Alicia Gardner, office services supervisor. I continue to be appreciative of the faithful attention and careful work of the editorial staff at HarperSanFrancisco.

James W. Cox
The Southern Baptist Theological Seminary
2825 Lexington Road
Louisville, Kentucky 40280

SECTION I.
General Aids and Resources
Civil Year Calendars

1996

JANUARY						
S	M	T	W	T	F	S
	1	2	3	4	5	6
7	8	9	10	11	12	13
14	15	16	17	18	19	20
21	22	23	24	25	26	27
28	29	30	31			

FEBRUARY						
S	M	T	W	T	F	S
				1	2	3
4	5	6	7	8	9	10
11	12	13	14	15	16	17
18	19	20	21	22	23	24
25	26	27	28	29		

MARCH						
S	M	T	W	T	F	S
					1	2
3	4	5	6	7	8	9
10	11	12	13	14	15	16
17	18	19	20	21	22	23
24	25	26	27	28	29	30
31						

APRIL						
S	M	T	W	T	F	S
	1	2	3	4	5	6
7	8	9	10	11	12	13
14	15	16	17	18	19	20
21	22	23	24	25	26	27
28	29	30				

MAY						
S	M	T	W	T	F	S
			1	2	3	4
5	6	7	8	9	10	11
12	13	14	15	16	17	18
19	20	21	22	23	24	25
26	27	28	29	30	31	

JUNE						
S	M	T	W	T	F	S
						1
2	3	4	5	6	7	8
9	10	11	12	13	14	15
16	17	18	19	20	21	22
23	24	25	26	27	28	29
30						

JULY						
S	M	T	W	T	F	S
	1	2	3	4	5	6
7	8	9	10	11	12	13
14	15	16	17	18	19	20
21	22	23	24	25	26	27
28	29	30	31			

AUGUST						
S	M	T	W	T	F	S
				1	2	3
4	5	6	7	8	9	10
11	12	13	14	15	16	17
18	19	20	21	22	23	24
25	26	27	28	29	30	31

SEPTEMBER						
S	M	T	W	T	F	S
1	2	3	4	5	6	7
8	9	10	11	12	13	14
15	16	17	18	19	20	21
22	23	24	25	26	27	28
29	30					

OCTOBER						
S	M	T	W	T	F	S
		1	2	3	4	5
6	7	8	9	10	11	12
13	14	15	16	17	18	19
20	21	22	23	24	25	26
27	28	29	30	31		

NOVEMBER						
S	M	T	W	T	F	S
					1	2
3	4	5	6	7	8	9
10	11	12	13	14	15	16
17	18	19	20	21	22	23
24	25	26	27	28	29	30

DECEMBER						
S	M	T	W	T	F	S
1	2	3	4	5	6	7
8	9	10	11	12	13	14
15	16	17	18	19	20	21
22	23	24	25	26	27	28
29	30	31				

1997

JANUARY						
S	M	T	W	T	F	S
			1	2	3	4
5	6	7	8	9	10	11
12	13	14	15	16	17	18
19	20	21	22	23	24	25
26	27	28	29	30	31	

FEBRUARY						
S	M	T	W	T	F	S
						1
2	3	4	5	6	7	8
9	10	11	12	13	14	15
16	17	18	19	20	21	22
23	24	25	26	27	28	

MARCH						
S	M	T	W	T	F	S
						1
2	3	4	5	6	7	8
9	10	11	12	13	14	15
16	17	18	19	20	21	22
23	24	25	26	27	28	29
30	31					

APRIL						
S	M	T	W	T	F	S
		1	2	3	4	5
6	7	8	9	10	11	12
13	14	15	16	17	18	19
20	21	22	23	24	25	26
27	28	29	30			

MAY						
S	M	T	W	T	F	S
				1	2	3
4	5	6	7	8	9	10
11	12	13	14	15	16	17
18	19	20	21	22	23	24
25	26	27	28	29	30	31

JUNE						
S	M	T	W	T	F	S
1	2	3	4	5	6	7
8	9	10	11	12	13	14
15	16	17	18	19	20	21
22	23	24	25	26	27	28
29	30					

JULY						
S	M	T	W	T	F	S
		1	2	3	4	5
6	7	8	9	10	11	12
13	14	15	16	17	18	19
20	21	22	23	24	25	26
27	28	29	30	31		

AUGUST						
S	M	T	W	T	F	S
					1	2
3	4	5	6	7	8	9
10	11	12	13	14	15	16
17	18	19	20	21	22	23
24	25	26	27	28	29	30
31						

SEPTEMBER						
S	M	T	W	T	F	S
	1	2	3	4	5	6
7	8	9	10	11	12	13
14	15	16	17	18	19	20
21	22	23	24	25	26	27
28	29	30				

OCTOBER						
S	M	T	W	T	F	S
			1	2	3	4
5	6	7	8	9	10	11
12	13	14	15	16	17	18
19	20	21	22	23	24	25
26	27	28	29	30	31	

NOVEMBER						
S	M	T	W	T	F	S
						1
2	3	4	5	6	7	8
9	10	11	12	13	14	15
16	17	18	19	20	21	22
23	24	25	26	27	28	29
30						

DECEMBER						
S	M	T	W	T	F	S
	1	2	3	4	5	6
7	8	9	10	11	12	13
14	15	16	17	18	19	20
21	22	23	24	25	26	27
28	29	30	31			

1

Church and Civic Calendar for 1996

JANUARY

1 New Year's Day
  The Name of Jesus
5 Twelfth Night
6 Epiphany
7 Eastern Orthodox
  Christmas
15 Martin Luther King Day
18 Confession of St. Peter
19 Robert E. Lee's Birthday
25 Conversion of St. Paul

FEBRUARY

1 National Freedom Day
2 Presentation of Jesus in
  the Temple
  Groundhog Day
3 Four Chaplains Memorial
  Day
12 Lincoln's Birthday
14 St. Valentine's Day
19 Presidents' Day
21 Ash Wednesday
22 Washington's Birthday
25 First Sunday in Lent
26 Eastern Orthodox Great
  Lent Begins

MARCH

3 Second Sunday in Lent
5 Purim
10 Third Sunday in Lent
17 Fourth Sunday in Lent
  St. Patrick's Day
19 Joseph, Husband of Mary
24 Fifth Sunday in Lent
25 The Annunciation
31 Palm/Passion Sunday
31–April 6 Holy Week

APRIL

4 Maundy Thursday
5 Good Friday
7 Easter
  Daylight Saving Time
  Begins
14 Pan-American Day

Orthodox Easter
25 St. Mark, Evangelist

MAY

1 Law Day
  Loyalty Day
  May Day
  St. Philip and St. James,
  Apostles
12 Mother's Day
  Festival of the Christian
  Home
16 Ascension Day
20 Victoria Day (Canada)
24 First Day of Shavout
26 Pentecost
27 Memorial Day (observed)

JUNE

2 Trinity Sunday
  Eastern Orthodox
  Pentecost
9 Children's Sunday
14 Flag Day
16 Father's Day
29 St. Peter and St. Paul,
  Apostles

JULY

1 Canada Day
4 Independence Day
22 St. Mary Magdalene
25 St. James the Elder

AUGUST

4 Civic Holiday (Canada)
6 The Transfiguration
14 Atlantic Charter Day
15 Mary, the Mother of Jesus
14 St. Bartholomew, Apostle
26 Women's Equality Day

SEPTEMBER

1 Labor Sunday
2 Labor Day

8 Birth of Virgin Mary
Grandparents' Day
Rally Day
14 Rosh Hashanah
17 Citizenship Day
21 St. Matthew, Apostle and
Evangelist
22 Christian Education
Sunday
Gold Star Mother's Day
23 Yom Kippur
28 Sukkoth
29 St. Michael and All Angels

OCTOBER

6 World Communion
Sunday
Child Health Day
13 Laity Sunday
14 Columbus Day (observed)
Thanksgiving Day
(Canada)
16 World Food Day
18 St. Luke, Evangelist
24 United Nations Day
28 St. Simon and St. Jude,
Apostles
31 National UNICEF Day
Reformation Day
Halloween

NOVEMBER

1 All Saints' Day

2 All Souls' Day
5 Election Day
10 Stewardship Sunday
11 Armistice Day
Veterans Day
Remembrance Day
(Canada)
21 Presentation of the Virgin
Mary in the Temple
24 Thanksgiving Sunday
Bible Sunday
28 Thanksgiving Day
30 St. Andrew, Apostle

DECEMBER

1 First Sunday of Advent
6 Hanukkah
8 Second Sunday of Advent
15 Third Sunday of Advent
Bill of Rights Day
Wright Brothers Day
21 Forefathers' Day
22 Fourth Sunday of Advent
24 Christmas Eve
25 Christmas
26 Boxing Day (Canada)
St. Stephen, Deacon and
Martyr
27 St. John, Apostle and
Evangelist
28 The Holy Innocents,
Martyrs
31 New Year's Eve Watch
Night

The Revised Common Lectionary for 1996

The following Scripture lessons are commended for use in public worship by various Protestant churches and the Roman Catholic Church and include first, second, Gospel readings, and Psalms, according to Cycle A from January 6 to November 28 and according to Cycle B from December 1 to December 31. (Copyright 1992 Consultation on Common Texts.)

EPIPHANY SEASON

Jan. 6 and 7 (Epiphany): Isa. 60:1–6; Ps. 72:1–7, 10–14; Eph. 3:1–12; Matt.

2:1–12 (Baptism of the Lord): Isa. 42:1–9; Ps. 29; Acts 10:34–43; Matt. 3:13–17

Jan. 14: Isa. 49:1–7; Ps. 40:1–11; 1 Cor. 1:1–9; John 1:29–42

Jan. 21: Isa. 9:1–4; Ps. 27:1, 4–9; 1 Cor. 1:10–18; Matt. 4:12–23

Jan. 28: Mic. 6:1–8; Ps. 15:1–5; 1 Cor. 1:18:–31; Matt. 5:1–12

Feb. 4: Isa. 58:1–9a (9b–12); Ps. 112:1–9 (10); 1 Cor. 2:1–12, (13–16); Matt. 5:13–20

Feb. 11: Deut. 30:15–20; Ps. 119:1–8; 1 Cor. 3:1–9; Matt. 5:21–37

Feb. 18: Lev. 19:1–2, 9–18; Ps. 119:33–40; 1 Cor. 3:10–11, 16–23; Matt. 5:38–48

LENT

Feb. 21 (Ash Wednesday): Joel 2:1–2, 12–17 (alt.); Isa. 58:1–12 (alt.); Ps. 51:1–17; 2 Cor. 5:20b–6:10; Matt. 6:1–6, 16–21

Feb. 25: Gen. 2:15–17; 3:1–7; Ps. 32; Rom. 5:12–19; Matt. 4:1–11

Mar. 3: Gen. 12:1–4a; Ps. 121; Rom. 4:1–5, 13–17; John 3:1–17

Mar. 10: Exod. 17:1–7; Ps. 95; Rom. 5:1–11; John 4:5–42

Mar. 17: 1 Sam. 16:1–13; Ps. 23; Eph. 5:8–14; John 9:1–41

Mar. 24: Ezek. 37:1–14; Ps. 130; Rom. 8:6–11; John 11:1–45

HOLY WEEK

Mar. 31 (Palm/Passion Sunday): Matt. 21:1–11; Ps. 118:1–2, 19–29; Isa. 50:4–9a; Ps. 31:9–16; Phil. 2:5–11; Matt. 26:14–27:66

Apr. 1 (Monday): Isa. 42:1–9; Ps. 36:5–11; Heb. 9:11–15; John 12:1–11

Apr. 2 (Tuesday): Isa. 49:1–7; Ps. 71:1–14; 1 Cor. 1:18–31; John 12:20–36

Apr. 3 (Wednesday): Isa. 50:4–9a; Ps. 70; Heb. 12:1–3; John 13:21–32

Apr. 4 (Thursday): Exod. 12:1–4 (5–10), 11–14; Ps. 116:1–2, 12–19; 1 Cor. 11:23–26; John 13:1–17, 31b–35

Apr. 5 (Good Friday): Isa. 52:13–53:12; Ps. 22; Heb. 10:16–25 (alt.); Heb. 4:14–16, 5:7–9 (alt.); John 18:1–19:42

Apr. 6 (Holy Saturday): Job 14:1–14 (alt.); Lam. 3:1–9, 19–24; Ps. 31:1–4, 15–16; 1 Pet. 4:1–8; Matt. 27:57–66 (alt.); John 19:38–42 (alt.)

SEASON OF EASTER

Apr. 6–7 (Easter Vigil): Gen. 1:1–2, 4a; Ps. 136:1–9, 23–26; Gen. 7:1–5, 11–18; 8:6–18; 9:8–13; Ps. 46; Gen. 22:1–18; Ps. 16; Exod. 14:10–31; 15:20–21; Exod. 15:1b–13, 17–18 (resp.); Isa. 55:1–11; Isa. 12:2–6 (resp.); Bar. 3:9–15, 32–4:4 (alt.); Prov. 8:1–8, 19–21;

9:4–6 (alt.); Ps. 19; Ezek. 36:24–28; Pss. 42–43; Ezek. 37:1–14; Ps. 143; Zeph. 3:14–20; Ps. 98; Rom. 6:3–11; Ps. 114; Luke 24:1–12

Apr. 7 (Easter Sunday): Acts 10:34–43 (alt.); Isa. 65:17–25 (alt.); Ps. 118:1–2, 14–24; 1 Cor. 15:19–26 (alt.); Acts 10:34–43 (alt.); John 20:1–18 (alt.); Luke 24:1–12 (alt.)

Apr. 7 (Easter Evening): Isa. 25:6–9; Ps. 114; 1 Cor. 5:6b–8; Luke 24:13–49

Apr. 14: Acts 2:14a, 22–32; Ps. 16; 1 Pet. 1:3–9; John 20:14–31

Apr. 21: Acts 2:14a, 36–41; Ps. 116:1–4, 12–19; 1 Pet. 1:17–23; Luke 24:13–35

Apr. 28: Acts 2:42–47; Ps. 23; 1 Pet. 2:19–25; John 10:1–10

May 5: Acts 7:55–60; Ps. 31:1–5, 15–16; 1 Pet. 2:2–10; John 14:1–14

May 12: Acts 17:22–31; Ps. 66:8–20; 1 Pet. 3:13–22; John 14:15–21

May 19: Acts 1:6–14; Ps. 68:1–10, 32–35; 1 Pet. 4:12–14, 5:6–11; John 17:1–11

SEASON OF PENTECOST

May 26: Num. 11:24–30; Ps. 104:24–34, 35b; Acts 2:1–21 or 1 Cor. 12:3b–13; John 20:9–23 or John 7:37–39

June 2: Gen. 1:1–2:4a; Ps. 8; 2 Cor. 13:11–13; Matt. 28:16–20

June 9: Gen. 12:1–9; Ps. 33:1–12; Rom. 4:13–25; Matt. 9:9–13, 18:26

June 16: Gen. 18:1–15 (21:1–7); Ps. 116:1–2, 12–19; Rom. 5:1–8; Matt. 9:35–10:8

June 23: Gen. 21:8–21; Ps. 86:1–10, 16–17; Rom. 6:1b–11; Matt. 10:24–39

June 30: Gen. 22:1–14; Ps. 13; Rom. 6:12–23; Matt. 10:40–42

July 7: Gen. 24:34–38, 42–49, 58–67; Ps. 45:10–17; Rom. 7:15–25a; Matt. 11:16–19, 25–30

July 14: Gen. 25:19–34; Ps. 119:105–112; Rom. 8:1–11; Matt. 13:1–8, 18–23

July 21: Gen. 28:10–19a; Ps. 139:1–12, 23–24; Rom. 8:12–25; Matt. 13:24–30, 36–43

July 28: Gen. 29:15–28; Ps. 105:1–11, 45b; Rom. 8:26–39; Matt. 13:31–33, 44–52

Aug. 4: Gen. 32:22–31; Ps. 17:1–7, 15; Rom. 9:1–5; Matt. 14:13–21

Aug. 11: Gen. 37:1–4, 12–28; Ps. 105:1–6, 16–22, 45b; Rom. 10:5–15; Matt. 14:22–33

Aug. 18: Gen. 45:1–15; Ps. 133; Rom. 11:29–32; Matt. 15:(10–20) 21–28

Aug. 25: Exod. 1:8–2:10; Ps. 124; Rom. 12:1–8; Matt. 16:13–20

Sept. 1: Exod. 3:1–15; Ps. 105:1–6, 23–26, 45b; Rom. 12:9–21; Matt. 16:21–28

Sept. 8: Exod. 12:1–14; Ps. 149; Rom. 13:8–14; Matt. 18:15–20

Sept. 15: Exod. 14:19–31; Ps. 114; Rom. 14:1–12; Matt. 18:21–35

Sept. 22: Exod. 16:2–15; Ps. 105:1–6, 37–45; Phil. 1:21–30; Matt. 20:1–16

Sept. 29: Exod. 17:1–7; Ps. 78:1–4; Phil. 2:1–13; Matt. 21:23–32

Oct. 6: Exod. 20:1–4, 7–9, 12–20; Ps. 19; Phil. 3:4b–14; Matt. 21:33–46

Oct. 13: Exod. 32:1–14; Ps. 106:1–6, 19–23; Phil. 4:1–9; Matt. 22:1–14

Oct. 20: Exod. 33:12–23; Ps. 99; 1 Thess. 1:1–10; Matt. 22:15–22

Oct. 27: Deut. 34:1–12; Ps. 90:1–6; 1 Thess. 2:1–8; Matt. 22:34–46

Nov. 3: Jos. 3:7–17; Ps. 107:1–7, 33–37; 1 Thess. 2:9–13; Matt. 23:1–12

Nov. 10: Josh. 24:1–3a, 14–25; Ps. 78: 1–7; 1 Thess. 4:13–18; Matt. 25:1–13

Nov. 17: Judg. 4:1–7; Ps. 123; 1 Thess. 5:1–11; Matt. 25:14–30

Nov. 24: Ezek. 34:11–16, 20–24; Ps. 100; Eph. 1:15–23; Matt. 25:31–46

Nov. 28 (Thanksgiving): Deut. 8:7–18; Ps. 65; 2 Cor. 9:6–15; Luke 17:11–19

ADVENT AND CHRISTMAS SEASON

Dec. 1: Isa. 64:1–9; Ps. 80:1–7; 17–19; 1 Cor. 1:3–9; Mark 13:24–37

Dec. 8: Isa. 40:1–11; Ps. 85:1–2, 8–13; 2 Pet. 3:8–15a; Mark 1:1–8

Dec. 15: Isa. 61:1–4, 8–11; Ps. 126; 1 Thess. 5:16–24; John 1:6–8, 19–28

Dec. 22: 2 Sam. 7:1–11, 16; Luke 1:47–55; Rom. 16:25–27; Luke 1:26–38

Dec. 25 (Christmas Day): Isa. 62:6–12; Ps. 97; Titus 3:4–7; Luke 2:(1–7), 8–20

Dec. 29: Isa. 61:10–62:3; Ps. 148; Gal. 4:4–7; Luke 2:22–40

Four-Year Church Calendar

	1996	1997	1998	1999
Ash Wednesday	February 21	February 12	February 25	February 17
Palm Sunday	March 31	March 23	April 5	March 28
Good Friday	April 5	March 28	April 10	April 2
Easter	April 7	March 30	April 12	April 4
Ascension Day	May 16	May 8	May 21	May 13
Pentecost	May 26	May 18	May 31	May 23
Trinity Sunday	June 2	May 25	June 7	May 30
Thanksgiving	November 28	November 27	November 26	November 25
Advent Sunday	December 1	November 30	November 29	November 28

Forty-Year Easter Calendar

1996 April 7	2006 April 16	2016 March 27	2026 April 5
1997 March 30	2007 April 8	2017 April 16	2027 March 28
1998 April 12	2008 March 23	2018 April 1	2028 April 16
1999 April 4	2009 April 12	2019 April 21	2029 April 1
2000 April 23	2010 April 4	2020 April 12	2030 April 21
2001 April 15	2011 April 24	2021 April 4	2031 April 13
2002 March 31	2012 April 8	2022 April 17	2032 March 28
2003 April 20	2013 March 31	2023 April 9	2033 April 17
2004 April 11	2014 April 20	2024 March 31	2034 April 9
2005 March 27	2015 April 5	2025 April 20	2035 March 25

Traditional Wedding Anniversary Identifications

1 Paper	7 Wool	13 Lace	35 Coral
2 Cotton	8 Bronze	14 Ivory	40 Ruby
3 Leather	9 Pottery	15 Crystal	45 Sapphire
4 Linen	10 Tin	20 China	50 Gold
5 Wood	11 Steel	25 Silver	55 Emerald
6 Iron	12 Silk	30 Pearl	60 Diamond

Colors Appropriate for Days and Seasons

White. Symbolizes purity, perfection, and joy and identifies festivals marking events, except Good Friday, in the life of Jesus: Christmas, Epiphany, Easter, Eastertide, Ascension Day; also Trinity Sunday, All Saints' Day, weddings, funerals. Gold may also be used.

Red. Symbolizes the Holy Spirit, martyrdom, and the love of God: Good Friday, Pentecost, and Sundays following.

Violet. Symbolizes penitence: Advent, Lent.

Green. Symbolizes mission to the world, hope, regeneration, nurture, and growth: Epiphany season, Kingdomtide, Rural Life Sunday, Labor Sunday, Thanksgiving Sunday.

Blue. Advent, in some churches.

Flowers in Season Appropriate for Church Use

January. Carnation or snowdrop.
February. Violet or primrose.
March. Jonquil or daffodil.
April. Lily, sweet pea, or daisy.
May. Lily of the valley or hawthorn.
June. Rose or honeysuckle.

July. Larkspur or water lily.
August. Gladiolus poppy.
September. Aster or morning glory.
October. Calendula or cosmos.
November. Chrysanthemum.
December. Narcissus, holly, or poinsettia

Historical, Cultural, and Religious Anniversaries in 1996

Compiled by Kenneth M. Cox

10 years (1986). *January 28:* U.S. space shuttle *Challenger* explodes after takeoff from Cape Canaveral, Fla. *February 7:* Haitians force President Jean-Claude Duvalier into exile. *April 28:* Soviet Union reports nuclear accident at Chernobyl power plant. *November 13:* National Conference of Catholic Bishops issues statement criticizing U.S. economic policies. *December 23: Voyager* aircraft lands in California after first nonstop flight around the world.

25 years (1971). *April 22:* Haiti's president Francois "Papa Doc" Duvalier dies, is succeeded by son Jean-Claude, who is sworn in as "president for life." *June 13:* The *New York Times* begins publishing excerpts from *The Pentagon Papers,* detailing U.S. involvement in Vietnam. *August 15:* President Nixon announces "New Economic Policy," imposing a ninety-day freeze on U.S. wages and prices. *September 9:* Inmates at Attica Correctional Facility in New York take over the prison; death toll reaches forty-three when police retake control. *Debuts:* Carole King's album *Tapestry;* Stanley Kubrick's film *A Clockwork Orange.*

40 years (1956). *May 21:* U.S. Atomic Energy Commission explodes first airborne hydrogen bomb. *June 29:* Congress passes Federal Aid Highway Act, authorizing construction of a 42,500-mile network of roads linking major U.S. cities. *July 24:* Italian passenger liner *S.S. Andrea Doria* collides with Swedish liner *S.S.*

Stockholm in the Atlantic Ocean off Massachusetts. *November 17:* Soviet premier Nikita Khrushchev tells visiting Western ambassadors: "History is on our side. We will bury you." *Debuts:* Sen. John F. Kennedy's *Profiles in Courage;* Eugene O'Neill's *A Long Day's Journey into Night.*
50 years (1946). *January 10:* United Nations General Assembly opens its first session, in London. *February 24:* Juan Perón is elected president of Argentina. *July 4:* The Philippines gain independence from the U.S. *September 30:* The Nuremberg Tribunal returns guilty verdicts against Hermann Göring, Rudolf Hess, and other leading Nazis. *Debuts:* Nikos Kazantzakis's *Zorba the Greek;* Roosevelt dime; Benjamin Spock's *The Common Sense Book of Baby and Child Care;* Timex watches.
75 years (1921). German-American evangelist Frank Nathan Daniel Buchman founds the Oxford Group at Oxford University. *Debuts:* Band-Aids; British Broadcasting Company; Emmet Kelly's "Weary Willy" clown; Rorschach ink-blot test.
100 years (1896). *January 4:* Utah admitted as forty-fifth state after agreeing to give up polygamous marriage. *May 18:* U.S. Supreme Court upholds racial segregation in *Plessy v. Ferguson,* permitting "separate but equal" facilities for education, transportation, and public accommodations; John Harlan's lone dissent states: "The Constitution is color-blind."

Debuts: Cracker Jack; Miami, Fla.; Nobel prizes; Tootsie Rolls; Volunteers of America.
125 years (1871). *January 18:* German Empire's Second Reich inaugurated at Versailles. *March 3:* Congress passes Indian Appropriation Act, making Indians wards of federal government. *October 8:* Chicago Fire ignited, destroying much of the city. Mormon leader Brigham Young, who has twenty-seven wives, arrested on polygamy charges. *Debuts:* Hymn "Onward Christian Soldiers."
150 years (1846). *May 13:* U.S. declares war against Mexico. *June 14:* California's Black Bear revolt begins. *June 15:* Oregon Treaty signed with Britain gives territory south of forty-ninth parallel to U.S. *Debuts:* Smithsonian Institution; New York's Trinity Church.
175 years (1821). *February 24:* Mexico declares independence from Spain. *March 3:* U.S. Supreme Court declares its power superior to that of any state court in matters involving federal rights. *Debuts:* electric motor; march "Hail to the Chief"; poker card game; *Saturday Evening Post.*
200 years (1796). *March 9:* Napoleon Bonaparte marries Josephine de Beauharnais. *May 18:* Congress passes Public Land Act, authorizing sale of 640-acre-minimum lots of government land on credit. *November 10:* Russia's Catherine the Great dies (b. 1729). *Debut:* Smallpox vaccination.

Anniversaries of Hymn Writers and Hymn-Tune Composers in 1996

Compiled by Hugh T. McElrath

25 years (1971). *Death* of Leslie H. Bunn (b. 1901), author "Happy are they, they that love God"; John Raphael Peacey (b. 1896), author "Go forth for God," "Filled with the spirit's power," and others.
50 years (1946). *Birth* of Frank Sawyer, translator "I've come to tell." *Death* of Henry E. Hardy (b. 1869), author "O dearest Lord, Thy sacred head"; Shepherd Knapp (b. 1873), author "Lord God of Hosts, whose purpose never swerv-

ing"; C. Austin Miles (b. 1868), author-composer "In the garden," GARDEN.
75 years (1921). *Birth* of V. Earle Copes, composer of FOR THE BREAD OF KINGDOM ("For the bread which you have broken," "Faith, while trees are still in blossom," and others), VICAR ("Hope of the world"); John Ferguson, author "Am I my brother's keeper?"; Hugh T. McElrath, author "We praise you with our minds, O Lord" and others; John W. Peterson, author-composer, "O what a

wonderful, wonderful day," HEAVEN CAME DOWN, "Surely goodness and mercy"; GOODNESS, TORONTO ("So send I you"), and others; James H. Wood, harmonizer BEACH SPRING ("Come, all Christians, be committed," "We are travelers on a journey" and others). *Death* of Edwin O. Excell (b. 1851), arranger NEW BRITAIN ("Amazing Grace"), author-composer, "Since I have been redeemed,"—OTHELLO, composer BLESSINGS ("Count your blessings"); William J. Kirkpatrick (b. 1838), author-composer, "Lord, I'm coming home,"—COMING HOME, composer, KIRKPATRICK ("He hideth my soul"), TRUST IN JESUS ("'Tis so sweet to trust in Jesus"), DUNCANNON ("Lead me to Calvary"), REDEEMED ("Redeemed, how I love to proclaim it"), JESUS SAVES ("We have heard the joyful sound"), CRADLE SONG ("Away in a manger") and others; Jessie B. Pounds (b. 1861), author "The way of the cross leads home," "I know that my Redeemer liveth" and others; Edgar Page Stites (b. 1836), author "Simply trusting every day"; Thomas Vincent Tymms (b. 1842), author "Our day of praise."

100 years (1896). *Birth* of Charles Jeffries (d. 1972), author "Speak forth your Word, O Father"; John Michael Peacey (d. 1971), author "Go forth for God," "Filled with the spirit's power," and others. *Death* of Edward White Benson (b. 1829), author "O Jesus, crowned with all renown"; Elisabeth Rundle Charles (b. 1828), author "Never further than the cross"; Allen W. Chatfield (b. 1808), translator "Lord Jesus, think on me" and others; Arthur Cleveland Coxe (b. 1818), author "How beauteous were the marks divine," "O where are kings and empires now," and others; Thomas Benson Pollock (b. 1836), author "God the Father, God the Son," "Jesus, in thy dying woes," "Jesus, Son of God most high," "Jesus, with thy church abide," and others; Thomas Hughes (b. 1823), author "O God of truth, whose living Word" and others; Harriet Beecher Stowe (b. 1811), author "Still, still with thee, when purple morning breaketh."

125 years (1871). *Birth* of Percy Buck (d. 1947), composer MARTINS ("Sing Alle-

luia forth"), GONFALON ROYAL ("The royal banners forward go") and others; James Weldon Johnson (d. 1938), author "Lift every voice and sing." *Death* of Henry Alford (b. 1810), author "Come, ye thankful people, come," "Forward be our watchword," "Then thousand times ten thousand," and others; Henry James Buckoll (b. 1903), author "Come, my soul, thou must be waking"; William Henry Burleigh (1812), author "Lead us, O Father, in the paths of peace"; Carlotte Elliott (b. 1789), author "Just as I am, without one plea," "My God, my Father, while I stray," "O Holy Saviour, Friend unseen" and others; Thomas Toke Lynch (b. 1818), author "Dismiss me not thy service, Lord," "Gracious Spirit, dwell with me," and others.

150 years (1846). *Birth* of William R. Featherstone (d. 1873), author "My Jesus, I love Thee"; Frederick Mann (d. 1928), author "My God, my Father, make me strong"; George C. Stebbins (d. 1945), composer ADELAIDE ("Have thine own way, Lord"), BORN AGAIN ("Ye must be born again"), CALLING TODAY ("Jesus is tenderly calling"), HOLINESS ("Take time to be holy"), JESUS, I COME ("Out of my bondage, sorrow and night") FRIEND ("I've found a friend, O such a friend"), and others.

175 years (1821). *Birth* of Sir Henry Williams Baker (d. 1877), author "The king of love my shepherd is," "O God of love, O God of peace," "Lord, thy word abideth," and others, translator "On this day, the first of days" and others, composer STEPHANOS ("Art thou weary, heavy laden") and others; Henry Martin Dexter (d. 1890), translator, "Shepherd of tender youth"; Edward H. Plumptre (d. 1891), "Rejoice, ye pure in heart," "Your hands, O Lord, in days of old," and others; Gilbert Rorison (d. 1869), author "Three in one, and one in three"; Jeannette Threlfall (d. 1880), author "Hosanna, loud hosanna"; James G. Walton (d. 1905), arranger ST. CATHERINE ("Faith of our fathers," "Jesus, thy boundless love to me," and others); Aaron R. Wolfe (d. 1902), author "A parting hymn we sing."

200 years (1796). *Birth* of William Hiley Bathrust (d. 1877), author "O for a faith

that will not shrink." *Death* of Felice de Giardini (b. 1716), composer ITALIAN HYMN ("Come, thou almighty king," "Thou, whose almighty word," and others); Joseph Swain (b. 1761), author "O Thou in whose presence" and others.

225 years (1771). *Birth* of Siegfried Augustus Mahlmann (d. 1826), author of original of "God bless our native land"; James Montgomery (d. 1854), author of "Angels from the realms of glory," "Be known to us in breaking bread," "Go to dark Gethsemane," "God is my strong salvation," "Hail to the Lord's anointed," "In the hour of trial," "Prayer is the soul's sincere desire," "Stand up, and bless the Lord," "The Lord is my shepherd," "O Spirit of the living God," and others; Sir Walter Scott (d. 1832), translator of original of "That day of wrath, that dreadful day." *Death* of Christopher Smart (b. 1722), author "Awake, arise, lift up your voice," "Hearken to the anthem glorious," "Where is this stupendous stranger," "We sing of God the mighty source of all things."

275 years (1721). *Birth* of John Bakewell (d. 1819), author "Hail, Thou once despised Jesus"; Edward Perronet (d. 1792), author "All hail the power of Jesus' name."

300 years (1696). *Publication* of the "New Version" of the Psalter by Nahum Tate and Nicholas Brady, source of "As pants the hart for cooling streams" (Psalm 42), "Through all the changing scenes of life" (Psalm 34), and others.

325 years (1671). *Birth* of Erdmann Neumeister (d. 1750), author of original of "Sinners, Jesus will receive."

375 years (1621). *Birth* of Georg Neumark (d. 1681), author-composer original of "If you will only let God guide you"—NEUMARK. *Death* of Praetorius (b. 1571), composer of ES IST EIN ROS' ("Lo, how a rose e'er blooming"), PUER NOBIS NASCITUR ("O splendor of God's glory bright," "That Easter day with joy was bright," and others).

425 years (1571). *Birth* of Michael Praetorius (d. 1621), composer ES IST EIN ROS' ("Lo, how a rose e'er blooming"), PUER NOBIS NASCITUR ("O splendor of God's glory bright," "That Easter day with joy was bright," and others). *Death* of Peter Herbert (b. unknown), author original of "Now God is with us, for the night is closing."

450 years (1546). *Death* of Martin Luther (b. 1483), author-composer "A mighty fortress is our God"—EIN FESTE BURG, "Out of the depths I cry to thee"—AUS TIEFER NOTH, "From heaven on high to earth I come"—VOM HIMMEL HOCH, and several others. *Birth* of Johann Steurlein (d. 1613), composer of WIE LIEBLICH IS DER MAIEN ("Sing to the Lord of harvest," "To worship, work, and witness," and others.)

1175 years (821). *Death* of Theodulph of Orleans (b. 760), author of original of "All glory, laud, and honor."

Quotable Quotations

1. Say what you like about the Ten Commandments, you must always come back to the pleasant truth that there are only ten of them.—H. L. Mencken

2. Amazingly, the word of the Lord of hosts is often not a statement, not a command, not an order, not even a declaration. No, God's word often comes to us a question: Where are you? Who do you say that I am? Who will go for us?—Arthur P. Boers

3. His safest haven was prayer; not of a single moment or idle, but prayer of long devotion . . . walking, sitting, eating or drinking, he was always intent upon prayer.—Thomas of Celano

4. A great fortune is a great slavery.—Seneca

5. This is the mission for which we are preparing: to go to hell, to find and walk the paths that lead to the places and conditions where evil is the strongest and the human need is greatest, and there to set people free to experience and serve the living God of righteousness who creates and loves them.

"Go to Hell," says God, "and I will go with you."—Hal Missourie Warheim

6. Help us, this and every day, to live more nearly as we pray.—John Keble

7. To say "Amen" is not just to utter a ritual word, but to make a serious commitment. God calls us to make our lives an *Amen* to his purpose, lives that say Yes! to God.—Arthur P. Boers

8. A great deal of talent is lost to the world for want of a little courage.—Sydney Smith

9. If mountains can be moved by faith, is there less power in love?—Frederick W. Faber

10. Real happiness doesn't lie in having power and influence. Real happiness lies in becoming servants, in opening our lives to the healing, loving power of God so that it flows through us and blesses everybody around us.—John Killinger

11. The great use of life is to spend it for something that will outlast it.—William James

12. No generation can claim to have plumbed to the depths the unfathomable riches of Christ. The Holy Spirit has promised to lead us step by step into the fullness of truth.—Cardinal Suenens

13. The strength of a nation is derived from the integrity of its home.—Confucius

14. We do not know whether the power of God will be shown by transforming our present circumstances, or by transforming our lives to make us people with the courage to remain faithful, no matter the cost, to the vision our God has given us.—James Ayers

15. You may learn about mercy from an essay, but it is better to learn about mercy from a merciful person.—Chevis. F. Horne

16. Expect great things from God
    Attempt great things for God.—William Carey

17. Admitting our limitations does not disqualify us from being witnesses; it is a part of being qualified. In our weakness we find God's strength.—Gary D. Stratman

18. If we could first, know where we are, and whither we are tending, we could then better judge what to do, and how to do it.—Abraham Lincoln

19. I have studied the great theologians and philosophers, and they have given me many insights into life. But Jesus offers a presence and a relationship I cannot define, much less describe, and never want to escape.—David E. Sumner

20. There is no wilderness so terrible, so beautiful, so arid, so fruitful, as the wilderness of compassion. It is the only desert that shall truly flourish like a lily.—Thomas Merton

21. The great thing in this world is not so much where we stand, as in what direction we are moving.—Oliver Wendell Holmes, Sr.

22. He stands behind the peril, and he determines how it is to turn out.—Eduard Schweizer

23. If that vital spark that we find in a grain of wheat can pass unchanged through countless deaths and resurrections, will the spirit of man be unable to pass from this body to another?—William Jennings Bryan

24. Christians who warm to the Damascus road experience must learn to appreciate the Emmaus type—and vice versa.—Stephen Cherry

25. All empty souls tend to extreme opinion.—William Butler Yeats

26. The true Christmas season for the writer and reader of the Gospels is one that leads not to consumption but to consecration.—Edmund S. P. Jones

27. In this world there are only two tragedies. One is not getting what one wants and the other is getting it.—Oscar Wilde

28. No life is so hard that you can't make it easier by the way you take it.—Ellen Glasgow

29. It is only by taking the fact of eternity into account that we can deliver thought from its slavery to life. And it is only by deliberately paying our attention and our primary allegiance to eternity that we can prevent time from turning our lives into a pointless or diabolic foolery.—Aldous Huxley

30. In Jesus' view, heaven is the projection forward—into God's time and space—of a life lived wisely, responsibly, and charitably here.—Robert McClelland

31. Old age is like a plane flying through a storm. Once you're aboard, there's nothing you can do.—Golda Meir

32. Life becomes, for many, a matter of barter. We sell ourselves to the highest bidder, never mind the consequences or the terms, for that matter, so long as the end figure totals up to expectations.—Thomas J. Gibbs, Jr.

33. Where there is great love there are always miracles.—Willa Cather

34. Dogmatism frames the picture of the truth with the view from our window and does not acknowledge there are other vistas from which to experience the reality of the living Christ.—M. Vernon Davis

35. Go into the wilderness, struggle with the question of the ages, but don't stay too long. God has work for you to do in the world!—Cheryl B. Rhodes

36. Loneliness is the most terrible poverty.—Mother Teresa

37. Jesus would have all of us examine ourselves as closely as we examine our neighbors, that we may be driven by the sight of our own sin back upon the mercy of God.—Bruce Hedman

38. A man is accepted into a church for what he believes and he is turned out for what he knows.—Mark Twain

39. We believe, amid all kinds of confusion, in the gracious providence of God. At the beginning and at the end of our often crooked ways, the perpendicular Word. In the beginning and at the end of human history, God.—Jan M. Lochman

40. Sooner or later you must bet your life on which is the deepest reality of all—the darkness so real you can almost taste it, or the fireflies of grace, the glimpses of glory that give hint of a deeper joy and peace than anything you have yet known.—Allen C. McSween, Jr.

41. Conscience: The inner voice that warns us that someone may be looking.—H. L. Mencken

42. Christian discipleship includes the freedom of Christians, who have only one ultimate sovereign, both to support and to challenge the assumptions that govern those lesser sovereignties that shape the world of politics, economics, education, and culture.—Allan M. Parrent

43. The devil can cite Scripture for his purpose.—William Shakespeare

44. William Blake was biblically correct . . . when he said that "everything that lives is holy." —Wendell Berry

45. Jesus Christ is our model—our guide. This is frightening as well as reassuring when we recall the nature of his unselfish love and its high demands of us.—William Powell Tuck

46. Nothing great was ever achieved without enthusiasm.—Ralph Waldo Emerson

47. If we understand that no artist—no maker—can work except by reworking the works of creation, then we see that by our work, by the way we practice our arts, we reveal what we think of the works of God.—Wendell Berry

48. We have come to this point: The gulf of injustice is so wide between the peoples of the earth that we don't even know who is on the other side.—Judith Lynne Weidman

49. A God who let us prove his existence would be an idol.—Dietrich Bonhoeffer

50. If we cannot comprehend the whole of God's being, we can comprehend what God has made evident through the Son who, for us, put on a human face.—Dana Martin

51. Though the mills of God grind slowly, yet they grind exceeding small; Though with patience He stands waiting, with exactness grinds He all.—Friedrich von Logau

52. On the eve of the end of the world, plant a tree.—Koran

53. Those of us who are believers believe in a God of hope, a God of miracles, a God who promises us that we can have a future completely outside the boundaries of our own imagination, that what comes in the future need not be what has come in the past, and that we have a responsibility to cocreate that future.—Al Gore

54. If God did not exist, it would be necessary to invent Him.—Voltaire

55. The special place of human beings in all that God made lies in their being

given a share in God's own concern and providence for the whole of creation. The Creator has entrusted the world to us, as a gift of responsibility.—Pope John Paul II

56. Love is, above all, the gift of oneself.—Jean Anouilh

57. I have never seen what to me seemed an atom of proof that there is a future life. And yet—I am strongly inclined to expect one.—Mark Twain

58. Those who do not remember the past are condemned to relive it.—George Santayana

59. Following Jesus requires that we risk faithfulness including, and gracefully beyond, a legal or moral formula.—Mary Zimmer

60. Consecration! Yes, it can be a glorious adventure, but at the same time it can also be the costliest thing in all the world.—Donald Macleod

61. The man with toothache thinks everyone happy whose teeth are sound.—George Bernard Shaw

62. A just cause is not ruined by a few mistakes.—Fyodor Dostoevsky

63. Not where I breathe, but where I love I live.—Robert Southwell

64. Callous greed grows pious very fast.—Lillian Hellman

65. A calculating love is no love at all! Religion that always acts within the safe bounds of reasonableness is a mutilated religion!—Don Affleck

66. All the things I really like to do are either immoral, illegal, or fattening.—Alexander Woollcott

67. We, not God, bear ultimate responsibility for the kind of world in which we live.—Sanford Ragins

68. The first lesson in prayer is: Just keep it up. Don't stop asking, don't stop seeking, don't stop knocking.—Ronald W. Higdon

69. Science without religion is lame, religion without science is blind.—Albert Einstein

70. This is the meaning of the gospel—a community of faith, a community of comfort, and a community of ministry.—Wayne Oates

71. The most savage controversies are those about matters as to which there is no good evidence either way.—Bertrand Russell

72. Love is a great beautifier.—Louisa May Alcott

73. Hypocrisy is the homage which vice pays to virtue.—La Rochefoucauld

74. All things are possible until they are proved impossible—even the impossible may only be so, as of now.—Pearl S. Buck

75. What makes the artist is his power to shape the material of pain we all have.—Lionel Trilling

76. Happiness is the interval between periods of unhappiness.—Don Marquis

77. The secret of happiness is not in doing what one likes, but in liking what one has to do.—James M. Barrie

78. No one can make you feel inferior without your consent.—Eleanor Roosevelt

79. A good End cannot sanctifie evil Means; nor must we ever do Evil, that Good may come of it.—William Penn

80. Marriage is three parts love and seven parts forgiveness of sins.—Langdon Mitchell

81. The cruellest lies are often told in silence.—Robert Louis Stevenson

82. Good human work honors God's work. Good work uses no thing without respect, both for what it is in itself and for its origin.—Wendell Berry

83. He who forgiveth, and is reconciled unto his enemy, shall receive his reward from God; for he loveth not the unjust doers.—Koran

84. The tragedy is not that things are broken. The tragedy is that they are not mended again.—Alan Paton

85. Experience enables you to recognize a mistake when you make it again.—Franklin P. Jones

86. I don't think Jesus simply told his disciples how to pray; I think he told them how he prayed. He prayed persistently. He prayed shamelessly; he didn't hold back anything. He poured out his heart to his loving heavenly Father whom he trusted—implicitly.—Ronald W. Higdon

87. People who fight fire with fire usually end up with ashes.—Abigail Van Buren

88. It is hard for a selfish or greedy person to be truly grateful.—Steven P. Vitrano

89. It is not well for a man to pray cream and live skim milk.—Henry Ward Beecher

90. God's list of hurts forms the agenda for our work.—David Allan Hubbard

91. A man's worst difficulties begin when he is able to do as he likes.—Thomas Henry Huxley

92. Sometimes, through the grace of God, we learn more in failure than we can learn at any other time.—Roger Lovette

93. Not failure, but low aim, is crime.—James Russell Lowell

94. Whether healing comes by medicine or by miracle, it is of God, for our God is a God of the ordinary and the extraordinary, of the natural and of the supernatural.—W. Clyde Tilley

95. Some people give time, some money, some their skills and connections, some literally give their life's blood . . . but everyone has something to give.—Barbara Bush

96. A good scare is worth more to a man than good advice.—Ed Howe

97. I am not young enough to know everything.—Oscar Wilde

98. To travel hopefully is a better thing than to arrive, and the true success is to labour.—Robert Louis Stevenson

99. However bad I may be, I am the child of God, and therein lies my blame. Ah, I would not lose my blame! In my blame lies my hope.—George Macdonald

100. There is no greater lie than a truth misunderstood.—William James

Questions of Life and Religion

These questions may be useful to prime homiletic pumps, as discussion starters, or for study and youth groups.

1. What assurance do we have of God's acceptance of us?

2. Does a sin separate us from God?

3. When does anger have a rightful place in our life?

4. To what extent can we be free from anxiety, worry, and fear?

5. What is the role of authority in the church and who has it?

6. Who or what determines the type of behavior that is acceptable in the Christian community?

7. What is the "bottom-line" belief that makes a person truly religious?

8. Does "blessing" people with our prayers and encouragement have positive results?

9. What are the spiritual and ethical implications of our kinship with all humankind?

10. In what areas of life is commitment a decisive force?

11. Is compassion weakness or strength?

12. Is an obedient Christian life a matter of compulsion or desire?

13. When does God judge us?

14. What are the ingredients of courage?

15. How do covetousness and legitimate desire differ?

16. Where do science and the biblical accounts of creation meet?

17. How does one realistically prepare for death?

18. What is the power of hope in human experience?

19. What are the demands of discipleship?

20. Is doubt a normal Christian experience?

21. Is it hard to forgive?

22. What can we do to help preserve the natural environment?

23. Are all people equal?

24. What is eternal life?

25. Where do we get our faith?

26. When is a belief false?

27. Is the family a friend or foe of faith?

28. What causes fear?

29. Is fidelity in marriage an option?

30. When is religion sick?

31. How do destructive sects arise?

32. Is absolute freedom possible?

33. How do friendship and evangelism go together?

34. Is personal fulfillment the goal of life?

35. How do our personal gifts or talents relate to God's plan for our lives?

36. Are there valid ways to determine the "good"?

37. What does the Bible mean by grace?

38. What do we have to be thankful for?

39. When does desire become greed?

40. What are the usual stages in the grief process?

41. How can we distinguish between real and imagined guilt?

42. Why is hate wrong?

43. Can prayers have a positive role in physical healing?

44. Who or what determines what is heresy?

45. Is honesty always the best policy?

46. What is hope, and what are its sources and sustainers?

47. Is true humility weakness or strength?

48. What are some contemporary examples of idolatry?

49. How can church and home working together overcome biblical literacy?

50. Why is our God characterized as a jealous God?

51. What is the difference between joy and happiness?

52. On what basis does God judge us?

53. Is life fair?

54. What makes killing wrong?

55. Are human knowledge and biblical teaching in necessary conflict?

56. Does "law" have a positive use according to the Scriptures?

57. What are the qualities essential for leadership?

58. Is all life precious?

59. Are there different ways of defining love?

60. How can we distinguish between love and lust?

61. How permanent should marriage be?

62. What can a third party do to reconcile differences?

63. Are there helpful guidelines for practicing meditation?

64. Why do we call Jesus the Messiah?

65. What is a miracle?

66. Why not let people have their own religion and not try to change them?

67. What are the chief motivators for Christian living?

68. Do older people have unique contributions for the enrichment of our lives?

69. Is Christian unity a "given" or something to be achieved?

70. When is God's patience exhausted?

71. Is peace in the world possible?

72. When does piety become offensive?

73. Is politics legitimate in church matters?

74. Is poverty a virtue?

75. Does God need our praise?

76. What does prayer accomplish?

77. How can we know when God is with us?

78. Is pride "pardonable"?

79. How sacred is a promise?

80. What is biblical prophecy?

81. What are the evidences for the providence of God?

82. Why could one call sin "stupidity"?

83. Are we punished by our sins or for our sins?

84. Is baptism a rite of purification?

85. How do repentance and remorse differ?

86. How is Jesus' resurrection related to his Crucifixion?

87. Is Christianity better explained by "revelation" or "reason"?

88. Are sacrifice and self-fulfillment in conflict?

89. How does God save us?

90. Which word best describes the Holy Scriptures—inerrant, infallible, reliable, or authoritative?

91. How secure is our salvation?

92. What are God's purposes for sex?

93. How do we know the leadership of the Holy Spirit?

94. What is the measure of our financial obligation to our church?

95. Does suffering have value?

96. Is tradition good or bad in religious practice?

97. Of what use are creeds?

98. What is the difference between wisdom and knowledge?

99. Why is worship necessary to a complete Christian life?

100. How might the "Space Age" relate to the plan of God?

Biblical Benedictions and Blessings

The Lord watch between me and thee, when we are absent from one another.—Gen. 31:49

The Lord bless thee, and keep thee; the Lord make his face to shine upon thee, and be gracious unto thee; the Lord lift up his countenance upon thee, and give thee peace.—Num. 6:24–26

The Lord our God be with us, as he was with our fathers; let him not leave us, nor forsake us; that he may incline our hearts unto him, to walk in all his ways, and to keep his commandments, and his statutes, and his judgments, which he commanded our fathers.—1 Kings 8:57–58

Let the words of my mouth, and the meditation of my heart, be acceptable in thy sight, O Lord, my strength, and my redeemer.—Ps. 19:14

Now the God of patience and consolation grant you to be likeminded one toward another according to Christ Jesus; that ye may with one mind and one mouth glorify God, even the Father of our Lord Jesus Christ. Now the God of hope fill you with all joy and peace in believing, that ye may abound in hope, through the power of the Holy Ghost. Now the God of peace be with you.—Rom. 15:5–6, 13, 33

Now to him that is of power to establish you according to my gospel and the preaching of Jesus Christ, according to the revelation of the mystery, which was kept secret since the world began, but now is manifest, and by the scriptures of the prophets, according to the commandment of the everlasting God, made known to all nations for the obedience of faith: to God only wise, be glory through Jesus Christ for ever.—Rom. 16:25–27

Grace be unto you, and peace, from God our Father, and from the Lord Jesus Christ.—1 Cor. 1:3

The grace of the Lord Jesus Christ and the love of God, and the communion of the Holy Ghost, be with you all.—2 Cor. 13:14

Peace be to the brethren, and love with faith, from God the Father and the Lord Jesus Christ. Grace be with all them that love our Lord Jesus Christ in sincerity.—Eph. 6:23–24

And the peace of God, which passeth all understanding, shall keep your hearts and minds through Christ Jesus. Finally, brethren, whatsoever things are true, whatsoever things are honest, whatsoever things are just; whatsoever things are pure, whatsoever things are lovely, whatsoever things are of good report; if there be any virtue, and if there be any praise, think on these things. Those things, which ye have both learned and received, and heard, and seen in me, do; and the God of peace shall be with you.—Phil. 4:7–9

Wherefore also we pray always for you, that our God would count you worthy of this calling, and fulfill all the good pleasure of this goodness, and the work of faith with power; that the name of our Lord Jesus Christ may be glorified in you, and ye in him, according to the grace of our God and the Lord Jesus Christ.—2 Thess. 1:11–12

Now the Lord of peace himself give you peace always by all means. The Lord be with you all. The grace of our Lord Jesus Christ be with you all.—2 Thess. 3:16–18

Grace, mercy, and peace, from God our Father and Jesus Christ our Lord.—1 Tim. 1:2

Now the God of peace, that brought again from the dead our Lord Jesus, that great shepherd of the sheep, through the blood of the everlasting covenant, make you perfect in every good work to do his will, working in you that which is well-pleasing in his sight, through Jesus Christ, to whom be glory for ever and ever.—Heb. 13:20–21

The God of all grace, who hath called us unto his eternal glory by Christ Jesus, after that ye have suffered a while, make you perfect, establish, strengthen, settle you. To him be glory and dominion for ever and ever. Greet ye one another with a kiss of charity. Peace be with you all that are in Christ Jesus.—1 Pet. 5:10–11, 14

Grace be with you, mercy, and peace, from God the Father, and from the Lord Jesus Christ, the Son of the Father, in truth and love.—2 John 3

Now unto him that is able to keep you from falling, and to present you faultless before the presence of his glory with exceeding joy, to the only wise God our Savior, be glory and majesty, dominion and power, both now and ever.—Jude 24–25

Grace be unto you, and peace, from him which was, and which is to come; and from the seven Spirits which are before his throne; and from Jesus Christ, who is the faithful witness, and the first begotten of the dead, and the prince of the kings of the earth. Unto him that loved us, and washed us from our sins in his own blood, and hath made us kings and priests unto God and his Father; to him be glory and dominion for ever and ever.—Rev. 1:4–6

SECTION II.
Sermons and Homiletic and Worship Aids for Fifty-two Sundays

SUNDAY: JANUARY SEVENTH

SERVICE OF WORSHIP

Sermon: The Choice We Will Face

TEXT: Josh. 24:14–18

Most people laugh when we talk about New Year's resolutions. The attitude seems to be: "What's the use to make them, we're only going to break them!" So we don't talk much about making New Year's resolutions. That could be a mistake. For one thing, it reminds us that there are areas of our lives that need to be improved.

The making of resolutions reminds us that we are responsible for what we make of our lives. If there are areas of our lives that need to be changed, we can make decisions about whether or not we want to change them. Growing toward maturity is learning to accept responsibility for our lives.

At one time in our lives, most of us have made this resolution. We resolved that we would be a Christian. In the year ahead, that resolution will be tested and tried. We will have to choose. Will we serve God or not? It is similar to the experience that Joshua had in this farewell speech when he told the people they had to make a decision. They would have to choose to serve God or not. In the days ahead, there will be several times when we will have to decide: Will we choose to serve Christ or not to serve him?

I. *Will we choose to serve Christ when temptations come?*

a. In Joshua's day, there were many voices calling for the allegiance of the people—many false gods. The problem with the false gods was that they looked enticing and promised so much. Joshua would say that in the end, they would deliver only boredom and emptiness. But they had to decide which god they would serve. Which God or god would they trust for life?

In our day there are many false gods calling our attention. They do look enticing, and their words are like honey, sweet to our hearing. They can easily persuade us that they know the key to life and the joy and happiness of it.

(1) *Materialism* tells us that the way to life is found in things: televisions, clothes, cars, and houses. It sounds so right, and many of us spend our lives in the pursuit of things.

(2) There is the god of *pleasure* who tries to convince us that life is just meant to be one big party. You've got to do what you feel, do what comes naturally, do what you want. Go ahead! Anything that brings us a blast, do it. That sounds tempting. We all want to have a good time. We all want to feel good. It's easy to follow that god.

(3) The god *success* tells us that making it to the top is all that matters. You need to make it no matter what the price: family, friends, even your own personal integrity.

(4) The *popularity* god tells us that being with the "in" crowd is where it's at. Just find the majority opinion and go with it. Nobody wants to be left out anyway. We all want to be part of something,

17

so we compromise and do what others want us to do because that's the way to life.

b. The gods call out to us. They sound so sweet, we can easily fall for their seduction. Then the voice of *God* comes to us and, in light of all of those other voices, the voice of God sounds so tame. God tells us that *things* won't bring us life. We must never come *under* the control of things, we must be *in* control of things. They will only bring emptiness. God tells us that to give way to our passions will lead to our destruction because we become a slave to our emotions instead of being in control. The pursuit of pleasure for pleasure's sake will one day leave us empty. God tells us that to be a success is not the goal of life: to be a servant is. It's lonely at the top. Life is found not worrying about being number one but worrying about being a servant. Being popular? God tell us that's not important. What is important is being right, being decent, being morally strong. When we get down to it, being popular can leave us empty and confused inside.

But we will have to decide. Sometime this year, those temptations will come. Will we keep our resolution to be his children?

II. *Will we choose to serve God when the testing comes?*

a. The children of Israel had to face that problem then. To live in the Promised Land would not be easy. When it was hard to serve God, would they still hold on to him? Their forefathers had some trouble with that. They had gotten to the edge of the Promised Land, scouted it out, and discovered that there were giants in the land, and they didn't like that at all. They wanted the Promised Land, but they wanted God to give it to them on a silver platter. They didn't want to have to work for it and to fight for it. These their children would have to decide. Would they stay with God when the battles came? Would they still choose him?

b. The times of testing may not come to all of us, but they will come to many of us. It may be the loss of a loved one. It may be some sickness that won't go away. It may be a terrible disappointment that

beats us down. Maybe it's a failure you can't seem to get over. Maybe a financial setback causes us to struggle just to make ends meet. Will we trust God in the midst of them or not?

c. Many don't. Many give up on God. God has not promised us that he would magically make all of our problems disappear. He *has* promised to be with us in the midst of them, to help us face them, and to walk through them. Will we still resolve to hold on to him, even when it's hard?

III. *Will we trust him and choose him when the triumphs come?*

a. One of the great problems of Joshua's people was their triumphs. Some of their greatest temptations came on the heels of some of their greatest victories. Pride in themselves overtook humility and dependence upon the grace of God. Eventually, this was to be their downfall. They quit depending on God until they woke up one day to discover that God had become a stranger to them. They were weak and could not go on.

b. For us, the same temptations will be there. When the storms come, it is easy to realize our need of God, but when the sun is shining, it's easy to forget our need of him.

Remember that the sun shines today, but the storms of life can come up so quickly. What you ought to remember is every day of our life is a gift from the hand of God, and every day when things go well it is because of the grace of God. You must remember that who you are and what you will become is because of who he has been to you and what he will be to you.

So the year lies ahead for us. Most of us have resolved to try to be Christian, and that resolve will be tested. We will have to live it, and Joshua said we must choose who we will serve. Joshua said, "I don't know who you're going to choose, but as for me and my house, we will serve the Lord" (v. 15).

And he did. Most of us have said, "That's us. We've chosen to serve him." Will we continue to chose to serve him when the temptations come, and the testings come, even when the triumphs come? In all of those experiences, will we still hold on to him?

Will it be a happy New Year? It depends on the choices we make. In spite of what happens to any of us in the year ahead, it can be a very happy, blessed, good year if we will choose every day of it to serve the Lord. But it is our choice. It's in our hands. What will we do?—Hugh Litchfield

Illustrations

THE DIFFERENCE. Cliff Harris, a well-known preacher, spoke in prison. A prisoner introduced him. He said, "Several years ago in the same neighborhood two boys grew up. They went to the same schools, played on the same ball team; they went to the same Sunday school and church. But one of those boys got smart and said he didn't need church and Sunday school anymore, and he quit going. Then he started choosing some things that were not good. The other one stayed in church and Sunday school and tried to do what was right." The prisoner continued, "It has been years since that time, and I am here to tell you that both of these boys are here in this prison tonight. The one who tried to do right is one who is going to preach to you in a few minutes. The one who thought he was smart and chose to do wrong is this prisoner who is introducing him to you."—Hardy R. Denham, Jr. in *Proclaim*

FREEDOM. All choice, when one comes to think of it, is terrifying; liberty, where there is no duty to guide it, terrifying.—André Gide

SERMON SUGGESTIONS

Topic: Hope Fulfilled

TEXT: Jer. 31:7–14

The Church, the new Israel through faith, will experience God's grace (1) in salvation, verses 7–8; (2) in parental consolations, verses 9–10; (3) in special providences, verses 11–14.

Topic: The Blessings Christ Brings

TEXT: Eph. 1:3–14 NRSV

(1) *Initiative:* What we enjoy in Christ as believers is ours because of God's eternal purpose. (2) *Inclusion:* Gentiles, as well as Jews, inherit God's gracious redemption. (3) *Intention:* God wills that in Christ we might "live for the praise of his glory." (4) *Inscription:* We are marked with the seal of the Holy Spirit, the pledge of our inheritance.

Worship Aids

CALL TO WORSHIP. "Praise the Lord, O Jerusalem; praise thy God, O Zion. For he hath strengthened the bars of thy gates; he hath blessed thy children within thee" (Ps. 147:13–14).

INVOCATION. Open our minds, O God, to the thoughts of thee and of thy purpose for us. Grant that we may never settle down in the familiar and the comfortable, so that we are not ready to rise up and follow the stars that lead us on and on. Help us in our life here on earth to start out on the great adventure of finding a way of life with our fellow men and women as we have been taught by our Lord and Savior, Jesus Christ.—Theodore Parker Ferris

OFFERTORY SENTENCE. "And Moses spake unto all the congregation of the children of Israel, saying, This is the thing which the Lord commanded, saying, Take ye from among you an offering unto the Lord: whosoever is of a willing heart, let him bring it, an offer into of the Lord" (Exod. 35:4–5).

OFFERTORY PRAYER. Gracious Lord, in this first Sunday of the New Year, let our giving be of such quality of spirit that gratitude motivate it and grace endue it unto good works for Jesus' sake.—E. Lee Phillips

PRAYER. We come to thee with penitence for the sorry failures that spoil our recollections of the year gone by. We have been thoughtless and unkind when goodwill would have helped a friend. We have filled other lives with our smoke, darkening days that else might have been sun-clear. Surrendering to our worst, we have made it difficult for others to live at their best. We are sinners, Lord, and we confess it. O God, grant us such sincere penitence and such effectual desire for amendment, that through the gateway of another year we may pass forgiven and empowered. . . .

If the Eternal were against us, then were all our works vain and our hopes empty. Thanks be to thee, O God, for the great tradition of our faith, the insights of the seers, the visitations of the Divine in our own hearts, and Christ above all, thy very word spoken to us in a life, assuring us that the eternal is not only great but good, and that where love is there God is also. Strengthen us with this faith renewed today for the year that awaits us. Undergird all the uncertainty of its perplexing days and its disturbed circumstance with a steady confidence in thine eternal Purpose. O God of goodness and of grace, be our God now!

Gather us all into thy sustaining care. The children with their eagerness and gaiety—let thy benediction rest on them. The youths with their growing strength—enrich their lives with worthy interests. The mature in the fullness of their power—may they use it with dedicated unselfishness. The aged who draw near the end of their journey—may the gates of death be to them open doors to an eternal morning. All of us, facing our temptations, trials, challenges, and opportunities—make us adequate for each day's living. So, beyond our power to ask or our right to deserve, minister thou in secret to our souls.

We pray in the Spirit of Christ.— Harvey Emerson Fosdick

LECTIONARY MESSAGE

Topic: Becoming a Child of God

Text: John 1:10–18

What is the relationship of the human race to God? All of the religions of the world address the issue, and they define what kind of God exists. Genesis begins by defining what kind of God exists and the nature of the relationship of people to God, as well as to the rest of creation.

John's Gospel takes up this same theme, explaining what Jesus Christ has to do with this relationship.

I. *We are not like God.* In a pluralistic world with rival religious views like that of the first-century Roman Empire, the Gospel of John takes pains to distinguish the claims of the gospel from other worldviews. As in twentieth-century America, a prominent worldview of the time claimed that people shared the divine essence and would remerge with the Oversoul at death. The gospel makes no sense in that kind of a world, for people would have no need of a savior. The Gospel assumes that people have a fundamental need for a quality of life that does not belong to them by nature or by birth. Rather than *sharing* the divine spark that constitutes divinity, people exist as creatures of God: they are born, they live, they die. Apart from "light" that comes from God outside themselves, people would live out their biological existence in "darkness." Despite the advances of technology, human experience indicates that the barbarity of the human race has changed little over the last five thousand years. If human morality reflects the divine essence, then whatever God is must be a dreadful being. John declares that the human race is so different from God that we do not even recognize the presence of the Divine when we come into the Holy presence (v. 10).

II. *God became like us.* By distancing the human race from the divine, however, one might construe a world in which God either does not exist, or God would be too holy to have any contact with humans. In distinguishing the claims of the Gospel from other worldviews, John describes the kind of God who not only exists but cares about the plight of the human race. The Gospel assumes a world in need that can be remedied only by the intervention of God. Through Jesus Christ, God intervened in the problems of the human race. The idea of the Divine becoming human represents an intellectual obstacle in a scientific world where what cannot be demonstrated by sensory experience has no valid place. It represented no less an obstacle for the philosophical community of the Hellenistic world, which could not conceive of pure spirit having anything to do with the flesh. John made no effort to defend the idea of the incarnation. He simply explained the kind of God who would care enough about the human race to enter the world of creation.

The Gospel assumes a world in which people do not have the power to take the initiative to become like God. On the contrary, the Gospel assumes a world in which people practice self-delusion concerning their relationship to God. By taking the initiative, God revealed the glory that he intended people to share. Through Jesus Christ, God revealed "the glory of the One and Only" (v. 14 NIV), which stood in stark contrast to the quality and character of life experienced by the human race. The Gospel of John tells the stories of people who encountered Jesus and became witnesses to the visitation by God to the human race. Rather than a mythical interpretation of natural events or a rationalistic interpretation of metaphysics, the Gospel of John builds on the experience of people to describe what difference it makes that God became like us.

III. *We can become like God.* Though people are different from God, people can become children of God. Being a child of God does not come from being human. Because people are different from God, people are not children of God by birth (v. 13). In an egalitarian society like the United States, which thinks in terms of entitlement, people may tend to think of relationship to God as a right. Though framed in an entirely different cultural context, the Jews of the first century would have considered their peculiar history with God as an entitlement. In further clarifying what kind of God exists, John made clear that the God of the Gospel is beholden to none. Nonetheless, the God who made himself known through the Law given through Moses offers grace to all through his son Jesus Christ (v. 17).

People become children of God through faith in Jesus Christ, who came to reveal his Father (v. 12, 18). The Gospel offers relationship with God. The God who created all things by his Word brought the possibility of a new form of existence by that same Word who became human. The whole idea is mere nonsense in every kind of world except one that was created. The Gospel of Jesus Christ is an expression of the character of the kind of God who would create a world and continue to care about it. The problems of this world derive from humanity's lack of faith in its Creator, but salvation comes through faith in that Creator who reveals himself fully through his Son.

Salvation begins by the willingness to rethink one's assumptions about what kind of God exists. The kind of God that exists determines what kind of universe exists. A universe God created is one in which God can move freely without violation of the natural order. By entering the world, God partook of the natural order. By virtue of being Creator, God has the freedom to extend the work of creation to make people into children of God.—Harry L. Poe

SUNDAY: JANUARY FOURTEENTH

SERVICE OF WORSHIP

Sermon: Unashamed

TEXT: Rom. 1:16a

Have you ever thought how some words having to do with our human feelings have almost disappeared from our vocabulary? I am thinking of the word "shame," which distinguishes human beings from the lower forms of creation. Sophocles, the Greek poet, said that the capacity to laugh was God's gift to humanity. One might say also that the feeling of shame is unique to every level of the human race. Phrases such as "hang your head in shame" or "blush with shame" do not apply to cows or cats or trees, but all of us can recall how seriously we were rebuked when a parent or teacher admonished us with the words, "Shame on you!" or "You ought to be ashamed."

What does it mean to be ashamed? Usually it means your emotional reaction to having done something "out of character." You betrayed your better self—the self others thought you to be—and now you knew it. Before a convention of news editors (1993), Dan Rather, the CBS anchorman, declared: "We should all be ashamed of what we have and have not done, measured against what we could do."[1] Every one of us remembers similar reasons for shame in our own lives. But the reason for feeling this way is not always a matter of lament, because it implies in some positive sense that we recognize that right is right, and in the light of this and of what we ought to have said or done, we are ashamed of ourselves.

Now although the word shame or a feeling of it rarely occurs in contemporary newspapers or magazines, and not at all in political messages, yet when we turn to the Bible it occurs in some form or another over a hundred times; and what is more, it is intimated again and again in many well-known evangelistic hymns. Listen to an eighteenth-century hymn:

Jesus! and shall it ever be
A mortal man ashamed of thee;
Ashamed of thee whom angels praise
Whose glories shine through endless days.
Ashamed of Jesus! sooner far
Let evening blush to own a star.

Over against these lines set Isaac Watts's hymn of affirmation.

I'm not ashamed to own my Lord
Or to defend his cause;
Maintain the glory of his Cross
And honor all his laws.

We are all told that in a great revival meeting led by the American evangelist

Dwight L. Moody, a young convert arose to give his testimony for what God had done for him in Jesus Christ. Unaccustomed to public speaking and somewhat overawed by the size of the crowd, the young man began to stammer and became almost incoherent. Just then a brash unbeliever turned to him and said, "You ought to be ashamed of yourself, standing there and mumbling like that!" "Yes," said the young man, "I am ashamed of myself, but I am not ashamed of Jesus Christ!" Here was a person who had seen and felt a new factor in his life, namely, the reality of the Christian gospel and, although he found himself to be insufficient in the face of it and was somewhat overawed by it, yet no one could point a finger at him, for the gospel and his acceptance of it were something greater that anyone could imagine or measure.

Now, this is what St. Paul was getting at in the first chapter of his letter to the Christian community in Rome about the year A.D. 58, twenty-five years after the Resurrection. In it he declared, "I'm not ashamed of the Gospel of Christ for it is the power of God for salvation to everyone who believes" (v. 16).

Time and again in his writings and sermons he acknowledged his own moral and spiritual weaknesses and failures and expressed how great a shame this was for him, but the negative was always erased by the positive, namely, the power of the gospel to make his life whole again. Thomas Hardy, in one of his poems, intimated that any consideration of the best deserves a look at the worst. Is it too much to surmise that in the early years of Paul's life, when he was persecuting the infant Christian Church, that he might have been ashamed to bring the gospel to Rome? But why should he?

Well, first of all, there was the nature of Rome itself. On every shore of the Mediterranean world the name of Rome symbolized glory and power. Its strong arm subjected sects and colonies to the emperor's stern control. Under its sway were the skills, the money, and the pagan superstitions of lieutenants and bond slaves of every kind. But inside this em-

---

[1] *Gentlemen's Quarterly*, April 1994.

orces of the millenniums and makes a iny crystal. And he takes the vision of Christ, the love and power of the Redeemer—for what? Just that he could make you and me new."

Think of the dimensions of the gospel Paul declared! Henry Ward Beecher of Brooklyn stated: "Paganism drags heaven into the mud of earth and makes gods into sinful men. Christianity raises earth to heaven and makes sinful men into children of God."

III. Let us now bring the matter home to ourselves. As you and I look out today on this rebellious, war-bloodied, and crime-ridden world, upon what do we take our stand? Are we ashamed of that faith and belief that produced such names as Paul, St. Francis, John Wesley, Albert Schweitzer, Dietrich Bonhoeffer, Mother Teresa, Billy Graham, to name a few? Are we ashamed of it, and therefore have we slunk back into a life of neutrality, indifference, and easy compromise? Do we take the dividend of the Christian faith but put nothing back into it? In this topsy-turvy world, are we afraid to show our colors?

Or, on the other hand, are we proud of the Christian gospel because, more than any other religion, it has proved itself by its power to set right what is wrong in the hearts of human society? If so, are we ready to show it? How? (a) It will mean that the Church, the community of God's people, must not rest with things as they are but will speak out unashamedly about what this gospel can do when you and I believe in it. (b) It will mean that older people, who have a large stake in the world of business and finance, will stand courageously by what they know to be right in the sight of God and unashamedly declare it to be the only true way to work and live. (c) It will mean that the younger generation will have done with all that is coarse, cheap, and unfair and will hold unashamedly to the highest moral principles as God's will for his world.

Such assignments will not be easy, and the price can be terribly high. But to be ashamed of our support of them is a badge we should blush to wear. Paul said

to his fellow evangelist Timothy: "I am not ashamed, for I know whom I have believed." Such a stand outthinks, outlives, and outdies this modern world, and by it the gospel is upheld, and joy and satisfaction will be registered in this world, and the next.—Donald Macleod

Illustrations

SHAME.   Professor George H. Palmer of Harvard used to tell of a boy lying in bed very late in the morning and being called by his mother. "Aren't you ashamed of lying here so late?" said the mother, and the boy answered, "Yes, mother, I am ashamed, but I had rather be ashamed than get up!"—Charles L. Wallis

GUILT AND INNOCENCE.   Schiller, in his biography of Frederick the Great, tells of the monarch's visit to a Potsdam prison. One prisoner after another assured him that he was innocent and the victim of a frame-up. Finally one man, however, looked down at the floor and said, "Your Majesty, I am guilty, and richly deserving punishment."

Frederick bellowed for the warden. "Free this rascal and get him out of our prison," he ordered, "before he corrupts all the noble innocent people here."—Bennett Cerf, *Laughter Incorporated*

SERMON SUGGESTIONS

Topic: Because of God's Grace
TEXT: 1 Cor. 1:1–9 NRSV
(1) We have been enriched with spiritual gifts. (2) We are being strengthened daily in view of Christ's return. (3) We can depend on the faithful God who has brought us "into the fellowship of his Son, Jesus Christ our Lord."

Topic: What John Saw in Jesus
TEXT: John 1:29–42
(1) A sin offering for all humankind, verse 29. (2) The one who baptizes with the Holy Spirit, verse 33. (3) The Son of God, verse 34. (4) A personal Savior, verses 35–42 and 43–51.

pire was a decaying and hapless moral order. Who would blame Paul if he were to shrink from bringing a gospel of love, grace, and purity to the gates of ancient Rome?

Then there was the nature of Paul's organization. What could he show before the efficient and legal machinery of Rome? His movement consisted of merely a loosely attached group of slaves and artisans, touching a new person here and there, meeting in fear and secrecy, behind bolted doors, and claiming they had a mission to change the world. How unpromising and impracticable would they appear before the institutions of Rome with its steady clout and uniformity! Could we blame Paul if he would hesitate to face the ridicule and contempt of Rome?

And, then, there was the nature of his leader. Let us remember that in those centuries the social and cultural essence of Rome was shot through with the worship of the emperor. At his command were the iron-clad legions akin to the Nazi and fascist military of our twentieth century. And here was Paul proclaiming the life and power of Jesus, a young Jewish idealist, born in a barn in an obscure village called Bethlehem, yet claiming to be truth *alive!* Nonsense! Rome would say. And then this young prophet gambled his whole life upon it, and Roman soldiers nailed him to a tree. What a far-fetched story to tell a skeptical and power-drunk generation at Rome! Yet, across the Adriatic Sea stood this eager and farsighted Jew, turning his face westward and saying: "I am ready to preach the Gospel to you at Rome, for I am not ashamed of the Gospel of Christ for it is the power of God for salvation to everyone who believes." Could this be anything but wildest presumption to face imperial Rome under the banner of a leader such as Jesus of Nazareth, whom Pilate had disgraced by crucifixion and whose followers made the amazing claim that he was now alive!

Not much here to go on, is there? Yet Paul had such strong convictions that nothing on earth could hold him back.

Let us look at two of them.

I. Paul was not ashamed of because of its secret. At its co ter, he maintained, was the God. Rome could parade its pa ers, its network of strangest go and ceremonies of ancient sup but at the nation's heart was frustration because all these could not remove the question garding the meaning of life or and goal of all their striving or th rity of love, faith, and living tru came, however, not with just blueprint for people to haggle ov to declare an *event;* something ha pened, as Professor H. H. Farme "God had gone into action for us ar salvation in one Jesus of Naza Therefore, Paul's message was not new program for living, not some made point of view, no welfare sc for a social order, but on the cont that there was one God of love whos lution to the human problem was "(so loved the world that he gave his son that whosoever believes in him will not perish but have eternal life." And this eternal recipe has changed for good the lives of millions of men and women everywhere for two thousand years.

During the war, a well-known singer lost his only son, and he said to a friend: "When a man comes to a thing like this, there are just three ways out of it. There is drink; there is despair; and there is God, and by his grace, it is God for me." A New York minister remarked to me that whenever he talked with people who had left off attending and supporting the Church and the strong emphasis of the Christian faith, not one of them ever said they did so because they found a greater Lord than Christ.

II. Paul was not ashamed of the gospel because of its dimensions. He knew it meant salvation not merely to any Roman citizen, but for him "it was the power of God to everyone who believes." Thomas Erksine of Scotland put it this way: "It is a dynamic power that sets *all* people right." George H. Morrison, also of Scotland, said: "God takes the sun and makes a daisy. He takes the gift of lice and makes an insect. He takes the mighty

Worship Aids

CALL TO WORSHIP.   "I waited patiently for the Lord; and he inclined unto me, and heard my cry. He brought me up also out of an horrible pit, out of the miry clay, and set my feet upon a rock, and established my goings. And he hath put a new song in my mouth, even praise unto our God: many shall see it, and fear, and shall trust in the Lord" (Ps. 40:1–3).

INVOCATION.   Lord of life, guide our worship that we may praise you with whole hearts and serve you with unfettered faith and love you with undiminished joy, through Christ our Lord.—E. Lee Phillips

OFFERTORY SENTENCE.   "Ascribe to the Lord the glory due his name. Bring an offering and come before him; worship the Lord in the splendor of his holiness" (1 Chron. 16:29 NIV).

OFFERTORY PRAYER.   Almighty God, you sent your Son Jesus Christ to reconcile the world to yourself: We praise and bless you for those whom you have sent in the power of the Spirit to preach the Gospel to all nations. We thank you that in all parts of the earth a community of love has been gathered together by their prayers and labors, and that in every place your servants call upon your Name; for the kingdom and the power and the glory are yours forever.—*The Book of Common Prayer*

PRAYER.   Our hearts are uneasy, O God, for though we are loath to confess that we have sinned, yet we know for a surety that all we have done has been far from good. We have lapsed from the best we have known, we have suffered our worst impulses to have their way, we have covered our shame with excuses that gave us a sense of comfort, false as it might be. We have been willing to do penance after a fashion, to pay for our ill-temper, to make up for our vicious ways, if in such things we were not forced to admit that we have been wrong. Take this blinding veil away from us, O God, that we may be honest with ourselves and no longer victims of our own deceit. Heal us and strengthen us that we may know how to stand in thy presence and receive thy judgment to the saving of our souls.—Samuel H. Miller

LECTIONARY MESSAGE

Topic: A Call For Service

TEXT: Isa. 49:1–7

Other Readings: 1 Cor. 1:1–9; John 1:29–42

There is a sound that is recognizable by young and old, office worker or farmer, policeman or teacher. It is the ringing sound of the telephone. Its message is simple. Someone is calling. Someone wants to get in touch with us.

There are times when the call is pleasant. Perhaps it is a friend whom we have not heard from in months or years. How good it is to reestablish friendships. Other times the sound of the ringing phone brings sorrow. An accident has occurred. Maybe a loved one has suddenly died. When the phone rings, we never know what message awaits. Not until we answer.

Paul's first letter to the Corinthians focuses on the call of God at least four times in chapter 1. Each call is a call related to serving God.

Paul announced his own personal calling in verse 1 of chapter 1. He was called by the will of God to be an apostle. God had chosen him for a special work in the kingdom of God. We are reminded by the prophet Isaiah that God knows us and who we are and what we can mean to his kingdom's work. Isaiah takes courage in knowing that "the Lord called me from the womb, from the body of my mother he named my name. . . ." God's call for our service is based on his complete knowledge of us. And his delight is to call us to be his servant even though the world may doubt or despise us. Our service to God takes on added importance as we realize the potential God sees in us for service in his kingdom.

God not only calls us to service individually as he did Paul and Isaiah but collectively as his body, the Church. Paul reminds us that we are "called to be saints together with all those who in every place call on the name of our Lord Jesus Christ, both their Lord and ours. . . ." We share in the work of the kingdom. Therefore, there is no room for pride. We need one another in this kingdom work.

Jesus knew that work in the kingdom would require a team effort. John tells us in chapter 1 that Jesus gathered around him those who could be counted on to help. John, in the midst of his popularity with the crowds and effectiveness in preparing the way for the Messiah, was willing to step aside and point to Jesus. He was content to watch his own disciples turn and follow Jesus. As a result, the tiny band of believers around Jesus grew and helped launch his work. It was a call to service that moved away from one individual to many.

The call of God in service is also one that provides the believer with certain promises. One is to remind us that God is faithful (1 Cor. 1:9). God does not call us to his kingdom's work only to leave us alone. It is God who furnishes the resources for us to do his work. Isaiah says, "I will give you as a light to the nations, that my salvation may reach to the end of the earth." Isaiah helps us to understand that it is the Lord who is faithful. We do not have to work in our own strength.

Another promise is that our calling to service will result in fellowship with Jesus. As we read John's record of the calling of the early disciples, we sense the fellowship that developed. No doubt the early disciples enjoyed every moment with Jesus. They learned from him. They laughed with him. They worked with him. It was a fellowship of love.

But to every believer this love is available. Not just to the early disciples or to the early Church but to modern-day disciples as well. All we have to do is to respond in love and obedience to the call of God. His service is never dull and boring. It is filled with the joy of life itself in Christ and with all the resources God alone can provide. When God calls may we say with willing hearts, here am I Lord. Send me.—Ronald W. Johnson

SUNDAY: JANUARY TWENTY-FIRST

SERVICE OF WORSHIP

Sermon: Why Be Christian Today?

TEXT: 1 Pet. 3:15

The words of our text come to us with striking relevance in our world situation today, for never in the whole history of the Christian faith has our faith been more rudely challenged or severely tested as now. Indeed, it seems that Christianity more than all the other great religions of the world has to be on guard against foes from without and enemies from within its own household. The facts are plain: Christianity finds itself presently thrust into a world one-half of which is shot through with spiritual indifference and cold secularism, where religion is treated as an option and handled on a take-it-or-leave-it basis; whereas in the other half the principles of the Christian faith are fighting for their life, struggling to sustain integrity and avoid being engulfed by systems that deny even the name of God. Now certainly events and circumstances differ from age to age and from culture to culture, but the underlying issues are surprisingly the same today as they were in the first century of the Christian Era. St. Peter, for example, remembering his fellow Christians who were scattered across Asia Minor and in constant danger of being absorbed or liquidated by their enemies, sent them this word of caution: "Always be ready to make a defense to anyone who calls you to account for the faith that is in you." In other words he forewarned his friends to be ready and equipped with adequate answers if and when they should be confronted with questions such as these: Why do you hold on to a hope you cannot see? Why are you Christ's men and women? Why are you Christian anyway?

And these same questions meet you and me in the common encounters of our common life today, and in the most subtle ways we are put on the spot concerning our faith and beliefs, and the answers we give will determine the quality of the Christian witness in our midst for generations yet to come.

Now, what do these critics say who challenge our beliefs and call our faith into question?

Some say Christianity is like a drug; it stupefies the poor, downtrodden and oppressed by promising them pie in the sky bye-and-bye. Others say Christianity is like a poisonous infection; it gets into one's blood and makes one too humble and tolerant, and hence its followers are less able to be masters than slaves. Some others, moreover, feel that Christianity is all right as a Sunday hobby or a cultural luxury for those who are interested in that kind of thing, but it should never be permitted to lay any claim upon us the other six days of the week.

The only thing, however, that such perspectives show is that these critics are not quite sure or clear about what Christianity really is. For them it appears to be a refuge for the socially dispossessed, or it provides a sentimental fellowship for those who like softness, or it is the means whereby our bourgeois culture is perpetuated and sustained. And they will go on thinking about Christianity in this way until they have looked at it squarely in the face in order to see it for what it is. And if they were to do so, they would see that Christianity involves total response somehow they feel they must. It can mean going all out for some end worthy of all their effort even though it involves dying to self in order to realize it. John H. Withers of Belfast, Ireland, remarked: "Christianity is not a philosophy, but a personal relationship which opens up for us the inexhaustible resources of God." As such, therefore, you and I cannot take any middle ground regarding it; we must be either for it or against it.

One day a minister overtook a man who lived in his parish but who gave no support to the Church or what it stood for. After they had walked some little distance, the minister turned to him and asked, "Jim, why are you not a Christian?" The man stopped for a moment and seemed at a loss for anything to say. Then he answered: "Well, I'll tell you and I'll tell you honestly: I'm not a Christian simply because I am not man enough." And there are thousands throughout the land who have nothing to do with Christianity or the meaning of the person of Christ for humanity simply because they are not big enough to face up to it or brave enough to accept it. For Christianity has never appealed to our weakness but to our strength; never to our foolishness but to our wisdom; never to the whims and notions of the featherbrained but to the consistent dedication of the courageous will. Indeed, the story of the Christian faith has proved, as Dean Inge of St. Paul's once remarked, that it has been always a religion for heroes and has no time or place for those good-natured little people who want everybody to have a happy time.

Peter wrote: "Always be ready to give an account to anyone who calls you to account for the hope that is in you." Why be a Christian today? If tomorrow at your place of work or business you were asked to defend the reason or integrity of your belief, what answer would you be inclined to give?

I. Initially and basically you ought to respond: *I am a Christian for my own sake.*

Joseph Parker of London's City Temple wrote, "Jesus never comes to make us less; he comes to make us more." Why, then, should we not be Christian for our own sake? Look through the chapters of the New Testament, and out of its pages there fairly tumble groups of excited men and women who had a peculiar radiance on their faces, whose hearts seemed thrilled by their good fortune, and whose minds were so dazed they could not find words to explain what had happened to them. Their whole life was different, and their lives were gloriously new. And the secret of it all was that someone had taken over their lives and had given them a new spiritual understanding. Mark Rutherford commented that if he were asked to add one beatitude to those already in the New Testament, it would be, "Blessed are those who give us back our self-respect." And the world of the first century was full of men and women who were yearning inwardly for such a blessed gift. For, in the face of a dismal sense of failure, their inner cry was, "If only I could make a new start." Then came this man, Jesus, and we see him moving among these crushed and crouching figures who had given up trying and he treated as persons who had souls and he gave them of his best. Then the strangest things happened: Zacchaeus, a crooked tax collector, was changed; Mary Magdalene, woman of the streets, was transformed; Nicodemus, a proud Jewish intellectual, found an entirely new center for his life; and a whole host of others discovered that they, too, were intended to become children of God. And they sang about it, reveled in it joyously, and witnessed to their tremendous experience. Moreover, no one of them would ever dream of going back to the dull and shabby life from which they came.

II. Then we ought now to say: *I am a Christian today for the world's sake*. On an expedition to the South Pole, Rear Admiral Richard E. Byrd became lost in the Antarctic at midnight, and later he said, "I knew I was lost and I felt sick about it away down inside." None of us can deny that there is another sense of lostness everywhere throughout our land today. In trying to account for it, some people claim it stems from a loss of faith in the leadership of those entrusted with responsibility in many areas of our common life. Others say the reason is not only that the old charts have been discarded and the ancient landmarks erased but that we seem to be moving out into strange areas of science and technology where risks are high and horizons unfamiliar and unclear. Some others blame the expansion of our knowledge of our universe, which has made human creatures appear like puny items in a cosmos of a trillion stars. But the reason is deeper than all these, and strangely enough, it lies much nearer home; it belongs in the category of a lost relationship.

Is there anything you and I today need more than this? On every hand we meet men and women who need desperately a new sense of life's meaning, direction, and purpose. And we must show them that it is only through a personal relationship to a Being who is greater than ourselves that their lives can discover this meaning and purpose. Moreover, the reality of this sense of purpose is always tested by the depth and integrity of our concern. Oh, yes, we can be like some people who fold their arms and indicate they couldn't care less. Or, like some others who are content to let the world drift. Or, as some others, embrace some humanistic philosophy that fills them with an air of sophistication that creates a chasm between them and the needs of humankind. But as Christian men and women we cannot—and indeed dare not—close our eyes upon the masses of people who need our light in their darkness, or to all the sinister threats to human freedom, or to the burning cruelties perpetrated by one nation upon another, or to the fact that as Americas we spend billions annually to amuse ourselves and only millions upon the moral and academic well-being of our children.

Sure the time is ripe and indeed emergent for us to cease haggling over peripheral matters and ask ourselves as Americans: Are we a people of a high purpose? Are we Christian for the world's sake? Let's face it: as Christians it is for us to declare unequivocally today that we believe this world belongs to God and that we're all headed for disaster if we leave him out; it is for us to teach that there is only one destiny for the world of men and women and that is to be found in obedience to the will of God; and it is for us to witness that it is only in Jesus Christ that we find out what that will is and only through him do we get the power to do it.

III. Further, we ought especially to say: *We are Christian for Jesus' sake*.

The president of one of our American universities was making his farewell remarks to the members of a graduating class and he concluded: "Be Christian and you'll always be successful!" How ordinary and trifling do such words read and sound beside these lines from the Gospels: "He who saves his life shall lose it, but whosoever loses his life for my sake and the gospels the same shall save it." For these words of Jesus take issue with every modern misinformed school of thought that sees religion as a means to an end; that considers Christianity merely as a door opening upon worldly success and personal influence; that thinks of Christian worship as merely a therapeutic exercise that makes everyone feel better. This kind of Christianity is unreal and cannot and will not stand up where all kinds of pagan and militant ideologies are hurled against it. But real Christianity began with the Son of God laying down his life for our sakes and with his call to everyone to a personal commitment for his sake. And throughout the New Testament on over a dozen occasions when he called men and women to follow him, it was "for my sake and the gospels." What did he mean by this? He meant for the sake of who he was; of why he had come; and of what he could make out of the lives of ordinary men and women. And, therefore, when you or I say, "I am a Christian for Jesus' sake," it means we have confessed Christ as the only one who can give purpose to life and meaning to human history; and that as he gave himself for us, so must we work and serve and pray in his name till all nations claim him as their own.—Donald Macleod

Illustrations

THERE'S HOPE FOR YOU.   I visited the office of my friend Ted, a successful Chicago businessman. On his desk is a plaque engraved with the words "There's hope for you!" I asked him if there was a story behind the plaque.

Ted told me about an excruciating failure he'd gone through in his business years before. He lost everything. At what he called "bottom below bottom," Ted was forced to face his economic plight and his spiritual emptiness.

Some Christian businessmen who met over lunch each Thursday in the Chicago Loop took him under their wing. One of the men always ended his conversation with Ted with the parting shot, "Ted, there's hope for you!" Eventually Ted began to believe it, and one day he committed his life to Christ.

Ted told me, "I was never a very hopeful person before meeting Christ. It's been nonstop hope ever since. I keep that plaque to remind me where I was and that I'm where I am today because of the Lord. It also is a good conversation starter. Everybody needs to be told, "There's hope for you."

Ted's Valley of Anchor had not been some terrible sin, or even poor management, but a series of tough circumstances in the oil industry that had caused his little equipment company to go belly-up. The key thing is that what *he* thought of in those dark days as dismal failure became a door of hope.—Lloyd Ogilvie

BELONGING TO JESUS CHRIST.   Howard Moffatt, one of our medical missionaries to Korea, told of the arrival of our American troops at Inchon on their way to Seoul in September 1950. The big guns had virtually wiped out a small Korean village, and as an act of vengeance the Communists were holding captive a young Korean Christian and they gave him a terrible beating. Then they offered him the choice of renouncing his belief in Christ or being shot. But gazing up from the ground while still dazed and bleeding, the young man said, "Alive or dead, I'm still Jesus Christ's man!"—Donald Macleod

SERMON SUGGESTIONS

Topic: When God Rules

TEXT: Isa. 9:1–4

Whether through direct intervention or through earthly powers, (1) God relieves oppression ("darkness"); (2) God brings joy (as "at the harvest").

Topic: God's Nearness

TEXT: Matt. 4:12–23

(1) Signified in the person and presence of Jesus, verses 17a, 18. (2) Signified in the message of Jesus: (a) "Repent"; (b) "Follow me"; (c) "Fish for people." (3) Signified in the practical compassion of Jesus, verse 23.

Worship Aids

CALL TO WORSHIP. "The Lord is my light and my salvation; whom shall I fear? The Lord is the strength of my life; of whom shall I be afraid?" (Ps. 27:1)

INVOCATION. What love, O God, you lavish upon us that we should be your children. For this privilege to be among your people in this holy place, we worship and adore you. For this opportunity to celebrate your word of grace in your mighty deeds in the history of Israel, in your coming in Jesus of Nazareth, in your presence in the Church, in the mystery of your coming in these moments, we praise you. Free us from all shame and pretense that we may worship you in spirit and in reality. Praise be to you—Father, Son, and Holy Spirit!—John Thompson

OFFERTORY SENTENCE. "Lay up for yourselves treasures in heaven, where neither moth nor rust doth corrupt, and where thieves do not break through nor steal" (Matt. 6:20).

OFFERTORY PRAYER. Lord, let us not give with reluctance, hesitancy, and resentment; rather teach us to give joyfully, liberally, gladly, as did our Savior who for the joy that was set before him, endured the cross, despising the shame, and is seated at the right hand of the throne of God.—E. Lee Phillips

PRAYER. Grant, O God, that every wrong thought we have had of Thee may be turned steadily right, and every poor and partial view of life which we have harbored be made steadily whole; open our eyes that we may see as Thou wouldst have us see, and not be blind; and bring us through all this changing pattern of the years to live our lives with Thee down the ways of Thy good and changeless will in Christ Jesus.—Paul Scherer

LECTIONARY MESSAGE

Topic: Division in the Church

TEXT: 1 Cor. 1:10–18

Soon after the Resurrection, some in the Christian community stressed the exalted Christ while they discarded the sheer nonsense of the Crucifixion. In this text Paul does not describe individual preferences for a mystical appreciation of Christ, nor a true knowledge of the Messiah nor, indeed, those who constitute Chloe's children. Paul abhors a *partisan faith* in those who would cling to his methods and indeed celebrate his baptismal activity. Whether or not Paul identifies baptism with the saving activity of God, here, at least, he is glad not to have baptized anyone. The party spirit that celebrates common experience at the hands of an incandescent leader finds no acceptance with our Apostle to the Nations. It is faith in Christ that Paul celebrates, not the inner ring of shared aspiration, mutual experience, or camaraderie that would exclude all others. So Paul excludes party loyalty in his preference for an undivided Christ. Paul was not crucified for them, nor were those at Corinth baptized in his name.

Divided loyalty would focus on the symbol or trophy of salvation to the exclusion of its power. J. B. Phillips translates part of our passage to the effect that Paul intends his brothers "to speak with one voice . . . a unity in thought and judgment." There is no endorsement in this passage for Paul's men or those who prefer Apollos, or, again, disciples of Cephas or even someone else who says, "I owe my faith to Christ alone." Paul was not sent by Christ to see how many he could baptize but to proclaim the gospel with power. The issue is not quantification of religious activity but power through preaching; not words of wisdom, but this cruciform foolishness of God that is wiser and stronger than men. Peter Taylor Forsyth has well said, "The King alone can make the Kingdom. . . . The power that makes the soul will make the church. . . . And the Gospel that made the book will bless the book. . . . This cross is the message that makes the preacher."[1]

The Savior triumphant on the cross, not merely *after* it, is the *power of God*. Preaching of that Crucifixion, claims Paul, is a matter of life and death. Clever words may create partisans but rob the cross of its power (v. 17). Paul's first letter at Thessalonica reminded the Thessalonians (2:1–13) that he had been entrusted with the gospel by God and that

[1] *Positive Preaching and the Modern Mind*, 49.

neither flattery, greed, desire for honor, nor dishonesty would accompany Paul's preaching to them. Such transparent motives would ensure time and again the reception of Paul's preaching as a power in their lives rather than as a mere human message. For the clever slogans of a skillful propagandist foster partisan group activity in the redeemed community. Power rather than party, life instead of death, proclamation with integrity—all of these animate Paul's exhortation that the gospel is "not the sacrifice we make, but the sacrifice we trust." Forsyth—Marvin Anderson

SUNDAY: JANUARY TWENTY-EIGHTH

SERVICE OF WORSHIP

Sermon: Christ Disclosed Through the Cracks in our Characters

TEXT: 1 Cor. 1:18–31

I. Our heroes tend to be persons who have survived life's hard knocks. It could well be that weakness frightens us. It's as though we've come to equate strength and true courage with the stubborn resolve to overcome every obstacle. Those who grit their teeth and bite the bullet are admired. And they're held in such high esteem because they are examples of that "pioneer spirit"—that rugged individualism so much a part of American folklore.

Much of the time, most of us look to protect ourselves from feeling pain, emotional or physical. And all too often we send up a smoke screen, calling it strength, in the effort to prevent others from seeing our weaknesses. After all, we wouldn't want others to peer into the cracks in our characters, now, would we? We begin, almost from birth, to fabricate a personal fortress that we hope will convince others that our character is strong. It soon becomes evident in every aspect of life. A massive build-up of military hardware. A burglar-proof alarm system in our home. The false security of financial success. A handgun hidden somewhere in the house or in the glove

compartment of the family car. An insurance policy to cover every angle of every ailment.

Sometimes we conceal our weakness behind the mask of personal power and the silly claim that we've managed to master our own misfortunes. And then there's our tendency to take advantage of the weaknesses of another. It all amounts to pretty much the same thing.

We often attempt to masquerade our deepest insecurities behind the caricature of courage or the paper-thin shield of a false sense of strength. Political posturing, the fascination with financial success, the abuse of personal power. In the end, they all fail as a feeble attempt to cover up our lack of genuine courage.

II. We all know that fears, anxieties, and apprehensions stalk us and set us in chains. And we also know how often we attempt to shield ourselves behind some pretty flimsy fortresses. But there are alternatives, you know. We needn't rely on the tactic of the stiff upper lip or the pretense to power,

Christ makes possible a difference kind of strength and courage. A courage that won't conceal the wounds and weaknesses of human existence. A courage willing to take up the chaos and confusion of life's crises. The kind of courage I once witnessed in a woman battling cancer. A courage I've witnessed in others as well. That courage that only Christ makes possible in his people.

And I remain convinced that this kind of courage is contagious! Someone once said, "Keep your fears to yourself, but share your courage with others." That may well be a bit of an overstatement. But I've little doubt that the courage of Christ in one life can beget a similar courage in the life of another.

III. And yet, such Christian courage is not to be measured simply by what we do but also by where and when we do it. So, if we should attempt to cover up our losses, to avoid disclosing our brokenness, or to hide our heartaches, we merely belie the fact that we haven't submitted to the strength of our Savior. Because human weakness is the very soil in which this Savior plants his seeds of strength and courage.

And maybe that's because it's the weak and wounded heart that can surrender all claim to self-sufficiency. When we're at our wit's end, when our backs are up against some wall, then all of those fortresses we've fashioned for ourselves begin to look pretty flimsy, don't they?

But that's the beauty of it all! We no longer need fashion fortresses to guard us from failure, or faults, or feeble faith. And there's no need to pretend that we can overcome our own personal pain, relying solely upon our own inner resources.

We needn't bite the bullet, fight back our tears, or make light of our troubles and fears. There's real freedom to be found in submitting to a Savior who already knows how desperately we need his strength. You see, the courage of Christ is the mortar in the cracks of our character! His power prevails through our weakness.

The apostle Paul once wrote to the Christians in Corinth, saying, "We preach Christ crucified . . . the power of God. . . . For God's weakness is stronger than human strength!" And even though I'm not certain exactly what Paul had in mind when he spoke of "God's weakness," I have some idea.

Perhaps Paul was referring to God's long love affair with humankind. It seems to me that this is one way to understand "God's weakness." He loved us enough to walk smack-dab into the heart of our hatred, our faithless ways, and our darkest fears. In fact, God loved us so much that he laid his life on the line for our salvation.

That brilliant military strategist, Napoleon, once remarked that "the empires of Alexander and Caesar and Charlemagne and myself have failed because they were founded by force; but the kingdom of Jesus Christ abides because it was founded upon faith and love." Which is what the apostle Paul was encouraging his brothers and sisters in the church at Corinth to see. They had made a mess of their communion in Christ. They had become divided over issues that really didn't matter. And they became puffed up with pride in their own individual convictions. Thinking themselves strong, they were actually quite weak.

And we run the risk of doing the same. There are certainly measures of courage and strength that run counter to those made clear in Christ. And yet, even after two thousand years of history, only the courage of Christ remains the most constant source of comfort and abiding strength to stretched and weary souls.

"For God's weakness is stronger than human strength." And God's weakness, said Paul, is revealed in the cross of a Galilean carpenter. That cross, and only that cross, holds the power to prevail over everything life can throw your way. Because that cross carries the Savior whose strength will sustain you.—Albert J. D. Walsh

Illustrations

THE WAY THROUGH THE CRISIS.   Fortunately, God uses many languages. If we do not listen to the "still small voice," he may express himself more urgently in storms and floods, and if we misunderstand him again, he may try to help us by unleashing the earthquake. The language that we understand best is suffering. That is why the mourners are blessed; and that is why suffering, either our own or our friends', suffering of which we may be a cause, is the best and most efficient goad toward self-education.—Fritz Kunkel

DIVINE SUPPORT. The limitless support that men so painfully lack is to be found only in God. Everybody knows that, even the atheists, who, whether or not they realize it, are just a little jealous of the believers, who have in God a last resort through which they can sometimes win victories that would have been impossible for them on their own, and to console them when they are disappointed in other people and with themselves. God is always there, always available, and for everyone, both small and great, unbelievers as well as believers, rebels as well as those who obey him. He is the only support on which we may always rely.—Paul Tournier

SERMON SUGGESTIONS

Topic: What Do We Have to Boast About?

TEXT: 1 Cor. 1: 18–31

(1) Is it human wisdom? (2) Is it human power? (3) Our proper boasting is "in the Lord." (a) God turned the cross to good. (b) God chose even "unthinkable" persons to do his work. (c) God is the source of all that is good in our "life in Christ," verses 30–31.

Topic: How to Face and Foil Temptation

TEXT: Matt. 4:1–11

(1) Don't let physical needs blind you to your duty to God (v. 3 and 4). (2) Don't presume on your standing with God, verses 5–7. (3) Don't imagine you are the recipient of a special revelation of God that will dispense you from rules that apply to other people, verses 8–10. (4) Expect to win the battle and receive from God what you need, verse 11.

Worship Aids

CALL TO WORSHIP. "Lord, who shall abide in thy tabernacle? Who shall dwell in thy holy hill? He that walketh up-

rightly, and worketh righteousness, and speaketh the truth in his heart" (Ps. 15:1–2).

INVOCATION. O God, help us in our struggle to be all that you intended that we should be. Let us not be discouraged by our many failures. Give us grace that will redeem the past, strengthen the opportunities of the present, and give victories in the days to come.

OFFERTORY SENTENCE. "You know the generosity of our Lord Jesus Christ: he was rich, yet for your sake he became poor, so that through his poverty you might become rich" (2 Cor. 8:9 REB).

OFFERTORY PRAYER. Gracious God, we are enriched far beyond all that we can compute, through what Christ has done for us. Grant that we, by his example, might enrich others through what we share of our witness, our work, our prayers, and our giving.

PRAYER. O God, you who are the God who calls. As you called Abraham at the dawn of recorded history, so you are calling us out of our history. With the dispatch that Abraham answered, may we respond. "He went out not knowing where he was going."

Your call is always a call to walk by faith—not by sight. You call us to the open road, to "go out not knowing where we are going," to live with expectancy, to embrace the untried, the not-yet, to perceive the new thing you are doing in our day. You call us to the windswept frontiers of existence, to venture and adventure, to live on the growing edge. You call us "to the road less traveled," for narrow is the gate and disciplined is the way that leads to life.

How we want a faith for the security of the familiar, but you call us to a faith for insecurity, the unknown. We want to tent on the old campground, but you are calling us with the dawn of each new day to break camp and move on. Your call is always to the unknown, to some land of your promise. With Abraham of old, we, too, are pilgrims looking for that city whose builder and maker *you* are.

You call us again and again. May we hear your call loud and clear in the Word spoken so discreetly in this hour. You are calling us to a renewed sense of mission—to "enlarge the place of our habitation," to embrace the inclusiveness of your love, to proclaim your salvation to those near as well as those afar. We pray for such commitment as to grasp with all our mind and heart and person the new day of opportunity that has dawned upon us.

How we thank you for Abraham and all those heroes and heroines of the faith who have modeled for us the pilgrim life! How we thank you for him who in these last days so responded to your call to faith that he chose your will even when it meant his own Crucifixion!

Let us now run with perseverance the course that is set before us looking unto Jesus the Pioneer and Validator of our faith, who for the joy that was set before him endured the cross, despising the shame, and is now seated at your right hand loving us, praying for us, cheering us on.—John Thompson.

LECTIONARY MESSAGE

Topic: Who Is on Trial?

TEXT: Mic. 6:1–8

"If you were charged with being a Christian would there be enough evidence to convict you?" This question asked by preachers for a long time sums up the thrust of this, one of the best-known Old Testament passages. The passage begins with one of many trials of God, implied charges by the people against God. With a Perry Mason flourish the prophet reverses the roles and the defendant becomes prosecutor. Let us, the Church, put ourselves in Israel's place. What would we offer in evidence of our faithfulness? Would we present the high tribunal our worship attendance record, our faithfulness to the communion table, our giving record, our pious language? What would satisfy the demands of God?

I. *God convenes court.* The first five chapters of Micah have addressed the fall of the nation. The nation has suffered the humiliation and physical abuse that is a part of military defeat. In chapter 5 the defeat of the enemy has been promised, but the Lord now moves from results to causes. A great deal of human suffering is self-imposed. God convenes a hearing to examine causes and fault and involves the natural order to serve on the jury.

a. God is not the culprit. Israel has cried out to God, blaming God for the adversity that has befallen them. Individuals and nations follow this pattern. It is so easy to lay at the door of a sovereign God responsibility for every sickness, every loss. God asks, "What have I done to you?" He proceeds with a history lesson, pointing out that God has done "for" and not "to." God redeemed Israel from bondage, sent bold and able leaders.

b. Guilt is obvious. The trial ends for all practical purposes. In true Perry Mason format the witness in the same breath must declare the innocence of the accused and confess guilt. The testimony ends. God is delivering Israel from a mess they have made. Let the complaining come to an end. Let justice prevail.

II. *God's justice.* Justice in the Bible is fundamentally related to righteousness, that is, to things conforming to God's order. God is more concerned with restoring things and persons to their proper relationship than in punishing offenders. The discipline of Israel was always oriented toward redemption, restoration, reconciliation. God reminded Israel who God had been to them in order to impress them with who God was to them.

Civil and criminal courts both strive to find the ideal and restore it. If someone damages your property, for example an automobile, he or she is expected to repair it to the condition it was in before the damage occurred or to pay you what the car was worth. In some cases, such as the denial of human rights, no compensation can restore lost dignity or remove pain and suffering. In criminal cases humans turn to retribution rather than restoration.

Israel sought to make right her wrongs

against God, the violations of the covenant, with ritual sacrifice. God rejected such offerings as worthless. Not even the pagan act of child sacrifice (v. 7) would placate God. God implies that the evil done cannot be undone—only forgiven. Instead of futile efforts to make up for the past, God seeks a fresh start.

III. *A conditional pardon.* God speaks through the prophet what will heal the broken relationship between God and people. God reveals "what is good," that is, the better way of one religion. What is most striking is that two-thirds of the formula for right relationship to God has to do with human relationships. "Justice" requires treating all persons as God treats you. One must respect the "image of God." Application is spelled out in the verses beyond our focal passage. Honesty in all dealings, truthfulness in all matters are essential for the people of God. There is a biting indictment of those who have dealt unfairly with others.

"Kindness" was a much stronger word to Micah's audience than to most people today. It implies love and mercy. We are dealing here with the two sides of the same coin. "Kindness" is justice in action. God asks of God's people more than justice. He requires justice that is tempered with mercy. What is suggested goes well beyond courtesy, to concrete acts of service. Kindness may mean a bedside vigil with one who is ill, food for the hungry, an act that requires inconvenience and sacrifice. It means more than not cheating or exploiting; it implies help and assistance to those who have been cheated or exploited by others.

The first two requirements of true religion—one might say in this case, of true repentance—are rooted in the third, "walk humbly with your God." It is in the continuing presence of God that one finds courage and strength to be just and kind. The new Testament calls us to "walk by the Spirit" (Gal. 5:16); to "walk in love" (Eph. 5:2).

Christianity is a matter of relationships. First, it is relationship to God in and through Christ. Secondly, it is living in right relationship with all of God's creation.—Raymond Bailey

SUNDAY: FEBRUARY FOURTH

SERVICE OF WORSHIP

Sermon: Loving the Obnoxious
TEXT: Hosea 1:2-3; 2:16-20

Among the leading religious news issues have been stories of sexual misconduct among the clergy. We thought that the wave of scandal was over when two prominent TV evangelists went down in shame. The Roman Catholic Church has been struggling with a combination of bad press and some bad priests. Legal advisories have been issued to churches about appropriate guidelines to protect their children. Those who read between the lines know that we are not immune. Hosea seems at home here, yet the scandal takes a different turn from your daily newspaper. I am tempted to take flight to the dreamy world of allegory, to suggest with a sigh of relief that Hosea's story was never meant to be taken literally— perhaps not even seriously. Surely God's servant could never be seen in a brothel—certainly not in search of a wife, certainly not at the command of God. Yet, the word is plain, even if the message suffers from disbelief. Hosea is an embarrassment. The prophet reminds me of the radio evangelist who claimed to have conceived a child of the Holy Spirit. Did the wayward wife come first and the explanation later? Is this about the typical human alibi: "I was just following orders?" Our puritan heritage tends to place sexual misconduct at the top of the hierarchy of sin. Here the offense was more than sexual infidelity. The message of Hosea is about a marriage between two people, but ultimately it is about the covenant relationship between God and Israel. The message is timeless. The love of God revealed in Hosea is epitomized in the suffering love of Christ. This is the kind of love that Christ expected in the kingdom of God. Hosea's love is both a possibility and a necessity for the Church.

I. *Physical and spiritual prostitution are related.* In this world of commerce, some things are not for sale. The attempt to market love is flawed at the foundation. The lewd images of city prostitution in news reports are both repugnant and pathetic. What would cause someone to choose a life of prostitution—drugs, greed, unemployment? What kind of desperation causes someone to seek companionship in the company of a prostitute? The ancient profession is beyond comprehension for most of us, but we have less difficulty understanding the marketplace of ideas and success. Anytime the Church sells her soul for financial gain, immoral social policy, or popularity, the effect is the same. Hosea's persistent love for Gomer reflects the steadfast love of God, but we need to be careful not to spiritualize the story too much. The allegory is not an escape from harsh reality.

Although the sexual behavior of Gomer was as offensive to the eighth-century residents of Israel as it is to us, our perception of the scandal lacks the religious overtones of Hosea's world. Canaanite prostitution was religion-based. It concerned rites of fertility to enhance agricultural production and to maintain control over nature. Gomer was not just another fallen woman; she was probably a temple prostitute. The message of the prophet is about morality; it is more about worship. The repugnance of prostitution is just a fragment of the scandal. Prostitution was a symbol of infidelity in worship. Israel's whoring after other gods seems like a crude form of expression, but it communicated the emotion as well as the fact of Israel's drift into the religions of her neighbors.

II. *Our natural tendency is to seek love in beauty.* Tennyson's "Northern Farmer: New Style" humorously portrays a father advising his son on marriage: Doant thou marry for munny, but goa wheer munny is!" while the horse beats out the rhythm of, "Proputty, proputty, proputty." A few years ago *Psychology Today* suggested a close kinship between "Beauty and the Best." The article indicated that external appearance has a tremendous impact on success and failure. Love, money, and grades seem to be drawn to the physically beautiful people. Who is to love the ugly people of our world? Even churches get caught up in the quest for the best. We were sent out to seek the lost sheep of this world, but we prefer to stay with the flock. Could we handle a visit from Gomer? More to the point, would any of us be likely to reach out to Gomer? We tend to center our attention on the fields that are easy to harvest rather than the fields where the need is greatest. We tend to love the lovely and the lovable and avoid the obnoxious.

Delos Miles remembers hearing someone at church commenting, "Delos will never amount to anything. Look who his father was!" His father was an alcoholic farmhand, and his family lived in dire poverty. Delos told his story in a book he wrote as a professor in a Baptist seminary, *Evangelizing the Hard-to-Reach.* He was among the unattractive people whom he identified as the "left-outs" who sense that "church people aren't like me."

III. *"Beauty is in the eye of the beholder."* The connection between Gomer and Israel has two significant snapshots. Gomer is not so fallen that she is beyond redemption, and Israel is not so redeemed that she is beyond falling. Hosea's personal experience communicates the horror of Israel's sinful chase after false religion, and it pictures the persistent love of God. The loving eye of God can find something beautiful to love even in one like Gomer. Hosea's love for Gomer was a redemptive love. Christian love has the power to bring out the best in the people we love. Christ spent much of his time "in haunts of wretchedness and need" where ugliness, immorality, and greed were more likely than beauty, holiness, and prosperity. He did not come to condemn the ugly but to love them. That sounds a bit like something he asked of us.

Wes Seeliger and Lymen Coleman have found the mission of the Church in a children's story about a handsome prince turned into a frog by a wicked witch. One day a beautiful young maiden came by and gave him a big kiss. Immediately he was transformed again into a handsome prince. The story has a sermonic observation: "So what is the task of the church? To kiss frogs, of course, what else!"—Larry Dipboye

Illustrations

THE INVISIBLY WOUNDED. The Reverend David Smith conducted for many years a column on personal problems in the *British Weekly,* and one question that came to him one day was how to deal with cranks. He replied with these wise and understanding words: "Never be unkind to anyone—not even a crank. When you are about to crush someone who has annoyed you, look before you strike, and when you see what you are about to do, you won't do it. In attacking a crank you may be striking a wounded animal."—Jack Finegan

TRANSFORMING GRACE. Some of the greatest saints had been some of the foulest sinners.

I was reading recently the life of a woman who had been for years anybody's "pickup," and today she is raised to the altar, entitled "saint," and receives the veneration of vast multitudes.

The God who took the foul-mouthed Peter, the bloodstained Paul, the lustful Augustine, and a million lost and undone sinners and made them not just "highly respectable" but made them saints will not deny his grace to you.—W. E. Sangster

SERMON SUGGESTIONS

Topic: Pious Pretense

TEXT: Isa. 58:1–9a (9b–12)

(1) *Situation:* We have an inborn desire to acknowledge and even worship a power greater than ourselves. As it was with the Israelites, tradition and circumstances may confirm and enhance that desire. (2) *Complication:* However, conflicting personal, family, community, or national interests can make our piety a hypocritical pretense (cf. Jer. 2:14–17). (3) *Resolution:* The answer is not more prayers and pious practices but practical, concrete acts or concern and care for others (cf. Matt. 25:31–46).

Topic: What Is Special in the Gospel?

TEXT: 1 Cor. 2:1–12 (13–16)

(1) It is not to be found in human wisdom. (2) It is to be found in God's wisdom: (a) which is God's hidden mystery; (b) which God made known to us; (c) which can be discerned and shared through God's spirit.

Worship Aids

CALL TO WORSHIP. "Praise ye the Lord. Blessed is the man that feareth the Lord, that delighteth greatly in his commandments. His seed shall be mighty upon earth: the generation of the upright shall be blessed" (Ps. 112:1–2).

INVOCATION. God of power, we come to worship this day, to catch the rhythms of grace, the threads of mercy, the directives of Providence, and the power of convictions that seek the salvation of all, through our Lord Jesus Christ.—E. Lee Phillips

OFFERTORY SENTENCE. "Whatever you are doing, put your whole heart into it, as if you were doing it for the Lord and not for men, knowing that there is a master who will give you an inheritance as a reward for your service. Christ is the master you must serve" (Col. 3:23–24 REB).

OFFERTORY PRAYER. O God, take that buried impulse to care for other people and make it grow until we care more and more about more and more people; until through us thine own care is made real and thine own arms support those who are falling.—Theodore Parker Ferris

PRAYER. O Lord our God, we are this morning filled with a sense of our need. And yet, with all this consciousness, how proud are we! How vain are we! We know ourselves to be unlovely; and yet, we walk as if we were monarchs. We know ourselves to be stained with evil; and yet, how do we look with contempt upon those who, around about us, are stained with evil! We are guilty of all manner of sin; and that we know; and yet how do we lord it over men! We wander in darkness and lose our way; and yet, how are we calling to one and another to follow us! We are blind leading the blind; and in the ditch we quarrel, where all of us have tumbled full often. And what is there in us that thou canst love when thou are looking with a feeling of justice? But there is that which is mightier than justice in thee. When thou dost look with refinement and taste, there is nothing in us that is pleasing to thee; but there is that which is mightier than art and beauty in thee. When thou dost look with thy great mother-heart upon us, and thou dost yearn for us, even as children, though we be disobedient children; yea, when thou dost take us in thine arms, and look upon us in the light of eternity, then thy love and thy compassion are mightier in thee than is summer in the earth. Then, though we are defiled, though we are filled with disputing qualities, though we are unlovely to ourselves and to our fellows, and before God, thou dost love us. And this is the mystery of the ages—how Love can love the unlovely. Thou knowest, O God, altogether, thyself and ourselves; and thou understandest what is this mystery hidden from ages. We do not; but we desire to repose in the faith of it utterly. We desire to rejoice that we have a God who is omnipotent by love, that by it he yet will overcome all evil on the earth, and purge it away, that by it he yet shall control the wandering spheres, and bring them back to harmony, and that by it he shall yet establish thy kingdom, and the city thereof whose Builder and its Maker shall be God, and whose name is Love.—Henry Ward Beecher

LECTIONARY MESSAGE

Topic: The Royal Law
Text: Matt. 5:13–20
How did Jesus propose to fill the Law

full? Would it be in the way that Jews had done for hundreds of years? Did Jesus propose to cancel the old Jewish law and introduce some type of libertine program? Matthew wants us to know that Jesus was calling us back to the original purpose of God in giving the Law. Over the years the Law had become a mixture of human and divine commandments.

I. *The will of the Father.* Jesus accepted the authority of the Law, but reserved the right of every rabbi to interpret these commands. He and the rabbis of his day did not always agree. Jesus desired to search and discover God's original purpose in giving the commandment. Once that was found, Jesus required an obedience to God's commandments. He did not teach a freedom from the Law that dominated later Gentile Christianity.

Filling the Law full includes being the salt of the world as well as its light. The Law for Jesus did not include some hyperpride in having kept the 613 Laws of Judaism. Obedience to God was always tied to service of fellow persons in his love. If one is salt, Christian faith preserves and adds zest to life. Your perspective is always directed to the world, and its hurts, finding ways to minister in the name of Jesus.

Light penetrates even into the darkest realms of the world. A power failure in New York City caused that bright metropolis to be shrouded in darkness. That was a frightening sight. The spiritual darkness of our time needs the bright light of God's love. What a surprise! Demonstrating light—showing God's love fulfills the Law.

II. *The Law is eternal.* Matthew, writing at a time when Pauline theology was being misunderstood by some of the Gentiles, is the only Gospel writer to pen these words of Jesus. As Christians we are not free from the Law. In fact, not one jot or tittle; the smallest letters in the Greek and Hebrew alphabet will pass away. Obedience to God's will is very important in the Christian faith. We often neglect this aspect of the Gospel—but it is there! As believers, we cannot rest upon the free grace that brings our salvation. The demand of God is always calling us to holiness, a truth that is emphasized in every book of the New Testament. Paul, in Romans, chides his enemies for stating that he teaches cheap grace. They were passing the rumor that he taught that one should go on and sin to give God the pleasure of forgiveness. With a strong phrase Paul indicated this was not the case! (3:5–6).

III. *Stricter than the Pharisees?* How could Jesus say that? To do righteousness is to do the will of God. Jesus called for a radical obedience to that end that would put even the scribes and Pharisees to shame. This latter group at times concerned themselves more with the outer forms of the Law and kept a checklist on external requirements. Jesus said it would be difficult if not impossible for a rich person to enter the kingdom—much as a camel going through the eye of a needle. There is a harshness to the call of Jesus that is sometimes covered over in pious platitudes.

The teaching of Jesus did not relax the commandments or will of God but rather intensified his hold on our lives. We are not called to an easy religion, nor can we rock our way into the kingdom of God. We are called to a royal law of Christian love and required to obey it.—James L. Blevins

SUNDAY: FEBRUARY ELEVENTH

SERVICE OF WORSHIP

Sermon: As Strangers and Pilgrims

TEXT: Heb. 11:1–3, 8–16

Strangers and pilgrims, strangers and aliens, strangers and foreigners—depending on the translation this describes how one ancient writer characterizes our forebears in the faith. Pilgrims and strangers, they wandered looking, yearning, searching for a homeland. "These all died in faith . . . having acknowledged they were strangers and pilgrims on earth."

What an allusion for us who live in the twentieth century. Strangers and foreigners to homelands form the staple of our time. And we know as we see the array of faces from every corner of the earth on the streets of our own city and delve a little into its history that Boston provides at least a way station for today's strangers and pilgrims.

Yet we know one does not necessarily need be driven from a homeland to live as a stranger and foreigner. We can feel that way at our own address, in our own hometown, in our own skins. Daw Aung San Suu Kyi, for instance, the winner of the Nobel Peace Prize in 1991, under house arrest in Myanmar for pursuing democratic values and polity, is an alien in her own land. And think of those Native Americans, and black men and women of our country, living here for centuries, perceived in so many ways as strangers, exiles, aliens—foreigners in their own land. Talk with a gay or lesbian person these days, and you will meet a human being with a sense of constant displacement.

I. You see, I believe all of us are strangers and pilgrims, regardless of our skin color, regardless of who we are, where we live, where we have come from. C.S. Lewis called this the inconsolable secret in each of us, "our sense of exile on earth as it is . . . the sense that in this universe we are treated as strangers." He goes on: "At present we are on the outside of the world, the wrong side of the door. We discern the freshness and purity of the morning, but they do not make us fresh and pure. We cannot mingle with the splendors we see!"

Is that so? Does beautiful music bring tears to your eyes? How come? Could it be we wish to mingle with the splendor we hear, yet find ourselves on the wrong side of the door? Why are the most wonderful moments of our lives edged with tears? Is there a sense, perhaps, that somehow we are touched by truth or beauty of the loveliness we yearn for—a homeland—just brushing us, yet out there leaving us strangers to its full embrace, pilgrims toward its inclusive welcome?

Just speaking simply about the nature of our lives, we *are* strangers and pilgrims on this earth. We do not like it very much and will try almost anything to deny the truth and ease the pain. Why else all that television, the reaching for a drug, or alcohol, the frantic social life? Having been the father of four teenagers awakening to their sudden realization of being strangers and exiles, Linda and I watched their strenuous, utterly bizarre contortions to prove to their parents and their peers that this is the one thing—*the one thing*—they are not, and if anyone is at home in this world, completely, fully, utterly, it is they.

And more personally, as Linda and I watched the film *Shadowlands*, the story of C. S. Lewis and his later years with Joy Grishom, I found myself struck, as an inveterate reader and near biblioholic, with the assertion, "We read to know we're not alone." Is that why we read? Is that why I read? Strangers. Exiles. And so we go about building our little securities, amassing insurance, forming our networks, keeping up with the latest rap and fashions, staying hip with the newest novel, throwing ourselves into solving the latest problem shrieking from the headlines of the *Globe* or the *Herald,* the *Times* or the *Wall Street Journal,* trying like crazy to master that remote-control gizmo on the VCR, its cousins and progeny—all this and more, so nobody will guess, least of all ourselves, that we are really not at home in this world, that we are strangers and pilgrims.

II. Now friends, here is the beauty part, and I suspect this may be a reason we find ourselves coming into church from time to time. Those who have been claimed by the biblical faith know they are strangers and pilgrims here, but when push comes to shove they are not really worried about it. As our author says, "These all died in faith . . . having acknowledged that they were strangers and foreigners on this earth." This marvelous evangelist, this author to the Hebrews, is trying to tell a group of struggling churchmen and women who face ridicule, contempt, and religious rejection, whose faith is collapsing and whose hope wanes, that the things tempting them, the afflictions threatening them, are but the passing hazards on a road whose destination lies ultimately in the love of God. They are always people of the Way. The problems facing them are simply those all passing travelers risk. They need to keep their eyes on the city without foundations. And when they settled down, guess what? They settled in what are known as "parishes." Parishes! Do you know what a parish is? Well, it is not a body of people who gather on the first day of the week—and, depending on your point of view, perhaps, a social club, a political club, a bevy of hypocrites, a covey of the psychologically crippled—hardly. A parish, as one commentator reminds us, comes from a Greek root meaning "a body of aliens in the middle of any settled community." Is that us? A "parish" on this corner, strangers, aliens, exiles amid this earthly city, ourselves pilgrims on the way to a city where we finally claim our citizenship, a city whose builder and maker is God?

I like the analogy of our life here as if we were pilgrims stopping by at a roadside inn, to be sure, perhaps even an ample and luxurious inn. Most of us know that experience, and most of us delight in it to the extent we know the inn as a stopping point on the way. But we know finally it can be terribly lonely without really a home awaiting us.

III. And living as strangers and foreigners, as our author would have it, does not mean shunning this world, going to a monastery, deciding the criteria for our Christianity is cutting our vices—as personally releasing as that may be. It really means that at the heart of our lives stands a relationship to God, a bridge to One who is really permanent, a connection to a core, a rock, an immovable anchor—what metaphor can we use?—a capital *P* person who counts the stars in the heavens and numbers the hairs on our heads. Grounded in God we find our abiding home. Everything else is transient. We keep our eyes on the enduring city, putting into proper perspective the hindrances distracting us. We find our rooting and grounding in One about whom St. Augustine confessed: "Thou hast made us for thyself and our hearts are restless 'til they find their rest in thee."

Oh, what a difference this rootedness, this citizenship in God can make in our lives! We see it in Paul, who because the gospel of grace rules his life, is able to take shipwreck and beating, jailing, persecution, and betrayal and say, finally, "Whether we live or whether we die we are the Lord's." Paul is at home in this world with all of its tribulation and distress only because he is first of all at home in the love of God that never lets him go. Paul is a stranger and pilgrim here; but it does not phase him in the least. He knows where his true home lies.

IV. Oh, friends, only as we come to know this earth is not our true home can we ever be at home here. Only as we ground our lives in the God of Jesus Christ and the promise of a new creation, setting on the margins the decaying, contingent, and crumbling securities we invest in now, only then can we find ourselves the true security able to bear us through, with joy and purpose, our current exile and alienation. I pray we, like those saints of old, may desire a better country, that is a heavenly one, that as strangers and pilgrims amid this glorious creation, we may look forward to the city that has foundations, whose architect and builder is God.—James W. Crawford

Illustrations

NEW WORLDS. It is an incontrovertible fact that a single happening may permanently change the tenor of a human life. John Keats, at the age of eighteen, was handed by a school friend a copy of Spenser's *Faerie Queene*. No sooner had he begun to read the poem than the soul of the youth was kindled with heavenly inspiration. Instantly, he knew that he was destined to be a poet.

John Masefield, a roving, seafaring lad of twenty-two, happened upon a copy of one of Chaucer's poems. He read it with absorbing interest. That poem became the means of introducing him into what he calls "a glad new world of thought in fellowship with Shakespeare, Milton, Shelley, and Keats."

Jenny Lind, a struggling young music student from Stockholm, one day discovered that she had a glorious voice. Her entire outlook on life was immediately changed. This is how she describes the experience: "I got up that morning one creature; I went to bed another creature. I had found my power."—John Sutherland Bonnell

READY TO GO. The Fiji Islands were called originally the Cannibal Islands. They were inhabited by fierce and treacherous tribes whose main object was to kill and devour their enemies. John Hunt, a young Methodist missionary, went there many years ago. As a young man in England he was studying for the ministry and had just agreed to go to Africa as a missionary. He was engaged to a young woman who was willing to go with him, and what was more difficult, had obtained her mother's consent. Then the missionary society called him one day and told him that they wanted him to go to Fiji. John Hunt was willing, but he wondered what Hannah would say. So he wrote her a letter and told her the change of plans and then waited for her answer. His friend saw how nervous and upset he was. Finally, John told him that he was unsure of Hannah. Then the letter came, and with a shout John burst into his friend's room with the news. "It's all right," he said. "She says she will go with me anywhere."

Something like this happens to men who commit themselves to Jesus Christ and his kingdom. Perhaps the most wonderful part of it all is the assurance that from that moment on, Christ will go with us wherever he wants us to go. It is this assurance that fills us with power and peace. We become partners with God in the tasks that he has to fulfill for our time.—Gerald Kennedy

SERMON SUGGESTIONS

Topic: A Simple, Crucial Choice

TEXT: Deut. 30:15–20, especially 19b

God requires of us, his people, (1) that we consider the options that he places before us—life and death, blessings and curses; (2) that we go the positive productive way: (a) loving God, (b) obeying God, (c) holding fast to God; (3) that we remember his promises to us.

Topic: Getting to the Heart of Things

TEXT: Matt. 5:21–37

Three levels of motivation, all of which are important: (1) public approval, (2) inner attitude, (3) the authority of Christ, verses 22, 28, 32, 34, 38, 44.

Worship Aids

CALL TO WORSHIP.   "Happy are those whose way is blameless, who walk in the way of the Lord. Happy are those who keep his decrees, who seek him with their whole heart, who also do no wrong, but walk in his ways" (Ps. 119:1–3 NRSV).

INVOCATION.   O God, you have marked out a way for each of us. Strengthen us in the assurance that your way, the way always of a pilgrim and often the way of a stranger, leads to you, to your blessing, and to your glory.

OFFERTORY SENTENCE.   "From everyone to whom much has been given, much will be required; and from the one to whom much has been entrusted, even more will be demanded" (Luke 12:48b NRSV).

OFFERTORY PRAYER.   By your gracious provision of our needs, O Lord, we have become more responsible for what we do with what we have. Help us, first, to share our love and, then, in sharing our love, to be more and more willing to bring that love to expression in our tithes and offerings that support and extend your kingdom.

PRAYER.   Strong God, God of love: Your Son Jesus told us that his church would be persecuted as he was persecuted. If we should suffer for righteousness' sake, save us from self-righteousness. Give us grace to pray for enemies, and to forgive them, even as you have forgiven us; through Jesus Christ, who was crucified but is risen, whom we praise forever. *The Worship Book*

LECTIONARY MESSAGE

Topic: The Consequences of Divisions: God Alone Counts in Christian Service

TEXT: 1 Cor. 3:1–9

Throughout the history of humankind and continuing throughout the church age, the problem of who will receive credit representing the division among various groups continues to persist. It appears that part of human nature is to align oneself with a particular group or movement. Especially when the Christians involved are not mature in their walk, more of a fleshly or worldly mentality will predominate. We as a people align ourselves with political parties, candidates, and various ideologies. Members of local congregations are even identified according to the pastoral leadership to which they feel most akin. The Church has known more than its share of conflict surrounding doctrinal positions of prominent leaders and scholars.

The apostle Paul, in addressing the church at Corinth in this first recorded epistle, is gravely concerned, maybe even burdened, by the apparent growing division in this church. The city of Corinth provided an appropriate setting for such a rising conflict. Located on the narrow isthmus between the Aegean and Adriatic Seas, Corinth was a port city and wealthy commercial center. To avoid the dangerous trip around the southern tip of Greece, ships were dragged across the isthmus. Many diverse influences had left an indelible mark on the culture and lifestyle of the city's citizens. Many would have described the city as an immoral place noted for everything sinful.

Division and conflict between the Church and the surrounding community was to be expected, but division in the congregation of faith caused Paul much pain.

As Paul writes, he is undoubtedly disappointed in their conduct. He had preached in Corinth on his second missionary journey. While living and working with Aquila and Priscilla, fellow tentmakers, he often preached in the synagogue until opposition forced him next door. Paul apparently remained in the city eighteen months, and according to Luke (Acts 18:8), "Many of the Corinthians, hearing, believed and were baptized." After leaving, Paul wrote the church a letter that has been lost (5:9), but disturbing news about the believers and questions they asked Paul in a letter they sent to him prompted the writing of 1 Corinthians.

One of the major consequences of their division was that their spiritual growth was being stunted. The Corinthians were choosing to remain in their carnal, fleshly, or infant states. As a result, many of the rewards, benefits, and blessings God promised were about to be lost. These Corinthian Christians are Paul's brothers and sisters in Christ, but as a result of their condition Paul cannot address them as spiritual, full-grown believers. Paul writes and literally speaks to them as persons who have not obeyed the things they have been taught. He addresses them as worldly, mere infants in Christ; baby Christians, if you will.

Indeed, one of the burdens of the present Church is that too many who should be full-grown, mature saints of God, some who have even evolved to positions of authority and leadership in the local fellowship, are yet babies in Christ. Immature Christians who are called upon to make mature decisions and discernments undoubtedly will cause major conflicts within the body of Christ.

Paul uses the Greek word *sarkinos*, which means "fleshly," or "of the flesh." Fleshly Christians are babies in Christ, undeveloped individuals who cannot understand the deeper truths of the Word of God and who are characterized by strife.

Paul writes, "I gave you milk to drink, not solid food; for you were not yet able to receive it. Indeed, even now you are not yet able" (v. 2). Paul scolds them for still living as persons who are not Christians. Apparently, there is still much jealousy and quarreling within this Corinthian church family. Various groups have aligned themselves with Paul's teaching. Others have decided that Apollos with his approach is more effective. Paul concludes that these Christians are conducting themselves as mere unspiritual persons. Factionalism is not of the spiritual person but is of the carnal fleshly nature.

Paul continues his rebuke of their behavior, as some claimed to be followers of Paul, others of Apollos. Who is Apollos? Who is Paul? They are only servants owned by God. Paul planted, Apollos watered, but it was God who kept it growing. Paul wants them to understand that the one who plants or the one who waters is not the important one. God is the important One. God alone is the One who makes it grow. The one who plants and the one who waters are alike. Each one will get his or her own pay. All who serve in the field at Corinth are fellow laborers or workers for God. They are not competitors but faithful allies. All are laborers together on God's property.

A growing, serious issue confronting the Church of today is a demonic competitive spirit. There is an ungodly aligning of believers in various camps. Camps centered on individual leaders. Camps focusing on theological differences. Camps idolizing denominational traditions and even camps that devalue the contribution of other legitimate Christian fellow laborers.

Paul would undoubtedly be gravely disappointed that the body of Christ still often operates as a very immature, narrow, and childish institution. We still major on the minor and often neglect the major.

It is immature. It is fleshly. It is carnal. It is childish to allow the division that continues to hinder the progress of the work of Christ on this earth. As we pray, "Thy Kingdom come, Thy will be done on earth as it is in Heaven," the kingdom's reality on earth is partly the responsibility of the body of Christ coming together to make the kingdom a reality in its fullest.

Division, strife, and jealousy will not be banished from the body of Christ without growth and maturity. Our spiritual food is without doubt the Word of God. Believers must consume and digest the Word. It is the spiritual diet that transforms babes into full-grown, mature colaborers with God.—T. Vaughn Walker

SUNDAY: FEBRUARY EIGHTEENTH

SERVICE OF WORSHIP

Sermon: A Day in God's Realm
TEXT: Mark 1:29–39
When Mark begins his Gospel, he wastes no time in telling us what is at stake. In this first chapter, he gets right to the point. It is the new world God sends; it is Jesus bringing it; it is you and I called to witness to it. And in this morning's lesson we get a vivid image of what God's new world, this so-called kingdom of Heaven, looks like. Mark shows it to us with punch and power.

I. In the first place, what Mark does in the passage is to describe a major portion of a day in the life of Christ. Though this particular passage does not include it, in the immediately preceding passage Jesus begins the Sabbath day teaching in the synagogue at Capernaum. He encounters a man with what Mark calls an unclean spirit. Jesus rebukes the spirit, commands it leave the man, and when all is done, those who witness this occasion remain stunned, for Jesus speaks and acts with a dazzling and radical authority.

Our passage begins when Jesus and his friends leave the synagogue and travel, perhaps for breakfast, to the home of Peter's mother-in-law. She is sick in bed, down with a fever, stricken, as Mark literally writes, with "fire in her bones." Jesus touches her, lifts her up, and she begins to minister to the guests.

Throughout the day crowds throng the stoop of her house. Jesus casts out demons, healing, restoring, renewing. He ends the day exhausted, only to wake before sunrise and retreat to a quiet place, there to commune with the One who offers him renewed strength and power. But those disciples will not let a good thing go. They search Jesus out, they plead with him to get on with the work he interrupted at Peter's house. Jesus will have none of it. He tells them they must be on their way, spreading the kingdom far and wide through word and deed. That is a day in the realm of God.

Now, with all this vivid imagery, with all this demon rebuking, healing, curing, lifting people up, what is going on? Take just the healing of Peter's mother-in-law, for instance. What is Jesus doing? Does he possess the power to kill the bacteria rocketing up his mother-in-law's temperature? Is he messing with her body chemistry? Did he destroy the virus igniting the fire in her bones? I am not sure. I will not deny it. But I think Mark is pointing at something at least as important as he describes for us this singular day in Jesus' life. He is depicting life in Christ's new creation. He is telling us about the purpose of God to affirm us, each and every one, as a full participant in a community of grace and love. He is telling us the dominion of God carries with it, right now, a communion of grace including us all.

You see, I think the clue to this passage is Peter's mother-in-law, rising at Jesus' touch, and, as the passage says, beginning to minister to them. I think the demon-possessed form a crush at her front door, not only because Jesus refutes and exorcises the demon but because Jesus promises to restore to fullness of human discourse those cut off by their illness. The sign of Peter's mother-in-law's healing is her full participation again in the common life of her community. Those crowding the stoop of her house perceive in Christ what Mark proclaims to be a community where disease, sickness, woundedness—whatever the symptoms of separation may be—are not barriers to the full embrace of the love and grace of God. That is life in the realm of God. That is why this realm of God comes as a gift to all of us. Jesus asserts this inclusive realm the very first day of his ministry.

II. What a message! Do you see what it means? The New Testament confirms something we know already: The things that really kill us are the things that cut us off from others. The things that do us in are the things that threaten to isolate, to stigmatize, to diminish our full humanity in the eyes of others and what we may believe to be the eyes of God. In the passage we read this morning, the chasm, the barrier, the wall, the barbed-wire fence dividing us from one another is disease. When Mark wrote this passage, disease sent a message of godforsakenness. Nothing could be worse than illness. It screamed alienation from the love of God. It triggered fearful and terror-stricken resistance and rejection of those afflicted.

So! What does Jesus do but march right into the middle of the diseased, and yes, no less importantly, the diseased as socially rejected. He drives out the demons, quenches that fire in the bones, and restores the marginalized, socially suffering, wounded hearts and souls to sure and certain security and embrace with the community of Jesus Christ.

So what? Who cares? Well, let me assure you this morning that should you be afflicted with some illness, some virus, some physical characteristic the general public either stigmatizes or counts a disability; let me assure you—while not changing the biological components of your condition—let me assure you the world may be against you, but God is on your side and so is God's Church.

But more, just as Mark picks the worst of isolating instances to illustrate the inclusive embrace of Jesus, so we need to be clear that the barriers we build separating us from one another are wiped out, dissolved, cast aside by the love and power of the God of Jesus Christ.

You see, in the realm of God, there is no disease, no prison record, no troubled, tormented ethical dilemma, no past history eating you up, no bout with drugs or alcohol, no blunder with sex, no anguished or even furious division with family or friend—nothing that can turn off the love of God for you regardless of your condition, your status, your mood, your thought, your action. You may be drowning in hell itself—but be assured even if you turn your back on God, the love yearning, searching, banging against your slammed door or trying to worm its way through the cracks around the jamb, clamoring to get to you, will never, never cease.

Hear that? It is why that crowd packed the front yard of Peter's mother-in-law. It is why we call this indefatigable love "good news." Mark crystallized its radical and redeeming consequences for us in a vignette illustrating one glorious day in the realm of God. What a day that was— for Jesus and for that unruly gang on the stoop of Peter's mother-in-law's house. But most especially, for you and for me.—James W. Crawford

Illustrations

GOD GIVES HIMSELF.

> We don't invent God:
>   he reveals himself.
> We don't give ourselves to him:
>   he's the one who gives himself.
> All he asks is that we receive Him—
>   receive him as he is:
>   poor,
>   loving,
>   hurt by our indifference,
>   anxious and attentive
>   to all that concerns us.
> We look for him,
>   and he's told us to believe he was
>   present all along.
> We think we're vanquishing him,
>   and he surrendered so long ago!
>   —Louis Evely

IMAGE OF MAGNIFICENCE.   When you remember the things that you have been striving for during the day and lying awake at night worrying about, most of these shrink into insignificance when they come anywhere near this image of the Man who is the image of the love of God.

When this happens, there begins to be a new life rising in you from below, or coming down from above. Unconsciously your soul begins to take on the form and shape of this Supreme Image of "magnificence."

An actor submits to the demands of a great role, a great character: Hamlet, for example. The actor lives and breathes as a man, yet as he surrenders himself to the character he is to portray, Hamlet begins to live in him, and toward the end of the play, it is Hamlet who speaks, Hamlet who acts, not the man. Paul said, "I live; yet not I, but Christ liveth in me."

Keep in your soul this Image of Magnificence, for this is the secret of the New Life.—Theodore Parker Ferris

SERMON SUGGESTIONS

Topic: Who Wants to Be Holy?

TEXT: Lev. 19:1–2, 9–18

(1) Today, the word "holy" carries certain negative meanings, as in "holier than thou." (2) The Bible, however, defines being holy in a two-fold way, positively and creatively: (a) "You shall love your neighbor [your own kind] as yourself" (19:18); (b) "You shall love the alien [someone different from you] as yourself" (19:34). (3) The reasons: (a) God is Lord and can demand it of us; (b) God is *our* Lord, and he wants us to be like him (19:2).

Topic: The Right Foundation

TEXT: 1 Cor. 3:10–11, 16–23

(1) Our faith and practice are founded upon Jesus Christ alone. (2) We, God's temple, are built carefully upon that foundation and are indwelt corporately and individually by God's Spirit. (3) Therefore, if all is right, everything in the Church is from God, with God, for God, and—derivatively—for us.

Worship Aids

CALL TO WORSHIP.   "Teach me, O Lord, to follow your decrees; then I will keep them to the end. Give me understanding, and I will keep your law and obey it with all my heart" (Ps. 119:33–34 NIV).

INVOCATION.   Do the powerful and mighty thing in us, O Lord, energizing us for service, ordaining us in the deeper avenues of prayer, motivating us to compassion and openness. Make true disciples of us that others may see God in us and glorify our God in heaven, whom now we worship and adore.—E. Lee Phillips

OFFERTORY SENTENCE.   "Honour the Lord with thy substance, and with the first fruits of all thine increase" (Prov. 3:9).

OFFERTORY PRAYER.   Eternal God, from whom we have received generously all things whereof we are glad, we worship thee not only with our substance but chiefly with the offering of ourselves to thee in service. Bless these gifts, the symbols of our sacrifice and toil; enlarge them in spiritual usefulness for thy causes and our needs throughout the world. In Christ's name we pray.—Donald Macleod

PRAYER.   Father of all mercies, whose amazing grace we dare to claim and whose boundless love we long to own, we bow before you in this holy place and plead with you to make us and use us as your will ordains. Ours is a life limited by fears and failures, uneven pledges and broken vows, feeble efforts and exploited goodness. We know what is right, but the will to champion it just is not within us. Lord, our need is for grace to come to us in Jesus, who alone can set us free and show us what to be.

We thank you for your endless kindness, which is constant and real for all who fear and accept your name. In all our thoughts about the long story of Christian living from age to age, we marvel at the certainty of your works of grace. In moments of despair, your grace has come with the gift of hope; in lonely hours of sorrow, the comfort of your favor has brought us through; and when remorse for sin has rent our souls, our way out appeared when we felt justified by your grace. Let praise resound now within this sanctuary as we worship and call upon the whole earth to adore your grace.—Donald Macleod

LECTIONARY MESSAGE

Topic: The Christian's Ultimate Challenge

TEXT: Matt. 5:38–48

The Sermon on the Mount has been called "The Christian Manifesto," "The Christian Decalogue," and by many it is considered the world's greatest sermon. The remarkable beatitudes depict the growth in Christian character. The metaphors of "salt" and "light" indicate the quiet but powerful influence that Christians can have on other Christians and on the world at large. The remainder of chapter 5 deals with challenges from our Lord to his disciples in their conduct with and among their fellow Christians.

Men and women have met and achieved great satisfaction in challenges they have faced.

The challenge given to Moses to lead the people out of bondage in Egypt was a heroic undertaking. And the challenge given to Joshua, upon the death of Moses, to lead the people to take possession of the land was accepted with courage and obedience.

In today's world we read of heroic achievements. The story of Sir Edmund Hillary of New Zealand and Tenzing Norkay of Nepal conquering the storms and bitter cold of Mount Everest on May 29, 1953, the first men to reach the top of the world. We could select men and women in all walks of life who have won their spurs in other fields and with other challenges. But more challenging to us are the words from our Lord given in our text.

Jesus said: "Think not that I have come to abolish the law and the prophets; I have not come to abolish them, but to fulfill them." He came to give them new and richer meaning. He wanted his followers to see the Law in a new light, to reverence the Law of God, for the Law was given to be our tutor to let us know right from wrong and to lead us to appreciate the good news of the gospel of Jesus Christ.

Look at the way Jesus applied this teaching:

I. *Retaliation and Revenge: The Principle of Nonresistance.*

Here again, our Lord presents the old way and contrasts that with this way. "You have heard that it was said, 'An eye for an eye and a tooth for tooth.'" It was the *lex talionis,* designed to help those ancient and primitive people know how to deal with one another and with the enemy. Not on the basis of no limit, such as was seen in the Middle East in the war between Israel and the Palestinians. When one person was killed among the Jews by the Palestinians, they would retaliate by killing five or ten, and then the other side would try to outdo the first.

The law given in the Old Testament was meant to help them to be fair in their justice system. If a man knocked out one's teeth, one had the right to have the offender's teeth knocked out. But he did not have the right to kill him for it.

Now, hear Jesus' way: "But I say to you, Do not resist one who is evil." His was the new and unheard-of way—nonresistance. Myron Augsburger in *The Communicator's Commentary* says of the words of Jesus in this passage (5:38–42) that it "contains the essence of the Christian ethic, and is the distinguishing characteristic of Christian conduct." One should also compare Romans 12:9–21. Who would listen to such as this? "If anyone strikes you on the right cheek, turn to him the other also; if any would take you to court and sue you for your shirt, give him your coat as well; if one (a soldier) forces you to carry his gear for a mile, go with him a second mile. Give to him that begs help, and do not refuse him that would borrow from you." There, in these brief words, Jesus had used illustrations from one's personal life, from the law court, from military life, and from the business scene.

Is it too far out? Is it so naive that you can't believe your ears? Yes, the Master is showing us a new way.

II. *Love and Hate: Another Challenge.*

Note the contrast again in the following: "You have heard that it was said, 'You shall love your neighbor and hate your enemy.' " A part of this is found in the Old Testament: "But you shall love your neighbor as yourself: I am the LORD" (Lev. 19:18b), but there is no word found in the Old Testament that says, "and hate your enemy."

However, the actions of the people toward those who were their enemies indicated there were bitter feelings of hatred toward one another. Our Lord was speaking clearly and strongly to his disciples about such feelings. That was the old way. "But I say unto you, love your enemies and pray for those who persecute you." And he set the example by praying for the ones as they nailed him to the cross. "He kept on praying. 'Forgive them, for they know not what they do.' " Stephen, one of the early leaders, prayed for his enemies even as they were stoning him to death: "Lord, do not hold this sin against them."

Love conquers all. We need it in our homes, in our churches, and in our business and political world.

III. *Be Ye Perfect: The Ultimate Challenge.*

Hear the Master: "You, therefore, must be perfect, as your heavenly Father is perfect." We make a mistake if we think this means sinless perfection in this life. Rather, the Master has given his disciples the perfect goal, the Creator, Redeemer, Sovereign God of the cosmos, for us to fashion our lives, and not some man as good as he might be.

We are to aim our lives toward perfection. We are challenged to fasten our spiritual eyes on the Perfect One. We are to attempt more perfect relationships with God and our fellow man and seek his power and grace to help us walk in his will and way. Our churches, our denominations, our communities of faith, are called to seek the mind of him who gave his all that we might become like him.

The ultimate challenge has been given to us by none other than our Lord Jesus Christ. The gauntlet is down. Who will pick it up and accept the challenge?

Robert Browning said it so well: "Ah, but a man's reach should exceed his grasp, Or what's a heaven for?" (from "Andrea del Sarto")—G. Allen West, Jr.

SUNDAY: FEBRUARY TWENTY-FIFTH

SERVICE OF WORSHIP

Sermon: Finding Our Roots

TEXT: Deut. 26:1–11

The unique contribution of Israel to the scope of world religion was the historical tie to God. When Moses inquired of the identity of God at the burning bush, the response was not only a name, "*I am who I am,*" but a history, "the God of your ancestors." This people had been robbed of their roots by the institution of slavery in Egypt. They needed something more than a new religion and a new destiny in life. They needed to know who they were. They needed to find the source out of which their lives flowed. Long after they had passed through the wilderness to the Land of Promise, the events of God's deliverance continued to be reviewed in song and story. Even their confession of faith in Yahweh reflected the events of the Exodus. Gerhard von Rad identified the confession of the faith in Deuteronomy as the oldest picture of Israel's saving history. This is Israel's root story. It contains no prayer, no invocation or petition to God. The basis of faith was in the events in which Israel was saved.

I. *Purpose grows out of history.* Genealogy has become the avocation of someone in almost every family. Perhaps changes in mobility and communication have improved the flow of information from the past, but the need to know who you are is a discovery most of us make somewhere in middle life. In discussion of the place that Israel learned to call home, the Land of Promise, Walter Brueggemann made the profound statement: "There are no meanings apart from roots." The Bible scholar spoke of Israel's obsession with a piece of dirt on the Mediterranean, but he discovered the failure of urban promise for people here who left home and family to find fortune on the other side of the fence. For Americans of the first half of this century, this usually meant leaving rural roots for an industrial promise in the city. Vance Packard and Peter Berger have chronicled the disillusionment of life in the city. Alvin Tofler labeled the rapid pace of change in the world as "future shock," but he identifies the rootless existence of corporate nomads as a major human obstacle.

The problem is commitment and sense of destiny, but most of our failure is at the bottom rather than the top, at the beginning rather than at the end. Purpose in life grows out of the ground of our existence. Alex Haley's exploration of *Roots* was more than a passing curiosity about the family tree. Haley addressed the struggle of the American black culture to find meaning in life. Slavery was more than a problem of personal freedom; it was a barrier to the past. Black culture in America had been cut off at the historical root. The novelist's reconstruction of his family history, although largely fiction, was an attempt to get to the root of his existence, to know who he was.

II. *Our roots bring us together.* Common roots are the essential ingredient of family. We know our siblings by our parents. Our kind and kin are a source of security in life, which links us to the rest of God's creatures. Genetic family is an essential ingredient to survival for animals that run in packs but also for Homo sapiens, who need the safety of a community where they are accepted and loved. Thus, family concerns not only the genes we share through the common ancestry that we can identify but the experiences we have in common. At the advent of home slides and movies a recurring gag began to appear. The scene is the distressed guest forced to be audience to the amateur photography of the host. This kind of humor links up with the memory

of being a captive audience to photography of someone else's family or vacation. A church anniversary can have a similar effect on the folks who did not experience the beginnings of the congregation.

We do not appreciate history until we have one. Youth is often bored with history. You know that you are getting older when you begin to enjoy remembering the past and you want to go back in place with hope to get a glimpse of a time you have left behind. Nostalgia is a highly personal yearning. It is limited and limiting. It is about you and yours. We feel like outsiders and sojourners when we were born in another place or another time from the history being celebrated, unless we are becoming family. We can get very interested in someone else's family history on the eve of a wedding. In-laws and outlaws can be equally threatening to family identity. Finding someone good enough for your son and daughter may be the concern at the surface, but down deep we realize at a wedding that this is the juncture where two families are joined. Where do these strangers come from?

Church is like that. We make so much noise about being family because we are not. A minor miracle at the root of our existence as a church is the wide diversity of the roots of this congregation. Geography was totally irrelevant in the making of this church. Family and regional differences had to be compromised, and a new center had to be found that was stronger than southern or Baptist. Everyone here was a sojourner, a stranger in a new country; but something changes when we bring our diverse experiences together if we are making a life rather than a visit. We can come together in celebrating a past event only if we are all included in the making of the family.

III. *Roots run deeper than the memory of one generation.* Historical roots gain in importance as personal history grows. In other words, the older you are, the more important history becomes, but the depths of our faith probe deeper than the life of any generation. We have to reach to the bottom of history. The organic metaphor applies. The longevity and stability of trees begin at the root. The longevity and stability of our faith begins at the root. Just as a tree cannot exist just out of last year's growth, the church cannot survive on last year's tradition. Sometimes conservative religion is not conservative enough. Much of what parades as conservatism among Baptists are ideas that have grown out of the recent experience of majority status. Like the historical credo that sustained Israel, the deep roots of our Baptist heritage are deeply planted in the cry for liberty. But just as the heritage of Baptists is deeper than the history of this church, the biblical heritage reaches to depths beyond the name of Christian. Even the traditions that begin at the beginning of our particular history are lacking in the kind of depth that transcends tribalism. We come together as family because we share the same parental root. Our parentage goes beyond Thomas Helwys and John Smythe, beyond Peter and Paul, beyond Israel and Abraham. We are the children of God.—Larry Dipboye

Illustrations

ANCESTRY.   There is no king who has not had a slave among his ancestors, and no slave who has not had a king among his.—Helen Keller

THEY STILL LIVE.   You may bury the bones of men and later dig them up to find they have moldered into a white ash that crumbles in your fingers, Justice Windom said. But their ideas won. Their visions came through. Men and women who gave all they had and wished they had more to give—how can we say they are sunk and buried? They live in the sense that their dream is on the faces of living men and women today. In a rather real sense the pioneers, old settlers, First Comers as some call themselves—they go on, their faces here now, their lessons worth our seeing. They ought not to be forgotten—the dead who held in their clenched hands that which became the heritage of us, the living.—Carl Sandburg, *Remembrance Rock* (Prologue)

SERMON SUGGESTIONS

Topic: Willing Victims
TEXT: Gen. 2:15–17, 3:1–7
(1) The serpent was the foil that exposed the "victims'" own desires: (a) for power, verse 5; (b) for pleasure, verse 6a. (2) Desires became deed, verse 6b. (3) Deed fostered disillusion, verse 7.

Topic: Adam and Christ
TEXT: Rom. 5:12–19
(1) The pervasiveness of sin and death through Adam. (2) The pervasiveness of grace and life through Jesus Christ.

Worship Aids

CALL TO WORSHIP.   "Happy are those whose transgression is forgiven, whose sin is covered. Happy are those to whom the Lord imputes no iniquity, and in whose spirit there is no deceit" (Ps. 32:1–2 NRSV).

INVOCATION.   Help us, O God, to be honest with you, confessing our sin. Grant that we many know the happiness of those whose sin is forgiven, plumbing the depths of your grace. Use this service of worship, we pray, that we may know who we are and whose we are.

OFFERTORY SENTENCE.   "Whoever shares with others should do it generously; whoever has authority should work hard; whoever shows kindness to others should do it cheerfully" (Rom. 12:8 TEV).

OFFERTORY PRAYER.   Now as we open our pocketbooks and billfolds, give us, Lord, a spirit of gratitude, generosity, and dedication, that we may be better Christians because of our stewardship and that Christ Jesus may be made known to many.—E. Lee Phillips

PRAYER.   Whom have we in heaven but you? And there is none we desire upon earth other than you. Our flesh and our heart fail; but you are the strength of our heart and portion forever.

"Great *is* thy faithfulness." Hearing your word proclaimed again on this occasion, we are assured that you are faithful according to all your promises.

From the beginning, your word is a word of grace. With the newness of every new day we are made conscious of the graciousness of your creation from the Garden of Eden to the glory of this morning hour. You did not forget your people in their bondage in Egypt but called a shepherd carefully schooled in the rigors of the wilderness to lead them out and through fifty years of wandering. However the story of their deliverance may be told, it is the story of your grace. For us living in these last days, the fullness of your grace is present in the person, the life, the ministry, the passion, the living again of Jesus of Nazareth. And it is your grace in him as the Messiah that delivers us from the bondage of our Egypt. That this story of your grace has been shared with us by loving parents, faithful teachers, concerned ministers, caring friends, we praise you and give you thanks.

When we contemplate the magnitude of the universe, the worlds beyond our world, the galaxies without number, unlimited space, time without beginning and without end, we find ourselves exclaiming with the Hebrew poet, "What is man that you are mindful of him?" But on second thought we rejoice that you are not only mindful of man, but of men, of persons. That you are not only the great God and the great King above all gods but you are the shepherd of every life. You are here as the Good Shepherd calling us each by name. May we not be so generous with the sermon that we fail to realize it is for us, for me. Your word of grace has our name written on it. Your mighty deeds of old, of today, and in every tomorrow are for our salvation. The story of your grace intersects with our story at the cross as no other place in human history, and we find ourselves praying—what else can we pray?

Nothing in my hand I bring,
Simply to thy cross I cling.

Through him, who is the measure of the faithfulness of your grace and is becoming our prayer.—John Thompson

LECTIONARY MESSAGE

Topic: The Warfare without Discharge

Text: Matt. 4:1–11

No one is safe in the constant warfare with temptation until one attains the crown. All humanity is in the wilderness with Jesus, but like him each must face the tests alone.

You and I are on probation until we have met the Satan that God allows to test us and have resisted him unto victory. Computers offer an illustration of morality. The great power of a computer arises from the choice, for each memory micron, of one of two states—either on or off, open or shut, zero or one. So in morality—good or evil must prevail. If something is not good, it is evil. We have commandments, laws, and ream on ream, book on book of the experience of others to guide us, and their mistakes may teach us. The one big advantage of human life over all others is the ability to profit from the experience of others and not have to experiment with poison to know that it kills.

I. *Temptation to satisfy physical needs.*

a. Jesus first recognized evil in the temptation to do a good thing at too high a spiritual cost. There are three elements a human body needs in order to survive: air, water, and food. In general, depending on present health and condition, one can survive about four minutes without air; one can live roughly four days without water; and one can survive without food for about forty days. After the forty days of fasting, Jesus would feel the pangs that make eating the most essential act possible.

b. But, to prove that he was the Son of God by turning stones to bread was not necessary either for him or for Satan. Satan knows about Jesus Christ. Only humans are foolish enough to question the divinity of Jesus. The test here is to misuse power for purely selfish ends, in violation of the purpose of Jesus' life. Satisfying hunger is natural, not sinful.

But perversion of a divine gift would have been sinful in light of that purpose.

c. Elsewhere, Jesus had been long without food, and his disciples urged him to eat. Jesus replied, "I have meat to eat that ye know not of. . . . My meat is to do the will of him that sent me, and to finish his work" (John 4:32, 34). Here, Jesus mentions the true purpose of his life (see Deut. 8:3), to live by God's word and help others do the same. The essential life is the one of the spiritual person, nourished by God's word, not the life of the body, dear as that is in the hierarchy of human values. Can all human beings ever learn to put the essential life that comes by God's word above the merely convenient and enjoyable? We say, "A person has to live," and that is true, if we mean the life of the spirit, the gift of God.

II. *Temptation to misuse and cheapen the Father's love.*

a. Jesus then revealed how evil it would be to make a purely wasteful show of power for useless and profligate demonstration. Jesus had no need to test the power, or the love, or the willingness, of God to protect him merely to satisfy Satan.

b. Jesus' answer was taken from Deuteronomy 6:16: "Ye shall not tempt the Lord your God, as ye tempted him in Massah." In Massah, the people tempted God, saying "Is the Lord among us, or not?" Can we, like them, not accept God's presence without a miracle? Here again is an example of the choice of good or evil. To live by faith is good; to live by waste, uselessness, and selfishness angers God and disproves faith. Whenever we expect provision by God in a miracle, or when we seek danger in order solely to be rescued from it, we are "tempting" God in sinful ways.

III. *The temptation of unworthily receiving power.*

a. Satan attempts to make Jesus believe that there are shortcuts to accomplishment, to influence in the lives of people, quick and easy control over wealth, goods, and services, without thought and hard work. Success in the acquisition of such "worldly goods" comes so readily to the one who studies and applies intelligent, persevering effort as to seem almost miraculous, without spurious, dishonest, soul-destroying service of evil as a means to shorten the process. "Selling out" is not necessary.

b. Satan did not then nor does he now possess such a world of wealth. His offer is a fraud. Yes, he is in the world. He is the agent of temptation that comes to every person. Graft and corruption, fraud and deceit, lying and cheating are found everywhere in government and business because he promises so much that is not his to deliver.

c. All the world belongs already to Jesus by God's promise (Ps. 2:7–8), but to possess it he would have the hard life of trial and death. And God has promised all things needful to all who put his kingdom and righteousness first. We qualify for the ministry of angels, as did Jesus, by the words of Deuteronomy 6:13, serving God. —John R. Rodman

SUNDAY: MARCH THIRD

SERVICE OF WORSHIP

Sermon: Beyond Rejection

TEXT: Luke 13:31–35

I. Preachers and sermons do not escape criticism. As a matter of fact, one of the classic critiques that I remember was very succinct and very withering at the same time. It went something like this: "First of all, he read it. Secondly, he didn't read it well. Thirdly, it wasn't worth reading." Now just in case we think that those who read such sermons are the only ones who come in for criticism, think of writers. Anyone who has written for publication knows something about critique.

There was a woman who wrote several chapters of a romance novel. She was convinced that this was her best work, so she sent it to a publisher. After what seemed an inordinate amount of time, she sent a wire to the publishing company inquiring about the status of her novel. The wire said, "Please report on my story. I have several other irons in the fire." Finally, there came a reply by wire, collect: "We have read your story. Please put it in with the other irons." Withering. In all walks of life we deal with such disappointment. I thought this week of the career mathematician. Here is a person who works with paper and pencil, sometimes for years, to work out one problem. When Einstein was five years old his father gave him a compass. And he was fascinated by the way it kept pointing north no matter where he stood and no matter how he turned it. From that point on his life was involved not just with the success of problem solving but the string of failures that come from trying one hypothesis after another. Every mathematician or physicist knows about finding rejection before there is success.

Now, you may have noticed that these simple illustrations come from what we call the three Rs; readin', ritin', 'rithmetic. Behind these three is a fourth R, and that R is rejection. If we live, we deal with rejection. It is a part of life we inherit in this fallen world.

II. Just in this past week, I interviewed several people from around the country, and I asked them, "What is the thing that you fear the most?" Almost to a person they said "Rejection." *Rejection*. One of those that I interviewed said, "Why do you think we spend so much time posturing and preening when we come into a new group? Or why do others coming into the same group insist on withdrawing and hiding? It's because we're afraid that we won't fit in, that we will be rejected." He added, "It's junior high all over again." He had a point. It seems to me that all rejection, imagined or real, subtle or dramatic, has a public face and a private face. In this last week, I spent some time with a married couple who are both Presbyterian pastors in southern California. We who pastor don't expect much notoriety; as a matter of fact, we hope we won't get any. Yet these folks lived through a nightmare in this past year. They found themselves in newspaper headlines and their story picked up by all the major networks. It started out so innocently. Their session had worked methodically and patiently toward a next step in their day-care program. They would now more fully incorporate it into the mission and ministry of their church. There would be chapel, there would be teaching about Jesus in an age-appropriate way. It all seemed so reasonable. They wisely allowed an eighteen-month transition for any staff member who did not feel at home with this philosophy to find other employment. Then it broke loose. The morning after the session decision, the reporters were on their front lawn. Soon they were accused of being bigots. Not only was the slander unbelievable, but there were bomb threats, threats on their lives, and they had to move their children from their home to the home of a neighbor. Yes, there was some public support. It came, interestingly enough, because one of the charges was anti-Semitism from the rabbis in that area, who championed their right to teach the faith in their own church. But it was still a nightmare. The worst part was not the public aspect but the private part of dealing with those whom they had trusted and invested themselves in, and they were now feeling from them rejection.

III. As I say these things this morning, I know that it does not fall on deaf ears. Many of you know rejection. Some of you have gone through a painful divorce and feel there is a large *F* hanging around your neck for "failure." Others have been forced to seek new employment. In both of these examples and many others your rejection is public. Coming out of your own experience of rejection we see, almost for the first time, the story of Jesus recorded in Luke 13.

In this scripture that we have read this morning, Jesus is confronted with public rejection. Within this very public arena he will not back down to the threat of rejection, denial, and even destruction. The threat is no less a public figure than the dreaded despot Herod. "Herod, that

fox." Fox means, first of all, a creature
who is sly. Herod, as you will remember,
was very sly and devious. Secondly, it
means one who wants to devour or destroy. The history of Herod clearly reveals that he would kill even his own
family to get what he wanted. Yet Jesus
does not knuckle under. "Fox" in the idiom of Jesus could also mean "insignificant." Even though he thought he was of
all men most significant, he could not
rule and reign over Jesus of Nazareth.
He says, "Go and tell Herod, that fox, I
will cast out demons, I will cure the sick,
yesterday, today, tomorrow and the third
day it is finished." It is completed. The
third day rings in our ears as an affirmation of Resurrection. It is a way of saying,
"I will come through, and God will vin-
dicate me." Did you notice it was the
Pharisees who gave the message that
Herod was after him? Maybe these Pharisees were on Jesus' side; that's entirely
possible. But isn't it also possible that
these Pharisees wanted to get Jesus out of
the way to get rid of him? Jesus seems to
say, Be it "foxes" or "vipers," I will not
take one day off of the ministry that God
has given me. So, we see that in the public face of rejection Jesus stands strong.
However, that strong stand leaves us with
a question: "In what form does that
strongest sense of rejection come?"
That's right, in the private sphere. Jesus
in a very private moment looks down at
the city he would have taken in his arms
and says, "Oh, Jerusalem, Jerusalem."
For this is the city that keeps him at arm's
length.

St. John's Gospel says, "He came to his
own and his own received him not." Do
you know of anything in this whole wide
world that hurts more deeply than coming to the people that you love the most
and being rejected. *He came to his own and
his own received him not.* "Oh, Jerusalem,
Jerusalem." We can hear him say, "I
yearned to take you my scattered children, as a hen takes in her chicks and
broods over them." This Jesus wanted
more than anything else. This was his
greatest yearning and desire.

The first story to illustrate the Gospel I
can remember my mother telling me was
about a farmer who walked out on his
land after a fire had taken that field. He
came across the charred remains of a
hen, and he kicked the hen out of the
way. Underneath were chicks, alive,
chirping and running in every direction.
The hen had given her life for her
brood. Jesus says, "Oh, Jerusalem, Jerusalem; I would have given you all if you
had come to me." This is the story of rejection.

It is more than personal rejection. It is
the rejection of God and God's kingdom.
Is the rejection of God and God's Messiah. If we can keep this in mind, we may
come closer to understanding the enigmatic saying at the end of the story. Jesus
says, "You will not see me until you say,
'Blessed is he who comes in the name of
the Lord.' " It makes sense only when we
realize that Jesus is quoting the heavenly
Father. God says to us, "You will not see
me until you say 'Blessed' or 'Welcome' to
the One who comes in the name of the
Lord, even the Messiah."

It is precisely at this moment that we
see Jesus' strength over rejection. He
who knew the greatest rejection in the
universe found himself linked with something greater and larger than all human
rejection. He found himself in the perfect will of God. It was not by accident,
but by constant intentional surrender to
the Father's will. It is the only way that
we overcome rejection.

IV. For now we see that we are the
ones who reject God. God has been seeking us, wanting us to know him in such a
way that we can enjoy him and know him
forever. We reject him. His invitation is
to all of us. We not only can overcome
the sting and agony of rejection but we
can also when we invite him into our lives
go beyond our unrecognized rejection of
Christ. This is a message also for those
who have already received Christ as Savior, because we run afar afield of God
when we forget that it is only in surrendering to him that we will know perfect
peace. For he is the One who will not reject us. "You will not see me until you
say, 'Blessed is he who comes in the name
of the Lord.' "—Gary D. Stratman

Illustrations

YOU ARE ACCEPTED.   Grace strikes us when we are in great pain and restlessness. It strikes us when we walk through the dark valley of a meaningless and empty life. It strikes us when we feel that our separation is deeper than usual, because we have violated another life, a life which we loved, or from which we were estranged. It strikes us when our disgust for our own being, our indifference, our weakness, our hostility, and our lack of direction and composure have become intolerable to us. It strikes us when, year after year, the longed-for perfection of life does not appear, when the old compulsions reign within us as they have for decades, when despair destroys all joy and courage. Sometimes at that moment a wave of light breaks into our darkness, and it is as though a voice were saying: "You are accepted. *You are accepted,* accepted by that which is greater than you, and the name of which you do not know. Do not ask for the name now; perhaps you will find it later. Do not try to do anything now; perhaps later you will do much. Do not seek anything; do not perform anything; do not intend anything. *Simply accept the fact that you are accepted!*" If that happens to us, we experience grace. —Paul Tillich

WHEN WE CAN LOVE.   I can love only when I meet you where you are, as you are, and treat you there as if you were where you ought to be. I see you where you are, striving and struggling, and in the light of the highest possibility of your personality, I deal with you there.

My own religious faith is insistent that this can be done only out of life of devotion. I must cultivate the inner spiritual resources of my life to such a point that I can bring you to my sanctuary, before his presence, until, at last, I do not know you from myself. The discipline of the heart and the mind and the desire may become a lung through which God breathes. Therefore, if I say I love God and don't love you—I lie. If I say I love you and don't love God—I lie. —Howard Thurman

SERMON SUGGESTIONS

Topic: The Father of Us All
TEXT: Rom. 4:1–5, 13–17 NRSV.
(1) Abraham's faith: His belief in God's promise was the most righteous thing he could do. (2) Abraham's descendants: All who believe—Jew or Gentile—are made righteous after Abraham's example by faith, not by works.

Topic: The Best Thing that Could Happen to Us
TEXT: John 3:1–17.
(1) Jesus' encounter with Nicodemus shows that all—even the most religious—need a birth from God. (2) John tells us how this birth happens: (a) It is because of God's universal love; (b) This love comes to us in Jesus Christ; (c) The miracle takes place when we simply accept what God freely offers in Christ.

Worship Aids

CALL TO WORSHIP.   "I lift up my eyes to the hills—from where will my help come? My help comes from the Lord, who made heaven and earth" (Ps. 121:1–2 NRSV).

INVOCATION.   We are here today, our God, to lay the past week before you:

· the good and the bad
· the beautiful and ugly
· the meaningful and the mundane
· our joys and our griefs
· our loves and our cherished hatreds
· our moments of deep, abiding peace and our devastating anxiety attacks.

Give us the grace to leave it with you. May we go from this place with the desire to please you in all that we do—confident that even that desire is pleasing to you.

Teach us to be the strong face of the Christ to one another. Give us ears to hear the pain of others, eyes to see the needs of others, hands open to help. Show us that only in sharing our mutual woes can we hope to bear our mutual burdens. —Nina Polland

OFFERTORY SENTENCE.   "The silver is mine, and the gold is mine, saith the Lord of hosts" (Hag. 2:8).

OFFERTORY PRAYER.   Lord bless everything about this offering, the giver, the recipient, the potential for God and good and let God's name be praised in its every disbursement and use; as Jesus would want.—E. Lee Phillips

PRAYER.   O God, in whom is neither near nor far, through Thee we yearn for those who belong to us, and who are not here with us. We would fain be near them to shield them from harm and to touch them with the tenderness of love. We cast our cares for them on Thee in this evening hour, and pray Thee to do better for them than we could do. May no distance have power to wean their hearts from us, and no sloth of ours cause us to lag behind the even pace of growth. In due time restore them to us, and gladden our souls with their sweet sight. We remember too the loved ones into whose dear eyes we cannot look again. O God in whom are both the living and the dead, Thou art still their life and light as Thou art ours. Wherever they be, lay Thy hand tenderly upon them, and grant someday we may meet again, and hear once more their broken words of love.—Tileston, *Prayers Ancient and Modern*

LECTIONARY MESSAGE

Topic: God Leads and Enables

TEXT: Gen. 12:1–4a

In the twelfth chapter of Genesis we find what could well be called the hinge of Old Testament salvation history. Almighty God has finished his work of creation, all of which was declared to be good. Then tragedy came as Adam and Eve chose to disobey Jehovah, a choice that brought a curse upon them and all creation. The human situation worsened until it reached its low point in the time of Noah. God wiped out sinful humanity in order to make a new start through Noah's family, but humankind again sank to the depths, as typified in their pride, arrogance, and sinful ambition that led to their constructing the Tower of Babel. It was at this point that Jehovah God set in place the great hinge, a redemptive process that the Lord initiated and has used ever since. He began the establishment of this crux by first of all calling Abram.

Notice! It is God who took the initiative. It is always thus. A caring Lord does not stand idly by when a situation develops that needs action. His creation has fallen into terribly destructive sin, so God moves redemptively to bring his creatures out of the morass of evil that has resulted from their rebellion. All through history this scenario is repeated. His people are suffering under grinding bondage in Egypt, so he initiates a process of deliverance through Moses. His servant, Paul, is languishing in a prison cell, so the Lord sends an earthquake that opens the prison gates. On other similar occasions, God simply sends other believers to encourage his apostle. And this great God is still moving today to deliver or to encourage us, whether in bereavement, loss of job, severe suffering, or some other situation. It was true for Abraham and it is true for us: The loving God responds redemptively to us in all our needs. Out of this reality comes our awareness that we as God's people are to follow the pattern set by him. Since he has taken the initiative to help us in time of need, so must we in relation to those around us.

The form of God's love toward Abram was a call to go to a place that the Lord would show him. No indication is given that Jehovah named any particular place. We know from 11:31 that Abram had earlier left Ur of Chaldea with his father, Terah, and headed for Canaan. They had stopped in Haran instead and remained there until Terah's death. Apparently, since God indicated no destination, Abram chose to head out again toward Canaan. The Lord repeatedly gives us experiences of calling. Some are dramatic and grand. Others are rather ordinary, but God regularly calls or leads us to new experiences of service and growth. He does not leave us to stagnate or to get stuck in a rut. This is one of the joys that belong to persons of faith. But never forget that underlying all of this is the redemptive purpose of the one who calls. And like Abram, we move in the direction that seems best, trusting God to show us his way.

Along with the Lord's leading in Abram's life came a clear promise: Jehovah would work with him in accomplishing the intended goal. "I will bless you," God said. He would even bless those that blessed Abram and curse those that cursed him, a dramatic way of saying that in obeying God's will Abram could always be sure of God's enablement. We, too, have that assurance. A thirty-seven-year-old father of four called his dad to say that God was leading him into the preaching ministry. His dad told him that was impossible, since he would have to

get college and seminary and had no savings. The son replied, "Do you think God would lead me into something and then not enable me to do it?" Indeed! Wherever God guides he always provides. The going may be rough and tumultuous, but the Lord will see us through somehow.

Not only did Jehovah promise to bless Abram, he also made it clear that the purpose of his blessing Abram was so that the blessed one would in turn bless others. All nations were included in this blessing. Abram must not selfishly enjoy the Lord's blessings but was directed to pass them on. In the teachings of Jesus (especially the Great Commission), we who follow him are given the same glorious mandate: to pass the gospel on to all the nations.—W. Bryant Hicks

SUNDAY: MARCH TENTH

SERVICE OF WORSHIP

Sermon: Questions about Sin

TEXT: Ps. 103:1–5; 10–14; 22, John 1:5–10

Many want to say that our conduct—how we live and how we act—is simply left up to us. Morality is fluid, they say. It is in motion. There is no such thing as right and wrong. Each decides for himself or herself what is right or what is wrong.

I. John was no stranger to that kind of attitude. He was dealing with a group of people who are called Gnostics. The Gnostics believed that they had a "special knowledge" about God and life. They asserted that they lived on a superior level to others because of this knowledge. They claimed that either they had not sinned at all or they had no responsibility for their sins, because they lived above them. John was writing to them about the reality of sin and the darkness that sin brings within one's life.

a. There are those who say: "Well, just let me make my own decisions. I will decide. My conscience will determine what is right and wrong for me. I do not need

any church, any God, anybody telling me how I should live or how I should act." I guess my problem with that approach is that I am troubled with some people's untroubled conscience. Some people's consciences will let them do anything anyplace or anytime. I am very troubled by those who want to say, "I will let my conscience by my guide," because the history of the world is filled with pages stained by blood based on individual decisions about right and wrong.

b. There is no question in my mind that some guidelines are essential for meaningful living. Yet, like the early Gnostics, we want to cry out and say, "I am not responsible for the sins of society. I am not responsible for my own sin. I am really free from blame."

In our society today some of us almost always want to say "not me." We point to somebody else for the blame. We are more sophisticated today. We know how to place some responsibility. We blame heredity. We blame the environment. We blame illness. We blame circumstances or emotions or somebody else. It is always somebody else's fault. We do this individually, and we do this as a nation. We continuously pass on our faults to somebody else.

II. Sin is the reality that leads, the Scriptures declare, to death. Sin, in all of its seriousness, creates death within our authentic self, death in our relationship with other people, and most profoundly it has separated us from God. The Scriptures are very clear about the darkness of sin. "The wages of sin is death" (Rom. 6:23). Sin threatens our sense of life's meaning, and our self-centeredness results in death. Death is the consequence of a meaningless life that has lost its sense of direction and purpose.

a. God has created the kind of universe in which sin is possible. When we sin, God doesn't reach over and say: "Ah, I saw you do that and I'm gonna get you." We crush ourselves instead against his laws. He has created a universe in which there are natural laws. There are also moral and spiritual laws. And when we violate them, we feel the repercussions of our actions. For example, suppose I drink too much and become intoxicated, then get into my automobile and drive down the highway at some breakneck speed without control because I am drunk. Whether I want to or not, the laws of motion and stability will be enforced. If I run into a tree, whether I want to or not, my car will crash and I may be hurt or killed. Or because of my high speed, I may kill other people.

b. God doesn't will that, but God permits it. He gives us freedom to do his will or to violate it. He gives me the freedom to abuse my body or to make it stronger. He gives me the freedom to try to learn to do good or to do evil. He gives me the freedom to try to live a moral life or to live an immoral life. God does not force me to conform. When I violate the moral and spiritual laws that are built into the universe, into my life, and into relationships, I often can get hurt. Or I may hurt other people.

c. Though we may receive forgiveness, and hopefully we will, that does not remove all the consequences that may have resulted from some sinful act. When the prodigal son came home, he was forgiven. But his forgiveness would not undo some problem he may have created in the far country. If he became involved with some young woman and she became pregnant, his forgiveness would not undo that act. Or if he was engaged in some fight, and he lost a hand, he could receive forgiveness from his father, but his hand would not be restored. God forgives us, but sometimes the consequences of our sinfulness may go on for a long time.

III. Sin has created a sense of brokenness within us between God, ourselves, and others. Sin has separated us from our true and authentic self. We have been distorted by sin, and sin has distorted our relationship with other people. But God, in his forgiveness, offers us an opportunity to build a new bridge, to restore our broken relationship with him, to help in the restoration of our relationships with others, and to help pull our broken self together. The word salvation means wholeness or fullness. God brings us back together as the authentic persons he has created us to be. His redemption restores us with the quality of life that we were created to have. He reveals to us what we can be through the power of his redeeming love.

a. Unlike persons to whom the Epistle of John was written, we do not want to set ourselves as the standard for morality. John wrote them, "If we say we have not sinned, we make him [God] a liar, and his word is not in us" (1 John 1:10). When we begin to say, "I will be the judge of what is right and what is wrong," that becomes very dangerous. That is partially what is wrong in our society today. We have allowed movies, television, and magazines to determine our standard of morality. And that standard has fallen to the lowest level. Our society has been pervaded with immorality. But that still does not make it right. Just because some say it's OK to cheat, or some say it's OK to steal, or some say it's OK to murder, that does not make it right. If all society begins to follow the direction of the lowest level or morality, then we will have chaos. Our society will break down, and life will have no meaning.

b. A higher standard, however, has

come into the world and provides guidance for our lives. Now we judge life not by our personal standards but by the morality of Jesus Christ. I think the Swiss theologian Karl Barth is correct when he says we begin measuring our life not by Christ. When we measure ourselves by Jesus Christ and his standards, then we begin to see how far short we have fallen. The same One, by whom we measure our lives, is the very One by whom we experience authentic life. Through his righteousness and love, we find forgiveness and grace, and we are able to go on. He has lifted before us the standard on how we should live. He has forgiven us when we have fallen short, but he continuously gives us the strength and courage to follow him.

c. The Psalmist exclaims in Psalm 103:2–5 that we might experience the forgiveness of God in a pit of perdition where we feel we have encountered complete ruin or irreparable loss. Or we may meet God's forgiveness in the depths of death itself. God comes to us and liberates us from our sin. He lifts us up to face life in a new way. Our sins are removed by God "as far as the east is from the west." When God's mercy and forgiveness have had opportunity to work in our lives, our sins are distanced from us.

IV. Our lives can sometimes be twisted, distorted, and broken. But, like clay, they are placed in the hands of the eternal God who is at work in our own lives. Through his loving, forgiving presence, he takes our life, which may be misshapen, distorted, twisted, broken, or annihilated. He reshapes it into what he has created us to be—full, authentic persons. Sin is serious business, but the marvelous good news this day and every day is that in Christ we have found forgiveness and we can begin anew. Let us go on with the journey.—William Powell Tuck

Illustrations

SIN AND IDOLATRY.   St. Paul, speaking of the perversion of man's life through sin, climaxes his argument by pointing to idolatry as the source of the trouble: "They exchanged the truth about God for a lie and worshipped and served the creature rather than the Creator." It was surely no accident but a very profound truth about the human condition that caused to be placed first among the Ten Commandments the injunction: "You shall have no other gods before me!"

Needless to say, idolatry is not just a kind of mistaken belief, a failure to understand "how things are." Like faith, it is an attitude of commitment, and indeed idolatry is a kind of perversion of faith. It has the same motivation—the inherent quest for meaning and selfhood. But idolatry can lead only to the stunting and distorting of the self, as was indeed seen very clearly in the Old Testament.—John Macquarrie

THE TIME FOR FORGIVENESS.   I was pastor once of a church that was located a few blocks from a college. We drew a number of university students to our church for worship. I got to know some of them well, and others were total strangers. One day I was called to the hospital to visit a young woman whom I didn't know. She had attempted suicide. I went to the hospital and talked with her. She had tried to commit suicide because she was pregnant and didn't know what to do. I talked with her at some length and persuaded her that the thing she had to do was to talk with her parents. I went back to the church and called a friend of mine who was pastor in the town where she was from. I asked him if he knew her parents. He did. In fact, they were members of his church. He told me that he had been playing golf that afternoon with the young woman's father. I asked him: "How will he react?" "I don't know," he said. "He has an explosive temper." "Tell them to come by and talk with me before going to see her," I suggested. They did. Then, they went to the hospital to see their daughter and embraced her and loved her. They knew that it was not the time for condemnation, not the time for rejection, but the time for forgiveness—the time for saying, "Let's begin again." The Scriptures declare to us that, although we are sinners who have all sinned and fallen short of the glory of God, God, nevertheless, reaches out his loving arms and draws us unto himself and says, "I forgive you."—William Powell Tuck

SERMON SUGGESTIONS

Topic: Is the Lord among Us or Not?
TEXT: Exod. 17:1–7, especially verse 7 NRSV
(1) Who asks such a question? God's own people. (2) Why do we ask such a question? (a) We may be afraid. (b) We may be suffering. (c) We may be disappointed. (3) What does God do about our plight? He goes on being the same gracious God: (a) caring for us even when we see no evidence of it; (b) sometimes giving dramatic answer to our complaints or prayers, undeserving though we are.

Topic: Why We Can Enjoy Peace with God
TEXT: Rom. 5:1–11
(1) Through God's grace we have been justified by faith. (2) We confidently expect to share the glory of God. (3) We are prepared to face anything with God's love in our hearts.

Worship Aids

CALL TO WORSHIP. "O Come, let us sing unto the Lord: let us make a joyful noise to the rock of our salvation" (Ps. 95:1).

INVOCATION. Enable us to realize that being here in this sacred place is a privilege, Father. Thank you for the freedom that allows our gathering. Thank you for the habits that bring us together. Thank you for the Lord, in whose name we pause and worship. Pray, may this not be an occasion when we are here in the body, but absent in spirit. Show us all how to bring our minds and spirits from the faraway places to which they so often wander, that we may worship you with all our faculties—mind, body, and soul. Remove all pretense from us and lead us to genuineness like unto our own.—Henry Fields

OFFERTORY SENTENCE. "Bear ye one another's burdens, and so fulfill the law of Christ" (Gal. 6:2).

OFFERTORY PRAYER. Lord, forgive us for withholding what we ought to share, thereby denying others the joy of knowing the presence, forgiveness and love of the Savior in whose name and love we give. . . —Henry Fields

PRAYER. Eternal God, Father, Creator of all things, we bow in humble trust this day. We acknowledge our weakness and sins and ask for your forgiveness. Give us the strength to live lives that reflect our devotion to you. We affirm the moral laws you have established and seek to live by them. With Christ as our example, we want to live our lives in love and concern for you and others. Guard our path, lest we stumble and fall into the alluring ways of evil. Fortify our backbone so we can withstand the temptations that call us away from your way. Increase our faith to trust you and your moral laws when persons all around us deny them and compromise them.

Strengthen this day those who are sick in body and spirit, those who bear the heavy loads of grief, those who long to serve you but lack the courage, those whose burdens of loneliness, pain, and personal struggle seem to have brought them to a dead-end street. Open a new door of grace and opportunity for them.

We come to meet you in this service. Feed us with the abundance of your grace. Sustain us by your eternal love. May we leave this place nourished by your abiding presence.—William Powell Tuck

LECTIONARY MESSAGE

Topic: What Is Worship?
TEXT: John 4:5–42 (21–24)
Religious people have applied the word *worship* to many different experiences, but have they truly worshiped in a biblical sense? Today some are construing religious entertainment as worship. The Samaritan woman whom Jesus encountered at the well in John's Gospel

based her worship upon the superstition that God is confined to a certain physical place. Even today there are those who isolate God to certain places where they have had a special spiritual experience. Religious services in many cases have degenerated to a spectator experience rather than one that seeks to encounter the mystery of God.

A key factor in understanding worship lies in the proper relationship of God to the individual. Some treat worship as a human endeavor that can take place anytime they please. Others approach worship as an opportunity to encounter God as the great mystery that moves and makes a difference in their lives. Worship is the response of the Christian to a self-revealing God.

I. *God in worship.* All true worship begins with the self-revelation of the Divine. It is God's idea to come to us. God is the prime mover, and we cannot meet the Divine on our own if God does not move first. Worship is an experience that is primarily with God and not other humans.

Søren Kierkegaard in *Purity of Heart* gave an excellent contrast of Christian worship and a performance of a public play. He stated that in a Danish production there were three main parts to a presentation: the people in the audience, the actors on the stage, and those who prompted behind the scenes. When it came to worship, Kierkegaard saw a reversal in the role of each participant. The worshiper was the actor and God was, to Kierkegaard, the audience. The worship leaders were the promoters that helped bring the two together. He felt that worship was not something done by the worship leaders for the sake of the worshipers; it was, rather, what the worshiper does for God out of a deep reverence. We must never forget that worship is directly related to God and the transaction that God initiates with the individual. Worship when it is focused first toward God becomes a life-changing experience.

We pause before God to adore and worship. Many do not know how to delight God. God loves us because of the great investment in us and not because of what we will return in response.

II. *The worshiper in worship.* In worship we must confess or declare our sins. We stockpile sin because we have not emphasized confession of sin. We many times just ignore our sins. If sin is an offense in the world, how much more is it an offense in the sight of God? Prayer and repentance comes before renewal. When we hold on to our sins we lose the joy of our salvation. If we confess our sins, God is faithful and just to forgive us our sins and to cleanse us from all unrighteousness. When one is forgiven of the heavy load of sin, life seems to explode with joy and gladness.

We hesitate to live God's way because we have not heard the Divine speak to us. A vital part of worship is being still and hearing the voice of God. Then we know what we should do to show our love for God.

Worship without dedication and commitment is empty. We need to consciously consecrate our lives to God. "Thy will be done" is part of real worship.

III. *The results of true worship.* God will commission and authorize us to go out and make a difference in this world. We will feel a new sense of urgency to begin something new and fresh.

Worship, when truly experienced, will become one of the most important transactions of our lives. We are to remember that apart from God we are nothing. Worship is in every sense a deep relationship with God.

It is a dreadful thing to fall into the hands of an angry God, but on the other side of the coin, it is a joy and blessing to be touched by the hands of a loving and caring personal God. God's mercy can be a significant experience for each of us.

Worship is not an insignificant way to spend time in our busy week. When you engage in worship, the reality of you and the reality of God interact, and hopefully something wonderful takes place in your life. Worship is a time when you are in communion with your Creator. It's a time when we come together.—William P. Cubine

SUNDAY: MARCH SEVENTEENTH

SERVICE OF WORSHIP

Sermon: Things to Remember
Text: Ps. 137:5–6
Much of Christianity has gone out of our Christian civilization. We can clarify our thought by going back to the words of a man who lived long ago. He was an exile and prisoner in Babylon. He soon found himself confronted with an inescapable problem. He lived in an unfriendly world. Nothing was conducive to his faith. Nowhere was there any support from social circumstances. The low level of his moral environment was a constant threat to his inner life. There was only one safeguard. It was his memory. He clung to it desperately. Every day he would enter upon the same act of consecration and say, "If I forget thee, O Jerusalem, let my right hand forget her skill. Let my tongue cleave to the roof of my mouth, if I remember thee not; if I prefer not Jerusalem above my chief joy." This act of remembrance became a holy ritual.

Is our situation so different? It is not easy to be a Christian. The social pressure is heavy. If we witness the decay and breakup of great institutions, is it not because of indifference of our day has infected us as though it were a virus? Is it not, in part, because we do not do what the Psalmist did in Babylon? Is it not because we will not perform this holy ritual of remembering, wherein we link ourselves again and again to the things we desperately want and seek to preserve? We have been lured away from the path on which we traveled. We have found new values and put a new esteem upon new practices. Many things have come between today and our early earnestness, until there has been created at the heart of this generation a blank; and neither nature about us nor human nature within us can tolerate a blank. It must be filled up. It has been filled up. What has happened is a tragedy. We have forgotten, and our yesterdays are shrouded by distance and indifference.

I. Consider the case of the children of this generation. It is an unpalatable fact that more than two-thirds of our children are brought up without any Christian teaching.

a. Who are the parents of these children? In most instances, they are nominal Christians. In many cases, they are members of our churches. Not only will they not teach their children the truths of our Christian faith; they are sufficiently careless that no one else may teach them. They have forgotten something. They have forgotten that not so long ago they stood in a church and gave answer to this question: "Do you promise in the presence of God and before these witnesses to bring up your child in the nurture and admonition of our holy religion?"

b. What has come between these parents and that other day? What other values have crowded in? What has obliterated "the memory trace"? Somewhere you discover parents who have been inordinately selfish. It will not do to say that they will not coerce their children religiously. It will not do to say that they refuse to indoctrinate their children. This is mere rationalizing. When you find yourself getting careless, enamored of your own wants, remember what you said then. "If I forget thee... If I remember thee not above my chief joy..." What you said then is something to remember.

II. Consider now the second fatality that has befallen our generation—our broken homes. To speak of them is not merely to give expression to a social phenomenon that is almost unique to this century and does violence to the whole spirit of our Christian religion.

a. Time was when divorce was an extremity; when it was release from an intolerable condition that threatened the soul of a man or woman. Now, in most instances, it has become an escape from boredom, or the refusal to bear responsibilities, or sheer flight from inconvenience. One wonders whether people who launch forth into divorces ever turn back to the day when they repeated their marriage vows. You remember them: "I... take thee... to be my wedded wife; And I do promise and covenant; Before God and these witnesses; To be thy loving and faithful husband; In plenty and in want; In joy and in sorrow; In sickness and in health; As long as we both shall live." Whatever tragedy has befallen people, whatever hardships have come near unto them, and however difficult married life has turned out to be, in that moment there was no question of insincerity. At that hour, people meant what they said.

b. Marriage is built upon the ability and upon the flintlike determination never to let the sun go down upon an angry word or a difference of opinion. Even married people cannot always see eye to eye. I have been told that there are married people who never have any differences of opinion, but I must confess that they have never lived in any community where I have been. Invariable agreement is not the secret of marriage. The secret of marriage, in this respect at least, is the ability to see things for what they are, to keep differences of opinion within the bounds of their meaning, and not to make molehills into mountains. Marriage is built upon the understanding that whatever transpires in a home belongs to two people—not to this one or that one only.

c. What has happened to people between today and that other day when they repeated these words: "In plenty and in want; In joy and in sorrow; In sickness and in health?" Shall we rationalize and say that difficult times make marriage impossible? Shall we say that too many were too young? It is good to be young when one is married, but there comes a time when young people must stop being adolescents and become adults. Or shall we insist that marriage is so slender an institution that it can no longer endure the strain of these disorganized days? Rather than stoop to recrimination in burdensome and trying times, turn back to that hour and to those words: "In plenty and in want; In joy and in sorrow; In sickness and in health." Say it often—say it, as you said it then!

III. Consider now the third fatality that has befallen our generation—the millions who have fallen away from the Church. What has happened to these millions is a story of unparalleled sadness.

a. No matter how large a congregation, one cannot help but wonder concerning the many who are not here and ought to be here. It will do no good to say that one ought to be content with the many that do come. That is cold comfort. Do you recall the story of Jesus concerning the ninety and nine who safely lay in the shelter of the fold? One was missing. It was that one that brought concern. It was that one that led that shepherd forth upon a heedless search.

b. Have those who have become so casual in their religion and in their relationship to the Church forgotten what they said when they took upon themselves the Christian vows? "I accept Christ as my Lord and Savior, and I do promise to be faithful in the observance of my Christian duties and to support the Church with my strength and my possessions." Were these words uttered in a momentary flurry of enthusiasm? Did they not then believe that it was good to walk in the Christian way?

c. No, the things we said yesterday were not empty phrases; they were not mere formulas; they were the symbols of holy intentions. They are still powerful factories, and, as we repeat them again and again, they may become the means of searching out our own hearts, and therein lies health.

IV. There are things to remember. I am speaking to you who are young—you who have crossed the threshold of marriage. Don't let life spoil it for you. I speak to you who are thinking of marriage. Weigh it soberly, this word you will be asked to repeat—then hold it in that shrine within yourself. I speak to you who have little children. Don't let life spoil your opportunity. Repeat these words that you uttered when you brought your child to be consecrated in baptism. I speak to all of you who sometimes grow careless about the inspiration you need to live. Cling to the Church.

You are the Church. For good or ill, for better or worse, you are the Church. And when the storms blow and the road is rugged, open the window toward the west and look out. There are things to remember. There really are.—Arnold Lowe

Illustrations

A COSMIC EVANGEL. Every ancient religious philosophy—however powerful and satisfying, to its initial devotees—gradually lost its grip. Inevitably, it just stepped down from one phase of influence to the next lower—a peculiar katabasis like that of radium. At first it was a religion, an inspiration; then a morality, an ethic; then a liturgy, a ceremony; then a relic, a fossil: a museum piece.

In the case of the gospel, there not only was no fading out of the philosophy of Jesus, but an increasing glow. He did not offer a gospel that was good for an era, or a localized area—a gospel that would presently become outmoded and obsolete. It was a cosmic evangel, with the flavor of eternity saturating it.—Lloyd C. Douglas

THE UNFORGETTABLE CHRIST. The healing touch of Christ upon your life and mine, the redemptive touch of Christ upon modern life and society, that is our great hope for casting out the false gods and for breaking every idol down. Jesus comes today to a society quite aware that "his word was with power," but that also prefers to evade the spiritual decisions he would urge upon it. He comes to fill the vacuum in your life, to heal its witheredness. Let his command quiet the fury of your life this day. Hear him speak peace to your turbulent soul. Greet him as the worker of wonders from Nazareth, ready to transform your tangled being; as the Holy One, ready to show you to moral victor; as the Redeemer of your soul, ready to deliver you from sin and death. Let the fame of him surge through your life, through your home, through your street, through your city. Why send him on—on to some neighbor's home, when yours is Christless? Why send him to an-other street, when your own needs his visit and work and presence? Why send him to another city, to another land, through your neglect, when through your response and obedience his fame can go through every place of our own region round about?—Carl F. H. Henry

SERMON SUGGESTIONS

Topic: A New Identity for You

TEXT: Eph. 5:8–14

(1) What you were—darkness. (2) What you are—light. (3) What you can do: (a) "Try to find out what is pleasing to the Lord." (b) Expose wrong for what it is. (4) What Christ will do: "Christ will shine on you." Cf. Matt. 5:16.

Topic: Deepening Insight

TEXT: John 9:1–41

Like the blind man, we may gradually experience richer insights into the significance of Jesus. (1) We may see him as a man, verse 11. (2) We may see him as a prophet, verse 17. (3) We may see him as a special person from God, verse 33. (4) We may at last bow before him as Lord of our own life, verse 38.

Worship Aids

CALL TO WORSHIP. "The Lord is my shepherd; I shall not want" (Ps. 23:1).

INVOCATION. Today, O God, help us to reclaim our heritage in Jesus Christ and his truth. We thank you for the provision for our spiritual needs in him, so that we lack nothing essential to a victorious life amid the seductions and perils of our times.

OFFERTORY SENTENCE. "Live in love as Christ loved you and gave himself up in your behalf, an offering and sacrifice whose fragrance is pleasing to God" (Eph. 5:2 NEB).

OFFERTORY PRAYER. Here are our offerings, O Lord. As we try to live in love, help us to find ways and means to bring our love to worthy expression. By your grace multiply what we bring that many may be fed the Bread of Life.

PRAYER. Compassionate God, you have taught us that you are love, and that those who abide in love abide in you. And you have taught us that if we say that we love you, and hate our brothers and sisters, we are liars, for if we cannot love our brothers and sisters whom we have seen, we cannot love you whom we have not seen. Save us from lives of hatred, the festering sores of old scores carefully kept; the brain-dead unresponsiveness to goodness and joy; the musty, dead air of lovelessness; the sulfurous, toxic stench of lives bathed in anger. Compassionate God, you are the true vine. Remove every branch that bears no fruit, and prune every fruiting branch that it may bear more fruit. You, in whom there is no darkness, enlighten us until we are altogether your sunward vines, and bear much fruit, more than anyone would have dreamed, anyone but you.—Peter Fribley

LECTIONARY MESSAGE

Topic: God and Human Leadership

TEXT: 1 Sam. 16:1–13

Most people at times question whether or not God is involved in history or provides leaders for human political or religious groups. Such questions are particularly intense in times of major historical crisis.

Israel faced this problem during the time of transition between the reigns of Saul and David. God removed his blessing from Saul and through Samuel anointed the shepherd boy David as Saul's successor. Even though elements of the story are far removed from our time and modern Christian standards of behavior, it teaches some valuable lessons about God's activity in history and his provision and expectations of leaders for the people.

I. *Leaders as servants of God.* In the divine ordering of history, leaders are the servants of God. It was a turbulent time in Israel. Saul had won a great military victory over the Amalekites. Strange as it is to modern ears, Saul thought that he had been commanded by God to kill all living beings, animal and human, and destroy the possessions of the defeated enemy. Yet Saul disobeyed God. He spared the life of King Agag and allowed his army to loot the material goods and keep the best of the animals. Samuel the prophet stormed onto the scene. He announced that Saul would be deposed as king and then himself hacked King Agag to death. Remorseful, Saul pled with Samuel to perform a sacrifice to the Lord. Following the sacrifice, Samuel and Saul departed, each never to see the other again.

The writer states that God grieved that he had ever made Saul king of Israel. Leaders anointed by God do not always do the will of God. Leaders, civil or spiritual, do not have a blank check to operate with impunity outside God's will for humanity and his redeemed people. In God's historical activity, the wheels of God grind slowly, but they grind exceedingly fine. Either in history or in eternity, God holds leaders accountable for their obedience to his will for the human family.

II. *God's provision of new leadership.* God, often working in mysterious ways, provides new leadership at the appropriate time. As Samuel was grieving over Saul, he was commanded by God to go to Bethlehem to anoint a new leader for Israel. Fearing Saul's vengeance, Samuel disguised the true purpose of his trip by taking a heifer for a sacrificial ceremony with the family of Jesse. The details are intriguing as Jesse fearfully met Samuel, Samuel performed the purification rites, the sacrifice was offered, and the sons of Jesse were paraded before Samuel. Finally, the young boy David was called out of the pasture. When David appeared, God disclosed to Samuel that this was the future king. Saul anointed him, and he was filled with God's spirit from that time on.

Still, it would take some years of growth before he would publicly assume his kingly role. Saul's madness had to work itself out in his final years. David became Saul's harpist, the vanquisher of

Goliath, the leader of Saul's army, and finally a fugitive from Saul's wrath—all before he succeeded Saul as king. During those last debilitating years of Saul's reign, David was waiting in the wings, maturing, developing his skills and wisdom, preparing to become Israel's greatest king.

Leaders are never indispensable. Saul is an example. God is mysteriously at work in the background or in the shadows preparing each generation's leaders. In God's own good time, they will be anointed and assume their role in the civil or religious worlds.

III. *God's criteria for leaders.* God's criteria for selecting human leaders differ from our human standards. Jesse must have been surprised that his youngest and smaller son was God's choice for Israel. The story notes the dramatic procession of Jesse's sons before Samuel. Even Samuel guessed wrong. When he saw Eliab, a man of impressive height and stature, Samuel was sure that he was God's choice. Then he heard the voice of God say, "The Lord sees not as man sees; man looks on the outward appearance, but the Lord looks on the heart" (1 Sam. 16:7).

Often great civil leaders or spiritual leaders have not possessed the most handsome looks, impressive intellects, social skills, or public charisma. In the case of David, he was ruddy, meaning perhaps that he was redheaded, and he had beautiful eyes and was handsome. But he was not as physically impressive as many of his brothers. That story has been repeated in many generations both in society and in the Church. When God chooses leaders, they often are a surprise to those who measure people by the world's normal standards. Some may be highly gifted. Others may not possess many qualities prized by society. There remains a mystery about how God raises up leaders.

IV. *God's anointing of leaders.* The best leaders depend not only upon natural gifts but upon the divine anointing. Even as a boy, David displayed unusual qualities as a sheepherder in protecting his flock against lions and wolves. When Israel was quivering in fear from the challenge of Goliath, David faced the enemy armed only with a slingshot and wearing no armor. He had many natural qualities—courage, physical strength, good looks, musical skill, and natural leadership ability. Yet many of his contemporaries must have had similar qualities. The decisive touch for this budding young king-to-be was that he was anointed by Samuel and received the power of God's spirit.

In a time when the general society does not consider spiritual depth an essential quality for public leadership, God works more subtly in the public arena as he uses people to do his will who may not even consciously be aware of God. God has often worked in that way, even through the enemies of his people. Although the Church cannot control the public arena in a secular society, we can pray that our leaders may somehow do God's will in the world.

However, in the Church, we can develop processes and sensitivity to God's leadership that can ensure the highest quality in church leaders. The one essential quality each spiritual leader must possess is the anointing by God's spirit and a consistent purpose to do God's will. Then it may be said to some degree of all God-anointed leaders as it was of David: "And the Spirit of the Lord came mightily upon David from that day forward" (1 Sam. 1:13).

With that promise, God's people can look to the future with hope, believing that in all the chaos and turbulence in the world and in the Church, God is still calling, preparing, and anointing leaders to lead his people to do his will on earth.—Richard B. Cunningham

SUNDAY: MARCH TWENTY-FOURTH

SERVICE OF WORSHIP

Sermon: Ambition

TEXT: Matt. 20:17–28

I.a. Everybody wants to be somebody. Nobody ever says "I want to be a bum." Over time, our ambitions may simplify somewhat; instead of president or rock star or CEO, we may just want to have enough to pay the bills and a little more. But we still want to be somebody. We don't want to be forgotten or overlooked. Even Jesus' disciples are this way. Look at James and John, who had been with Jesus since the beginning. Ever since Jesus had started preaching in Galilee, they had been around to listen and to help. They were, with Peter, the closest of the twelve to the Master. But that wasn't good enough; "Two out of three ain't bad," but it could be better. Instead of being two of the three most famous, they wanted to be the two most famous. They wanted crowns. They wanted to be in charge of the rest. They wanted fame as the leaders who took over after Jesus. Ambition, hot burning desire to be better, to be known, to be remembered: That's what was behind their request.

b. "Let us have thrones on either side of you when you come into your kingdom. We've earned it; we've been with you from the beginning. Peter makes a lot of noise, but you can't depend on him when the chips are down. Sure, he tried to walk on the water with you, but he sank, didn't he? And just the other day, when you were talking about dying, he said the wrong thing, and you called him Satan, didn't you? So name us top dogs. Let us have the chief two chairs."

1. In the first place, their request is unrealistic. They have no notion of Jesus' own goals. He has just gotten through telling them that when he gets to Jerusalem, he's going to be handed over to the authorities and put to death. He's headed for a cross; they ask for a throne and a crown. He's headed for humiliation and disgrace; they ask for fame. They want to follow Jesus, but they don't know where he's going. Their request is just not realistic.

2. In the second place, even if they had been asking for the right thing, they were asking the wrong person. Not only were their goals wrong, but their source was wrong. Jesus tells them that it is not in his power to grant their request. "You'll have to take that up with God, guys; but when the kingdom does come, he'll have someone in mind for the spots on either side of me, and I don't know who it will be." And finally, even if they had asked for the right thing, and even if they had asked the right person, the way they asked shows that they know they're doing something shady. James and John, so loud and crazy that Jesus nicknamed them "Sons of thunder," did not have the courage to come and ask Jesus themselves. They sent their mother to ask for them: "Please, Jesus, do this for my two boys—boys, come up here and stand so Jesus can see you—they're such good boys." Wrong goals, wrong source, wrong method: three strikes, and they're out!

c. Jesus helps to get them back on course. First boys, let's get your starting point right. Everybody in the world wants to be in charge. The world is power hungry; you must be different. The world wants not just to rule, but to "lord it over" other people: you must be different. If you want to end up right, you've got to start by separating yourself from the desires of the world.

Millard Fuller was a high-powered lawyer in Montgomery, Alabama. He had made a million dollars while he was a student at the University of Alabama, and he and his partner were well on their way to becoming some of the wealthiest, most influential people in the South. Then one day he thought about how unhappy he was, how his family was coming apart, how his children were strangers to him. And he decided instead of trying to be the wealthiest and most powerful, he'd try to be the one who did the most good. He dropped the desires of the world; he chose a starting point; and his organization, Habitat for Humanity, has built homes for homeless people all over the world. Is your ambition to follow Jesus? Then you have to start in the right place. The world wants you to try to be the most powerful, the one in charge; you must be different.

II.a. OK, so I must be different in order to follow Jesus. But which direction do I turn? If I turn away from one direction on the compass, there are still three choices left. Which way do we go? Jesus tell us: "If you want to be great, you must be a slave of all the rest." Now, that's different. Everybody wants to be somebody; nobody says, "I want to be a bum; I want to work at minimum wages all my life." Nobody wants to be a slave. We are upwardly mobile, headed for more money, more power, more control; born in a log cabin, but then elected president—that's our national story, a story of ambition upwards, not downwards.

Deuteronomy says that if you own a slave, you cannot force him to serve you for life. After seven years, you must let him go out of your house. But maybe he likes working for you and wants to stay. Then you take him to the doorpost and pierce his ear, and from that moment on he is part of your household. He cannot leave you, and you cannot sell him. You belong to each other. That's the picture Jesus is painting here.

b. Think about it: If we want to follow Jesus, then our goal is not to become first or leader. James and John want the thrones and the crowns. Instead, Jesus says that the best position in the Church is not president or king but slave. Try to become bond slaves to each other, he says. That's the top position; that's what to aim for. It goes against everything we have been taught, but there it is.

How do we know if we're really heading for that goal? We want to follow Jesus, and we understand about turning aside from the world and heading for servanthood. But we need guidance in making sure we are keeping to the path. We need measurements along the way; a road sign occasionally, with the name of our destination on it, so we're certain we haven't turned off by accident somewhere.

c. The guideposts, Jesus says, are simple: "The Son of Man came not to be served but to serve, and to give his life as a ransom for many." Are you serving? Look at your life and think about it for a minute: Whom do you help by what you do everyday, besides yourself? We each have to take care of ourselves; there's no shame in that. But whom else do you serve?

Mother Teresa lived as a missionary teacher in Calcutta, India, for twenty years thinking that there was nothing she could do for the poor around her. For twenty years, she looked out the window of her room, and pitied the poor, and prayed for them. Then one day she realized she had to act; she looked out her window and saw Jesus standing in the middle of the poor people sleeping in the street, beckoning her to come outside. And she did.

Whom do you serve? There's no shame in taking care of ourselves; but if we follow Jesus, we will serve others, too. Service is one guidepost. The other is the last part of that verse: Jesus came to give his life for the many. A wise man once said that the only force that can really give in this world is love, and that the only thing that love can truly give is itself. "Are you able to drink the cup I will drink?" Jesus asked, and James and John thought they could. But to follow Jesus means to give ourselves for the many, to offer ourselves as gifts to others.

Do we want to follow Jesus? It's not the most glamorous life in the world. You don't get to be king or president by following Jesus; you don't live in luxury; you're more likely to be crucified than crowned. But if that is your ambition, then his hand is out to you, too, motioning to you to follow him.—Richard B. Vinson

Illustrations

THE SIN OF PRIDE. Christianity traces *hubris* back to the root sin of pride, which places man instead of God at the center of gravity and so throws the whole structure of things onto the ruin called judgment. Whenever we say, whether in the personal, political, or social sphere,

I am the master of my fate;
I am the captain of my soul

We are committing the sin of pride; and the higher the goal at which we aim, the more far-reaching will be the subsequent disaster. That is why we ought to distrust all those high ambitions and lofty ideals that make the well-being of humanity their ultimate end. We cannot make ourselves happy by serving ourselves—not even when we call self-service the service of the community, for the community in that context is only an extension of our own ego. Human happiness is a by-product, thrown off in our service of God.—Dorothy L. Sayers

TWO POWERS. The terrific red-blooded power that inspired Alexander's legions to sacrifice their lives on the battlefield, and the other power, the shining love which filled the Christian martyrs with joy when they were torn by beasts in the Roman arena, these two powers shake and illuminate our own world even now. And they seem to be as young and dynamic as they have ever been. We must study them, understand them, deal with them; indeed, we must choose between them or we shall be lost in the chaos.—Fritz Kunkel, *In Search of Maturity*

SERMON SUGGESTIONS

Topic: A New Life Is Possible

TEXT: Rom. 8:6–11.
(1) We face an unavoidable choice—whether to allow ourselves to be dominated by "the flesh," our lower nature, or by "the Spirit," the work of God in Christ within us. (2) The consequences of both are awesome—"death" with the flesh; "life and peace" with the Spirit.

Topic: Life Giver

TEXT: John 11:1–45, especially verses 25 and 26.
(1) He raised Lazarus, a sign of his lordship over death and life. (2) He raises

us to a new quality of existence in God: (a) that brings abundant blessings here and now (John 10:10); (b) that survives all the ravages of time.

Worship Aids

CALL TO WORSHIP. "Out of the depths have I cried unto thee, O Lord. Lord, hear my voice: let thine ears be attentive to the voice of my supplications. If thou, Lord, shouldst mark iniquities, O Lord, who shall stand? But there is forgiveness with thee, that thou mayest be feared" (Ps. 130:1–4).

INVOCATION. Like the Psalmist, O God, we need your forgiveness, and, like him, we believe that you do forgive us when we acknowledge our sin and forsake it. Let this service of worship help us to search our hearts and discover new depths of your love to help us scale the heights of obedience and service.

OFFERTORY SENTENCE. "Every good and perfect gift is from above, coming down from the Father of the heavenly lights, who does not change like shifting shadows" (James. 1:17 NIV).

OFFERTORY PRAYER. Thank you, Lord, for your steadfast love, demonstrated in your daily providences. Help us to find our pattern of stewardship in your good gifts.

PRAYER. God of silence, we bring our noisy hearts to you. And into your healing quiet we cast the confusion of another week. Some of us have talked when we should have listened in these days. Some have been angry when we would have better tried to understand. Some have merely muttered when we should have spoken out loud and clear for you. Forgive us, Lord, for the noise. Touch our lips with the coals of fire that cleansed Isaiah, so that we might know how to speak and when to keep silent.

Nurturing God, we bring you our weakness. Some are tired today. Tired of trying. Tired of coping. Weary from grief, or anxiety, or disappointment. We need your gentle embrace, your loving smile, the spiritual food only you know how to prepare just right. In these moments lead us, we pray, to the feast of your sovereign realm.

Almighty God, we ask for your leavening in our world. We're here because we believe life is better when you are in control. We know that that leadership begins with each of us, and so we offer ourselves as your workers in this town. And we ask that your spirit move powerfully among our leaders. We pray for our president, for our governor, for our mayor, for the men and women of the police and fire departments, for the teachers in our schools and for all those in places of responsibility. We pray for the powerful movement of your spirit among us all.

Capable God, we pray for your help for the suffering people of the world. We ask for your blessing on all those who tell your story in places where your name is not yet known. And we thank you for loving us before we knew to pray, for hearing our prayers even when we do not know how to speak them, and for answering even our smallest cries of faith through Jesus Christ.—Ronald D. Sisk

LECTIONARY MESSAGE

Topic: The Valley of Dry Bones
TEXT: Ezek. 37:1–14

Many years ago a brilliant minister was led away into exile as a war casualty. As he made the long journey from Jerusalem to Babylon, he passed through a valley where a battle had been fought. When the battle was over the armies left the battlefield, leaving their dead lying unburied in the large valley. The bodies deteriorated and the sun bleached the skeletons. Historically, the valley became known as the Valley of Dry Bones. The minister who is presented with the challenge in this valley is Ezekiel. This depressing scene undoubtedly reminded Ezekiel of the deplorable state of his nation, Israel. Like these dry, dusty, and divided skeletons in the valley, Israel, a victim of deportation, was a divided and defeated nation in Babylon. Ezekiel's commission is to revive and encourage

the Jewish exiles and renew their hope and confidence in their returning to their own land. Psalm 137:1–5 is a vivid picture of Israel's hopelessness. One of the most glaring evidences of morbidity in our world is the absence of hope. When hope dies, purpose and meaning are lacking. When hope dies, the stream of excitement dries up. When hope dies, suicidal thoughts escalate. When hope dies, the stars fall from the silvery sockets of life and the sun of life fails to bathe its golden head in the pool of the morning.

Ezekiel took a visual survey of the Valley of Dry Bones (v. 2). There is a change in divine proceedings (v. 3). The omniscient God who is the Creator of everything asks a finite creature, "Can these bones live?" The One who took Job to the classroom of nature and baffled him with the all-surpassing knowledge of the Holy One now condescends and asks Ezekiel, "Can these bones live?" Ezekiel did not respond with a pessimistic no! Neither was his reply that of a blind optimist. Ezekiel's answer revealed his faith in the God whose knowledge penetrates the innermost recesses of the bosom of mystery and wonder. He simply said, "O Lord God, thou knowest." The human family faces many crises for which there are no logical explanations. What kind of explanation can be given for a seventeen-year-old son murdering his parents and two teenage sisters in response to a disciplinary measure issued against him by his parents? The funeral for these four persons was held at the Florence Christian Church in Florence, Kentucky, on Sunday, May 29, 1994, and they were buried the next day (Memorial Day), May 30, 1994. Ezekiel's reply is the appropriate one for this inexplicable tragedy and other unexplainable events: "O Lord God, Thou knowest."

The situation looked hopeless. As far as Ezekiel could see, dry bones covered every inch of the valley. Is there any hope for Israel? Is there any hope for our nation and world today? The human race is on a collision course with destruction. The lives of the youth are frayed, fragmented, and fractured by drugs, sexual promiscuity, and alcohol. Corruption has tainted the halls of all of our national authoritative establishments. Is there no brighter day for the human race on the horizon? The hope lies in the activity of divine-human instrumentality. God commands Ezekiel to prophesy to the bones (v. 4–8) and to prophesy to the winds (v. 9). When Ezekiel did his part in prophesying, God fulfilled God's part in providing breath and life for the revived and resuscitated house of Israel (v. 10–11). God could have revitalized the valley without resorting to the enlistment of human agency. However, God chose to enter into partnership with Ezekiel. God had employed this method in several instances during Israel's pilgrimage to the Promised Land. Moses lifted up his rod, and the waters of the Red Sea divided and stood up in attention like retainer walls as the Israelites marched through them. The Israelites marched around the Jericho walls one time a day for six days and seven times on the seventh day before the prodigious walls fell down flat. In this passage, Ezekiel does his part and prophesies to the bones and tells them to hear the word of the Lord (v. 7). Ezekiel receives a response from his preaching: noise, movement, unity, organization, and form. However, after Ezekiel's initial preachment, the human forms lay lifeless throughout the valley. It was only after Ezekiel prophesied to the four winds and they entered the nostrils of the human forms that they began to breathe and rise from the dust of desolation as a mighty army of God.

Is there any hope for tomorrow? Can these bones live? Will the human race survive in this nuclear age? But it will take the activity of divine-human instrumentality. Humanity has reached its extremity. We are coming apart at the seams. The foundations of our society are being removed. We must enter into a partnership with God if there is to be a *human renewal.* The wind is blowing again. In scripture, wind is a symbol of the Holy Spirit. If we are to experience life in the church, the wind of the Spirit must blow again as on the day of Pentecost. Then and only then will these bones live!—Robert Smith, Jr.

SUNDAY: MARCH THIRTY-FIRST

SERVICE OF WORSHIP

Sermon: Already Late

TEXT: Mark 11:1–11

I. "And Jesus entered Jerusalem, and went into the temple, and when he had looked around at everything, as it was already late, he went out to Bethany with the twelve." The imagination begins to focus on the scene. The little demonstration is long over. The crowds and their signs have all gone home. The palm branches are all scattered about the roads. The sun is getting over the hills, and the long shadows of evening are beginning to stretch over the walls of Jerusalem. Now after all of the excitement and the celebration and the cheering, things have grown very quiet. The crickets have begun their evening serene, and Jesus comes into the Temple. He looks around the building, he looks at the stalls for the sellers of the sacrifices. He looks at all of the gradual accumulation of stuff that gathers in the holy places. There is the memorial chair to Rabbi Smith, and the hand-painted picture by the rabbi's wife that has a brass dedication plaque on it. There are the specially designed and built holding pens for pigeons, made and dedicated by the carpenter's association. All these things that are given in great love, but that so slowly begin to clutter our lives and our worship. He looks at the board on the wall of the names of the people who have died in the Maccabean revolution. He looks at the different courts into which the people who go to worship get filtered. There is the outer court, where the God-fearers can stand. There is the place for women. There is the place for men. There is a different place for the priest, and there is the Holy of Holies into which only the high priest can go. He looks at the place where the Torah is kept, and perhaps his mind is struck by the contrast between the Torah and all of the laws and judgments that have been made based on the Torah that now have been imposed on the faithful. He looks around, and because it is already late, he retires from the city and spends the night outside with his disciples in Bethany.

Already late. Late in the day, yes. Jesus knew how much there was still to be done and yet so little time, but there was no sense in trying to start it now. Wait until tomorrow! The thrill and the excitement of the Palm Sunday parade was wonderful, but what was that parade when compared with how much was left to be done and how little time was left? Already it was late in Jesus' ministry. He knew the hour had come for the Son of Man to be glorified, and there was still so much to be done. Was the parade an event of hope or was it just another case of misguided expectations? Did his disciples really get the difference in the kind of kingdom Jesus was bringing by his entrance or did they still expect him to be crowned with Caesar Augustus's crown? Already late in his ministry, was Palm Sunday a day of hope and encouragement that his message had been heard by those who had been with him so long or another day of disappointed expectations and his failure to live up to their vision and dreams?

II.a. Palm Sunday begins with excitement and promise. Jesus sent two of his disciples into a village near Jerusalem to secure transportation: an ass and a colt. This was a very deliberate choice. Jesus had decided that the time had come to make public what he had already been trying to explain to his disciples. It was not time to do something to declare that Jesus was God's Messiah, come to bring a new kingdom of God upon the earth in a way that no other kingdom was brought on earth. Up until this time he had been the one who had told his disciples, told the demons, told those who had been healed by him, not to tell anybody who he was. Because it was already late it was now time to go public. The Old Testament prophet Zechariah had predicted that the Messiah would come riding upon

an ass. So Jesus, picking an ass and riding it, was making a very clear statement to the people. And when they saw Jesus coming, the people, at least some of them, understood, and began celebrating, "Blessed is He who comes in the name of the Lord." "Hosanna in the highest." And using what they had around them, their garments and the tree branches, they began to lay out the royal welcome.

b. Palm Sunday starts out with a deliberate act of faith, a declaration of identity, an act of courage and hope, and a public profession by Jesus to be the agent of God. If you don't think it takes some courage to claim that you are an agent of God in history, try standing up at work and say that God told you to do something and see what kind of response you get. It is one thing for all these people to come and say, "Good teacher, how must I be saved?" It is one thing for others to say about him that when he talks we think we hear the voice of God. It is another for Jesus to come out and say, "I am one whom God has sent to be the Messiah." So Palm Sunday begins with Jesus making his declaration of his identity.

c. And we welcome this day in our Christian life as a day of great joy and celebration. It is "All glory, laud, and honor, to Thee, Redeemer, King." It is a parade day. A day of delight and balloons if you want, bands, and songs, and joy, because for us as part of the people of God, we take great courage and hope in this act of Jesus, because we, like the disciples of John, come to Jesus and say, "If you are the Christ, tell us plainly." And this parade of Jesus on the ass is about as plain a declaration as Jesus will ever give us. Parades are so often how we welcome those we recognize as special. So the Palm Sunday parade is how we recognize and acknowledge that Jesus Christ is the Messiah of God. With songs and psalms we affirm that the God who was known to prophets in time long past has crossed over the threshold of human sight and hearing and is now present in our midst of history riding upon the ass rather than riding upon the white horse of the military hero. Coming as the servant and not one to be feared.

III.a. Yet Palm Sunday is not all party and celebration. The cheering stopped. The people went home. The world continued to spin. And the darkness that is ever about us, driven back for a moment, settled back over the community, and time moved on toward Good Friday. Palm Sunday is the straightforward courage of the Christian faith. It is the model of our Christian hope and courage. It is not simply a day of happiness. It is not just a bit of fluff to entertain the troops. It is not a day of partying to distract people from the misery of their lives. Palm Sunday is a day of joy of "Blessed is he who comes in the name of the Lord" because it knows how late it always is for all of us. Palm Sunday is no blind, "Pollyanna" good time. You and I know how silly sounding Bobby McFerrin's "Don't Worry, Be Happy" song is. Don't worry, be happy, when our honored and exalted political leaders are sent to make decisions for us about the important issues in our lives and they can't find the courage to do it.

b. The parade of Palm Sunday is the day when we raise our hymns of joy to the one who comes riding on the donkey, who comes riding in willing to declare his identity, knowing full well that we are fickle people who get tired of parades and go home, that we do not like to miss our evening meals or the Jeopardy game; who comes riding in knowing full well that religious leaders like things neat and tidy and have a holy hatred of those who meddle with their holy things, knowing that the humble speaker of truth can quickly be shouted down by the mob, knowing us so well that he knew that we would quickly sell our souls for a small handful of silver, knowing that even good friends would go to sleep while he suffered. Jesus comes riding in knowing full well all of that. Palm Sunday is one bright and glorious moment in human history when the ultimate power of God came riding humbly, sitting on a donkey, making a costly demonstration of his great and unexpected love for all creation. It is a bright and glorious day when love came forward as courage and proclamation, as integrity and hope, and became a small parade headed for the gallows.

Perhaps Palm Sunday might go down in the theater of life as a tragedy. Jesus Christ comes as the Messiah, makes his declaration of who he is and what he has come to do, and yet he knows that it is already late, that the events lead on to the cross, but his love for us will not enable him to change its course. "Blessed is he who comes in the name of the Lord."—Rick Brand

Illustrations

THE WHY OF REJECTION.   Here without doubt is one reason why Jesus gives offense to many today. It has to be remembered that while some people reject Christ because they cannot understand him, others reject him because they understand him only too well. They know that his demands are stringent and exacting, that they involve a cleaning up of the inner life, the substitution of self-denial for self-interest, the subordination of the material to the spiritual, and they are not prepared to toe the line or pay the price.—Robert J. McCracken

ENTERING THE MYSTERY.   On that first Palm Sunday all Jerusalem was stirred, saying, Who is this? The answer was not fully available. Jesus was in the process of making an answer. We know him or may know him as the ironical, whimsical, and mysterious one, not simply the prophet from Nazareth of Galilee. For in the cross he everlastingly identifies himself for those who will stop to see, to gaze, to ponder, and to learn. In the cross of his entire self-offering he is, in the centurion's words of dawning and fulfilled realization, truly the Son of God. So, likewise, if we can come to see, and with the centurion at the foot of the cross, enter somewhat into the mystery that is embodied there, we will be better able than the pilgrims on that first Palm Sunday to declare: "Blessed is he that cometh in the name of the Lord."—Robert E. Cushman

SERMON SUGGESTIONS

Topic: The Qualities of Servanthood
TEXT: Isa. 50:4–9a
(1) Preparation to help others. (2) Teachability. (3) Willingness to suffer in the course. (4) Confidence in the vindication and victory of God.

Topic: "Who Is This?"
TEXT: Matt. 21:1–11
(1) It is a question of prophecy. (2) It is a question of history. (3) It is a question that requires a personal response.

Worship Aids

CALL TO WORSHIP. "O give thanks unto the Lord; for he is good: because his mercy endureth forever" (Ps. 118:1).

INVOCATION. We are, all of us, children of your mercy, O God, and even now we look to you for your loving kindness as we raise our hearts to you in confession, adoration, and supplication. Forgive our sins, accept our praise, and grant our petitions for Jesus' sake.

OFFERTORY SENTENCE. "The children of Israel brought a willing offering unto the Lord, every man and woman, whose heart made them willing to bring for all manner of work, which the Lord had commanded to be made by Moses" (Exod. 35:29).

OFFERTORY PRAYER. Lord of life, give new resolve and strength to our stewardship, deepen and broaden our commitment because the world needs what God offers in Christ and what the Church provides in fellowship to all who will believe.—E. Lee Phillips

PRAYER. O God, most holy and most gracious, we bless you for the Church as the school of virtue and godly living; for the sacred Scriptures that bring to us the story of your redeeming will; for all the wise and saintly men and women of the past and the present; for the goodly fellowship of the prophets, and the noble army of the martyrs; for the great cloud of witnesses from whose faith and hope we would take courage in our struggles and trials. We rejoice to believe that you are always overruling trouble and temptation and sin and disappointment, and out of them are making stepping-stones to bring us nearer to you. Forbid that we should know your grace in vain. Rather may your goodness bind us anew to loyalty and to faith, and constrain us to a life separate from evil, and consecrated to goodness.

We would not be selfish in our prayers. We cannot come into your presence without bringing in our hearts the tears, the pain, the longing of our brothers. O God, our sympathy with them is but the broken reflection of your sympathy. Come to the burdened, the wretched, the grief stricken, those who have been made sad by others, and those who have brought sadness upon themselves. May they hear, by faith, the still voice of your sympathy! May they feel the beating of your great heart of compassion! May they take comfort in the assurance that you suffer in and with them and yet abide in everlasting blessedness! Hear our prayers on behalf of all those who are struggling against the power of evil.

Call the sinning and the suffering into fellowship with Christ that they may find in him the secret of victory over the evil of the world; that he may rise in their souls, a star burning brightly through the long night unto your perfect day.—Adapted from Samuel McComb

LECTIONARY MESSAGE

Topic: Activating the Mind of Christ
TEXT: Phil. 2:5–11
Most people become aware of the power of the human mind only when it cannot work properly. When a person's brain malfunctions, sometimes electric shock can facilitate its recovery.

St. Paul's exhortation to the Philippians, "Let the same mind be in you that was in Christ Jesus" (NRSV), conjures the ideas of pushing the button to allow a shuttle to launch from the pad, dropping a substance in the test tube that will lead to a chemical reaction.

Congregations that are "coasting" in maintenance ministry, functioning only as chaplains for the faithful, need the command to activate their mind of Christ so that they can be transformed into apostolic churches seeking the hurting and lost humanity and guiding these people to a mature attitude of service in the kingdom. The path to genuine service requires activating the mind of Christ.

I. *Relinquish your rights* (v. 5–6). Paul appeals to the Philippians, urging them to have the mind of Christ as a guide for their relationships with one another. The disposition or mind that governed Christ also should govern his people. Their mind and attitudes have been influenced by Christ, but arrogance and a self-seeking attitude raise their ugly heads. The appeal is that they activate Christ's mind in their relationships with one another.

Founding Church members and pastors think they have rights. The Philippian church was started amid travail and conflict. The membership reflected in its beginning stages a diverse rainbow of socioeconomic classes. Acts 16 depicts the "founding members" of the congregation: a wealthy merchant, Lydia; a middle-class Roman soldier, the jailer; and a dependent youth, the slave girl whose demon Paul had exorcised in the market place. The founder of the Church was not Paul but Christ.

II. *Serve sacrificially* (v. 6–8). "Emptied himself" probably means that Christ gave up his privileged estate in heaven for a humble one of privation and sacrificial service on earth. The phrase refers to Christ pouring out his life to God in humble, obedient self-denial, refusing in any way to act selfishly. His *kenosis* (emptying) was not the surrender of divinity but the acceptance of servanthood. The essence of that mind was his disposition not to grasp at equality with God but rather to be "obedient unto death, even death on a cross."

Cross bearing and servant mind-set run against aggressive self-expression and "assertiveness training." The sports dictum that "winning is everything" has supplanted Christian principles, especially in making Church growth the measure of success in some expressions of American Christianity.

Jesus took a course opposite to that of the first Adam. Adam grasped the equality with God; Christ renounced equality with God to become a man. Whereas the first Adam tried to snatch equality with God, Jesus (the second Adam) emptied himself or "poured out his life" to God in the service of humankind.

When former President Jimmy Carter visited New York City in 1985 to assist in the Habitat for Humanity building projects, he demonstrated the Christian virtue of sacrificial service. He lodged in rudimentary quarters of the Metro Baptist Church and assisted the members to move chairs from the fellowship hall to the sanctuary for the midweek prayer service. The media expected him to lodge at the Waldorf Astoria Hotel and could not understand why he "did not pull rank." The congregation located in the area of the city known as "Hell's Kitchen" demonstrated their gratitude and placed a plaque with a hammer in the foyer to honor the genuine service of a Christian statesman to a needy city.

III. *Worship in awe* (v. 9–11). That "every knee shall bow and every tongue confess" means that God's kingdom will be absolute in that the lordship of Christ must eventually be acknowledged everywhere. The passage does not guarantee universal salvation. It does promise universal lordship of Christ, his enthronement.

Paul previews the "leveling of the field" at the end time. The Philippians are assured that when they activate the mind of Christ as the guiding light for Christian living, then they will rejoice over being counted with the righteous as Christ is crowned Lord of lords and King of kings.

We catch a glimpse of what it may mean to bow our knees to the exalted Lord when during the performances of Handel's *Messiah* we stand up reverently to join in adoration as the choir sings the "Hallelujah" chorus. Instead of our petty desires, Christ becomes the center of worship and in our "bowing the knee" we gain a true perspective.

The Church of the twenty-first century can be fruitful to represent the kingdom of the Second Adam if she can activate the mind of Christ.—David F. D'Amico

SUNDAY: APRIL SEVENTH

SERVICE OF WORSHIP

Sermon: The Resurrection of Our Lord

TEXT: Luke 24:34

I. Very near the place of the Crucifixion there was a garden belonging to Joseph, of Arimathea, this being the name of a little country town from which he had come. He was a man of wealth, as no other could have owned a garden just outside the walls of a great city. He, too, was a man of elevated social position, for excepting the high priest there was no higher position possible for a Jew than to be a member of the Sanhedrin. He was a disciple of Jesus, but "secretly, for fear of the Jews." This gentleman was afraid of losing social caste, and afraid of losing a distinguished position, and so he had not been able to declare himself a disciple of Jesus before the world.

a. In the Sanhedrin Joseph appears to have opposed the vote by which Jesus was condemned, and we may suppose that from this garden of his, near to the place, he had looked out with mournful interest upon the scene of the Crucifixion. Perhaps as his eye wandered, it fell upon the new tomb he had caused to be cut from the solid rock in the garden, preparing it for the entombment of himself and his household, but in which no one had yet been laid. It is one of the contradictions that are perpetually occurring in our Lord's life that he died as a despised malefactor, and yet he was buried like a man of the greatest distinction. Another member of the Sanhedrin, Nicodemus, who three years before had visited Jesus by night, also went to Golgotha. No expense was spared by those distinguished and wealthy men in expressing love and admiration for the body of the prophet.

b. This interment was witnessed, we are told, by two women—Mary Magdalene, and another Mary, the mother of Joseph. They stood at a distance and so did not see that Nicodemus had brought those spices. Now as the sun was going down, and the stone was rolled to the mouth of the sepulcher, the women went to the city planning what they would do when the Sabbath was past.

II. The hours went on, and when the sun set on the Jewish Sabbath, which was Saturday evening, the women went to the shops, which were opened at sunset, to buy their spices. When the early morning came, they went to the tomb. On their way there occurred to their minds a difficulty. The two women had observed that it was a very large stone that was rolled against the tomb, and it occurred to them that they would not be able to remove it. But they pressed on, and when they arrived at the sepulcher, the stone was rolled away. Immediately the thought came, not that he was risen, but that the body had been removed by some friend or some enemy. So one of them, Mary Magdalene, rushed back to the city to the residence of John, where Peter also was, to tell them about it. The other woman remained. And presently looking into the sepulcher they saw two angels, who spoke to them and said: "Why seek ye the living among the dead? He is not here, he is risen. Go tell his disciples that he is leading the way to Galilee and they shall see him there."

a. Soon after the women left, here came Peter and John, eagerly hastening at the news Mary had brought that the sepulcher was opened. They saw the linen cloths that had wrapped the body lying, and the napkin that had been wrapped about the head was folded and laid apart. John, telling the story afterward, says that he "saw, and believed." Those accustomed to dealing with evidence know that among matters of importance, very slight circumstances will sometimes clinch the whole thing and leave no doubt about it. Here was such a slight circumstance. It could not be that friends had borne that body away, for they would have carried it away with the cloths; and enemies would not have left the cloths folded and neatly laid away. Their presence there and the tokens of order and loving care satisfied John that the Master was risen indeed. It meant reality. He saw and believed.

b. But Jesus was not there, and they knew not what to do nor to think, and so they went soon away. However, Mary Magdalene had followed them to the tomb, and was now standing without and weeping. After a little she stooped timidly and looked into the tomb, and again the angels appeared and said, "Woman, why weepest thou?" Still she had no thought that he was risen. She said, "They have taken away my Lord, and I know not where they have laid him." Then she turned around and through her tears saw a man standing by, who she took it for granted was in charge of the garden, and she said, "Sir, if thou has borne him away, please tell me where thou hast laid him?"

Do you remember what followed? Ah! she heard a voice, a voice that years before had spoken, and the dread demons that possessed her fled away. She heard that voice as he said, "Mary." And she turned and said, "My teacher!"

Sometime after, Jesus appeared to the other women and gave them commissions with his own lips likewise. As the morning went on these women told their story, and the disciples would not hear a word of it. They said it was all idle tales. With that magnificent, supercilious superiority with which men often speak as regards women, they said it was all women's idle tales.

c. As the day went on, our Lord appeared to Simon Peter, not to condemn him, but as a condescension to poor fallen Simon, because he had fallen so low. Then in the afternoon, he came to two men walking toward Emmaus, talking sorrowfully together. They had believed that this Jesus of Nazareth was the Redeemer of Israel, and now that belief was all gone.

What a scene it was when breaking bread their eyes were opened and they knew him, but for one brief moment, and he vanished from their sight. Then as they came back to Jerusalem, they said the Lord had risen indeed and had appeared to Simon and they told their story.

As they talked about it with the doors shut for fear of the Jews, suddenly he stood in their room and in his old loving way he said, "Peace be unto you." And he said "Why are ye troubled? See, it is not a spirit! Look at the wounds in the hands and in the side. Give me food." They gave him food, and he ate it before them. Their incredulity broke down. They had been told that the Messiah was to be despised and rejected and to die and to rise again. There was nothing hard to believe about it if they understood the Scriptures, but the fact came first and they were obliged to believe the fact. Then their hearts were opened to see that the fact had been predicted long before by the prophets.

III. We have reached the Lord's day evening. You remember how a week later he overcame the incredulity of Thomas, how he appeared in Galilee and then back in Jerusalem, and at length in the presence of the disciples ascended into heaven. Without following those appearances I wish to make certain observations respecting the Resurrection of the Son of Man, even the Resurrection of Jesus Christ as an unquestionable reality.

a. My friends, if I do not know that Jesus Christ rose from the dead, then this world has no history. I do not know anything in the past if I do not know that. If a man will look carefully and thoughtfully over all these incidences, will note the slowness of belief of these men, their intelligence, will see that they were not prejudiced enthusiasts, will see how when they had fairly been convinced of this they gave their lives for it, if a man will put all circumstances together including the traditions and discrepancies of the experience, I am satisfied that he will see, if he is willing to see, that the fact shines out clearly.

b. The second observation is that the Resurrection of the Lord Jesus establishes the truth of Christianity. The apostle Paul says he is declared to be the Son of God by the Resurrection from the dead. It was the sign manual of the Deity, it was the seal of the sovereign of the universe affixed to his claim, it declared him to be all that he had ever professed to be, and so it establishes the truth of all his teachings and the truth of the whole Christian society.

c. The third observation is that the Resurrection of Christ consummated his work of redemption. This is a view I think does not appear to come often within the sight of Christian teachers at the present time, and yet was much in the minds of the first disciples. Paul says "Who was delivered for our offenses and was raised again for our justification." He laid down his life, and took again for us. He rose triumphant over death and over sin and over Satan in our behalf.

d. The fourth observation is that the Resurrection of Christ is the pledge of the resurrection of his people. "Now is Christ risen from the dead and become the first fruits of them that slept." The sheaf of barley that they weighed as the first fruits of the harvest was regarded as a pledge that the rest of the harvest would come in its time and Christ's Resurrection is the first fruits, the pledge of Resurrection. And so the apostle wrote to the Thessalonians, "But I would not have you to be ignorant, brethren, concerning them which are asleep, that ye sorrow not, even as others which have no hope."

e. Yet a fifth observation. The Resurrection of Christ is celebrated by us on the Lord's day. I have no time to go into the argument that is here involved, but we believe from slight intimations in the Acts of the Apostles and in Revelation that show conclusively that the Christians of that time held religious meetings on the first day of the week, and from the light that is shed back upon it, and from known facts we learn that the apostles had authorized that the Sabbath should be transferred to the first day of the week.

f. Finally, the Resurrection of the Lord Jesus is a pledge to his people to live a risen life. You remember what the apostle says to the Romans: "Know ye not that so many of us as were baptized into Jesus were baptized into his death; therefore we were buried with him by baptism into death, and, like as Christ was raised from the dead by the glory of the Father even so we also should walk in the newness of life." Oh, ye Christian people, when you first set out in Christ's service, you did by a solemn ceremony declare that by faith in Jesus Christ you had died to sin and risen to a new life and were going to live always afterward a new life. Has it been so with you? Does your heart smite you with the painful thought that it has been but very partially so? O friends and brethren, then God has given you a time to set out afresh.—John A. Broadus

Illustrations

UNFINISHED EASTER.   If anyone asks why this very religious generation is not battering at the doors of the churches instead of wandering through the corridors of the occult, gathering in charismatic groups, or taking the mystic road to Kathmandu, my answer would be that, on the whole, we have failed to present the gospel as a living experience. We have become reporters of the religious experiences. We have become reporters of the religious experiences of others from Abraham to Bonhoeffer, rather than catalysts of the living Christ. Instead of bringing people into vital contact with him, and conveying the excitement of life in the spirit, we have tended to offer what I might call an ABC of theology and an NBC of current affairs. We are suffering from the blight of the second-hand-honoring of someone else's God, interested in someone else's Jesus, keeping the gospel at one remove from the center of our lives. So Easter may become nothing more than an exercise in religious nostalgia to the sound of the trumpets—David H. C. Read

HE APPEARED ALSO TO ME. He appeared also to me in the face of a friend in a restaurant not long ago. He said to me, "I am afraid of the word *cancer;* I am not afraid of the word *death.* I *am* concerned about possible loss of vitality or change in personality. How do I meet it like a man?" Well, he is meeting it like the tremendous man that he is. He is making plans. He is living with confidence and courage to face whatever comes. He is an Easter man. I admire him; I love him.

He appeared also to me in a hospital room this week in the face of a man who has been seriously ill. He pointed to a vase with a long-stemmed rose in it and told me that someone from the church had brought it to him. Then he said quietly to me, "There is a great message in that rose. It says a lot." It said a lot to him of the love of God and his friends in the church. He was not alone, but his friends were with him, and the spirit of Jesus was in his room.—Robert A. Raines

SERMON SUGGESTIONS

Topic: God for Everybody

TEXT: Acts 10:34–43

(1) *The question:* Does God accept people from all ethnic and religious backgrounds? (2) *The response:* (a) God sent the good news of peace in Jesus to Israel; (b) The recipients of the message rejected and crucified Jesus; (c) God raised Jesus from the dead; (d) Witnesses testified to facts of the faith and preached the good news. (3) *The objective:* the forgiveness of sins through Jesus Christ.

Topic: Setting Our Course

TEXT: Col. 3:1–4

(1) Our status—"raised with Christ." (2) Our direction — toward "things above." (3) Our security—"hidden with Christ in God." (4) Our destiny—"with him in glory."

Worship Aids

CALL TO WORSHIP. "This is the day which the Lord hath made; we will rejoice and be glad in it" (Ps. 188:24).

INVOCATION. Though many high and holy experiences fade soon from our hearts and leave a lingering sadness, grant, O God, that we may know this day the exultation of those who have risen with Christ and are seeking the things that are above, where Christ is, seated at their right hand.

OFFERTORY SENTENCE. "Ye ought to support the weak, and to remember the words of the Lord Jesus, how he said, It is more blessed to give than to receive" (Acts 20:35b).

OFFERTORY PRAYER. Gracious Father, we have opened our mouths, and thou hast filled them with good things. Now open our hearts to others, we pray, that we may help bring fulfillment to their hopes and prayers. Bless these offerings and direct their use, so that nothing be wasted.

PRAYER. Eternal Father, because our Lord lives today, we live. But some of us have not felt the lifting power of that truth. We go about as those who know that our Lord was crucified, but hardly knowing that he was raised from the dead. We have been told that thou hast caused us to sit together in heavenly places with him, yet the sights and sounds and smells of earth are still too much with us. May we hear in thy word the trumpet blast of victory and rise with confidence, wide-awake to what we are and what we should be doing. Help us to live on this earth as those whose citizenship is in heaven, but as those who are eager to bring life of heaven to this earth. Grant strength to those sorely tempted every day to live as if this world were all. Grant concern and tact to those who see others tempted and wish to help. And give us all a knowledge of thy comradeship with us in our pilgrimage.

LECTIONARY MESSAGE

Topic: Seeing Is Believing?

TEXT: John 20:1–18

Other Readings: Acts 10:34–43; Col. 3:1–4

"Seeing is believing," or at least this is the common statement. In the familiar account of the Easter events in John 20:1–18, there are vignettes that tell of three people who saw the same things, but their responses differed. "Seeing" is a theme of these verses, for some form of "see" or "look" appears at least eight times. Let us consider these stories of those who saw—perhaps we will find ourselves in the accounts.

I. Mary Magdalene was one of the "blessed women" who witnessed the Crucifixion of Jesus. She came early to the tomb, no doubt with a mixture of emotions—hope, fear, sorrow, curiosity. As Mary approached the cave she was startled to see that the stone had been moved away from the entrance. Without stopping to examine the cave, she ran to tell Simon Peter and the Other Disciple. Although Mary had not actually investigated for herself, she concluded that "they" had taken Jesus away and placed the body somewhere else. We can identify with Mary, for "jumping to conclusions" is a popular activity. As someone has remarked, this is the only exercise some people get!

II. Mary's report to the two disciples generated action—they both ran to the burial place. For whatever reason, the Other Disciple arrived at the tomb first, but he did not enter. It remained for Simon Peter, the impetuous one, to examine the inside of the cave for himself. The grave clothes were arranged neatly, probably in the same position as when they were on the body. Robbers would not take such care, or more likely, they would have taken the linen and spices, for these had value. But even with the evidence at hand, Simon did not really believe in the Resurrection of Jesus until later. We can identify with Simon Peter, for we may act on religious impulses at times, but full faith in the resurrected Christ comes later.

III. The Other Disciple entered the tomb, after his initial hesitancy, and he saw the same evidence as Simon. But he "saw" more, for verse 8 tells us that he believed. He saw not only the physical evidence but also a deeper meaning. Even

his faith was not complete, for there was more to learn about the Resurrection of Christ as that event related to Scripture. But the Other Disciple believed as best he could and as much as he could, and we can identify with him. Sometimes we must say, "Lord I believe, but help my unbelief, correct my faulty belief, complete my inadequate belief."

IV. So we have three stories of the reactions of three people to the open tomb. But there is more, certainly for Mary. She is the first person to have the privilege of meeting the risen Lord. When Mary returned to the tomb, she saw something the two disciples had not seen—two angels sitting where the body of Jesus had been placed. Mary gave the same response to the angels as she had to Simon Peter and the Other Disciple. But there was someone else near the tomb, and in her grief and confusion Mary thought the stranger was the gardener. He would know where the body had been taken, because he would have supervision of the burial places. Only when the stranger spoke her name, "Mary," did she realize that he was indeed the Lord. Just as he had promised, the Good Shepherd called the name of his sheep.

V. But what about us, gathered here on an Easter Sunday far removed from those first Easter events? The responses of the people in the three stories are typical of the ways people respond today. Some are convinced that Easter is some sort of fraud or hoax—someone has stolen the body. Some are aware of the Easter story, but they want more evidence. To these groups, we ask, "What more evidence is needed to convince you that Jesus really did rise from the dead?" In addition to the eyewitnesses, consider those who have lived and died for the sake of Jesus. Consider all the places of caring which have been built in his name. Consider the countless acts of love performed for the sake of the Risen Lord. If this is not enough, if you listen carefully, you may hear him call your own name.

There is one more group, those who consider the evidence and believe. For this group, there is a blessing. When the Risen Christ appeared to the disciples, in response to the confession of Thomas, Jesus said, "Because thou hast seen me thou hast believed; blessed are they that have not seen, and yet have believed."— Paul M. Debusman

SUNDAY: APRIL FOURTEENTH

SERVICE OF WORSHIP

Sermon: Human Interference

TEXT: Exod. 17:1–7b; Ps. 78:41; John 15:9–17

In 1936, Col. George Wingate died. He was an officer in the British army in India and had stayed on afterwards to found a mission for evangelism and medical service among the natives. His eldest son, Orde, was a somewhat independent and willful person, but he had remained faithful to the fine traditions of the family. One day a friend asked him this question: "Tell me, Orde, when you say one man is good and another bad, what exactly do you mean?" "Why," replied Orde, "I use these words in the biblical sense: When I say one man is good, I mean he lives to fulfill the purposes of God; when I say another man is bad, I mean he lives to frustrate the purposes of God."

Here are suggested two distinct types of persons whose natures are clearly etched by the fact that while one tries to do the will of God, the other gets in God's way. One belongs with those people who throw their lot in with God and his purposes, but the other is identified with those who are always at cross-purposes with God. But someone interrupts now and asks: If God is sovereign Lord of the universe, holding the whole world in his grasp and directing the destiny of his creation, how can mere persons, single human beings, get in his way? Now the person who puts the question in this way indicates that he or she has a wrong notion of the sovereignty of God. He is not a sovereignty of naked power, but he is one who is free to act toward us on his own terms rather than ours. And those terms are exercised in a way that is consistent with his spirit of love and grace.

Our text is the Psalmist's reflection upon the conduct of a people at a particular point in biblical history: "Yea, they turned back and tempted God, and they limited the holy one of Israel." (Ps. 78:41). The words are said about the children of Israel, a pilgrim people, who seemed completely involved in God's purposes and of whom the verdict of history was that they were an instrument in his hands. But when we read their story, it is marked by rebellion, stubbornness, and shame, reflected by their continually getting in God's way. And the basis of it all lay in the poverty of their faith and their inadequate understanding of God's power and grace.

Look, for example, at the evidence: At the beginning, when they saw the Red Sea before them and heard the clattering chariots of the Egyptian army behind them, remember how they turned on Moses and shouted, "It were better for us to serve the Egyptians than to die in this wilderness!" They failed to realize how big God was as compared with their small whimpering and stumbling faith. Or, again, just six weeks out from Egypt with their food gone, they curled their lips scornfully and asked: "Can God prepare a table in the wilderness?" And then later on, they had no water to drink and they cried out angrily: "Why have you brought us out of Egypt to kill us and our children and cattle from thirst?" It was on account of these attitudes and actions that the Psalmist put down this unusual verdict: "They limited the Holy One of Israel!" They limited God.

All this may be dismissed by many as a chapter of ancient history, but the principle involved here is as up-to-date as this morning's sunrise. Even the most casual glance at the way people are living today shows us that they still limit God. They still get in his way. They still fence God in. Human interference is real. They do so whenever they place limits upon his love, his claims, his purposes, and his power. And the most grievous evidence of it is when we permit the size of our lives to determine the size of our God. God has a high purpose and intention for all of us as a nation, as a Church, and as individuals. Shall we, then, get in his way? Will some future generation say of us, "Yea, they turned back and tempted God and they limited the Holy One of Israel"?

Let us bring this principle now into the everydayness of our common life.

I. We get in God's way, first of all, when we limit the boundaries of his influence.

Lord Melbourne, who was Queen Victoria's first prime minister, was heard to murmur on coming out of church one Sunday morning, "Religion is all very well, but it is going a bit too far when it claims to interfere with one's private life." Now this is our most frequent and common way of limiting God. You and I are willing to let God have his way with us for one hour on Sunday morning, but all too often we cut him off after the benediction, and during the rest of the week our philosophy of life is: "Business is business and religion is religion and never the twain shall meet." We limit God when we fail to see that religion is not merely worship, but worship that determines, molds, and shapes our daily life. And what our world yearns to see today is not a God who is confined within the walls of any one church, but a God who is active in the home, among the professions, in the world of business, and *that* because you and I have encountered his holy being in a meaningful act of worship in church.

But the matter goes deeper than this: We try frequently to make this God we worship in church into our own pet pattern and claim him exclusively as our own. As soon as we think of the only true Christian as a Methodist, Episcopal, or Presbyterian Christian, we get in God's way, and we create a situation the religious pioneers of our country had to fight against. And incidentally, this is a problem created by our own attitude to our creeds. Now creeds have been useful expressions of the Church's thinking on certain theological issues and problems at a given time in history, but creeds were never meant to fence God in or to be the final word about him. Whenever any Christian denomination seemingly says: "If you jump through our hoop ... if you sign on our dotted line ... we'll arrange for you an introduction to *our* God." That attitude promotes "churchiness" in its worst form, against which Jesus in his own day hurled the most vehement denunciation. The only religion that can attract and challenge the world of our time is that which produces in you and me the highest form of moral and spiritual character. And this comes not from a God whom we encase within the boundaries of our own making, but one whose greatness fills the horizon of our life.

During a European war a young English soldier lay dying in no man's land and the Roman Catholic chaplain hurried to his side. "But," protested the boy, "I do not belong to your Church." "No matter," said the chaplain, "you belong to my God."

II. We get in God's way when we refuse to give him his chance with us. In any Gallup poll concerning religious convictions, most Americans will say they believe in God. But the quality and integrity of that belief is shown in the degree to which they permit God to exercise his presence in their lives.

There are those irregular believers who call on God eagerly when they face a crisis or get into a jam, but for the rest of the time they prefer to run their life in their own way. There are those who believe in God for a dividend. Like the children of Israel, they hold on to God when things are going well, but when their flimsy faith does not pay off, they shake their fist in God's face. Or there are those superficial believers who acknowledge God's everyday attributes—his love, power, and grace—but when they are face-to-face with life's exacting demands, they fret, worry, and despair like forlorn orphans of the human race.

Now, all these have one thing in common: They do not let God have a place or action in their lives. They get in his way either by superego or whimpering complaints. George Buttrick told of meeting a friend in Grand Central Station, New York City, and, noticing a new spring and jauntiness in his step, George asked him about his new, seemingly unconscious vitality, and his friend answered, "George, I've just resigned as general manager of this universe and it's amazing how quickly my resignation was accepted."

This points up a major flaw in the exercise of our religious belief today. God has become something to be possessed and used for personal advantage, to guarantee success, or to get us always to be number one. But in this thinking we fail to see that life consists not in our possessions but in our being possessed. We flaunt our high standard of living and say, "All this belongs to us," but we do not go on to further the question: To what do we belong? Life consists in our being able to be possessed by something infinitely greater than ourselves, to which we give freely all our zeal and passion, and thereby find the true secret of living. To allow God to have his chance with us involves openness of mind and heart, and this begins when we ask ourselves seriously: What claims my life? To whom or what do I give the highest allegiance of my soul and will? Only God is big enough to claim the whole of your life and mine. St. Paul testifies, "I live, yet not I, but Christ lives in me; and the life I now live in the flesh, I live by the faith of the Son of God who loved me and gave himself for me" (Gal. 2:20).

III. This leads to a final thought: We get in God's way when we limit the greatness of his love. After a disaster in a Welsh coal mine where many lives were lost, someone scribbled on the wall of a public building, "Welsh disaster! Where was God? There is no God!"

In the great crises and tragedies of life, like the children of Israel, we are all too ready to conclude that God's love has run out; that he has ceased to care. But God is never the author of tragedy. He stands faithfully within each tragedy where he can undergird his own. We limit God when we cast doubts upon his love, for his love is like any other love; it can always be measured by the amount it is ready to give. And God gave everything, because no one of us is beyond the scope of his love. John Henry Jowett at the close of his ministries in New York and London said, "I proclaimed always that everyone is in the love grip of the eternal." And many of us have found that when life seemed to have tumbled in and we were at the very edge of things, the love of God was all we had left and it was all we needed to have anyway. Should we presume, then, to limit God?—Donald Macleod

Illustrations

BELIEFS THAT MAKE US BRAVE. Behold the sufferer who through long illness has kept her kindness and patience. Does she doubt the goodness of God? No. Those who might seem to have most reason for disbelieving in divine goodness shame us with their sunny confidence, while the most pessimistic writings have been done by parlor critics in comfortable situations. The teachers who toil patiently in the schoolroom and are tried by the thoughtlessness of youth are not the ones who prate about the prevalence of morons. The devoted social workers who serve in the slums and see the seamy side of life somehow sustain their faith in the worth and future of the common man.—Ralph W. Sockman

IT MAKES A DIFFERENCE. When Charles T. Leber was secretary of the Foreign Mission Board of our Presbyterian Church, he told us about a famous institution in Westphalia, Germany, where medical care was given to epileptics, especially young children. One day a wealthy businessman was being shown about the hospital in hope that he might support it financially. He asked a young doctor, "How many children are helped sufficiently to live normal lives again?" "About one in a hundred," came the reply. "What?" retorted the businessman.

"One in a hundred! Why, it isn't worth it!" "Maybe not," said the doctor, "but suppose one boy in a hundred were your own son."—Donald Macleod

SERMON SUGGESTIONS

Topic: And the Thousands Said Yes!
TEXT: Acts 2:14a, 36–41

(1) A solid affirmation, verse 36. (2) A fitting response, verse 37. (3) A requisite plan of action, verse 38a: (a) Repentance; (b) baptism in the name of Jesus Christ. (4) A heartening promise, verse 38b: (a) the forgiveness of sins; (b) the gift of the Holy Spirit. (5) An essential imperative, verse 40b. (6) A happy conclusion, verse 41.

Topic: From Fear to Faith
Text: John 20:19–31

(1) Fear and the locked doors, verse 19–23. (2) Doubt and the closed mind, verses 19–29. (3) Faith and the open door, verses 30–31.

Worship Aids

CALL TO WORSHIP.   "I have set the Lord always before me: because he is at my right hand, I shall not be moved. Therefore my heart is glad, and my glory rejoiceth: my flesh also shall rest in hope" (Ps. 16:8–9).

INVOCATION.   Eternal Lord our God, in whom we live and breathe and have our being, grant us a meaningful worship, a cleansing confession, and a life-shaping vision of that will which to do is the heart's delight and the soul's joy, through Christ our Lord.

OFFERTORY SENTENCE.   "You are so rich in everything—in faith, speech, knowledge, and diligence of every kind, as well as the love you have for us—that you should surely show yourselves equally lavish in this generous service" (2 Cor. 8:7 REB).

OFFERTORY PRAYER.   Our heavenly Father, whose bounty is beyond our com-prehension, whose goodness is beyond the utmost reach of our imagining, we thank thee for thy boundless love. Now we give our gifts of love and gratitude and praise to thee, in the spirit of Christ.— Lowell M. Atkinson

PRAYER.   Our heavenly Father we come into thy presence with expectant hearts knowing of the wonderful power that belongs to thy spirit, and the trans-forming grace that can make such a difference in our own lives when we come face-to-face with thee. We come into thy presence eager for fresh fellowship with thee and a new experience of thy won-derful love. We would truly place our lives in thy keeping and put our hand in thy hand and follow thy leading along our life's way. We thank thee that thou canst lift us up from the distress of help-lessness and set us on our way with strength and vigor. We thank thee for that thou dost quicken the mind and challenge our courage, illumine our spir-its, give peace to our troubled souls. The experience of our life's history bears wit-ness that thou art a true God, able to in-spire and to invigorate and to redeem to the utmost. We would renew ourselves in loyalty to thee in this hour. Grant that we may so receive thy blessing that we may be given greater enthusiasm for thy king-dom. With eager spirits and with stron-ger and sturdier step, may we move with assurance into the coming week.

We ask thy blessing upon all the fam-ilies and homes of this parish. Grant that thy Holy Spirit may truly bring light and joy and strength and peace into every heart. Wilt thou be with the people of this community to whom this church would minister and who are not here to-day? Grant that ours may be an increas-ing witness and ministry of outreach that will bring a challenge and hope to those who are not yet in a living fellowship with thee.

We lift our prayer for those who work for Christ in every land of this earth. We rejoice in the thought of this far-flung fellowship, which gives us courage as we work where we are. Wilt thou grant power to thy people as with happy hearts and unquenchable resolve they hold high the banner of Christ in every place and in every land?

We ask that thou wouldst bless especially those who have a special need of thee because they must walk in life's shadows. To all who experience the pain that is our common lot, grant a full measure of thy grace to bring strength and consolation and comfort.

We thank thee for the privileges that make us glad. We thank thee for the demanding responsibilities that make us mature. We thank thee for the need to do and to endure, to sacrifice and to serve. Make us strong and dauntless servants of that suffering Servant who endured all for us. Grant that we may walk worthily in his steps. For we ask it in his holy name who is our Redeemer and Savior forever, even Christ the Lord.— Lowell M. Atkinson

LECTIONARY MESSAGE

Topic: A Joyous Living Hope

TEXT: 1 Pet. 1:3–9

The prayer of praise that opens the book of 1 Peter presents a powerful picture of the Christian life.

I. *A living hope.* Peter writes to the persecuted Christians of his day to remind them that they have been reborn by the mercy of God. It is a rebirth to a new life—one that is filled with a living hope. It is a new life, not like the old one based on merely human aspirations, resources, and strengths. It has come as a gift of God's mercy and grace. Its power is found in "the Resurrection of Jesus Christ from the dead." It was this in-breaking of God into human history in Christ's Resurrection that made the new birth possible and made its new life qualitatively different from the natural life—a new life filled with a living hope.

The Christian life is characterized most essentially as a "life of hope." This is set over against the merely human, earthly life, destined ultimately to decay and perishing. It is a living hope. A living hope means that it responds to the forces brought to bear upon it from the outside. It is a growing hope. It is a hope that in itself renews life. It is set over against the earthly hopes that are based merely upon human strength, wisdom, or worldly resources.

The Christian life is a life characterized by hope. Even in the midst of difficulties, trials, suffering, perplexities, even persecution, the Christian life is sustained by an unbreakable hope. Even illness and the last enemy of death cannot take away the steadfast hope that Christ has placed at the center of the reborn life of the Christian.

II. *An imperishable inheritance.* Peter also reminds the Christians that God has given them "an imperishable inheritance." It is an inheritance of infinitely greater value than the richest material inheritance that anyone could receive from their earthly parents or other relatives. The Christians have a glorious future before them. It is an eternal inheritance, one beyond anything this world has to offer. The riches and pleasures of this world are all destined to perish, but the inheritance of the children of God is everlasting, of ultimate beauty and value.

III. *A life of joy.* It is the living hope in the life of the Christian and the assured imperishable inheritance that lead the Christian to live a life of joy. This joy is ever present in the new life because despair and the feeling of futility have been swept away by the in-breaking of the grace of God. So the Christian can even rejoice in the midst of his or her temporal suffering and persecution. This is so because of the assurance of the ultimate triumph of the living hope in their lives, and the gift of the imperishable inheritance that God has promised to them. The genuineness of their faith, hope, and persevering will redound to their praise, glory, and honor in the revelation of Christ at the end of time. Even their trials and sufferings become the means of blessing, not because of the sufferings themselves, but because of the way the sufferings are dealt with by the Christians.

Even a greater blessing comes in knowing that they are guarded by God's power. So their daily living is characterized by an "unutterable and exalted joy."

It is the joy of knowing that the mercy of God and the response of their faith in a living hope leads them to eternal salvation. This is the salvation that is the glorious consummation of God's promises of victory over all man's enemies and is the gift of eternal life. It is the promise that is to be revealed in all its fullness at the end of time. It is the acceptance of this promise and steadfast faith in the God who made the promise, that brings to the Christian the living hope, the imperishable inheritance, and the life of joy.—Ronald F. Deering

SUNDAY: APRIL TWENTY-FIRST

SERVICE OF WORSHIP

Sermon: Forgiveness of Sins

Text: Mark 2:9

The only persons to whom this message is addressed are those conscious of moral wrongdoing. If there is any hearer with no uneasy stirrings of conscience about his attitude toward anything or his relationship with anybody, then this sermon is not for him. For we are going to talk about forgiveness of sins.

This morning in particular I stress the difficulty of forgiving sin. So often pardon has been presented as an easy gospel, as though one lightheartedly could cry, Come, everybody, and have your sins forgiven! No, it is hard to forgive sins—hard for us; hard for Christ. "Which is easier," said Jesus in the story of the palsied man, "to say, Thy sins are forgiven thee; or to say, Arise and walk?" You see what the Master implies there. It is easier to tell a palsied man to walk—it is easier to meet any other human need—than to say, Thy sins are forgiven.

At first that sounds strange from Jesus. We should have thought it easy to forgive. He said so many glorious words about forgiveness; he exhibited it so marvelously in his life; he made it forever memorable on the cross. One would think forgiveness spontaneously overflowed from him. But no; it was hard for him to forgive, as it always ought to be. And a lesson is there that we modern Christians need to learn.

I. Why, then, was it hard for Jesus to forgive? In the first place, because he took sin seriously. It is easy to condone sin, to make light of it; but when one takes it seriously, it is hard to forgive.

a. Frederick W. Robertson, the English preacher, walked down the street in Brighton once with a face terrific as the Furies and grinding his teeth in rage. He had just heard a man plotting the ruin of a fine girl whom he knew. He took that seriously and it was hard to forgive.

When, therefore, you hear anyone talking about forgiveness lightheartedly as an easy matter, you may be sure of this: He is not forgiving sin; he is condoning it, and that is another affair altogether. There is plenty of that without our adding to it. To say that sin does not matter, to make light of it, to take it easily, to be gracious and tolerant about it—there is plenty of that. But that is not forgiveness. That is moral looseness. Sin does not matter—tremendously! To condone sin is easy; to forgive it is hard.

b. Here lies a familiar difference between two kinds of mothers. Some mothers have no moral depth, no moral seriousness. A superficial affectionateness distinguishes their motherhood. They have an instinctive maternity for their offspring, such as bears have for their cubs or birds for their fledglings. When the son of such a mother becomes a prodigal and wallows in vice, she will receive him again—will receive him, condoning his sin, making light of it, saying that it does not matter, making up more excuses for it than he ever could himself concoct. But some of us had mothers who never would have forgiven us that way. They would have forgiven us, but, alike for them and for us, it would have been serious. They would have borne upon their hearts the outrage of our sin as though they had committed it themselves. They would have forgiven us, but it would have turned their hair gray. That is forgiveness. It always means self-substitution. He who gives forgiveness gives himself. And it is not easy. That is forgiveness, and it is not easy. "Which is easier, to say, Thy sins are forgiven thee; or to say, Arise and walk?"

II. In the second place, Jesus found it hard to forgive because he loved people. Ah! you say, the love of people makes it easy to forgive. No, you miss the point. When you love someone deeply and another's sin hurts that person, it is hard to forgive.

a. Joseph's brothers dropped him into a pit, hauled him out again, sold him as a slave to a band of Midianite merchantmen bound for Egypt, dumped his long-sleeved cloak in the blood of a goat, and carried it back to the father, Jacob, trying to persuade him that Joseph was dead. Now suppose they had grown conscience stricken, remorseful, and, unable to stand it any longer, had gone to Jacob, confessing their sin and asking his pardon. Can you not feel the first question that would have risen in the father's heart in a storm of anxious and indignant grief—Where is Joseph? What, then, has become of Joseph? You ask me to forgive you, but your sin is not simply between me and you. Where is Joseph? Somewhere in a distant land, in miserable slavery he may be today. How can I forgive you until I know that all is well with Joseph?

When you love people, it is hard to forgive sin.

b. So in the Gospels you find it hard for Jesus. He was tremendously severe upon the scribes and Pharisees, you say, and truly he was. But what is the reason? Does it not reveal itself in verses like this, "Beware of the scribes . . . they that devour widows' houses, and for a pretense make long prayers"? His mother was a widow. When, therefore, he was hard on scribes, one surmises the figure of his mother in the background of his mind. "They that devour widows' houses"—that made it hard to forgive.

c. My friends, forgiveness is the miracle. The first thing that we are sure of in this universe in law. Someone has said that we can no more have sin without punishment than we can have positive electricity at one end of a needle without negative electricity at the other. And it would take more than a lighthearted chatterer condoning sin to convince me that there is anything else here. Too cheap! Too easy! But when I face Christ I face one whose plummet reached to the bottom of sin. That is the miracle: that he taught forgiveness, that he practiced it so marvelously that no poor human wreck was beyond the reach of its benedictions; and that throughout Christian history the glory of the gospel has been men and women reclaimed by pardon to a reestablished fellowship with God. Never take it lightly. "Which is easier, to say, Thy sins are forgiven thee; or to say, Arise and walk?"

III. In the third place, Jesus found it hard to forgive because forgiveness is such a terrific experience for the man who is forgiven. Rather, I hear someone saying, it is glorious to be forgiven.

a. To do somebody wrong, to be alienated from him, to be ashamed of yourself, and then by free forgiveness to be restored to the old friendship and trusted again—surely that is the most humiliating experience that a proud man can go through. If there were any other way out of the remorse and guilt of sin, who wouldn't try to find it? For you see, there is just one thing that forgiveness does—one thing only. Forgiveness does not take away the fact of sin. Forgiveness does not take away the memory of sin. Forgiveness does not and cannot take away all the consequences of sin. That great thing forgiveness does—and to have been thus alienated and then reconciled through forgiveness—is about the most searching experience that the human heart ever goes through.

b. Is not that what Christians have always meant when they associated forgiveness with the cross of Christ? I do not know what theory of the atonement you may hold, and I might almost say I do not care whether you have any theory at all, but recognize this fact: Behind all the explanations of atonement that have arisen and taken form and faded away in the history of Christian thought, this conviction has lain deep—the cross means that it was not easy even for God to forgive. It cost. And that is true to life.

c. When, therefore, the gospel has invited men to forgiveness, it never has invited them to a lighthearted place where sins are condoned. It has called them to the cross. And they have always heard the cross saying to them that it was hard even for God to forgive. It cost. It cost just what it always costs when men forgive: love putting itself in our place, bearing on its innocence the burden of our guilt. For whether a mother forgives a son or God forgives us, a cross is always at the center of it, and it is not easy.

IV. Everything that we have said this morning has been leading up to this final and climactic matter: No man's sin ever is done with until it has come through this process of forgiveness. Either your sin has been forgiven or else it is yet in you as sin. I think that is about the solemnest fact in human life.

We know that most clearly when we are at our best. We have gross, brutal hours, when we forget our unforgiven sins, lock them in the hold, let the roar of the world fill our ears until conscience cannot be heard, but ever again the finer hours return, when we know that unforgiven sin still is here because unforgiven. Any minister who takes preaching in earnest cannot look out over congregations like this, Sunday after Sunday, without thinking of all the unadvertised needs that must exist beneath our respectable exteriors. Who can sum them up in their infinite variety? But deepest of all, the unforgiven sins! There must be many here this morning. Go down into that secret place. Unlock that hidden door. Take out that unforgiven sin. For your soul's sake, get rid of it! But there is only one way. Whatever theology you hold, it is the way of the cross—penitence, confession, restitution, pardon.—Harry Emerson Fosdick

Illustrations

WHO MAKES FORGIVENESS POSSIBLE? *Christ can make it possible for you to forgive* *what now seems to you to be unforgivable!* A pagan may be able to overlook his mate's sin or to ignore his fault, but the reason may well be that his love for the other does not run very deeply. A halfway Christian may be able to bypass the sin of his spouse, but he will keep it smoldering just beneath the surface, so that now and again he will cut the other with nasty little words and deeds. The completely Christian attitude is entirely different and, in fact, out of reach for the unbeliever. The Christian can say to his or her spouse, "This *we* have done." If we are really "one flesh" are we not partly to blame for the sin of the other? The Christian also knows that God's forgiveness is real and complete for himself, so that he can truly forgive and forget the sin of his loved one in gratitude to God for his own forgiveness.—Richard E. Boye

WHY WE HOPE.   There is a throne room, and on the throne sits no dictator or lord of the assize, but a Father. There is a workroom where the Potter is molding to shapes of beauty the clay submitted to his hands. There is a Holy of Holies, where stands a cross to speak of sacrifice and love and forgiveness; where the greatest saint may bow beside the greatest sinner to pray, not as the Pharisee but as the publican, "God be merciful to me, a sinner."—Herbert Welch

SERMON SUGGESTIONS

Topic: Living as Strangers
TEXT: 1 Pet. 1:17–22 NIV
(1) Because we are subject to an impartial judge. (2) Because life is empty if it is only earth-centered. (3) Because of Jesus Christ: (a) who redeemed us, verses 18–19; (b) who regenerates us, verse 23; (c) who releases an unworldly love in our hearts, verse 22.

Topic: Sight and Insight
Text: Luke 24: 13–35
(1) *The story:* The risen, incognito Christ was recognized by two believers. (2) *The meaning:* God's truth dawns upon

those who seek him. (3) *The application:* Truth dawns (a) when disillusionment prevails; (b) when least expected; (c) when faith alone must carry the load of the future.

Worship Aids

CALL TO WORSHIP. "The stone which the builders refused is become the head stone of the corner. This is the Lord's doing; it is marvelous in our eyes. This is the day which the Lord hath made; we will rejoice and be glad in it" (Ps. 118:22–24).

INVOCATION. Because you have the broken, spoiled, and rejected things, O Lord, and make them useful and honorable, we dare hope in your forgiveness and in your willingness to use us in your service. Deepen our faith today and give us the joy of your salvation.

OFFERTORY SENTENCE. "And Jesus sat over against the treasury, and beheld how the people cast money into the treasury" (Mark 12:41a).

OFFERTORY PRAYER. These coins and bills are yours, Father. We take them for our given wealth and lay them before you, thankful that we have the opportunity to be a part of eternal enterprises. Multiply their effect as they are used for your glory around the world.—Henry Fields

PRAYER. Large voice of beyond, by your word spoken, creation and all its wonder came forth, and you declared it good.

Holy voice from above, by your inviting whisper, human beings were created in your image and given breath of your lips, and you declared us very good.

Loving voice from beginning, in the fullness of time the Word of your heart became flesh and lived and served among us, and you declared him your beloved son.

O redemptive voice of forever, by the power of your awakening Word, Christ was spoken forth to resurrected life, and you declare eternal victory.

Still small voice from within, you call us to life, full and abundant in Christ, and in Christ's death and Resurrection, you call us to eternal resurrection and hope. Thanks be to God.

O grand voice of God, we lift our hearts and voices to you in praise and adoration. This Third Sunday of Easter, we continue to proclaim, Jesus Christ is risen, Alleluia, Jesus Christ is Lord, Alleluia.

God of all time and space, your creation is voicing her resurrection and new life of spring. Alleluias are bursting forth in the green carpeting of the fields, the heavy leafing of the trees, the glorious blossoms of dogwoods and azaleas, the nodding colorful faces of tulips and daffodils, the choirs of birds singing their alleluias, and the brilliant rising of the sun, even this Lord's day. God of wonder, who touches earth with beauty, make us beautiful and lovely too. May we blossom forth in the smile and mystery of the Resurrection.

Embracing Presence, for those devastated and displaced by violent weather, we pray; for those wounded and abandoned in war zones, we pray; for those held hostage by the grip of fear and gunfire, we pray; for those whose voice has been silenced, and for those who have never had voice, we pray. And as we worship and pray this day, may we go forth to live and speak as resurrection people, alive in the Christ in whom we pray.—William M. Johnson

LECTIONARY MESSAGE

Topic: The Old Fashioned Gospel

TEXT: Acts 2:14a, 36–41

My major interests as a teacher lie in the area of church and community. Because of this I often find myself involved in conducting surveys or reading surveys conducted by others. I remember rather vividly one parishioner's response to a survey of his church concerning the types of sermons the members felt needed to be preached from their pulpit. Ignoring all the options, he wrote in the margin. "I just like to hear the 'Old-Fashioned Gospel.' " He didn't elaborate, but experience has taught me to believe that he meant the preaching of the very basic story of Jesus the Christ. He is not alone in his preference, for it is the repeating of this story that continually brings new and renewed commitment to a salvation experience. Call it an evangelistic sermon, an Easter sermon, or the "Old-Fashioned Gospel," it is essential to the lives of God's people. The preachers in the book of Acts knew this, and they preached it often.

Peter's sermon at Pentecost contains all the basic elements of the *kerygma*, the form the story took in the early church. When Peter's rehearsal of the story is completed, it brings immediate response. Being "cut to their hearts" the listeners are led to ask with anxious voices, "Brethren, what shall we do?" William Willimon notes in his commentary on Acts, "The kerygma has the power to evoke that which it celebrates." Peter's response in verses 38–39 is applicable to inquirers across the centuries. It involves action on the part of the individual seeking answers and a reciprocal action from God.

I. *Repent*. The story of Jesus carries with it a power of persuasion that rhetorical ability cannot rival. The presence of the Holy Spirit brings individuals into a direct encounter with the holy God, and conviction results. Human beings are called to respond to this encounter through repentance. According to Peter, repentance, a change of mind and action, is first and foremost. And although the verse is difficult to interpret at this point, other scriptures lead us to understand that it is repentance, not baptism, that leads to the remission of sins.

Although our sins of the past are forgiven, it must be made clear that the consequences of sin are not wiped out. We may have to live with that which we have done to others and to ourselves that cannot be undone. Maybe a remembrance of our mothers will help us to understand. Do you remember an occasion you did something that deeply hurt your mother? Then later she took you into her arms and hugged you and forgave you, and the relationship was restored. Things between the two of you were right again, but it did not nullify the consequences of your act. The same is true in our repentance before God.

II. *Be baptized*. To be baptized is not the crucial element here for the forgiveness of sin, but it is an essential element in one's willingness to commit to discipleship. Being baptized in the name of Jesus Christ is a visible expression of an inward change. Even here the grace of God is present to strengthen the resolve to a new way of life in Christ Jesus.

III. *Receive the gift of the Holy Spirit*. The day of Pentecost began with the coming of the Holy Spirit in power to the assembled apostles, and now the day ends with the promise of reconciliation and the gift of the Holy Spirit to all who repent. Other passages in Acts make it clear that Luke sees God as the source of the gift of repentance and the gift of the Holy Spirit (see 5:31–32, 11:18).

The telling of the story of Jesus had produced results, and there were three thousand added to the kingdom that day. God had taken the initiative. God had drawn those present that day unto himself. The biblical doctrine of election was realized, not in the choice of one person instead of another person but God's choice of all who would respond in repentance.

Those filled with the Spirit would now manifest the fruit of the Spirit: love, joy, peace, patience, kindness, goodness, faithfulness, gentleness, and self-control (Gal. 5:22–23). By repentance and receiving the Holy Spirit and expressing this through the act of baptism they (as the passive imperative verb in Acts 2:40 indicates) were letting themselves be saved. The Church of the living Christ was alive and growing.

Verse 39 was a promise to the recipients of the book of Acts, but it is also a continuing promise to every generation. Forgiveness of sins and the gift of the Holy Spirit is available to everyone whom the Lord calls. How will you respond to the "Old-Fashioned Gospel?"—John Dever

SUNDAY: APRIL TWENTY-EIGHTH

SERVICE OF WORSHIP

Sermon: Do You Find Things Hard?

TEXT: 1 Pet. 2:20a–21

Peter says what *he* thinks. God calls people to suffer. It's a bold enough statement. We wonder why God allows suffering: to Peter somehow it seems part of the plan. You hear God's voice, and you stop dead in your tracks. You turn around and shout back, "All right. What is it?" And it's a headache he has for you! Or a heartache, which is worse. Very good, answers this old fisherman who used to be so peppery; take it patiently. Jesus did! Quit reviling. Don't threaten. "For even hereunto were ye called," he writes: to make a great go of a hard life!

I. Let's say two things about that. To begin with, let's say this; one discovers it sooner or later: that whatever else we are here for, we are not here to be as we say "happy!" Not in the common, popular definition of the word. That isn't the end and goal of existence.

a. Take any hard life; and most lives are hard in patches if not all over! You can see for yourself that nothing will ever come of resenting it. You may be fed up with the difficulties, as we are in the world just now. Pessimism, despair, 140,000 suicides every year in the United States; it doesn't seem very fruitful! My guess is that we weren't intended to resent the difficulties. So let's take a more moderate course.

Try renunciation. They did that in the East. Turn back on this dreadful thing called life, have nothing to do with it. Cool down all your passions. Work up the cult of oblivion. Say that Heaven itself is a forgetting. And you'll fare no better! Living isn't supposed to forget, to run off and hide its head in the sand like an ostrich, until "all discords die away, all babblings cease."

It amounts to this: You can't get anywhere by damning the struggle; you can't get anywhere by dodging it; and you can't get even that far by trying to do away with it, as some in our time would like.

b. It makes thoughtful people sick to have this happiness theme dinned into their ears from morning to night! Shelves are filled with books of near-psychology about it. Motion pictures glorifying it. Turbaned and unturbaned swamis lecturing on it. As if it were somehow everybody's divine right! When we weren't made for it. We were made for whatever it is that comes up out of the hard soil of effort, out of the creative struggle of human souls, out of the throb and hurt of sacrifice, and the deep tension of forgiveness and hope and an undiscourageable will! There is an "antagonism at the heart of the world"; so that conflict is of the essence of life. These mighty opposites, these contraries, with their forbidding faces, keep us alive. They are our breath, and the marrow of our bones.

A hard life, you say, but say what you will, we were made for it! "Hereunto were ye called!" If you'll start with that, you'll see what happens. You'll see that whatever else Christianity is for, it's not intended primarily to make life easier! I'm eternally afraid of that notion; I'm afraid of it because the first thing that occurs to us when we begin to talk about religion is how glorious it is to be assured of God's love. What light comes from him to shine on the darkest path! What power is ours for the asking! And it's true; it's all true. It bolsters us up when we fail; of course it does! It keeps us confident of our own worth under Heaven. It gives us courage when death comes. But there's so much more than to sit in the sun and bask on that beach! More in life than this smoothing of fur, this padding of cells! More than this surplus of sugar-coated plums that some of us look for, straight from the pantries of the sky! We are tremendously surprised now and then when religion doesn't work that way; and there are those who are ready to chuck it out!

II. But it doesn't. There's that other half of it that we clean forget. The half that's supposed to take hold of ugly situations, as God took hold of chaos, and make something of them. The creative half. And that's painful. Here is the second thing we need to say. It calls for some kind of suffering. You have to give up something to build the kingdom of God in your home or at the office. Really you do. Maybe pride. Maybe success. Something. It's not easy. You don't do it and avoid putting yourself out.

a. It isn't even a thing you have to endure with resignation. "Thy *will* be *done!*" Like a man groaning! It's something to be obeyed, always something to be wrought. "*Thy* will be done!" Like a man shouting! That will is aiming at the redemption of human life, and the redemption of human life is a bitter job. Get in line with it and see. Go to Calvary and look around. And when your eyes are full of it, whisper this, as Peter did: "Hereunto were ye called!"

b. I can't quite tell you how much this means to me at the moment, seeing how God lets us go on being knocked about by the world, and by the people in it; by poverty and accident and death, contempt and greed and war. It's no doubt true, as it has been suggested, that if any man were to permit the things God permits, having power to prevent them; if any government were as bad as his government at times appears to be: we'd put the man in prison, and overthrow the government! I suppose there's no use making any bones about it.

c. I would only ask, what's the good of talking about anything else? I don't know why there's this ghastly mess humanity is facing; unless the answer is just human sin. One can say that without any thought of defending the Almighty. He isn't apt to need our defense. We don't have to carry around in our hands fifty-two easy explanations of why things are as they are, dealing out a few, like so many cards from a pack, every time something goes wrong down here on this sad little planet! I don't know the why of these difficulties you're facing; unless somehow most of them are just part of the same terrifying picture.

Let's be outspoken. We'll not come through the fire of this unknown future that nobody can dodge, and get away as in the past without even the smell of smoke on us! We can take no easy view of God any longer, trifle with him and suppose it won't make a great deal of difference; that he will let us do pretty much as we please, then come in and strike a neat balance in our favor.

III. We have been doing pretty much as we please: letting old habits cling when we could be rid of them—just make us a big enough offer and see! Paying no attention to God when we're angry, or hungry for a little advantage, or lustful for a little pleasure; laughing him out of court and business and politics. Going to church or staying at home, what matter; helping or hindering as the mood takes us; shrugging him off every time the bugle calls, and we are minded to make one more effort to wipe out our name with our own blood. And it won't do.

"If when ye do well, and suffer for it, ye take it patiently, this is acceptable with God. For even hereunto were ye called." It may well be.—Paul Scherer

Illustrations

THE ULTIMATE ANSWER. Faith is an elusive thing. It cannot be programmed. There is nothing we can do to make it happen, or even to prevent its occurrence. Faith is the ultimate answer to the question of suffering, but we humans cannot bring about faith in anyone. Only God can do that. We can try to remove as many barriers and open as many doors as possible between God and the sufferer so that the Holy Spirit is not impeded in its work. We can share our own faith as far as we understand it. We can make available those biblical resources through which God has promised to give insight and strength. But we cannot make another person believe. Sometimes it happens and sometimes it doesn't.—Daniel J. Simundson

DRAWING THE LINE. My wife and I had spent three years in Atlanta, talking with youths such as these—young black men and women trying, in the face of adversity, to forge a better life for themselves. These were more outspoken and self-assured individuals than the ones we had known in the early 1960s. They were quick to describe themselves as "job-hungry" and as full of determination, willfulness, hopeful anticipation. They were not, though, uninterested in some of the refinements of psychology I had heard discussed in New Hampshire and Illinois: "There's success and success. It's not only getting there, it's *how* you get there. If you have character, that means you keep trying, no matter how hard it is, and you don't lose your soul while you're doing that. You have to say to yourself, 'I'll go far and no farther.' You have to draw the line, and if you do, and you can hold to it, you've got character."—Robert Coles

SERMON SUGGESTIONS

Topic: Getting Down to Business

TEXT: Acts 2:42–47

In the early Church, believers in the risen Lord: (1) got themselves informed about faith and life as Christians; (2) did everything needed to keep the fellowship intact and healthy; (3) saw a favorable response to their conduct.

Topic: Whom Shall We Follow?

TEXT: John 10:1–10

(1) *Situation:* People need leadership, and many individuals have attempted the task. (2) *Complication:* False messiahs and false prophets (a) have deceived and led astray many; (b) have been rejected by a remnant of God's people. (3) *Resolution:* Those who are attuned to God (a) find salvation in Jesus Christ, "the way, the truth, and the life," (b) experience a wholesome freedom, verse 9b, (c) enjoy life in its fullness, verse 10b.

Worship Aids

CALL TO WORSHIP. "Surely goodness and mercy shall follow me all the days of my life: and I will dwell in the house of the Lord for ever" (Ps. 23:6).

INVOCATION. Today we are here, O Lord, through your goodness and mercy.

Let the encouragement and joy of this day speak to us reassuringly of things to come, whatever the circumstances of our lives may be.

OFFERTORY SENTENCE. "Then he said to them all, 'If any want to become my followers, let them deny themselves and take up their cross daily and follow me' " (Luke 9:23 NRSV).

OFFERTORY PRAYER. Gracious Lord, you are kindness incarnate in Jesus of Nazareth, from you come all good and perfect gifts, and with your empowering loveliness all our gifts are transformed, transfigured, and shine. We thank you for the joy of who we are and all that is ours. Receive our gifts and receive us; teach us how to receive one another, and especially how to receive ourselves. For if you have great hopes for us, how can we have less?—Peter Fribley

PRAYER. Eternal God, Maker of this and every day, in the sharp cool of this spring morning, we find our way toward your warm and inviting presence. As we gather to worship, steady and make sure our presence. Even as we gather from different streets and neighborhoods, we come also from different places and avenues of life; but we are here now in this moment, and we seek your glad welcome, your kind embrace, your unconditional love and acceptance, we seek your face, O God in Christ.

Gracious Redeemer, author and source of all cleansing and forgiveness, we confess the choking sin in our lives; our hands are dirty with evil, our hearts are hard with hate, our minds traffic in destructive thoughts, our wills succumb to less than good. In this resurrection season, cleanse us from the death of our ways and raise us to newness of life and love in thee.

Wondrous Creator, ever making things and persons new and whole, on this day as we prepare to hear of wholeness in your Word, we bring you our brokenness, all the fractured pieces of our wounded lives—they are many. Again, we have been told, earth has no sorrow that heaven cannot heal, but we wonder and doubt. Does God really know the ache and emptiness of my heart, the chaos of my life? And does God even care? Many of us, O God, did not expect things to be as they are at this point in our lives. Seemingly, someone has stolen all the bases, taken away the foul lines, thrown asunder the rule book. And we awaken each day to that uninvited friend, called pain and sorrow, ashes for breakfast, again.

O Christ in God, we bring our broken selves to you this day, desperately seeking your touch of healing and your invitation toward wholeness. Hear each of our cries for help and come in your Holy Spirit to surround and comfort us with redemption and grace. Amid our anguish and tears, we humbly tremble our pray in the name of Christ. —William M. Johnson

LECTIONARY MESSAGE

Topic: The LORD is my shepherd; I shall not want

TEXT: Ps. 23

Psalm Twenty-three is probably the most familiar passage in the Old Testament. Even some who have very little church background are likely to know the familiar cadence, "The LORD is my shepherd; I shall not want."

L. J. Kirby was a valued lay leader in a church I served in North Carolina. He was semiretired and had the time and desire to make visits for the church. His all-purpose biblical passage to use with those individuals he visited was Psalm Twenty-three. To the patient in the hospital facing surgery, Psalm Twenty-three was a word of assurance; to the family who had just lost a loved one, Psalm Twenty-three was a word of comfort; to a family who was unchurched, Psalm Twenty-three was a testimony of his faith. He found a way to use that passage in virtually every visit. And at his funeral, I could do no more and no less than recite Psalm Twenty-three. That psalm epitomized his faith as it does for many for us. No interpretation could do justice to what that psalm meant to him. Yet, familiarity

brings difficulty in addressing the text afresh.

"The LORD is my shepherd." In Hebrew this opening phrase has only two words: YHWH the-one-shepherding-me. YHWH is the personal name of God, the name that epitomizes the covenant relationship between God and God's people. This is no God who has created the world and now stands off at a distance; God is personal and relational. And this personal God, this Yahweh, is the-one-shepherding-me. God is not merely one bearing the name of shepherd, or holding the role of shepherd. The participle indicates the active nature of Yahweh's relationship with us. As early as Genesis 49:24, God has been referred to as Shepherd of his people. Shepherding includes all the nurturing, protecting, and providing images of the verses that follow. God is not just a transcendent deity, he is immanent and active within our lives. Even more to the point in this regard, YHWH is *my* shepherd. God is eminently personal and relational.

If David is the author of this psalm as a long-standing tradition assumes (apart from the traditional ascription of the entire Book of Psalms to David, seventy-one psalms, including Psalm Twenty-three, bear the title "A Psalm of David"), we note a double implication. David himself was a shepherd (1 Sam. 16:11, 19; 17:15, 34); he knew well the needs of the sheep and the difficulty of caring for them. He also as king was one who was called a shepherd (Ezek. 34, and often), a ruler. So he might doubly use the metaphor of shepherd for himself. But in this psalm, David notes that he also *has* a Shepherd. There are many times in our lives, when we need that nurturing and protecting of a Shepherd. YHWH *is* that Shepherd to us—nurturing, providing, protecting!

"I shall not want." Almost all the English translations of the Tyndale tradition down to the New Revised Standard Version have this translation. And in Elizabethan English, that translation worked quite well. However, in our modern idiom, we want much, much more than we have. Our wants, our desires, are often fueled by advertisers creating new "needs." We want the latest model car, the newest labor-saving appliance, the most recent style of clothes, the "in" toy. We want it all, and we want it now. This verse seems strangely quaint to our life-style. If we can't afford our "want," we simply put it on the credit card so that our wants can be met. A few recent translations such as NIV, Jerusalem Bible, and Revised English Bible (and one old one, the Bishop's version of 1568) translate this phrase as "I shall lack nothing." Not only does this give a good rendering of the Hebrew, but it also communicates well to our modern idiom. With YHWH as the one shepherding us, we lack nothing.

This understanding of the nature of God is quite common in the Old Testament; it is closely related to the Exodus and Wilderness tradition. Deuteronomy 2:7 expresses the thought well: "Surely the LORD your God has blessed you in all your undertakings; he knows you're going through this great wilderness. These forty years the LORD your God has been with you; you have lacked nothing." God's presence and provision (lacking nothing) go together in that passage, and in this psalm. Our God is sufficient; "If God be for us, who can be against us?" (Rom. 8:31). The LORD is my shepherd; I shall lack nothing. — Joel F. Drinkard, Jr.

SUNDAY: MAY FIFTH

SERVICE OF WORSHIP

Sermon: Release from Resentment

TEXT: Luke 6:27–31, 36

I. Are you familiar with the biblical story of the prophet named Jonah? One day, so the story goes, Jonah received a call and commission from God.

a. Well, if you're familiar with the story, you already know Jonah's response. He hopped a ship headed in the opposite direction. However, as is always the case, the hold the Lord had on Jonah's life was unyielding. And so, this half-hearted prophet *himself* repented, headed for Nineveh, and held a citywide tent revival. Needless to say, Jonah's crusade brought in far more converts to the faith than he'd expected.

Perhaps we'd expect him to break out in a song of praise! Ironically, Jonah didn't think this such a joyous occasion. Just the opposite!

b. The magnitude of God's mercy proved displeasing to this prophet. Then, the story says, Jonah became angry with God. Imagine that!

What fascinates *me* most is this *attitude* Jonah displays. Because, frankly, I don't think it's all that foreign to each of us and all of us. Jonah would have perceived the people of Nineveh as his enemies. And what we want for our enemies is certainly

not that they be *blessed* with God's bountiful mercy and goodwill. Rather than see our enemies redeemed, we'd much prefer to have them go to wrack and ruin.

II. And you recall the parable Jesus once told about the young man who one day approached his father, requested his inheritance, and then made a complete mess of his life in some foreign field? Having fallen on hard times, he finally came to his senses, remembering both his home and father. And so, he headed for home. "But while he was still far off, his father saw him and was filled with compassion; he ran and put his arms around him and kissed him."

a. As you probably already know, this young renegade, who returned home with egg on his face, had an older, more stable, more responsible brother. After a hard day handling his father's business, this older brother came home only to hear "dancing and music."

It appears that "good ol' dad" was throwing a big bash for his *wayward* son. And the older brother "became angry and refused to go in." Now that sounds like Jonah, doesn't it?

b. It's a kind of jealousy that wants nothing less than to set very strict limits to God's love! We assume this position every time we expect the Lord to be more severe in judging the sins of others than we anticipate for ourselves. And we often find it difficult to delight in the repentance and redemption of those *we* define as "gross sinners." We'd rather see them *burned* than *blessed!*

III. Someone once glibly remarked that we should "act nothing in furious passion" because, after all, it's like "putting to sea in a storm." But still, we do, don't we?

a. It feels so right to retaliate when we've been wounded. Nothing is quite so bittersweet as the taste of revenge. We willingly exchange blow for blow with those we perceive to have broken trust with us. And how quickly we look for ways to pay off old scores whenever former friendships turn sour.

Do you recall feeling that way? Are you, even now? Painful, isn't it? It's also problematic! And that, for any number of reasons.

b. The most obvious being that such bitterness—such unchecked resentment— has this way of making us mean-spirited and even malicious. With time, over time, it begins to harden the heart, as a callous of indifference encases our character. Sooner than we think, we can become the kind of person other people hope to avoid!

And there are occasions—certainly we already know this, don't we?—there are occasions when such "storms" result in doing irreparable damage.

c. Maybe we attempt to "patch things up." But between ourself and the other, things are never again quite the same. Time after time the hope of any genuine reconciliation breaks up on the rocks of an abiding resentment. A resentment just beneath the surface of all that we think, and do, and say. So. Some breaches widen until, it would appear, no bridge will ever be built to last.

IV. That, you understand, is at least *one* reason we should be grateful for the "gospel." And in particular, that portion of this morning's lesson in which Jesus has said:

a. "I say to you that listen, Love your enemies, do good to those who hate you, bless those who curse you, pray for those who abuse you. . . . Do to others as you would have them do to you. . . . Be merciful, just as your Father is merciful!"

Sounds terribly "idealistic," doesn't it? For many—if not *most*—of us, this apparent command of Christ is beyond our reach. How could he ever expect *us* to live up to such unrealistic demands?

b. Perhaps we should begin with the recognition that these words of Christ are "gospel." That is to say, they're *good* news! In other words, they're not so much about what *we* are capable—or, incapable!—of accomplishing under our own wind. They *are*, however, about that which *Christ* makes possible in the power of his Holy Spirit!

c. Jesus tells us *exactly* what he means in those now famous words: "Do to others as you would have them do to you. . . . Be merciful, just as your Father is merciful."

d. Christians—living under the Lordship of Christ!—are empowered to *act*, and not simply *react!* We just can't afford to allow our affections and attitudes to be shaped and determined by the hatred and hostilities unleashed on us. What we *can* do is commit our wounds to Christ and then *release* our resentment, and bitterness, and desire for retaliation into his nail-scarred hands.

IV. Look. As God's people, we seldom quarrel with him about the measure of mercy he extends to us. But isn't it surely the case that we cringe, and smile through clenched teeth, at the mere suggestion that God might display a similar mercy to those we detest?

a. I'll tell you what I think is at issue here. Apparently God's gracious and forgiving treatment of others leaves the work of judging unattended. So, guess what?

Well, we assume that *we* must take up the slack. That's what! We're not all that comfortable in a kingdom where parties are thrown for wasteful prodigals. And we're not all that at ease with a God whose graciousness exceeds all reasonable limits.

b. So, if we want our world to be different, I suppose we'd better release our bitterness and resentments into the hands of our Redeemer. Whenever, however frequently we feel them. It's just not possible on our own. We must submit to the spirit of him who knows absolutely *nothing* of retaliation, and *only* of redemption.

c. Ridiculous? Not really! Redemptive? Most assuredly! In fact, an embittered woman once responded to these same words of Christ by saying, "But, Pastor, they're hard; they're painful!" And I said in response, "You're right! They are! And Christ has the scars to prove it!"—Albert J. D. Walsh

Illustrations

SELF-TRANSCENDENCE. Most people who have been soundly in love have had that overpowering desire to make the beloved happy, even if it requires some sacrifice. The sacrifice does not seem to matter, because they are getting their happiness from seeing the pleasure of the people they love. When this happens in your own relationship, you have experienced not only one of the greatest ecstasies possible in this life but also a perfect example of the Christian ethic at work. You have transcended your self.—Alan Loy McGinnis

ENOUGH IS ENOUGH. Haven't we seen enough hatred, enough bitterness, enough hostility, resentment, and retaliation? Why, even in the Church, it happens far too frequently. One has a disagreement with some other; and two years—or even *ten* years—later, they're still angry and avoiding each other. I suppose we need to be reminded: "Act nothing in furious passion; it is putting to sea in a storm!" —Albert J. D. Walsh

SERMON SUGGESTIONS

Topic: What It Means to Be Chosen by God

TEXT: 1 Pet. 2:2–10 NIV

You have a chance to grow (verse 2), because (1) you have status, verses 9a, 10; (2) you have a mission, verse 9b, 5.

Topic: Why We Listen to Jesus

TEXT: John 14:1–14

(1) He gives us assurance about the life to come, verses 1–3. (2) He makes life's ultimate possible, verses 4–7. (3) He reveals God to us in an incomparable fullness, verses 8–10.

Worship Aids

CALL TO WORSHIP. "In you, Lord, I have found refuge; let me never be put to shame. By your saving power deliver me" (Ps. 31:1 REB).

INVOCATION. Sometimes, Father, we feel that we are wanderers and strangers in this world, folks just making a journey from we know not where and back again. Then we catch glimpses of purpose in life, feel akin to something majestic and eternal and for a brief moment understand that we are part of a family whose heritage is grounded in eternity. This morning give us the perception and sure knowledge that we are your children, one and all. Deliver us from being like sons and daughters who have gone into the far country and forgotten home and father and family. In this sacred hour of worship recall us to you, that our assurance of belonging may be personal and we may be given courage to live bravely for our individual family as well as the larger family of mankind.—Henry Fields

OFFERTORY SENTENCE. "Thanks be to God for his indescribable gift" (2 Cor. 9:15 NIV).

OFFERTORY PRAYER. Gladly we bring our tithes and offering before you this morning, Father. May they be used across the world to express the royal law of love for neighbor because of love for God, we pray in Jesus' name.—Henry Fields

PRAYER. Lord, you call us to worship you, and you give us diverse gifts for diversely fitting praise. To some you give the ministry of music; to some the ministry of administration; to some, teaching; to some, charitable acts; and with some you have blessed the world with their gift of simply being there.

Receive these your diversely gifted people, and whom you receive, forbid that we should refuse. Open our hearts to one another, not to receive the gifts we want; not to receive the gift we think we cannot live without, but to accept the offering of great price placed before us from the heart of another.—Peter Fribley

LECTIONARY MESSAGE

Topic: Stephen: Full of Grace and Power

TEXT: Acts 7:55–60

Stephen is described as full of grace and power in Acts 6:8. Being full of grace and power did not make Stephen invincible. After his Resurrection, Jesus pledged that his disciples would soon receive power. The Holy Spirit will come upon them (Acts 1:8) and will enable them to preach anywhere and in any circumstance. It is this power to preach even with death staring him in the face that propels Stephen. God does not give disciples the power to win over others but the power to win them over—to transform the enemy, not to destroy the enemy.

I. Full of Power

a. *To proclaim fervently.* When a person is arrested in the United States, the law requires police to read him his rights. We have seen it acted out on TV shows. A police officer nabs a culprit and runs through the litany of rights: "You have the right to remain silent." When Christians are delivered up for their faith, they do not have the right to remain silent. Instead, they have the privilege of speaking the truth to their persecutors. The episode of Stephen's stoning shows how dangerous that can be.

Jesus had warned his disciples that they would be hated by all for his name-sake and would be handed over for trial. He comforted them that when this happens they need not worry—about what to say, that is. Apparently, he believed that they would be more anxious about what they might proclaim in such frightening circumstances than they would about the fact that their very lives were endangered. They need not fret about a feeble testimony. He assures them that he, Jesus, will be speaking through them (Luke 21:17). Stephen's sermon in the face of a lynch mob is a perfect example of the fulfillment of Jesus' promise. Stephen does not try to rebut the accusations brought against him but turns the prisoner's dock into a pulpit.

b. *To challenge fearlessly.* It is easy to leave the stiff-necked and callous alone and not to challenge them. If they get riled they inevitably strike back. Most persons therefore would prefer to play it safe by avoiding them altogether, or by giving them innocuous, lemon meringue sermons that will not rouse their fury. But love cannot leave them alone. The herald needs to confront them with their sin, though it might mean certain death. Love does not turn away from the hardhearted or cower before their wrathful opposition. It leads Stephen to proclaim fearlessly so that some might be won over. Perhaps there is a Paul in the audience who though breathing threats and murder may yet be conquered by words and actions proclaiming God's love and grace.

c. *To challenge daringly.* Stephen had been brought up on charges that he spoke against this holy place, the Temple, and their holy theology with all of its implications. He does not back down from his proclamation of the truth but daringly attacks their fatal delusions. In his sermon, he attacks the two most precious things for Jews—the holy land and the national shrine, the Temple. He not only affirms that God can get along fine without either, he hints broadly that they have turned them into idols. He traces a direct line of apostasy from Israel's rejection of Moses for the idolatry of the golden calf (7:39–41) to the worship of planetary powers resulting in the exile (7:42–43) to the present idolatry of the Temple (7:48–50). The movement of God's spirit is bigger than any nation, and Stephen's sermon marks the beginning of the initial movement that has been centered in Jerusalem and is destined to move beyond. If they circle the wagons around their idols, they will be left behind and will surely perish.

II. Full of Grace

Stephen's concluding words, "You stiff-necked people, uncircumcised in hearts and ears," do not seem to be the best way to end a sermon. They sound vitriolic and unloving. They also can get him killed. But the end of the story reveals that these strong words are tempered by the deepest love. As life ebbs from his body, Stephen cries out to God that these stiff-necked, hard-hearted murderers be forgiven for this deed. He dies preaching with a vision of the glory of the Christ he proclaimed and Christ's words of forgiveness for the people (see Luke 23:34) on his lips. He dies a seemingly powerless death, but his assailants could not repress the power of his testimony. After every beating in Acts, the Christians get up again to preach the same things again; or if they do not get up again, others show up to take their place. It is a strange proof of God's grace.—David E. Garland

SUNDAY: MAY TWELFTH

SERVICE OF WORSHIP

Sermon: Shining Lights from Biblical Homes

TEXT: Exod. 10:20–23

I never could remember coming home to a dark house. Our white frame house, standing at the end of a gravel street in a small Mississippi town, always had a bright shining light in the window.

Now older, more analytical and appreciative of the home place, I count that consistent and dependable light as one of the great blessings of home. Yet, it seems I am less enamored by the literal light and more cognizant of the heritage symbolized in the shining light. After all, God does not expect certain shining lights to burn in the homes of his people. The primary precedent for God's shining home light is recorded in the Exodus narrative. As the heavy and haunting plague of darkness shrouded Egypt, Moses recorded, "There was a thick darkness in the land of Egypt three days . . . but all the children of Israel had light in their dwellings" (Exod. 10:22–23). Those flickering lamps offered hope to God's frightened people, people who were always strangers in a foreign land. What light should be shining forth in homes of God's people today, especially in an age of many darknesses?

I. *The light of freedom and responsibility.* Isaac and Rebekah prayed for a child. Their prayers were answered with the birth of twin boys, Jacob and Esau. Esau grew with a drive to explore the outdoors. Bold and aggressive, he matured into a skillful hunter. Jacob enjoyed home around the family tent. The Bible never attempts to hide Rebekah's favoritism for Jacob and similar feelings by Isaac for Esau. Nevertheless, we must award these well-meaning parents credit for allowing their sons freedom to develop their natural abilities and gifts. The twin boys matured as individuals. Appreciation for the precious commodity of personal freedom should originate in the home. But how much freedom? What about the other side of the coin—responsibility? Freedom must be extended in correlation to the manner in which responsibility is accepted. If responsibility is shelved, freedom can be proportionately lost. In the far country, the prodigal son irresponsibly wasted the substance his father freely gave him. Irresponsibility always results in a loss.

II. *The light of cooperation.* The Bible strongly celebrates the united effort of people with varying abilities. Moses' home illustrates this truth. His sister protected him as a baby. His brother became his spokesperson. Later, Moses' father-in-law offered wise counsel. The family participated in the making of a leader. Every member of a family must know he plays an essential role, contributing to the joy of the home. Each must know he gives a special something to the family no one else can give. Such cooperation testifies to a family-shared conviction of the

God-given value of each individual. This contribution to the mutual welfare of each other forms a basis for effective personal relationships later in marriage, in Church activities, and in the work world.

III. *The light of loyalty.* I asked, "What is love? The nine-year-old replied, "Love is something you give to someone you care for because you want them to have it more than you want to keep it." In his own way, he combined love and loyalty. Naomi freed Ruth to leave her. Ruth's bond held her close to the aging mother-in-law. "Don't urge me to leave you or turn back from you. Where you go I will go, and where you stay I will stay. Your people will be my people and your God my God. Where you die I will die, and there I will be buried" (Ruth 1:16–17 NIV).

Loyalty under God is even more essential for the family. In the memorable words of Joshua, "As for me and my house, we will serve the Lord" (Josh. 24:15). In an age of periodic moves that always result in loss—a lost, broken, or changed relationship—a sense of true family loyalty produces an increasingly valuable stability for the family.

IV. *The light of the presence of Christ.* One day Jesus visited in the home of Simon Peter and healed the fisherman's mother-in-law (Matt. 8:14). One evening Jesus relaxed in Matthew's house and used the occasion to show his care for sinners (Matt. 9:10). Following a fatiguing time with a multitude, Jesus went into a certain home and began to teach. When Christ is present in the home, life changes for the better.

One of the greatest realities of the Christian faith includes the power of the risen Christ to invade all aspects of a life. We can know his life-changing presence. A family can include just husband and wife; or parents and children; or single parents and children; or parents, children, and grandparents; or a single person; or a family can include any combination of these plus the presence of the living Christ.

An old and often-told preacher's story pictures Robert Louis Stevenson as a young lad gazing out into the dark night from his bedroom window. His nanny inquired, "What are you doing?" He answered, "I am watching a man punch holes in the darkness." The old village lamplighter was methodically making his way down the dark streets, lighting the streetlamps.—James Porch

Illustrations

LOVE NEVER FAILS.   Paul Scherer tells of how he went one day to look up the Crimean War with its charge of the Light Brigade, its drums and guns, its death and suffering. He wanted to put against her proper background one lone woman, a lantern in her hand, going from bedside to bedside in the hospital barracks while soldiers kissed her shadow as she passed. He could remember her name, all right—it was Florence Nightingale; but he couldn't remember for the life of him what that war settled. Can you? What is permanent in this world? What is really lasting? Only love—which never fails.—Edmund A. Steimle

THE BATTLE WON.   John the Evangelist, who is praised for his charity, once induced his mother to use political influence, and on another occasion, when the city of the Samaritans rejected our Lord, he and his brother, James, asked our Lord to rain down fire from the heaven and destroy the city. This was not charity. In fact, there must have been a tendency to hate in John, for not without aptness did his Master call him who wanted to send down lightning, a Son of Thunder. But sometime or other in John's life, he seized upon the weak spot in his character, namely, want of kindness to fellow man, and through cooperation with grace, be became the great apostle of charity.

The temptations of the saints were for them opportunities for self-discovery. They revealed the breaches in the fortress of their souls that needed to be fortified, until they became the strongest points. This explains the curious fact about many saintly people, that they often become the opposite of what they seemed to be. When we hear of the holiness of certain souls, our first reaction is: "I knew him when. . . ." Between the "then" and the "now" has intervened a battle, in which selfishness lost and faith won.—Fulton J. Sheen

SERMON SUGGESTIONS

Topic: "Do Not Fear What They Fear"

TEXT: 1 Pet. 3:13–22, especially verse 14b

Suffering of one kind or another, to one degree or another, is unavoidable. (1) However, faithful believers do not have to fear: (a) painful consequences of wrongdoing; (b) a sense of the meaningless of existence; (c) guilt for bad behavior. (2) Rather, innocence in suffering is redeemed and: (a) can be a blessing, verse 14; (b) can magnify Christ as Lord, verse 15a; (c) can provide an unparalleled opportunity to witness for Christ, verses 15b–16.

Topic: We Have a Helper

TEXT: John 14:15–21

(1) Our need: someone like Jesus Christ—to be with us, to reassure us, to teach us. (2) Our provision: the Holy Spirit—who is the Spirit of Jesus, our advocate, the catalyst of the teachings of Jesus. (3) Our access: through obedience to Christ's commandments.

Worship Aids

CALL TO WORSHIP. "Bless our God, O peoples, let the sound of his praise be heard, who has kept us among the living, and has not let our feet slip" (Ps. 66:8–9 NRSV).

INVOCATION. Holy Spirit, strengthen us in trial, comfort us in sorrow, encourage us in well-doing, and in every way possible lead us to an uplifting worship, a holy confession, and a righteous dedication to the purposes of the Lord, our God.—E. Lee Philips

OFFERTORY SENTENCE. "The earth is the Lord's and the fullness thereof; the world, and they that dwell therein" (Ps. 24:1).

OFFERTORY PRAYER. All things and all people belong to you, O God, and for that we are glad. Give us the grace to acknowledge your lordship in the right use of the things within our power and in the proper respect and love we show toward those you have made in your own image and likeness.

PRAYER. Almighty God, our gracious Redeemer and Lord, we lift up our hearts to thee in joy and gratitude for all the things that touch our hearts and fill us with passion and hope, for all the things that break through layers and the wall we build around ourselves in the pretense that we can take care of ourselves. For all the rapid and dramatic changes in the temperatures, for the steady coming of the seasons one after another, for the mighty winds we cannot tame and the rush of spirit in the face of the warmth of the sun, for all the ways in which nature and the elements around us penetrate into our lives and change the way we feel, think, and act, so that we know we are not always of our own emotions. Rainy days and Monday get us down.

We rejoice and give thee thanks for the constant stream of little deeds of kindness, acts of mercy, sacrifices of selves that penetrate the veneer of cynicism that says that life is a dog-eat-dog existence and you have to attack before you are attacked. And yet, despite all the wicked and evil things around us, there are still the "costly demonstrations of unexpected love" that touch our souls, bring tears to our eyes, melt the coldness of our hearts, and sustain us far beyond the cruel pragmatism of the daily rat race.

O gracious God, there is so much that can make us ill, we rejoice and give thanks for every moment of health and healing that we see. We give thanks for the excitement of the games we play, for even the passion of the fan is evidence that we are not as cool as we pretend and that something matters and some things are more important than others to us. We pray for that same passion to touch our lives in the pursuit of justice and mercy and the kingdom of God.

Grant thy peace and power to those who are burdened by commitments that have not turned out as they had hoped, those who have taken mates who have disappointed them, those who have wanted family and do not have them, those who have chosen careers that have not gone as they had hoped. Bless with thy power and peace those who are burdened by old wounds and old deeds that cannot now be changed or fixed. Words spoken to loved ones who are now dead. Business promises that were not kept and that cannot now be repaired. Talents and training that never got used or appreciated. O gracious God, fill us with the vision of thy kingdom, that where we come into the fullness of thy glory, we can be reconciled, we can restore love to its proper place, we can enjoy the fullness of our gifts and the gifts of all others as they were meant to be. Bless and keep us and enable us to live more and more in thy Spirit as thy people.—Rick Brand

LECTIONARY MESSAGE

Topic: Paul in Athens

TEXT: Acts 17:22–31

Paul in Athens! The leading Christian evangelist debates the leading philosophers of the Greco-Roman world! This famous encounter long has captured the imagination of the Church.

I. *The Scene*

The text at hand records Paul's sermon on that day in Athens. But first let's set the scene. During his second missionary journey, and his first evangelist venture into Europe, the apostle Paul apparently found himself alone in Athens, "waiting" (Acts 17:16) for Timothy and Silas to join him. He appears to have had no plans to undertake a missionary effort in Athens. Luke invites us to picture Paul wandering around the ancient city, looking at its historic cultural sites, its famous university, and its numerous pagan religious centers and shrines. Paul finds himself unable to remain a mere tourist, however. "Deeply distressed" (v. 16) by his encounter with the city's verdant but deeply confused religious scene, Paul plunges into dialogue with the intellectuals and philosophers of

Athens, "proclaiming the good news about Jesus and the resurrection" (v. 18).

Always up for a good intellectual debate (see v. 21), some of the philosophers take Paul to stand "in front of the Areopagus" (v. 22). It has never been clear whether this is a reference to the city council, known by the name Areopagus, or to a hill near the Acropolis also called by that name. If the former is the case, Paul may have been asked to appear before the council in their official capacity as the supervisory body in charge of religious and cultural affairs. But if the latter is true, we should imagine a more informal setting in which philosophers, students, and anyone else who was interested gathered to debate the new traveling philosopher. In either case, the situation appears relatively unthreatening, unlike in so many other cities that Paul visited. There would be no flogging, no jailing, no mob violence. But perhaps it was precisely this oh-so-calm response that was the real problem Paul faced that day in Athens.

II. *The Sermon*

You have to know your congregation and find a way to connect with them. Every preacher knows this. But what a congregation Paul faced that day in Athens! He was speaking to the elite, the leading thinkers of a civilization whose intellectual and cultural exploits remain formative for our own culture to this day. This was not the kind of sermon he would have preached in the marketplace in Corinth or the synagogue in Tarsus. But it was the kind of sermon he felt he needed to preach to the philosophers and intellectuals in Athens.

Paul opens by noting "how extremely religious you are in every way" (v. 22). Some interpreters have sensed a note of irony or even a hint of sarcasm in these words; but perhaps Paul was simply trying to begin by finding some common ground with his listeners. Paul is affirming their religious instincts, their desire to know the truth and to know the Divine. He has a great announcement to make—their quest is over. The god they have described as unknown (v. 23—a poignant statement, to be sure) is in fact the one true God. Paul describes this God first as Maker and then as "Lord of heaven and earth" (v. 24). God is the One who "gives breath," and everything else, to humankind, no person or group excepted (v. 25–26). Here we see a clear affirmation of the unity of humankind, a doctrine the Stoic philosophers embraced and justified by an argument from nature. Paul affirms the idea but grounds it instead in the one Creator of every human person and group.

On the foregoing basis Paul offers a critique (remarkably gentle, really) of all pagan "shrines" and forms of worship, as well as of icons of gold, silver, and stone (v. 29). The apostle calls his listeners to trade in their many images and imagined gods for the one, true, unimaginable God. Moving into more explicitly Christian preaching (though never once mentioning the name of Jesus), Paul announces that this one God has inaugurated a new age, an age marked by the resurrection from the dead of "a man whom he has appointed" (v. 31). "Now" is the time when God commands "people everywhere" to repent their former ignorance and turn from their idols. A day has been set for the judgment of the world; this judgment has been delegated to the man whom God has raised from the dead.

III. *The Scoffers*

Observers have noted that nowhere did Paul's preaching of the gospel meet with less success than in Athens. Luke tells us that Paul's sermon is met by scoffing; others vaguely express interest in further conversations sometime (v. 32). A handful of others are described as "believers." But Paul apparently was not able to found a Christian community in Athens, and he soon moved on to Corinth, leaving the intellectual mecca of the Greco-Roman world behind for good.

Yet no proclamation of the gospel is in vain. Certainly this account has profoundly affected the Christian approach to dialogue and intellectual interaction with the world around us. Paul's encounter with his world's philosophers sets the precedent for our encounter with the philosophers and intellectuals of our own time, and with their ideas. His attempt to connect with the groping, partially true but confused religiosity of even the pagan informs our attempt to do the same in our own time and setting. We cannot retreat into our comfortable Christian ghettos. We must go to Athens and preach the gospel of Jesus Christ in terms that Athens can understand.— David P. Gushee

SUNDAY: MAY NINETEENTH

SERVICE OF WORSHIP

Sermon: Some Laws of Spiritual Work

TEXT: John 4:32–38

The disciples must have been very much astonished at the change they observed in the Master's appearance. They left him, when they went away to a neighboring city to buy food, reclining beside Jacob's well, quite worn out with the fatigue of their journey, following upon the fatigues of long spiritual labors. And here now he is sitting up, his face animated, his eyes kindled. He has been at work again.

Now, from this passage with its images,

I have wished to discourse upon *some laws of spiritual work*. For we are beginning to see, in our time, that there are laws in the spiritual sphere as truly as in the mental and in the physical spheres. What are the laws of spiritual work the Savior here indicates? I name four:

I. Spiritual work is *refreshing* to soul and body. "My food is," said the tired, hungry one, who had aroused himself, "to do the will of him that sent me, and to accomplish his work."

a. We all know the power of the body over the mind, and we all know, I trust, the power of the mind over the body; how any animating theme can kindle the mind until the wearied body will be stirred to new activities. So there is suggested to us the thought that we should learn to love spiritual work. If we love spiritual work, it will kindle our souls; it will even give health and vigor to our bodies.

b. How shall we learn to love religious work so that it may kindle and refresh us? Certainly, the only way to learn to love spiritual work is to *do* the thing. The only way to learn to love spiritual work is to keep doing it until we gain pleasure from the doing; until we discern rewards in connection with the doing; and to cherish all the sentiments that will awaken in us that "enthusiasm of humanity." Then that will refresh both mind and body.

II. There are *seasons* in the spiritual sphere—sowing seasons and reaping seasons, just as there are in farming. "Say not ye," said Jesus, "There are yet four months, and then cometh the harvest?"—that is to say, it was four months from that time till the harvest. They sowed their wheat in December; they began to reap it in April. "Say not ye, There are yet four months, and then cometh the harvest? Behold, I say unto you, Lift up your eyes and look on the fields; for they are white already to harvest."

a. In the spiritual sphere it was a harvest time then, and they were bidden to go forth and reap the harvest that waved white and perishing. The like has been true in many other seasons of Christianity; there have been great reaping times, when men have harvested the fruits that come from the seed scattered by others long before.

b. This principle is true in individual churches, that there are seasons of sowing and reaping. It has to be so. If you expect that piety will go on with even current in the Church, that there will be just as much sowing and reaping at any one time as at any other, then you will certainly be disappointed. That is not the law of human nature. That is not possible in the world. Periodicity pervades the universe. People have their ups and downs.

Oh! do you want to see a great season of harvest among your own congregation? What are the conditions but deepened spiritual life in your own individual souls, stronger spiritual examples set forth in your lives, more earnest spirituality in your homes, a truer standard in your business and social relations to mankind, more of heartfelt prayer of God's blessing, and more untiring and patient and preserving effort, in season and out of season, to bring others to seek their salvation?

III. Spiritual work *links the workers in unity.* "Herein is the saying true," said Jesus; "One soweth, and another reapeth. Other men have labored, and ye are centered into their labors."

a. We stand upon the shoulders of the past, and thereby we are lifted up in all the higher work of mankind; and we ought to be grateful to the past, and mindful of our duty to the future; for the time will come when men will look back upon our inventions, our slow travel, our wonderful ignorance of the power of physical forces and the adaptations of them to physical advancement, and smile at the childishness with which, in the fag end of the nineteenth century, we boasted of ourselves and our time.

b. And now it is not strange that this same thing should be true of spiritual work? When you undertake to do some good in a great city like this, you might sit down and say, "What can I do with all this mass of vice and sin?" But you do not have to work alone. You can associate yourself with other workers, in a church, with various organizations of workers, and thereby reinforce your own exertions; you can feel that you are a part of a mighty force of workers, of your own name and other Christian names. Grace be with all them that love our Lord Jesus Christ in sincerity and are trying to do good in his name! And it will cheer our hearts to remember that wide over the land and over the world are unnumbered millions of workers of the army to which we belong. They tell us that the International Sunday School Lessons, which most of us study every Sunday, are actually studied now every Lord's day by at least ten millions of people all studying on the same day the same portion of the Bible. That is but one fact to remind us that we are members of a great spiritual host, doing a great work in the world.

c. My brethren, there is nothing like Christianity to individualize mankind. It was Christianity that taught us to appreciate the individuality of men: "Every man must give account of himself unto God." Men were no longer to lose themselves in the state, as classical antiquity taught them to do, but to stand out in their separate personality and individual responsibility and individual rights and duties. But at the same time much of what we can do that is best in the world we must do by close connection and interaction one with another. Let us rejoice to act through others.

God be thanked that we cannot only do good in our individual efforts, but we can do good through others! Let us cultivate this, let us delight in this, that we can labor through others. Whenever your pastor may stand before the gathered assembly, he can speak with more power because of you, if you do your duty to him and through him.

IV. Spiritual work *has rich rewards.* "And he that reapeth receiveth wages," saith Jesus, "and gathereth fruit unto life eternal."

a. Spiritual work has rich rewards. It has the reward of success. It is not in vain to try to do good to the souls of men through the truth of God and seeking his grace. Sometimes you may feel as if you were standing at the foot of a precipice a thousand feet high and trying to spring to its summit, and were all powerless. Sometimes you may feel as if you had flung your words against a stone wall and made no impression at all. Somehow it does good to somebody, it does good at some time or other; it shall be known in earth or in heaven that it did do good. Comfort your hearts with these words: It is not in vain to try to do good.

b. We talk about doing nothing in the world. Ah, if our hearts were in it! We do not know what we can do. That tiger in the cage has been there since he was a baby tiger and does not know that he could burst those bars if he were but to exert his strength. Oh, the untried strength in all our churches, and the good that the people could do if we would only try, and keep trying, and pray for God's blessing. My friends, you cannot save your soul as a solitary, and you ought not to dare to try to go alone into the paradise of God. We shall best promote our own piety when we are trying to save others. We shall be most helpful to ourselves when we are most helpful to those around us. Many of you have found it so; and all of you may find it so, again and again, with repetitions that shall pass all human telling. "For he that watereth shall be watered also again."

V. Spiritual work shall also be rewarded in the Lord of the harvest's commendation and welcome. Ah, he will know which was the sowing and which was the reaping. The world may not know; we may never hear, but he will know which was the sowing and which was the reaping, and who tried to do good and thought he had not done it, and who was sad and bowed down with the thought he had not done it, and who was sad and bowed down with the thought of being utterly unable to be useful, and yet was useful. He will know, he will reward even the desire of the heart, which there was no opportunity to carry out. He will reward the emotion that trembled on the lip and could find no utterance. He will reward David for wanting to build the Temple as well as Solomon for building it. He will reward all that we do, and all that we try to do, and all that we wish to do. O blessed God! he will be your reward and mine, forever and forever.—John A. Broadus

Illustrations

UPS AND DOWNS. Returning from Germany after World War II, I was sailing in the hold of a troop ship. A violent storm shook the vessel, and the ship pitched up and down violently. The other soldiers and I were frightened. Suddenly, the ship seemed to rise higher than before and plunged down into the ocean. We feared the worst. Almost at once, driven by panic, all of us stormed from the deck.

Even as we did, the calm voice of the captain came over the loudspeaker: "Now hear this. Now hear this. Every soldier is ordered to return to his bunk immediately." The command was repeated several times.

Having been trained to obey orders, we returned to our bunks, cringing with fear and apprehension. We found out later that the ship was in no danger, nor were we. Gradually, the fear and anxiety vanished, and peace was restored in their place.

Sometimes calamity strikes us, and we may think the joy of the Lord has taken a sabbatical.

What good would the joy of the Lord be if it flowed into people's lives only when all was peaceful, calm, and successful? Our Lord meant for his joy to reign in good times and bad. This thought almost reminds me of wedding vows—"in sickness and in health, in poverty and in wealth."—Carlton Myers

THE RIPENING PROCESS.   I love to eat fresh garden fruits and vegetables in the summertime. Allowed to ripen in the sun, they have an indescribable texture and flavor. They are so unlike the pitiful things we buy in the grocery store in January. While the store may call that spongy, hard, tasteless thing a tomato, it does not have the quality it would have had if it had remained on the vine to ripen in the sun. When the Spirit first begins to produce fruit in a Christian, it does not appear in its perfected form. Instead, spiritual growth comes through a ripening process. Too often, Christians remain content with the first appearance of spiritual fruit in their lives. Apart from close contact with Christ, the process stops like the tomatoes picked before they are ripe. By abiding in Christ, a Christian's life matures like ripening fruit.—Harry L. Poe

SERMON SUGGESTIONS

Topic: Planning for the Future

TEXT: Acts 1:6–14

(1) Wishful thinking, verses 6 and 7. (2) Practical promise, verse 8. (3) Ultimate hope, verses 9–11. (4) Interim preparation, verses 11–14.

Topic: "Don't Be Surprised!"

TEXT: 1 Pet. 4:12–14 NRSV

(1) When you have to suffer for your convictions and commitments. (2) That solidarity with Christ and his people in suffering will result in ultimate joy. (3) That even now there are compensating blessings (cf. Matt. 5:11; Luke 6:22).

Worship Aids

CALL TO WORSHIP.   "You are awesome, O God, in your sanctuary; the God of Israel gives power and strength to his people. Praise be to God!" (Ps. 68:35 NIV).

INVOCATION.   Gracious Lord, you know the sighing of a contrite heart before it is uttered. Make us, we pray, the temple of the Holy Spirit, that we may be defended by the shield of your celestial goodness, through Christ our Lord.— After the *Sarum Breviary*, A.D. 1085

OFFERTORY SENTENCE.   "And he said to them, 'Pay attention to what you hear; the measure you give will be the measure you get' " (Mark 4:24).

OFFERTORY PRAYER.   For the warmth of the sunshine, the smell of the flowers, and the laughter of children we give thee thanks. For we know that all good and perfect gifts come from thee. No measure of gratitude could express the debt of love we owe for the gift of thy incarnate Son; but I implore thee to receive these meager tokens as symbols of our devotion to thee from this time forward. We offer all that we own and all that we are for the strengthening of this fellowship and the glorification of thy name. Hear our prayer because we ask in the name of Jesus, our Savior and our Lord.—Michael E. Berryman

PRAYER.   Thank you, Father, for establishing us in the close relationships of home and family. Living as we do with one another, give us the grace to be kind and thoughtful, caring and helpful to each other. Enable us to develop attitudes that discourage self-seeking and encourage Christlike selflessness. Make us brave enough to bear one another's burdens and sensitive enough to know when others must walk their personal road alone. Grant every parent the wisdom to respect their children even as they seek to instruct and guide them toward maturity. Generate a spirit of respect in children for parents and make parents aware of their need to earn that respect by their lifestyles and self-discipline. Inspire all within the framework of the family to walk the pathway of faith, that they may manage the present and anticipate the future with ever renewed hope. May our homes send forth spiritually strong and faithful people to meet the world with a knowledge of Christ and a spirit of Christlikeness because such has been found in the relationships and sharings of our families.

Thank you for the family of faith, the Church, Father. As we live together in this family may we determine to be more faithful to Christ, the head of the Church. Inspire us with a desire to learn of him and follow him as we make daily decisions about small and great matters in our lives. Build within us a desire to share the goodness of God with others as we rub shoulders with fellow human beings in the marketplace, on the job, and in casual meetings by the wayside. Lead us into a lifestyle that, by its very difference, draws others to him who is Lord of all of life. Give us redeeming words to speak to our fellow pilgrims of life as they struggle with the ravages of sin, the pain of being sinned against, and the spiritual lostness that leads to present emptiness and eternal separation from your love and presence. May this family of the faith never forget that our primary purpose is to preach salvation, bring deliverance to the captives, so that every person's hell may be changed into a heaven of purpose, joy, and love and light. To the end that such may happen with us we commit ourselves to you in worship, with expectation, waiting for the powerful movement of your Spirit among us with his calling and cleansing and leading to all that you want us to be and do in Jesus' name.—Henry Fields

LECTIONARY MESSAGE

Topic: About the Meaning of (Eternal) Life

TEXT: John 17:1–11

What is the meaning of life? This is not only a philosopher's question echoing through the infamous ivory tower of philosophical speculation. It is an age-old question and, for that matter, a genuinely human question. It might be a question that is asked in despair or in hope, out of cynicism or out of sincere curiosity and a deep desire for goals and guidance in life. Be that as it may, the question about the meaning of life—the meaning of *our* life—is perhaps *the* most human question.

The answer to the question, according to Jesus, has to do with God, with us, and with our knowledge. The meaning of eternal life, says Jesus in his prayer for the community of his disciples, is that we know the one true God and Jesus Christ, the one whom God sent (v. 3). The meaning of life is found in knowledge of God and God's redeeming activity through Christ.

Does that mean that the answer to the question is back in the court of religious philosophers, of professional theologians, intellectual giants who have figured out the divine mind and the ways God works in this world, and who can tell us all about it? We might indeed come to this conclusion if we apply our modern understanding of what it means to "know." Biblical wisdom, however, offers another avenue of understanding Jesus' words. "Knowing," in biblical understanding, is not primarily an intellectual or cognitive activity, a movement of the mind, but is rather a relationship, a movement of the heart. It is an intimate and transforming bond between the knower and the known. Knowing has to do with participation, with connection, with taking the risk to be deeply affected by that which is known. "To know another," in biblical language, can even mean erotic and sexual intimacy. Knowing, as Parker Palmer puts it, is the practice of relatedness.

To know God in Jesus thus does not mean to know *about* God and the doctrines of the Church. Jesus did not refer in his prayer to the social elite of his times that was educated in religious matters. Rather, he referred to the small band of companions who had shared the last years of his life and his ministry, the people he called his friends (John 15:15). Knowledge of God has to do with being a friend of Jesus. The answer to the question about the meaning of life is found in friendship, in the space that is created by a faithful and steadfast covenant relationship in which we find ourselves known, gracefully received, accepted, and empowered by a loving and forgiving God.

Such is the knowledge of God that Jesus is speaking and praying about. Life that is grounded in such knowledge is eternal, not only because God's faithfulness transcends even the boundaries of death but because this knowledge restores in us the image of God. In knowing God in Christ we come to know ourselves in the mirror of grace as those who have been eternally intended for fulfillment in relationship with the Creator of life and with each other as fellow creatures. The reflection in the mirror reminds us of the beginning when we were free for God and for each other. And, at the same time, it promises a new beginning, a new creation, a transformation from self-will to community, from dividedness to reconciliation, from going astray to finding a place where we belong with God and with each other. The promise is ours when we enter the gracious space that Christ has opened for us, the covenant space of forgiveness, healing, and discipleship.

The question regarding the meaning of eternal life, then, does not point us beyond this earthly life or beyond death. Eternity does not have as much to do with endlessness as it has to do with essence. In reminding us of the beginning, the question points us toward the middle of life, toward the incarnate Christ who embodies both the glory of God and the true meaning of humanity. The meaning of eternal life is found this side of paradise. It is found as we are being found by God and as we find each other in this world where we live together as sojourners. That we know God through Christ as a passionate and compassionate friend, and that such knowledge draws us into community with each other and empowers us to participate together in the liberating movement of God's dominion, that is the meaning of eternal life.— Frank Milstead Woggon

SUNDAY: MAY TWENTY-SIXTH

SERVICE OF WORSHIP

Sermon: The Distinctive Design of the Church Christ Builds
TEXT: Acts 2:1–41

The book of Acts talks about the lifegiving force of the spirit of God indwelling the people of God and creating the Church of God. The greatest need today is not a beautiful building in which to worship. The greatest need today is a contemporary Pentecost.

A pastor of a church in California who also has a nationwide television program decided to take a poll of his listeners. He sought to find out their deepest needs and questions. A large number of the responses had to do with a lack of enthusiasm and excitement in their lives and in their churches. The word *dull* was repeatedly used as a description of numerous churches across America.

The need revealed in this national survey is the same for us today. We need the spirit of God transforming us, giving us life and vitality. The Pentecostal experience of the early Church needs to be recaptured by us as we occupy this new sanctuary.

I. The first chapter of Acts describes three ways in which the energy of the Spirit transformed those early disciples from a group of fearful followers into a group of fearless, exuberant followers of Jesus Christ. The Spirit manifested himself in the form of wind, fire, and a filling.

a. *Acts 2:2 describes the manifestation of the Spirit as a mighty rushing wind.* As I sat in my study reading these words, I contemplated how I could illustrate the blowing of the wind. Out of the sky came an illustration. I heard the sound of a mighty noise. Crack! Boom! The lights flickered and then went out. As I reflected on my experience, I realized the opposite happened at Pentecost. They heard a sharp piercing noise, but the lights came on for them. The wind blew; and instead of the power being turned off for them, the power was turned on. We, in the Church, need the wind to blow, giving us power.

The wind can be destructive or constructive. Several years ago while living in Alaska, I experienced the constructive power of the wind. The temperature had been subzero for weeks. We longed for warmer weather. I awakened one morning and heard what sounded like rain. I went out and soon realized what I heard was water dripping from the roof. During the night a chinook—warm winds from the south—had blown in, raising the temperature from minus-twenty degrees to plus-forty degrees. That's what we need. We need a chinook. We need the warm winds of the Spirit blowing in our hearts, filling us with his power so that we might truly be the Church.

The distinctive design of the Church Christ builds is a Church where the wind of the Spirit blows. The true Church is not built by human hands. The true Church is built by Jesus Christ. Now that we have built a building, we need to allow the wind of the Spirit to blow in this place, energizing us to be his Church. For unless the wind blows, this is nothing more than brick and mortar, paint and plaster. Unless the wind blows in this place, the people who gather here are lifeless.

If everything else is perfect—the building, the people, the organization—and the wind of the Spirit does not blow, then we are nothing more than dull Christ-ians—lifeless forms in need of burial. But if the wind blows, we become full of life and vitality.

Our prayer as we enter this new building is this: "Let the wind blow again, O Lord. Let the wind blow."

b. *The second dynamic of the Spirit at Pentecost was fire.* Acts 2:3 says: "And there appeared to them tongues as of fire, distributed and resting on each one of them" (RSV). Fire is a metaphor used in the Bible in various ways. It is used to describe the judging, purging power of God. John the Baptist proclaimed one characteristic of fire when he said: "His winnowing fork is in his hand, to clear his threshing floor, and to gather the wheat into his granary, but the chaff he will burn with unquenchable fire" (Luke 3:17 RSV). The Church needs the purging fire of the Spirit. We need the Spirit to burn away anything that would cripple us in his service.

The Spirit is a refining and inspiring fire. Like a smelting fire, the fire of the Spirit burns off the dross and leaves pure metal. The fire of the Spirit rekindles enthusiasm, warmth, and spontaneity in the Church.

How we need the fire of the Spirit to purge us, judge us, refine us, and inspire us for service!

c. *Third dynamic of the Spirit at Pentecost was a filling.* Acts 2:4 says, "And they were all filled with the Holy Spirit and began to speak in other tongues, as the Spirit gave them utterance" (RSV). Let's not jump the track and focus only on the "other tongues."

They were filled with the Holy Spirit. Notice when it talked about the wind coming, the wind filled the place. Now it says the Spirit filled the people. As we come to worship in this new place, we need the Spirit to fill both the place and us.

The Spirit filling the lives of Christians is as important as the breath of life. The Spirit is the life-giving force to the Church. Our need is for the wind to blow and fill the room and for the Spirit to come, giving us life. For if he does not, we are empty. We are dull. We lack enthusiasm.

A pastor friend of mine made a comment in his church newsletter that bears repeating. He said: "We talk a lot about empty pews, but empty pews are not our problem. Our problem is the empty people who are in the pews."

Sometimes we stress filling these pews with people. That is important. We have more pews now than we have ever had before, so that challenge is before us. We must reach out and involve others in the life of this church. But there is something far more important than filling these pews, and it is for those who are in the pews to be filled with the Spirit.

The distinctive design of the Church Christ builds is for the Spirit to invade every facet of our being. Those first disciples were transformed energy that filled the place and the people evidenced itself in the form of a mighty wind, a refining fire, and a filling Spirit.

The revitalization was only a means to an end, though. It was not an end in itself. Sometimes the Church confuses the two. Sometimes we mistakenly think we need to be filled with the Spirit for ourselves, but that is only the beginning.

II. Three things resulted in the early Church when the place and the people were filled with the Spirit. The disciples experienced the miracle of communication, the boldness to witness, and a new way of relating to each other in generosity and openness. All three of these things pointed outside themselves.

I do not fully understand the phenomenon described in Acts when the disciples proclaimed the good news in their own language and others heard in a different language. The miracle that occurred was one of communication, pointing outside themselves.

They had a boldness and a courage to bear witness to others about Jesus Christ. This boldness never occurred until Pentecost. Look at a before-and-after picture of Peter. At the Crucifixion, Peter denied his Lord three times. At Pentecost, he stood proclaiming the gospel, and three thousand persons came to know Christ.

Generosity and openness became the order of the day. Here again, the result of the filling of the Spirit was outward.

The Spirit energized those first disciples, and he energizes us—not for ourselves, but for others. We do not build the Church; Christ builds the Church. He infuses it with life—the life-giving Spirit of God so that we, his people, can serve him.

The miracle of Pentecost can happen again. As we enter this new building we have some needs. Our greatest need is not that we have a beautiful place to worship. Nor is our greatest need to fill this place with people. Our greatest need is for the people to be filled to the top with the Spirit.

Our prayer today is that the wind of the Spirit would fill this place, that the fire of the Spirit would judge and inspire our lives, and the breath of the Spirit would breathe life into this church. Our prayer is that, as the Spirit so fills us, we would be empowered to communicate Christ's love boldly, ministering in his name.—M. John Lepper

Illustrations

A SPIRIT OF FELLOWSHIP. In the New Testament the Holy Spirit is in an especial manner the Spirit of the "community" of Jesus, the "Church." For the Holy Spirit is a spirit of fellowship, bringing individuals out of their isolation, making "one body" of them. To be sure, there is for the most part little evidence of this in our churches, a sign of how little the Holy Spirit is alive within them. As the fire is to be known by its brightness and warmth, so the Spirit of God is to be known by the fellowship it produces. And as fire kindles fire (what looks like fire but does not spread is probably only pyrotechnical display), so life kindled by the Holy Spirit must spread and ignite all with its burning. It was in this way that the Church of Jesus Christ spread, it was in this way that the Reformation set all Europe on fire within a few years. It is the Spirit's way of working. The Holy Spirit is God at work now, redeeming, coming to us in the word concerning his Son, the "triune God."—Emil Brunner

AT ROCK BOTTOM. Here on the day when David miserably felt he had reached rock bottom, he suddenly discovered that he had reached the Rock of Ages. In the moment of his despairing cry, "Take not Thy Holy Spirit from me," he was nearer the heart of God than he had been for months. This, I repeat, is the Gospel shining through; and it means that when you have touched the depths, you have touched the everlasting arms.

Take any of us here today. How comes it about that we are here? Surely our broken vows, our frequent failures, would long ago have justified God in removing his Spirit from us once and for all. And yet—the very fact that we are here in God's house is evidence of his spirit still operating in our lives. And therefore to the most discomfited soul here today the word of the Lord would be precisely Jesus' word to his disconsolate disciples long ago: "Look up, and lift up your heads, for your redemption has come nigh!"—James S. Stewart

SERMON SUGGESTIONS

Topic: If All the Lord's People Were Prophets

Text: Num. 11:24–30, especially verse 29.

(1) Would the world be overrun with preachers? No! People can speak for God in different ways and situations. (2) Would they all necessarily be certified and conformist? No! Sometimes the independent voice is more in tune with the voice of God. (3) Would there be a true revival of religion? Yes, provided that: (a) principle is before personality; (b) it is recognized that the Spirit of God is given to the Church and not to leaders only.

Topic: Ingredients of Pentecost

Text: Acts 2:1–21

(1) Unity of persons, verse 1. (2) Unity of purposes, verse 11. (3) Unity of messages, verse 21.

Worship Aids

CALL TO WORSHIP.   "I will sing unto the Lord as long as I live: I will sing praise to my God while I have my being. My meditation of him shall be sweet: I will be glad in the Lord" (Ps. 104:33–34).

INVOCATION.   Throw open the floodgates of glory, Lord, and pour out your Spirit upon us, as we wait, as we pray, as we expectantly seek the infilling that proclaims Jesus as Lord.—E. Lee Phillips

OFFERTORY SENTENCE.   "But ye shall receive power, after that the Holy Ghost is come upon you: and ye shall be witnesses unto me both in Jerusalem, and in all Judea, and in Samaria, and unto the uttermost part of the earth" (Acts 1:8).

OFFERTORY PRAYER.   Holy Spirit of God, work in us and through us, by our living and by our giving, as well as by our personal testimony, so that Jesus Christ may be known everywhere. To that end, receive us and our offerings just now, we pray.

PRAYER.   Father God, you are the same yesterday, today, and forever. We thank you and praise you for keeping your word and for honoring every promise that you make.

We bring to you today our many hurts, scars and painful, open wounds, which have been inflicted upon us by the broken and unfulfilled promises of family members, friends, and countless others on whom we have depended. Heal our hurt and disappointment. Help us to forgive those who have failed to keep their promises to us, especially those unfulfilled commitments that continue to burden our daily existence.

Forgive us for failing to always keep faith with our own promises: for the things we said that we would do, but never did; for the things we promised we would never do, but did anyhow; and for the things we denied doing, even when the responsibility was completely our own.

Let truth, integrity, and peace rule our hearts and our homes, our places of work and worship, and all our relationships. In the name of Jesus, who never taught us anything that was not the truth and who has never made us a promise that he is unable to keep, we pray.—Gary C. Redding

LECTIONARY MESSAGE

Topic: Happy Birthday to the Church

TEXT: Acts 2:1–21

The author of Luke-Acts must have really enjoyed birthday parties! The Gospel of Luke begins with Gabriel's annunciation to Zechariah regarding the birth of John the Baptizer, the joyous "Magnificat" of Mary, and the actual experience of John's birth. The second chapter of Luke provides the most popular and certainly the most eloquent telling of Jesus' nativity. Now, here in the second chapter of Acts, the first book of Church history, the author chronicles another important birth—the birth of the Church! Once again, a time of great joy and thanksgiving.

I. *Announcement.* The apostles and "devout people from every nation under heaven" (v. 5) had gathered in Jerusalem, fifty days after the Passover, celebrating the grain harvest (Feast of Weeks), a time of joy and thanksgiving. In Jewish tradition this time also commemorated the giving of the Law to Moses seven weeks after Passover. Even though the apostles had been instructed to wait in Jerusalem, neither they nor the multitudes that had gathered for the Jewish festival could have anticipated the life-changing event that was about to take place—the official inauguration of the new law of Love proclaimed by Jesus.

The author's announcement of this new day, the birthday of the Church, is steeped in Jewish imagery. Wind and fire were often the material in which the presence of God had been experienced throughout the Old Testament. And while there has been much debate over the proper understanding of the tongues of flame and the utterances of the disciples, there can be no doubt about the aim of the writer to harken back to the Babel story. This new wind and this new experience of utterances reversed the Babel experience, proclaiming a new existence unified by the power of love. This is not some theological treatise recording the mind of humanity working out the concept of the Holy Spirit, but rather the joyous, thankful acknowledgement of a gift.

II. *The Gift.* It is the power of the Holy Spirit working upon the lives of people that makes possible the birth of the Church. This is the gift of the Holy Spirit. The author employs, at least in part, a bit of the apologetic, once again using the words and imagery of Jewish tradition. The Church is not out to destroy Rome or Jewish institutions. Christianity is, instead, the fulfillment of Jewish prophetic tradition and has no concern for any type of power that would interest Rome. Utilizing the words of the prophet Joel, the author emphasizes that the pouring out of God's Spirit "upon all flesh" (v. 17) is a clear sign of the Messianic Age. This is a time of immediacy and exception of "a great and epiphanous day" (v. 20).

Certainly the apostles and "devout" people had experienced the presence of the Holy Spirit in their lives on previous occasions, but here, at this time of Pentecost, they experienced for the first time the *power* of the Holy Spirit. No longer must they cower under the Law or what must have seemed the failure of the cross; rather all people could now rejoice in the power of the Resurrection. It was the power of the Holy Spirit that enabled Peter and the others to begin their active missionary work. It is the power of the Holy Spirit that enables the people of God in all ages to act beyond one's self and participate in this new life.

III. *Invitation.* A new day had dawned, a new wind had blown, and with them came a new invitation. No longer would only kings, prophets, or judges experience the power of God's Spirit; rather all people would be empowered to prophesy, see visions, and dream dreams. No longer would God be known only through the parochial experiences of circumcision and observance of laws. A new and universal invitation had been given: "And it shall be that whoever calls on the name of the Lord shall be saved" (v. 21).

Birthdays are about new life, and that is what the New Testament experience of

Pentecost celebrates. The life of the Church is vitalized by the power of the Holy Spirit and guided by the new law of love made manifest in the life, death, and Resurrection of Jesus. What remains is the Church's continued response to this birthday party and God's invitation to new life.—Ronald L. Loughry

SUNDAY: JUNE SECOND

SERVICE OF WORSHIP

Sermon: The Man Who Came by Night

TEXT: John 3:1–16

I. Nicodemus was a conservative Jew of considerable prominence. Seventy-one men sat on what we would call the Supreme Court of Jerusalem. It was the Sanhedrin. Its function was both legislative and judicial, and it heard both civil and religious cases. Its influence in local affairs was enormous, even during the hundred years of the Roman occupation. Nicodemus was one of those men. In other words, he was a pillar of the establishment.

a. The man from Galilee was in town, so Nicodemus went to see him, at night. Why did he go at night? Why didn't he go honestly in the daylight? Obviously, he didn't want to be seen by his colleagues in the company of Jesus. He was something like the man who visits a friend on the shady side of the street but goes in by the back door.

b. This much can be said in favor of Nicodemus: He had the courage to meet Jesus face-to-face; he did not stand on the edge of the crowd so far away that he couldn't really see the look in his eye, or catch the tone of his voice. He made the move and went to see him.

He was not only a conservative by nature; he was also courteous and began the interview with a compliment. He said, Rabbi, we know that you are a teacher sent from God. This is the approach of an open-minded conservative; reasonable, not fanatical; courteous, but cautious.

II. Jesus, on the other hand, wasted no time with formalities; he went straight to the point. He began to talk at once about the necessity of rebirth.

a. You can't make a few alterations here and there. You can't do it by making minor repairs or even major ones. You can't do it by amendments to the Constitution. It must be a completely reconstructed life. You must be born again.

Nicodemus took in a literal sense the words that Jesus used in a figurative sense. Nicodemus asked, How can a man be born when he is old? Yet before we move on, we must remember that there are many who do just what Nicodemus did.

Many people in this congregation, for example, as I put the bread in their hand at the communion rail and say, "The body of our Lord Jesus Christ which was given for thee," later ask, How can that little piece of bread be the body of a person who lived two thousand years ago? They are not stupid people, but they often fail to see that the literal meaning of the word is not always its only meaning. So, we are not too far removed from Nicodemus, not even the brightest among us.

b. Jesus went on to describe the kind of rebirth he meant. First, it was a birth of *water,* and it is reasonable to assume that he had in the back of his mind the baptism of John the Baptist. It was a clean start, beginning with a frank recognition of mistakes made in the past, an open acknowledgment of them; and being washed in the river Jordan, muddy as it was, by the waters of forgiveness and starting a new life with a clean slate. To turn over a new leaf.

It was also a birth by *spirit.* You must be born of water and of the spirit, Jesus said. In other words, it is something that happens to a person when something "comes over him." It just happens; suddenly he is a different man, a new person.

c. With his feeling for the beauty and

imagery of poetry, Jesus said that it was like the wind. You know what the wind is; you hear it, you see what it does, but you don't see the wind itself. This birth of the spirit is something like that. It is not a physical thing; it isn't repeating once again the physical process of birth; it's something that happens in a different realm.

Whatever it is, one thing is certain about this rebirth: It is not contrived; it is not planned. It is nothing that you can set out to do. It is, in the words of the Bible, "from above." It means something that happens to you; something that gets hold of you and does something to you; it is not the result of anything that you yourself do; it comes when you're not looking, from a source you cannot locate.

III. Then Nicodemus asked one of those stupid questions that I am sure was for the purpose of the dialogue. He said, How can these things be? Jesus was surprised. He said, I'm surprised at you, Nicodemus, that a man of your standing in the nation, of your intelligence and training should ask that question. This is a familiar sight in everyday life. I have used familiar words to describe it—birth, water, wind—all things that you know and see.

a. Jesus then went on to speak of things that Nicodemus might not be expected to understand. He then went down deep, or up high—whichever you prefer—to say what God did to make this new life possible. At that point Nicodemus dropped completely out of sight. The dialogue continues as a monologue by John, whom the spirit of Jesus uses as a mouthpiece.

b. He plunges right into the heart of the subject and says, "God so loved the world, that he gave his only Son to the end that all who believe in him should not die, but have everlasting life" (John 3:16).

IV. Remember that to the woman at the well Jesus said, *God is spirit.* To Nicodemus he says, *God loved the world and gave his Son.* The first is a statement about the nature of God; the second is a statement about the action of God. To know that God is spirit is important; let no one ever underestimate it and try to put him

in a box, or a building, or a system of thought. But to know that God loved so much that he gave himself to save men from a living death, that is quite a different thing.

a. How in the world could John say a thing like that about God? How could anybody know anything like that about God? John could say it because he had seen it happen; it had happened to him. He saw Jesus live; it was no ordinary life. He saw Jesus die; it was no ordinary death. It did something to him; he felt in that death something that was deep in the nature of things: the desire, the will, to give, to spend, not for gain but for love.

He came to see that God's nature is not only to be but to give, to love; and that man finds his life not only in existing day to day—though thousands of people are trying to do that—not existing from day to day, but in responding to that love like an echo.

b. He went on to say that whatever may be the final judgment on a man's life, the man brings it upon himself. His judgment will be the response he makes to the light that he has seen. It may be the light of a fact, which requires him to change all of his former assumptions. It may be the light of his conscience. It may be the light of the cross. Whatever the light may be, his response to it will be his judgment. If he withdraws from it, if he turns his back and runs away from it—denies the facts, drugs his conscience—he is lost. If he is drawn toward it, he finds life. But that is the subject of another sermon!

V. What happened to Nicodemus? There he is, the sympathetic observer, the man who stood on the sidelines, the man who had the courage to go and see for himself, the man who did more than most of his colleagues; but for one reason or another never made the plunge. Do you see anything like yourself in Nicodemus? I do.—Theodore Parker Ferris

Illustrations

CHANGED!   A young man was an alcoholic for a long time. Everything was done that could possibly be done; he tried, his wife tried, his family tried, without any success whatsoever. He was brilliant. His employers tried, they made every allowance. Then one day, because he lived in a state that did not take this sort of thing lightly, he was arrested for driving under the influence of liquor and was put in jail for six weeks. We all thought that that might be the end of him. He never has taken a drink since. It was years ago; he was reborn.—Theodore Parker Ferris

CHRIST IS ABLE.   When "Chuck" Colson accepted Christ as Savior in 1973, reporters greeted the news with skepticism. In *Time* magazine, a writer said: "Of all the Watergate cast, few had a reputation for being tougher, wilier, nastier or more tenaciously loyal to Richard Nixon than one-time presidential adviser Charles W. Colson." On June 21, 1974, Colson was sentenced to a prison term largely because of his conviction that he should tell the truth about his role in disseminating derogatory information about Daniel Ellsburg. Today, he serves as chairman of Prison Fellowship, an organization that he founded in 1976. What those skeptical reporters did not understand in 1973 was that Christ's power to change lives is not limited by the depths of a person's sins.—Lucien Coleman

SERMON SUGGESTIONS

Topic: Creation

TEXT: Gen. 1:1–2; 2:4a. (1) It was orderly. (2) It was progressive. (3) Its apex was humankind—male and female—created in God's image. (4) Its author from first to last was God.

Topic: Paradoxes of the Christian Mission

TEXT: Matt. 28:16–20

(1) Doubters and believers. (2) Earthly powers and the authority of Jesus. (3) Human frailty and disciplined discipleship. (4) The lonely journey and the faithful presence of the living Lord.

Worship Aids

CALL TO WORSHIP.   "O Lord, our Lord, your greatness is seen in all the world! Your praise reaches up to the heavens; it is sung by children and babies. You are safe and secure from all your enemies; you stop anyone who opposes you" (Ps. 8:1–2 TEV).

INVOCATION.   God of all time and every place, help us to truly worship you today. Here in this very room, let us come face-to-face with your eternal glory, your overwhelming holiness, your everlasting strength, your tender love, and your healing touch.—Gary C. Redding

OFFERTORY SENTENCE.   "Each of you has been blessed with one of God's many wonderful gifts to be used in the service of others. So use your gift well" (1 Pet. 4:10 CEV).

OFFERTORY PRAYER.   Before you we bring gifts of tithes and offerings—hard currency. Pray, turn it into bread, housing, words of eternal life and starvation; and use it to bless the world in Jesus' name.—Henry Fields

PRAYER FOR MEMORIAL DAY WEEKEND: A LITANY OF THANKS AND PETITION

L: For Memorial Day's quiet, a time with family and friends, a time with our own thoughts, a time simply to feel and be;

R: *We give you thanks, O Lord.*

L: For the blessed memory of the dead, ministering spirits, mediated in Christ, friendly ghosts who call;

R: *We give you thanks, O Lord.*

L: For the company of flowers: peony and lilac, iris and geranium, their silent laughter that lances sorrow, their sorrow that lightens and eases our own;

R: *We give you thanks, O Lord.*

L: For the privilege and dignity of a decent burial; the strength of caring and kindred spirits;

R: *We give you thanks, O Lord.*

L: For the buoyant, uplifting truths of the Christian faith, inwardly heard and truly lived, that transcend all barriers;

R: *We give you thanks, O Lord.*

L: That there may be peace and domestic tranquility, founded upon fairness and compassion and the opportunity of a decent life for all;

R: *Hear our prayer, O Lord.*

L: That we bind up the wounds of those whom life has treated harshly, and that we may, with goodwill and true helplessness, teach, and learn, that caring accountability that gives life;

R: *Hear our prayer, O Lord.*

L: That with hearts truly fixed on you, and uplifted by all ministering spirits, we may work for those blessings for which we have prayed, and not grow weary beyond renewing;

R: *Hear our prayer, O Lord.*—Peter Fribley

LECTIONARY MESSAGE

Topic: A Message from a Christian Friend

TEXT: 2 Cor. 13:11–13

Few things are as challenging as joining a story in the middle. When late to the movie, theater, or flipping the TV dial after the fifteen-minute commercial message, it's hard for most of us to pick up the story line.

Today's lectionary text gives us only the last few sentences of Paul's Corinthian correspondence. His arguments with the members of the church he planted in Corinth are somewhat known to most of us; but these final brisk words collect the positive values of the Christian faith for Corinthian believers. Paul was saying "good-bye." What he says here outlines what he believed to be most crucial about our Christian faith.

I. Whatever you have experienced in life, "Rejoice!" This is a commandment, not just an idle word. Joy is the proper response to the good news of the gospel of Jesus Christ. Surely Paul did not mean that life was all pleasant. Life's burdens and disappointments, agonies and pains, evil activities or pleasant experiences are known by all of us. Paul insists in the face of these that the sure gift of God in Christ is forgiveness for sin and the strength to "lift up our hearts" in every situation. In Christ, Paul says, "You have not been forgotten by God." This message from an often imprisoned, beaten, and abused missionary pastor would not be missed by his readers.

II. The second message has two parts.

a. "Mend your ways." The grace and mercy of God through the Holy Spirit has given us yet another chance to "pull ourselves together" while still in this life. The ways we spend our lives together are vital and important to God. When we fail, God has sent the Holy Spirit as encourager, so that we may try again. With God, we always get another chance! Thank God for another chance and for the companionship of the Holy Spirit, whose constant presence nurtures us in this task.

b. The believer's mind is another part for mending. "Be of one mind" is a powerful corrective to the severe words elsewhere in this letter. Differences in ways to express faith will continue to fuel conflict between fervent believers. However, the hallmark of the Christian faith is not only to believe, but to join our minds to the mind of Christ. We are to "be of one mind" in faith. The good news of the Gospel is that believers can be reconciled to believers by the same grace that reconciled believers to God. It is a profound work of the Holy Spirit to nurture us both in the mending of our ways and in enabling us to become of one mind with fellow believers.

III. Paul's third admonition, "be at peace," requires little explanation to those who "rejoice" in Christ and whose lifestyle is constantly "mended" under the guidance of the Spirit. They know daily celebration. However, those missing the joy of Christ and mending by the Holy Spirit will be locked out of the experience of the peace of God. When you can live on the island of peace with the creator, sustainer God and in harmony with your most intimate friends, then an inner state of comfort or peace is one of your rewards. Here, Paul describes the Christian faith as superior to the ancient Hebrew goal of "shalom." The God of love and peace becomes a routine presence for Christian believers.

Notice the trinitarian form of Paul's admonition. Life's experiences themselves are "trinitarian." With Christ to save, the Holy Spirit to guide, and God as loving parent, the ancient doctrine of the Trinity becomes a process of our living faith. How then can anyone avoid knowing the trinitarian nature of God?

Ancient Christian theologians attempted to define the Trinity through the theological creeds, doxologies, and dogmas of the Church, using terms like *substance, person, equality,* and *duration.* Others used simple object lessons to assist Christians to understand the paradox of one, yet three.

There is a legend, of uncertain origin, that Patrick, a fifth-century missionary bishop, was sent by Pope Celestine I to convert the pagan tribes of Ireland. Consistently the Irish had mistreated, impris-

oned, and murdered other missionary priests. Patrick was fully aware of his danger. When interrogated by Laoghaire, high king of Ireland, Patrick was required to define the Trinity. If, said the high king, you give me an adequate definition of the Trinity, I and all my people will become Christians. If not, you will die. Without hesitation, Patrick stooped to pluck a green shamrock from the grass in front of the king and said, "As your Irish flower grows from one stalk and expresses its beauty in three leaves, so God is one and beautifully expresses himself as Father, Son, and Holy Spirit."

By clear object lessons or through the trials and tribulations of personal experience, glimpses of the mystery of the doctrine of the Trinity are given to those of us who are believers. We can give thanks that Paul's last words to the Corinthians are true for us today: The grace of the Lord Jesus Christ, the love of God, and the communion of the Holy Spirit *is* with us, Amen. —Walter C. Jackson III

SUNDAY: JUNE NINTH

SERVICE OF WORSHIP

Sermon: Called to Be Saints

TEXT: Rom. 1:7

A favorite term was invoked by the apostle Paul in describing members of the Christian community; he called them "saints." The New Testament letters of Paul bestow this title over three dozen times. The apostle says things like this: "The saints salute you"; "Contribute to the needs of the saints"; "You are fellow citizens with the saints and members of the household of God"; "To all God's beloved . . . who are called to be saints." And so the references go. Paul was entirely comfortable with that designation, "saint."

But if Paul was comfortable with it, probably we in this later day are not. At least, saint is not an ordinary word in our vocabularies. If we think about it at all we have images of stained-glass heroes with

long beards and halos. Saint is not a word or concept given much currency among us.

Even in translations of the Scriptures this is so. Out of nine modern-speech versions of the New Testament, five of them avoid as often as possible a literal translation of the Greek word, *haglos,* which means "holy, consecrated," or (as we would say) "saint." Take that greeting of Paul found in the opening verses of his Epistle to the Romans. An exact translation says, "To all those who are in Rome beloved of God, *called saints:* grace to you and peace from God our Father and the Lord Jesus Christ." Rather than use that word "saints," here is how some of the contemporary translations read: one version substitutes the words, "dedicated people." Another says, "holy people"; still another, "God's people." Dr. J. B. Phillips uses the phrase, "Christ's men and women," while Dr. Goodspeed chooses simply "people." Care is taken, it seems, to spare us from having to think of Christians as saints; the preference being for a more egalitarian term like "people."

II. Why this aversion? What do the translators think we are afraid of? Being so concerned to communicate in understandable language, some of the current Scripture translations leave us unaware of the full import of the biblical message, at least on this subject. (The New Revised Standard Version of the Bible happily uses the word "saints" in the Romans reference I have just mentioned.)

There is one explanation to offer, although it has less and less validity in this ecumenical age. In our zeal to be distinguished from Catholics, we Protestants historically (and even presently in some areas of the globe) have shed words and practices that seem to us unwarranted. Protestants are most uneasy with the Catholic veneration of saints and the election of certain men and women to Sainthood, spelled with a capital S. The word "saint" thus appears to confer almost superhuman status upon ordinary mortals. It is this that Protestants reject. Sadly, in the process, we purge our Bibles of a very important concept. Not reading that we are called to be saints (as Protestants), we fail to see or think of ourselves as those who are specifically set apart for God's service.

Yet that is what "saint" means, as Paul employed it. The saints are those set apart for God's possession, God's use, God's service. Paul described himself as "separated [or set apart] for the Gospel of God." He was not talking about perfection nor about sanctimoniousness. Paul was a very practical, down-to-earth person. When he said that Christian believers are called to be saints he was dealing with *discipleship*. He was saying that Christians are those who have taken seriously the attempt to follow in Christ's footsteps. They have not arrived, but their pilgrimage had begun.

III. Our Protestant confusion over this matter is evident in a story about the church elder who spoke one day to a businessman in the congregation.

This elder, representing the spiritual concerns of the church, said to the man, "As the fish perishes on dry land, so you perish when you get entangled in the world. The fish must return to the water and you must return to the Spirit." The businessman was aghast. "Are you saying that I must give up my business and go into a monastery?" "Definitely not," the elder answered. "I am telling you to hold on to your business and go into your heart."

When we hear the word "saint" we jump to the conclusion that it is all about monasteries and otherworldliness. Not so, as the elder would say. It has to do with searching your heart, and setting your course, and trusting Christ. "Saint" is a title suggesting faithfulness and consecration. As our worship began we sang a glorious hymn that provides a definition for us if we heed the words. William How was the author of that hymn; he has us extolling "all the saints, who from their labors rest." These are the people, the next stanza tells us, who by faith confessed before the world the name of Jesus. They are likened to soldiers, faithful, true, and bold. Their hearts are brave; their arms are strong. These are the saints, a countless host. Alongside that hymn I would place a children's refrain that begins, "I sing a song of the saints of God. . . ." It concludes by saying, "I mean to be one, too."

IV. We could name this, our Christian vocation. We are called to be saints. That means, we are consecrated people—and any holiness or virtue that attaches to being saints is because of God's grace and God's calling. As saints, our lives focus upon such things as prayer, service, and building up the body of Christ. Philosopher Friedrich Schleiermacher in a totally different context wrote that the "special calling . . . of a person . . . is the melody of that person's life." Our special calling is to be saints, and our resulting faithfulness to God becomes the melody of our lives. In a wedding ceremony the minister says, "Marriage is an honorable estate." So it is! Living as saints likewise qualifies as an honorable estate. This is the proper description of a Christian's life, the life that you and I—all of us—are called to lead.

Once again, that life of the saint is in the midst of the world, not in some monastery or out of the mainstream of experience. An Old Testament verse can be appropriated as a guideline here. It says, "I will rise now and go about the city, in streets and in the squares; I will seek him whom my soul loves." If we identify God as the one our souls love, then our daily walk, in the city streets and squares, is a constant witness to him. We seek him whom our souls love.

We shall pray to be strengthened in our service as the people of God. In all of this we shall be acting to fulfill our Christian vocation, our calling to be saints. And when you think about it, there is a certain legitimacy in relating the idea of "saint" to a stained-glass window. Instead of making saints aloof and ethereal, their image in stained glass carries a richer meaning. A little child explained it when he sat in a great cathedral observing the faces etched in colored glass on every side. When told that these were pictures of people called saints, the youngster's eyes brightened and he said, "Now I know what saints are. They are people who let the light shine through."

That's it. That is a worthy description of our lives, of each one here who is called saint. Through you, through me, the light of God can shine.—John H. Townsend

Illustrations

GOD'S HOLY PEOPLE.   "Saints." A subtle danger of misunderstanding lurks near that word. When we hear the term "saints," our thoughts are prone to move in a moralistic direction. We think of an ethical quality in man, perhaps even approaching sinlessness. But it must be affirmed that all such thoughts are false to Paul's meaning. He knows no "saints" in the Roman Catholic sense of the term. He does not mean to apply the term only to such Christians as have advanced far in personal sanctification. *All* Christians, without exception, are saints. But it is not by virtue of their own efforts or their eth-ical quality that they are such. They are saints only by virtue of God's call. Thereby they have been taken out of this world and set apart as God's own. Through God's call and election they have become members of God's holy people. Therein, and alone therein, their holiness lies.—Anders Nygren

BECOMING A CHRISTIAN.   What makes a person a Christian, however, is something particular that happens precisely to him. He becomes a Christian through the Word of Jesus Christ that is spoken to him specifically in the power of the Holy Spirit. Without ceasing to take part in the being of the world, he is called by this Word, that is, awakened, enlightened, and liberated, to being as a member of the community of Jesus Christ. By this Word, spoken particularly and distinctively to him, he is separated from the rest of the world. Though he still belongs to it, he is set over against it as one who knows and bears witness to the objective self-declaration of God.—Karl Barth

SERMON SUGGESTIONS

Topic: The Best by Faith
TEXT: Rom. 4:13–25

(1) *The Abraham story:* God promised Abraham universal blessing through his descendants (Gen. 12–17). (2) *The meaning:* God's promise is fulfilled, not by good works but by grace realized through faith. (3) *The implications:* (a) God can and does do the "impossible" (v. 17); (b) Though *doing* is important, *believing* is of first importance (v. 22); (c) The most significant focus of *our* faith is in "him who raised Jesus our Lord from the dead" (v. 24).

Topic: Jesus' Puzzling Behavior
TEXT: Matt. 9:9–13, 18–26

(1) Traditional practices of the Pharisees. (2) Unsavory associations of Jesus. (3) Divine justification for Christian compassion, verse 13.

Worship Aids

CALL TO WORSHIP.   "Let us all the earth fear the Lord; let all the inhabitants of the world stand in awe of him. For he spoke, and it came to be; he commanded, and it stood firm" (Ps. 33:8–9).

INVOCATION. O God, maker of the heavens and the earth and all that is in them, grant that this service of worship may continue your work of creation, making us into the kind of people that you would have us be—saints, no less; your own special people to do your will in this world.

OFFERTORY SENTENCE. "Good people produce good from the store of good within themselves; and evil people produce evil from the evil within them. For the words that the mouth utters come from the overflowing of the heart" (Luke 6:45 REB).

OFFERTORY PRAYER. Mighty God, you have called us together, and, by your Holy Spirit, made us one with your Son our Lord. We thank you for the Church, for the power of the Word and the sacraments. We praise you for apostles, martyrs, and brave people who have witnessed for you. We are glad you have joined us in friendship with all Christians, and that you sent us into the world full of the Holy Spirit to say that you are love; through Jesus Christ our Lord.—Adapted from *The Worshipbook*

PRAYER. O God, our Father, you alone can enable us to accept and to obey your commandments and to do your will.

Increase our faith.
Help us,
To trust you when the skies are dark;
To accept that which we cannot understand;
To be quite sure that all things can work together for good to those who love you.

Increase our hope.
Give us
The hope which has seen things at their worst,
and which refuses to despair;
The hope that is able to fail,
and yet to try again;

The hope which can accept disappointment,
and yet not abandon hope.

Increase our love.
Help us,
To love our fellow men as you love them;
To love you as you have first loved us;
To love loyalty to our Lord above all other things.

Help us so to love you that your commandments will never be a weariness and a burden to us, but that it will be a joy for us to obey them, so that in obedience to you we many find our perfect freedom, and in doing your will our peace.

So grant us,
To fight the good fight;
To run the straight race;
To keep the faith,
that we may win the glory and the crown.

Hear these our prayers for your love's sake. Amen.—William Barclay

LECTIONARY MESSAGE

Topic: The Family of God

TEXT: Matt. 9:18–22

I. Religious leaders today often hold up the family as a kind of cultural and religious icon, arguing that "decline" in the family has led to moral decay in the nation and membership losses in churches. The solution, it is proposed, is to strengthen the traditional family. Such an attitude, however, tends to exclude those from less traditional families and those without families and prevents them from feeling a part of the life of a congregation. Many who are single parents, widowed, divorced, and lifelong singles feel excluded from Church life and less than adequate—as though they just don't quite measure up. The question confronting our Church is this: "Will we develop a biblical understanding of what a family is or continue to exclude what is becoming an increasingly significant proportion of our Church membership?" We can begin to answer this question only when we recognize that it is the Church—not a biological family unit—that God intended to be the first family of all Christians.

II. In today's Scripture passage we encounter a woman who had suffered from a hemorrhage for twelve years. In her culture, this woman could not have suffered from a more terrible or humiliating disease. It isolated her from all human contact. Everything and everyone she touched was infected with her uncleanness. She was completely shut off from the worship of God and the fellowship of other believers. Her life was an unending existence of isolation and loneliness.

So isolated was this woman, so ostracized from Jewish society, that she could not muster confidence enough even to approach Jesus directly. Surely someone so unclean could not talk to the great Teacher. Besides, if anyone in the crowd recognized her they would immediately cry "unclean," and she would be banished from his presence. No, the best thing was to approach him unobtrusively. She had heard of his great miracles. Perhaps if she touched just the hem of his cloak, that would be enough to heal her. Everything else had been tried; what was there to lose?

With trembling fingers, this poor woman reaches out and touches Jesus. She immediately feels power surging through her weakened body and knows that she has been healed. Jesus, too, knows that power has gone from his body and demands, "Who touched me?" Jesus does not wish to expose the woman but to continue the healing that has begun in her. The restored woman, fearful of losing her newfound health, steps forward with great trepidation. Rather than receiving the rebuke she fears, she instead is blessed by the great Teacher. Recognizing the shame and isolation that has been her only companion for twelve years, Jesus calls her "daughter."

We cannot imagine the impact this one word would have had on that poor suffering creature. "Daughter" is a relational word. To be a daughter is to be in relationship. It is to be a part of a family. Jesus not only healed her; he brought her into his family—the family of God. She who had been excluded, ostracized, shunned, is now a part of a family. She has brothers, sisters, mothers, and a Father. She belongs. She is included. She is a part of something. She is in relationship.

Then, as if to put a seal on all that has taken place in this woman's life, Jesus tells her, "Go in peace and be free from your suffering." Jesus confirms that she is now a member of his family. She need never walk alone again. Her suffering, both physical and spiritual, is ended.

III. Is this true of our family? Is our Church a place where no one need walk alone, where everyone feels wanted, needed, and loved? Or do we exclude those who may not be like us, whom we don't understand, or who don't live up to our expectations? It is only right that everyone who enters the walls of this church will feel as this woman did—a loved and needed member of God's family.—J. Richard Jackson

SUNDAY: JUNE SIXTEENTH

SERVICE OF WORSHIP

Sermon: My Father, My Teacher

Text: Deut. 6:1–13; Eph. 6:1–4; Luke 15:11–32

We are not perfect, but we also know that there is something very important about being a father. As a matter of fact, when the phrase "my father" comes into my mind, the words that complete the thought is "my teacher." *My father, my teacher.* A colleague of ours in the Presbyterian ministry has written "For Fathers Who Aren't in Heaven." That's us. We're not perfect, but there is a real sense in which we are always teaching. There is never a moment, as mothers and fathers, guardians and grandparents, that we are not teaching. It may be at the very moment that you think you are not teaching that you are teaching the most. By our absence, by our presence, by the things we stress, by the things we avoid, we are always teaching. We will find no better curriculum than the one that is here in Deuteronomy 6. We give a lot of lip service in our country to the Judeo-Christian heritage, but we had better give more than lip service, for it is the basis of our entire society and every institution in it.

At the heart of that tradition is Deuteronomy 6. The sum of Moses' address to the Jewish people is, "Now if you go into the promised land you must teach your children and your children's children." According to Deuteronomy 6 there are three things we must teach our sons and daughters: The first is that we teach God. Secondly, we teach about grace. Thirdly, we teach guts. That's right, I said it, guts. Some of you parents will have to straighten your children out later. The preacher should have chosen another word, but nonetheless it will probably stay in your mind. Guts, grace, God.

I. This passage begins by saying that we are to love the Lord our God with *all* of our heart and soul and strength. "Shema O Israel"; hear, O, Israel. It is saying, "Listen, this is all that will make a difference when your children come to you and are worried about death, destruction, disease, and other enigmas." At those moments easy answers and pat responses do not suffice. Have you taught them that there is God beyond yourself? One of the greatest pits that we fall into as parents is the preening and posturing that suggests we've done it on our own and there is no one beyond us. When we point beyond ourselves we have given our children a greater gift than any formed by loom or lathe. We either teach that we are the center of the universe or that there is One who has called us into being and will be with us each step of the journey.

Long before my father was reconciled to the church I remember watching him at night. He would kneel beside his bed and pray. Years later my father's faith in Christ was strengthened, and there was a new sense of commitment. But before that I remember, more than anything else, seeing my father kneeling beside the bed. To this day that is my most vivid impression of my father. It shows me strength more than beating somebody into subjection. It means he knew enough of himself to know he needed to kneel before almighty God and pray for his family, his work, and his life.

Douglas MacArthur said that he was probably known best as a soldier, but it was not his most important work. His important work was as a father because as a soldier he dealt in destruction, but as a father he dealt in building up. And the most important time he ever spent as a father was when his son would kneel with him to pray daily: "Our Father, which are in Heaven . . . " The most important thing as mothers, fathers, grandparents, aunts, uncles, neighbors we ever teach our children is that God is, and *God is* to be worshiped, enjoyed, and served forever.

II. The second truth that we have to teach is grace. Did you notice that in this passage from the sixth chapter of Deuteronomy Moses says to the people, "You will go into land that I will give you"? *I will give you.* "You will then come into houses that you did not build. You will drink out of cisterns that you did not dig out of the ground. You will, indeed, enjoy vineyards that you did not plant." The most important thing we can give our children is a sense of grace. I didn't earn it, possess it, build it myself. The very fabric of the universe is a gift. God has given us health, opportunity, and salvation in and through Jesus Christ. What we are called to do is respond; for the only response to grace is gratitude. The lives that are strong and enduring beyond time are those that have learned that grace begets gratitude, and gratitude is a way of living that cannot fail.

One of my fathers in the faith, Elton Trueblood, has said that we come to a new understanding of living when we begin to plant trees under whose shade we will not sit. It is gratitude for God having given us so much that impels us to plant trees that we will never sit under. I think we have gotten ourselves into such an ecological mess because we have not taken the biblical injunction seriously to be caretakers of the earth, not just for ourselves but for our children and our children's children. Grace leads to gratitude, and gratitude leads to a responsible stewardship of the earth's resources.

III. Then, finally, there is need to teach "guts." In verse 12 it says when you get into the land you must fear the Lord. It sounds harsh to us. Yet if we fear the Lord we will fear no one else. If we fear and love the Lord we can stand up to all others who say, "You must do it our way or perish." To stand up against all the conventional wisdom of this "present age" takes guts. He goes on to say, "And you shall serve the Lord." It takes courage to serve the Lord instead of ourselves or the despots of this present age. You may call it gumption, but what we need to communicate to our children more than anything else is that there are a few important principles on which we will stand and on which we must continue to give all of our life's energy. We stand *here;* God help us, we can do no other. We can communicate to our children that there is a God who loves us and calls us in Jesus Christ. To stand against the "go-with-the-flow" materialism is to bear witness that life is grace and we are given so much so that we may be a channel of God's blessing to others. Think of "guts" as the fortitude to stand when others would easily sit down. We have found that which is worth standing for and passing on to future generations. When we do it we are teaching "guts."

Like a good textbook this passage not only gives us three subjects that we should teach children, but it also tells us how. It says, "Teach your children diligently." First of all, when you sit in your house. Secondly, when you walk on the road, and thirdly, in your rising up and your lying down. The first suggests that the most important ways in which we teach our children are not in teaching Sunday school or sending our children to Sunday school. I watch my children,

and you know what I discover? They are watching me. They are watching me *all* of the time. The times they seem most open to learn are not when I have on my preacher hat. Oh, no, it's when I'm trying to get them to bed. *Then* all of the "great" questions come up; yet some of these questions are important ones. This is a reminder of the importance of what we teach when we are *sitting in our houses.* Indeed, if we're sitting at home but thinking about work we're not fully there when our children talk to us. We are teaching them something then when we are half listening to them. Yet, when we overcome other pulls on our time and are fully present for our children, we are preparing the way for all we might teach them of one who commands us to listen, "Hear O Israel."

We are given the opportunity to teach our families about God, about amazing grace, about the guts it takes to stand and live. We do it in our sitting, in our walking out on the roads of our vocation, and also in our rising up and in our lying down. Think for a minute how you teach in that way. If you begin the day by saying in a horrified tone, "Good God! It's morning" instead of "Good! God, it's morning!" you've already begun to set the mood. We begin in our rising up and then also in our lying down. I think about how we end the day some days. Last night was one of those times when the best way you can end the day is in the forgiveness of sins. It is saying, "I blew it, I didn't do the best as a father." It is hearing the confession of our children and believing that God forgives us, builds us up, and give us a renewed vocation; God calls us in and through the family.— Gary D. Stratman

Illustrations

WHEREVER WE GO.   We're also teaching when we're on the road. How we live our lives outside the home is so important. Believe me, our children will pick it up. Arthur Miller, the playwright, has given us several plays the truth that what we do in our life outside the home will influence our children. In the play *All My*

Sons a wartime industrialist wanted his children to respect him more than anything else, but in his work he cut corners. Because of cutting those corners in his industry his own son was killed. What he said he wanted most was lost. In another of Miller's plays, *Death of a Salesman*, Willy Loman wanted his sons to respect him and honor him. Yet his self-esteem was so low that he thought he needed an affair to bolster it. His son found out about that affair, and the one thing he wanted more than anything else, the respect of his son, he lost. We do teach our children "when we walk on the road," for what we truly honor and value is often seen in our life outside the home.—Gary D. Stratman

LISTENING AND IMITATING.　　Children have never been very good at listening to their elders, but they have never failed to imitate them.—James Baldwin

SERMON SUGGESTIONS

Topic: "Is Anything Too Wonderful for the Lord?"

TEXT: Gen. 18:1–15 (21:1–7), especially 18:14a NRSV

(1) The ancient story demonstrates that God is resourceful beyond our imagining. (2) Yet, we today share Sarah's initial skepticism: (a) in our prayers; (b) in our planning; (c) in our everyday, blind secularism that fails to see God at work even miraculously in our material world. (3) Nevertheless, God shatters our skepticism by what he *does* and *is*.

Topic: From Faith to Glory

TEXT: Rom. 5:1–8

(1) Peace with God. (2) Through Jesus Christ. (3) To the end that we have "hope of sharing the glory of God."

Worship Aids

CALL TO WORSHIP.　　"What shall I render unto the Lord for all his benefits toward me? I will take the cup of salvation, and call upon the name of the Lord" (Ps. 116:12–13).

INVOCATION.　　Help us now, O Lord, to pay our vows to you in the presence of all your people. And let this day mark the beginning of a new and better life with you and for you and for those who have been given to us by you to love and cherish.

OFFERTORY SENTENCE.　　"But my God shall supply all your needs according to his riches in glory by Christ Jesus. Now unto God and our Father be glory for ever and ever. Amen (Phil. 4:19–20).

OFFERTORY PRAYER.　　Lord, help us in this offering so to prioritize our values that we can distinguish the important from the transitory and thus give to feed the soul in Jesus Christ's name.—E. Lee Phillips

PRAYER.　　O God, whom to be with is to be at home:

The very idea of family was born out of the fellowship of the Holy Trinity. We thank you for the general idea and its embodiment in specific persons.

Whether through natural birth or by means of adoption, you have brought persons together to love and care for one another. We express gratitude for such nature.

Understanding God, please do not hear us unappreciative if we confess that families have problems. Certainly that is not your fault. You have given us good models. You have guided our steps. But there are problems even among families who worship you regularly.

We have the capacity (sometimes a strong tendency) to mess up that which you have intended as good. Brothers and sisters quarrel with each other. Husbands and wives fail to get along. Grandparents are forgotten. Cousins become vicious competitors. Family members even abuse one another—mostly by manipulation and language, but sometimes by physical and psychological violence.

O God, help us—enable us to recognize and deal with the fatigue that allows us to destroy our loved ones.

Spare us that torrid, selfish drive to

success that causes us to ignore and hurt those with whom we live.

Still the surges of jealousy and competitiveness that fill our lives but empty meaning from our relationships.

Teach us understanding, patience, forgiveness, and reconciliation.

Help us love again.

We desire for ourselves and request from you families that emulate, at least in part, your family, O God.—C. Welton Gaddy, *Prayers* (Judson Press)

LECTIONARY MESSAGE

Topic: You Are Important

Text: Matt. 9:35–10:8

The grand theme of the life of Jesus was his emphasis upon persons.

The reader of Matthew 9:35–38 observes that the author does not report specific facts and effects. He paints a picture of the Messiah's traveling from village to town with scenarios of interpersonal relationships.

The first Gospel of the New Testament described the travel of Jesus, especially painting pictures of persons, all kinds of persons whom he encountered. There is a remarkable similarity between the persons and the problems of those cities and those of today.

Matthew noted that crowds evoked the compassion of Jesus because he viewed them as "sheep without a shepherd." Sheep are notoriously helpless animals, totally dependent upon a shepherd for guidance and protection.

Sheep and shepherd are familiar metaphors in the Old Testament, describing leaderless people. No wonder God instructed Moses to choose Joshua as successor, "that the congregation of the Lord would not be as sheep which have no shepherd."

I. *God initiates his love.* Following the Genesis creation narratives God created mankind. Why? God, best described as "love," created mankind upon whom he could lavish his love. From "the beginning" God revealed himself as One who is love and concerned for all his creation.

II. *God works through people.* Matthew described the calling of the twelve disci-

ples to become the instruments of God's grace. The harvest, therefore, depends upon individuals willing to be his ambassadors. Integral in this mission is the ministry of compassion.

III. *God calls helpers.* Throughout holy Scriptures God called men and women to communicate his love to individuals and nations. Matthew delineates the calling of the "twelve" and their training to minister in the name of Jesus to harassed, helpless people.

One of the responses of Jesus to sheep without a shepherd was his recruiting helpers to share the good news of his grace.

Is it not interesting that the words of Jesus were heard when and where there was a glut of religious practitioners, amid multiplied religious activities, synagogues in every village, six thousand Pharisees, twenty thousand lower priests, a small, powerful group of Sadducean priests, a large group of Essenes? This is hardly different from our current era, inundated with religion, yet folks are lonely, helpless, and empty.

Jesus sent "missionaries," chosen representatives of himself.

The first helpers were called disciples, learners. Because those early followers had the capacity to be disciples, the Teacher shared his authority to teach, heal, and defeat evil. Thus, the embryonic group of helpers became apostles, ones sent, commissioned.

IV. *God cares for all.* The good news is that God cares for all the sheep, the lame and those without a shepherd. He cares about their fears, one of which is their fear that he will abandon them. People are afraid because they imagine that it would be easier for God to leave them than to care for them.

The compassion of God is straightforward and not patronizing. People are brothers and sisters among humankind, not cases, unfortunates, not even disadvantaged, and certainly not disenfranchised. Jesus Christ identifies with each person, on the level with and face-to-face.

Consider some examples of his universal ministry of loving compassion: to an outcast woman, John 4; to a Pharisee, John 3; to a representative of the "IRS," Luke 19; to a youth who "had everything," yet experienced emptiness, Mark 10; to an attorney seeking truth, Luke 10; to a scribe who was evaluating his priorities, Mark 12; to a mother-in-law who was ill, Mark 1. Each individual was important to Jesus.

V. *You are important.* As Jesus traveled through Palestine he stopped dead still for individuals and groups in need, sheep without a shepherd. Consider an illustration from the third Gospel.

Luke 15 is a microcosm of the life of Jesus. Three stories, including one about a lost coin, a lost son, and a lost sheep, focus upon compassion. The three parables place emphasis not upon the flock but upon one sheep; not the fortune, but one coin; not the lost family, but one prodigal away from home and the other prodigal at home. Individuals are important to Jesus.

As my young son accompanied me on a preaching tour, we talked about Matthew 6:24–34, the sparrows and the lilies, and God's love for all his creation. An elementary pupil, he caught the great sweep of the Creator by his simple translation, "How much more important are you than all God's creation, much better by far." So it is that people, like sheep—harassed, helpless, and without a shepherd—are important to God, "much better by far."—Edgar Earl Hatfield

SUNDAY: JUNE TWENTY-THIRD

SERVICE OF WORSHIP

Sermon: The Story of the Iron Gate

TEXT: Acts 12:1–19

I. This is a story about a gate. It is an iron gate that leads to a prison. There it stood, shut, locked, forever closed, save when someone had a key to open it.

Inside the prison was Peter. Peter got himself into serious trouble and was imprisoned by the order of one no less than Herod. As far as Peter could see, and as far as his friends could see, there was no escape possible. Then, one night something totally unexpected happened. There was a light in the cell as if from nowhere. There seemed to be someone with Peter. He roused him out of his sleep.

"Get dressed," he said, "put on your shoes, wrap your cloak around you." Peter did so, and as he did his chains fell off. Then the strange visitor said, "Follow me," and they went through the halls of the prison, passing one guard after another. Finally, they came to the gate. It was severely, impenetrably closed; yet, when they actually approached it, it opened for them of its own accord! Now this is not a fairy story but a miracle story, and I hope the difference will appear as the sermon proceeds.

II. There were at least two influences at work that may have had something to do with the opening of the gate.

a. The first was the prayers of Peter's friends. The story says that "there was a continual stream of prayer going up to God from the church on his behalf"—a continual stream of prayer going up from all the other people who were associated with him in the new resurrection movement. There is hardly any other strength so sustaining in time of trouble as that—to know that hosts of people who care about you are lifting you up in their prayers.

But Peter must have said to himself, "It is all very well to have that reassuring strength, but what good can those prayers possibly do me under these circumstances? You might as well match a butterfly with a bulldozer, or expect a zephyr to blow down a skyscraper as to expect a stream of invisible, intangible prayer-thought to have anything to do with, or make any impression upon, a prison wall." And yet, we know that in life spiritual forces are continually mastering material situations.

I wonder, to us modern people that a

stream of prayer coming from sincere, devout people, rising up to God on behalf of someone whom they know to be good and honest and true, why does it seem strange to us that that great spiritual power and force could do something? The longer we live the more we believe from experience that prayer has power; and the more we appreciate what Martin Luther meant when he wrote that he would rather have an army against him than a hundred men and women praying. That is one of the influences that was very probably at work on the iron gate.

b. The other is the angel of the Lord, for the Bible describes the strange visitor in Peter's cell as an "angel." As far as I can see, angels as they appear in the Bible are the personification of laws beyond the range of our present understanding. From time to time that other world breaks in upon this world; when that happens, we see strange and marvelous things. The angels are those who dwell in the margin of mystery by which our life is bounded; and from time to time they come into our world like unearthly visitors, and then strange things come to pass.

To think of it in more purely personal terms, here is a man who has used up his reserve energy and he knows that he has come to the end of his resources. He is spent; he has overdrawn his account. As he faces a difficult assignment, he shrinks from it because he knows that according to all the laws of his own nature he will not have the strength to meet it. And then, when he gets to it, the strength flows into him. He has the strength, not according to any laws that he knew previously, but according to other laws that have been set in operation. It is as though there were an angel strengthening him.

c. So, there were these *two* influences at work in the case of the gate that opened of its own accord. Up from the earth came the stream of prayer. Sometimes think of that when you are in trouble; think of that constant stream of vitality rising up as if to touch the skies. And then, from the other direction, from the other world of mystery and power, coming down from above, was an angel

of the Lord, like a flash of light. When these two things come together it is no wonder that something unusual happens and that the gate opens of its own accord.

III. This is a story with a moral. In fact, there are two morals.

a. The first is that nothing is impossible. We live in an unrestricted universe in which spiritual forces can master material situations. They do not always do it, granted. The angel does not always come, and the gates do not always open. We are ready to grant that. But it can happen; *and it is more likely to happen when we believe that it can happen.*

Sometimes you feel like a hopeless individual. I know you do because some of you tell me that you do. At least, you feel as if you were in a hopeless situation. You look around and you see not one single opening or way out. You feel just as confined as Peter did in his cell, although you have the freedom of the city of Boston, or the whole countryside in which you live. You say to yourself, "I am a hopeless case. I know the laws that operate in my case, and I know that they cannot be changed. This is my fate and I will grit my teeth and bear it."

Never say it! There are no hopeless cases, for no one knows when, without violating any of the laws that are operating now in your situation, some new law may be brought to bear from above that will completely change your situation and release you, liberate you, and set you free.

As I said before, I am not prepared to say that miracles always happen, and the man who counts on them is bound to be disappointed. Sometimes people get into a jam, and they apparently stay there for a long time and nothing happens. But living in the kind of universe that we do, our task is to keep our minds open to the possibility that anything *may* happen, not counting on a miracle, but ready for it if it should happen; for when the streams of prayer begin to go up, and the flights of angels begin to come down, then you can expect a miracle.

b. The other moral is this. Nothing is so hard as you think it is going to be. We have a way of looking into the future, and as we do, we can see all sorts of obstacles, tremendous hazards, things that we think we never can possibly meet or overcome.

Then we find that when we get there, they are not so bad as we thought. We stand looking at them, and as we do, we dread them. I am willing to confess that I, and I am sure you too, have wasted more energy in dreading the things that were ahead than doing any amount of work that I was called upon to do. As you look as them and weigh them in preparation, they seem so heavy that no human shoulder could ever carry them; but when you pick them up, they are not nearly so heavy as you thought they were going to be.

Think how much time you spend dreading the future. I am frank to say that I have even dreaded going to the dentist and when I got there, I found it not pleasant, but the way was open and the ordeal of no such magnitude as I had foolishly imagined it. When you begin to shoulder the task, in shouldering it the weight is diminished.

So, when we get to these gates that seem to be so impenetrable and so thoroughly closed, they have a strange way of seeming to open of their own accord. Even the gates of death, I have learned, which seem to be so fastly closed and so terrible to anticipate, when you get to them they open as if to welcome a friend, and you go through without any fear or any dread.

IV. What I am asking you to do now is to face frankly the fact that there is something in your future that you dread. I wish I knew for my own satisfaction if there is anyone who has nothing in the future that he dreads. It may be disease or old age, embarrassment, failure, disappointment in love. Whatever it is, take that thing out and look at it and then say to yourself, in secret, in the presence of God, "I am never going to dread that again. I am going to do everything I can to prepare to meet it and then I am going to forget it, because I know that when I get there, the gate will open of its own accord." You can never force the gate open; it will not respond to the battering of impatient men. All you can do is to move steadily toward it.

As the curtain falls on this story of Peter and the gate, we see Peter going down the street after he has been released from prison; he goes just one block, and the angel leaves him. It is as though when we need strength to meet some great emergency in life, the strength comes, and when we go through the gate and are set free once more into the ordinary paths of life, the angel leaves us and lets us go on our own free way. But we go with the reassurance and the remembrance of the time when the going was hard, and the angel of the Lord visited us, and there was a light in the cell, and the gate opened of its own accord!—Theodore Parker Ferris

Illustrations

A WAY OUT.   In 1812 there was a small boy in a French village playing in his father's saddle shop, and he put out both his eyes when he fell with an awl in his hand. He grew up a blind boy, and when he became an adult he wrote to his father, "The blind are the loneliest people in the world. Only books can free the blind. But there are no books for the blind that are worth anything." That idea impressed itself upon his mind and kept working upon him until one time he saw a French army captain with a code of dots and dashes that were raised so that they could be read in the dark. He took his clue from that, and in five years he printed a book that the blind could read. He was Louis Braille. The idea that was in his mind that only books could free the blind did free them and did open their prison door. Here then is another instance in which spiritual forces master material situations.—Theodore Parker Ferris

THE PEACE OF GOD.   The peace of God with which Paul's letter to the Romans concludes is no cushion on which to rest. Rather it is a height toward which I must stretch. I myself have not yet reached that height. This becomes clearer to me every time I submit this self-examination to the scrutiny of God.

But I am also one who has been laid hold of. A hand has touched me. And regardless how often I have failed, how much despair I suffer, failure and despair cannot harm me. I am called by my name and my name is written in the book of life. That simultaneously becalms and disturbs me; for the peace of God does not lull one into drowsiness and sleep. Rather, God's peace is a mover and shaker without compare. God's peace is the power with which we go forth, outside, before the gate, into the world.—Helmut Thielicke

SERMON SUGGESTIONS

Topic: Yet God Was with Them

TEXT: Gen. 21:8–21

(1) *The Story:* In a cruel turn of events, Hagar and Ishmael became victims in a domestic political struggle in which God intervened with grace. (2) *The Meaning:* God's justice and love operate above and beyond human control. (3) *The Application:* (a) God is generous. Abraham provided a bottle of water; God gave Hagar and Ishmael a well; (b) God is present. Abraham exiled them to the unfriendly wilderness and loneliness; God gave Hagar and Ishmael his very presence.

Topic: What It Means to Be a Follower of Jesus

TEXT: Matt. 10:24–39

(1) We may be ill-treated as he was. (2) We are assured of our worth to a loving heavenly Father. (3) We will be acknowledged as belonging to Jesus in the final judgment. (4) Meanwhile, we have a cross, a sometimes extremely costly cross, to take up in order to follow our Lord where he goes.

Worship Aids

CALL TO WORSHIP.   "Give ear, O Lord, unto my prayer; and attend to the voice of my supplications. In the day of my trouble I will call upon thee: for thou wilt answer me" (Ps. 86:6–7).

INVOCATION.   Lord, get through to us today. Pull out all the stops. Seal your Word in our hearts and your will in our souls. Stir us up and let us be found faithful in sacrifice and service. Don't let us go.—E. Lee Phillips

OFFERTORY SENTENCE.   "You are so rich in all you have: in faith, speech, and knowledge, in your eagerness to help and in your love for us. And so we want you to be generous also in this service of love" (2 Cor. 8:7 TEV).

OFFERTORY PRAYER.   Lord, allow us to be as faithful in giving as are your blessings to us, that by sharing we may learn the worth of receiving, in the kingdom of joy built on giving itself away in God's honor.—E. Lee Phillips

PRAYER.   Eternal Father of all mankind, we thank you this morning for the opportunity of free worship in a free land. We thank you for the great moral and spiritual heritage that is ours and for those who in past times purified and sustained true worship for future generations. This morning as we stand in the long line of the faithful, grant us your presence to inspire us, to keep us, and to direct us as we keep the faith that has been entrusted to us.

Forgive us, Father, for not always being true to the faith and heritage that we have received. Too many times we have lost sight of you and your high calling as we have become lost in the arguments and debates concerning fine points of religion and theology. So often we have failed to see Jesus and looked instead for ways to magnify our brothers' and sisters' weaknesses. We have been quick to criticize and slow to support evident strengths. We have been quick to find fault in what is being done but slow to lend a hand to do the work better. We have sought to make excuses into reasons for lack of cooperation in kingdom service. Too often we have sat on the sidelines finding fault with those hard at work in the fields when you have called us to be in the midst of the harvesters gathering in your name. Father, we have injured our souls, discouraged others, and erected selfish barriers that need to be torn down. Forgive us and lead us toward a personal and churchwide great awakening that will lift, encourage, bring light, and save all lost souls within the dominion of our responsibility.

Help us to see our task as a great unfinished opportunity for Christ. Help us to read the Bible as a living book and to seek you through prayer. As a living savior help us to find true liberty and truth and adventure in the local church. Help each of us to accept our church membership with loyal devotion and to grow in grace as we serve our Lord day by day.

Now may your peace and love and healing and joy, your forgiveness, redemption, and salvation come to all who stand in need of your personal presence in their lives and situations.—Henry Fields

LECTIONARY MESSAGE

Topic: Participation in Christ

TEXT: Rom. 6:1b—11

I. *Participation versus pinballism.*

a. According to an important sociological study, many of us in the United States see ourselves as self-contained individuals—no more profoundly related to others than a pinball in a pinball machine is related to the bumpers it bounces against—self-contained spheroids with a shiny, reflecting surface, bouncing toward the goals we hope for ourselves.[1] If that is true of us, we will surely misunderstand what Paul is saying to us here. Paul is talking about being baptized into Christ, dying with Christ, being raised with Christ, being united with Christ, being conformed to Christ's likeness, walking in the newness of the life of Christ. We are not isolated individuals; we are participants in the death and life of Jesus Christ.

b. How do we participate in Christ's death and Resurrection? (1) By the grace of God, who showed his love for us in Christ's dying for our disobedience and being raised to make us no longer enemies of God but friends (Rom. 4:24–25 and 5:8–11). (2) By the peace with God, which we have because Christ has given us access to God (Rom. 5:1–2). (3) By the love of God, which pours into our hearts—love toward God and toward others (Rom. 5:5). (4) By our baptism into Christ (Rom. 6:1–11).

II. *Participation in baptism into Christ.*

a. Baptism is our identifying with Christ in his death and Resurrection. In the early Church, converts were taught for two years the way of discipleship—living that follows Christ. Then they faced Rome and renounced the worldly way of life; they faced Jerusalem and professed the way of discipleship they would walk in. They "took off their garments of simple 'penitential' cloth . . . , and were immersed three times in the name of the Holy Trinity." They were given "the garment of new life . . . . Baptism was a declaration of 'no' to one way of life and 'yes' to another . . . ."[2] It was a drama of participation in Christ: not only burying the old sinful self but also raising up the new self to live and breathe in the Holy Spirit.

b. Some experience the death of the old self and the resurrection of a new self in Christ as we face our own limits and commit ourselves to a faithful life of service; or let our pride and prejudice go and love another who is hard to love; or admit we are not in control of our own lives and submit to God's grace and control; or take the bread and the wine as participation in the death and Resurrection of Christ.

III. *Participation in the body of Christ.*

a. Romans is symmetrical. The first eight chapters have their mirror image and climax in the last eight chapters.[3]

---

[1]Robert N. Bellah, et al., *Habits of the Heart: Individualism and Commitment in American Life* (New York: Harper & Row, 1985), 78 et passim.

[2]Larry Rasmussen, *Moral Fragments and Moral Community* (Minneapolis: Fortress Press, 1993), 157–59.

[3]Each section in the first eight chapters argues toward a conclusion in the last eight chapters:

1:1–8 = ch. 16 (Paul, apostle for the gospel: grace and peace to *all*).

1:9–15 = 15:22–23 (travel plans and prayer).

Chapter 6 prepares the way for the climax in chapter 12. There we see that dying to sin and rising to new life means giving our bodies as a living sacrifice and being transformed into a life of love and peacemaking. It means affirming the different gifts of members of the body of Christ and living together in Christlike love. It means not thinking of ourselves

---

1:16–17 = 15:14–21 (service to the gospel and faith/obedience of the Greeks).

1:18–4:25 = 14:1–15:13 (all are sinners saved by grace, so don't judge or boast but make peace with one another).

Ch. 5 = ch. 13 (peace, love, hope).

Ch. 6 = ch. 12 (dying/sacrifice; living a transformed life in Christ).

Ch. 7–8 = ch. 9–11 (misery of Paul's sin and Jews' unfaith; God's deliverance of Paul, Jews, and Greeks—no separation).

too highly but preferring one another. It means obeying the new standard of teaching, taking peacemaking initiatives toward enemies (compare 6:17 and 12:14–21).

b. So it is all participation in Christ. If we live our lives as self-contained pinballs rather than as participating in Christ, then we hear Paul's words merely as urging us to try harder. That is not good news; we fail too often. But if a new life, a new body, and a new participation have been given to us, then we are part of a team, welcomed into a new family, pulled along by the Spirit. When we fail on some plays, other teammates support us and try to make up for it. The big play that makes up for all our miscues is Jesus' death and Resurrection. We have been given a part in that crucial play.—Glen H. Stassen

SUNDAY: JUNE THIRTIETH

SERVICE OF WORSHIP

Sermon: God Has Said Yes to You!

TEXT: Gal. 3:26–29

My wife and I knew a man who, as a small child, was found on the street. Someone gave him a fictitious name and an approximate birthday. He became an outstanding teacher and has filled a very responsible post well. But all of his life it has troubled him that he knows nothing about his early life and his parents. Of course he had a father and a mother, but he has lived his entire life as if he had neither.

I. All of us are God's children, whether we want it that way or not. God has created us, and we belong to him. But that is not the divine filial relationship that Paul has in mind in Galatians. Our sonship remains completely empty and unproductive until we know our Father, until we live with him and let him guide and comfort us. If God does not go with us into our office, into the nursery and bedroom, on the vacation and to the hospital, and finally to the deathbed and the cemetery, it really makes little difference whether we declare, "There is no God," or declare, "Of course, there is a God."

This is what Paul means when he says to us, "For in Christ Jesus you are all sons of God, through faith." He has this special relationship in mind. To be children of God is to be in a faith relationship to God through Christ. It means something real. It comes alive when our life seems empty, bleak, useless, and when happiness and love of life are almost gone. As children of God we live our life with him step-by-step. In times of crisis, he stands inquiringly before us with his commands, and in time of trouble, he holds us close to himself.

However, we can no longer take such a relationship for granted. We are not obedient, trusting children; we go our own way. What is really important to us? Vacation spots, business deals, passing examinations, engagement, children, music, boating, mountain climbing, and a hundred other things. And God? Most of us would say, "He stands above everything else, of course." But the question is not what we *say* but what we *do* about what we say. Often God is banished from our lives, though we hold him in reserve for emergencies, for times of illness and bereavement, and perhaps even for the occasion of a wedding and the birth of a child.

II. But once more Paul has something quite different in mind. What makes us God's children? "For as many of you as were baptized into Christ have put on Christ." That is to say, by means of our baptism we have put on Christ. What a remarkable picture! Let's ponder it a bit. You may dream, especially when you are young, a typical anxiety dream. You walk down the street at noon and suddenly notice that you have on only a nightshirt. Everybody stares at you, and it is dreadful to appear so scantily clad among the people. Behind this dream, apparently, lurks a characteristic way of feeling about ourselves that often overwhelms us—the feeling of being betrayed to everyone, of being exposed to all eyes, so that we can find no place to hide, while everybody laughs at us. But if, in this dream, all at once a man should stop in the public square and put a topcoat on us, completely covering us, we would be free from anxiety.

What Paul is saying is this: In baptism, Christ clothed us. How we would like to hear it said to us: "You all *are* sons of God!" "You *have* put on Christ!" Indeed, that *has* happened. It doesn't matter whether *our* faith at the present moment is strong or weak or perhaps so shriveled up that we imagine we have none, for Paul says to us: Becoming children of God, putting on Christ *has* happened to you. Christ goes with you as an enveloping cloud. You do not see it, perhaps you do not even think about it anymore, yet it is there.

In the medieval legends of the saints, it is reported that on one occasion the brothers suddenly beheld a saint enveloped in a brilliant cloud of light. He knew nothing about it himself and did not see the cloud, yet the others were permitted to see it for a fleeting moment. Paul has something like that in mind. He has been permitted to see the phenomenon. And this is how he describes it: The cloud of light *is* about you; you *have* put

on the Lord Christ in your baptism; you *are* clothed in him for as long as you live.

III. What are we to make of what he says to us in our text? For obviously understanding something and believing it are decisive. Through faith in Christ Jesus, he has told us, we are children of God. Perhaps the third sentence gives us a bit more help: "There is neither Jew nor Greek, there is neither slave nor free, there is neither male nor female; for you are all one in Christ Jesus."

You are a man or a woman, superior or subordinate, religious or irreligious, or something else that goes without saying. Of course, that is what gives us so much trouble—the notion that we are just what we are. "A typical man," your wife may say of you. "Hopelessly pagan," you may say of yourself. We would concoct a thousand different labels. They might shade into every variety of praise and self-satisfaction or reproach and depression. Depending on our temperament and mood, we would then find the result most gratifying, tolerable, or horrible.

But at that point Paul walks among us to say: Everything positive or negative that might be said about you is now very unimportant. For God has not loved you because you have earned an 8 percent dividend. Nor has he loved you because you are a deluxe edition of the religious man. Nor does he love you a little bit better because you have had a harder time than someone else. It makes no difference. To sum it all up: You are precious to God for the sake of Jesus Christ. For that is the meaning of the extraordinary life and death of Jesus of Nazareth. In him God has said to us, and said it for all times and peoples: I *will* you men; I do not let you blithely go your own way into the hell of catastrophe. I stay by you.

That is the word that God thrust into this world when Jesus sat down with the tax collectors, when the prostitutes ran after him and dared crouch at his feet, when he quietly and without a trace of hatred let himself be crucified, and when he appeared to his disciples at Easter as the ever-living One who at that very moment was alive among them.

IV. Paul appeals to us to believe that. But what does it imply? Perhaps our big mistake today is that we regard having faith and holding-to-be-true as one and the same thing. Certainly intellectual assent is important. Naturally, God would like for us to pay attention and listen to what Paul has to say to us today because we hold it true. But probably having faith is much more important for us now. That is to say, it is more important that Paul's two sentences go with us and begin to live in us.

Sometimes that can happen long before we are able even to say *yes* with our intellect. Perhaps, it is beginning right now in a rather small, unimportant matter. Perhaps, so simple that the Lord Christ may be in it when we spend our pocket money next week, and may be permitted to show us for once a human being more needy than we ourselves. Perhaps, it is beginning in such a way that I can learn to be a little bit more trusting and not constantly overburdened and anxious about what might happen tomorrow. Perhaps, it is beginning in such a way that I learn to laugh at my inferiority complexes or even at my self-conceit. And what is beginning is nothing other than the belief that God in Jesus Christ is saying *yes* to me and does not ask me first what I have offered.

But now we must say something further in conclusion. In the course of this century, things have happened in our Church that make it difficult to learn to look at faith in this way. Paul tells that we are all one in Jesus Christ. He says not only that we are one but that we have become one single man in Jesus. By this he wants to say to us not just that every individual of us has "put on" Jesus Christ but rather that in baptism we have become a member of the Church that is already embraced by Jesus Christ and lives by him. Precisely at that point, it seems to me, we must learn something else that is not only to be spoken, heard, and believed, but also permitted to take form.

Four hundred years ago our churches were quite small, and the individual was still recognized in the worship service and had vital fellowship. But since then, we have grown so much that this is no longer possible. In spite of that, it is true, of course, that we belong together in Christ as one individual man. But it is no longer realized among us. For that reason, misunderstanding grows and grows until every man may regard the verse of the Bible as true for himself alone and limit faith to that. So the efforts to live together with one another as a community—in a youth group, at a church banquet, or at a spiritual retreat—are all very significant. Moreover, in every worship service, the word that has been delivered to us, the songs that we sing together, and the prayers that we pray together all bring us together in Christ. We must also train ourselves to do this wherever we are able to form this oneness in a humanely visible way.

According to a promise penned by Jeremiah five hundred years before Jesus Christ (Jeremiah 31:7–11), God would redeem a great multitude and bring them together from all parts of the world as a single flock under one shepherd. What Israel was as the descendent of Abraham in the Old Testament—God's own nation, which was upheld and clothed by the love of God—this great community out of all nations is supposed to become. Paul tells us that this has been fulfilled: "And if you are Christ's, then you are Abraham's offspring, heirs according to promise."

My dear friends and fellow Church members, by this miracle God wants to tell us today that we are his children and may live as his children because in Jesus of Nazareth, who lived, died, and was raised again nearly two thousand years ago, he has said *yes* to us. Now we may go to our homes, covered by this word that God has presented to us as a parting gift. We are no longer unprotected, no longer abandoned to go our own way in everything; we are completely enveloped by Jesus Christ himself. Though we often find it hard to believe, we *can* know that we are members of the community that is completely enveloped and upheld by its Lord Jesus Christ.—Eduard Schweizer

Illustrations

OUT OF THE DEPTHS.   Suffering does not sabotage the plans of God, nor does it contradict the promise of our Lord. Rather he has taken it into his calculations, and it is the profoundest reality in the kingdom of God. Only through suffering can we enter into glory. More than that, only in suffering do we become aware of the glory of God, because it pleases God to have men cry to him out of the depths and to send his only begotten Son into the depths.—Helmut Thielicke

THE BATTLE WON.   When the Bible insists that whoever you are, whatever the past, you are this day set free, it means that for the first time in your life perhaps you are free to fight your way through all that, rid of everything that would narrow your life down to what it has been or hem it in with what you call its possibilities. Give the enemy what name you like beyond flesh and blood, speak of principalities and powers: but know that the odds are no longer over there; they are over here, where you are. It's a battle that's been won and that you never have to lose. The question is, do you realize that, and do you ever thank God for it?—Paul Scherer

SERMON SUGGESTIONS

Topic: Is It OK to Sin?
    TEXT: Rom. 6:12–23
    The topic is not a foolish question. By their actions and words some ask it seriously—since God is merciful and forgiving. (1) The answer is no, for sin is a death-dealing slavery. (2) The answer again is no, for righteousness is paradoxically good slavery, bringing: (a) sanctification and (b) eternal life.

Topic: On Encouraging the Good
    TEXT: Matt. 10:40–42
    (1) Those who attempt to do God's will, whether they represent God or try to avoid drugs and illegitimate sex, are up against tremendous and subtle pressures.

(2) They can be strengthened in doing what is right by personal and moral hospitality. (3) Those who thus encourage the vocationally and morally embattled will be rewarded by God himself (see Matt. 10:32).

Worship Aids

CALL TO WORSHIP.   "I have trusted in they mercy; my heart shall rejoice in thy salvation. I will sing unto the Lord, because he hath dealt bountifully with me" (Ps. 13:5–6).

INVOCATION.   Eternal God, whose presence can be ours when we call upon thee in spirit and in truth, hear our prayer as we come with believing minds and hearts to see the glory of thy face. This is a day of rest and peace, and only those who live near to thee are true heirs of these blessings from thy gracious hand. Enter now the temple of each waiting life before thee and make us into a company of people who know and serve thy holy name. Take out of our inner being the strain and stress of daily care and may each of us in this place become still and give in and admit that thou alone art God. O thou helper of the helpless, come to us, for we need thy help. In Jesus' name we pray.—Donald Macleod

OFFERTORY SENTENCE.   "Bear ye one another's burdens, and so fulfill the law of Christ" (Gal. 6:2).

OFFERTORY PRAYER.   Lord, let us not withhold the best part, rather may we be willing to give all we can so others can know the victory we have found through Christ Jesus. Then grant us that which the world cannot give: joy without measure.—E. Lee Phillips

PRAYER.   O thou invisible God, whom we cannot see and yet whom we know, help us to see the reflection of thy goodness and power in the things that thou hast made. Give us the will and the mind to read thy messages that have been preserved for us in the Bible, and hold before us continually the picture of thy everlasting love in the face of Jesus Christ. Give us the grace in the midst of the confusion and disquietude of this world to stop from time to time whatever we are doing to think about thee.—Theodore Parker Ferris

LECTIONARY MESSAGE

Topic: Testing and Blessing

TEXT: Gen. 22:1–14

Every human life, the life of humanity and the life of the people of God, is marked by repeated testing in relationship to God as Creator and Redeemer. Such testing characterizes the divine-human encounter. This dialectic of testing and blessing marked Abraham's initial call by God (Gen. 12:1–3) and the course of his life as the father of Israel, God's chosen people. At the critical juncture when Abraham lacked an heir, God promised that his heir "shall be a child of your own body" (Gen. 15:4). In that "Abraham put his faith in the Lord," the "Lord counted that faith to him as righteousness," and he represents for both covenants the father of the faithful.

In our text, Abraham is put to a radical test by God. Instead of disobeying and then evading God's call as did Adam and Eve as the first among equals in the human family, Abraham listened to and obeyed God's call and injunction. The call to sacrifice his beloved son, Isaac, the child representing the fulfillment of God's promise and Abraham's heir, was both radical and incomprehensible. Kierkegaard referred to this command as the "teleological suspension of the ethical."

Unlike the editor of our text and his readers past and present, Abraham did not know how God could or would fulfill his covenant promise to him or through him apart from Isaac, the heir of the promise. Unlike Adam as the representative of each of us who call in question or seek to qualify God's clear injunction, Abraham responded in faithful obedience. We might ask: "Would he not have had sufficient reason to refuse such a command from God?" "Is not such a command immoral and unethical?" Our text provides no information regarding why Abraham was so certain that God's command was to sacrifice Isaac as a sign or test of his ultimate allegiance to God. It was the absolute test of Abraham's faith. It required him to surrender the son he loved above all things, who at the same time was the heir of God's covenant promises. Was Abraham's love for Isaac greater than his love and devotion to God? Were ties of family, blood and kinship of greater worth than fulfilling the obligations of being the father of God's covenant people?

Clearly, there is no basis for universalizing God's command to Abraham. God's call and commands are always specific within a particular historical context. For Abraham, it was sufficient that God's command was clear. It called for action: "Take ... go ... offer ... sacrifice." Abraham would not be remembered as the father of the faithful had he been content only to hear God's word or to confess his faith in God without acting upon it. Biblical faith is always coupled with obedient action. When God spoke to Moses on Mount Sinai, he said: "I keep faith with thousands, with those who love me and keep my commandments" (Exod. 20:6 NEB). Jesus said: "Not everyone who calls me 'Lord, Lord' will enter the kingdom of Heaven, but only those who do the will of my heavenly Father" (Matt. 7:21 NEB). Calvin saw this clearly in emphasizing that "all true knowledge of God is born of obedience." When faith is made synonymous with feelings, it easily degenerates into an unhealthy subjectivism.

Abraham's obedient response to God's command involved a three-day journey marked by increasing solitude and the "dark night of the soul." After leaving his servants behind, Abraham places the wood for the fire on Isaac's back and carries the "fire and the knife" himself, and "the two of them went on together" (Gen. 21:6–7). The silence is broken by Isaac's heart-rending question to his father, "Where is the young beast for the sacrifice?" (Gen. 22:7). With empathy but without foreknowledge of the depth of the truth he utters, Abraham answers: "God will provide himself with a young beast for sacrifice, my son" (Gen. 21:8).

All conversation ceases. Abraham is the sole actor; he builds the altar, arranges the wood and binds his son, Isaac, the victim to be sacrificed. As he is about to kill his son, God's angel calls Abraham by name and commands: "Do not raise your hand against the boy; do not touch him. Now I know that you are a God-fearing man. You have not withheld from me your son, your only son" (Gen. 21:12). At the climax of Abraham's testing, God honored Abraham's faithful obedience and spared his son, the heir of the promise. God blessed Abraham after he had tested him so radically. The provision of the ram for the sacrifice "instead of his son" was the confirmation of God's ap-proval and blessing of Abraham. "God works in mysterious ways his wonders to perform." Paul says of Abraham: "No distrust made him waver concerning the promise of God, but he grew strong in his faith as he gave glory to God, fully convinced that God was able to do what he had promised" (Rom. 5:20–21).

Abraham's faithfulness was rewarded and surpassed by the greater faithfulness of God. God's covenant love manifest in the calling and sustenance of Abraham reached its true fulfillment in Jesus Christ, his Son, who was perfectly obedient through all trials and testing (Heb. 2:13). For this reason Paul proclaims: "He who did not spare his own Son but gave him up for us all, will he not also give us all things with him?" (Rom. 8:32; cf. 6:13).—David L. Mueller

SUNDAY: JULY SEVENTH

SERVICE OF WORSHIP

Sermon: When the King Refuses

Text: Matt. 20:21–22

May I remind you of facts? According to St. Matthew, the mother of the sons of Zebedee—that is, Salome—came asking for chief places for her two sons in Christ's kingdom. Perhaps they got their mother to make this request on their behalf. After all, she was the sister of Jesus' mother, and she did help the apostolic band. But whatever the reason, I used to despise James and John for this. I used to count them the fathers of all those ecclesiastical "place seekers" whom I despise. But I have changed my mind. Not about place seeking in the Church, but about James and John. What I think they wanted was not a comfortable seat but a spectacular piece of service. They wanted to burn themselves out. They wanted a task of outstanding size. After all, they were men of action. They had energy, and to spare. They longed to call down fire from heaven and sweep in the kingdom of God. And what had they been offered? Following Jesus around villages! Watching him heal the sick! Witnessing his restoration of the weak willed! "O Master," they cried in effect, "let us *do* something for thee." "O mother Salome, you bid Jesus let us do something for him." And so she goes, not without maternal pride, I think, "Grant that these my two sons may sit, the one on thy right hand and the other on thy left in thy Kingdom."

Now here is a remarkable fact. She wasn't rebuked by Jesus! She did not, as far as we are told, receive any answer at all. St. Matthew only put that in out of reverence for James and John; but I doubt it. Anyway, James and John received the answer. Maybe Jesus saw it was a "put-up job." And the answer they received hurt. It hurt terribly. Jesus said, "Ye know not what ye ask." It hurt because they thought they knew very well. But his next words cut deeper still. "Those two places are reserved for others." Doubtless they retired crestfallen. They had offered for heroic service in Christ's kingdom, and they weren't wanted! Doubtless Salome, their mother, went away crestfallen, too. Her two sons weren't wanted!

II. Did it ever occur to you, I wonder,

that God might not want our service? That's a new view of the sovereignty of God. I cannot say it occurred to me till I considered this scripture. We grow so accustomed to the idea that all the calling to God's service is on God's side and all the refusing is on our side; but the Bible has a knack of turning upside down preconceived notions. Sometimes God does not want our heroic service. Our allegiance? Yes, God always wants that. But quite often nothing startling from us, nothing life giving, nothing tremendous, only patient following in the routine acts of life; going to the city, working patiently, and coming home by the same bus. . . .

I think this is difficult. I think it is far easier to live the heroic life when you are out in the limelight, when people will notice what you say and observe what you do. My heart goes out to James and John. I know how they felt. It is so much easier to live the Christian life when we are called to some big and challenging task. But when we are called to occupy some insignificant platform in life, or scarcely any platform at all; when young people have to stay at home to look after aged parents; when routine jobs occupy so much of our waking hours and we are growing older without seeing the sunny parts of the earth, then it is we grow rebellious against the smallness of our lot. I say I sympathize with James and John, more especially when their offer went unaccepted.

III. Is this why our Lord wasn't hard on these two men? But the other disciples were. The Scripture says "they were moved with indignation." They certainly read the question of James and John as place seeking. And on that account were given corrective teaching by Jesus. He showed that there have to be leaders in the Christian Church; but there is a difference between leadership there and leadership in the world. In the former, it is a primacy of service. He who is accounted great is he who does most for other people, not he for whom other people do much. In the Church, the supreme leader should be the supreme servant. And if he thoroughly understands this he can seek a chief place. Je-

sus understood it. He had chief place, but it meant service unto death, or, as he put it, "Even as the Son of Man came not to be ministered unto, but to minister, and to give his life a ransom for many."

IV. Come back to James and John. Come back to their mother's request: "Command that these my two sons may sit, one on thy right hand, and one on thy left in thy Kingdom." Come back now and look at these men with all the resentment and indignation and envy taken out of your eyes. Learn instead this lesson about unanswered prayer. Salome asked, "Command these places for my sons in thy glory." And Jesus refused. He did not answer that prayer. He said those places were in fact already allotted. He also added, "Ye know not what ye ask." And this is what I am inclined to think, that whenever God does not answer our prayers it is because we do not know what we ask. And here you have it in black and white: "Command that these my two sons may sit, the one on thy right hand and the other on thy left in thy glory" (St. Mark's word). But the day came when, standing by the foot of Christ's cross, Salome saw what coming in his glory was. It was crucifixion. And to think that she had asked *that* for her two sons! How she must have wanted to tear the tongue out of her mouth! There *was* one on his right hand! and another on his left! Malefactors they were, dying in agony! Oh, if only she had known! But Jesus knew. Therefore he did not grant her request. Perhaps that is why he does not always answer our requests. We do not know what we ask. But God does.

And I am sure some have prayed to God with all their heart, "O God, let me out, let me out, I cannot stand this routine another day. I shall scream if I see that wretched office desk again." And God has said "no" to our prayer; and we've had to go back and the routine has had to go on. But we shall be making the mistake of our lives if we are sullen in consequence. We know not what we ask. We may have been asking for crucifixion without knowing it. . . .

Once more we look back at these men. We don't know exactly what happened to

John. But we do know what happened to James. With bewildering brevity the end of his life is described in the book of the Acts of the Apostles. "And Herod killed James the brother of John with a sword." Did Salome remember then? Did she remember how Jesus had said, "Ye shall drink of my cup and be baptized with the baptism that I am baptized with." Jesus had been baptized in blood. Did Mary mother of Jesus run to Salome her sister then? "They did it to my son, now they have done it to yours." Did they sit long hours each trying to comfort the other? We do not know. But this we know. James did in the end get what he asked. Perhaps he was ready for it then. And someday for us God may grant our prayer though he denies it now. We shall be ready then. But till then we must be patient, very patient, believing that God knows best what we can manage. . . . —D. W. Cleverley Ford

Illustrations

THE WILL OF GOD.   In 1792 William Carey preached a moving sermon on the text "Enlarge the place of thy tent," using it to plead with his congregation, "Expect great things from God, attempt great things from God." Thus was born the Baptist Missionary Society: Carey himself went as missionary to India, and the congregation supported him, despite any who may have argued that it was God's will that the heathen should die in ignorance. But let warning be given: though the prayer means "Thy will be done" through me, there is still prime need to pray the prayer. For we easily substitute our will for God's will; and, though it is God's will that a swamp should be drained, it is not his will that the land thus reclaimed should be the site of a factory to manufacture burglar tools.— George A. Buttrick

PROVIDENCE AND PRAYER.   We have to reckon with the universal testimony of Christian experience that, when God is believed to intervene providentially at all, he always intervenes "exceedingly abundantly above all that we ask or think, ac-cording to the power that worketh in us." That is to say, the Christian, when he believes he discerns the workings of Providence, sees, not an occasional wand waving from the hand of an omnipotent magician, but the infinitely ingenious becomes the infinitely creative power of "the only wise God our Savior" (Jude 25). —Geddes MacGregor

SERMON SUGGESTIONS

Topic: The Story of a Marriage
TEXT: Gen. 24:34–38, 42–49, 58–67
(1) *Then:* By a circuitous route, Isaac in the providence of God found his wife Rebekah. (2) *Always:* Through the ages, God has worked through and in spite of many customs to establish homes. (3) *Now:* (a) We can be sure that God is pleased when a man and a woman properly find each other and marry; (b) We can be equally sure that God wills that the two love one another and make the marriage a mutual blessing, verse 67.

Topic: Our Blessings in Christ
TEXT: Eph. 1:3–14 NRSV
(1) Election—God took the initiative for our salvation. (2) Sanctification–God chose us "to be holy and blameless before him in love." (3) Adoption—God has brought the Gentiles into his family of faith. (4) Inheritance—God grants us redemption, salvation, forgiveness through the blood of Christ. (5) Assurance—God seals, confirms us as his own, by the Holy Spirit, a down payment on all good things to come.

Worship Aids

CALL TO WORSHIP.   "I will make thy name to be remembered in all generations: therefore shall the people praise thee for ever and ever" (Ps. 45:17).

INVOCATION.   From the rising of the sun until the going down of the same, your name is to be praised. This is the new day you have made fresh with the morning showers—alive with all the possibilities of your creative love. We praise you for Christ who makes all things new through your abounding grace. Let us live these moments—this day—on tiptoe to see the wonderful fulfillment you will for us and for all your people. Enrich our minds and hearts with your word of grace, inspire us with your Holy Spirit that in thought, word, and deed we may glorify you. Praise be to you—Father, Son, and Holy Spirit.—John Thompson

OFFERTORY SENTENCE.   "Do not forget: thin sowing means thin reaping; the more you sow, the more you reap" (2 Cor. 9:6 JB)

OFFERTORY PRAYER.   O God, we have been reaping all our lives from what others have sown, and we are blessed beyond all our deserving. Continually give us the grace to see what we give and the generosity with which we give will be rewarded in an abundant harvest of blessing for others.

PRAYER.   You, the God who calls, called Abraham at the dawn of history to go out knowing where he was going—to leave the security of familiar places and to live by a faith for insecurity. You called the young man Isaiah in the face of the tragedy of his day to proclaim new shoots of hope springing from dead stumps. You have called us to be your people in this time and place—faithful stewards of the Word of life in the face of all the deaths that we die. You call us to the windswept frontiers of existence to be discerning of the new thing you are doing in our day. We have heard your call in your word; may we respond with the dispatch of the young Isaiah: "Here am I, Lord, send me." Renew in us a sense of world mission to which your love in Christ calls us. You call us to go into all the world and all the worlds of persons—to be the light of your love in all the dark corners of existence.

We pray for leadership in Church, community, nation, world that invests wisely today in leadership for tomorrow. May we so practice our goals as not to squander the future tense of humankind.

As in this congregation we seek to foster a community of faith, a laboratory for spiritual maturing, and a fellowship of Christian love, grant to us an eagerness for learning, a readiness for discipline, and a concern that makes for true comradeship.—John Thompson

LECTIONARY MESSAGE

Topic: Will You Dance or Will You Cry?

TEXT: Matt. 11:16–19

Jesus faced animosity almost from the word go. It seems that people who seek to make a real difference in the lives of others have always faced difficulty—and probably always will. While coming in many different shapes and sizes (ignorance, skepticism, unbelief, unwillingness, deceit, and even outright persecution), hostility was habitually part of Jesus' lot. The parable of the "Children in the Market Place" occurs within a section of Matthew's Gospel chronicling such opposition to Jesus (11:2–12:50). The parable itself (11:16b–17) is preceded by an introductory question (v. 16a) and followed by its application to the ministries of Jesus and John the Baptist (v. 18–19a). By concluding the parable with a wisdom saying (v. 19b), Jesus calls to us, asking what our response will be.

I. *A children's game.* The parable features a simple children's game. One group of children would begin by playing a tune, and the rest of the gang was supposed to respond by mimicking the joyous dance at weddings; the first group would then play a dirge, and their playmates were to feign the mourning at graveside. What the game lacked in imagination it made up for in imitation (children love to copy adults), repetition (children never tire of the same series of events) and a sense of expectancy (children are addicted to the end of the game).

The cackles and cries of children in a busy market hardly qualify as a startling or unexpected scene. The parable's playful, innocent and lifelike character lulls its audience, both ancient and modern, into a (false) sense of security. However, the solemnity and gravity of weddings and funerals—legitimate times of great human joy and sorrow respectively—should slow us in our rush to trivialize the story. Further, the children's outright refusal to play the game gives us pause; silence can be an ominous sound.

II. *More than just a game.* A closer look at the parable confirms our suspicions. The historical references that drive its plotting and application transform a harmless story about frolicsome children into a severe warning about the most important of all human decisions and the most important time in history.

"This generation" (v. 16) positions the Jews of Jesus' day within Israel's history and necessarily invokes the story of God's dealing with the world through Israel. "We wailed" (v. 17) echoes the Gospel witness to John the Baptist's harsh message of judgment, while "neither eating nor drinking" accurately portrays John's peculiar lifestyle. "He has a demon" (v. 18) was surely an accusation brought against John, though we have no record of such charge. The title "Son of Man" (v. 19) was Jesus' favorite designation. In contrast to John, Jesus came "eating and drinking" (v. 19) and thus was falsely maligned as a "glutton and drunkard" (v. 19; cf. Deut. 21:20). Slandering Jesus as a "friend of sinners and tax collectors" (v. 19) was triggered by the character and intent of his ministry.

We are asked to see that what really drives the parable is nothing other than what had actually occurred in the ministries of John and Jesus. Further, we are invited to discover ourselves within the parable as it unfolds the plan of God for the world. Herein lies the rub.

III. *Time will tell.* By adding the wisdom saying (v. 19b), Jesus completes the narrative framework: there is a past (the previous generations in which God explained the rules for responding to him), a present (the controversial ministries of John and Jesus) and a future (a day in which wisdom will be justified). While solemnly repenting at a harsh message of judgment or joyously receiving a wonder-filled message of forgiveness may seem like foolishness now, there comes a day of vindication—and of judgment.

IV. *Lessons from the parable.* (a) God's grace can be experienced by accepting his calls for repentance and his invitations to celebrate. (b) The parable underscores God's creative patience; despite the lack of response, he continues to send messengers. (c) While the messengers may be different, the message remains the same: the servants give multiple tellings of the very same story. (d) The story includes both judgment and forgiveness; to neglect either is to rip asunder what God has joined together. (e) Danger always exists for us to refuse the offer of forgiveness and ignore the possibility of repentance. (f) Any decision to respond now will be vindicated later; any decision to ignore now will be regretted later.

The ultimate failure is not to live according to the plotting of God's game. It may require us to sing and dance; it may require us at times to mourn and cry; but whatever response be required, becoming lost in God's purposes is the only way to become a child.—Carey C. Newman

SUNDAY: JULY FOURTEENTH

SERVICE OF WORSHIP

Sermon: Jacob's Ladder

TEXT: Gen. 28:10–17; Ps. 91

I. I want to suggest to you that Jacob was an impostor. His story is one of the most completely drawn in all of the Bible. You know what kind of a person he was. You know that he wanted his father's blessing more than he wanted anything else in this life, and he strove hard to get it. He cheated his brother in order to get it. Over the years, he became increasingly crafty and clever; a cheater. He gets what he wants and becomes enormously wealthy. But he is still restless. He is still looking for something that his cleverness cannot get him.

a. Jacob is the person who, no matter how successful he is, still fears that he is a failure. And no matter how much he is loved, still fears he is unlovable. And no matter how much in charge of this life he pretends to be, he fears that he is not really in control of his life, not ultimately.

And to that extent, I suggest that we are all like Jacob. We are all impostors. We like to give the impression that we are on top of things, that we have arrived. But we still sense that something is missing. And all of our knowledge will not discover it, nor will our sophistication guarantee it, nor our wealth or our power garner it, nor our righteousness earn it.

b. So eventually we have to admit that it is beyond us. Jacob had to come to that point. He surrounded himself with material things, trying to prove that he was somebody, but beneath that facade he knew that there was something missing still, something that all of this furious activity could not gain for him.

And that's the revelation in this story. What he really wanted was God's blessing, and all of this activity, this restlessness, is an attempt to find it. That's the point of the story of Jacob's dream at Bethel.

II. The text says, he came to a "certain place." He rested there that night. He laid down on the ground, got a stone for a pillow, and dreamed that there was a ladder set up from earth to heaven and that there were angels descending and ascending the ladder.

a. God speaks to Jacob first to renew the covenant that he made with Jacob's ancestors, Abraham and Isaac.

And then God says three words, and I want you to hear this because I believe these are the words that God speaks to all of us. He says to Jacob:

Behold, I am with you, and I will keep you wherever you go. And I will not leave you until I have done that which I have spoken to you.

Then Jacob awoke and said, "Surely God is in this place. And I did not know it." That's the message of the Bible from the beginning to the end. And that's what was revealed to Jacob at Bethel. "Behold, I am with you. Wherever you go I will keep you."

b. It's amazing. Thousands of years ago some hustler named Jacob heard these words spoken to him by God, and we have remembered them ever since. Do you know why we have remembered them? Because we want to hear them ourselves. Have you ever heard them?

I long to hear them. And along my journey I have heard them, and I long to hear them again. I live off the memory of that experience of God's presence. And that's why I come to church, I guess, to hear them again. "I am with you, and I will never leave you."

III. And then the text says that Jacob took the stone that he had used as a pillow and built a shrine at that place. He called that place "Bethel," which means "the House of God." And later Bethel would become a special shrine in Israel and a temple would be built there. And people would flock there because that's where Jacob heard the words, "I am with you and I will never leave you."

a. Churches are shrines. Churches are bethels, holy places, where we come to meet God. That's what we are here for. This is the House of God. We gather here and sing:

Abide with me; fast falls the eventide;
The darkness deepens; Lord, with me abide!
When other helpers fail and comforts flee,
Help of the helpless, O abide with me.

It can happen. And it can happen here while we sit quietly and listen.

b. But the story of Jacob is here also to tell us that it can happen anywhere. Surely, God is in this place. This strange place out in the desert between Haran and Paddan-aram. That's where he met God. It happened to Jacob when, for a moment, his striving ceased, and he slept, and dreamed. And it happened.

IV. I long to experience a sense of not being totally alone, a sense that God is with me now, and will always be. And I wager that you yearn to have that experience, too. You may doubt that it will ever happen to you. You may feel the way Jacob did, that it is not going to happen to you. And when it happens to other people, you may say that it was only a dream or it came as the result of some sensory deprivation. Or you can say that it's just due to primitive, enlivened imagination. You can say that. And you can say, "I'm going to make it on my own in this world. I don't have need of divine influence."

a. But if you are honest, you will also say that you want to stop the striving, the struggling, you want to stop pretending to be somebody. You want to hear God say to you, "Behold I am with you. And no matter what happens in the future, I will always be with you."

b. Jacob didn't believe that could ever happen. He believed he was all alone in this world. Therefore, it is all up to him. So he scrambled, he connived, he struggled, he pretended, and he cheated. And do you know what? It came to him anyway, as a surprise, without his expecting it.

Think of how much easier and sooner it will come to you if you ask for it.—Mark Trotter

Illustrations

THE "LADDER." But "ladder" as a translation is not quite accurate, not as we use the word. A ramp is really a better translation of the Hebrew. And therefore, the image is that of a ziggurat. A ziggurat was a tower made of earth—wide at the bottom and narrow at the top. It looked something like a pyramid. Ziggurats were a common sight in ancient Mesopotamia where the patriarchs originated. Ziggurats had a ramp around the outside that allowed the priest to ascend from the earth, where the people lived, to the top, to the symbolic heaven, where God lived.

And so this dream, while it appears to have strange images in it, was for Jacob, and those who lived in the Near East in that ancient time, a familiar image. The way a church would be a familiar image in a dream for a modern person.—Mark Trotter

GOD THINKING OF US. Sometimes during the last war my students wrote me from the battlefield, and one sentence came up again and again in countless variations: "I am so exhausted from marching, my stomach is so empty, I am so plagued with lice and scratching, I am so tormented by the biting cold of Russia and so dead tired, that I am totally occupied, without the least bit of inner space for any speculative thinking. I haven't only forgotten Hölderlin and the other authors I read in school, I'm even too weak to leaf through the Bible. I am even lazy about the Lord's Prayer. My whole spiritual life is disorganized and ruined, I just vegetate."

How should I answer these young men? I wrote them, "Be thankful that the gospel is more than a philosophy. If it were only a philosophy, you would just have it as long as you could keep it in mind and it could afford you intellectual comfort. But even when you can no longer think about God, he still thinks about you."—Helmut Thielicke

SERMON SUGGESTIONS

Topic: How We Mess Up

TEXT: Gen. 25:19–34

(1) *Then:* The twin boys Esau and Jacob were locked in a struggle from their beginnings, and Esau forfeited his birthright through a foolish bargain. (2) *Always:* History confirms by recurrent examples that we humans, when we are desperate with desire, will forfeit permanent or ultimate happiness for immediate satisfaction. (3) *Now:* We see this today: (a) in marital infidelity; (b) in financial dishonesty; (c) in simple unwillingness to do the difficult thing to succeed in any endeavor.

Topic: Audience Response

TEXT: Matt. 13:1–9, 18–23

Why do people respond as they do to the message we share? (1) *Jesus' Parable:* A man sowed a seed that fell into different kinds of soil, and some types of soil yielded no harvest, but one type yielded an abundant harvest. (2) *The Meaning:* (a) Some people hear words, but fail to understand their meaning for them. (b)

Some like some things about what they hear, but they will not follow through when the going gets rough. (c) Some let worldly preoccupations usurp their spiritual vitality. (d) However, others hear the message of God clearly, take it to heart, and by the grace of God bring forth in spite of all discouragements a surprising, incredible harvest.

Worship Aids

CALL TO WORSHIP. "Thy word is a lamp unto my feet, and a light unto my path" (Ps. 119:105).

INVOCATION. As you illuminate our pathways every day, if we have eyes to see your light, so shine upon us today in this service of worship through your word spoken, sung, and remembered.

OFFERTORY SENTENCE. "Therefore, as opportunity offers, let us work for the good of all, especially members of the household of faith" (Gal. 6:10 REB).

OFFERTORY PRAYER. We do not give, Lord, to be noticed or praised, we give because we want to give, for there is joy in giving that shares the message of salvation in Jesus Christ, our Savior.—E. Lee Phillips

PRAYER. In the hushed stillness, ever attending God, as the gentle rain quenches the thirst of a dry dusty earth, may your spirit come as refreshing rain and touch the deep hunger and thirst of our parched lives. In the stillness, may we remember that you are God, that you have made each one of us uniquely so; that we have not made ourselves; and, most of all, that we belong to you, and that you have given us life, name, call, and redemption. Free us from all the vain things that charm us most and turn our hearts toward home, toward you, our dwelling place in all generations.

Master of mercy and forgiveness, in your holy presence our sin is ever between us. Hear our confessions, receive our repentance and sorrow, and cleanse us to believe and to accept our suffered forgiveness. And as we accept forgiveness, O God, may forgiveness flow from us to others.

Generous Creator and Redeemer, turn us from our obsession to get more, and make us pause to remember how blessed and rich we are. As we whisper thanks, we voice but a few simple joys of life. Thank you for consoling music that reaches beyond words into the pit of our pain and sorrow. Thank you for sunrises and sunsets that awake and bid farewell to the light of each gracious day. Thank you for the young adults that have celebrated their love and committed their fidelity to each other. Their marriages offer us hope and gladness. Thank you for our daily bread, for the whisper of a memory, for the crafty raccoon at camp, for the sacredness of a name, for the gentle stir of a breeze.

Lord of the deep, even for the darkness and the pain, we halt and stutter a thanks, for in the agony we draw kinship with you in suffering, and we learn that your Spirit will pray our prayers too deep for words. O Holy Spirit, hear the sighs and groans of our hearts. And, most of all, thanks for the Christ, Jesus our Lord, in whom we live and give thanks, and worship and pray.—William M. Johnson

LECTIONARY MESSAGE

Topic: Turning From, Turning Toward

TEXT: Rom. 8:1–11

It is not difficult to visualize sin and death. Television beams these images straight into our living rooms in living color: politicians indicted almost weekly; genocide in Bosnia; terrorism in the Middle East; bombings in Northern Ireland; kidnapping, murder, drugs, and drive-by shootings all over the United States. Bombarded by shots as terrible as these, we are tempted to turn away in disgust, scream out in anger, or isolate ourselves in fear, but few would deny that death and destruction are alive and well in our time. Fortunately, these pictures are simply images from a box that we can shut off. Usually, we conveniently ignore the larger world. After all, we did not pull the trigger or explode the bomb. How smugly self-satisfying it seems, at first, that Paul provides us with a text of assurance that seemingly lets us off the hook: "There is now therefore no condemnation for those in Christ Jesus." But be careful; Paul often confronts us with words of assurance that have a bite to them. He explains why there is no condemnation for those in Christ (8:1–4). He draws some careful distinctions about what it means to be "in the Spirit" or "in the flesh" (8:5–8). Finally, he confronts us with the full implications of life in the Spirit (8:9–11).

I. *No condemnation for those in Christ (8:1–4).* In addressing the Roman Christians, Paul says, "The law of the spirit of life in Christ Jesus has liberated me from the law of sin and death." For Paul, "the law of sin and death" (8:2) did not simply refer to life without God. Paul speaks of Old Testament law, which demonstrated humanity's inability to attain righteousness before God. Paul thus articulates one of the foundational tenets of Christianity: We are not capable of earning salvation. God, by sending his own son, accomplished what the law could not accomplish (8:3) because it was weakened by the flesh.

II. *"Fleshing out" distinctions (8:5–8).* Paul delineates the characteristics of two contrasting approaches to life. Those who live according to the flesh set their mind on the flesh (8:5), a lifestyle that leads to death (8:6). They are hostile to God (8:7), incapable of submitting to God's law (8:7), and they cannot please God (8:8). By contrast, Paul states that those who live according to the Spirit set their mind on the things of the Spirit (8:5), which leads to life and peace (8:6). Doubtless, no Christian knowingly strives to perfect a "life in the flesh" as described by Paul. Yet Paul clearly indicates that those who do not walk in the Spirit are indeed walking in the flesh. Like the old adage says: "If you are not for me, you are against me." Ironically, while no Christian knowingly strives to live according to the flesh, few of us claim to have attained total concentration on things of the Spirit, which result in life and peace. We recognize the fallacy of a life in the flesh but neglect the power of life in the Spirit. We have demonstrated we are willing to turn from the things of the flesh, but we are often unwilling to turn toward things of the Spirit.

III. *Where are you? (8:9–11).* We have a lot in common with the Roman Christian community. Paul does not write them simply to pass the time. He invokes the language of admonition with a strong reminder: "You are not in the flesh but in the Spirit." Paul reminded the Romans, indeed he reminds us, that we are not called to live a life of aggression against God, we are called to live a life in the power of the Spirit of the one who raised Jesus from the dead. We are not called to live a life of apathy toward the things of the Spirit; we are called to live life in the power of the Spirit of the one who raised Jesus from the dead. We are not called to live a life of fear, afraid of what others might do to us; we are called to live life emboldened in the power of the Spirit of the one who raised Jesus from the dead. How does the spirit of life in Christ Jesus liberate you? Liberation from the law of sin and death requires that we turn away from things of the flesh, but also that we turn toward things of the Spirit.—James D. Nogalski

SUNDAY: JULY TWENTY-FIRST

SERVICE OF WORSHIP

Sermon: The Lights

TEXT: Gen. 1:16

It is evident from this poignant verse that the three levels of light described were created with varying powers for different purposes insofar as giving light to planet Earth is concerned, and that each of these levels of light is expected to perform its light-giving function in keeping with its capacity. The function of the sun in giving light to our earth, for instance, is much greater than the light-giving function assigned to the moon; yet, it matters significantly that both lights perform according to individual capacities to fulfill the light-giving mission assigned.

"And the stars, also!" Insofar as giving light to planet Earth is concerned, the contribution of these stars seems quite small to the nonscientific observer; yet, we know that God's plan for his universe needs every one of the stars, even the ones that, because of their remoteness, seem so small to us. Small though some of the stars may seem to you and me, it matters greatly that each star live up to its candlepower.

Now, let us look quickly into the parable of talents in Matthew 25:14–30 for a stimulating parallel. To his servants the departing Lord gave talents according to their varying abilities: to one man he gave five talents, to another he gave two, and to a third he gave one talent. The parallel is interesting: greater light, lesser light, "stars also"; five talents, two talents, one talent.

With God-created lights and with God-created people it is unmistakably evident that the Creator expects his creations to live up to individual candlepower and to perform according to capacities committed. The thing that matters most is not how much light power or talent power the individual possesses; rather, the great determinant of God's pleasure or displeasure toward us is whether or not we live up to the amount of power entrusted to us individually. It matters greatly to God that you and I live up to our candlepower!

I. Are you a five-talented Christian?

If you are one of God's greater lights and are not actually living up to your candlepower in the matter of sharing your abilities in witnessing and serving, primarily through your church, I wonder if you know the threefold blessing that is being missed?

a. First, *you* are missing the tremendous blessing that the sense of joy in your own heart would bring. The sense of

knowing that you have been a good steward to God-given abilities would make your fellowship with God a warm, smiling, joyous blessing. The knowledge that, through a complete sharing of your abilities in Christian witnessing and serving, you are facilitating the world's most important enterprise, the fulfillment of the Great Commission, would bring you joy. Too, the knowledge that the use of those God-given abilities had helped to strengthen others spiritually would bring to your heart a sense of gratification.

b. Second, *God* is missing the joy for which his heart yearns. The great, compelling hope of God's heart is that the world be reconciled to him through Christ. Your performing to the limit of your abilities automatically strengthens the work of the Church and the outreach of its main mission of winning men to God. Your failure to live up to your candlepower robs God's heart of great joy.

c. Third, *others* are missing the inspiration of the dedicated example of a talented life if you are not doing your best in witnessing and serving. Because you are a greater light in ability, the impact of your humble, happy dedication of those abilities to Christian service and witnessing "packs an extra punch," inspiring other multitalented Christians and even less talented ones to begin to do their best. Thereby you do bring inspiration, strength, and joy to others in living up to your candlepower.

II. Or are you, perhaps, a lesser light, a two-talented person? You would love to do solos in the choir, but you know that there are other voices better suited to solos than yours; therefore, you sing with radiance and faithfulness in the chorus.

a. What would our choruses be with only solo voices? What would our orchestras be without their second instruments? What would drama be if there were no supporting characters? Subordinate and supporting roles are indispensable to music, drama, and life!

b. In Christian service, some of the most valuable and Christlike participants through the centuries have been the lesser lights—people who have performed with love and devotion to the limit of their lesser abilities, never asking for the spotlight, never waiting to be publicized and praised, never stopping to demand gratitude. Many of these two-talented people have demonstrated more Christian grace and spirit than their more talented associates.

III. But if you are, honestly, a one-talented person, an "also" of the light creation, it matters so much that you, too, shall give your best in witnessing and serving, however small your best may be.

a. Lest someone dismiss these ways as being insignificant, let it be said with emphasis that if they constitute *all* the contribution possible for you to make, they will be honored of God and warmly appreciated by your church. Instead of complaining that you cannot preach or teach or preside or sing or conduct or direct, why not search for the lesser things you can do, and do them with all your power?

b. For instance, you can *attend* with such faithfulness that your name will be mentioned among those who can be counted upon to be present, regardless of the difficult circumstances.

You can *listen* with such radiant attention that those who do preach or teach or sing will find in your devoted listening a source of inspiration to them to do their best.

You can *pray* for those who will be in leadership, both prior to their hours of performance and during their times of service.

You can *invite* people with such radiance and constancy that some will attend whose lives may receive enrichment, even transformation.

You can *smile* with the love of God behind your smile, so that people's hearts will be blessed by the radiant happiness of your face.

c. Little things? They are not little things if they constitute the maximum talent of a Christian; and God will bless the giver of these apparently minor contributions with great joy and usefulness for living up to his candlepower.

IV. Have you ever seen a star through a telescope? It is the most beautiful of all the heavenly lights. God looks at the "lit-

tle" people through the telescope of love and truth, and they are beautiful beyond description—most of all, because, despite their littleness of size and scope, they are living up to their candlepower!

Regardless of the level at which you appear in the galaxy of lights or in the range of ability, are *you* living up to your candlepower?—Chester Swor

Illustrations

GOD'S DESIGN FOR US. God among his other functions must be a tireless activity toward an end. Everything he calls into being works toward that end, I myself with the rest. I am not a purposeless bit of jetsam flung out on the ocean of time to be tossed about helplessly. God couldn't so will an existence. It would not be in keeping with his economy to have any entity wasted. As our Lord puts it, the sparrow cannot fall without him; without him the lilies are not decked; the knowledge possessed by his infinite intelligence is so minute that the very hairs of the head are numbered. My life, my work, myself—all are as much a necessary part of his design as the thread the weaver weaves into the pattern in a carpet.—Basil King

QUIET FAITHFULNESS. Thousands of alumni of a southern university remember with affection a janitor whose labors of love to the limit of his ability were immortalized at his death by a bronze marker on the campus. Thousands of readers of newspapers in the spring of 1960 were thrilled by an account of a custodian in a school: his completely on-the-altar life of service brought to him such love and gratitude that the 1960 school yearbook was dedicated to him. Many will recall the devotion of a large church to a girl whose life was limited in more ways than one but whose complete devotion to her church won such love that at her funeral the flowers and attendance matched similar tributes paid at times of death of the city's leading citizens. The quiet, faithful, listening, praying, loving ones who strengthen thousands of churches with humility and goodness have brought a legacy of great inspiration and strength.—Chester Swor

SERMON SUGGESTIONS

Topic: An Unrecognized Presence

TEXT: Gen. 28:10–19a

Can we claim the Jacob story as our own? (1) We, too, are wanderers: we face a life filled with uncertainties. (2) We, too, may become aware of God's presence and providence where we least expect them. (3) We, too, will acknowledge in appropriate ways what God, newly experienced in our life, now means to us.

Topic: Where the Spirit Is at Work in Us

TEXT: Rom. 8:12–25

(1) We will abandon a life of sin, verse 13. (2) We will become aware of belonging to the family of God, verses 14–16. (3) We will live in confident expectation of the triumph of God in his creation and in our personal lives, verses 18–25.

Worship Aids

CALL TO WORSHIP. "Search me, O God, and know my heart: try me, and know my thoughts: and see if there be any wicked way in me, and lead me in the way everlasting" (Ps. 139:23–24).

INVOCATION. In this house of worship we long to be met by your transforming spirit, Father. So we ask that as Father of all mercy, you have mercy upon us today. As Father of light, shine in our hearts. As Father of goodness, deliver us from evil. In our weakness be our refuge and strength. In our loneliness be our ever present companion, and in our lostness be our Savior. Father of love, teach us to love one another as you love us.—Henry Fields

OFFERTORY SENTENCE. "From everyone to whom much has been given, much will be required; and from the one to whom much has been entrusted, even more will be demanded" (Luke 12:48b NRSV).

OFFERTORY PRAYER. Lord, because we have been given much, of us much is required, so we give as we are able, seeking to be faithful stewards, who make a difference in spreading the gospel of Christ our Lord.—E. Lee Phillips

PRAYER. O God whose presence is light, hear the praise of your people. For we who have known the darkness of despair find it difficult to adjust to the light of promise. Teach us to sing before we see, and hope before we are healed.

We are thankful that hope is not rooted in statistics, won-lost records, performance ratings, or bank statements. Thankful are we that in the midst of hopelessness, even the hopelessness of Gethsemane and the cross, Christ says to us: "I have overcome the world."

O Lord, deliver us from the conviction that it is we who have been overcome by the conditions of this present age. Be with those in this congregation who know the pangs of separation. May your presence be light and hope to those we love who are in nursing homes, hospitals, or jails, and help us not to forget those who find themselves without loved ones no matter how distant. Renew our ministries, O Lord, to the orphan, the widow, and the poor. Enable us to seek justice for the nameless as well as for friend or relative. We pray especially for our government; may truth win the day and your justice and mercy go beyond party spirit and narrow nationalism.

O God, bless our parents, whom we remember this day. Grant us, their children, sensitivity to their needs and burdens. Bring comfort to any person who feels pushed out of family, work, and the fellowship of friends. We know you are nearer than hands and feet, but we pray for the courage to be your hands and feet in ministering to those who feel excluded by age or illness. Relying on your Spirit to go where we cannot, we pray in the name of Jesus.
—Gary Stratman

LECTIONARY MESSAGE

Topic: Creation's Longing
TEXT: Rom. 8:12–25

"All things are connected." You hear that phrase a lot these days. You see it on T-shirts. It sums up the current emphasis on protection of the environment. All the natural order is seen to be linked. Destruction of any part poses a threat to the whole, whether it be tropical rain forests, the ozone layer, or African elephants. Far from a current fad, this idea has roots in the Bible and in the doctrine of creation.

I. *A biblical teaching.* In the creation narrative, nature and humankind are tied closely together. Humans are given dominion over all God's creation (Gen. 1:28) and human sin brings with it the fall of nature itself (Gen. 3:17–19). Paul had this in mind when he spoke of the "futility" of creation and its "bondage to decay" (Rom. 8:20–21). If nature's fate is thus tied to humanity's fall, it follows that nature's restoration likewise depends on human salvation.

II. *A future hope.* The prophets envisioned God's future "age to come" as a time when nature's "fallenness" will be reversed, when God's original purposes for creation will be realized. All nature, animate and inanimate, will be in perfect harmony. The leopard will lie down with the lamb and the toddler will play unharmed over the hole of the poisonous snake. Suffering and destruction will cease, for the knowledge of God will pervade all of creation (Isa. 11:6–9).

Paul picked up on this vision in Romans 8:19–23 when he linked the "eager expectation" of the created world with the "redemption" of the children of God. His idea was that the freedom and perfection of nature itself is somehow dependent on the salvation of humanity. This statement on creation occurs in the context of a larger treatment of the Holy Spirit's role in the life of the believer. The Spirit is our guarantee for the future life of glory, strengthening us to endure this present world of imperfection and suffering. In the life to come, the children of God will no longer experience the sin, decay, and suffering of this world. What applies to humanity applies equally to the created order. No wonder creation groans and longs for humanity's redemption! All are bound together, the renewal of humanity and the natural order alike.

III. *A present reality.* Romans 8:18–23 is, of course, a grand confession of faith—a confession of the utter seriousness of human sin and the ultimate triumph of God's grace. Paul never intended it as a scientific treatment. And yet, modern science has placed us in a position to appreciate the truth of Paul's confession. Human sin can have profound effects on nature. Greed can lead to rape of the earth, bringing flood, drought, or famine in its train. But cannot human redemption bring about a reversal in the pattern? Surely those who have died to self and been raised to a new life in Christ can begin to bring about some reconciliation between nature and humanity.—John B. Polhill

SUNDAY: JULY TWENTY-EIGHTH

SERVICE OF WORSHIP

Sermon: Getting Up out of the Dumps
TEXT: Ps. 42–43

Life treats us all "with difficulty" sometimes. You can be sailing along, quite serenely, enjoying the experience of living, when some urgent crisis abruptly precipitates you down in a dizzy descent that can leave you spiritually breathless. Or some emotional current tugs at you, unexpectedly dragging you down into a vortex of despair and discouragement.

In such a situation you must kick off in faith immediately if you are to survive! This was a lesson David learned and recorded for us in Psalms Forty-two and Forty-three. Here we find David "down in the dumps." Cast down suddenly in the midst of life's experiences, he reminded himself that he must get back quickly to the place of life and safety.

When life dumps us into a season of melancholy and disquiet, we too become anxious, troubled, worried. Fears of the future and feelings of hopelessness about the present tumble us about in an agitation that increases its power over us every extra minute it keeps us under before we surface. How do we get up out of the dumps?

I. *Memory is a way up out of the dumps.*

a. The first five verses of Psalm Forty-two form a tear-stained page of David's autobiography. In loneliness and conflict he became depressed with his vision of himself and frustrated by his distorted vision of God. The questions he asked in the first half of verse 5 he answers with affirmations of trust in the second half of that chorus. And such a response came only as he traced through his former times of blessing and used this memory as a ladder to lift his sagging spirits.

b. All persons know feelings of depression, despondency, and dejection. Sometimes feelings of deep misery well up out of our human nature in reaction to situations beyond our control in spite of all we do to avoid them. God delights to use ordinary people. He takes us with all our built-in blemishes and promises to lift us up again when we get down. And he uses the memory of former blessings as a path to lead us up out of the dumps.

c. Of course, many times we forget that our spiritual lows arise from emotional and physical pressures around us. The young may feel down in the dumps because of too much study or too many late nights out on the town. The old may be depressed from the loneliness and weaknesses that come with age. If you are single you can be down in the dumps because you long to share your life intimately with another. If you are married you may be down in the dumps because you have grown tired of involvement with others and long to be independent.

When we are down in the dumps, it is not really that God is any different. Circumstances and situations change; and we change as life ebbs and flows around us. This is the time to remember God's faithfulness and former blessings.

II. *Faith is a way up out of the dumps.*

a. No experience can be so deep that we get beyond God's reach or beneath his support. Sorrow, affliction, depression, and accident may cast us down to the depths, but never past the eternal arms of God! So the prayer of verse 9 in Psalm Forty-two brings him into the calm of verse 11: "Why art thou cast down, O my soul? and why art thou disquieted within me? hope thou in God: for I shall yet praise him, who is the health of my countenance, and my God."

b. The act of faith, wherein we express our belief in the fact that God is with us, can lift us up again. We are sometimes so happy in the green pastures that we forget that if the way leads through the valley of the shadow, he still leads, he still travels with us to comfort and to sustain.

We may too easily act as if God had left us when we fix our eyes upon the situation, the circumstances, or our feelings. Yet all the time his faithfulness remains, and we can find the support he has provided if we will only look for it and expect it.

c. Psalm Forty-three, verses 1–4 is the third stanza of David's mighty hymn. Before the chorus (in v. 5), for the third time he pled his case before God in prayer, recognizing his own self-pity and reaching out in praise to lift his soul up again. And he cried, "O send out thy light and thy truth: let them lead me" (v. 3a) to the holiness and joy expressed in verse 4. So memory and faith are ways up out of the dumps.

III. *Light and truth are ways up out of the dumps.*

a. They lead. They point the way upward. When you are in the dumps you need to look for God's light and God's *truth* to lift you out! It is never wrong to ask why you are cast down and disquieted within, but it is always wrong to ask it only of yourself and not of God! When you search his Word for the light and truth that are there, you can hear him answering your questions with the memory of past blessings and the support from his immediate presence as a strength to faith. But his Word is the key. You will struggle to see the light and find the truth, remaining in ignorance and error if you only search your own heart. But when you find out what God says to you in his Word, light and truth become pathways to lift you up from the dumps.

b. God has never promised to keep us out of trouble but to keep us from falling when we get into it. He gives no special hedge of protection for his children to claim as shelter from all the common woes of life. But he promises us that he will work at all things, even the bad things, to get the good out of them for those who love him and are called within his eternal purpose. He grants no special insurance against us falling into the dumps; but he guarantees our security while there and promises that he will work things out in his own way and at his own time if we will trust him.

c. Let us then have patience with the patience of God. He has not promised us that the sun would always shine, that the billows of life would gently caress us in calm and quietness. But he has promised, "I will never leave thee, nor forsake thee. So that we may boldly say, The Lord is my helper, and I will not fear" (Heb. 13:5–6).—Craig Skinner

Illustrations

THE PROBLEM OF EVIL.   There is the problem of evil, which no philosopher has yet been able to solve, evil that slips in everywhere and has also twisted the divine meaning of adventure. There are adventures that are proud, cruel, deceitful, destructive, and stupid. But when we read the Bible carefully we discover a great mystery: that God reigns over evil, nevertheless without ever being its author or resigning himself to it; God's purpose is worked out not only through man's obedience but also by his disobedience.—Paul Tournier

HANDLING THE PAST.   Remember, above all: The past is the past. It has no magical, automatic effect on the present or future. At most, your past habits make

it harder for you to change than to remain stationary. Harder, but not impossible. Work and time; practice and more practice; thinking and doing; these are the unmagical keys that will unlock almost any chest of past defeats and turn them into possible present and future victories.—Albert Ellis/Robert A. Harper

SERMON SUGGESTIONS

Topic: The Deceiver Deceived
TEXT: Gen. 24:15–28
(1) *The story:* Laban deceived Jacob by giving him the wrong daughter in marriage. (2) *The lessons:* (a) Sometimes we experience the same kind of unpleasantness we have foisted on others, as did Jacob the deceiver; (b) God continues his purpose amid the weaknesses and wrongs of his people.

Topic: The Paradoxical Kingdom
TEXT: Matt. 13:31–33, 44–52
(1) The kingdom of heaven in its expansion, verses 31–33. (2) The kingdom of heaven in its narrowing focus: (a) like a hidden treasure, verse 44; (b) like a choice pearl, verses 45 and 46. (c) like a separation of good and bad, verses 47–50.

Worship Aids

CALL TO WORSHIP.   "O give thanks unto the Lord; call upon his name: make known his deeds among the people" (Ps. 105:1).

INVOCATION.   You have given us so much to thank you for, O God. We confess that we are slow in seeing what you have done, and we let ourselves descend into frustration and disappointment and even despair. Open our eyes that we may see; then open our mouths that we may speak of your goodness.

OFFERTORY SENTENCE.   "It is not that you ought to relieve other people's needs and leave yourselves in hardship, but there should be a fair balance—your surplus at present may fill their deficit, and another time their surplus may fill your deficit" (2 Cor. 8:13–14a NJB).

OFFERTORY PRAYER.   Now, Father, we let our pocketbooks tell the truth about real dedication. No words, no deeds, just parting with some of our wealth for your service. May our pocketbooks speak of large dedication, we pray.—Henry Fields

PRAYER.   O, Father, you are the source of all life and the light of all seeing: we acknowledge with joy and reverence that the world is your creation, and that life is your gift. Lift up your thoughts from the littleness of our own works to the greatness, the majesty, and the wonder of yours, and teach us so to contemplate your glory, that we may grow into your likeness.

May that love be real to us through which we call you, "Our Father." Teach us the meaning of your grace: to love in the presence of hate; to forgive in the face of malicious slander; to celebrate life in the presence of death; to be a lightbearer in the midst of darkness.

As the oyster takes a grain of sand and turns it into a pearl, may we be as creative in using the irritation that comes to us in fashioning a life to reflect your glory. May the promise of your love be realized in all of our relationships. May we not turn from the cross but seek faith and courage to choose your will in all of life.

O Father, the mystery of intercessory prayer we cannot fully fathom. But our hearts cry out in behalf of others, for we sense the intimacy with which our lives are set—that no one lives and dies unto herself or himself. For youth, in their aspirations to make a better world and for parents, in their desire to be responsible to their sons and daughters, we pray understanding and love, so that high idealism may be nurtured to responsible action. For those in mature years, we pray the fulfillment of your purpose in all of the uniqueness of their personalities and opportunities. Encourage those in bereavement with a grasp of the meaning of eternal life and an awareness of your love from which even death cannot separate. Bless those who are ill and the families who patiently keep vigil.

From the celebration of your presence in this place may we be enabled to celebrate your presence in the peculiar circumstances in which each of our lives is set in the days coming. In all things may we discover that the greatest joy in life is to do your will and that in your service is perfect freedom.—John Thompson

LECTIONARY MESSAGE

Topic: "But How Can I Know?"

TEXT: Romans 8:28–39

I. Sooner or later we all have to deal with the issue of suffering. The "health and wealth" preachers with their triumphal, painless interpretation of the Christian life do us a disservice by pretending that we don't suffer. That kind of theology is too easy.

II. No, sufferings of every kind remain a part of life—even the lives of believers. Paul presents us with a catalog of sufferings, sufferings that he himself knew firsthand (see 2 Cor. 4:7–12; 11:21b–29): from physical want (hunger, nakedness), from the mortal enemies of Christianity (persecution, sword), from unseen spiritual forces (angels, principalities, powers, height and depth—technical terms pertaining to the apogee and perigee of heavenly bodies or astrological powers), sufferings associated with the death throes of this present age (tribulation, anguish), sufferings associated with the uncertainties of human existence (life, death, things present, things to come), and, in case he left anything out, he adds "anything else in all creation."

Paul was no stranger to suffering. Neither are we. And in the midst of suffering the Christian has a harder time than the unbeliever. The unbeliever can say that suffering is random, senseless, and the best we can do is make the best of it. But the Christian must ask the God question. Where is God in the midst of my suffering? What (if anything) does my suffering mean, theologically?

The God question is vital, but the answer is often elusive. Some who dare to face the question end up in disbelief.

Most are left simply wondering *what* to believe. How can I know that God is with me and not against me? How can I know that God is working all things together for the good? How can I know that my sufferings won't get the best of me? How can I know that everything is going to be alright?

III. This passage suggests several bases for confidence. First, we can know because God has already been at work on our behalf. Look at what God has already done for us in bringing us to salvation: we have been foreknown, predestined, called, justified, and glorified. These short verses provide us a panoramic view of the plan of God for his elect. And let us not forget how costly this plan was for God. He did not spare his own Son but gave him over for our sake. A God who would go to such lengths to reconcile us to himself could never turn against us.

Second, we can know because our suffering identifies us with Jesus. Paul quotes Psalm 44:22 (in v. 36) and makes allusion to the binding of Isaac (Gen. 22:16 LXX, in v. 32). Jewish exegetes before and after Paul applied these very passages to those who suffered persecution rather than renounce their faith. By reminding us of this aspect of traditional piety, Paul assures us that affliction and trouble is part of what it means to live out one's commitments to Christ in a hostile environment. Rather than signs of God's displeasure, this kind of suffering is in fact an emblem of the close connection we have with our crucified Lord.

Third, we can know because of the surpassing love of God in Christ Jesus. It was this love that sent Jesus to the cross, and it is this love that will bring us to him in glory. God's love is greater than any earthly trial, and it relativizes the impact of the sufferings we face (see Rom. 8:18).

IV. Therefore, in the midst of all these things, we more than prevail. Just think of those who have prevailed in the midst of sufferings. They are often more inspiring than those who seem to experience a pain-free life.

V. This passage really does speak of the Christian's victory in the face of suffering. It doesn't reject a triumphal interpretation of the Christian life, but it contextualizes it. We prevail not *over* our sufferings but *in the midst* of them.

We cannot know beforehand the specific outcome of any trial or temptation we may face, but we can know that God is at work, finding the good (sometimes there isn't much!) and bringing it out. Therefore, Paul can conclude with a resolute "I am convinced" (v. 38). And there is ample reason to be convinced of God's loving purposes. When we are, we will have our answer. How can I know that everything is going to be alright? I can know this because I know God.—Darrell J. Pursiful

SUNDAY: AUGUST FOURTH

SERVICE OF WORSHIP

Sermon: Nevertheless I Am Continually with Thee

Text: Ps. 73:23

My dear brothers and sisters, for you I will try, briefly, to clarify what we have here. You will see that each word is significant.

I. "Nevertheless" is the opening word. Nevertheless means "in spite of." It stands for defiance. It is a war cry against a threatening power, a dangerous interference or affliction. These take the form perhaps of an almost irreparable loss; perhaps of "circumstances," as we say, caused by others if not by ourselves in most cases; perhaps of one or more individuals whom we cannot stand because they are in our way; perhaps even of our own personalities, of ourselves such as we are individually.

Sorrow is your plight, and so it is mine. We suffer here within the walls of this house, and so do the people of this city, even of the whole world. Behind the sorrow of each individual there lies the sorrow of a world in disorder, of a harassed, dark, and dangerous world. There also lies the sorrow of man as he is: not good, but haughty and lazy, a liar and a poor wretch, not well off, but living in misery.

What a great thing it would be were we able to throw in the face of all these adversities the defiant "nevertheless"!

II. "Nevertheless I *am*" would then mean: In spite of everything I live! I will swim against the stream! I will not give in! I will not despair, I will not drown! Rather, I will persevere and, what is more, I will have confidence and hope! I will keep above water and not be submerged! Truly, he who could freely master his own great and small troubles, and the plight of the world and of mankind, might rejoicingly exclaim: "Nevertheless I *am!*"

III. "Nevertheless I am *continually*" implies: at all times and in all circumstances, whatever happens, through thick and thin. Hence, not only occasionally, not only in the morning, but also in the evening when the darkness deepens and the night falls, not only in good times but also in bad times, not only when the good news pours in but also amidst the steady flow of distressing news, even in the grip of disappointment and dejection.

Dear brothers and sisters, the Bible where these words are written is one great invitation extended to us all. Whenever we gather for worship, as we do right now, the invitation is addressed to us. As worshipers we can and we may repeat in our hearts: "Nevertheless I am continually!" Do you realize that the Bible is a *book of freedom*, and that divine worship is a *celebration of freedom?* In worship, my brothers and sisters, we celebrate the freedom to proclaim that "nevertheless I am continually."

IV. a. But at this point we need to watch out. I would bet a hundred to one that all of us, were it a matter of choice, would continue: Nevertheless I am continually—*with myself!* I stand by my mind, by my opinion, by my point of view, by my rights! I stand by my aims and by my claims! "Nevertheless I am continually" would thus imply reliance on our own strength in defiance of all and every-

thing. The Bible calls it *sin* when man wants to be with himself. Certainly where this is the case there is no freedom.

b. In the Bible, the book of freedom, we read differently: "Nevertheless I am continually *with thee.*" My friends, picture for a moment a man groping in the dark who suddenly sees a light, or another who is starved and suddenly receives a piece of bread, or one who is dying with thirst and is offered a cup of water. This is what happens to us when we leave behind the "with myself" and break through to the conviction: "nevertheless I am continually *with thee.*"

What kind of a "thou" is this? Is it a *man*? Yes, indeed, someone with a human face, a human body, human hands, and human language. One whose heart bears sorrows—not simply his own, but the sorrows of the whole world. One who takes our sin and our misery upon himself and away from us. One who is able to do this because he is not only man, but also *God*, the almighty Creator and Lord who knows me and you much better than we know ourselves, who loves me and you much more than we love ourselves. He is our neighbor, he is closer to us than we are to ourselves, and we may call him by his first name.

Do you know who he is? The hymn gives us the answer:

> Christ Jesus is his name,
>   The Lord Sabaoth's Son;
> He, and no other one,
>   Shall conquer in the battle.

Brothers and sisters, we are now all invited to talk to him instead of talking to ourselves. We are at liberty to say to him: "Nevertheless I am continually *with thee.*"

V. At this point your question will surely be: But how can we accomplish this? Let me hasten to answer that *we* cannot do this. Yet there is something much more excellent than what we can do. Here it is written: *Thou dost hold my right hand.*

a. Therefore, I hold on because *you* hold me. I am continually because you are with me. Because you hold me, I say: "Nevertheless I am continually with thee." I say so because evidently my sorrow is not my own, but yours; because you have taken my sorrow and the sorrow of all mankind to your heart, have borne them in your life, and vindicated them in your death on the cross; because "in soul and body, whether I live or die, I am not my own, but I belong unto my most faithful Lord and Savior Jesus Christ."

b. One more thing remains to be considered. The text states: *Thou dost hold my right hand.* The right hand is man's strong and skillful hand. It is the hand to work, to write, and, if necessary, to fight with. We give the right hand of fellowship when we greet one another. The right hand symbolizes ourselves, indeed ourselves where it counts, where we mean business, where our heart is. We are not asked to extend the right hand of fellowship to the Lord God. There is no need for it whatever. The gesture is belated. *He* holds us by our right hand, he takes us seriously where it counts to be taken seriously. This is our situation.

c. Let me conclude with a question. Who are you? Who am I? The answer is: one whom God holds by his right hand, on whose heart and lips God has laid the confession of faithfulness and the great comfort: *Nevertheless I am continually with thee.* Glory be to the Father, and to the Son, and to the Holy Ghost. Amen.— Karl Barth

Illustrations

GOD'S SILENCE.   The silence of God is part of his gracious discipline that seeks our spiritual maturity. It springs out of his patience with our waywardness and folly. Our Lord had to keep many things from his disciples. He had to be silent in his love for them. "I have many things to say unto you but you cannot bear them now." But he also said, "If it were not so, I would have told you." The silence of love, the fact that God does not as a rule interfere in any outward way, has developed our characters. He gives us enough light to carry us through. He gives us a lamp, though it be only to our feet: the darkness remains round about.—John Bishop

COMING TO FAITH.   Let us imagine the case of a small child, a little boy, entrusted to the care of a nursery governess. When she arrives, the little fellow is taken into the room where she is and left in her care. But she is strange to him, he does not trust her, but looks distantly at this strange woman from the opposite corner of the room. She knows that she cannot do anything with him until she has won his confidence. She knows she has to *win* it. The little boy cannot manufacture it, cannot make himself trust the governess. His faith in her is something that he cannot create—only *she* can create it. And she knows that she cannot create it by forcing it; she has to respect the personality of the child; and to try to take the citadel by storm would be worse than useless, and would produce fear and distrust instead of confidence.

She sets about her task gently, using various means—words, gestures, and smiles, and perhaps gifts, all of which convey something of the kindness of her heart. Until at last the little fellow's mistrust is melted away, she has won his confidence, and of his own free will he responds to her advances and crosses the floor to sit on her knee. Now that her graciousness, using all these means, has created his faith, she can carry on the good work she has began.—D. M. Baillie

SERMON SUGGESTIONS

Topic: "Supreme above All"

TEXT: Rom. 9:1–5 REB, especially verse 5b: "May God, supreme above all, be blessed for ever."

To be blessed: (1) because he chose a people to represent him to the world; (2) because he sent the Savior Messiah through these chosen people.

Topic: God's Care of His Own

TEXT: Matt. 14:13–21 NRSV

(1) In extraordinary circumstances: "He had compassion for them and cured their sick." (2) In ordinary circumstances: "And all ate and were filled."

Worship Aids

CALL TO WORSHIP.   "I am called upon thee, for thou wilt hear me, O God: incline thine ear unto me, and hear my speech. Shew thy marvelous loving kindness, O thou that savest by thy right hand them which put their trust in thee from those that rise up against them" (Ps. 17:6–7).

INVOCATION.   Lord, we desire thy courts and would do thy bidding. Thy inner sanctuary is a place where our hearts long to reside. To do thy will is our joy. Speak to us again and reveal thy glory through the Spirit and the Son.—E. Lee Philipps

OFFERTORY SENTENCE.   "On the first day of every week, each of you is to put aside and save what ever extra you earn, so that collections need not to be taken when I come" (1 Cor. 16:2 NRSV).

OFFERTORY PRAYER.   Lord, our God, allow this offering to represent our belief in the love of God, salvation in Christ Jesus, the mission imperative of the Church, and the power of the Holy Spirit, that your name may be glorified forever.—E. Lee Philipps

PRAYER.   In unhurried silence, heavy with wonder, deep in misery, we venture into your inviting and glad presence, Holy God, seeking to worship you as Creator, Sustainer, Redeemer, and Lord of all. Receive our willing presence and sincere praise as offerings of our worship.

In the beginning of time, Creator God, you called the earth out of darkness into light. And, it was called good. In the passing of time, Sustaining God, you sent faithful servants to declare your words of life and light. And, in the fullness of time, Redeemer God, you gave the best gift, for in Christ, you called the world from darkness and death to marvelous light and eternal life. Thanks be to God.

Accepting and Forgiving God, we confess the shadows of our public lives and private selves. Forgive the darkness of our hearts, closed and cold, leaning hard against the warmth and wealth of love's pure light. Pardon the darkness of our minds, shaping and harboring evil that sabotages our relationships and injures our commitment to you. Forgive the darkness of our deeds; all that hurts and harms your children and brings tears to your eyes and brokenness to your heart. Cleanse our lives and shine the light of forgiveness upon us all.

God of wholeness, we offer prayers of thanksgiving for healing experienced by many this week past. God of comfort, cradle tenderly those for whom healing has not come and those for whom it will not come in this life. God of all faithfulness, lead us to be faithful too. Breathe the breath of Pentecost Spirit on us and stir us to places of service for the kingdom to come and for your will to be done.—William M. Johnson

LECTIONARY MESSAGE

Topic: Wrestling with God

TEXT: Gen. 32:22–31

Brothers like to wrestle. Upon coming to Rome from college for vacation, not realizing my brother had grown so much, I tried to intimidate him. He extended his arm, now longer than mine. I ran into his fist. A big black eye was the result. The younger brother gained my respect thereafter.

Jacob was a wrestler. He wrestled with his brother in his mother's womb. He wrestled with Isaac, his father, and Esau, his brother, for the family birthright and blessing. He wrestled at Luz in a dream of a ladder to heaven with the Lord standing above it and angels ascending and descending. He exclaimed, "The Lord was in this place and I did not know it." He called that place Bethel, "the House of God" (Gen. 28:19).

He wrestled for fourteen years with Laban, his uncle, for Rachel and Leah, his wives, and six more years as a herdsman. Now he is wrestling with the fear of meeting Esau and facing his anger. An angel of God instructed him for his return to Canaan (Gen. 31:11 ff). "And the angels of God met him" at Mahanaim (Gen. 32:1).

Upon learning that Esau was approaching with four hundred men, Jacob, terrified, prayed for God's deliverance. He reminded God of his promises at Bethel. A cunning design was devised. He divided the flocks, herds, camels into two companies, so that if Esau struck one the other would escape. Three different droves at spaced intervals were sent as gifts to Esau to appease him with presents and to arrange a friendly meeting.

After the presents were sent, in the night Jacob took his immediate family over the brook Jabbok for safekeeping. Upon returning he "was left alone." Then came the life-changing experience: "A man wrestles with him until the breaking of day" (Gen. 32:24).

This psychic documentary in Jacob's life leads us through our own wrestling with both known and unknown challengers. The wrestler is first identified as a man. Later, Hosea speaks of the Night Stranger as an angel (Hos. 12:4). Jacob concluded that the Strong One was God, "For I have seen God face to face, and my life is preserved" (Gen. 32:30).

It is time for us to personalize Jacob's wrestling experience into our own with man and God. And to know the difference.

I. *The Trial of Desolation.* "Then Jacob was left alone" (v. 29).

a. There is a cosmic loneliness that haunts the human heart. In this darkness we wrestle with life's greatest issues.

Jesus faced this in Gethsemane and Golgotha as he cried out at the great mysteries of life and sacrifice.

b. "And a man wrestled with him" (v. 24). We, too, wrestle in the night hours. Who was this man? Was he a demon of the dark side of the soul, a ghost haunting the desert places as Azazel, the spirit of the wilderness? Or was the man Jacob himself? His own conscience?

c. There are many men with whom we wrestle:

(1) The man of fear: Jacob was afraid of Esau. We continue to wrestle with our fears and gripping guilt.

(2) The man of greed: Jacob had burned with desire for Esau's birthright and blessing. He still wanted more.

(3) The man of jealousy: Jacob was second born and wanted to be first born.

(4) The man of sensual passion: It is at night our physical fantasies take captive our imaginations, our self-control, and our moral strength. It is before battle that the strongest urges arise. The physical anticipates the spiritual.

d. But the stranger had supernatural powers. He was a man of strength and a messenger of portending events. He was more than an angel. He was God.

The apostle Paul spoke of wrestling against principalities, powers, rulers of darkness, spiritual wickedness in high places (Eph. 6:13). In our aloneness and desolation we are wrestlers crying out for a blessing. And God comes.

II. *The Tenacity of Desperation.* "I will not let you go unless you bless me" (v. 26).

a. All night long the struggle continued. In desperation Jacob kept holding on. In extreme straits strength comes with a surge.

The man struck Jacob in the hip to subdue him. We are stricken in our bodies and zeal to gain our attention and surrender. Even in human heroism one must be hurt to realize the blessing desired and awaiting. "No pain, no gain" is the modern parlance.

b. Jacob wanted a third blessing. Two had been given: the first from Esau in the birthright won by trickery; the second from God at Bethel won by bargaining. Now Jacob besought the third by tenaciously praying.

In our desperation of physical injury, life-threatening illnesses, family breakups, financial reverses, we are thrown out of joint, and we limp with pain. We cannot win by trickery, by bargaining, but by prayerful surrender. The antagonist was not a Night Shadow but one with the power to bless. It was in the human hurt the Divine Man revealed himself. Now Jacob was no longer the supplanter but became the suppliant.

c. What was the blessing Jacob so desperately sought? Could it have been for protection and peace with Esau? Could it have been for more flocks and lands in Canaan? Could it have been for renewal of the covenant made at Bethel?

d. What is the blessing we seek? We not only seek a second or third blessing from God, we seek to hold on to him until we know with whom we are wrestling and see him face-to face (Peniel) in loving companionship.

Jesus instructs us that Christian persistence will have its proper reward (Luke 11:5–13).

III. *The Turning Point of Confession.* "What is your name?" and he said, "Jacob" (v. 27).

a. The man asked Jacob to identify himself. The man did not attack on a chance meeting as a robber stalking his prey. This was a proof test to bring Jacob to spiritual submission, to elicit his surrender to be God's instrument for God's plans for a chosen people.

b. There are times we have to confess who we are. In identifying ourselves the great changes are permitted to happen. "Jacob." The name depicted the character, identification, self-incrimination. He was the supplanter, the "heel grabber" (Hebrew etymology), the trickster, the traveler, the trader, the hustler.

In giving his name he confessed he was the hurting one, the selfish one, a nobody: Jacob, the sinner.

c. At the turning point of confession, the strong man gave Jacob a name change, "You are no longer Jacob but Israel." No longer the "heel grabber" but one who struggled and "prevailed with God." You are a Son of God, a prince with God. In the confession there comes the coronation.

The biblical name change not only symbolizes a character change but a choosing for service (Abraham, Peter, and Paul). He was to be the father of nations and kings. His descendants bear his name today.

d. We ask today, "What is your name?" Is your name thief, liar, trickster, adulterer, renegade, runaway. Confess your name. Let God give you a new name such as "a son of God," "a prince of God," "a patriarch for the family of God."

e. Jacob asked the wrestler, "Tell me your name?" The answer: "Why do you ask my name? You know who I am." Jacob was satisfied. The man blessed him there (v. 29).

Jacob's life was spared. The hip injury memorialized the happening of God's touch and smile (face-to-face). After the reunion with Esau, each with forgiveness and joy turned to his respective land for expanding destinies.

IV. *The Triumph of Destiny.* Jacob named the place Peniel (the face of God), "For I have seen God face-to-face and my life is preserved" (v. 30).

a. We remember the place when and where God came to us. It is a sanctified place always in our memory. Peniel and Bethel will always be.

But how do we see the face of God? His visage may appear shadowy in the terror of the darkness. As we hold on to him the night flees in the light of his resurrected presence.

Jacob goes back to Bethel. "I will make an altar there to God, who answered me in the day of my distress, and has been with me in the way which I have gone" (Gen. 35:3).

b. Jacob is no longer a wrestler. He is the worshiper. He eternalizes his pilgrimage. His limp, no longer a handicap, strengthens him for the new walk with God. He becomes the father of nations and kings (Gen. 35:11).

c. The irony of history has been that many of the descendants of Jacob-Israel still wrestled with God through the ages. They wanted to be blessed but would not accede to his purpose for their heritage. God's man came to them. Instead of saying, "Bless me," they crucified him. The darker nature of Jacob, "the heel grabber" comes out again. Enmity rather than friendship still is strong.

d. The triumph of our destiny comes as we hold on to God through faith in Jesus Christ. The day breaks and we see God in the face of Jesus (John 1:18; 14:9). He knows us and we know him. The threat of death given to Moses for looking on God's face is no longer applicable (Exod. 33:20).

e. Our new name is Christian. We are the new Israel, leader, and patriarch to those whom God has entrusted to us.

Our destiny, though limping or crucified, is to hold on to the Divine visitor, our Lord. He will meet us again face-to-face. We go on our journey with reconciliation and rejoicing to Bethel (the House of God) and to our Heavenly Home.—Eugene I. Enlow

SUNDAY: AUGUST ELEVENTH

SERVICE OF WORSHIP

Sermon: Questions Without Answers

TEXT: Rom. 8:35–39

Throughout his long history, man has asked questions and found answers. His doubts and inquisitiveness have been spurs goading him to ask more questions and find more knowledge. There is nothing on this earth that has been excluded from his concern.

There are times when he asks questions not because he is thirsting for understanding but because he is rebellious. Whenever life makes spiritual and moral demands upon us, we grow restless, and then ask questions, not because we want to know but because we want to express resentment against the manner in which the universe has dealt with us. Most of these questions are asked in an angry mood. We rebel against life's demands; we resent the disciplines circumstances foist upon us. We hate what life is doing to us, and so in a spirit of defiance we demand to know. The questions are thrown back at us again and again. There is no answer for the simple reason that we know the answer.

I. Let me put this in a way in which all of us have experienced it. As we read the Scriptures, we suddenly come upon a word like this: "Cast all your anxieties upon him because he careth for you" (ARV). We read, and almost laugh.

a. We remember too many moments when life was cruel and fitful in its vagaries. We remember when it seemed as though some evil hand were toying with us, when life sank its grasping tentacles into our hearts.

We remember how life appeared to move in circles, and circles within circles, until we lost all sense of direction. We remember when difficulties and troubles piled up until they became so overpowering that we could no longer cope with them. We recall the tragedies and heartaches when we were churning in our misery.

b. As we remember, the soul is on fire with anger. It is an anger that grows out of disillusionment and harsh memories. And so we read again, "Cast thy burden upon the Lord, for he careth for you." And now we ask, "When did he care?" But there is no answer, and we need none, for we know the answer. We have known it all along. We know that he did care, else we would not be here at all. We know that he did care, else we would not have found strength to come through fiery trials. We know that he did care, else we would have been consumed by our hurts and loneliness.

II. Somewhere else we read, "Let him who standeth take heed lest he falleth." How we rebel against that. This seems to be the essence of foolishness.

a. Why, we want to know, should we live as though life were a prison house? Why can't we let go and live naturally and follow the bent of our desires? Why should we act as though every coming moment were charged with terror? It is not true that we are always standing on a precipice. Why, then, be on guard and strain against the times?

b. And so we read again, "Let him who standeth take heed lest he falleth." And now, resentful of what we read, we ask why. But even as we ask, we know the answer. We have known the answer all along, for all along we have known that the soul is in greatest danger, not when things go to pieces about us, but when we stand on enchanted ground.

III. Again we read, "If any man would come after me, let him take up his cross and follow me."

a. Let someone tell us why we should take that road. Here lies the source of conflict within the heart. We have other thoughts and other purposes. We have other wants and other desires. Why must we do this when everything within us cries for something else? Why must we be generous and noble and courageous? Why must we go upon the sorrow road? Why upon the road of humility and forgiveness? We are human; we are hurt; we are bruised; we have pride. Why must we humble ourselves? Why must we live with others constantly in our thoughts?

b. And even as we ask, we know the answer. We have known it all along. All along we have known that we must go on that road, or have no peace. All along we have known we must go on that road, or find no rest. All along we have known that we must go upon that road, or we cannot walk with strength before others, but will be torn within ourselves.

IV. We turn to one other passage in our Bible and we read: "No one cometh unto the Father but by me."

a. We know how good he was and how great. We know how readily he yielded to the needs of those about him. We know how well it will be with us, if we pattern ourselves after him. But this exclusiveness! This saying that we cannot know God unless we know Christ first! This insistence that we cannot reach God unless we first touch Christ! Against that we rebel.

Why must we choose Christ? Is not God, God whether there be a Christ or not? Are there not other ways of living—good ways, decent ways, respectable ways?

b. So we ask and we want an answer, and there is no answer. We have always known that we shall never touch the heart of it, but even as we ask, we know. We have always known. We have always known that we shall never experience his abiding love unless we see Christ first. We have always known that we shall

never understand God's strength or God's mercy, God's holiness or God's goodness, unless we look at Christ.

Then all grows quiet within us. Then we know that we will want him—want him more than we have ever wanted anything else.

V. And suddenly this whole matter is turned around, and it is no longer we that ask, seeking an answer; now it is Christ who asks, "Lovest thou me more than these?" Then, like Peter long ago, we must say, "Why do you ask? You know the answer. You have known it all along."

Yes, therein lies our hope, that he does know the answer—and now we know it, too. And if we have ever said this before, we say it again, only this time, the ring of joy is in it:

Who shall separate us from the love of Christ? shall tribulation, or distress, or persecution, or famine, or nakedness, or peril, or sword? . . . Nay, in all these things we are more than conquerors through him that loved us. For I am persuaded, that neither death, nor life, nor angels, nor principalities, nor powers, nor things present, nor things to come, nor height, nor depth, nor any other creature, shall be able to separate us from the love of God, which is in Christ Jesus our Lord.

That is the only answer.—Arnold H. Lowe

Illustrations

WHEN DANGER LURKS. When the skies are bright, when the waters are not churned by angry storms and the sands of the desert are not sucked up into dark funnels of smoke, then our souls are in peril. When all goes well with us, when there are no enemies about, no unfriendly waves washing upon our shores, when life speaks generously to us, then we are in danger. When we are safe, when we have plenty, and when our guard is lowered, then we are in peril. We remember those words from Ecclesiastes: "In the day of prosperity be joyful, but in the day of adversity consider." What freedom from danger can do to our hearts! When our guard is lowered, how slothful we become, how easy of mind, how careless in our habits, and how inattentive to our deepest needs. —Arnold H. Lowe

COMING TO AWARENESS.   A little while ago I talked with a man who had been a "good church member" all his life and lived an exemplary business and social life. But for some reason he had never found an inner meaning and power promised by the New Testament. He felt somehow cheated and empty. He accepted an opportunity to study the Bible with a few others and entered with them upon a corporate search for truth and meaning in the New Testament. As these people became friends and began to share their experiences as well as their ideas, the tempo of the man's questions accelerated, a light came into his face, and I could almost watch the scales dropping from his eyes. He was "getting it"; or it was "getting through" to him. Over a period of some months a crucial realization and turning point had come to him. He spoke to me about it:

"For years I knew intellectually with my mind that God loves me and all men, but for some reason it didn't do anything to me, nothing happened in me or to me; it just didn't make any difference. But in this study group, as I came into close contact with other persons who knew this forgiving love of Christ personally, it began to rub off on me until I caught it too!"—Robert A. Raines

SERMON SUGGESTIONS

Topic: God's Plan Unfolds
TEXT: Gen. 37:1–4, 12–28
The Psalmist said, "Human wrath serves only to praise you" (Ps. 76:10a NRSV). God's plan unfolds: (1) despite envy and jealousy, verses 1–4; (2) despite murderous intentions, verses 12–24; (3) despite greed, verses 25–28.

Topic: Salvation Is for All
TEXT: Rom. 10:5–15
(1) It is for those who have tried to save themselves and failed. (2) It is for those who have faith in Jesus Christ. (3) It is for all without distinction who call on the Lord.

Worship Aids

CALL TO WORSHIP.   "O give thanks unto the Lord; call upon his name: make known his deeds among the people. Sing unto him, sing psalms unto him: talk ye all his wondrous works" (Ps. 105:1–2).

INVOCATION.   We do call upon you, O Lord, even as we thank you for all your mercies, asking for the faith, hope, and love that would make our lives and words witness to your greatness and love.

OFFERTORY SENTENCE.   "Now stewards are required to show themselves trustworthy" (1 Cor. 4:2 REB).

OFFERTORY PRAYER.   Help us, O God, to realize that we indeed are stewards, not only of the divine mysteries, but of the manifold gifts of your providence. May we, therefore, find joy in the responsible use of what you have given to us, and may others be blessed by what we return to you even now.

PRAYER.   Father, the burdens of life grow heavy as we travel along the road. Often we long to lay our burdens down and once and for all be free. Yet, in our rational moments we know that burdens give strength that we would never have had, had they not been a part of life. As we meet in your presence we pray that you will renew our strength that we may "mount up with wings as eagles, that we may run and not be weary, that we may walk and not faint." Open windows through which may come the sunshine of your love. Open avenues along which we may pass to fulfill your purpose for our lives. Open opportunities through which we may express your love to people in the world around us.

Among us are those whose lives have been invaded by devastating circumstances. Family struggles and disagreements create havoc for some. Illness beyond human ability to heal limits life for others. Economic struggles cramp the dreams of many who would like to help make the world a better place for all. Overt and blatant sin claims too many, shutting out the wonder and glory of your purpose for them. In a hundred ways and more, Father, our lives are at the mercy of limiting circumstances, keeping us from being all that we desire to be and feel that you want us to be. While we cannot explain this mystery of limitation, we know that you can take the events of life and, working through them, bring us to where you want us to be in spite of them.

So, we ask that we be granted an encounter with the Lord that will renew our faith, give us resurrected hope, open our eyes to a higher vision of your purpose, and save us from our limiting sins. Meet us, Lord Jesus, as we are, often worried, many times frustrated, sometimes confused, and at times fearful and lost. Remind us always of your power to save, your love to sustain, and your presence to encourage. And in that knowledge send us out when this hour is done to be your ambassadors to the least, the last, and the lost at every level of life.—Henry Fields

LECTIONARY MESSAGE

Topic: Wobbling on the Water

Text: Matt. 14:22–33

Our Lord Jesus walks on the water, but most of us are like Peter. At best, we wobble on the water! This well-known miracle of Jesus serves as a testimony to the Lordship of Christ over the natural world. On a more personal level, it serves to remind us as Christ's disciples of where we need help in our pilgrimage of faith.

The striking contrast between the peaceful mountain of prayer and the tempestuous sea of struggle calls us to remember our own quest for a spiritual "still point" in the midst of a frantically turning world.

I. The Mountain: The Preparation of Praying (v. 22–23). Jesus "made the disciples get into the boat" (v. 22). They want to stay around the site of the miraculous meal (v. 13–21) and bask in the glory of the moment. They certainly would have enthusiastically supported the political clamor for Jesus, the "loaves and fish" king (cf. John 6:15).

Jesus avoids this popular acclaim, for it misunderstands his mission. He dismisses the crowd. Instead Jesus seeks the solitude of the mountain to gain clarity about his calling.

Jesus' disciples prove to be of no help. He must rely upon God alone for guidance and direction. When the stresses of life and ministry threaten to overwhelm us, we need to follow the example of our Lord and retreat to the mountain of prayer to regain our perspective on life and ministry.

II. The Waves: The Miracle of Walking (v. 24–27). The disciples were following Christ's commands and yet ran into the storm. Obedience does not mean exemption from suffering. When the disciples earlier encountered a similar storm (8:23–27), they had the blessing of having Jesus in the boat with them. He was swiftly awakened and, despite their "little faith" (8:26), calmed the tempest.

Now, however, Jesus is no longer physically "in the same boat" with them. Yet, even when Jesus is not physically present with his disciples, he is interceding for them. His comforting presence is spiritually available. This promise of Christ's continuing presence has sustained Christians in difficult straits throughout the history of the Church.

When the disciples are in need of Jesus, he comes to them. It is "early in the morning" (v. 25; cf. Exod. 14:24)—literally the fourth Roman watch, between 3 and 6 A.M. In moments of personal and spiritual "stuckness" these lonely hours before the dawn can often be the time of greatest desperation. This is crisis time!

Jesus is the Lord of nature who constrains his powers in order to assist those "battered by the waves" (v. 24). Christ does what is naturally impossible in order to provide the help and courage his storm-tormented disciples desperately need.

"But when the disciples [see] him walking on the sea" (v. 26), they fail to recognize him. As Matthew Henry sadly comments, "These disciples said, 'It is a Spirit?'; when they should have said, 'It is the Lord.' " What the disciples need to end their ghost-haunted terror is the simple recognition of the presence of Christ.

These same disciples will later face persecution for their faith in Jesus. Their memories of this night, recorded in Scripture, will offer them great comfort. Perhaps in their suffering they could glimpse again the shadowy figure of the Lord, coming to them with words of encouragement. For the reality of Christ's presence gives Christians courage to overcome their fears.

III. The Wind: The Struggle of Wavering (v. 28–33). Peter impulsively challenges Jesus to include him in the miracle (v. 28). In response to Jesus' one-word invitation Peter launches out on faith and begins "walking on the water . . . toward Jesus" (v. 29). Peter is a tough fisherman who typically is not afraid of jumping into the sea and swimming ashore (John 21:7). Yet, when he notices "the strong wind" (v. 20), he suddenly is paralyzed by fear.

This incident is like a "rehearsal" of Peter's famous denial of Christ (Owen).

The same fear that later would drive him to deny Christ (26:69–75) after boldly proclaiming his loyalty (26:33–35) now causes Peter to start to sink beneath the angry waves. His "little faith" (v. 31) needs to be purged of its self-confidence.

Nevertheless, in this life-and-death situation Peter's "little faith" shows its true colors, for "in the moment of his failure he clutched at Christ" (Barclay). He cries out to the Lord for salvation.

We do not have to struggle alone against the contrary winds of life. Jesus comes with his hands reaching out to us. When we feel that we are drowning in the storms of life, it is our hope in Christ that enables us to keep our "heads above water."

"Christ does not fail even those who fail him" (Stagg). He reaches out and holds those who belong to him. For Jesus Christ is the Son of God, the One who "trampled the waves of the sea" (Job 9:8). After their experience of doubt and fear, the disciples are ready to worship Jesus (v. 33).

When Christ along with the wobbly Peter enters the boat, the frightening wind ceases (v. 32) and the peace begins. We need to welcome Christ into our own little boats, as we seek to cross "to the other side" (v. 22).—Charles J. Scalise

SUNDAY: AUGUST EIGHTEENTH

SERVICE OF WORSHIP

Sermon: Reckoned

TEXT: Rom. 4:13–25

What is all this fussing and arguing over anyway? What difference does it make what a person believes? All that really matters is how they treat other people, right? Well, that is what all this fussing and arguing has been over for more than two thousand years. This will be a boring sermon to most of you because you have heard it over and over, and you know that it is not the law and obedience to the law that earns salvation as it is the righteousness of faith.

I. Earlier in this letter to the emerging

Church at Rome Paul has quoted one of the great models of faith, David; so David pronounces a blessing upon the man to whom God reckons righteousness apart from works: "Blessed are those whose iniquities are forgiven and whose sins are covered; blessed is the man against whom the Lord will not reckon his sins."

The question Paul is attempting to deal with, and the question that is still central to all religious striving, is, "How can one enter into a right relationship with God so that one may inherit the blessings of God?"

a. There has been a lot of blood spilt over that question. There is still a lot of blood being shed in that debate. It is this question that is still at the heart of every debate over moral and ethical behavior. Does the having of an abortion exclude you from a right relationship with God? Does being a homosexual make it impossible for you to enter into a right relationship with God? How does one enter into a right relationship with God so that one may inherit the blessings of God?

b. As in so many fights there are lots of different positions, but more often than not they all get bunched together into one side or another. We tend to force issues to be black or white, yes or no, America: love it or leave it. Liberal or conservative. How do we enter into a right relationship with God? One side ends up being described as those who say you get on God's good side by obedience. You enter into a right relationship by doing what God says. The children of Israel were God's elect people and were blessed they had been given the Law.

II. Well, now, Paul's side sees it different. Paul had tried the Law, and he knew that in his own case all that Law ever did was make him angry, infuriate him because no matter how much he did, he always saw the Law as there convicting him of failure. So Paul says that one enters a right relationship with God by that wonderful gift of the promise of God's free grace and the human faith that simply takes God at his promise. It is not by works of obedience, but one enters by faith into a relationship with God, which by God's grace and promise already exists for one to come into by trust.

a. Abraham is the prime example of this relationship of faith and trust. Abraham believed, trusted, hoped, lived in confidence in God, and that is how he became the father of many nations. Not the Law, because for one thing Abraham didn't have the Law when he was called out of Ur. It wasn't because of circumcision, because he hadn't been circumcised when the promise of blessings was given. It isn't the law because law always takes the personal out of it. If the blessings came by the law, then the blessings are our dues and it is kind of mechanical. If it is on the basis of the law, all the law can

ever do is mark iniquity; the law never brings joy.

b. Paul makes his argument that the promise to all of us rests on faith because only by grace and faith can we really talk about it being a promise, only on the basis of grace and faith can the promise be offered to all those who believe and not just the Jews and the circumcised, and the law never seems to produce a promise but only wrath. On his side Paul puts the nature of promise, a promise made out of the generous and loving heart of God, not the requirement of a code book.

c. On the opponents' side Paul puts the Law, which can only mark wrong but cannot bring the desire to do better. He puts transgression, for only when you make a law do you make a criminal. This is the argument that only by making drugs illegal have we made a lot of criminals. And wrath, for when you have violations you have anger that wants to punish and anger at oneself for failing to measure up.

III. That is the old debate, and there is still value in talking about this great divide between law and grace, between faith and works, between convictions and attitudes and deeds. For the Christian faith Paul's positions had held the day, and yet even as we still affirm the central conviction that we are redeemed by grace through faith and not by works, we are living more and more in a community and a culture that has accepted the position of Paul's opponent.

a. If Paul is right that our relationship with God is to be fashioned on the basis of faith in the promises of God that have been given by grace, and in that relationship we are to find our lives enriched and blessed and how we live and act will flow out of that relationship, then we ought not to be surprised that we now are out of step with our culture.

b. We are brought into a dynamic and vital relationship with God, and it affects all of our powers and choices and decisions, our hopes, our fears, our expectations for the future, the dreams we have, and the monsters we hide from, and the challenges we rise to. Faith is that throwing of one's whole self and total person into a relationship of trust and love with God. But the life of faith is always a hope against hope, a trusting in a God-given hope when our human hope is gone. A God-given hope of resurrection, when our human hopes have been crucified.— Rick Brand

Illustrations

AMAZING GRACE.   Paul wrote of a higher righteousness that comes from God himself and never depends on our doings. Whenever we know that righteousness of God firsthand, it always changes our lives. One man tells that one day he blundered into an affair with someone else's wife. He was weak and vulnerable, and in his weakness he became involved with another woman. The guilt and wrong of what he had done against God, his family, and this woman and her husband were too much for the man to bear. Finally, at great risk, the man decided he had to talk to the woman's husband. The husband came and sat quietly as the guilt-ridden man poured out the story of his adultery with his friend's wife. And the confessor reported that when he was through, he sat there ashamed and weeping, not knowing what to do, wondering what the betrayed husband might do. The betrayed man got out of this chair, came around behind the desk, and put his arms around the friend who had destroyed his family. The two men wept for a long time. The remorseful man concluded: "He could have killed me, but instead he did for me what nobody else had ever done in all my life. He graced me. He affirmed me, and it changed my life."—Roger Lovette

FORGIVE YOURSELF.   Yes, we must forgive ourselves—not glibly, not hastily, but nonetheless truly. So long as a thing done or said in days gone by has power to hurt us emotionally, it is dangerous. If not dealt with, it can tear us to pieces; if pushed down into the mind, it may explode later.

An example in point is Dostoyevsky, the great novelist of older Russia. It is an exaggerated case, due to his tempera-

ment, but for that very reason it lights up the truth. He hated his father, and while a student, due to a pitiful allowance, suffered many financial embarrassments.

Just when he had finished a sharp letter to his father, that "senile egoist," demanding money, news came that his father had been killed. A terrible sense of guilt gripped him as though he himself had struck the blow that killed him because he had wished it. A spasm shook him, he fell to the floor foaming at the mouth, and he was never a well man to the end.

As I say, it is an extreme example, but it does show in a heightened form that we must forgive, and be forgiven, if we are to live. It is here that religion comes to our rescue with its glorious truth of forgiveness. No matter what we have done, it is not hopeless; it can be cleansed, and our souls set free. Else there would be no hope for any of us, unless we are better than the best man knows himself to be or just morally insensitive.—Joseph Fort Newton

SERMON SUGGESTIONS

Topic: A Merciful Imprisonment

TEXT: Rom. 11:29–32, especially verse 32

(1) After attempting to explain how Jesus and Gentiles are related to salvation in Christ, Paul acknowledges the impossibility of knowing God's judgment and ways (11:33–34). (2) However, the centerpiece of his faith is in the words: "that he may be merciful to all" (v. 32): (a) God's mercy in the history of God with the Jews; (b) God's mercy in the Christ event (John 3:16); (c) God's mercy in receiving the Gentiles.

Topic: How Christ Rewards True Faith

TEXT: Matt. 15:10–20, 21–28

(1) Not always immediately: he allows our faith to be tested. (2) Never with rejection: he has a purpose in the course of our faith. (3) Ultimately with reward: (a) he may change our attitude toward what we desire; (b) he may give us something

better than what we wish; (c) he may give us exactly what we wish.

Worship Aids

CALL TO WORSHIP.   "How very good and pleasant it is when kindred live together in unity! It is like the precious oil on the head, running down upon the beard, on the beard of Aaron, running down over the collar of his robes. It is like the dew of Hermon, which falls on the mountains of Zion" (Ps. 133:1–3 NRSV).

INVOCATION.   Gracious God, Father of our Lord Jesus Christ, you have brought to us in fullest expression your gracious, undeserved acceptance. Strengthen our faith to believe it and live by that fact, as we lift our hearts to you in prayer and praise.

OFFERTORY SENTENCE.   "I will freely sacrifice unto thee: I will praise thy name, O Lord; for it is good" (Ps. 54:6).

OFFERTORY PRAYER.   O God, we can buy nothing from you by our gifts; we can only bring the tokens of our gratitude for the blessings of your grace and favor. We love you because you first loved us, and so we give.

PRAYER.   In the midst of summer's life we come together with hearts thankful for people who are there when we need them to see us through some troublesome and hard time, some devastating illness or event that clouds life with shadows and fears, some loneliness which leaves the heart sad and the spirit broken. Thank you, Father, for people who meet us with no preplanned agenda, who have the time to listen to our story and by so doing call away from foolish action as they call us back from the brink of disaster.

Thank you for the many ways in which you come to us in tough times through some stream of notes as artist's fingers fall on keys, or sound the trumpet or present some immortal melody that is like an island in the midst of our surging sea, an island of peace where hope is restored. Thank you for the remembrance of some strong voice that has carved a channel into the geography of our soul to water the dry desert in which we wander, as a word fitly spoken in other times to illuminate the moment and refresh our lives.

Thank you for ways to escape the demanding routines that so often burden our hearts, for books that open new worlds and point us toward new kingdoms to enter; for the momentary Sabbaths that come in a few minutes of silence and stillness; for the coolness of summer shade on a blistering day to remind us that there is promise in the midst of the toil and sweat and tears.

Thank you for those sacred spots on this earth that visited, even in memory, steady us in our wavering struggles: a special hill, a row of trees, some skyline at morning, a house where time and again our spirit returns to get its bearings, so that we know anew that we are loved and rediscover who we really are and what we are about in this world.

Thank you for the Scriptures, those sacred words to which we return again and again to restore our souls, meet our Savior, understand our God, find direction for our journey, and encounter lasting peace in the midst of our tumultuous life. Thank you Father, for being with us all the journey.—Henry Fields

LECTIONARY MESSAGE

Topic: God Brings Life out of Hatred

TEXT: Gen. 45:1–15

The emotional climax of the story of Joseph and his brothers comes in this self-disclosure scene. The brother whom they had sold as a slave turns out to be the master of the land of Egypt. The son whom their father believed to be dead now holds the power of life and death over his family. The brother whom they had hated (37:4) now weeps loudly as he makes himself known to them. No wonder the brothers are dumbfounded. They do not speak until the end of the passage.

I. "I am your brother Joseph, whom you sold."

Joseph had recognized his brothers on their first meeting (42:7), but he had kept his identity secret, manipulating them from his position of authority. He had accused them of spying (42:9). unjustly imprisoned them (42:17), held Simeon hostage (42:24), framed them as thieves (44:1–5), and tricked them into an oath that could have cost Benjamin his life (44:9). This elaborate manipulation appears to have been a sort of test, to see if the older brothers would treat Benjamin and their father any differently than they had treated Joseph. Judah has just made an eloquent speech, offering to take Benjamin's place as a slave so that their father Jacob will not die of grief (44:18–34). Joseph's self-disclosing speech could have been full of anger, revenge, judgment, or proud boasting, but it is not. Joseph, the wise man with the God-given insight into the meaning of Egyptian dreams, can also discern the meaning of the lives of Jacob and his sons. In the person of Joseph, newly revealed to them, the brothers learn how God had been at work to save lives.

II. "God sent me before you."

Joseph had last seen his brothers when they sold him to traders on their way to Egypt (37:25–28). His speech refers to that part of his suffering (v. 4b) and to the remorse he had heard his brothers express (42:21), but only within a word of reassurance: "Do not be distressed . . . because God sent me ahead of you to save lives." The rest of Joseph's story, how he was falsely accused and unjustly imprisoned, and how his administrative skills and gift for interpreting dreams brought him to the attention of Pharaoh, is subsumed under the simple acknowledgement, "God sent me."

God had sent Joseph to Egypt to save lives. Joseph's plan for storing up grain in the years of abundant production enabled the Egyptians and surrounding nations to survive (41:53). Among those nations lived the family of Jacob. By keeping Egypt and her neighbors alive, God has made it possible for the Israelite ancestors to survive and, eventually, to become "a great host" (v. 7). God's special care for Israel is part of God's provision for humankind.

III. "God made me ruler."

Joseph's elevated status enables him to take special care of his father's household. Because of his intelligence, skill, and God-given discernment, Joseph had gained the highest position in the land of Egypt (41:38–46). Although God had made him "father" to Pharaoh, one who counseled Pharaoh and provided for the needs of his house, Joseph was ready to become a son to Jacob again (v. 8–9). His message to Jacob is an invitation to bring the whole family to settle in Egypt. There they would be fed and could escape impoverishment during the five remaining years of famine (v. 11). Joseph would be near them as son and brother again.

Joseph understands the events of his life according to God's call and leadership. He is able, therefore, to act out of true humility. He gives up the secret identity that had enabled him to manipulate his brothers and relinquishes the opportunity to carry out his revenge against them. He uses his power as one who is "father" to Pharaoh in order to be a loving and dutiful son to Jacob. Finally, he does not demand obeisance from his brothers but gives them his embrace of welcome instead. Joseph discloses himself not as the victim of his brothers and others but as one sent by God to save lives.— Pamela J. Scalise

SUNDAY: AUGUST TWENTY-FIFTH

SERVICE OF WORSHIP

Sermon: The Word Is Forgiveness

TEXT: Col. 3:1–17

I. If one were to make a list of the significant words Christians live by, right up near the top would be the word *forgiveness*. More than we realize, our lives of faith and our day-by-day interaction with other people depend upon forgiveness. This gift and blessing provide the context in which we live and move and have our being. By the grace and mercy of God we are a forgiven people. By the command of God we are a forgiven people. We are to be forgiving in our relationships with one another.

Some consciousness raising is important here. Forgiveness, sadly, is not always foremost in our thinking or acting. It is almost like a secret thought. Do you remember the early days of television when Groucho Marx held forth with a kind of ridiculous interview show? One of the features of that show was "the secret word." If a contestant inadvertently spoke a certain word (which the audience already knew), buzzers sounded and commotion reigned and the surprised contestant won a monetary prize. "Forgive" is too often like the secret word. Yet, for Christians, forgiveness is how God breaks through our guilt and how you and I repair broken relationships with each other. It really might help if some buzzers and gongs sounded occasionally, to call our attention again to the word and experience of forgiveness. This fundamental component of Christian life deserves more expression than it usually receives.

The Hebrew Scriptures of the Old Testament have three words that today we translate as "pardon" and "forgiveness." One word literally means "cover"; another means "lift up, carry away"; and the third suggests "let go." Modern dictionaries hardly improve on those meanings. The dictionary says that forgiveness is an act of forgoing any attempt to get even or pay back a wrong. It is the giving up of resentment, the letting go of penalties for obvious offenses. It has to do with pardon, with excusing faults or foolish behavior. We might add, it is a big order. To forgive on these terms is to reach out in a bold and powerful way.

II. That is precisely what has happened to us. God has reached out with forgiving love. To be Christian is to be a person whose wrongs are wiped away, whose faults and offenses toward God have been lifted up and carried off. No divine resentment of anger toward us remains. Our rebellious behaviors, once a barrier between ourselves and God, have been cast aside; our sin has been removed. A human perception of what this means was recorded in bygone years on a tablet in the chapel of the Peking Union Medical College. That tablet had been placed in memory of a certain Dr. Hall who had died of plague infection while attending to his patients. One Chinese patient said of Dr. Hall (and these were the words on the memorial tablet): "He took my sickness into his own heart." God, by forgiving us, has taken our sickness (our sin) into his own heart.

We are freed from it, as a result. Talk about a day of independence! Politically, such a day is vitally important to us as citizens of this land. But spiritual independence—referring to freedom from sin because of God's forgiveness—that is an endowment deserving equal or even greater celebration. The New Testament likens it to breaking out of bondage, to escaping enslavement. That freedom, that independence, is the hallmark of each Christian, a direct result of the bold and powerful act of God in forgiving us.

There is a condition, however. Forgiveness throughout human experience is conditioned upon *repentance*. Repentance quite simply involves a change of mind and intention. Turning about is one way to define it, reversing directions is another. When our repentance is real, when we grieve for the mistakes we have made before God, the result is restoration of a right relationship with God. Alienation is overcome, the barrier that sin imposed is broken down. Divine forgiveness serves to loose or to send away all that stands between ourselves and God. Repentance is our step; forgiveness is God's. It may be a faltering, hesitant step on our part. But it is a swift and ready response from God.

III. If forgiveness based on repentance forms the crux of our relationship with God, it follows that forgiveness is meant to be operative in human experience as well. We begin to realize the magnitude and grace of God's forgiveness when we attempt to be forgiving ourselves. Because forgiveness often is costly to us emotionally and hard to express, we sometimes do its opposite: we add guilt to the other party and in the process, of course, add it to ourselves. A friend of mine talks about giving the gift that lasts forever: guilt. Most of us know what he means. Instead of increasing feelings of guilt, instead of pretending a problem does not exist, instead of creating alienation between people, our concentration needs to be upon forgiveness. The New Testament guideline could not be more plain; we read, "Just as the Lord has forgiven you, so you also must forgive."

Jesus told a dramatic parable to this effect, a lesson we rightly can turn to again and again. It seems that a certain man owed ten thousand talents to his king. (One talent was worth more than fifteen years' wages of an average laborer.) This man could not pay. When he was threatened by the prospect of being sold into slavery, along with his wife and children and all of his possessions, he begged his master for forgiveness. He promised that somehow he would make restitution. The king listened and responded mercifully; he actually forgave the entire debt. What an incredible release! The man who owed more than he ever could repay was freed from that bondage. His was a true day of independence.

But Jesus' story was not ended. This same man, released from his burden, forgiven and free, happened to encounter a friend who owed him a hundred denarii. (The denarius was the wage for one day's labor.) Seizing this fellow by the throat, the man demanded, "Pay what you owe." "Have patience with me and I will pay you," pled the friend. But the first man refused and saw to it that this unfortunate debtor was thrown into prison.

Before long, word of this incident reached the king. He summoned the worker whom he had forgiven, calling him a wicked slave. Said the king, "Should you not have had mercy on your fellow slave, as I had mercy on you?" In his anger, the master consigned the unforgiving man to torture and to full payment of his debt.

This stern parable was Jesus' response to a question from his disciple, Peter. Peter had asked, "Lord, if someone sins against me, how often should I forgive? As many as seven times seven?" Peter thought such a number was a magnanimous response to personal injury, and it in fact reflected the wisdom of the time. But Jesus had another answer. "Not seven times," he said, "but, I tell you, seventy times seven." Limitless is the nature of forgiveness, was Jesus' message. There is no counting, no keeping score. There is only grace, and love, and a desire to repair relationships, broken for whatever cause.

The full Scripture verse from which I quoted earlier says this (and these are teachings of the apostle Paul): "Bear with one another, forgive each other; just as the Lord has forgiven you, so you also must forgive." Paul then speaks of clothing ourselves with *love* "which binds everything together in perfect harmony." Love, clearly, is the moving force behind forgiveness. There is no real forgiveness apart from outpouring love. In saying this we obviously are addressing the central issues of Christian life and faith. Forgiveness born of love represents the essence of all that we are and do.

IV. Every time anyone enters this sanctuary, he or she sees the mark and emblem of divine forgiveness: the cross of Jesus Christ. Someone has named the cross God's "plus sign." What Jesus gave us by his sacrifice on the cross has added meaning and cleansing and hope and empowerment to your life and mine.

That makes it a "plus sign," indeed. But it also is a minus sign—for Jesus' sacrifice on the cross subtracted from our life experience the guilt, the wrong, the sin, and bondage that would ever act to destroy us. The cross adds forgiveness even as it subtracts our sin. What great good news that is! It gives us reason to shout and sing, to give thanks to God forever more.

What better way to celebrate our resulting spiritual independence than at the table of our Lord. At this table we remember the love of God in Jesus Christ, a love that was declared to all the world upon the cross. These moments of communion allow us opportunities for reflection, and yes—repentance. Sorrow for our sin can find expression, opening us to the forgiving love of God. It then remains only for us to accept God's acceptance of us, God's forgiveness. We shall leave this place, because of that, with new resources in our souls. The word, my friends, is forgiveness.—John H. Townsend

Illustrations

GOD'S ENDLESS QUEST.   A yacht landed one evening at the wharf of Inverness, Scotland. Two young men disembarked and set out upon a walking tour. They got lost. Late that night they knocked at the door of a farmer's cottage; but though they plead that they were both hungry and cold, the farmer kept the door shut in their faces. They went to another cottage a mile or more away. This farmer was more hospitable. Though it was past the midnight hour, he opened his door. To his surprise he found that one of the young men desiring to get into his humble home was a prince who later became beloved George V of England. What must have been the shame and humiliation of this neighbor when he found that all-unwittingly he had shut the door in the face of his king. It is your king that is knocking at your door. It is your king that is seeking for you.—Clovis G. Chappell

FORGIVING ENEMIES.   During one of the persecutions of the Armenians by the Turks, an Armenian girl and her brother were closely pursued by a Turkish soldier. Trapped at the end of a lane, the soldier killed the brother before his sister's eyes. The sister escaped by leaping over a wall and fleeing into the country. She later became a nurse.

One day a wounded Turkish soldier was brought into the hospital where the young woman worked. She recognized him as the soldier who had killed her brother and had tried to kill her. The soldier's condition was such that the least neglect on the part of the nurse would have cost him his life. But she gave him painstaking and constant care.

As he recovered, the soldier recognized her as the girl whose brother he had killed. He asked her why she had taken such good care of him. He had killed her brother. She said she had a religion that taught her to forgive her enemies.—James E. Carter

SERMON SUGGESTIONS

Topic: And God Was Standing in the Shadows

TEXT: Exod. 1:8–2:10. (1) Israel—a story of oppression and growth. (2) Moses—a story of danger and opportunity.

Topic: A Timeless and Timely Appeal

TEXT: Rom. 12:1–8 NRSV

(1) To do what? To present our entire self to God. (2) For what reason? In consideration of the mercies of God toward us. (3) In what way? By choosing the right world to identify with. (4) To what end? To discover God's will for our lives.

Worship Aids

CALL TO WORSHIP.   "Our help is in the name of the Lord, who made heaven and earth" (Ps. 124:8).

INVOCATION.   Powerful in creation, powerful in your love, O God, make us anew in your Son Jesus Christ, so that your love known in him may be made known by us to friend and foe alike. To that end, use this service of worship to draw us closer to you and make us more nearly what you would have us to be.

OFFERTORY SENTENCE. "Wherever your treasure is, there will your heart be too" (Matt. 6:21 NJB).

OFFERTORY PRAYER. O God, who has blessed us abundantly with inner joy and an outer supply of all good things, we bring you now our gifts in response to the message of your Word and in gratitude for your help in our poor attempts to do your will. May these offerings become streams of influence from this church to build and nurture your kingdom and to redeem our broken world; through Jesus our Lord.—Donald Macleod

PRAYER. Our Father, we beseech of thee that thou wilt set the truth home to every heart. We thank thee that so many have ceased to be reluctant, and have closed with the offers of salvation, and are blessed. We thank thee that so many are scattered along the path at various stages, all tending upward, working out their salvation with fear and trembling. We beseech of thee that those who stand looking wistfully forward may be persuaded. Grant, we pray thee, that those who hear the call of God afar off may listen until its articulations become distinct, and they hear the Savior saying, "Give me thine heart. Love me more than all others." Oh! grant that this love, beginning, may purge away all impure affections; all gross pleasures; all habits of selfishness and self-indulgence. Oh! that thou wouldst lift us to a higher plane; to a nobler conception of life; to a more urgent and earnest determination to acquit ourselves honorably. And when we shall have passed through trial and discipline and instruction and persuasion in this life, bring us to thyself, prepared to dwell with thee. And to thy name shall be the praise for evermore.—Adapted from Henry Ward Beecher

LECTIONARY MESSAGE

Topic: The Remembered Christ

TEXT: Matt. 16:13–20

"Who was Jesus?" Often interest in Jesus' identity does not signal a serious searching, but indecision, skepticism of the Christian claim, or a protest intended to invent a new picture of him. New books regularly appear on the market, new movies arrive in the theaters claiming to offer fresh insights into who Jesus was. Generally one learns more about the authors or the movie makers than one does about Jesus from such projects. In the midst of such flights of the imagination, the Church is called to a steadfast confession of the apostolic witness. We serve and follow not a reimagined but a remembered Christ.

I. *The finality of Jesus.* Curiosity about Jesus is not new. Peter's confession that, "You are the Christ, the Son of the living God," was made in the midst of a confusing welter of opinions, all of them interesting, none of them demanding. His confession stands apart from the rest because it ascribes finality to Jesus as the Christ. Peter affirms that Jesus is no mere prophet but "the Messiah, the Son of the living God," the unique and the sole mediator of the one true God's saving purposes, before whom he, a monotheistic Jew, will later bow in worship (Matt. 28:17).

II. *The particularity of Peter.* The continuing life of the Church here and now is inescapably tied to the apostolic witness, Peter's confession of Jesus there and then. Just as Peter affirms the uniqueness of Jesus, Jesus singles out Peter from all others of his followers. Of course, there was nothing special about Peter himself. Jesus' words of response attribute Peter's insight entirely to the work of God, "Flesh and blood did not reveal this to you, but my Father who is in heaven." And Peter was yet to fail tragically in his faithfulness to this confession. Nevertheless, the confessing Peter stands as the rock on which Jesus promises, "I will build my Church." Jesus went to the cross, not as a revolutionary, nor as a mere prophet, but as the one who affirmed Peter's confession that he was the Christ, God's Messiah. The Resurrection vindicated Peter's confession, and Jesus' acceptance of it. The community of Jesus' followers, the true people of God, has its origin not in visions or enthusiasm, not in the "Easter faith" of anonymous disciples, but in Peter's confession of Jesus as Christ as Caesarea Philippi. As Jesus promised, this confession has sustained and will continue to sustain Jesus' followers in the face of violent hostility, even to "the gates of Hades," martyrdom itself.

III. *The exclusivity of faith.* Jesus' response to Peter contains yet another claim, scandalous in its particularity, itself the cause of much persecution. He promises to give Peter the "power of the keys," the right to include in or exclude from participation in the coming kingdom. Again the tenor of the passage indicates that it is not Peter in and of himself, but Peter in his confession of Jesus as the Christ to whom this authority is given. Jesus provides the grounds here, not for the papacy, but for the exclusive claim that Luke later ascribes to Peter: "There

is salvation in no other, for there is no other name given among human beings by which we must be saved" (Acts 4:12). According to Matthew, Jesus gives the same authority to the entire community of those who follow him (Matt. 18:15–20). Obviously, with these words Jesus is not condoning a judgmental or critical spirit in his followers. Nor does he want his disciples to force him upon others as Messiah. His closing admonition to the disciples in this section reveals that Jesus was not seeking popularity but faithful confession from his disciples that would lead through the cross to the Resurrection ("Then he commanded his disciples to tell no one that he is the Christ"). Peter had confessed the finality of Jesus as God's Christ. Jesus now not only affirms that confession but draws out its implications, making an unequivocal claim to supreme authority. The world will tolerate boundless speculations about Jesus, but it cannot endure the believing confession Peter made at Caesarea Philippi. Are we presently faithful in word and action to the apostolic witness to Jesus as the Christ?—Mark A. Seifrid

SUNDAY: SEPTEMBER FIRST

SERVICE OF WORSHIP

Sermon: Six Ways to Tell Right from Wrong

TEXT: 1 Tim. 1:12–13

Our thought starts with the plain fact it is not always easy to tell the difference between right and wrong. Behind a great deal of our modern immorality is not so much downright badness as sincere confusion as to what is right. In many a dubious situation how we wish that someone would tell us that!

Today I propose talking about this matter with homely practicality to my own soul and to yours. We may take it for granted that we would not be here in a Christian church if in general we did not desire to do right. But we had better take it for granted also that this general desire to do right and this general acceptance of the Christian philosophy of life do not

solve our problem. So this morning I invite you to a practical land journey as we set up six homely guideposts to the good life.

I. In the first place, if a man is sincerely perplexed about a question of right and wrong, he might well submit it to the test of common sense. Suppose that someone should challenge you to a duel. What would you say? I would advise you to say, Don't be silly! As a matter of historic fact, dueling, which was once a serious point of conscientious honor, was not so much argued out of existence as laughed out. The common sense of mankind rose up against it, saying, Don't be silly!

a. What we are saying now is that this is a healthy thing for a man to say to his own soul before somebody else has to say it to him. One wonders how many here would be affected by it. You do not really care anything about drink, and left to yourself you would not drink at all, but it is so commonly offered to one nowadays and is so generally taken as a matter of course that you are drinking too much. Don't be silly! Or you may have in your hands today a choice between promiscuous sexual liaisons and a real home where two people love each other so much that they do not care to love anybody else in the same way at all; where romance deepens into friendship and overflows into children; where, as the sun grows westerly, the family life becomes every year more beautiful. And with that choice in your hands you are playing with promiscuity. Don't be silly!

b. That is the first test, and, alas! twenty years from now somebody here this morning, listening to this and paying no heed to it, will be looking back on life and saying the bitter thing. "God be merciful to me, a fool!"

II. In the second place, if a man is sincerely perplexed about a question of right and wrong, he may well submit it to the test of sportsmanship. Now the essence of sportsmanship is that in a game we do not take for ourselves special favors that we deny to other players but, making the rules equal for all, abide by them.

a. There is no doubt why it is wrong to cheat the government with petty smuggling or to join whispering campaigns about people when you do not know the facts, or to treat contemptuously a person of another race or color. Play the game! In all such cases we know well that we would not wish to be treated ourselves as we are treating others and that if everybody acted on that principle, it would not be well for all. Sometimes one thinks that half the evil in the world is simply cheating. People do not play the game.

b. Do not, I beg of you, restrict the application of this test within the limits of individual behavior. There are ways of making money in our economic system, not simply illegal but legal, speculative gambling with the securities of the people, using public utilities as a football to be kicked all over the financial field in hope of making a goal of private profit

with it, or betting day after day on stocks that represent genuine values that honest business once created but that now can be used merely for a gambler's chance without creating anything. If everybody acted like that, there would be no values even to gamble with and no welfare for anyone. Be sure of this, that this rising tide of public indignation against economic wrongs has this much justification: We have a right at least to ordinary sportsmanship, and in wide areas we have not been getting it. The Golden Rule, my friends, is a grand test. Husband and wife, parents and children, employers and employees, black and white, prosperous and poor, Occident and Orient—what if we did not cheat! What if we did as we would be done by! What if we played the game!

III. In the third place, if a man is sincerely perplexed about a question of right and wrong, he may well submit it to the test of his best self.

a. Notice, I do not say to his conscience, for the conscience merely urges us to do right without telling us what the right is, but deeper than conscience and more comprehensive is this other matter, a man's best self. There is the passionate self. There is the careless self. There is the greedy self. But deeper than all these is that inner self where dwells the light that, as the fourth Gospel says, lighteth every man coming into the world.

b. Be sure of this, that if, in large ways or small, any one of us does help to ennoble our society and build a better nation for our children and their children to be born into, it will be because we have taken our secret ambitions up to the tribunal of our finest self. There is something in us like a musician's taste, which discriminates harmony from discord. There is something in us like a bank teller's fingers, which distinguish true money from counterfeit:

. . . To thine own self be true,
And it must follow, as the night the day,
Thou canst not then be false to any man.

IV. In the fourth place, if a man is sincerely perplexed over a matter of right and wrong, he may well submit the question to the test of publicity. Strip it of secrecy and furtiveness. Carry it out into the open air, this conduct we are unsure about. Submit it to the test of publicity.

a. How often in politics, in church life, in business, in personal character we see things that remind us of a claque at the theater hired to applaud a play! They can get away with it as long as the public does not know it is a claque. It depends on secrecy for its success. What a test publicity is!

b. I know one business firm in this city that in a few weeks will crash into a receivership under the tremendous blow of a righteous court decision. Ten years ago that firm did a secret thing that would not stand the test of open knowledge. For ten years those men have lived in deadly fear that it might be known. And now the light has fallen.

Things that cannot stand sunlight are not healthful. There is a test for a perplexed conscience. How many here do you suppose would be affected by it? Imagine your behavior public.

V. In the fifth place, if a man is perplexed about a question of right and wrong, he may well submit it to the test of his most admired personality. Carry it up into the light of the life that you esteem most and test it there.

a. My friends, it is the beauties and the personalities that we positively have loved that set for us the tests and standards of our lives. Why is it, then, that conduct that seems to some people right seems to some of us cheap and vulgar, selfish and wrong? It is because for years we have known and adored the Christ. There is a test for a perplexed conscience. Carry your behavior up into the presence of the Galilean and judge it there.

b. If someone protests that he does not propose to subjugate his independence of moral judgment to any authority, not even Christ's, I answer, What do you mean by authority? There are all kinds of authorities—ecclesiastical, creedal, external, artificial—against the imposition of whose control on mind and conscience I would as vigorously fight as you. But

there is one kind of authority for which I hunger, the insight of the seers.

VI. In the sixth place, if a man is perplexed about a question of right and wrong, he may well submit it to the test of foresight. Where is this course of behavior coming out? Every course of behavior has not only a place where it begins but a place where it comes out.

a. Life is like a game of chess. Some youth is here this morning with all his pieces on the board and freedom to commence. They tell me, however, that when a man has once played his opening, he is not so free thereafter. His moves must conform to the plan he has adopted. He has to follow the lead with which he had begun. The consequences of his opening close in on him until at last checkmate is called. See! says the expert, when you choose those first moves you decided the end. Well, with what gambit are we opening our game?

b. We really do not need to be so perplexed about right and wrong as we sometimes are. To be sure, there is nothing infallible about all this. I call you to witness that in all this I have not been imposing on you a code of conduct; I have been appealing to your own best moral judgment. Alas for a man who neglects that! For though, as in Paul's case, one may come out at last to a good life, it is a better thing to have to look back and say, A blasphemer, and a persecutor, and injurious—such was I—ignorantly.—Harry Emerson Fosdick

Illustrations

JUST CHECK IT OUT! In Robertson's *Short History of Christianity,* this rationalist author makes a fair case for his theory that of all stupid people, religious people stand far in the forefront. The brutalities, the persecutions, the prejudices, and the suspicions of which they have been guilty seem to belie the affirmations of a God of Love and of a Prince of Peace.—Charles P. Robshaw

•

TIME TO GROW. When you come out of the river, you bring some of the river water with you. The water clings to you until enough time has passed to dry it up. Likewise, you come out of a worldly social order when you become a Christian. But some of the worldly ways cling to you. Time, instruction, and prayer are necessary for you to grow beyond such things into mature Christian character.— Herschel H. Hobbs

SERMON SUGGESTIONS

Topic: The Way of a Genuine Christian
TEXT: Rom. 12:9–21

(1) It is a way of love. (2) It is a way of harmonious living. (3) It is a way of creative nonretaliation.

Topic: Jesus' Cross and Our Cross
TEXT: Matt. 16:21–28

(1) Jesus' suffering was a necessary part of God's plan. (2) Our willingness to suffer for the sake of Jesus is God's plan for us. (3) In both cases, there are salutary results: (a) Jesus was raised from the dead; (b) we shall find true life.

Worship Aids

CALL TO WORSHIP.   "Seek the Lord, and his strength: seek his face evermore" (Ps. 105:4).

INVOCATION.   Hope of all souls that seek you, strength of all souls that find you, guardian of the souls of all of us, cause us to hear your loving kindness in the morning, for we trust in you. Cause us to know the way wherein we should walk, for we lift up our souls to you as we gather in these sacred moments of worship and praise. May our expectation be met with your reality. May our hopes be fulfilled in your wisdom. May our lives be directed for your purpose.—Henry Fields

OFFERTORY SENTENCE.   "God, who supplies seed for the sower and bread to eat, will also supply you with all the seed you need and make it grow and produce a rich harvest from your generosity" (2 Cor. 9:10 TEV).

OFFERTORY PRAYER.   Gracious Father, we do not understand all the ways of your providence, but we know it is your purpose to take our gifts, our tithes and offerings, and use them to bless others. We thank you for the blessings that we ourselves receive in the very attitude and act of giving.

PRAYER.   O Lord, our God! Thou knowest who we are: human beings with a good or with a bad conscience, some content and others discontent, some secure and others insecure, convinced Christians and nominal Christians, believers, half-believers, and unbelievers.

Thou also knowest where we have come from the bonds of family and friendship or from great loneliness, from peaceful prosperity or from manifold adversities and troubles, from happy, tense, or broken homes, from the core of the Christian community or from its fringe.

Here we are gathered now in thy presence: in all our diversity equally unrighteous before thee and before each other, equally subject to death, equally lost without thy mercy, yet also equally sharing the promise and the gift of thy grace to all in thy dear Son, our Lord Jesus Christ.—Karl Barth

LECTIONARY MESSAGE

Topic: The Liberating God
TEXT: Exod. 3:1–15

In our contemporary world peoples and individuals seek release from the oppression that enslaves them, be it political, economic, or spiritual. Is there no way out, no Exodus? Does God see? Does God know? Does God care? And the servants of God wonder about their responsibility in the struggle to set people free. This episode in the life of Moses shows that the main actor in the Exodus story is not Moses but God. God took the initiative, showed compassion, made the promises, and provided a way out. This reality encourages the contemporary observer to try to identify God's liberating work in today's events.

I. *God takes the initiative (3:1–6)*. Moses was not looking for God on this occasion.

He had become a fugitive in the eastern desert, wanting nothing more than to be unrecognized and unreported.

But God came looking for Moses. There was work to be done that would be worthy of the man's whole life. God confronted Moses in an unforgettable theophany, revealing to him that the one speaking to him was the God of the ancestors. Moses' past had caught up with him and he was afraid.

So God follows us to our hiding places, refusing to allow a life to be wasted in flight. We cannot escape life with its responsibilities and challenges. God takes the initiative to call us, to commission us, and to equip us to come to grips with our past and to focus on our usefulness for the future.

II. *God understands (3:7–9)*. How differently God sees and responds to human need! When Moses saw the burdens of his people, he lashed out and killed an abusive Egyptian. When God saw the people's affliction, he set in motion a plan for liberation. Note the piling up of the verbs: I have seen, I have heard, I know, I have come down to bring them up. The situation called for, not vengeance, but correction based on genuine compassion.

Biblical testimony is consistent that God is on the side of the oppressed and that the cries of the afflicted are heard. God is not untouched by human infirmity or tragedy. God sees situations clearly and acts to liberate the oppressed, and so must we.

III. *God commissions Moses (3:10–11)*. When God determined to liberate the Israelites, God did not say, "I will set them free immediately." God said to Moses, "I have seen the oppression . . . and I will send you that *you* may bring out my people." God did not need Moses; God chose to involve Moses and gave him the promise of divine presence and a confirming sign.

A part of the glory and dignity of human life is that God has consistently issued the gracious invitation to people to participate in the divine plan. Human weakness and reluctance are met with the divine promise, "But I will be with you." Countless servants of God have been undergirded by that promise and have found it to be trustworthy. God continues to call humans to great tasks for human betterment, and heeding that call is the glory of life.

IV. *God reveals the divine name (3:13–15)*. How much is in a name! Personal names were commonly thought to reveal character or to sum up the essence of a person. Moses asked God, "Who are you, really? What is your name? Why should I do what you ask me to do?" The reply was enigmatic: "I am who I am." That says all and reveals less than everything. The reply can also be translated: "I am who I was," or "I will be who I was." God's complete character was not revealed, but enough was revealed to answer Moses' objection. God was revealed again as the God of the ancestors, and thus the new act in history would be a new episode in the ongoing divine purpose. The servant of God can never claim that God has promised or revealed less than what was necessary for the completion of the task.

V. *God continues to liberate*. God's hand is not shortened that it cannot save. Oppressive regimes may have their day, but the cries of the oppressed are not unheard in heaven. God is the author of freedom and continues to call men and women into the service of freedom. Those who work and pray for the liberation of the oppressed and who trust in God's promises of divine empowerment may say with ancient Israel: "The eternal God is our dwelling place, and underneath are the everlasting arms" (Deut. 33:27).—Thomas G. Smothers

SUNDAY: SEPTEMBER EIGHTH

SERVICE OF WORSHIP

Sermon: Another Snake Story

TEXT: Num. 21:4–9

I. This serpent story comes near the end of a long, long story of the flight from Egypt to the Promised Land. The children of Israel continue their pattern of complaint with incorrigible persistence. Just three verses above this story of the serpents, God had come and given the children of Israel the victory over the king of Arad, and they called the place Mount Hormah, the mountain of destruction.

a. But now when the children of Israel went to start toward Moab they are told they will have to go around the long way. More red tape. For a hundred miles the route for Israel goes through a wilderness of countless pebbles of basalt and flint with a few patches of clear sand and here and there a yellowish streak of withered grass. Little food is available; terrible sandstorms afflict the region. This path was the corridor along which the hot sirocco winds blow. Their animals would have perished. All that would retard the progress had to be discarded.

b. When does it get any easier? When does it get to be our turn to have things go our way? The heat, the tiredness of the body, the exhaustion of their spirits all combine to bring out the old song and dance. "Why did you bring us out here? We had it so much better where we were." There is no talk of holy things here.

II. The story says that the march shortened their souls. "Their souls were shortened." They became short-tempered. The heat and exhaustion gave them a short fuse and they exploded. They lost their ability to control themselves.

a. The Israelites complain, We don't have any food. Oh, you mean that you have nothing to eat? Oh, we have this worthless light manna stuff, but it is horrible. You mean the gracious miracle of God that has sustained you—manna—you are calling worthless? We have no water. Oh, you mean that the water that God just miraculously gave you out of the rock of Meribah is all gone and you don't believe he can do it again?

b. Complaining is always a subversive event. When we complain, we are ultimately taking our issue before God. To take on a critical posture toward the way life is unfolding is ultimately to challenge the divine wisdom and providence of God.

III. The story is just another of the age-old stories of humanity's rebellion against God's way with life. And when we rebel, then life turns sour and God and life become a snake in the grass for us. In fact, this whole journey is a record of this constant refusal to accept God's way and to try to substitute the children of Israel's way. And the result is judgment.

a. The complaining children of Israel run into an area of mountain where there are herds of serpents. God brings punishment by the serpents. The snakes bite and kill. These snakes are God's judgment upon them for their rebellion, and they repent. Repentance is always the purpose and intention of God's judgments. The chastisement of God's wrath is for the purpose of redemption of his people.

b. The serpents are not removed, but "salvation" is provided by the very object that brought the judgment. The serpents, which are the punishment for sin, become objects to be viewed for salvation. God takes the results of evil and makes them into the means of redemption.

IV. God works in the cross of Christ, where the power of evil is most clearly visible in the death of Jesus, and that death becomes the event toward which we look to receive our hope, our redemption, our healing. Even as Moses lifted up the serpent of judgment on the sin of rebellion so that the serpent could become by God's love the symbol of salvation, so shall the Son of Man be lifted up on the cross in an act of rebellion and pride to become the agent of redemption and hope and salvation. That which is the result of the work of evil becomes the means by which evil is overcome. The cross of Christ brings forth the victory over the evil of the cross.—Rick Brand

Illustrations

FORGIVENESS.   A prominent man was asked by a reporter if he remembered an incident in which a friend had hurt him deeply. He quickly replied, "No, I specifically remember forgetting it." Not only has God forgiven our sins, he has forgotten them as well. He will not dig up the incident once he has forgiven it. He buries it in the deepest ocean (Mic. 7:19) and puts up a sign that says "No Fishing."—Wayne Rouse

TRANSFORMATION.   Snake Man used to work in an orange grove in Florida. His real name was Walt, but for a long time no one knew it. His friends called him Snake Man because he always would catch snakes and scare everyone with them.

One day he picked up a ground rattler and waved it at some of the workers. The snake twisted in his hand and bit him on the thumb. Snake Man's arm began to swell horribly, and he was rushed to the hospital, where it looked as if he might die.

Several weeks later, he returned to work looking pale and weak. One of the men called to him, "Snake Man! It's good to see you back!"

Snake Man looked at the group and announced, "I'm not Snake Man anymore. My name is Walt."[1]

Each of us has been bitten by sin. The wonderful story of redemption, however, is that Christ removes the sting of death from us, heals the fatal wound, and gives us a new life and a new name.

In Christ, you are no longer *Loser* or *Outsider*. You have been forgiven and your name is *Child of God*.—Mark Sutton

[1]John McPhee, *Oranges* (New York: Noonday Press, 1966), 53.

SERMON SUGGESTIONS

Topic: Remembering Forever
TEXT: Exod. 12:1–14

(1) Remembering together. (2) Remembering God's protection in a time of danger and upheaval. (3) Remembering with hope for the future. (4) Remembering in simplicity and humility (12:26–27).

Topic: Our First Duty—and the Others
TEXT: Rom. 13:8–14

(1) Love for neighbor sums up all the commandments: (a) love negates anything harmful to others; (b) love produces positive good for others. (2) This style of living is urgent: (a) Time is running out; (b) The world needs our true and light-giving witness.

Worship Aids

CALL TO WORSHIP.   "Praise the Lord. Sing to the Lord a new song, his praise in the assembly of the saints" (Ps. 149:1 NIV).

INVOCATION.   Gracious Father, give us a fresh vision today of your redemptive power. May our songs and our praise be as joyful as on the first day of our dawning faith in you. If circumstances have clouded our way, sweep away the darkness and doubts and renew the joy of your salvation within us.

OFFERTORY SENTENCE.   "Each of you is to bring such a gift as he can in proportion to the blessing which the Lord your God has given you" (Deut. 16:17 REB).

OFFERTORY PRAYER.   Lord, let not the treasure we have rust on earth or be stolen or so possess us that we miss the treasure that outlasts the moment and gives the soul unfading joy.—E. Lee Phillips

PRAYER.   We thank you, God, that through Jesus Christ our sins can be forgiven, our lives can be changed, and by your grace, we can start all over again. We thank you that evil desires can disappear, that hatred can be changed to love, that bitterness can be overcome by gratitude, and that guilt can be replaced by a sense of cleanliness and well-being. We thank you that your power can seize the soul and change the heart of stone and callousness to one of compassion and sympathy. We thank you that all of this is available to all of us today.

Father, finish the work of salvation that you have begun in us. May the power of Jesus Christ, which can conquer weakness, overcome prejudice, heal shattered hearts, mend broken relationships, and give birth to authentic joy, be more and more evidenced in the lives of those who claim to have been touched by your love and grace. And in the lives of those who have yet to experience the peace of God which passes all understanding, let your Holy Spirit begin the process of salvation even now.

We accept your invitation to come with our sins and our sinfulness. Make us clean and new from tip to toe, inside and out, through Jesus Christ our Savior and Lord.—Gary C. Redding

LECTIONARY MESSAGE

Topic: The Spirit That Disciplines in Order to Reinstate

TEXT: Matt. 18:15–20

There are many virtues in Christianity. However, forgiveness of sins is the very heart of being a Christian. The forgiveness of sins is evidenced through our salvation, our faith, and our eternal life as Christians.

There was an individual who was looking for a perfect church. This individual could not find that perfect church, and therefore stopped going to church altogether.

Even in the Church, the problems of sinners and sins, hypocrites and hypocrisy are realities. We strive to be Christlike, but all too often fall short of that goal. Some of the most important aspects of a church are those of human relationships and human fellowship.

In Matthew's Gospel, Jesus is telling the community as a whole how to handle the situation of another person sinning. Although we cannot be judgmental (and Christ does not desire us to be so) we must point out to persons, privately, transgressions that may hurt that individual and/or the Church. Jesus says that when there is sin among Christians, including our own, we must attempt to eradicate that sin. Confrontation is one way of doing that. It is a good rule not to speak of our Church members' faults to others until we have first spoken to them ourselves. The offended person is responsible to initiate action for reconciliation. This calls for initiative and deliberate action rather than a defensive attitude. Here Jesus suggests that a person is not to pass judgment but rather is to convince the offenders of their sin. The point is not to score points over them but to win and reinstate the erring persons into fellowship. Jesus assumes that the individuals who personally confront others will do so with true humility. If he hears you, you have gained your brother; you have helped to save him from sin and ruin, and it will be to your credit and comfort (see James 5:19–20).

Not everyone, however, will respond honestly to compassionate personal confrontations. The second step, if the first step does not prevail in the situation, is that you take with you one or more people (v. 16). If he will not hear you, yet do not give him up as in a desperate case, but go on in the use of other means.

The presence of one or two other brothers or sisters not only adds witnesses but also protects the sinner in the negotiations, if your demands for correction are misguided or excessive. This preserves openness in the process. The individual who takes one or two bystanders thus creates a group of two or three witnesses, thereby fulfilling the command of Deuteronomy 19:15. Let God's work be done effectively, but the main goal, however, is to resolve an individual's conflicts by intervening with as few other people as possible.

Thirdly, if the offender will not hear the several persons in step two, then it will be necessary to take the issue to the congregation. Why should we tell it to the church? Because problems are never solved by going to the legal court. Going to law merely creates further trouble. It is a feeling of Christian love, Christian care, Christian prayer, and Christian fellowship that personal relationship may be solved. The plain assumption is that the Church should seek to judge everything, not in the light of rule and regulation, but in the light of Christian love.

Jesus says that even if that does not work, the person who has wronged us is to be treated as a Gentile and a tax collector. The first impression is that they must be regarded as irreconcilable and hopeless, but that is precisely what Jesus cannot have meant. He never set limits to anyone's forgiveness. In the light of Jesus' consistent compassion for pagans or tax collectors, certainly he must also want Christians, individually, to continue to reach out these people and call them to repentance.

Many churches avoid the problem simply by ignoring Jesus and making no attempt to pursue his principles. Application also proves difficult because, today, church members who are disciplined often leave one congregation for another that accepts them with no questions asked. But without this application, sin in the congregation will continue to compromise the harmony of God's people.

Finally, there is the saying about loosing and binding. It is a difficult saying. It cannot mean that the Church can forgive sins, and so settle a person's destiny in eternity. What it may well mean is that the relationships we establish with our Christian brothers and sisters last not only throughout time but into eternity. Thus, we ought to get them right.—John U. Chung

SUNDAY: SEPTEMBER FIFTEENTH

SERVICE OF WORSHIP

Sermon: Philip: The Matter-of-fact Man

Text: John 1:35–51

What different roads men take to reach the truth! Here was this man Philip, dull, prosaic, plodding in all his methods! He had seen the Lord, but he was not jumping up and down about it in an ecstasy of feeling. He came to his friend Nathaniel and said to him, "We have found him of whom Moses in the law and the prophets did write, Jesus of Nazareth, the son of Joseph."

"Can any good thing come out of Nazareth?" Nathaniel said with a smile of incredulity. In his patient, plodding fashion, he replied, "Come and see." He would not venture upon any statement that might prove excessive. He would let everyone judge for himself. "Come and see"—he kept his feet always on the ground.

Let me study with you the general method, the limitations, and the positive value of this matter-of-fact type of man!

I. First, his method! He was as careful in his attention to detail as the paying teller in a bank. He never overlooked anything.

a. The day came when Jesus saw before him a company of people who were hungry. Jesus said to Philip, "Whence shall we buy bread that these may eat?" Instantly the mind of this bookkeeper-like man went off into careful calculation as to the probable cost of an adequate food supply for all those people. In a moment he replied, "Two hundred pennyworth of bread would not be sufficient for them, if everyone would take a little."

It was just a question of buying bread, and there were no bakeries at hand. He recognized the things that were seen and temporal, but he overlooked the things that were unseen and eternal. It would never have occurred to him to take five thousand people on a picnic until he was entirely sure that there was food enough in sight to feed them all. He was matter-of-fact to the core.

b. Philip was in Jerusalem on that first Palm Sunday. They were tremendously excited over the entrance of the Messiah into the capital city of their country.

There were certain Greeks among those who came up to worship at the feast. They wanted to know this religious leader from Nazareth who had made such a stir. This eager interest of theirs was a kind of first fruits of that mighty spiritual harvest that the gospel of Christ would finally reap among this wide-awake people. "Sir, we would see Jesus."

But Philip saw nothing of all this. Philip therefore went off to consult Andrew. "There are some foreigners out here," he said, "who want to see Jesus." Now Andrew was a man quick to decide. He saw the promise in that inquiry, and he promptly brought those Greeks to Jesus. The Master saw at once the deeper meaning of it all. He cried out in grateful joy: "The hour is come that the Son of Man should be glorified. I, if I be lifted up from the earth, will draw all men to me." Jews, Greeks, Romans—everybody! It took vision and imagination to see all that. This matter-of-fact man missed it.

c. Philip was there in the upper room that night when Jesus took bread and broke it.

What an hour of high privilege! It was enough to lift any prosaic soul from the dead level of ordinary feeling into the mountaintop of spiritual experience. Any man with sensibilities would have been caught up into the third heaven, not knowing whether he was in the body or out of the body.

But Philip, matter-of-fact even in that high hour, said calmly, "Lord, show us the Father!" He wanted to see something, something more, something definite and tangible, like the Statue of Liberty in New York Harbor or the Matterhorn from Zermatt or Mount Everest from Darjeeling. "Lord, show us!"

This was the method of this matter-of-fact man.

II. In the second place, notice the limitations of that method! Man cannot live solely by visible, tangible, demonstrated facts. We know in part. We have to take the rest of it on faith and press forward to the realization of those vaster hopes that make life worth living.

a. "How many loaves have you?" Jesus said to his disciples that day when Philip was making his calculation as to how many pennyworth of bread would be required to feed that hungry crowd.

They were doing their little sums in arithmetic, leaving out of account the most significant fact in that whole situation. They were adding up their little columns of figures like children at grammar school, just as if there had been no Lord Christ upon that hillside. They needed to learn another kind of arithmetic.

b. We live and move and have our being in the presence of the everlasting mystery of the expanding, enlarging, dominating power of life. How can a man fling away a bushel of seed wheat in the spring and then four months later, because that seed wheat has been wrought upon by the mysterious forces of soil and sunshine, of rain and dew, go out and harvest thirty-, sixty-, a hundred-fold? How can these things be!

The same beneficent hand of power and of wisdom that works in the wheatfield and among the potencies of cell and tissue was there at work that day by the Sea of Galilee when the hungry multitude was fed. This dull, prosaic, matter-of-fact man would have missed all that if the Lord had not opened his eyes that he might see.

c. How many loaves have you, Philip? How many loaves of knowledge as we face these world problems, vast, intricate, baffling? Not many! We do not know just how all these problems are to be solved in those great, hard years that lie ahead.

If you sit down with pad and pencil to figure it all out in a matter-of-fact mood, leaving him out of the account, you may well despair. You will all be saying: "Show us! Show us! Let us see the end from the beginning, that we may walk not by faith but by sight!" This is the everlasting of that whole method.

III. In the third place, the value of these matter-of-fact people for the kingdom of God!

a. Man does not live by bread alone nor by hard facts alone. Neither does he live by visions, dreams, and enthusiasm alone. He lives by all the great words that proceed out of the mind of God.

Thou shalt love the Lord thy God with

all thy heart in the desires you cherish, and with all thy strength in the deeds you do, and with all thy mind in the thoughts you think. It is for every man to seek for the joy of intellectual fellowship with his Maker by thinking his thoughts after him and by sharing with him in his wise, beneficent purposes for mankind.

b. Here are men in all our churches who might not add up very large in a prayer meeting! Their religious experiences are so plain and simple, so lacking in romance and picturesqueness, that they would not seem worth telling. Narrow-minded evangelists, intent upon one particular type of spiritual experience, sometimes try to make these men feel that they have no rightful place in the kingdom of God, that the religion of our Lord is not for them.

Yet these very men, matter-of-fact though they may be, are exceedingly useful in the life and service of the kingdom of God. They could tell you exactly how much bread would be needed for the annual dinner of the Men's Brotherhood. They are exceedingly valuable in planning and directing the financial side of church life. And even though every church should see visions and dream dreams, there are bills to be met that will have to be paid in dollars and cents.

c. Bear in mind where the prophet placed his climax in his portrayal of spiritual efficiency: "They that wait upon the Lord shall renew their strength. They shall mount up with wings like eagles. They shall run and not be weary." And then, last of all, "They shall walk and not faint."

Flying, running, walking—three modes of advance! The fliers, the bird-men with their aëroplanes, move across the sky at the rate of two hundred miles an hour. The runners in the hundred-yard dash move along the cinder track with almost incredible swiftness. But the main part of the world's work is being done by men and women who walk. The matter-of-fact people like Philip are not much given to flying nor to running, but they can walk in the way of everyday duty and not faint. Heaven be praised for the steady

contribution they make to human well-being!

IV. Philip wanted to be shown—"Show us the Father"—and he was shown. When he had been given time to think himself through and to see yonder in the distance the true object of Christian effort, he put himself into the task and moved straight toward the goal.

He was not on the Mount of Transfiguration with Peter, James, and John when the Master's face shone like the sun and his raiment was white as light. But he was there in the valley when five thousand hungry people were to be fed, helping his Lord, as soon as his eyes were opened to the greatness of the occasion, to meet that need. In the Father's house are many abiding places. The Father's house is not all roof garden, where privileged people can look off with impeded vision toward the stars. The Father's house has in it also kitchens and cellars. Philip will often be found there, seeing to it that they are well stocked and that the necessary work is being done with thoroughness and skill.—Charles R. Brown

Illustrations

CORRECTING A MISTAKE. There is a legend that was made current by Clement of Alexandria, one of the early church fathers, that Philip was one of those men who begged off at first when Jesus asked them to become his disciples. The Master said to a group of men, "Follow me." One of the men replied, "Lord, I will follow thee, but suffer me first to bury my father."

There is nothing to indicate that his father was dead at that time. He wanted to wait until his father had died and the property had been divided up and the estate all settled. Then he might be willing to give some attention to the claims of Christian discipleship.

The Master did not care for such postponed allegiance, and he said frankly, "No man having put his hand to the plow and looking back is fit for the Kingdom of God." It may not have been Philip, but if it was, he saw his mistake at once. He came in thoughtfully, deliberately, with no waving of banners, but as an honest, wholehearted friend of the Master.— Charles R. Brown

REBUILDING CHARACTER. As the world must be redeemed in a few men to begin with, so the soul is redeemed in a few of its thoughts and works and ways to begin with: It takes a long time to finish the new creation of this redemption.— George Macdonald

SERMON SUGGESTIONS

Topic: On Being Answerable to God
TEXT: Rom. 14:1–12, especially, verse 12

(1) This means that we must respect the convictions of other believers. (2) It also means that we must give proper attention to our own convictions.

Topic: Forgiveness Unlimited
TEXT: Matt. 18:21–35

(1) Forgiveness of our fellow Christians is a problem. Otherwise, Peter would not have asked his question. (2) Forgiveness is a larger obligation than we may have realized. (3) True forgiveness comes from the heart, verse 35.

Worship Aids

CALL TO WORSHIP. "Tremble, thou earth, at the presence of the Lord, at the presence of the God of Jacob; which turned the rock into a standing water, the flint into a fountain of waters" (Ps. 114:7–8).

INVOCATION. Almighty God, our Father, we are awed by your majesty and your love. At the same time, we are being taught to trust you for all our needs. So we look to you for renewal of faith and hope as we pray and sing and open our hearts to your word.

OFFERTORY SENTENCE. "Let the giving of thanks be your sacrifice to God, and give the Almighty all that you promised. Call to me when trouble comes; I will save you, and you will praise me" (Ps. 50:14–15).

OFFERTORY PRAYER. We now give thanks to you, O God, with our lips and with our offerings, gifts far too small in return for all your blessings. May all our promises and good intentions be fulfilled in our tokens of gratitude.

PRAYER. Hear us as we lay before you the intercessions and petitions of this community of your people. Lord, restore and save our world and its people of every realm and nation. Teach them that it is only by grace they can be reclaimed for good and while from you it is a gift, for them it works according to the quality of their faith. Give all of us the faith to believe that your grace is sufficient for us, for your strength is made perfect in our weakness. Let us not depend for our salvation upon the merits of what we say or do, but may we nurture those inner responses that your grace brings to birth in our souls. May that same grace spring into action by your Spirit descending to the places where daily we move and live. It is by your grace people become kind, respect and cherish one another, take upon themselves someone else's pain and tears, and, like a cord, bind each other's heart to their own and yours. Grant, dear Lord, that whenever Christian believers see in the Gospel the living streams of your grace, may their debt to Jesus be the sounding note of their praise:

> I once was lost, but now am found,
> Was blind, but now I see.
> 'Tis grace has brought me safe thus far,
> And grace will lead me home.—Donald Macleod

LECTIONARY MESSAGE

Topic: Egyptians Dead on the Seashore: Faith Confirmed by Sight
TEXT: Exodus 14:10–31

Phillips Brooks (1835–1893), a famous American preacher, entitled one of his sermons: "The Egyptians Dead on the Seashore" (Exod. 14:30). Brooks used his text as the basis for expounding on the topic of the human experience of passage from one set of experiences, frequently traumatic, to another. The dead Egyptians marked the end of a long experience of captivity and the beginning of a new trek. Brooks wanted to express his confidence that struggles, even when they seem interminable, finally do end! Tyrants eventually lie dead on the seashore, and the power of old masters is apparent only in their cold faces, "set and stern, but powerless in death."

Brooks's reading of the text undoubtedly has its validity, but I want to focus the interpretation somewhat differently. The Egyptians lying dead on the seashore are testimony to the saving work of the Lord and his servant, Moses. The terrible scene was vivid confirmation of the Lord's power to do what he purposed to do. The death of the Egyptians in the sea marked the end of a spectacular series of mighty acts by the Lord to break the grip of a world power on a group of people he had chosen to be his own.

The story begins in chapter 1 of Exodus and continues through the harsh bondage of the Israelites under the oppressive rule of the Egyptians. Determined to liberate the Israelites from their bondage and make them his own people, the Lord called and sent Moses back to Egypt to be his agent in rescuing them from the hand of the Egyptians and to bring them up out of that country to a fine land, one spacious enough for a good life: a land "flowing with milk and honey"—a vast Garden of Eden, luxuriant and fertile (Exod. 3:7–8). The task was difficult, however. The Egyptians did not yield their control easily, and the Lord struck them with devastating plagues until their will to resist was broken.

Finally the exodus from Egyptian bondage became a reality (Exod. 12:37–41, 50–51). However, the Egyptians recovered their will and were dismayed to discover their error: "What have we done? We have let the Israelites free from their bondage!" The Egyptian king, known by the title Pharaoh, and his advisers were set upon keeping the Israelites from escaping from Egyptian territory and pursued them with a large force of soldiers and chariots. Caught between the oncoming Egyptians and the sea, the terrified Israelites were comforted by Moses:

Do not be afraid, stand firm, and see the deliverance that the LORD will accomplish for you today.... The LORD will fight for you, and you have only to keep still (Exod. 14:13–14 NRSV).

Subsequently the Egyptian force rushed into the divided sea, only to find themselves driving headlong into the water when it surged back over them. The Israelites, crossing dry-shod, saw the confirmation of Moses' message in the dead bodies of their foes on the shore.

A pause is in order at this point. We are properly shocked at the appalling brutality of the pictures in Exodus 14–15. The dead bodies of drowned Egyptians are an unpleasant sight, which should disturb us. However, we must remember that in these stories the Egyptians and their Pharaoh are representative of the world powers confronting the saving will of God. They are the rulers and the authorities, representative of "the cosmic powers of this present darkness" and "the spiritual forces of evil in the heavenly places" (Eph. 6:12). The salvation of God involves struggle with the power of domination systems and evil oppression, both in suprahistorical and historical formations. Primary emphasis should not be put on the actual historical nature of the Egyptians. The biblical texts make it clear that the judgments of the plagues and the deliverance at the sea were aimed at the gods worshiped by the Egyptians and embodied in them (see Exod. 12:12; Num. 33:4). Other people could be substituted for the Egyptians in the long history of domination systems: Assyrians, Babylonians, Persians, Greeks, Romans, Germans, French, Russians, Japanese, British, Americans—and even Israelites themselves when they become like the nations. Further, we should remember that it is God's intention to redeem and save the great powers along with his chosen people. In the visions of the future in the Book of Isaiah, the Egyptians will be called "my people" by the Lord and pronounced "blessed" along with the Assyrians, who are described as "the work of my hands"; both in a redeemed troika with Israel, "my heritage" (Isa. 19:24–25).

Now, back to the confirmation of faith explicitly stated in Exodus 14:30–31. Seeing the Egyptians dead on the seashore, the Israelites "put their faith" (REB) in the Lord and in Moses. Sports commentators sometimes refer to the "physicality" of an athletic team; referring, I suppose, to the team's ability to use bodily strength and size rather than mental prowess and technique. This sports neologism may be used of faith: the "physicality" of faith. A mature faith manifests "physicality" in at least two ways. First, faith involves the body; it is not confined to the spirit or the "soul" of a person (see 1 John 1:1–4). Second, faith seeks for "physicality" in the sense that it finds fulfillment in the realm of the physical. The Book of James declares of Abraham that his "faith was active along with his works, and faith was brought to completion by the works" (James 2:22 NRSV).—Marvin E. Tate

SUNDAY: SEPTEMBER TWENTY-SECOND

SERVICE OF WORSHIP

Sermon: Where Evil Is Evil

TEXT: Ps. 73:1–28

I. Whenever I read the Seventy-third Psalm I find myself wanting to make it required reading for at least two kinds of people: those who reject religion as futile; and those whose religion does not mean much to them or to anyone else. The first have missed the meaning of religion altogether; the second are losing their grip on it.

a. I wish I could have known the writer of the Seventy-third Psalm. He sounds like a good neighbor and friend. He was human, honest and devout. And he was having the same kind of trouble with this religion that we have with ours: It had run out of power. He had reached the point where, so far as he could see, many of its counsels were in error, many of its promises untrue. Having made this appealing discovery, he felt honor-bound to proclaim rather than to hide it.

For example, he had been taught that the righteous prosper while the wicked suffer. That, he says, is not the way I see the facts. The wicked prosper; they sleep well; they have power, wealth, and respect; they do as they please; and they die in peace. The righteous suffer from doubts within and poverty and hardships without. No matter how carefully they obey the law, they cannot escape suffering in some serious form or other. The Psalmist's first impulse was to lift an outraged protest against the way his faith had deceived him in this matter. He seems even to have toyed with the idea of exposing the deception to his children, but the thought of doing that, in his own words, "was too painful for me."

b. It was a deeply troubled man who entered the Temple, stood before the altar, and lifted his heart with his hands to the God of all, seeking light and peace on this matter. His own description of what happened there cannot be improved upon: It was "as a dream when one awaketh"—though "nightmare" might have been a better word. As he awakened, one thing towered above all else: Evil is evil at all times, in all places, and in all people. Evil is evil because it is a violation of the will of God for life. No matter how successful it seems to be in terms of power, wealth, or anything else, evil is still evil in the sight of God, and the wise man will accept that grim fact at face value.

c. Jesus would agree with two of the three steps taken by the Psalmist in his approach to evil: First, identify it—evil is evil now and always. Second, grapple with it, renounce it, repel its efforts to conquer you and all others. Then comes the radically different third step. Whereas the Psalmist would say, "Meet evil in others by calling down the wrath of God on them in judgment and punishment," Jesus would say, "Overcome evil with good, by identifying yourself with the evildoer, seeking the redemption of his soul and the transformation of his life by your love and your help."

II. If our religion is worth its salt, it ought to help us when and where we most need help—the moment of moral choice, when we must distinguish between right and wrong, good and evil. It ought to help identify these moral alternatives, to call them by their proper name, and to be guided by that fact.

a. It is true that Christianity does not hand us a code of morality complete in every detail, but it is likewise true that Christianity is a flaming faith in One whose will is the moral order of the universe and who asks that we find our way in his will.

"How," you may ask, "does that help us? On the one hand you say we are to believe in the reality of a moral order; on the other you admit we have no specific moral codes on which to base judgments of good and evil, right and wrong. Yet you say if our religion is worth its salt, it will help us make such judgments! Pray tell how!"

b. This is a fair challenge—one that must be met. How did the experience of the Holy in the sanctuary help the Psalmist in his judgment of good and evil, as obviously it did? So far as I can see the help came through the realization that so long as there is a God there is a right and a wrong, and so long as there is a right it ought to be sought and chosen. His experience of God gave him a firm foundation for moral judgments. Once sure of the reality of God, he was sure of the necessity of making clear moral judgments.

c. Men are building moral codes all the time—must build them if they are to live together. Some are built on the worship of tradition or of state, or of our way of life. The Christian faith bids us worship the God of the universe and find therein the true foundation of a morality that is universal in its scope and concern. In a world done to death by partisan and provincial moralities aimed to benefit a few at the expense of the rest, it is high time we sought and found again one that is interested in the will of God for all men everywhere.

III. Nor can the Christian Church shrink from her duty in this crucial task. Yet as she assumes it she will need to change some of her deeply ingrained habits. She will stop trying to please people and will take seriously her call to serve God.

a. The Church—*this* Church—must seek to be the Church of God, the preacher of the gospel, to all men, but this is far from saying that she must be all things to all men. She must be *one thing to all men*. She must seek one thing: to preach the gospel that in Christ we have our clearest revelation of the will of God for man. She must measure all life by that standard. Therefore, she must both believe in the reality of evil and speak of evil, sin, judgment, and other unpleasant facts. But she will not be content with this—for her gospel is positive—she will speak of good, salvation, of the love of God and of the kingdom of God.

Men in search of a purpose for life, men aware of the aimless, patternless, purposeless lives they live from day to day, men sick to death of the confusion and compromises that blur their vision of life and duty, will welcome the clear witness of the Church no matter how austere and difficult it may seem. A person who knows himself to be seriously ill is ready for serious treatment.

b. The Psalmist found the matter too painful for him until he went to the sanctuary—then he knew!

Knew what?

Knew that God alone is the Lord of Life; knew that because of that fact good is good and evil is evil; knew that even as they are different in God's world, they are different in our life and must be distinguished in our life; knew that no matter how sleek, comfortable, prosperous, and powerful evildoers may seem to be, they continue to be evildoers whether they are someone else or are ourselves and are not to be envied by one who seeks to find his way in faithfulness and righteousness.

c. Having been humbled by the experience of meeting God, of seeing ourselves in the perspective of his will, we are prepared to renew our confession of loyalty to him and to call good good and evil evil. We are ready then to draw some proper moral inferences for our life and times—still calling good good and evil evil. That is the religious background of our social creeds, our many efforts to cope with the injustices and evils in our common life. We call evil evil and grapple with it.

IV. The final movement in Christian ethics is not the identification and rejection of evil; it is the identification of ourselves with the evildoer in an effort to save him. All vital Christianity is finally *vicarious* and *redemptive*, doing all we can do for another that we together may find and serve God.

Without faith we can do nothing, with it there is nothing we dare not try to do. It is the faith that overcomes the world.—Harold Bosley

Illustrations

WHO IS A CHRISTIAN? A Christian is a person who confesses that, amidst the manifold and confusing voices heard in the world, there is one Voice that supremely wins full assent, uniting all his powers, intellectual and emotional, into a single pattern of self-giving. That Voice is Jesus Christ. A Christian not only believes *that* he was; he believes *in him* with all his heart and strength and mind. Christ appears to the Christian as the one stable point or fulcrum in all the relativities of history. Once the Christian has made this primary commitment, he still has perplexities; but he begins to know the joy of being used for a mighty purpose by which his little life is dignified.—D. Elton Trueblood

NEW SPLENDORS. The scene of the death of Christ was the scene of new splendors. Wherever the cross has been planted in the soil of human life, it has always made a garden of it. Jesus was mistaken by Mary on Easter morning for a gardener, and as Spurgeon says, there is a deep truth in this superficial error. Christ is the true gardener of human souls, and wherever the cross has been

uplifted there have bloomed around it the passion flowers of repentance, the roses of love, and the lilies of purity.—John Bishop

SERMON SUGGESTIONS

Topic: The Bread God Gives

TEXT: Exod. 16:2–15

(1) *Situation:* God brought his people out of Egypt under the leadership of Moses. God delivers his people today from various kinds of bondage. (2) *Complication:* God's people were at risk in various ways as they began their trek of faith and indeed encountered life-threatening hardship. Those who follow Jesus today often find themselves in dire straits as they take cross-bearing seriously. (3) *Resolution:* The Israelites found the resources for resolution of their frustrations, not in human ingenuity, but in the Lord. Today our help is in the risen Lord who promised to be with us always.

Topic: God's Surprise

TEXT: Matt. 20:1–16, especially, verse 16

(1) That he should accept the Gentiles on the same terms and with the same standing as the Jews. (2) That he should accept sinners, as Jesus did, on the same terms and with the same standing as those who had considered themselves good enough for God. (3) That he should give a place in his kingdom to one who, like the penitent thief, repents at the last moment.

Worship Aids

CALL TO WORSHIP. "You descendants of Abraham, his servant; you descendants of Jacob, the man he chose: remember the miracles that God performed and the judgments that he gave. The Lord is our God; his commands are for all the world" (Ps. 105:5–7 TEV).

INVOCATION. We bow before you, O God, encouraged by your mighty acts in days long gone and by daily tokens of your providence in our own lives. Make us aware of your expectations of us, and strengthen us now to do your will.

OFFERTORY SENTENCE. "One who is kindly will be blessed, for he shares his food with the poor" (Prov. 22:9 REB).

OFFERTORY PRAYER. Take us outside ourselves, O Lord, and let us walk in imagination into all places and among all persons where there is need, and help us to feel and share in your loving Spirit. To care as you care is to be blessed.

PRAYER. This is the day that you have made, Father, so let us rejoice and be glad in it. It is a day of celebration and anticipation. Father, may it all be for you.

We are ashamed to confess that not everything we do in your name and in this sacred place is always for you! Sometimes, habit motivates out for you. Sometimes, we delude ourselves into thinking that you are grateful for whatever we do because you need us so much—your Church would not thrive and your kingdom could not expand without us and what we do. Forgive us, God, for forgetting that we are the ones who can do nothing without you. Sometimes, we do what we do merely because of the expectations of others. A friend asks us to help and we don't want ever to let anyone down. Lord, you know the truth about us. Help us to admit the truth about ourselves: about how much of what we do, we really do for you.

So, let this day be a turning point in our relationship with you. Reveal yourself to us in powerful, unexpected ways. And most of all, change us—our lives and our ways—so that our hearts might be truly filled with love for you, and that our love might be the reason we serve and worship you, through Jesus Christ our Lord.—Gary C. Redding

LECTIONARY MESSAGE

Topic: A Church United
TEXT: Phil. 1:21–30

Every leader strives to achieve unity. Coaches want their teams to be unified.

Conductors want their orchestras to be unified, and certainly pastors want their churches to be unified. All wise leaders know unity is essential to success.

The apostle Paul also recognized the value of unity. From his own sufferings in Philippi he knew the infant Church in Philippi faced determined opposition. In verses 28–30 Paul warned his friends of "opponents, suffering, and conflict" soon to come. He also knew the Philippian Christians needed to unite in order to proclaim the gospel effectively in their city. Therefore, Paul made a threefold appeal for unity.

I. *United in purpose.* Groups succeed when the members agree on their purpose and work together to achieve it. Even a mediocre team can win the championship if the players all work together. Paul challenged the Philippians to unite in their purpose. First, he called on them to be worthy of the gospel. He exhorted the Philippians to behave in such a way that credit came to the gospel instead of discredit. Second, Paul encouraged them to uphold the gospel. That purpose should unite any congregation. Upholding the gospel involves both proclamation and demonstration. Christians should tell the gospel, and they should also live the gospel. Ultimately, a Christian's purpose is to glorify God (Matt. 5:16).

II. *United in attitude.* Paul called on the Philippians to unite in "spirit." This does not refer to the Holy Spirit, but rather to their attitude. Paul wanted them to be like the early believers in Jerusalem who "were of one heart and soul" (Acts 4:32). This reflects not only unity of purpose but also unity of heart.

Unfortunately, churches often fail to achieve this unity. Charles Swindoll tells the story of two declining congregations in a small town. After struggling to maintain their churches for several years, the two churches voted to merge and form one stronger congregation. Everyone agreed it was a good idea, but they were too petty to accomplish their purpose. What was the problem? They could not agree on how to recite the Lord's Prayer. One group wanted "forgive us our trespasses," while the other demanded "forgive us our debts." So, the local newspaper reported that one church went back to its trespasses, while the other returned to its debts!

Sadly, many congregations are like those two. The people may agree on the Church's purpose, but they cannot agree on how to get it done.

III. *United in action.* Paul challenged the Philippians to unite in purpose, attitude, and in action. In fact, he exhorted them to strive "side-by-side." This phrase comes from the Greek athletic arena. In team sports the members of the team have to cooperate and help each other. If they don't, they are sure to lose. Paul longed to see the Church members working side-by-side to present the gospel to their city.

A missionary told of a village in Africa where a little child wandered away from home and was lost in the tall grass. The villagers searched all day, but they could not find the child. The next morning they formed a line, joined hands, and walked through the grass side-by-side. Soon they found the child, but the child was already dead. In her grief and anguish the mother cried, "If only we had held hands sooner."

Like the believers at Philippi, Christians today must join hearts and hands to uphold the gospel. When they share a common purpose, display a common attitude, and act in unison, the gospel will be upheld, people will be saved, and God will be glorified.—J. Mark Terry

SUNDAY: SEPTEMBER TWENTY-NINTH

SERVICE OF WORSHIP

Sermon: Get The "Red" out of Your Eyes: Anger

TEXT: Ps. 103:8–9

The human mind is a phenomenal thing. What massive powers it has! Never is that more true when something happens that upsets and angers us.

Red is a color. It is a bold color—easily recognizable. When we are embarrassed we blush red. When we are humiliated, we flush red. When we speak of something being torrid, we say it is "red hot."

We have also been known to associate the color red with anger. "He is red with anger." Maybe we say that because anger seem to cause the pigmentation of the skin to show redness. Something in our body fluid tints the skin for the time being, and one can see our anger even in our skin tone.

Anger is an emotion that is almost as natural as breathing. Anger occurs in varying degrees of intensity. Anger has been called the chief saboteur of the mind.

I. *Anger in the Bible.*

Over and over in the pages of the Bible, there are references to divine wrath and human anger. The Bible tells us that anger is one of God's attributes. We certainly know it to be one of our own, don't we?

What are we to think if anger is one of God's attributes? We must conclude that in and of itself anger is not bad. Since God is completely good, there is a way that anger can also be good. God became angry—but when? His anger was directed specifically against those individuals, institutions, and nations whose evil acts and overt expressions of injustice created suffering, death, and deprivation for their innocent victims.

Jesus gave us a vivid picture of that which received the wrath of God in the cleansing of the Temple (John 2:13–15). There were two things contained in this incident that tell us something about the anger of God.

a. *The disdain of holiness.* The sheep and oxen that were being sold by the Temple leaders were not those "without spot or blemish." The people were taking advantage of the pilgrim worshipers who had come in from faraway places. The Temple would not receive their coinage, so changers of money sat in the Temple area to exchange the foreign currency.

The people would then buy their sacrifice. Their journeys had been so long they could not bring the sheep and oxen with them to make sacrifices.

A disrespect for the house of the Lord and the worship that transpired there was a display of disrespect for the Lord God himself. It was more than Jesus could take. The anger of God was intense.

b. *The place of the incident.* The "sale" was taking place in the Court of the Gentiles. For a long time, the Jewish nation had failed in carrying out God's plan for the ages. They were to be a "light to the nations," but instead they withheld the light from the nations. There was a token accommodation of the Gentiles in giving them a "courtyard" for their place of worship in the Temple complex. But even that was being made unusable for worship by those who made a marketplace for it.

Injustice has always provoked the wrath of the Almighty. It makes no difference what kind of injustice it is. Abuse of those who are helpless to defend themselves—the poor, the hungry, the children—these elicit the wrath of God.

II. *Some important facts about anger.*

a. *Human anger is normal and not necessarily sinful.* Let us think of anger as a response to emotional pain. When one strikes one's thumb with a hammer, it is quite natural for one to respond vocally with some expression of pain.

"Mature people don't get angry." Of course mature people get angry. Why shouldn't they get angry if there is a reason for anger? Anger can be a healthy response to emotional pain just as a cry might be a healthy response to emotional pain or a natural response to physical pain. One should not feel guilty because of feeling angry.

b. *Human anger can be harmful.* Many good things can be abused. Anger can be a good thing, but anger can also be abused. A thin line separates anger from being healthy or harmful. How can anger be harmful?

(1) *By the ventilation of it.* "Blowing up" is the common expression we use. Exploding. When one blows up, one's emotional energies are sometimes out of control.

If we're angry when punishing a child, often the punishment is more severe than we might like. Parents can easily lose control of their muscles and strike harder than they intended.

(2) *The internalization of it.* That's the opposite of ventilation of it. Instead of "blowing up," "we clam up." People who feel anger but don't express it often mope, pout, sulk, and allow their anger to eat them up internally. Ulcers can be one of the products of such treatment of anger.

In the final analysis anger probably does do more harm to the one who possesses it than to the one toward whom it is directed.

c. *Human anger often results from distorted perception.* Our tendency is to see almost everything from our own biased perspective.

Isn't it true that we become angry over some things without having full benefit of the facts? And if so, isn't it a proper thing for us to be "slow to anger"? Anger might be a right posture to take, but let's not rush into it with blinding speed. Walk into it slowly.

d. *Human anger often leads to sin.* Anger can become a doorway through which we walk into sinful behavior. It can create bad attitudes, bitterness, a spirit of vengeance, hatred, and other diseases of the spirit.

Our lives have profound effects upon the lives of others. Our words—what we say and the way we say them—can bless or curse the life of another person. Even the way we express our justified anger can be either positive or negative, righteous or sinful.

e. *Human anger can be controlled.* How can we learn to control our anger? Here are some suggestions:

(1) *Admit to yourself and to the one who has prompted your emotional pain that you are angry.* Identify the specific cause of the anger. Deal with the problem at hand. Handle it on its own merit. Don't add others to it.

(2) *Learn to restrain your emotions.* Emotions have to be expressed, but they need

to be put under control. Many of our differences could be resolved if we went about solving them in the right way. Instead, they are worsened by the hostile manner in which the confrontation is made.

III. *Anger needs some restrictions.*

a. Paul gave two restrictions on anger.

(1)"Do not let the sun go down on your anger" (Eph. 4:26).

(2)"Do not give the devil an opportunity" (v. 27).

In the first statement the word "anger" might be better translated as "exasperation." Do not go to sleep at night exasperated. There are some things about which we might say, "Why don't you sleep on it?" But this is not one of them.

The expression that speaks of nightfall is a way of saying that you and I should seek to resolve the situation that produces anger as quickly as possible. Anger can be a cancer that eats away at a person's spirit and even at one's body. Physical symptoms ranging from mild headaches to heart attacks can be a result of undiminished anger. Psychological reactions such as anxiety, fear, tension, and depression come as a consequence of anger.

The will of God for us is not to harbor grudges, resentment, malice, and hatred for others. Love cannot dwell where hatred resides. Jesus counseled us to give a coat when a shirt is taken, to go two miles when one is compelled, and to love our enemies (Matt. 5:40–43).

b. The second piece of Paul's advice is an interesting one. "Do not give the devil an opportunity." An opportunity for what? An angry person is vulnerable to Satan. All the assassinations, murders, and wars have come about through angry people—people who felt they were being mistreated and abused by someone.

Cities have been burned by those who felt their cause had been neglected. The cheaters and the cheated have responded with anger and have stabbed one another to death. Families have been hopeless when anger had alienated one member from another. And the beat goes on.

IV. *The way to victory over anger.*

How can one become the victor over such a monster as anger? How can God get the "red" out of our eyes and enable us to win the battle in this tense emotional war of feelings of bitterness?

a. *He can give us a proper outlook on life.* The Bible characterizes all the members of the human family as sinners who have fallen short of God's intention. Because we are sinners, we fail. That means that people will do things and say things that are not good for them to do or say. People will hurt one another intentionally and unintentionally. If I'm looking for perfection in the way I am treated, I will continually be disappointed.

Kindness is still the best behavior. Nonretaliation is still God's advice to us. Confrontation might be necessary if we are able to resolve the issues that divide us, but that should be done in a spirit of love and goodwill.

b. *He can give us more patience with people.* And that is exactly what we need with some people. Our temptation is to "throw out the baby with the bath water." We make hasty judgments of others, write them off, and reject them too quickly.

We need to give people a chance. Their action that provoked our anger might have been as a result of something totally unrelated to us. Of course, people need to communicate those facts to us.

People usually have their reasons, right or wrong, for expressing their anger and hostility. Sometimes they receive healing in being able to tell their story to one who will not reject them. Be a good listener.

Even if you and I are the ones toward whom the anger is directed, we might be able to be agents of healing by not fighting fire with fire. "A gentle answer" is the way the wise man expressed it. Another translation describes it as a "soft answer."

c. *He can give us the victory when we surrender completely to him.* We can't control some things. Some events in life have hurt us deeply. Some people have crushed us with their words or actions. Revenge is not the answer. Retaliation will do neither us nor them any good. "Vengeance is mine, I will repay. And again, 'The Lord will judge His people'" (Heb. 10:30).

Let us leave it at that. Turn it over to

God. He has the ability to enable us to get on with life. People who have surrendered themselves to the lordship of Christ receive their share of rejection, abuse, and injustice, but they handle them better. God's grace enables them to live the abundant life. God gets the "red" out of their eyes.—Jerry Hayner

Illustrations

CONSTRUCTIVE ANGER. You and I would do well to get a little angry over the same things. A bumper sticker had these words: IF YOU LOVE JESUS, SEEK JUSTICE. ANYONE CAN HONK. Amen to that. At times Christians need to kick over a few tables and chairs. How long shall we sit idly by and allow the poor to get poorer, the minorities to continue to be rejected, and others to be treated as second-class citizens?—Jerry Hayner

DESTRUCTIVE ANGER. Of the seven deadly sins, anger is possibly the most fun. To lick your wounds, to smack your lips over grievances long past, to roll over your tongue the prospect of bitter confrontations still to come, to savor to the last toothsome morsel both the pain you are given and the pain you are giving back—in many ways it is a feast fit for a king. The chief drawback is that what you are wolfing down is yourself. The skeleton at the feast is you.—Frederick Buechner

SERMON SUGGESTIONS

Topic: Putting God on the Spot
TEXT: Exod. 17:1–7, especially verse 7
(1) All of us have needs, many of them profound and even life threatening, as with the Israelites. (2) The urgency of our need and our distrust of God may drive us to make rash demands on God to prove himself with some sign agreeable to us. (3) Jesus pointed the way for us when he was tempted to perform a rash act "for the glory of God." (see Matt. 4:5–7).

Topic: The Conquest of Arrogance
TEXT: Phil. 2:1–13 NRSV

(1) *The problem:* Selfish ambition or conceit. (2) *The solution:* (a) by regarding others better than yourself; (b) by looking to the interests of others as well as your own interests. (3) *The example:* (a) Jesus' self-emptying; (b) Jesus' reward.

Worship Aids

CALL TO WORSHIP. "Give ear, O my people, to my law; incline your ears to the words of my mouth. I will open my mouth in a parable; I will utter dark sayings of old, which we have heard and known, and our fathers have told us. We will not hide them from their children, telling to the generation to come the praises of the Lord, and his strength and his wonderful works that he has done" (Ps. 78:1–4 NKJV).

INVOCATION. God of the sparrow, we pray for ourselves, singly and as a church, in the nurture of our young people, in the support of their parents and teachers, and in our role in society: that we may show compassion, and apply our hearts to wisdom, nor lack Jesus' outrage, nor fail to hear his judgment, when youth be wronged or failed.

For these living tasks before us we give you thanks, and for them we pray you give us heart. God of the sparrow, hear our prayer.—Peter Fribley

OFFERTORY SENTENCE. "He will always make you rich enough to be generous at all times, so that many will thank God your gifts which they receive from us" (2 Cor. 9:11 TEV).

OFFERTORY PRAYER. O Christ, thou who didst come to take all fear from our hearts, help us to produce an order in which fear will have no place. We could do it if we knew how to love.—E. Stanley Jones

PRAYER. Your love is an everlasting love, Father. From the moment we were born, you have cradled and sustained us. And even when we pass from this life into your kingdom, your love will keep us, protect us, and provide for our every need throughout eternity. Teach us how to love each other with that same kind of faithful endurance. We ask for the compassion of our Lord toward those whom we do not even know—those who are hungry and homeless and helpless.

But most of all, we ask that you would help us truly love those with whom we live and work day in and day out. Help us to be patient with people even when they are foolish and silly and annoying. Make us at all times courteous and thoughtful and kind. Help us never to look at another person with contempt or disrespect. Help us never to begrudge other people their possessions or successes, but to be as glad for them as if they were our own. Lord, keep us from sulking when we do not get our own way. Help us not to be irritable and difficult to live with.

Our life, the world we live in, and the relationships we cherish are gifts, Father, and we thank you for them. Forgive us for the times when we do not see the wonder of it all—when our pride, our self-centeredness, our worries, and our fears blind us to your amazing grace. Mold us more in the image of Christ our Lord, who never lost sight of the gift.

You have loved us without limit, O God. Teach us to how to love like that.—Gary C. Redding

LECTIONARY MESSAGE

Topic: Choosing the Lesser Evil

Text: Matt. 21:28–32

Nobody likes to pay taxes; but if you don't, the government may find out about it, and then the fine and the interest would be far more than the original taxes were. So even though we dislike it, we pay the taxes: it's the lesser of evils. The dishes are dirty and need to be washed. We're tired and really ready to go to bed. But if we leave them until morning, we'll have to face them when we're trying to fix breakfast, and the food will be stuck on that much tighter. So even though we dislike it, we wash the dishes: it's the lesser of evils.

Jesus had the Temple authorities breathing down his neck. He had come into Jerusalem, with people screaming out his name and hinting that he might be the Messiah. He had gone into the outer court of the Temple and had preached some outrageous nonsense about the Temple being a house of prayer for filthy Gentiles. He had hung around with the worst sort of crowd, sinners and tax collectors, and had told the Pharisees they were hypocrites because they wouldn't do the same. The Temple authorities had had enough; they wanted to know what he thought gave him the right to do such outlandish things.

Jesus wouldn't answer their question directly because it was a dumb question. It's a little bit like this: A fire breaks out in one of those buildings up the street. You happen to be walking along and notice the smoke and flames. You run across the street to get the fire-fighting equipment and start fighting the blaze. If the fireman comes along and says, "Why are you doing this? What gives you the right to fight fires?" then you'd be entitled to say, "That's a dumb question—the real question is why you aren't helping me." So Jesus doesn't answer the question straight on. Instead, he told a story about the two sorry sons of a certain Palestinian farmer.

The farmer knows that today is the day to get in the grapes. It's too big a job to do all by himself, so he calls in his two sorry sons. To the oldest he says, "Son, I need you to work in the vineyard today." "No!" says the first son. "I'm not working in that hot, dirty vineyard. You get grape juice all over you, and then the bugs start tormenting you, and the brambles stick you, and besides all the bending over makes my back ache. I'm not going." So the father goes to his second sorry son. "Son, I need you to work in the vineyard today." "Certainly, dear father, I'd love to work all day long in your vineyard—whatever you say—you just go on out there, and I'll be right along, just as soon as I've finished breakfast." Later, when we return to the little family scene, the father and the first son are in the field working, but the second son is in the house watching a football game.

Neither one of these guys is very admirable. The first is disrespectful and disobedient, the second is a lying hypocrite. Neither of them wants to help their father. Neither one feels responsible for helping, neither one thinks about how the job must be done if the family is to survive. Both of them really intended to skip out on the work—the first one was just a trifle more honest, but you'd still want to slap him for his smart mouth. But if you had to choose, which one is the lesser of evils?

Jesus asked that question to the Pharisees: "Which sorry son did the will of his father?" and they answer correctly, "The first one. Even though he was rude and surly, he did go out to the field." And Jesus says, "Right! God likes sinners who repent far more than he does so-called righteous people who think they need no repentance." No matter how pious the second son sounds, he isn't in the field in the end of the story; no matter how rough the first son sounds, he is, and that makes him more valuable.

Who is Jesus talking about here? Obviously, he's pouncing on the Temple authorities. They want to know why he thinks he has the right to try to reform the Temple; they want to know why he thinks he has the right to question all these bright teachers of the Law; why he has the right to be called Messiah. And what he wants to say is, "The real question is, why aren't you guys in the fields working? The kingdom of God has started here, and things are moving. Sinners are repenting, demons are being cast out, the dead are being raised, and you guys are still on the sidelines worrying about what authority I have. Why aren't you doing this? If you're so all-fired spiritual, why aren't you helping me?"

If they had been given a chance to answer in this story, I think their answer would have been that they thought they were doing the right thing. They were trying their hardest to be obedient to God. Like the Pharisee in the parable: "God, I thank thee that I am not like other men, extortioners, unjust, or even like this tax collector. I fast twice a week, where others do it only once a year; I give tithes of everything I own, not just

from the profit, like others." Their answer would have been that when God looked at them, he would see that they were better than others.

They were not liars or cheaters or adulterers; they were better than average. That's what the Temple authorities would have said: God is pleased with us, because we're better than the average person, and tons better than any of the scum you hang around with, Jesus.

The Egyptians used to think about dying and going before the great judge of the Underworld. You'd stand there before him, wearing only your soul, and he'd weigh your soul to see how virtuous you had been during your life. And you were supposed to confess to him: "I have never mistreated cattle. I have never lied in church. I have never used God's name in vain. I have never cheated a poor man. I have never fished in the temple pond. I have never stolen a child's milk," and so on—thirty-six separate things you were supposed to say you'd never done, and if that were true, you could go to heaven. I'm pretty good, God; certainly better than average, certainly good enough to get to heaven.

Lots of Christians think that's what will happen to them, too. Only it won't be the Egyptian God Osiris who judges you, but St. Peter, or Jesus. They'll stand at the pearly gates and look at a long list of your deeds, and see if your good ones outweigh your bad ones, and if they do, you can go into heaven. People, that's not Christianity—not at all. God is not interested in picking the lesser of evils from this world. He is not going to take only the better-than-average people into heaven.

Instead, Jesus says, he's going to look at two things: Did we repent? Did we see ourselves as we truly are—perhaps not the worst sinners in the world, but sinners nevertheless? And did we believe— did we give ourselves over to God's gift of forgiveness in Jesus? It's a story of judgment, to be sure: as Jesus says, there will be a lot of surprised people on judgment day, people who think they have been good enough to be admitted to heaven, who discover too late that being good enough was not the point at all. But it's also a beautiful story of hope. There's nothing admirable about that first sorry son, but because he repented and gave himself to the will of his father, he was admitted to the vineyard.

There's an interesting tradition about the royal family in Vienna. The Hapsburgs were fabulously wealthy and built glorious castles. When one of them would die, the funeral procession would go from the castle to the basement of a certain church. The priest inside would hear a knock at the door: "Who is it?" "His Imperial Majesty, the Emperor of Austria," but the priest would answer, "I don't know him." A second knock, with the same answer. Then the third knock: "Who is it?" "A poor sinner," and the priest would open the door. So God opens the doors of heaven, the gates of his vineyard, to all who will repent honestly, and give themselves to the grace offered in Jesus.—Richard B. Vinson

SUNDAY: OCTOBER SIXTH

SERVICE OF WORSHIP

Sermon: Why Are We Here?

TEXT: John 13:3–4

I. It's an old riddle, this business of living. Men have been trying to solve it for a long while without any notable success.

Why in the name of everything that makes our going on intelligible do we live at all? And ever and again, though frequently they will not confess it, they feel themselves weighed down under a haunting sense of defeat and utter pointlessness because they have no answer to it. The result of it is, and you may see it all around you, that the quality of their lives reflects their uncertainty.

But Jesus took life up in his hands and made men want an eternity of it! It seemed unspeakably great to him. You couldn't see it as he saw it and flick it off as though it were a speck of dirt. Jesus said once that the angels of God would stop what they were doing to celebrate the return of a lone straggler worse off than the swine he had been feeding. He said that a man could set the whole world down on the credit side of his books and not be able to balance the account if his own soul were over there in the debit column. And so you have it: the human race, a big ditch, and a gentle shove; or a publican wavering on the brink of eternity, without lifting up so much as his eyes unto heaven, and Jesus Christ all a-tremble about it! Take it or leave it; it's just the way he looked at it, this poor uneducated carpenter who never has seemed to some people to know what he was talking about.

I wonder if we can come at the secret of life? What was it about one's being here that made it so purposeful and so great?

II. It seems to me that a good deal of our bewilderment, ancient and modern, much of this haunting sense of futility that plagues human life, is merely the result of not knowing where we come from and not being very sure where we're going.

a. Well, then where did we come from? The trouble is that what we call our knowledge—and sometimes we pride ourselves on it—doesn't help us much. We know very little about the origin of human life. They tell us it came out of very humble beginnings. Genesis talks about a bit of clay, and biologists talk about an ape, and a reptile, and a fish, and a bit of protoplasm. There isn't much choice between them. Somebody has said that the alternative is mud or monkey. Neither lineage is very proud. We need not expect any assistance at all in the solution of our problem from what men assert they have discovered about the past. The only thing they say with any assurance is that we have been coming along slowly for a million years or so. And that's no very great illumination.

b. But what about the future? If modern knowledge will not help us to read our riddle by telling us where we come from, will it help us by telling us where we're going? Again the answer is, "No, not much." You hear now and then such pronouncements made as this, of Mr. Darrow: "There is no goal in living. If we knew where we were going we could pick out the road. But so far as science, philosophy, or history can throw any light on the subject, we are not going anywhere." That's about the sum of it, I suppose.

c. And so we come back pretty much empty-handed to this puzzle of ours: Why are we here? The knowledge of what is behind us is of little use, and there is no knowledge of what is in front of us. And that is the equipment with which the man of the twentieth century who has no religion sets out to solve his problem. I am not surprised that thousands give it up and ask, "What's the answer?" The best they can do is just to go about their business and make what they can out of an unintelligible situation. All they can insist on is that none of it matters, where they come from or where they are going. While they are here they must try to build up some worthy standard and live by it. They must strive to be socially minded and pure minded; these things are biologically necessary. They owe it to themselves to give expression to the best that's in them. Beyond that there is nothing.

d. I leave you to be the judge of whether or not this solution is strong enough to bear the weight of human life. How much of permanence can there be in the life either of a civilization or of an individual where no more meaning than that is attached to living? Of itself it knows nothing of its destiny, and it knows nothing of the purpose it is intended to serve. You cannot rear anything on such a foundation.

III. The only adequate light that is thrown at all is the light that is thrown by the religion of Jesus Christ. It is not that I demand an explanation from Christianity. Christianity is not supposed primarily to furnish us with explanations. But it does have a distinct message that it puts before you for you to accept or reject. It is a message that is not only lovely enough to be becoming from the lips of One Who is Eternal, and Worshipful, and Lifted Up: it's a message that is reasonable enough for anybody to proceed on, and practical enough to transfigure the life that starts out with it for a fact. "Jesus knowing that he was come from God and went to God took a towel and girded himself, and began to wash the disciples' feet." What if that were the meaning of all this mysterious world of human life? What if God were the source of its strange pilgrimage and the white, assured goal of its ongoing, with only space enough between for some towel-girded ministry to feet that are weary and journey-sworn?

a. "Knowing that he was come from God." There is the place to begin. I wish that men would spend a little more time exploring the capacities that establish their kinship with the Infinite and a little less groveling around in sandpits for some evidence that will link their strain with the beast. It is all very well to be related on one side to my Mother Earth; I am considerably more concerned about my relation on the other side, whether or not it's to my Father God!

That's the consciousness you and I need to have. We need to set about winning it if we have lost it. And no one can say us nay to it. There is something filial in human nature, which, if given its chance, will answer to God as an echo answers to a shout. Humanity at its best has always lifted up its head with a strange sense of its high heritage. All that is best in its achievement it has wrought with that conviction upon it. And whenever and wherever that conviction has lost its hold, there has passed away a glory from the earth.

b. "Knowing that he was come from God and went to God." Will you let that too be true for lesser lives? I have fallen out of love with all our curious questioning about the form and circumstance of that life which is to come. By the very nature of human experience the terms of that existence are unintelligible to us. Because I believe in man and am not ashamed of my faith; and because I believe in God; because I believe in the value of my neighbor's life as in my best moments I believe in the preciousness of my own; and because I believe that there is a dependable Factor in the Universe, revealed to me as my Father in Jesus Christ, whose power I can rely on to take care of this that he has done—because I believe these things, I believe that nothing shall pluck my life out of his hands forever! "Knowing that he went to God." We are not going anywhere? Before the face of Christ I will not put my hand to that. We are going home to God, every step, today, tomorrow, sleeping, waking, resting, toiling—all the way home to God; and God is *here!* We are under "sentence of life," and we will not "petition that it be commuted to death"—life running Godward through eternity!

And now I wonder if you will believe in the sheer loveliness of this conclusion? "Jesus knowing that he was come from God and went to God took a towel,"—what a sequence it is!—such knowledge followed by such a ministry!—Paul Scherer

Illustrations

A POWERFUL TESTIMONY. In a church in New York City at the seven o'clock service one morning a disheveled lad crept into a back seat after a night of wandering the streets battling with doubt of his faith. He was seeking a haven of rest; he was wondering if there could be anything to the idea that religion could do something with a man. He was a student at Columbia University. As his eyes wandered over the congregation at this early-morning hour, he saw one of his idols, a great scientist, a great teacher in Columbia, under whom he had had a class. He knew that man's spirit and his mind, and there he sat with head bowed. So said the boy to himself, "If a man like that can believe in the God and Father of our Lord Jesus Christ, I can too." —Paul Quillan

FOR DOUBTERS. If you have doubts about the existence of God or misgivings as to the kind of God he is, I do not think your need will be met by argument. It will be met only by an act of trust on your part. You must be willing to be found by the pursuing love of God that will not let you go; to face the challenge that is relentless; to move out fearlessly from your narrow, self-centered life into a new, wide, spacious life with Christ at the center—trusting not in yourself but in the all-sufficient love and power of God.—Leslie J. Tizard

SERMON SUGGESTIONS

Topic: Getting There
TEXT: Phil. 3:4b–14
(1) Paul's résumé, verses. (2) Paul's renunciation, verses 7–11. (3) Paul's reward, verses 12–14.

Topic: The Jesus Story in a Parable
TEXT: Matt. 21:33–46
(1) *The parable:* A landowner sought produce from his vineyard and was rebuffed by wicked tenants who went so far as to kill the landowner's son; whereupon, the landowner punished the wicked tenants and leased his vineyard to more promising tenants. (2) *The pointed meaning:* The kingdom of God would be given to the Gentiles. (3) *The predictable reaction:* The Pharisees reacted with anger, but feared to do anything to Jesus because of the crowd's support of Jesus as a prophet. Later, the Pharisees and others had a part in the killing of the Son of God. (4) *The promising outcome:* Now all of us, Jew, Gentile, or whatnot, are beneficiaries of God's wisdom and graciousness.

Worship Aids

CALL TO WORSHIP. "Let the words of my mouth, and the meditation of my heart, be acceptable in thy sight, O Lord, my strength, and my redeemer" (Ps. 19:14).

INVOCATION. O God, may the words of the Psalmist be our prayer now, as we enter this hallowed place of our worship of you and enjoy fellowship with one another as believers. Help us to present to you our bodies as a living sacrifice and serve you here and beyond the walls of the sanctuary.

OFFERTORY SENTENCE.   Verily, verily, I say unto you, he that believeth in me, the works that I do shall he do also; and greater works than these shall he do. And whatsoever ye shall ask in my name, that will I do, that the Father may be glorified in the Son" (John 14:12–13).

OFFERTORY PRAYER.   You have given all of us work to do in your kingdom, Lord, and our offerings are an important part of that work. May we not despise this opportunity or substitute it for other important service. Use these gifts, we pray, for your glory; and use us, body, soul, and spirit, to that same end.

PRAYER.   Holy God, high above all, yet in us all; Mighty God, power beyond all, but in us all, we turn aside from the calls of the world to enter your sanctuary, breathe your presence, and voice our praise and worship to you. Generous Maker, we give thanks for the glory and beauty of this day, for the invigorating coolness that kisses us refreshed, for the bright sunlight that lights our paths, for the goodness and mercy that follows us. Thanks be to God.

Including God of us all, Lord Jesus Christ, who prayed for the disciples that they would be one, even as you are one with the Father, today we pray for the unity of the Body of Christ. You have called us not to be one as each other but to be one in the Spirit, one in you. So may it be, O God, we pray.

Merciful Redeemer, God of the crucified Christ, the pain and starkness of the cross reminds us of our oneness in sin. All of us fall short, miss the mark, tarnish your image upon us, dishonor your touch within us. Forgive pride that divides us, our lack of charity and understanding, our practiced selfishness, our comfortable narrow-mindedness, our cherished bitterness, our assumed divisions. Lord, forgive us, we pray.

Receiving God, arms open with abiding welcome, you always set a place at the table for us . . . and for each of your children. As there is room at the cross for us all in forgiveness, so at the table there is reconciliation and renewal. In your body being broken, we are made whole; in your body being given, we are made one. So may it be among us this hour and in the days ahead. Come, Holy Spirit, unite our voices, our hearts, our lives, our service for you.—William M. Johnson

LECTIONARY MESSAGE

Topic: Love Is Stronger Than Law

TEXT: Exod. 20:1–4, 7–9, 12–20

RELATED TEXTS: Phil. 3:4b–14; Matt. 21:33–46

In most of contemporary society, the word *law* has a negative connotation. With an extreme emphasis upon individual freedom, society views "law" as the enemy. "Watch out, or the 'law' will get you!"

In the biblical world, law had a very positive connotation. Coming from the Hebrew verb *yarah*, to point or show the way, the noun for law (*Torah*) carried the meaning of guiding one safely through a dangerous journey. It was like an accurate road map, a dependable guide to help the traveler reach his destination safely.

I. *God's grace precedes God's law.* When people have tried to post the Ten Commandments in public classrooms or courthouses, they assume that these are self-evident moral laws that will help to curb the violence and evil in our society. This overlooks the fact that these "Ten Words" (not commandments) were spoken by the Lord to the people he had already delivered from Egyptian bondage. These are not universal moral laws that any society or even any intelligent individual person is compelled to accept, like the law of gravity in the natural order. Instead, these "Ten Words" express the covenant response the Redeemer God expects from his redeemed people!

When President Harry Truman made the laudable statement that he tried to run the government by the Sermon on the Mount, he overlooked the fact that the sermon is directed to disciples who have already left everything and committed themselves to following Jesus. This act of faith was the presupposition of the demands placed upon his disciples.

While law can give guidelines and establish boundaries for human conduct, it does not provide the motivation for *obeying* the law. In fact, the law becomes a challenge and a hindrance to be circumvented unless the people who make the laws are committed to living by them. Since the Garden of Eden and the fall of human beings into sinful obedience to God, they have always pressed the limits of any restriction upon their behavior. We see it in little children; we observe it in the violence on our streets; we feel it in ourselves. Law challenges us to test its limits: "The commandment came, sin revived, and I died!" (Rom. 7:9). Without the grace that claims our hearts and engenders a desire to obey, the law itself becomes a part of the problem. It can never provide the change of mind and heart that is required to obey the law. The law cannot save!

II. *Love fulfills the law.* Augustine's famous dictum, "Love God and do as you please!" grasps this basic law of human behavior. A grudging obedience to a coercive commandment would never fulfill the purpose of the law. Only a change of will by the love of God can achieve that goal. We obey God not because we want to earn God's love and salvation but because we have experienced God's gracious love. We obey out of *love,* not out of *fear!*

III. *Sacrificial love is the power which rules the universe forever.* John's vision of the "Lamb which had been slain" standing in the midst of the throne room in the apocalyptic vision of Revelation 5, is the biblical confirmation of this great truth: Neither military power nor technological achievement will rule this universe ultimately. Suffering love, the greatest power on earth, the very nature of our Creator-Redeemer God will claim the throne forever and ever!

This power drives the nonviolent dimension of all efforts to achieve justice in racial, gender, or class conflicts. In short, it is the power of the cross, the only power that can "lead us home."

Like many other servicemen, I left my new bride on the California shore when I flew out to the Pacific with my air-rescue squadron. During the long months of separation, I faced temptations too powerful to describe. My great-grandchildren will feel the vibrations.

But knowing the Ten Commandments by heart was never my help in the time of temptation; it was her face in my heart. I would have died rather than hurt her and break her heart.

Love is stronger than law. It always has been, is now, and always will be, for *God is Love!*—Wayne Ward

SUNDAY: OCTOBER THIRTEENTH

SERVICE OF WORSHIP

Sermon: Saints in Strange Places

Text: Phil. 4:22

Few people would go looking for saints in the luxurious licentious palace of an emperor! For that reason, Paul's closing words in the Philippian letter grab our attention. "All the saints greet you, especially those of Caesar's household." One might as well look for saints at a raucous political convention, a bartender's association, or an adult movie house.

Who were those saints of whom Paul wrote? They were persons serving in some capacity within Caesar's household.

Evidently, the "saints" were part of the church of Rome, a church neither Paul nor Peter founded. The presence of a little band of saints in Caesar's household impresses a number of significant facts upon our minds.

I. *Adversity is no deterrent to the gospel.*

a. Planting the Christian faith in the heart of the Roman Empire was a bit like anchoring the battle flag at the enemy's post.

Think of the courage required to confess faith in the Lord Jesus when loyalty was demanded by lord Caesar! It puts us to shame because of our tepid Christianity, our easy church membership in a land where religion is popular, or our refusal to hear or take seriously the commands of Christ.

b. Small wonder that Paul and the saints in Caesar's household got along so well. They knew what it was to live dangerously. Adversity failed to break their spirit or deflect them from loyalty to their Master. Surely there were times when they felt fear or even discouragement. The best of God's children have moments like that. Momentary fears and doubts, however, do not destroy great souls.

Indeed adversity makes the person stronger and sturdier, like the wind that toughens the oak. God never produces saints in hothouses, carefully sheltered from heat or storm. It is in the crucible that the gold is refined and the dross consumed. Some persons cannot be understood apart from the role that adverse circumstances have played in shaping their lives.

c. Adversity equips us to help persons who themselves stumble upon hard and trying times. This is one thing the fellowship of the saints can do for us. Did that little *ekklesia* (church, or called-out ones) in Rome seek out Paul to befriend him and bolster his spirit? Or, caught up amid the pressures of Caesar's household, did they seek comfort and guidance from an elderly Christian who had lived for years with persecution and tension? Most likely, the contacts were mutually beneficial.

d. Not only does adversity equip persons for ministry, it provides opportunity for witnessing to Christ. Persons who handle their difficulties and sufferings with courage make a profound impact on others' lives. Death was lurking in Paul's cell, waiting only for the emperor's word. But no fear of death could keep the apostle from witnessing to the soldiers, slaves, and other persons about him.

II. *Adequacy of the gospel.* Saints in Caesar's household clearly attest the adequacy of the gospel. If the power of Christ can reach persons in the emperor's palace, there is hope for all of us.

a. Let us make clear the fact that saints are not out of this world. They are plain people who are mightily involved in changing this world. The New Testament view of sainthood sets the record straight, and in doing so challenges some of the ecclesiastical definitions of saintliness. One of those definitions observes that a saint is "one who is in enjoyment of the beatific vision and has been presented by the Church for the public worship of the faithful." There are no such persons in the New Testament! Saints are not people with halos. Nor are they perfect persons, sitting in self-righteous judgment of others.

b. Why, after all, does the New Testament call Jesus' followers saints? It is one of the most common designations used of them. The term *hagios* applies to a person worthy of veneration or reverence. That veneration is not self-generated. Rather, a saint is one who has a connection with God. God alone makes one "holy." Further, saintliness is maintained by association with God. God has exclusive rights to the life of the saints. They are set apart for his service.

c. Saints are plain people made over again by divine grace. They share the simplicity of their Master who went about doing good and healing those oppressed by the devil (Acts 10:38). How quickly we forget the origins of the humble Galilean carpenter and his identity with Palestine's toiling masses! Jesus came from the peasant class and appealed to the common people. They heard him with gladness and hope. Now see what we have done with him. We have hidden him within elaborate rituals, obscured him by ornate clerical grab and costly temples, and buried him beneath dogmas and creeds. Where is the carpenter clad in working garments, the plain-speaking teacher people loved to hear, the big-hearted man whose compassion allowed him to overlook none?

III. *The saints travel the victory road.* That sounds unbelievable. How could that small group of Christians in Caesar's palace or the little pocket of believers in

Greco-Roman cities be viewed as victors in anything?

a. They are linked with the power that creates and controls all things. They are sons and daughters of a heavenly Father and have access to him at all times. Caesar has his royal family and his court. Christians are a royal priesthood, "a kingdom and priests" to God (see 1 Pet. 2:9; Rev. 1:6). Every believer is a priest and a king! That is what the biblical writers are saying. Even the pauper is a king, made so by "Him who loves us, and released us from our sins by His blood" (Rev. 1:5).

b. Our victory consists of an imperishable heritage. The world may deprive us of fortune, home, job, friends, or even reputation. But nothing can "separate us from the love of God, which is in Christ Jesus our Lord" (Rom. 8:35–39 KJV). God does not lose or cast aside his trophies. Through his great mercy, he has granted us "an inheritance which is imperishable and undefiled and will not fade away" (1 Pet. 1:4). That fact undergirds our hope and puts iron in our blood. We are kept by the power of God—nothing can destroy us.

c. God's people at their best make an impact on society. Caesar might have sneered at the little band of Christians, but, in time, Christianity undermined and destroyed the old order. The strategy used is still a viable one: Drain off a few million souls by the attraction of a new and higher allegiance. We know the story. Under the Emperor Constantine, in A.D. 312, Christianity was made the state religion. That, however, might never have happened but for one fact: A small group of Christians lived like saints in Caesar's household, long before Caesar became friendly to their faith.—Nolan P. Howington

Illustrations

COMPLETING THE JOURNEY. Did you ever walk a swinging footbridge above a torrent of water? My first experience of that came near Frankfort, Kentucky. I was a student at the Southern Baptist Theological Seminary in Louisville and served a small rural church on weekends. Some kind church member would provide me a prophet's chamber each Saturday night. The road to many farmhouses crossed a creek. In the absence of a bridge, the creek was easy to ford except in rainy seasons. Then the driver would park the car, cross on an elevated footbridge, and walk to the farmhouse. Once I found myself on such a footbridge, carrying a heavy suitcase. The combination of high, rushing water and the swinging of the bridge shook me up. I felt near panic! I realized I could make it only by setting the suitcase down and pushing it with my feet while I held to the sides of the bridge. What helped even more was looking up and across at the destination I hoped to reach. When I fixed my eyes on that target, I found help in completing my journey.—Nolan P. Howington

HEAVEN'S INHABITANTS. We are unwise to limit heaven with earth's measure. A kind of selfishness makes us narrowly draw its confines and restrict its inhabitants to the few who suit us. But that fair land is spacious beyond comprehension, with twelve gates, never closed, into which streams a multitude that no man can number, from all tribes and peoples and tongues (Rev. 7:9). The mathematics of eternity is such that terrestrial geometry does not apply. The many rooms of the Father's house must extend in infinite corridors, like the images in a double mirror, through "caverns measureless to man." How else except by faith can one come to comprehend with all the saints what is the breadth and length and height and depth, and to know the love of Christ which surpasses knowledge (Eph. 3:18–19).—D. P. McGeachy III

SERMON SUGGESTIONS

Topic: How to Stand Firm in the Lord

TEXT: Phil. 4:1–9

(1) Harmony in the service of the Lord Jesus Christ. (2) Rejoicing in the Lord in all circumstances. (3) Preoccupation with whatever is excellent and praiseworthy.

Topic: The Wedding Banquet

TEXT: Matt. 22:1–14

This somewhat unrealistic allegory makes true and significant points. (1) Special invitation to the feast of the gospel of Jesus Christ had been sent to the Jews, that is, to those, above all others, expected to come to the feast. (2) Since the Jews rejected the invitation, the doors were opened wide to all who would come, "both good and bad." (3) However, those coming must be willing to put on the proper moral and spiritual attire in keeping with the special, elect occasion.

Worship Aids

CALL TO WORSHIP. "Praise ye the Lord. O give thanks unto the Lord; for he is good: for his mercy endureth for ever" (Ps. 106:1).

INVOCATION. Wherever we are, O God, we would praise you and give thanks to you, for your mercy not only endures forever, your mercy extends everywhere. Yet it is especially fitting that we praise you here, in this place dedicated to your worship and service. So, fill our hearts and loosen our tongues and lift up our voices that we may glorify you.

OFFERTORY SENTENCE. "We then that are strong ought to bear the infirmities of the weak, and not to please ourselves" (Rom. 15:1).

OFFERTORY PRAYER. As we are strengthened by your everlasting mercies, O God, so may we lend hope and strength to others. Use our offerings to that end, as they support the proclamation of the good news of Jesus Christ to the ends of the earth as well as in the dark corners of our own community.

PRAYER. Holy God, our Lord, majestic Name above all names, you are ever mindful of us and abidingly care for us; we praise and adore you! Eternal Presence, unfailing faithfulness, to cast our imaginations upon your grandeur and goodness is to find ourselves lost in wonder, love, and praise.

Holy, holy, holy, Lord God Almighty, early in this morning let our glad song rise to you. Ever attending Redeemer, we confess the shadow of our turning from you. The darkness then overwhelms us; our choices defeat us; we become sore afraid; we grieve your heart, harm others, disappoint ourselves. So, from your compassions that never fail, but are new every morning, unclench our hearts, cast away the darkness from our paths, soften our spirits with gentle grace, bind our wounds, touch our brokenness; open our angry fists, remove the cherished stones, lance the poison of unforgiveness from our souls. Restore us to full communion with you, with others, with ourselves.

Generous Parent to all these your children, where can we begin to thank you? How can we voice our gratitude? The alphabet of thanksgiving has no end. So accept our humble thanks for penguins and peacocks and polar bears, for psalms and prophets and parables, for pizzas and peppermint, for petunias. Thanks for Passover, for Pentecost, for the promise of paradox; for simple pleasures, for pain, for patience. We are grateful for paintings and pianists and poets. Thanks for prayer and peace, for your holy presence. And, in Christ, thanks for the firm promise of paradise.

We pray today, timeless God, for all those honoring the seasons in their lives, acknowledging your fresh bidding to them. And to every season there is a time. So teach us to know better what time it is in our lives, to apply our hearts to wisdom, our hands to service; to offer our all to you, for the kingdom and for your will. So may it be, in Christ.— William M. Johnson

LECTIONARY MESSAGE

Topic: It Is Hard to Wait!

TEXT: Exod. 32:1–14

Moses had been gone for some forty days. That is a long time to wait in a wild and desert place. The people were restless. They wondered if Moses was coming back at all. It was hard to wait, especially without a hint of their goal or the way to get there. Even the thunder on the mountain had ceased.

God was gone. Moses was absent. So this enterprising people called for Aaron to do something: "Make us gods for us to follow!" They took up a collection and Aaron made the image. Now they didn't have to wait anymore. They had a god. They said the right words: "These are the gods that brought you out of Egypt." And they had a party—to the Lord, of course.

It is so hard to wait. It seems easier, better, to do something, anything, than to have to wait—even if it requires making your own gods.

God understands impatience. He has his share of it. He had waited a long time to have his own people on the way to his land. And now they have already proved unworthy. He hadn't given them many rules to this point. But they could not keep even the most simple and basic rule: "No images!" He is ready to write them off, to wipe them out and start over.

Moses pleads for patience, for prudent patience. God had already done so much to bring the people this far. Why risk the bad publicity among the nations? He begs for God to change his mind, to cool his anger, to remember Abraham, Isaac, and Israel and his oath to them to put their descendants in God's own land. The words are cogent. God recognizes it. He does change his mind.

It is hard to wait. Hard for a people who cannot see the future. Hard for God who sees all too well the weaknesses and stubborn unwillingness to listen to him. But waiting is the name of the game.

God has worked and waited so long. His patience will not last forever, but amazingly he continues to wait. He took the long view in calling Abraham. Israelites at Sinai are just one stage in the long journey. Jesus tells of a king's marriage feast for his son (Matt. 22:1–14). He invited neighbors and friends, but they were too busy to come. He had to send out for others to be guests. Even among them one insulted the king by failing to dress properly. Jesus said that the kingdom of heaven is like that.

God is patient and merciful beyond measure. But eventually everyone must respond to the invitation or suffer the consequences of refusal.

Paul counsels with the Philippians about the problems of waiting for the Lord's return (Phil. 4:1–9). "Let all men know your forbearance. The Lord is at hand." Waiting for the great day of His return is hard.

But Paul admonishes them (and us) to be at peace with each other, to rejoice in the Lord, to pray and not be anxious. In this way waiting can bring the experience of the peace of God beyond all understanding, which makes waiting a joy.

Waiting is a time for reflection on all the good, the honorable, the pure, the gracious things. He promises that the God of peace will be with them. If only the Israelites at Sinai could have had Paul's instruction.

But we do have Paul's words. While we wait, do we do as he says? Or do we make our own gods and have a party? —John D. W. Watts

SUNDAY: OCTOBER TWENTIETH

SERVICE OF WORSHIP

Sermon: Grace: Love Beyond Meriting
TEXT: Eph. 2:1–10

I often think of the beautiful and rich words in our Christian vocabulary. They not only stimulate our minds, they move our hearts. We use such words as *light*, *love*, and *life*. But I sometimes think that

grace is the most beautiful of them all. It sets our hearts singing.

Grace pierces the heart of our faith. It is very comprehensive, gathering many other truths around it, and it reaches out in various directions. If, for some strange reason, we should be denied the use of all our theological words except six, grace would certainly be one of the six we would keep. It is that important.

I. *The centrality of grace.* Grace is central in our faith and the gospel we preach. Let me say five things about its centrality.

a. God is a God of grace who acts graciously. Both the Old and New Testaments bear witness to this. We sing "God of grace and God of glory."

This is no sentimental view of God. As we have already seen, God is just, executing his justice in judgment. His judgment can be fierce like the hot, blasting winds from the desert. His justice is in his hands of love, his judgment is in his hands of grace. His judgment is bent toward our salvation. He wounds to save, he cuts to heal.

b. Grace is central in Jesus Christ. The birth, life, death, and resurrection of Jesus are supreme expressions of God's grace. Jesus was the embodiment of perfect love, the expression of pure grace.

Paul's blessings to those early churches were essentially benedictions of grace. He gave one threefold (Trinitarian) benediction: "The grace of the Lord Jesus Christ and the love of God and the fellowship of the Holy Spirit be with you all" (2 Cor. 13:14). The grace of Jesus Christ comes first. Usually grace was sufficient within itself. He says it simply: "The grace of our Lord Jesus Christ be with you" (Rom. 16:20). He gave this simple blessing six different times.

c. Grace is central in the life of the Church. Not only does God save us by grace, but he calls us together as his people by grace. The Church must be a fellowship of grace. We are to live our lives in grace, we are to be a gracious people.

The Church should be one of those points of our world where the love of God is poured forth for the healing of our brokenness, where the grace of Christ overcomes our estrangement and alienation.

d. Grace is a great reality, linking the Old and New Testaments together. The God of grace is active in both, but he expresses his grace most savingly in Jesus of Nazareth.

The Book of Revelation tells of the consummation of history with the new heaven, the new earth, and the new city. As the epilogue comes to an end, a great invitation of grace is given: "The Spirit and the Bride say, 'Come.' And let him who hears say, 'Come.' And let him who is thirsty come, let him who desires take the water of life without price" (Rev. 22:17).

e. Paul is primarily responsible for making grace so central in our faith and in our vocabulary. He perceived it more clearly and spoke of it more forcefully than any other person.

Why this intense concern about and clear articulation of grace by Paul? It grew out of a dramatic and radical deliverance from the bondage of the law. For the first time Paul experienced the peace for which he had long sought but that had always eluded him. For the first time he felt forgiven and accepted by God. He was no longer caught in the meshes of law, he was free. What else could he do but talk about grace, and, as he did, he put it right at the center of the Christian vocabulary.

II. *Grace and human situation.* It is a grace that is not aloof and detached. It gets involved. It gets hurt and wounded. It is not cheap grace; it pays a price. It is grace that speaks to the human situation and addresses us in our need. Let me speak of three of these needs—frailty, sin, and death.

a. As human beings we are very weak and fragile. Paul talked about some weakness or handicap he had. He called it a thorn in the flesh. He said he asked Christ three times to remove it, but rather than removing it Christ gave him strength to accept it and live with it. But what was the enabling strength Christ gave? Grace. Christ said to him: "My grace is sufficient for you, for my power is made perfect in weakness" (2 Cor. 12:9a).

Grace and power, and it helped Paul accept his weakness. But it did more: Grace turned his weakness into strength.

b. Not only are we weak but we are sinful. Sin separates, alienates, and destroys. What is the answer to our sin? Grace.

One of the most wonderful verses of

Scripture is Romans 5:20. "But where sin increased, grace abounded all the more." There is more grace than there is guilt. There is enough grace in Jesus Christ to cover all the sin in the world. There is more forgiveness than there is condemnation. That is good news!

c. Not only are we weak and sinful but we are mortal. We die. And all things we create are like us. We build our mortality into everything we touch. Is there any answer to our mortality? Yes, grace is the answer.

Paul makes the same claim for grace: It gives life. "As sin reigned in death grace also might reign through righteousness to eternal life through Jesus Christ, our Lord" (Rom. 5:21).

There is a mystery that hangs over the New Testament idea of eternal life. It seems so elusive, so hard to grasp and understand. But maybe it is more simple than it seems. What if grace restores a broken relationship with God who is the primary source of life? That is what grace does. It puts us in touch with the spring of life from which sin has cut us off, and nothing can ever break that relationship again. That is to have eternal life.

III. *Grace when it is not called grace.* The reality of grace occurs often without the term. Grace is often found in the Bible without the word. While a concordance is indeed a helpful tool, here is one of its great weaknesses: It depends on key words to find the truth. But where the truth occurs without a pivotal word, the concordance is helpless.

Let us look at some of those passages where grace is present but the term is missing (see Isa. 1:18, 55:1).

a. Consider the parable of the workers in the vineyard (Matt. 20:1–16). There is a strangeness about grace. The story sounds odd to us and doesn't seem quite right. We feel that those who worked all day got cheated. But what we forget is that grace is not common, it is uncommon. The order of grace lies beyond the order of justice, yet is constantly intersecting it. On those levels of life that matter most, we live by grace. When it comes to love, forgiveness, reconciliation, and

salvation, we are like those men who worked for only one hour in the cool of the day. We are recipients of grace.

b. Another example is the prodigal son. He was a bad boy. He had squandered his wealth, had been reckless and immoral, besmirched his name, and brought disgrace to his family. When at last he stood before his father he was a pitiable and tragic figure. The father began by saying: "This is Joseph. He has been away from home for a long time and I thought he was dead. But he has returned home. Rejoice with me." And a long, loud applause went up. It was all grace, yet the word *grace* does not occur.

IV. The Christian religion is a religion of grace, although we are shocked to see how often we Christians keep slipping back into legalism.

Let us look at a religion of law versus a religion of grace as seen in Jesus. We will look at one of his stories.

a. Let us return to the prodigal son. The father accepted the prodigal boy back into the family freely, spontaneously, and lovingly. He laid down no laws, insisted on no restitution, and did not put his son on probation.

But how different with the elder son. The story ends with him, who had stayed home and had been so dutiful, a slinking, sulking character standing in the shadows of the banquet hall within the sound of the music and dancing. And the father did not dispute his word. It was all true. Yet, he did not know the meaning of grace. His legalism had made the elder brother proud, censorious, and judgmental, drying up the milk of human compassion in his heart.

The story comes to such a strange end. The bad boy is saved, the "good" boy is lost. And the difference was grace. The bad boy was humble enough to accept it, and the "good" boy was too proud to receive it.

b. We are constantly being tempted by legalism. One of your most important tasks will be to prevent yourself from slipping into it and help keep your people from falling into it.

We have to ask: What makes legalism so appealing? It makes us harsh, proud, and judgmental, drying up our compassion. We get caught in its meshes of requirements like a fly in a spider's web, and the more we struggle to go free the more entangled we become. It enslaves us and then it destroys us.

c. There is only one answer to legalism and that is grace. Jesus knew this and Paul found it out. Every generation has to learn that answer again.

Grace is such a wonderful and surprising thing. Maybe preaching, more than anything else, is announcing the surprises of grace.—Chevis F. Horne

Illustrations

A FREE GIFT.   I remember as a young boy slipping into my uncle's house early one morning before the day's work on the farm began. My uncle and aunt were the first people in our community to own a radio, and I was endlessly fascinated by it. There was a miracle before my eyes! That morning I got a sermon, and the preacher was using as his text Romans 6:23: "For the wages of sin is death, but the free gift of God is eternal life in Christ Jesus our Lord." He was not a good preacher, but he had a great text, which he repeated over and over again. That great truth cast a spell over me from which I have never gone free. Indeed, I don't want to be free of it. I can still feel its power. It spoke of eternal life as the free gift of God. It is of grace.— Chevis F. Horne

GRACE IN ACTION.   Out of the Armenian atrocities comes the story of a young woman and her brother who were pursued down the street by a Turkish soldier, cornered in an angle of the wall, and the brother slain before the sister's eyes. She dodged down an alley, leaped a wall, and escaped. Later, being a nurse, she was forced by the Turkish authorities to work in a military hospital. One day the same Turkish soldier who had slain her brother was brought into the ward. He was very ill, and a slight inattention would ensure his death. One side of her nature cried "Revenge"; the other "Love." The better side conquered, and

she nursed him as carefully as any other patient in the ward. The soldier recognized her, and finally, unable to restrain his curiosity, he asked the nurse why she did not let him die. When she replied, "I am a follower of him who said, 'Love your enemies and do them good,' " he was silent for a long interval, then at last he spoke: "I never knew that there was such a religion. If that is your religion, tell me more about it, for I want it."— Frederick Keller Stamm

SERMON SUGGESTIONS

Topic: The Great Mystery
TEXT: Exod. 33:12–23, especially verses 20–23
(1) God does not put himself at our disposal, so that we would be able to surround him with our intellect. (2) However, God has disclosed all we need to know about him in his revelation through prophets and seers and in a fullness in his incarnate Word. (3) Also, it is through the Holy Spirit that this revelation becomes real and personal in our experience.

Topic: When the Good News Does Its Work
TEXT: 1 Thess. 1:1–10 NRSV
(1) It comes in power, in the Holy Spirit, and with full conviction. (2) It is received with joy inspired by the Holy Spirit, in spite of persecution. (3) It makes those who receive it worthy and inspiring examples to others.

Worship Aids

CALL TO WORSHIP.   "Exalt ye the Lord our God, and worship at his footstool; for he is holy" (Ps. 99:5).

INVOCATION.   Holy, holy, holy, Lord God of Hosts. We worship and adore you, we draw near to catch your whispers and contemplate your teachings. Show us the way and help us walk in it, our Maker and our God.—E. Lee Phillips

OFFERTORY SENTENCE.   "Give unto the Lord, O ye kindreds of the people, give unto the Lord glory and strength. Give unto the Lord the glory due unto his name; bring an offering, and come into his courts" (Ps. 96:7–8).

OFFERTORY PRAYER. Lord Jesus Christ, you for the joy set before you, endured the cross, despising the shame. Give us the faith and the vision to see beyond our difficulties and self-denials and contemplate the joy that service and sacrifice can bring. Grant that we may find joy in what we do even now.

PRAYER. We thank you, Father, that you are always nearby, watching over us even when our restlessness leads us away from you. We all wander away from time to time. Sometimes it takes entirely too long for us to realize what we've done and how far away we've strayed before we turn around. We are grateful that you patiently wait for us to come to our senses, that you never give up on us, you never stop loving us, you never stop longing for us to return—no matter what we've done, where we've been, and how much we've tested your patience.

Every day we live, Lord, we are reminded that our thoughts are not your thoughts and our ways are not your ways. We are affected more by the standards of our world than by the demands of your Word. We worry about money and property—that we may not have enough. We're anxious about the economy—about taxes and inflation. We don't know what we'll do, how we'll get by if times get much harder. We don't know how to reconcile your Word with the harsh realities of life as we find them every day. We don't fully understand all that you say that seems to contradict the way life really is: like losing life in order to find it; and, that the way to honor is through humility; and this Word about giving generously and liberally leading to true wealth.

We really want to honor you with our lives, Father. But we confess that we've not learned yet to depend upon you to meet our needs. We've not learned yet to rely wholeheartedly upon your promises. Forgive us, God. In many ways, we are

good people. And yet, in so many ways we are still unredeemed. Hear us now, as we pray for the freshness of your Spirit to renew our faith, to brighten our hopes, and to finish the work you have begun in us through the power and the blood of Jesus Christ our Lord, in whose name I pray.—Gary C. Redding

LECTIONARY MESSAGE

Topic: God and Caesar

TEXT: Matt. 22:15–22

I. By this point in his ministry, Jesus had alienated the most powerful people in Palestine. The Pharisees, the dogged protectors of orthodoxy, hated him for rejecting their understanding of the Law and accusing them of hypocrisy. To discredit him with the masses, they conspired with the Herodians, with whom they had little in common. While the Pharisees avoided Gentiles whenever possible, the Herodians aided the Roman occupiers by supporting the Herod family, their puppet regime in Galilee. The Pharisees and Herodians disliked each other intensely, but they disliked Jesus even more. After piling on the flattery, they asked him a not-so-simple question, one they were certain would undercut his popularity no matter how he answered it: "Is it right to pay taxes to Caesar or not?"

The question was about the annual poll (or head) tax that Rome assessed on every Jewish man and woman. The Jews (with the exception of the Herodians) hated the tax for two reasons: First, on political grounds, they resented having to finance their own oppression; and second, on religious grounds, they believed that paying the tax had blasphemous and idolatrous overtones. Roman tax collectors would accept only the silver denarius on which was stamped the emperor's image and the inscription "Tiberius Caesar, Son of the Divine Augustus and High Priest." Devout Jews feared that using the coin was against the Mosaic Law's ban on "graven images" (Exod. 20:4). When the tax was first imposed in A.D. 6, Jews rioted in protest; and some twenty-five years later, most Jews still hated paying it.

It is easy to see Jesus' dilemma and why his enemies thought they had him either way: If Jesus said that it was wrong to pay the tax, then the Herodians could report his treason to their Roman allies; but if he endorsed paying the tax, the Pharisees could undercut his standing with the Jewish people.

Jesus immediately understood what they were trying to do. "Hypocrites," he replied. "Show me the coin used for paying the tax." Quickly—and somewhat sheepishly, we assume—the Pharisees produced the idolatrous coin. "Whose portrait is this? And whose inscription?" When they answered, "Caesar's," they found themselves ensnared in their own trap. "Give to Caesar what is Caesar's, and to God what is God's." There was nothing else to say, so they went away, amazed at Jesus' deftness.

II. A clever answer, to be sure, but what was Jesus getting at? His meaning is especially important now, when so many Christians are struggling with questions about the relationship between church and state and the loyalties that believers owe to God and government.

One thing we can be sure of: Jesus is not here arguing for two equally legitimate but separate spheres in human life, the social/political and the religious. I once heard a successful businessman interrupt a lecture on Christian ethics in the marketplace with the statement, "Religion is religion, but business is business." Others might be tempted to say, "Religion is religion, but politics is politics." Students of contemporary culture know that one of the characteristics of "modernity" is the "privatization of religion," the tendency to shove religious convictions to the margins of life and make them nothing more than a matter of personal preference with no significance outside the self. But the God of history and the nations is not so easily set aside or sequestered into some private zone far removed from the public square. Jesus did not mean that Caesar and God have equal claims on our lives or that when it comes to things political, God has no rightful claims at all.

What amazed the Pharisees and the Herodians about Jesus' response was how he refocused the issue to something much bigger than they had intended. In essence Jesus said, Give Caesar what he has coming, a silver coin with his image on it. It's already his anyway, so let him have it back. But give back to God all that God deserves, which is *everything, including yourselves*.

If we are right about Jesus' intentions, then we must not try to develop a full-blown political theology from his words or use them to answer all the practical questions we may bring to the text. From this passage we cannot learn how or when to turn Christian convictions into public policy or how to vote in the next election. The fact of the matter is that Jesus did not say much about such things; and the rest of the New Testament provides different perspectives on the believer's relationship to human government. In Romans 13 Paul paints a positive picture of the role of government and commands Christians to obey it; but in Revelation 13 the author describes a government gone demonic and warns believers to resist it unto death. According to the Book of Acts, it did not take Jesus' followers long to discover that "we must obey God rather than men" (Acts 5:29).

What we owe to God is infinitely more than we owe to Caesar. The words of I Peter 2:17 help put the issue into perspective: "Fear God, honor the king." There is a world of difference between those two obligations, no matter where we draw the line between God and the government. In the last resort, then, Caesar is Caesar, but God is God.—Timothy Weber

SUNDAY: OCTOBER TWENTY-SEVENTH

SERVICE OF WORSHIP

Sermon: The Sin of Prayerlessness

TEXT: 1 Sam. 12:19–25

I.a. A thousand years before the birth of Jesus, a man named Samuel stood before his nation. Forty years earlier, in one of the darkest periods of Israel's history, he had assumed national leadership. The government was corrupt, and the people were morally degenerate.

He was a man of strong, dominating personality. But Samuel was preeminently a man of prayer and intercession. Throughout 1 Samuel, you can read his incessant, impassioned prayers for his nation.

As Samuel grew older, the people became anxious for a change! They did not merely want a replacement for Samuel. They demanded comprehensive government reform. They were tired of being led by a prophet. They wanted to be like all the other nations. Give them a king!

Reluctantly, Samuel yielded to the people's demand and anointed Saul to be king of Israel. But, as the transition in governments was being made, the people became aware of the Lord's disfavor upon what they were doing. So, they asked Samuel: "Pray for your servants to the Lord your God, that we may not die; for we have added to all our other sins this evil, to ask for ourselves a king" (1 Sam. 12:19).

And, Samuel replied: "Far be it for me that I should sin against the Lord by ceasing to pray for you. . . ." (1 Sam. 12:24).

It's an absolutely remarkable statement. In essence, Samuel said: "I have always prayed for you, and I will never, never, never, never give up—even when I disagree with you, when I'm peeved and frustrated with you! To ever quit praying for you would be a sin against the Lord!"

Samuel believed that there is no more significant involvement in another person's life than prayer. And if that is true, prayer is more powerful in its positive impact upon your children than anything you can give them, including money, car, and college tuition. Prayer is more helpful to your co-workers than a compliment, more encouraging to your friends than any thoughtful act or gesture you can imagine, and demonstrates more love for your husband or wife than a tender embrace!

b. I doubt that in a congregation like this, there are many people who do not pray at all. However, prayerlessness is not only the complete disregard for power. It also means the failure to pray less than we need to, less than the Father desires, and less than we know we should. And that definition cuts a wide swath that includes us all!

Why do we fail to pray as we really should—especially for those for whom we care so genuinely—our children, our husband or wife, our friends at the church, our neighbors next door, our co-workers? Samuel viewed the problem as radically more serious than a mere character flaw, personal weakness, or indication of an overcrowded schedule and poor time-management skills.

If you and I are able to explain away our prayerlessness with the same alibis we use to make allowances for forgetfulness, short tempers that flare up without warning, chain-smoking, or dependence upon Valium or other relaxing substances, we will likely never become prayerful individuals. Self-improvement programs simply do not strengthen all the areas of weakness and failure in our life.

II. Samuel identified prayerlessness as sin!

a. It is sin because it is a violation of God's command. Jesus said: we "ought always to pray and not lose heart" (Luke 18:1). The word "ought" implies a moral obligation, a sacred duty. It is, then, a responsibility placed upon every Christian by the Lord himself.

There are many things we *ought* to do. We *ought* to give our money regularly and generously to support his work (1

Cor. 16:2; 2 Cor. 9:6–7). Giving is a sacred duty.

We *ought* to obey God rather than other people (Acts 5:29). If we are ever forced to choose between obedience to God and obedience to men, we must be true to God. It is a spiritual obligation.

Husbands *ought* to love their wives as Christ loved the Church (Eph. 5:25–28). As Jesus died for the Church without murmuring and complaining, men ought gladly and joyfully to sacrifice for their wives. Most marriages and homes would be radically changed if men would obey this command.

These are just a few of the *oughts* of the Christian life. And the obligation to pray is just as much a duty, a responsibility, as any of these *oughts*. Just as surely as we ought to give, and we ought to love, and we ought to live right, and we ought to help people, so we ought to pray.

b. Prayerlessness is sin because it is opposed to the purpose and plan of God. What God does in the world and individual lives, he does through prayer. The apostle James wrote: "Pray for one another. The prayer of a righteous man has great power in its effects. Elijah was a man just like us and he prayed fervently that it might not rain, and for three years and six months it did not rain on the earth. Then he prayed again and the heaven gave rain, and the earth brought forth its fruit (James 5:16–18).

Prayer has great power. It can change life. Prayer can save a soul. It can revive a church. Prayer can empower a person. It can turn a life around. Knowing what power there is in prayer, it is a sin to fail to use it.

c. Prayerlessness is sin because it denies pleasure to God. The wise man of the Old Testament wrote: "The prayer of the upright is his delight" (Prov. 15:8). Imagine that! God enjoys my praying! Besides all the benefits I derive from praying, God also finds joy!

d. There is another reason why prayerlessness is sin: It defeats the power of God. Because he was a man of prayer, the apostle Paul could write: "I can do all things through Christ who strengthens me" (Phil. 4:13).

To the Romans, he confessed that he did not always know how or what to pray. But in those moments, "the Spirit himself intercedes for us with sighs too deep for words.... The Spirit intercedes for the saints according to the will of God" (8:26, 27). And because Paul never, never, never gave up praying for those whom he loved—even when he did know how or what to pray—he had a confidence that "in all things we are more than conquerors through him who loves us" (Rom. 8:37).

(1) If you pray, God will give you the strength to keep getting up and starting over every time Satan knocks you down. But if you pray, and never, never, never give up praying, by God's grace, you shall eventually be able to stand your ground, hold your position, and ultimately win the victory over sin.

(2) What's more, you will even be able to influence the outcome of similar struggles in others' lives. The apostle Paul endured many hardships as a missionary. His life was often threatened, and he faced constant danger as he preached the gospel. But he wrote to thank his Christian friends by saying, "You have helped us through your prayers" (2 Cor. 1:11).

You need to see that. Prayer is a way to help people. Is it any wonder, then, that Paul urged us to pray for everyone? (1 Tim. 2:1).—Gary C. Redding

Illustrations

SUPPORT FOR PRAYER. Support for intercessory prayer at times comes from the most unexpected sources. The practice of prayer as meditation has been a characteristic of Catholic mysticism, and belief in prayer as petition has been professed much by Protestant pietism, but theological support now appears in some forms of process theology. Process philosophy, as existential philosophy, may be atheistic, but the emphasis on process as reality often opens new perspectives for belief in God and prayer. Both God and man are so involved in the creative process that it becomes logical to believe that prayer may change not only things and persons but even God himself! Objective ideas are potentialities or possibilities that God may accept or reject as concrete actualities. Skepticism, then, not science, is the greatest hindrance to prayer.—Dale Moody

THE FAITHFULNESS OF GOD.   The Christian apprehends God's working preeminently in the life, death, and Resurrection of Jesus Christ, and in him it discerns God's weakness and God's strength. Here is Love that suffers, but here also is Love that triumphs. Tragedy itself, accepted, endured, transfigured, and redeemed, ministers to a new and richer life. Sin, suffering, and death are woven into the pattern of divine providence. Contrary to his will they are rendered subservient to his will. So faith discerns, and hope is renewed. Love will have its perfect way. God's kingdom is, and is to come.—Peter Baelz

SERMON SUGGESTIONS

Topic: Moses: The Summing Up
TEXT: Deut. 34:1–12
(1) He was able to see what God had accomplished through him. (2) He was appropriately honored and mourned when he died. (3) His work was carried forward by Joshua, whom Moses had appointed to continue the task.

Topic: Paul's Courageous Service to Christ
TEXT: 1 Thess. 2:1–8
(1) It was in spite of heavy opposition. (2) It was not motivated by greed. (3) It was with tender, caring, self-giving devotion.

Worship Aids

CALL TO WORSHIP.   "Lord, thou hast been our dwelling place in all generations. Before the mountains were brought forth, or ever thou hadst formed the earth and the world, even from everlasting to everlasting, thou art God" (Ps. 90:1–2).

INVOCATION.   Almighty God, in our mortality we stand in the presence of your eternity. Except for your redeeming love and care we would seem to be utterly insignificant. As we contemplate your towering greatness, may we at the same time always remember your condescending love. We worship you now: help us to trust you always.

OFFERTORY SENTENCE.   "Thy prayers and thine alms are come up for a memorial before God" (Acts 10:4).

OFFERTORY PRAYER.   We know, our loving Father, that you delight in our prayers and that you are pleased with our deeds of mercy. But we are assured that you desire that we do the less dramatic thing also, as we bring our offerings from week to week to this place, so that the many important works of your kingdom may be supported. We thank you for this privilege.

PRAYER.   In the face of tragedy, O God, we do come confessing that we do not know how we should feel, or how we should pray. But, yet, in our better moments, we sense that you are calling us to feel—to feel deeply—and to pray—to pray earnestly. We do find ourselves wrestling with the strange mystery of your grace and the faithfulness of your love for all the world and for every person.

In our perplexity we discover ourselves in good company, for when the apostle Paul attempted to fathom the mystery of your grace, he could but exclaim: "O depth of the riches and wisdom and knowledge of God! How unsearchable are his judgments and how inscrutable his ways!"

May we realize with the apostle that we are not being called to explain the inexplicable, but to obey your word of love, which has been revealed, in Christ.

In the needs of our sisters and brothers we hear your call: "Whom shall I send, and who will go for us?" May we respond with the dispatch of young Isaiah when to the needs of his day, he committed: "Here am I, Lord, send me!"

We praise you, O God of all comfort, for all the compassion being expressed by so many both near and far. Strengthen in us and in all peoples the sense of the community to which you have been calling humankind from the beginning and is now present in the coming of your kingdom in Christ.

We praise you, on this occasion, for the beautiful and faithful witness of our youth and are grateful for the Church that fosters for them growing experiences.

We pray for those who teach in our schools, colleges, and universities that they may see their profession as a high calling. May these men and women be persons with creative minds and loving hearts awakening the minds of students to challenging thoughts and enlarging their hearts with a noble purpose.

Grant to our sons and daughters and our grandchildren an enthusiastic grasping of their opportunities to learn that this year may be invested wisely.

For those among us suffering the threat and pain of illness, we pray courage and a sense of wholeness that defies any disintegration of the physical.

For those of us lonely in bereavement we pray the companionship of the Good Shepherd to strengthen and encourage.

For those wrestling with difficult decisions, we pray the Light of your presence.—John Thompson

LECTIONARY MESSAGE

Topic: The Greatest Commandment

TEXT: Matt. 22:34–40

The time had come for the greatest teacher to tell us the greatest commandment.

Jesus had become a problem to the Jewish authorities and the professional religious community. He was an outsider with a growing following. He was teaching, performing miracles, and answering questions. In controversy with some of the leading figures of his day, Jesus was confronting them and debating with them, and the crowd thought he was wonderful.

An expert in the Law was selected to test Jesus with a difficult question. The religious authorities wanted to trap Jesus into making a controversial statement so they could discredit him. They believed themselves to be experts in the Law and were sure they could outwit Jesus.

The question was to name the greatest commandment in the Law. Since there were hundreds of laws and relative importance had been given different laws, any answer would be contentious.

But Jesus did answer. He combined two Old Testament commandments and added a remarkable teaching that made "love" the fulfillment of all the commandments and laws.

"Love the Lord your God with all your heart and with all your soul and with all your mind." Jesus gave this as the greatest commandment. Then he added a second, "Love your neighbor as yourself."

Love is the key word in both commandments. Love is most often understood as a way of responding to something that appeals to us. This love comes into being because something is lovable and evokes love in relation to it. When we love something of beauty or value, we want to acquire it.

But the love in both commandments is not this type of love. This is a radically different concept of love that grows out of biblical revelation. This is the type of love that is directed by our will and can be commanded as a duty. God showed us ultimate divine love, since Christ died for us. We are in return to love even our enemies.

Every week we hear of evil events in a number of locations. How can we break this curse of destruction? How can we relate to the unlovables in our midst? The power of this new type of love can overcome evil. We must learn to reach out with the gift of love.

Jesus then summarized the two commandments in a new and wonderful way. "All the Law and the Prophets hang on these two Commandments." Taken together "the Law" and "the prophets" include the entire Old Testament. Jesus has combined and enlarged upon all Old Testament teaching.

We all desire a relationship with God that is deeply personal and intensely satisfying. To experience this means paying the price to walk with God. The joy of knowing Jesus is followed by the realization that many of his instructions require us to give the gift of love to someone who is unlovable.

We have heard the Lord's instructions about the two "love commandments." We have heard that all the Law and the prophets hang on these two commandments. This requires us to forget about self and trying to make a good impression, to direct our efforts to loving others, and to grow and direct our thoughts to loving God with all our hearts and souls and minds.—Burton Van Dyke

SUNDAY: NOVEMBER THIRD

SERVICE OF WORSHIP

Sermon: Something to Live By

Text: Isa. 38:16

Something to live by? Let us look at life for a moment and ask ourselves: What are the things by which some people try to live?

Here is a person who claims he lives by sheer luck.

Here is another person who claims she lives by her wits.

Here is still another person who claims to live by his successes.

Now in some quarters and among some people, these may appear as sensible and satisfactory ways to live, especially among those who have become involved so frantically in the means of life that they have lost sight of the ends. But what happens when for some reason a person's luck runs out; or she comes to her wits' end; or his grand escalator of success hesitates and grinds to a sickening halt. By what then does any one of us live?

Our text brings us to one of those great and moving human experiences that only the Bible seems able to present. It takes us way back almost 2,700 years and about 750 years before Christ was born, when Hezekiah, king of Judah, was gravely ill and moving near to the gates of death. He had been a good king and had instituted many worthy reforms, but now it seemed that the bottom had dropped out of everything. All around his little country other nations were boiling in trouble and revolutions, and even in the best of times, Judah was threatened by the grim shadow of the Syrian army. And now, double trouble was on Hezekiah's doorstep: he had no son to succeed him on the throne—always a calamity to any Jewish king—and what was more, he himself was only in midlife, with a faultless record of faithful service behind him, but ahead, only the grim reminder of the prophet Isaiah, "Set your house in order, Hezekiah, because you are going to die."

So, as the king lay upon his bed through all these feverish hours, he was confronted with stern realities: the shortness of life, the suddenness of death, and the dark mystery of the unseen. No wonder he turned his face to the wall and prayed to God and wept, and seemingly asked the age-old question: why? Then the word of the Lord came to Isaiah to go to tell the king that God had heard his prayer and the prayers of his people and that he was going to live! Out of the valley of the shadow Hezekiah came with a song of thanksgiving in his heart and upon his life this glorious testimony: "O Lord, by these things men live!"

But, today, what word does Hezekiah bring to inquiring minds and anxious hearts as we worship in our contemporary sanctuaries? What did he bring back from this experience, from this brush with the unseen, from this crisis that had brought him to the very edge of things? What did he mean really when he declared, "O Lord, by these things men live"?

I. Hezekiah learned: *We simply cannot live without God.* Can't you picture Hezekiah as he basked in the prosperity of his kingdom? He had it made, so to speak. Comfortably ensconced in his royal palace, surrounded by a magnificent collection of art and sculpture, he had nothing to fear, especially from his own people, for his reforms had rendered them amiable, docile, and quiet. But then the blow fell and the king was brought face-to-face with death. Yet, out of this painful and shattering encounter, he learned a new meaning to life, namely, the ultimate reality of all life is God. And out of the king's bedchamber, where steps had been quiet and words were in low whispers, the voice of Hezekiah was heard: "God himself has done it. He loved my soul out of the pit of destruction. O Lord, by these things men live!"

How true can this experience be for you and me today! Are we not inclined to go through life light-heartedly, absorbed with our business, our successes, and our hobbies, and frequently the least of our concerns is he who made it all?

But then suddenly, life goes to pieces: a loved one dies and the house is sorely empty; a little one has an accident and you have to watch him hobble and stumble all his days; or a person in whom you trusted proves unfaithful and leaves a bleeding gash in your soul. And you turn your tear-streaked face to the wall and you long for the clutch of a hand that is strong, warm, and true, but everything the world offers seems so insufficient, disappointing, and helpless. Moreover, any speculating about God being the "ground of being" leaves you more deeply wounded and hurt. Everything that is in you cries out for a conscious fellowship; not that of the crowd, but of some *other one;* not as an avenue of escape, but someone with whom you can meet the issue head-on. As Karl Barth remarked, "Communion with God is not a dash into security, but a walk towards reality." And that reality that you and I cherish as a personal God will always respond when we trust him; will always meet our loyalty with his loyalty; and whenever you and I are in the dark, he is the only power that can help, deliver, and gladden our souls.

II. Hezekiah learned: *We cannot live without God's forgiveness.* Just as Hezekiah learned that God was the primary neces-

sity to all living, so also only God could give him a fresh start, because only God could forgive. He said, "Thou hast cast all my sins behind thy back" (v. 17). Now he was to have a new beginning, but it was to come through a new sense of God's forgiveness.

Now, regardless of what some people think and feel today, no one of us can ride roughshod over life. No person can presume that his or her will is absolute. None can stride across the world and truculently demand their own selfish rights. Life consists of sunshine and shadow, of give and take, of mountain peaks and lonely valleys, of strange reverses and new beginnings. And every act of forgiveness is for you and me a new start. And it is in and through these fresh beginnings that you and I really live.

No one can go on, day after day, adding to the ball of tangled tensions within them, without facing up to the need of a "soul washing" every now and then. And this comes when you strike the impossibility of being able by yourself to go on, and you stumble to your knees at the throne of grace and say, "Nothing in my hand I bring; simply to thy cross I cling." And God comes then to you and says, "Your sins are forgiven. Go and sin no more." "O Lord, by these things men live."

III. Hezekiah learned: *We cannot live without God's love.* The English writer D. H. Lawrence has a story called "The Man Who Loved Islands." It tells of a man who hated other people and who bought an island in order to be totally excluded from them. But he found there no satisfaction, so he bought and moved to another island, and then another and another, until finally he lost his mind. How very much we, too, do love our islands! We were made for life together, but too often and too long we stew in the misery of our isolation. We do not see that what we really need is to acknowledge and accept the fact that there is someone who loves us; someone who is trying to break through to us and tell us: You are my concern; you are of the highest value to me; your spiritual good is the burden of my spirit.

This is the thing by which we live! And this is what God alone can give you and me. We urge people to love God, but what a difference would occur if all of us were to acknowledge truly that God loves us. Every soul in the far country is there because of a broken relationship with the Father's love. For no person can be at war with God without being at war with himself or herself, with the community, and everything in the environment. A woman once said, "I accepted the love of God, and now I am able to love people as I never did before." This is the key to reconciliation between God and his world. This is the only way to that sisterhood and brotherhood that transcends race, color, and creed.

God's reconciling love does not deal with one side of life and neglect the other; nor embrace one group and overlook the other; nor focus upon one evil and ignore the other. God's love is pitted against sin in whatever form it takes. And only when you and I accept and know and *live* this love of God, will we learn how far it reaches; how many it includes; how deep it goes; and how much it costs.

Jesus said: "God so loved the world that he gave his only begotten Son, that *whosoever* believes in him should not perish but have everlasting life." "O Lord, by these things men live."—Donald Macleod

Illustrations

IMPETUS FOR LIVING.   Every person wants a big faith, for every normal person wants to make the most of his experience on earth. *But a big faith begins in belief that this is a spiritual universe.* Belief has its intellectual value. William James said in his great Gifford lectures that the average person in middle age who does not believe in a God who answers prayer and who ensures personal immortality after the grave, will grow sullen, caustic, melancholy, and even bestial. It was only a belief in a God who cared that saved Leo Tolstoy from suicide and gave him his impetus for his heroic attempt to live the Christian life.—Thomas S. Kepler

MORE THAN WE CAN SEE.   A man once saw a boy flying a kite. Observing something a little peculiar about the way he walked with the string, he approached and found the lad was blind. "Do you like flying your kite?" he asked.

"Oh, yes, sir," was the reply.

"But how is that, when you cannot see it?" was the next question.

"I can't see it," said the boy, "but I can feel it tuggin'!" —John Trevor Davies

SERMON SUGGESTIONS

Topic: How to Know That God Is with Us

TEXT: Josh. 3:3–17

(1) Some helpful ways: (a) Certain kinds of success may encourage us, verse 10; (b) A miracle may confirm our confidence, verses 11–17. (2) The best ways: (a) the coming of God in Christ to us (see Matt. 1:23); (b) personal experience of the Holy Spirit (see John 14:15–17).

Topic: The Making of a True Minister

TEXT: 1 Thess. 2:9–13

(1) Through selfless labor and toil. (2) Through blameless conduct. (3) Through active "parental" concern for the spiritual growth of those in one's care.

Worship Aids

CALL TO WORSHIP.   "O give thanks unto the Lord, for he is good: for his mercy endureth forever. Let the redeemed of the Lord say so, whom he hath redeemed from the hand of the enemy" (Ps. 107:1–2).

INVOCATION.   We are here, O Lord, to praise you and to seek how better to glorify you in our lives. Give us such discernment that we may see clearly how you have blessed us, and help us to share our faith with others.

OFFERTORY SENTENCE.   "Let the beauty of the Lord our God be upon us: and establish thou the work of our hands upon us; yea, the work of our hands establish thou it" (Ps. 90:17).

OFFERTORY PRAYER.   God of all good, you have rewarded our labors, and we acknowledge with gratitude your favor and do now dedicate a share of our material gains to the even more satisfying ministries of the Spirit.

PRAYER.   Eternal Father, we gather to rediscover ourselves and to rededicate ourselves to Jesus Christ.

Because we are involved in the sights and sounds, the struggles and confusions of the day, we need an hour dedicated to spiritual concentration. For the moment, at least, enable the salesman to relax and forget his urge to sell. Let the worried businessmen drop their burdens and kneel before the cross. Let executives forget tomorrow's decisions. Let office personnel lay aside their coming schedules, and cause concerned parents to experience a resurgence of hope and love. Let the confused find clarity; the sad, comfort; the weak, strength; the unsuccessful, courage; the successful, humility; and the doubter, faith.

Father, you have abundantly provided for our every need. Help us to recognize the needs and inequities in the world and bend our fortunes and energies to setting them right.

We ask that you bless your Church with perseverance and power, love and loyalty to Jesus. Keep us pure in our intentions, open to the leadership of the Holy Spirit and compassionate in our dealings with one another. In times when our souls are tired and tested, give us knowledge and the will to remain faithful and serving in Jesus' name.

May our stewardship constrain us to put more into the Church than we take out. Help us to see and grasp the unlimited opportunities that are ours to do Christian service. Cause us to be thankful for the privilege of supporting the Church, and save us from equating stewardship with charity. In all that we do may we never underestimate the importance and potential of those who love and serve the Lord and are faithful to his Church.—Henry Fields

LECTIONARY MESSAGE

Topic: Christ's Kind of Leader

TEXT: Matt. 23:1–12

"Hello, Reverend." "Hey, Padre." See ya, Parson." Anybody who has been a preacher for any length of time has heard every possible title—honorific or humorous. Our Gospel text for today makes us preachers a bit uneasy with such titles, as well it should. But is this just a warning against usurping terminology that rightly refers to the Divinity?

The nicely phrased maxim in verse 12 indicates that there is more to this teaching than nomenclature. When Jesus says, "All who exalt themselves will be humbled and all who humble themselves will be exalted" (NRSV), he points to something much deeper than titles. Don't you hear echoing in that statement the beatitude, "Blessed are the meek, for they will inherit the earth"?

Once again we hear Jesus reminding us that his is a dominion of humility. To be a follower of Jesus means to be a servant, at the disposal of others. When we consider the whole lesson, we see that it is not a matter of terminology; it is a matter of accountability.

I. *To be disciples of Jesus we are to be accountable first and primarily to God.* It is only appropriate that we strive to be faithful to the God who has been faithful to us—the God who in Christ was faithful "to the point of death—even death on a cross" (Phil. 2:8 NRSV). Jesus also points out that our activities directed toward God should not draw attention to ourselves.

All this talk about phylacteries, fringes, and the best seats must have been recalled and retold by the early Church (it appears also in Mark and Luke) for more than their enjoyment of Jesus' attacking the scribes and Pharisees. This was addressed to disciples to remind them and us that the praise of God and the obedience of God are parts of the disciple's accountability to God and so should not draw attention to ourselves. God is our primary point of reference.

II. *To be disciples of Jesus we are to be accountable to ourselves.* Jesus warned those first disciples against the tendency, as people today put it, to talk the talk but not walk the walk.

We find it all too easy both to explain away the harder teachings of Jesus and to justify our moral lapses. The early Church recognized the radical nature of the expectations Jesus held for his followers. Their righteousness was to exceed that of even the scribes and Pharisees (Matt. 5:20). They were to be perfect, as their heavenly Father is perfect (Matt. 5:48). The lives of the followers of Jesus should be characterized not by explanation and justification but by consistency and integrity. That is our accountability to ourselves.

III. *To be disciples of Jesus we are to be accountable to our fellow human beings.* "Servant" is not a very attractive concept in our culture. However, its meaning has changed little since Jesus said, "The greatest among you will be your servant" (v. 11 NRSV). He had used an even stronger term earlier (Matt. 20:27–28) when he told the twelve, "Whoever wishes to be first among you must be your slave," which he followed up with, "just as the Son of Man came not to be served but to serve, and to give his life a ransom for many."

To follow *that* leader means to serve others, whatever such service might demand of us. Our Lord's call comes to us whenever, wherever, and however there is human need we can fill.

Such service is humble work. This does not mean that Christians are to have inferiority complexes. Once we recognize that in the sight of God we are worth the life of Jesus and that God makes it possible for us to live lives of integrity, we should be able to find personal satisfaction in humble service. And then words like Paul's can ring true on our lips, too:

"You remember our labor and toil, brothers and sisters; we worked night and day, so that we might not burden any of you while we proclaimed to you the gospel of God. You are witnesses, and God also, how pure, upright, and blameless our conduct was toward you believers. As you know, we dealt with each of you like a father with his children, urging and encouraging you and pleading that you lead a life worthy of God, who calls you into his own kingdom and glory" (1 Thess. 2:9–13 NRSV).—Bruce E. Shields

SUNDAY: NOVEMBER TENTH

SERVICE OF WORSHIP

Sermon: The Greatest Teachings of Jesus: Faith

TEXT: Mark 4:35–41; John 20:26–29

A conference of noted professors, industrialists, and government leaders was held at Cambridge University. Its purpose was to address the question, What causes certain persons to become visionaries or achievers in society? Do you know the conclusion reached by the people at the conference? It was very simple: The greatest visionaries and achievers live as though seeing another world. They live very much in this world, but they appear to have some other world in their sights, and everything they do is governed by that other world.

This would certainly apply to Jesus, wouldn't it?

When he talked about it to his disciples, he called it "faith." Later, one of his followers would say that faith is "the assurance of things hoped for, the conviction of things not seen" (Heb. 11:1).

As he talked about faith and belief, it became apparent that there are three stages of the way we experience it.

I. *First, God is.* There was not a lot of argument about this in Jesus' day. The existence of God was not even considered debatable. As the book of James, which was possibly written by Jesus' brother, says, "Even the demons believe—and shudder" (James 2:19).

The same is basically true today. Most of us are inherently theistic; we accept the probable existence of a divine being.

Jesus knew that most of the people of his day had faith of this kind, faith of the most elemental variety. But that was not enough, he told his disciples. They must have more. They must move on to the second stage of faith, and believe that God cares about them.

II. God cares. You must trust this, said Jesus, and thus allay your anxieties about what you shall eat or drink or wear. Behold the prodigality of nature: the birds find food and the lilies are clothed more regally than an ancient king (Matt. 6:30). "O men of little faith." That was his constant reprimand to the disciples (Matt. 8:26; Matt. 14:28–32).

These stories are reminders of the way it is with our own faith. It is not hard to have faith, or to think we have it, when there are no particular storms or dangers in our lives. But when troubles come— when the water hose on the car breaks, when there is illness, when friends desert us, when we lose our jobs—then it is easy to doubt the very existence of God.

Your commitment must be so solid, said Jesus, that you believe even when everything is going against you. He himself held fast by such belief, even when nailed to a cross. "Father," he prayed as he was dying, "into thy hands I commit my spirit!" (Luke 23:46).

III. God is; God cares; and God is still acting in creation to bring the world and all his children into harmony with himself. This is the final level of faith Jesus talked about, the very highest kind of faith, in which believers so completely lose themselves in the hope of the kingdom of God that miracles begin to happen around them. It is a degree of faith that makes many people uncomfortable, for it goes beyond the conventional limits of religious practice; and yet the teaching of Jesus on the subject is truncated and incomplete without it.

When you totally align yourself with God, said Jesus, there is no limit to what may happen through the instrumentality of your faith (Luke 8:50; Mark 11:22–23; Luke 17:6–7 JBP).

Now, it is my personal opinion that the Master was not commissioning all his followers to go out and become instant miracle workers, raising the dead, healing the sick, and rearranging the mulberry groves of the world; but he was speaking

of the extraordinary power that belongs to the heavenly Father who is still acting to bring his kingdom to birth in this world, and of the incredible things that will happen in our lives and in our vicinities when we surrender ourselves absolutely to this vision.

Sometimes the miracles are quiet and almost unnoticed; but they are nevertheless miracles.

David H. C. Read, the noted minister of Madison Avenue Presbyterian Church in New York City, has written in his autobiography of a moment of near despair in 1940, a few months after he had been captured with his Scottish battalion and interned in a Nazi war camp. Conditions were at their very worst, he said. Letters from home were not getting through. The potatoes that had been the men's staple diet had gone rancid. The war news reported great victories for the Nazis. Read went for a walk around the inside of the wire. His eye fell on a newspaper whose headline said, LONDON EIN EINZIGES FLAMMENMEER—"London One Great Sea of Flames!" His wife was in London, and the news was heartrending. "Yet," he writes, "a few minutes later, as I stood looking out over the river, I was overcome by an indescribable sense of peace and a strange joy, as if the angels were singing through the barbed wire and reaching deep inside me."[1]

How can we account for this peace and joy at such a moment? There is only one way. It is faith—faith in the God who is still acting in the world, despite wars and hatred and destruction, despite disease and death and crucifixion, and who will ultimately establish his eternal kingdom on the very campsites of the enemy! Somehow Read knew, despite all the negative signs, that God was still in charge of human destiny.

When Jesus appeared to Thomas and the other disciples in an upper room after his death, Thomas fell down and cried, "My Lord and my God!" "Have you believed because you have seen Me?" said Jesus. "Blessed are those who have

---

[1] *This Grace Given* (Eerdmans'), 116.

not seen and yet believe" (John 20:28–29).—John Killinger

Illustrations

PROVING GOD.   A few years ago, a professor at the University of Mississippi spent most of a class hour working through a somewhat complicated philosophical proof of the existence of God. In the end, feeling quite pleased with himself, he looked at a student in his class and asked, "Miss Green, have I proved to you that there is a God?" "Oh, you didn't have to prove it to me," replied the coed, who had not been at all intimidated by the esoteric line of reasoning. "I knew it all the time."—John Killinger

BOLD BELIEF.   After Sir Walter Raleigh was beheaded in the tower, they found in his Bible these true and striking lines, written the night before his death:

Even such is time, that takes in trust
Our youth, our joys, our all we have,
And pays us but with age and dust;
Who in the dark and silent grave,
When we have wandered all our ways,
Shuts up the story of our days.
But from this earth, this grave, this dust,
My God shall raise me up, I trust!

All the things of this world he had lost, but he had kept his faith; and faith spoke to him of a hope and life beyond the grave.—Clarence E. Macartney

SERMON SUGGESTIONS

Topic: Encouraging Words for You

TEXT: I Thess. 4:13–18

(1) Death, contrary to the hopelessness of the unbelieving world, is not the end. (2) The return of Jesus Christ in glory means: (a) reunion with those who have preceded us in death; (b) being at home with the Lord forever.

Topic: Ten Bridesmaids and You

TEXT: Matt. 25:1–13

(1) *The parable:* For certain reasons, half of the welcoming party missed the big event because they were not on time with their preparations and the door was shut when they arrived. (2) *The meaning:* (a) We may be unprepared for the coming of the Son of Man for final judgment—if we assume that we have unlimited time for preparation; if we are careless and preoccupied with matters of lesser importance; (b) We may be prepared if we keep on the alert; or, better, if we so commit ourselves, once for all, that we will be always ready for any surprising event in God's unfolding scheme of things.

Worship Aids

CALL TO WORSHIP.   "Give ear, O my people, to my law: incline your ears to the words of my mouth. I will open my mouth in a parable: I will utter dark sayings of old: which we have heard and known, and our fathers have told us. We will not hide them from their children, shewing to the generation to come the praises of the Lord, and his strength, and his wonderful works that he hath done" (Ps. 78:1–4).

INVOCATION.   Gracious God and Father, help us to be attentive today to all that you have to say to us, and by your grace give us understanding of what we hear and see and feel. Beyond that, give us, we pray, faith in you, even when we do not understand.

OFFERTORY SENTENCE.   "Be ye steadfast, unmovable, always abounding in the work of the Lord, forasmuch as ye know that your labor is not in vain in the Lord" (1 Cor. 15:58).

OFFERTORY PRAYER.   Lord, may our offerings go about doing good in spite of the strange confusing ways of a world so riddled with drug abuse, crime, war, poverty, injustice, and crippling greed. And let that good be multiplied by the power of the Holy Spirit, for Jesus' sake.—E. Lee Phillips

PRAYER.   May we who would invoke your presence realize that you are already turned toward us in the eternity of your love. That in a universe where there are worlds beyond worlds, galaxies, seemingly without number, you would invade this planet with so great a love, blows our minds. There is a mystery here—the mystery of your grace—out of which the cosmos was created and the ways of life established.

How can we appear before you except in praise: "Lord, you have been our dwelling place, in all generations. Before the mountains were brought forth, or ever you had formed the earth and the world, from everlasting to everlasting you are God."

In the beginning your Spirit brooded upon the depths and order was created out of chaos and so your Spirit hovers over your creation in every generation, seeking to lead your people to that order that leads to life—where there is a waiting according to your word. We praise you, O Father, that in every generation you have been faithful according to all your promises.

That we have been brought to the knowledge of the gospel and are privileged to share the life of the Church in this time and place is of your abounding grace. We marvel at the mustard seed sown in that first century that strangely came to life, and today its branches reach through the whole world. We pray that we may fulfill Christ's commissioning to be the light of the world and the salt of the earth.

Renew us, O God, in such a sense of mission that we do not allow housekeeping duties to keep us from ministry to all the world and all the worlds of people to which you are calling us in the height, the depth, the length, and the breadth of your love in Christ.

In the full dimensions of your love, he was "a man for others." So may we live and love. Where there is any brokenness among us—of mind, of body, of spirit—we pray for the healing to make whole. We pray not only for the ill among us but for those caregivers who with love, understanding, and patience minister so faithfully. Strengthen and encourage them according to the demands of day and night calls.

We pray for the brokenness of this world. You have created a cosmos, but through self-serving ways we often render it a chaos. We pray for those who in the face of much danger seek to bring peace to areas where humans' and earth's resources are squandered by hostility and armed conflict. Grant to all leaders in church and state the wisdom of your truth and the faith and courage to answer its call according to their opportunity and responsibility.

We pray through him in whom all things cohere and who is among us as living Lord.—John Thompson

LECTIONARY MESSAGE

Topic: Memories of God

Text: Josh. 24:1–3a, 14–25

"I wish my grandfather could see me now." It was a young minister sitting across from me who said these words. He had been rebellious as a youth, and no one expected much good from him. In the years since his grandfather's death, this man had gotten his life straightened out, earned a college degree, then a Master of Divinity, and was now called to pastor a church. His grandfather had loved him dearly and had believed in him. This young man remembered his grandfather, the love that was so wonderful, and was shaped even now by that memory.

I. In the same way, God's people, whether Jews or Christians, are people of memory. These memories are sacred memories, full of meaning for those living by faith.

a. For example, there are memories of places that stir our spirits. The Jews remember with awe Haran, Bethel, Egypt, the wilderness of Sinai, the Jordan River, and the entry into the Promised Land. Christians are moved by the very thought of Bethlehem, Nazareth, Jerusalem, Philippi, Ephesus, and Rome, all places of sacred history dear to our hearts. All have places sacred to their own lives.

b. There are memories of people who participated in God's story and still live in our memories. We recount from Sunday school and sermons the stories of Abraham and Sarah, Moses, Ruth and Naomi,

Hannah, David, Simon Peter, and Paul. In my family there were my grandmother, who went to sleep reading her Bible at the table many nights, and my father, whose quiet faith and Sunday school teaching inspire me.

c. But most of all, these are memories of God. The people and places are a part of God's story, and that is why we remember. We remember where and when God met us, what happened, and how our lives were changed.

II. Joshua called the people together at Shechem and demanded a new decision from them. Now that they were in the Land of Promise and the long journey seemed over, would they stray from God? When things had eased up a bit and dependence on God did not seem such a necessity, their decision he recounted their sacred history. He called up their memories of all the way they had come, and how it was that God had delivered them, how God had been faithful, good, and powerful in their behalf. He reminded them of the decision, a covenant at Sinai, which their ancestors had made, and how God sought fidelity and loyalty in their lives. Memories of such sacred acts of God and covenants remain at the heart of our faith.

III. Memories are a source of God's continuing self-revelation. One who reflects seriously and deeply on the stories of Abraham and Sarah, Jesus, or of one's baptism is likely to encounter God in the stories in a familiar yet new way.

IV. Memories inform our decisions in a powerful way. When the Israelites remembered God's delivering them from the powerful and cruel Egyptian Pharaoh, they knew that God was in their lives, leading them, calling them to purity of life, and claiming them in all their circumstances.

V. Our memories give us identity. Just as one suffering from amnesia is the same person yet does not know who that person is, so the Jews at Shechem recited their history with God, and knew they were the people not of just any god, but of this God, Yahweh. Christians are people of Christ, one in Christ, one in baptism, one in faith, one in hope. We send our children from home to college or work and hope they remember who they are and live out of their sacred and family memories.

VI. Memories help us meet the demands of life. They give us direction, focus, and strength. When adversity comes we can remember, just as the Israelites long ago remembered and our ancestors in the faith remembered, that God is present, no matter what the situation, and that nothing is impossible with God. Memories help us to be thankful, gracious, and loving, for we know what we have received from God, and we remember the promises to us. The minister who reads the Twenty-third Psalm at a bedside is gathering the people together and calling to mind this great God who has acted in our memories and who is present in the Word and who calls to us even now to remember our covenants, to be faithful, and to choose between God and all that would be gods in our lives.—Stuart G. Collier

SUNDAY: NOVEMBER SEVENTEENTH

SERVICE OF WORSHIP

Sermon: The Place of Understanding

Text: Job 28:12, 14

Job had a problem on his hands. And Job's problem was the problem of ill health. The physical aspects of it didn't worry him a great deal; the moral aspects of it worried him tremendously. It was a troubled mind that he had, which anybody knows is worse than a sick body!

For what ailed him, he needed wisdom most of all. He could scrape his boils, but he couldn't appease his own soul!

I. Take one or two of our modern human problems, for instance;

a. First, there is funk, which is a kind of ingrowing fear that makes you "hectic and fussy and worried." There is something that has to be done, and you are dreading lest you can't make good.

b. Or perhaps it's frustration. That's a new name for an old disorder. Circumstances have hemmed you in and kept you from being the whole self you could have been. Until now the wind is out of your sails, and you go around trying to make up for it by being offensive. You could have been something too, if it hadn't been for the boils, or whatever it was that stopped you.

c. Or perhaps it's conflict. There's another new way of saying an old thing. Some evil in your life is at war with your ideals. It makes you despise yourself. You try to put the whole business out of your mind; but it trickles down on the lower levels, into the unconscious, and raises the mischief out of sight.

II. Now there is very little profit to be had out of taking that sort of self to the seashore, or getting into the great out-of-doors, or tucking a tennis racquet under its arm, or slinging a golf bag over its shoulder. There is very little profit to be had out of trying to forget about it, or going to the movies, or occupying your mind with something else. "The depth saith, It is not in me; and the sea saith, It is not with me." "Where shall wisdom be found?" That's what a man needs then! "And where is the place of understanding?"

a. There ought to be some medicine for the soul.

Some us believe there is. We believe that the religion of Jesus Christ is just that; not at its highest, but at its lowest! It's intended at least to make sick people well—I mean people who are spiritually sick; after that, it's intended to make them strong and able, with the strength of God!

Job, back there on the other side of the centuries, was sure that the process began in the place that he called the place of understanding; and no modern psychologist has ever got any further.

I do not believe that we have come beyond it. The longer one deals with human nature and with all those disorders that make it so strange and difficult a thing, the more firmly is one convinced of the amazing relevancy, the almost incredible aptness, of the Christian religion. To my knowledge, I have never stumbled upon a single instance, either in my experience or in my reading, of anxiety, of restlessness, of what we call plain, ordinary "nerves"—not one that wasn't the result of flouting that religion, consciously or unconsciously; and not one the cure of which did not lie well within its province.

b. It doesn't matter what sort of stress or strain it is that disturbs your peace. If it's some understanding of yourself that you need, Christ can bring you to that. He'll show you the worst, and then he'll tell you that that doesn't even begin to prejudice the best that he keeps talking about. If it's forgiveness, you may have that, if you'll just reach yonder and lay your hands on it, and know that you have it. If it's courage you lack because failure and disappointment and hopelessness have made you feel that you can't face life, then the only fight you have is the fight with your own doubts that "the mighty gifts of this God are yours for the taking!" These fears that haunt you: lie down quietly at night on your bed and for fifteen minutes say aloud to yourself, "In him that strengthens me, I am able for anything!" See what happens to them when you work at them, instead of spending all your time trying to cling by your fingernails to what little religion you have left. Christianity is no facile optimist that comes to these two people and says with a foolish, vacuous smile, "Cheer up!" Christianity breaks its heart over them in an agony of hope, with its eyes wide open and wistful in the knowledge of what God can do with them in spite of it all if they'll let him! Let him, I repeat.

III. And so I come to the last word that this religion of ours has to say in the hearing of all troubled souls everywhere: Give yourself somehow, somewhere, to that long, human cry for help that rings daily in God's ears. There are men and women in the world who are so busy healing the minds and bodies of other people that they have no time left in which to be mentally or spiritually sick themselves! It isn't without its significance that the sort of ill health of which we have been thinking together so frequently goes hand in hand with those ways of life that do not occupy themselves very much in the service of other life. In moments of high devotion there is no room for brooding uneasiness.

"As the Father hath sent me, even so send I you." There isn't much time for being anything but well when folk are continuously about the biggest business there is in the world! Is that the answer?—Paul Scherer

Illustrations

FORGIVENESS AND PEACE. Weatherhead, in his *Psychology in Service of the Soul,* tells of a woman who came to him on the verge of a breakdown. She was in a pitiable state, manifesting all the physical symptoms of great distress. It was hard to get behind her mind to see what was the matter. But at last it came out. There had been a rift between herself and her brother. Natural love and acquired hate had set her soul in opposite camps, warring against itself. The solution of it, and of the sleepless nights that went with it, came as if by magic; but it wasn't magic: it was Christ's answer to Peter's question! "How oft shall my brother sin against me, and I forgive him? Till seven times?" And the secret was whispered back: "Seventy times seven!" She sat down and wrote her brother a letter, inviting him to her home, and the ugly chapter in her life came to its close.— Paul Scherer

SPIRITUAL DRYNESS. I know by my own experience that he who determines to pray, not much heeding either immediate comfort or dejection, has got into one of the best secrets of prayer. Let no one weary or lose heart because of aridity. The Hearer of prayer sometimes comes very late; but at last he comes, and rewards the soul for all her toil and dryness and discouragement.—Saint Teresa

SERMON SUGGESTIONS

Topic: When Others Laugh

TEXT: Ps. 123

(1) Be sure that it is not because you are doing what is plainly stupid. (2) Put your trust in the God of justice, who can turn hostility into blessing (see Matt. 5:10). (3) Continue to hope and pray, verse 2b.

Topic: Something to Stay Awake For

Text: 1 Thess. 5:1–11

In contrast to the unbelieving world, true believers are: (1) prepared for "the day of the Lord," verses 1–5; (2) prepared to wage a creative war of faith and love, verse 8a; (3) prepared to receive salvation in the world to come, verses 8b–10.

Worship Aids

CALL TO WORSHIP. "Unto thee lift I up mine eyes, O thou that dwellest in the heavens" (Ps. 123:1).

INVOCATION. Lord of all, may we be tender, teachable, pliable this day, so we do not miss the power of your Word, the wisdom of your purposes, and the wonder of your glory.—E. Lee Phillips

OFFERTORY SENTENCE. "Keep your life free from love of money, and be content with what you have; for he has said, 'I will never fail you nor forsake you' " (Heb. 13:5 RSV).

OFFERTORY PRAYER. Lord, save us from greed while we pursue our livelihood, and open our hearts to the needs of others. Help us to trust you enough, for we need personally to be spared the blight of envy and discontent.

PRAYER. Spirit of the Living God, fall fresh on us this morning as we quietly wait in your presence for a word, a thought, a guiding insight to guide us in our journey. Reassure us anew of your eternal faithfulness, which we so often forget in the heat and turmoil of daily living. Remind us that your timetables are not synchronized with ours and that our frustration and impatience reflect our inability to wait on the Lord more than they do your absence from us. In our more sane and reflective moments we realize that you are always faithful and we are the faithless, the ones struggling in the far country. This morning call us together and inspire us to truly seek you with all our heart. For we know that when we engage in such a high adventure, we shall ever surely find you.

Give us this morning a clearer vision of the Lord Christ. Assure us that the morning of new beginnings has broken and that we can find in him all we need to live worthily and freely from sin and death. Open our ears and eyes that we may see the ministries that Christ calls us to perform and that we may hear the cries of the least, the last, and the lost; the weakest and the ones furthest away. Quicken our hearing to the words of our adversaries, not that we may engage in useless argument, but that we may learn from them and find ways to enrich the kingdom of Christ through their efforts and concerns.

Give us a clear vision to see the needs of those closest to us, Father. Often they are the last to receive our love and care; our sensitivity and concern. Keep us from ignoring them while we seek to help others in their relationship with the Lord and his world.

Now give us a clear insight into your word, that from it we may garner such truth that life will be done differently and we will strive for your high purpose as found in Jesus.

Heal the brokenness among us, brokenness of the heart, the mind and the spirit. Save us from being lost, and set our feet on the high road of faith that leads to our eternal home.—Henry Fields

LECTIONARY MESSAGE

Topic: Gifts and Investment

TEXT: Matt. 25:14–30

He was a master of the keyboard. As his fingers sped over the glistening ivory keys, sounds were produced that spoke to the many moods of the spirit. Soft sounds whispered to the quiet corners of memory, calling forth cherished thoughts. Crashing chords challenged the adventurous spirit of the soul with invigorating power. Soothing melodies calmed the sorrowing spirit of loss and pain, granting glimpses of renewed hope and joy. "Mine is a gift of God," he said. "It is my responsibility to use it for his glory."

He had read well Jesus' parable of the talents and had learned to practice its highest meaning. From that parable come much needed lessons for our generation.

I. The parable implies that each of us receives a special gift from God. Not all gifts are equal. Not all people have the same number. Yet each has the special one needed to accomplish God's purpose through his or her life. Since our talents are a gift from God, it is our first responsibility to recognize and accept that talent with all its implications. To covet the talents and gifts of another is to degrade our own and question the wisdom of the giver.

II. Once we recognize and accept our gift, we have an obligation to invest it for the glory of God and the betterment of others. Two beneficiaries in the parable understood the responsibility of their gift and invested it well. Others in the Bible, such as Deborah, the charismatic judge of Israel (Judg. 4:1–7), recognized their gifts and, investing them to God's glory and humanity's good, gave powerful examples of God's care that will forever be a part of our history and faith.

Still, many follow the example of the man who received the one talent and refused to invest it but rather buried it in the soil of uselessness.

III. Why do so many refuse to invest their gift, their talent?

The basic reason is simple fear. Some fear the giver. The parable ends with the one-talent man saying that he knew the giver was a hard man and he did not want to risk the wrath that might come from the master if the talent was not returned intact. This would be accompanied by a fear of failure. There are no guarantees that gifts and talents invested will produce a return. It is ofttimes easier to hold on to what one possesses than to fail by taking the risk of investment.

Jesus' answer to such reasoning is simple. What we do not use we lose. Said the Master, "Take the talent from him and give it to the one who has ten talents" (Matthew 25:28 NIV). Loss always follows the refusal to use a talent. Singers who cease to sing soon lose the ability to sing well. Pianists who cease to play lose their touch. Linguists who cease to review their languages soon forget the words, sentence structures, and nuances of the language. What we do not use, we lose. It takes courage to act boldly with an entrusted gift when we know that full accountability for it is going to be required by the giver.

IV. The parable reminds us that investment of our gifts and talents brings reward. Rewards may not be measurable by human standards, but they are invaluable when measured by Christ's standard. Investing our God-gifts in Christ's work will invariably produce Christ-followers and Christ-rewards.—Henry Fields

SUNDAY: NOVEMBER TWENTY-FOURTH

SERVICE OF WORSHIP

Sermon: Now Thank We All Our God

Thanksgiving is distinctly an American holiday; there is nothing like it elsewhere in the world. It celebrates neither a savage battle nor the fall of a great city. It does not mark the anniversary of a great conqueror or the birthday of a famous statesman. It does not commemorate the writing of a historic public document or the launching of a new constitution. The American Thanksgiving Day is the expression of a deep feeling of gratitude by our people for the rich productivity of the land, a memorial of the dangers and hardships through which we have safely passed, and a fitting recognition of all that God in his goodness has bestowed upon us.

It is the custom of members of some religious fellowships to use a rosary as an aid in fixing in the mind those things of which St. Paul spoke as true, just, pure, lovely, and of good report. Dr. Henry N. Wieman has suggested that each individual should make a mental rosary of his most precious memories, including the beauty he has seen, the fellowship he has enjoyed, and the good gifts that life has brought him. Then he suggests that each person frequently count the beads of his rosary and give thanks to God for each separate favor.

In early New England it was the custom at Thanksgiving time to place five grains of corn at every plate as a reminder of those stern days in the first winter when the food of the Pilgrims was so depleted that only five grains of corn were rationed to each individual at a time. The Pilgrim fathers wanted their children to remember the sacrifice, suffering, and hardship that made possible the settlement of a free people in a free land. They wanted to keep alive the memory of that long sixty-three-day trip taken in the tiny *Mayflower*. They desired to keep alive the thought of that "stern and rock-bound coast," its inhospitable welcome, and the first terrible winter that took such a toll of lives. They did not want their descendants to forget that on the day in which their ration was reduced to five grains of corn only seven healthy colonists remained to nurse the sick, and nearly half their numbers lay in the "windswept graveyard" on the hill. They did not want to forget that when the *Mayflower* sailed back to England in the spring only the sailors were aboard.

I. The use of five grains of corn placed by each plate was a fitting reminder of a heroic past. Symbolically it may still serve as a useful means of recalling those great gifts for which we are grateful to God. The first grain of corn might stand for that wonderful beauty of nature that is all about us.

Thus we can say: Now Thank We All Our God for the beauties of nature that are all about us.

II. Our second grain of symbolic corn reminds us of the great men and women of the past. They have lived in every age and in every country. In our own land great men have stepped forward to lead the people through difficulties and to inspire others by their vision. The dream of Woodrow Wilson of a united world has not yet come true, but his vision beckons men forward, and we can trust that in the future his hope for a brotherhood of man will be a reality.

Now Thank We All Our God for the great men and women of the past!

III. Our third grain of corn might stand for the work of the world that must be done, some portion of which will fall to each one of us. At times we all indulge in wishful thinking and dream that the good things of life may be ours without any real effort. But it is only in castles in Spain that the plumbing never leaks! Will Rogers said, "We don't have roses at our door unless we plant them there." Nor do any values and goods of life come to us without hard, conscientious work.

Work seems to be a squirrel cage for some who are forced to spend their days in hard, monotonous tasks that crush the human spirit. An English child who saw the miners of the Rhonda Valley during the last depression exclaimed, "Their eyes look like vacant windows." Our work does not need to be a squirrel cage. It may be a doorway through which we may go to serve and to bless those about us. The nurse may use her skill to help the sufferer in his hour of desperate need. The traveling salesman may use his work to move goods sorely needed by his fellow men. The teacher may use his subject as a start in reaching boys and girls who need advice and direction. The engineer may leave behind him good roads, well-constructed bridges, newly developed oil fields, and a multitude of machines that will take the drudgery out of the lives of others. If we choose our work wisely, we shall be able to say as did Thomas Edison, "I never worked a day in my life, it was all fun."

Now Thank We All Our God for the work of the world that waits for our hands to do.

IV. Our fourth grain of symbolic corn may stand for our friends and loved ones. We do not wear our hearts on our sleeves, nor do we talk much about our friends and those at home. But within ourselves we know what joy we take in our friends.

Our friends teach us to learn the meaning of that ancient Greek motto, "Know thyself!" Sometimes they are frank and brutal, pointing out our mistakes in no mincing words. They may speak of trivial things such as the slant of a hat or the color of a tie; but they also warn us of imperfections in our ideal and our attitudes. To them we are grateful for the frequent renewal and glorification of life. By their sympathy and understanding they help us in our day of defeat and discouragement. By sharing our small victories they double our pleasures. On those dark days when bitter sorrow has been our lot they have transmuted the bitterness and blunted the arrow that otherwise might have pierced our strongest armor. Emerson wrote, "Friends are not only for vacation times, but for days of shipwreck; not only to be with us on our pleasant rambles, but to be with us as we travel over the rough roads of life."

Thus we can say, Now Thank We All Our God, for our friends and loved ones.

V. Only one symbolic grain of corn remains. Can we do better than to dedicate it to God? It is not hard to see why the ancient writer of the Law of Israel cried, "The Lord, our God, is the great God, the mighty and the terrible, who regardeth not persons, nor taketh rewards. He doth execute justice for the fatherless and widow. . . . The Lord is merciful and gracious, slow to anger, and abundant in loving kindness and truth." It is not difficult for us to recognize the power of God. Every crack of thunder, every earthquake that stirs the earth to its depth, every comet's tail that streams across the sky, all testify to the power of God.

It is not difficult to appreciate the aesthetic quality in God when he has made so much of beauty all about us. It is not difficult to see that only a rational power could create the universe with all its wonders revealed by microscope and telescope. Power, beauty, intellect—all are revelations of God. But these qualities do not satisfy the hungering heart of man. The glory of God in the eyes of man is Creative Love. Much of what God is must always remain a mystery to us, since our minds are finite; but this we know, the quality in the personality of God is Creative Love. We all know something about human love; we have seen it, we have experienced it, it is the most wonderful thing in the world. But God is greater than man; in him love is raised to the nth degree, it is the dominant factor in the reality of God, the ruling principle.

St. Paul wrote to the Colossians: "Christ who is the image of the invisible God." We can see God in beauty, power, and mind. We can see God dimly in men and women at their best; but in Jesus Christ we see something more. His life is the expression of complete service and love. In Jesus we see revealed as nowhere else that same quality that is the chief characteristic of God—Creative Love.

And if the core of the universe is Creative Love, God's kingdom will yet come; a kingdom of peace, harmony, goodwill, and abundant life. Thus with grateful hearts, mindful of the beauty of nature all about us and the greatness of the leaders of the past; thankful for the work of the world that must be done and conscious of what we owe our friends and loved ones, we can but add our voices to all those who sing "Now Thank We All Our God!"—Bliss Forbush

Illustrations

GIFTS AND THE GIVER. Someone has suggested that "humanity is like an enormous spiderweb, so that if you touch it anywhere, you set the whole thing trembling."

One place where this enormous spiderweb is set a-trembling constantly is in the common, everyday experience of saying, "Thank you" and "You're welcome." We do it ten—a hundred—times a day as we touch another's life or another's life touches ours. Usually we do it so casually that the implications of the ordinary words of gratitude and response escape us.

Underneath the casual words there is a deep urge within us to be grateful and to express it. Someone holds a door for us, a waitress serves a drink, the driver of a car amazingly holds up so that we can break through the line, and we are grateful, because this is the way life should be—full of courtesy and thoughtfulness, reminders that we are all dependent on each other. And we respond casually, but actually out of the depths of our being: "Thank you." Of course if someone is thoughtless or rude we can use the same words in anger: "Well, thank you for that." Which is a way of crying out against the lack of recognition that we are all dependent upon each other.—Edmund A. Steimle

GRATITUDE. Thomas Gray once attended a sale of books with a friend. One lot particularly appealed to him: an elegant bookcase containing a collection of finely bound volumes of French classics. The hundred guineas demanded, however, was far beyond Gray's means, and his disappointment on learning the price was obvious. The Duchess of Northumberland, who had witnessed the incident and was acquainted with Gray's companion, asked the identity of the disconsolate bibliophile. Later the same day, Gray was overwhelmed with delight to find that the coveted bookcase had been delivered to his lodgings. The gift was accompanied by a note from the duchess, in which she apologized for making so small an acknowledgment of the intense pleasure she had derived from reading Gray's "Elegy Written in a Country Churchyard."—Clifton Fadiman

SERMON SUGGESTIONS

Topic: The Shepherd King
TEXT: Ezek. 34:11–16, 20–24
(1) The role is in the character of God

himself. (2) The role was illustrated by David and his successors. (3) The role was and is ideally fulfilled in Jesus Christ (see John 10:1–18).

Topic: Why One Man Prayed

TEXT: Eph. 1:15–23

(1) Heartfelt gratitude, verses 15–16.
(2) Hopeful supplication, verses 17–19.
(3) Humbling recognition, verses 20–23.

Worship Aids

CALL TO WORSHIP.   "Make a joyful noise unto the Lord, all ye lands. Serve the Lord with gladness: come before his presence with singing. Know ye that the Lord he is God: it is he that hath made us, and not we ourselves; we are his people, and the sheep of his pasture. Enter into his gates with thanksgiving, and into his courts with praise: be thankful unto him, and bless his name. For the Lord is good; his mercy is everlasting; and his truth endureth to all generations" (Ps. 100:1–5).

INVOCATION.   Gracious Lord, in whom we live and move and have our being, through whom we enjoy the blessings of this life; give to our worship gratitude, to our gratitude appreciation, and to our appreciation a dedication in stewardship that honors the Lord in all we do.—E. Lee Phillips

OFFERTORY SENTENCE.   "Blessed be the Lord, who daily loadeth us with benefits, even the God of our salvation" (Ps. 68:19).

OFFERTORY PRAYER.   Let us give thanks to God our Father for all his gifts so freely bestowed upon us. For the wonder of your creation, in earth and sky and sea, we thank you, Lord. For all that is gracious in the lives of men and women, revealing the image of Christ, we thank you, Lord. For our daily food and drink, our homes and families, and our friends, we thank you, Lord. For minds to think, and hearts to love, and hands to serve, we thank you, Lord. For health and strength to work and leisure to rest and play, we thank you, Lord. For the brave and courageous, who are patient in suffering and faithful in adversity, we thank you, Lord. For all valiant seekers after truth, liberty, and justice, we thank you, Lord. For the communion of saints, in all times and places, we thank you, Lord. Above all, we give you thanks for the great mercies and promises given to us in Christ Jesus our Lord; to him be praise and glory, with you, O Father, and the Holy Spirit, now and forever. Amen.—*Book of Common Prayer*

PRAYER.   O Lord, we lift before thee now in humble intercession the whole wide world in all its struggles, toil, and tears. Remove the things that make for war and strife and through the message of thy gospel give all humankind a higher goal to aim for and a clearer meaning in going on. Draw near to our country in these years of doubt and perplexity and save us from foolish pride and selfishness. Help us to restore those ideals that are fed by true religion. Make those who govern us responsible to our people and to thee, and as we and they serve "under God," may honor, truth, and justice have dominion in and over all things. Keep us strong in our will to uphold the heritage we have received and, as each national Thanksgiving comes and goes, may we continue to live in faith and trust as heirs of those who loved thee with all their heart and strength and mind. To thee—Father, Son, and Holy Spirit—be all glory now and always, world without end.—Donald Macleod

LECTIONARY MESSAGE

Topic: Christ Incognito

TEXT: Matt. 25:31–46

Reading the New Testament can be as disturbing as it is comforting. Especially is this the case in relation to the truth contained in the Gospel text for today.

In his parable of the great judgment, Jesus speaks unequivocally of the mystical union that exists between him and people in need. The critical question in this entire section of Scripture is, "But, Lord, when did we see You?" The answer to that inquiry relates directly to persons in need. Jesus indicated that he was present in a hungry man, a thirsty woman, a homeless stranger, a bedridden sick person, and a prisoner. In fact, an individual's reaction to these people in need revealed that individual's stance toward the reign of God. The very criteria for the final judgment involve acts of compassion expressed toward the Christ who appears in the form of persons in need.

Doesn't that truth prompt discomfort? Would it not be better if we could predict precisely where Jesus can be found—in worship, in Scripture, in confessions of faith? Is it not unsettling to think that Jesus can come to us incognito?

The truth of the incognito Christ breaks down neat, mutually exclusive divisions of life.

I. *Humanity and Divinity.* Life would be far more predictable and faith more comfortable if hard-and-fast distinctions could be made between relationships with God and interaction with other people; spiritual activities and involvements in business, social action, and politics. However, Jesus tolerates no such division of loyalties, totally erasing any neat line of demarcation separating God and humankind.

Piety is related to social activity. Spiritually includes the horizontal as well as the vertical dimension of life.

Christ's identification with all people results in a "high anthropology." No person is an individual abstraction of humankind or a worthless entity. All people have value in Christ. All people. Every person.

In one of her published prayers, Mother Teresa of Calcutta asks God to help her recognize Jesus when he comes to her hidden behind an unattractive disguise. We do well to pray likewise. It is precisely in relation to the ugly people with whom society has the most problems that we most clearly demonstrate our devotion to God.

II. *The Sacred and the Ordinary.* Jesus' teachings about the incognito Christ fuse the sacred and the ordinary. The present moment becomes decisive, even holy. Common, ordinary acts are filled with spiritual significance.

Attempts to be spiritual cause one to embrace the practical. God is loved by loving people in need. God is served by housing the homeless, comforting a person dying of AIDS, and clothing an ill-clad family. Actions that seem simple and unimportant take on the significance of a holy event when done for Christ.

Jesus snatches divine judgment from some distant future and sets it squarely in the middle of the present moment. A person's destiny is decided as that person meets the heavenly judge in the needs of a neighbor. Any final judgment that occurs simply confirms the verdict forged in the present.

III. *Worship and Service.* A trust vision of God is accompanied by a careful look at the needs of our neighbors. Worship sensitizes us not only to the transcendence of God but to the eminent presence of Christ who comes to us as a stranger.

Worship cannot be replaced by ethics and social action. But social action and ethical behavior can become expressions of worship. While serving people in need we meet the incognito Christ and bring glory to God.

A realization that Jesus can appear anywhere at any time in the form of anyone is disturbing. The incognito Christ disrupts a rigid compartmentalization of life. Those who understand know that if we are to serve Christ we must help hurting people around us.

Albert Schweitzer paid tribute to this truth with his life and in his writing. Schweitzer wrote that Jesus "comes to us as One unknown" and, to those who obey him, reveals himself in "the toils, the conflicts, the sufferings" that people pass through.

Let us pray that when we encounter this Christ, we serve him without hesitation and that in such service we come to know the promise of the "ineffable mystery" to which both Schweitzer and Jesus pointed, learning in our "own experience Who He is." The incognito Christ is our Savior and Lord!—C. Welton Gaddy

SUNDAY: DECEMBER FIRST

SERVICE OF WORSHIP

Sermon: Role Play

Text: Matt. 19:27—20:16

I. There are three roles to play today in this little drama, and I'd like us to try them out to see if we can be comfortable in them. The first characters are the first group of laborers. These were poor people who did not have a steady job. They did not own their own farms or businesses; they did not have skills that were in demand. They worked day by day; they were paid at the end of the day, and the next morning they went out and looked for another job. They stood around the city gates, and the farmers who needed extra help would come and hire them by the day.

How do they feel as they are standing there at daybreak? They are hopeful, perhaps; this is the time for harvesting grapes, and so there's a good chance they'll find work today. They are resentful, perhaps; they talk among themselves and complain about the rich people who seem to get richer. One of them used to own his own farm. Then a few years back there was a dry year, and his crop didn't make it, and he had to borrow money to buy seed and feed his family through the winter. When the next year was dry, too, he had to sell his farm to pay his debts. Now he's standing there every day, hoping to work for somebody else.

Then the vineyard owner comes: It's old man Moishe Ben-Asher! He's a good man; he pays a fair wage. The first group of workers are the ones who push to the front. He promises them a denarius: that's like the minimum wage for a day's work. That's fair, and if Ben-Asher promises a denarius, he won't try to cheat you at the end of the day. So they push to the front, they make noise, and he hires them. And they go off. They are grateful for the job, and a little proud, too: He hired us instead of them. We got the job; we'll put food in the house for our families. Nothing like real, honest work to give a person some self-esteem. You feel like you're pulling your own weight.

During the day, though, their pride turns ugly. When the vineyard owner hires some more people, the first group thinks to themselves, "Poor jerks; we'll get a denarius and have food on the table, but they won't even make enough to buy bread for supper—they haven't worked enough." And when they see that old man Ben-Asher pays the latecomers a denarius, too, they are angry. "We worked all day long in the hot sun for you, and you give those lazy bums the same pay? You didn't pay us a denarius an hour. We worked harder than they did, and you made them equal to us."

Can we feel like they feel at that moment? Can we feel comfortable in this role? Sure we can. We know what it's like to feel that somebody else is getting special treatment but we aren't. We know what it's like to feel anger when things are unfair and to feel jealousy when somebody else gets a bonus. Unfortunately, the role feels all too comfortable. We can feel just as they do at this moment—but the story tells us we shouldn't. Listen to the owner: "Friend, I am doing you no wrong; did you not agree with me for a denarius? Now, take what belongs to you, and go home; I choose to give to this last as I give to you."

It is so easy for our gratitude to turn into selfishness; for "Thank you for my good fortune" to become "It's mine, all mine." "Now I lay me down to sleep; I pray the Lord my toys to keep; if I die before I wake, I pray the Lord my toys to break so the other kids can't have 'em." We don't have to learn this role. We're born knowing how to play it. The trick is to learn how to act like something else, so let's turn to the second set of characters.

II. Ben-Asher's vineyard was very large. He hired the first gang of workers early in the morning, and they were doing a good job, but he saw that he needed more help to get all the grapes in before they turned too ripe. So he went back to the city to get some more folks. He found a very despondent-looking group. They had not been hired in the early morning, and they knew the chances of getting work were slim. Even if they found it, they wouldn't get a whole day's wages—what were they going to use to feed their families? Looks like the kids will go to bed hungry again tonight. That must be the worst feeling in the world. Your family is counting on you, but you can't support them. But then Ben-Asher came again, and hired them, and their despair turned a little. Maybe we can at least buy some bread for supper.

Then at the end of the day, as the sun was going down, Ben-Asher called a stop. Everyone gathered at the gate and the paymaster got out the money bag. "Let the last workers come to the front of the line," the boss said, and to everyone's astonishment, he gave them a whole day's wages. They can't believe it. Can you imagine looking in your pay envelope and finding double what you were expecting? You know it's got to be a mistake; but the boss says no, that's what you should get. It's Christmas, it's birthday, it's all good things in the world rolled into one incredible moment, and all they can think to say is, "Thank you, Reb Ben-Asher, thank you very much."

Can we feel like these people do? Can we be comfortable in that role? Can you imagine the sense of getting something we didn't really deserve or work for, the sense of gratitude for a very generous gift? The New Testament has a word for this, the word *grace.*

Now, Peter's dumb question that sparked this wonderful story shows that he's looking for a wage, a reward: "Lord, we have left everything and followed you. We've earned our salvation, haven't we? What are you going to give us in return for our sacrifice?" And in this parable, Jesus is saying that the kingdom of God isn't like that. Jesus says essentially what Paul said in another place: "You are saved by God's grace through faith. It is not the result of anything you did; it is purely the gift of God, so don't brag about how you deserve it." Can we play the role of the second group of servants, who simply accept the free, generous gift of the vineyard owner? Let us hope so, because that is what the Bible means by "Christian."

III. One more role to look at—the part of the vineyard owner. Old man Ben-Asher. He's an interesting character. He's a seeker. He doesn't wait for the workers to come to him; he goes out and finds them and invites them to his farm. He's a man of integrity, a man of his word. He promised the first group a denarius, and that's what he paid them. Other owners held back wages, but he never did. He was also a generous man. He knew those latecomers were going to have to feed their families, too. So he did something beyond the expected, beyond even honesty and integrity. He was gracious, even loving, to a group that did not expect it.

The vineyard owner in the parable represents God, does he not? Our heavenly Father reaches out to all people; God takes in the strays and feeds them; he takes pity on the poor and the helpless. I wonder: Can we play this role? Can we act the way God acted in this parable? Can we treat all as equals? Can we reach out in love to people who have no claim on our love? Can we be a seeker, a person of integrity, and a person of grace?

I think we can. Look at Peter, whose question sparked this marvelous story. When he asked the question "What are you going to give us, Lord?" he was thinking simply of reward. He learned to step out of that role and to give himself for his Lord. He, too, complained at first when the Gentiles came into the Church—"They aren't the right kind of people, Lord, and you're making them equal to us!" But he learned to set aside the role of bigot and play God's role, where everyone is a person of worth. Peter learned to shed his old roles and play God's part in life's drama. And you and I can, too. We can put down our grudges, put down our prejudices, put down our envies, and play God's part.—Richard B. Vinson

Illustrations

THE OTHERS. Listen to any impromptu pulpit prayer in church and ask yourself how much of that prayer is for the people inside your church and how much of it is for others. You will discover that nine-tenths, or perhaps ten-tenths of the prayer you hear is for "us in this church." The minister will defend himself by saying that he is voicing the heart's desires of the people before him in the pews, that he is ministering to their need.

But, I ask, is that all his people *ought* to desire? Don't they need to pray for others? They are supposed to be grown Christians. They are supposed to be helping God save the world. This prayer that ends in self reveals something that must pain God: It reveals that the people's major obsession is *not to save the world but to save themselves* from their own troubles.—Frank C. Laubach

LOVE'S PROOF. This great proof of God's love is a fact and not a word or theory. Love must be proved by deeds and not by words. The loudest protestations may be empty. No mere profession of the lip will ever satisfy the heart that longs to know another's love. Love's argument is service. Love's commendation lies in sacrifice. The self-forgetful service of the lover wins, as the words of warmest passion never would. And the proof of deeds is needed above all, when by the proof of deeds love seems disproved. If you or I by any act suspect that we are hated, it is not any word, however warm, that will ever blot that suspicion out. It is only some deed of love, clear, unmistakable, that will have power to do that. When there are facts fighting against the thought of love, nothing but facts can prove it. See, then, the wisdom of our God. It is the facts of nature and of life, of history and of experience, that make it so hard to believe his love. He knows it all, and so the proof he offers of his love is a fact too. Facts must be met by facts. And all the dark facts in life God overwhelms by the one proof of the greatest fact in the world's story. Yes, God so loved the world, not that he said or

thought, but that he gave.—George H. Morrison

SERMON SUGGESTIONS

Topic: A Cry for Help

TEXT: Isa. 64:1–9

(1) That God once again demonstrates his awesome presence in a blasé world, verses 1–3. (2) That God forgives and recreates his sinful people, verses 5–9.

Topic: Christ's Unfinished Task

TEXT: Mark 13:24–37

(1) Gathering his scattered people, verses 24–27. (2) Calling us all to final account, verses 32–37.

Worship Aids

CALL TO WORSHIP. "Turn us again, O God, and cause thy face to shine; and we shall be saved" (Ps. 80:3).

INVOCATION. Expand our minds today, gracious God, that we may know the scope of your love; and deepen our commitment to what we know to be true and right.

OFFERTORY SENTENCE. "The Lord is good to all: and his tender mercies are over all his works (Ps. 145:9).

OFFERTORY PRAYER. Our loving Father, help us to realize that in good times and bad you are the same gracious God, yesterday, today, and forever. Strengthen our faith so that we can believe, even when we cannot see, that your tender care enfolds us all. When material blessings abound, keep us from forgetting you. When things are scarce, may we still be faithful.

PRAYER. O Giver of immortal gladness, fill us with the light of day. O Father of all light, who into the darkness of chaos commanded, "Let there be light," and there was light; and did shine into the world at Bethlehem in the light of the fullness of your love, shine into our minds and hearts and persons that we may be heralds of the coming of your kingdom in this day and place.

We worship and adore you, O Father, in that a common place like Bethlehem is the scene of your advent—that every place is a Bethlehem—the house of God—the dwelling place of the Most High—that our common, everyday experiences are pregnant with the birthing of your kingdom. We rejoice that your coming is so firmly rooted in the terra firma of man's history that we are not alone on this planet but that we are kept by a love that will not let us go.

At Bethlehem may we so discover the signs of your coming that we do not miss your coming in the least of those among us. At Bethlehem we do come to know that all of life is pregnant with your grace waiting to be born in and through us that we may be heralds of the light of your presence in all the dark corners of this world.

We pray for the joy of your coming—the peace that can heal any brokenness for all of those among us broken by the loneliness of death—those broken by life-threatening illnesses—those weakened by any sickness or infirmity of body, mind, or spirit.

O you, who did consecrate the family by your advent here, grant to us a renewed commitment to the sanctity of the home, that it be the sanctuary of your love that you have ordained and the seedbed for all that is true, beautiful, and of real worth.

As a nation, O God, keep us from the arrogance of power that blinds one to his own need for your grace that alone can save, so that we may not miss the day of our visitation.

Through him who is your gift of love in Christmas and is present among us as our living Lord.—John Thompson

LECTIONARY MESSAGE

Topic: Blameless

TEXT: 1 Cor. 1:3–9

I. Have you noticed recently that no one is at fault; at least no one admits being at fault for anything? There's plenty of blame to go around but no one to take it. It's causing quite a problem, this backlog of guilt. The conservatives make fun of the liberals; the liberals rail at the conservatives. Blame is a hot potato. No one wants to catch it.

One of the characters in the "Family Circus" cartoon is a juvenile phantom named "Not Me" who is blamed for everything that goes wrong. Alas, "Not Me" isn't confined to the Sunday comics and the world of children. He's seen often in various disguises in the company of adults.

a. "Not Me" affects personal morality. He's standing behind many of those who parade across daytime television and exchange their particular perversity for fifteen minutes of fame and the cash that goes with being on a syndicated talk show. Rarely do any of them exhibit remorse. Each has set his or her personal needs and desires as the standard of morality. On the occasions when they do recognize their behavior is unacceptable, they resort to blaming others or some childhood trauma.

b. "Not Me" affects public life, too. He's been spotted from the lowest to the highest echelons of government, among both Democrats and Republicans. "Mistakes were made," said Ronald Reagan, speaking about the Iran-Contra debacle. The passive voice gives the impression the mistakes happened of their own volition. No human was responsible. There was no one to blame. "Not Me" is endearing in children but annoying or worse in adults.

II. St. Paul had a different idea about guilt. In his early years he exerted himself to be blameless. He had been a zealous Pharisee, keeping every jot and tittle of the Mosaic Law (Acts 26:5). He knew what a struggle it is to be a moral person in an immoral world. In his letter to the Romans he described his failure to live a godly life. "For what I do is not the good I want to do; no, the evil I do not want to do—this I keep on doing" (Rom 7:19). Notice that Paul didn't pass the blame to someone else. He had learned to trust someone greater than himself for his salvation.

a. The church at Corinth also was familiar with the full range of life's temptations and struggles. Factions divided the church. Sexual immorality among the Corinthians would make a modern TV talk-show host blush. An early ancestor of "Not Me" must have paid them a visit. And yet, Paul thanked God for the Christians at Corinth and spoke positively about their future, including their eternal future. How can this be? How can Paul, who knows very well his sinful nature and that of the people of Corinth, be so assured of his and their salvation?

b. The answer is simple. Paul knows that salvation is not dependent on his near-perfect obedience to the law, nor is it thwarted by the Corinthians' moral failures. Their assurance of salvation, and ours, is based on the faithfulness of God. Human frailty and faithlessness cannot cancel out the power and faithfulness of God. The Corinthians may be, at times, uncharitable, fanatical, or immoral in their behavior, but they have put their faith in the One who makes up for our shortcomings. Christians are justified by the death and resurrection of Jesus. As a result they need not fear to stand before the Judge on the Last Day. We all are justified—that is, found not guilty—by faith rather than our works.

c. The kind of evasive talk that admits only "mistakes were made" erodes the body politic. It destroys faith in government. Our personal excuses have the same effect on the body spiritual. They ruin Church fellowship and destroy personal faith. The remedy is not to talk our way out of responsibility with clever language. Rather, we talk our way into forgiveness by confessing our sins. We may be tempted to "save face" by calling black white, but our real need is to face the truth. As John wrote long ago, "If we claim to be without sin, we deceive ourselves and the truth is not in us. If we confess our sins, he is faithful and just and will forgive us our sins and purify us from all unrighteousness" (1 John 1:8–9).

The day of our Lord Jesus Christ will be sudden and unexpected, but believers have no reason to fear. The One who has called us will keep us strong to the end. If you don't now share this assurance of your salvation, today is a good day to join the redeemed of the Lord. —Alan Hoskins

SUNDAY: DECEMBER EIGHTH

SERVICE OF WORSHIP

Sermon: Trying to Live on Negatives

TEXT: 1 Sam. 14:46

These words deal with Saul, the first king of Israel, his violent warfare, and his final failure. Saul is a strange figure from a far yesterday, yet with a close relationship to some of the moods and life of our time.

He was a valorous man of war. He was the great anti-everything of his time, anti-Moabite, anti-Gibeonite, anti-Hittite. But he had no inner shrine of his own devotion. He is a portrait of a person trying to live on negatives.

Today, around us, there are millions like Saul in that respect. When we ask, "What are your positive values, what are you *for?*" the true answer would be something like this, "I'm against the 'isms.' I'm against Communism, or radicalism, or against racial equality, against the Jews or Catholics or Protestants." If we kept at our questioning, the answer would be the echo of an empty room.

All our current movements, which thrive on the whipping up of hatred and contempt, are examples of trying to live on negatives. To take the hiss out of our thinking and acting today is to move from negative hatreds to positive devotions.

I. This is true in our religious life. Any Christianity worthy of the name must live on positives. The great days in the history of the Church have been those in which great answers have been given to the question, "What are you for?"

a. Here is the heart of the Christian

faith—"God was in Christ reconciling the world to Himself." The great positive is a personal apprehension of that revelation, to say, "I know in whom I have believed." Beside that, we can say truly, all else is trivial. To receive that truth, to proclaim it in word and life, is to center life on the great positive.

b. The positive must mark the whole life of the Church if it is to be more than a debating society. A real danger of Protestantism is that it may confine its efforts to protests against that in which it does not believe. It may forget that the syllable "Pro" in its name means "for" something. Even its great watchwords may become empty phrases. What does the priesthood of all believers mean if the believers never act as priests and never lift up a prayer? What does salvation by faith mean if we do not exercise that faith? What does freedom of speech mean if we have nothing to say?

c. A so-called faith that has more of amiable good wishes and shrewd moral advice in it than it has of a core of theological creed is inadequate for man's plight. If men are to be new creatures, there must be new power. St. Paul looked out on the Roman and Greek world of his day and brought in a terrifically negative report. It still sears the pages in the seventh chapter of Romans. But he had more than negatives. He had this: "If any man is in Christ Jesus he is a new creature."

II. It requires only the briefest mention of this truth in its application to the international situation. When we confine ourselves to criticism and hate, that gives the enemy the center of the stage. It puts the initiative into his hands. We must have a vibrant dynamic democracy in which we believe more strongly and love more dearly than we hate any totalitarianism. Such a faith in our positive values, implemented and supported by aid to democratic forces in the world, would accomplish far more as an alternative to despotism than we have been able to accomplish by supporting, through fear, such ugly totalitarianisms.

III. One great positive of Christianity is the compulsion to struggle against the evil forces of the world. No negative preoccupation can compensate for the withdrawal from active fighting against what St. Paul called the "struggle against the ruling spirits of this dark age."

a. One of the most striking differences between some sections of the Church today and the Christian fellowship pictured in the New Testament Church is that the New Testament Church was fighting something. The Church of the New Testament never thought of itself as being in a rest camp; it was obviously on a battle line. The weakness of some parts of the Church today is the loss of that positive quality of life. It lies in the fact that many people who ought to be struggling against social wrong are not so much fighters as like dear old ladies in snowy white caps, sitting in rocking chairs, not really knowing that any fight is going on. The Church pictured in the Book of Revelation was fighting a "Beast." Today some of us, instead of fighting a Beast, stroke it and pet it and say, "Nice pussy!"

b. Our lives and our words lack sting. They have no dangerous positive commitments. Such a result was described with unconscious satire in an entry in the journal of Samuel Pepys: "A good sermon of Mr. Gifford at church upon 'Seek ye first the kingdom of God.' A very excellent and persuasive, a good and moral sermon. He showed like a wise man that righteousness is a surer way of being rich than sin." O lovely gospel!

c. But wherever there has been present among Christian people the great positive inheritance of a real fight against the exploiting powers of injustice that measures men in terms of profits and uses them as means to an end, there has always followed an enrichment of life and an intensity of spiritual experience. It was true in the first century. It is true in the twentieth.—Halford E. Luccock

Illustrations

"PSYCHIC NUMBING." Al Krass has some insightful things to say about what may cause parishioners to slump even when the preacher feels the Word has been preached with fiery enthusiasm. It's not that they just don't care, says Krass, it's that they care too much; they are numbed by fear of all the structures that may be coming unglued or are glued together in ways that perpetuate evil. It's that they care so much—as the terrorist bullets fly and the farms fail and the tropical rain forests give way to slash-and-burn and the sky threatens to flare with a glow not the sun's—that they dare not approach the shores of the ocean of internal feeling that is their caring. If they did, they might fall in and drown. Krass mentions psychologist Robert Jay Lifton, who worked with survivors of Hiroshima, and suggests that we, like the Japanese when faced with a world filled with actualities and possibilities too frightening to bear, repress our feelings. We are afflicted by "psychic numbing."—Ronald J. Sider/Michael A. King

WHERE WE BELONG.   A man's religion is the audacious bid he makes to bind himself to creation and to the Creator. It is his ultimate attempt to enlarge and to complete his own personality by finding the supreme context in which he rightly belongs.—Gordon W. Allport

SERMON SUGGESTIONS

Topic: A Message of Comfort

TEXT: Isa. 40:1–11 NRSV

(1) *Exegesis:* A message of comfort for God's people assures them that their punishment in exile is over and that God is returning in triumph on the royal road to Jerusalem. (2) *Exposition:* In the salvation history of God's people, there are declines and falls followed by resurgences of faith and hope because "God comes with might," and his people are comforted and rewarded. (3) *Application:* (a) Do not be surprised or dismayed when God allows suffering and deprivation, whether as a consequence of sin or in innocence, verses 6–8a; (b) Cling to God's promise never to leave or forsake, verses 8b and Josh. 1:5. (c) Praise God both in hope and in fulfillment, verses 9–11.

Topic: "If You Are Eager to Do What Is Good"

TEXT: 2 Pet. 3:8–15a NRSV, especially verse 15a

(1) There are affectional virtues you will embrace, verse 8. (2) There are destructive evils you will avoid, verses 9–12. (3) There are powerful incentives you will follow for doing what is right, verses 13–14. (4) There is a compelling secret you will discover in the entire process, verse 15a.

Worship Aids

CALL TO WORSHIP.   "I will hear what God the Lord will speak: for he will speak peace unto his people, and to his saints: but not let them turn again to folly. Surely his salvation is nigh them that fear him; that glory may dwell in our land" (Ps. 85:8–9)

INVOCATION.   We await your word, O God, your strengthening good news. Speak to us of your goodness, your purpose, and your redeeming presence.

OFFERTORY SENTENCE.   "Let the beauty of the Lord our God be upon us: and establish thou the work of our hands upon us; yea, the work of our hands establish thou it" (Ps. 90:17).

OFFERTORY PRAYER.   God of all good, you have rewarded our labors, and we acknowledge thankfully your favor and do now dedicate a share of our material gains to the even more satisfying ministries of the Spirit.

PRAYER.   Eternal God, Lord of all seasons, time of Thanksgiving past has turned our hands and hearts upward to you in gratitude. We have remembered your generous call and blessing upon us, and we give thanks. Forever God, Lord of all time, with grateful and open spirits we embrace this holy moment in time: Advent. It is a season for silence, for preparing, for waiting, for expecting and receiving the wondrous gift of the Christ. O Come, O Come Immanuel, and in our hearts, do dwell.

Gracious God, Master of kind forgiveness, we confess that our lives are not ready to receive this best gift. Our hearts are in the wilderness, so cleanse us from our rebellious wandering. The rough spots of our lives plead for the smoothness of your tender healing. Our crooked ways yield to your mending, in making straight our paths. Bring low our mountains of prejudice and pride; lift up our valleys of despair and defeat. Merciful God, cleanse our wounds of sorrow and loss with your comforting touch, and clothe us in your certain and abiding hope, Jesus Christ our Lord.

All-knowing and loving God, as we ready our spirits to offer acceptable gifts to you and to others this holy season, may we first seek gifts that only you can provide. Gentle Center of quiet presence, we pray for the gift of silence. Like Mary and Joseph, we have much to ponder deep in our souls. Liberate us from our affliction of and addiction to noise, and in the silence, surround us with your redeeming peace and Word. Patient Presence, we pray for the gift of waiting. With the Psalmist, let us wait for you and hope in your Word; to wait and discover enduring strength and clearer direction; to wait and find our harmony in being in step with you.

Abiding Holiness, we pray for the gift of kneeling; to find again the sacred posture of bent knees and bowed heart. In kneeling we see your world differently and find the Christ again in unexpected places and unfamiliar faces. God of all faithfulness, grant us the gift of hopeful expectancy that we may lean forward and onward in our lives and with gladness and delight, to make way, make way for your joyful arrival and stay. Blessed is the Christ who comes in the name of the Lord, for in him we hope and worship and pray.—William M. Johnson

LECTIONARY MESSAGE

Topic: Called to Be Different

Text: Mark 1:1–8

On the stage of history occasionally there appear figures who seem to be from another time. Their thoughts, their dress, and their actions are out of sync with the way the rest of the world does business. John the Baptist was just such a figure.

Instead of wearing the fine woven cloth that was then available, he wore a rough shirt of camel hair and a leather skirt. Instead of eating the traditional foods of the region he subsisted on grasshoppers and wild honey. And instead of settling down in a normal occupation he became an itinerant preacher like the prophets who had not been seen around there in two hundred years.

But the strangest thing of all about John the Baptist was his message: "Repent, for the kingdom of heaven is at hand." If there was anything about him that really seemed to be out of another time, it was those words. It had been a long time since someone had sounded so convinced that God was going to break into history in a powerful way.

Now this is nothing more than historical speculation, but do you suppose John really enjoyed making such a spectacle of himself? Do you think he liked spending all of his time facing the dangers of the wilderness instead of living in a comfortable city? Don't you think he might have felt just a little bit silly going around dressed in animal skins? And that diet probably did not do his digestive system any good either. This is all just supposition, but what if John felt just about the way you and I would feel if we had to do all of those same things today? If that were true, why would he have done them?

The answer to that question may seem simplistic, but it is the only one that fits: He did them because God told him to. If you think about it there have probably been times when you have felt just as silly. If John lived in an age that was just beginning to understand civilization and culture, we live in an age that has perfected it. Perhaps the worst sin one could commit today, or at least the worst social faux pas, would be to offend people's sensibilities by being in any way different.

Yet do we not face the same dilemma as John the Baptist? God has called us to be different, perhaps not so much in the way we dress or what we eat but in the way we think and in the way we act.

It may provide some comfort, however, to realize that, in spite of his differences, people still flocked to hear John the Baptist preach. Perhaps people kept coming back because they sensed that what he said was true. There was a conviction in his voice and a certainty in his eyes that led them to believe that they really had better repent because the kingdom of heaven was just around the corner.

Now if that is true, if people came to John because he convinced them that his message was the genuine article, let me ask you a question: Why do you suppose it is that people pay so little attention to us when we tell them that we are Christian? I am afraid it is because they really don't sense any difference between them and ourselves. They sense that we do feel silly about our Christianity and maybe a little embarrassed, and they don't want to get involved in anything that would cause them any embarrassment.

We must be realistic about this, however. For the most part, people may not be hearing our message because it lacks conviction, but there are also people who don't hear our message because it does have conviction, and the ones it convicts are those people. In all the crowds that came out to hear John the Baptist there was a group of Pharisees and Sadducees. These were the men who already had a lock on the positions of religious power, but they could not afford to let something like this go on without at least checking it out for themselves.

What they got was a little bit more than they bargained for. They got in line to be baptized just like everyone else, but John called a halt to the proceedings. He said, "You bunch of snakes, who told you to get in on this act? You think that just because you are good Jews that is going to be enough to save you from the wrath to come. Don't you know God can grow Jews from rocks if he wants to do it?"

Now admittedly John was not being very polite, and he would probably never get a job in a modern church if he did not learn how to be less blunt about it, but the Pharisees and the Sadducees could not argue with the fact that everything he said was true. They just didn't want to hear it.

The same thing is true today. Many people don't hear our message because they just don't want to. It strikes too close to home.—James M. King

SUNDAY: DECEMBER FIFTEENTH

SERVICE OF WORSHIP

Sermon: To Live Bravely

TEXT: 2 Cor. 3:12–18

We want clean, honest biblical interpretation. But we can't impose *our* standards on Paul. His tradition of Bible use *was* a little different than ours, and I think it was because he saw himself as a bridge-person or a hinge-person between an old era and a new one.

George Beasley-Murray, British New Testament scholar, says the Old Testament didn't become the New Testament ... but it *did* become a *new* Old Testament for Paul. As a Jewish Christian, he began to see in those Scriptures things he'd never seen before. (Remember, the Old Testament was the only Bible Paul had; nobody had suggested a New Testament yet!)

So, what does he do here? Well, in Exodus 34, there is a story about Moses coming down from Mount Sinai with his *second* set of tablets and commandments (he broke the first set). Exodus also says he came down with a *shining face*. So Moses wore a veil, a covering, over his face for a while. He took it off when he addressed God inside the tabernacle and when he came out to speak to the people. But he wore that veil to protect the Israelites from the shining brightness that made everybody afraid to get near him.

Paul gives a different twist to that story. Moses *really* wore that covering, he says, so the Israelites couldn't see the *fading glory* on Moses' face . . . because something bigger and better was on its way to us in Jesus Christ! And those who won't believe that have a covering over their minds and hearts. These Corinthian teachers are still holding to some of that veil . . . too much of the old revelation, too little of the new.

Moses had a limited and transient understanding of God. That's what Paul says. In Christ we have received a more full, more personal understanding—*not* as wrong overtaken by right but as the incomplete taken over by the complete.

The Exodus story doesn't say this, of course, so Paul was either drawing on some later-than-Exodus information that we don't have or his rabbinic influence has switched on.

In fairness to Paul, I think his conclusion is on target. When you experience life in Christ, as Paul has done, you're convinced that it's fuller and brighter than *any* other tradition—no matter how well anchored in the past.

In Paul's case, coming to Jesus Christ *was* like the lifting of a veil . . . like the shining of a brighter light. And it's not that Judaism and the Law and the traditions of the past were untrue; it's that Paul has found something in relationship with Christ that is more true for him and these Corinthian Christians.

So, he writes words like these to say, "Move on into your future with Christ . . . don't retreat into a past you've already left. God's Spirit calls you boldly forward!"

And there's the key to living bravely—it's in verse 17: "Now the Lord is the Spirit, and where the Spirit of the Lord is, there is freedom." The Spirit of the risen Christ, the Holy Spirit, lives *in* you. Christ is not someone *back there* in history . . . he lives in the midst of his people. I think that means that each of us has the freedom to do two things.

I. *First of all, we have the freedom to turn from the fading.*

What's that? It may be the undertow of condemnation and guilt about your past sin. Whatever your crimes and failures, let them fade in the blinding light of God's forgiving grace.

Emil Brunner said, "The most important thing about the devil is this: Jesus Christ has conquered him." Substitute any other word for devil—sin, failure, shame—and the truth still stands: Jesus Christ has conquered it. In Christ, you are forgiven and free . . . don't keep wallowing in yesterday's shame and regret. Let that fade . . . *you* are called to live ahead, boldly.

But—there are a lot of other "fading splendors" in our world, and there are an awful lot of people who don't know that yet. They may be the things you heard about in high school and dreamed about in college, the things you've been chasing all these years: power and influence and status and wealth. You see them and you get them reinforced every night on your television screen.

Then there's the job and the organization and even the code of ethics . . . and all of this is supposed to be the *bright, enduring* center of your life.

But they've turned out like the Jewish Law in some of Paul's experience. He says various things about the Law. One thing he mentions often is that the Law shows us how we *ought* to live and *want* to live but gives us no power to live that way. It gets us in touch with demand, but not in touch with strength to meet it. It creates a hunger that it cannot satisfy.

So many things we give *our* time and energy to leave us with a sense of emptiness and disappointment. "*This isn't it!* This job, this wealth, this influence, this ambition, this code of behavior—all of this was supposed to be the bright and shining center of my life . . . the permanent purpose around which I could build my existence, but it's fading, and I don't know where to turn. I'm still as hungry and empty as ever."

A lot of us here who've come to faith in Jesus Christ would say to you this morning that there's an unfading brightness there that this world can neither give *nor* take away. It's amazing now how dim and fading are those old splendors!

"Where the Spirit of the Lord is, there is freedom" to turn from the fading.

II. *There's a freedom also to turn toward the fresh.* Here's what that means: "All of us, with unveiled faces, seeing the glory of the Lord as though reflected in a mirror, are being transformed into the same image from one degree of glory to another" (v. 18).

Toward the likeness of Christ—*that's* where we're headed, and that's the focus of our living. Furthermore, it will always be fresh, not fading, because you cannot exhaust the mystery of God ... and Christian growth is a lifelong opportunity.

Paul talks about looking into a mirror here. He's talking about our looking at ourselves compared to Christ, and that keeps us changing and growing. But remember that mirrors in Paul's world were not made of glass but of polished metal, so you might get an inexact or even a distorted image.

That's a good way to talk about our growth as Christians. We *do* have distorted images of Christ that we need to outgrow.

Let's be honest—there are distortions of Christ and ourselves that must be cast aside and outgrown. Sometimes Christian faith suffers more at the hands of its friends than its enemies. But being changed into Christ-likeness is still a worthy and wholesome goal.

How can you live bravely? By turning *from* the fading and *toward* the fresh. There's the power and freedom to do that in relationship with Jesus Christ. Maybe this is just what you've been looking for!

Life in Christ begins in a moment of choosing. Faith gets born as you decide not to let life happen to you but to choose a life center for yourself.

How can you live bravely in this kind of world? How can you know freedom when there are so many limits? Paul's answer is the right one: "Turn away from what is fading, turn toward what is forever fresh." It is the risen Christ who beckons us forward and who will be with us every step of the way.—William L. Turner

Illustrations

ONE PERSON COUNTS. Basil King and Channing Pollock were sitting together in a restaurant when a woman at an adjoining table said to her companion, "It's a disgraceful state of affairs, but what can one man do?" The author of *The Conquest of Fear* looked at the man who wrote *The Fool* and asked, "Shall we tell her that everything of importance in the world was begun by one man—or one woman?" Under the title *One Man Power,* Channing Pollock went on to describe the abolition of slums, the reform of prisons, the beginning of the American Red Cross, the origin of the Braille system, the rise of Tuskegee Institute, and many another such things, pointing out that again and again it has been a single man or woman who has raised a banner lonehanded, behind which eventually thousands have enlisted.—Charles F. Kemp

THE ADVENTURE. Bruce Larson remembers how it was with him at the end of World War II. He and his comrades were waiting in Stuttgart, Germany, to come home. And waiting is mostly what they were doing. Some were waiting to go back to sweethearts or wives ... some were waiting to go back to college ... some were waiting to return to jobs. But waiting was what they were about, and they dreamed up ways to kill time and mark the days.

There was one group, however, who lived beyond the inertia and the apathy. They were a Bible-study group led by a regimental chaplain, and in their fellowship there was a sense of present-day vitality and future hope.

"The witness of this handful of men changed me," says Larson. He knelt in the bombed-out apartment building where they were stationed, committing his life to Jesus Christ. "I didn't know all that was involved," he says, "but I gave him all my life, whatever that meant. That was the beginning of the adventure and I am still on it."—William L. Turner

SERMON SUGGESTIONS

Topic: Is This What We Find in Jesus?

TEXT: Isa. 61:1–4, 8–11 NRSV

(1) Good news, verse 1. (2) Grace, verse 2a. (3) Comfort, verses 2b–3. (4) Renewal, verse 4. (5) Justice, verse 8. (6) Recognition, verse 9. (7) Salvation, verses 10–11.

Topic: Simple Directions for Living in a Complex World

TEXT: I Thess. 5:16–24 NRSV

(1) "Rejoice always"—let the Spirit fill you. (2) "Pray without ceasing"—do not give up in discouragement. (3) "Give thanks in all circumstances"—some of God's choicest blessings come when least expected.

Worship Aids

CALL TO WORSHIP.   "They that sow in tears shall reap in joy. He that goeth forth and weepeth, bearing precious seed, shall doubtless come again with rejoicing, bringing his sheaves with him" (Ps. 126:5–6).

INVOCATION.   Today, our Father, we come into your presence, as usual, from many walks of life, each of which has its own burdens. Some of us may be near the breaking point. But your word assures us that you do care for us and tells us that you do invite us to bring you into our struggles. Take your rightful place among us, gracious Father, and work with us even at the cost of pain and sacrifice on our part to make us what you would have us to become.

OFFERTORY SENTENCE.   "Bless the Lord, O my soul, and forget not all his benefits" (Ps. 103:2).

OFFERTORY PRAYER.   Gracious and ever-creating God, we praise you that you have placed us in this lovely, this enchanted place; for we believe that, for all that is wrong here, for all that desperately wants changing, it is the beauty of where you have set us that we cannot comprehend. The beauty of sunrise and sunset, of moon and moving arc of stars, the beauty of the seasons of our life and of the seasons of our friends.

And upon this earth you have called us to be stewards. Stewards of water and soil, stewards of air and ozone, stewards of energy; stewards of creatures at our mercy, large and small. Stewards of vulnerable people whom you call special. Stewards also of ourselves, who also are special.

Show us the work you call us to do and the people you call us to be. Keep us useful, keep us dedicated, but remind us now and then that the most useful things we can do may be to be who we are. Make us loving stewards of the mystery of our own souls, gentle with ourselves, that, in great and centered quiet, we may hear our very own angel whisper, Blessed are those who are gentle with themselves, for they shall inherit the earth. They shall know shalom.—Peter Fribley

PRAYER.   Gracious Lord, you ever call your disciples to be fishers of humanity, and in your son Jesus and all who mirror him you ever hold up to us the living center in whom all our efforts find their source and friend.

When too much does not work out, when too much seems to come to nought, and our hearts are heavy, grant us there to hear your present word, and in faith to cast the net once more, where and when you will, and to find ourselves made strong in the casting, glad and faithful disciples, patient and refilled with hope, men and women, children and youth, whose tank of hope is by no means on empty.—Peter Fribley

LECTIONARY MESSAGE

Topic: Sent

TEXT: John 1:6–8, 19–28

One of the earliest lessons in leadership involves getting the right person to do the job. We can wait for volunteers or we can proactively seek out that one person who will get it done. When God has an important assignment, he carefully selects the person he sends. Like many others before him, John was chosen for a special mission to a specific people. He was sent by God to serve others by seconding Jesus.

I. *Sent by God.* When God does call us, we can either go willingly or reluctantly. Many have tried to decline, but few have succeeded. Moses claimed inadequacy. Jonah cited theological differences. Neither was able to convince God to send someone else. On the other hand, John appears to have accepted willingly. He looked with honor upon his mission to fulfill prophecy.

Our response to God's summons will depend upon the disposition of our hearts. We go where we find reason to go. I have a friend who hated to go shopping until his girlfriend began working at the market. Now he finds any excuse he can to show up at her checkout. Where his "treasure" is, there is his "heart" also. Because John wanted to be the voice that prepared the way for the coming of the Lord, he accepted the call to serve others.

II. *To serve others.* When we are served in a restaurant, the food is placed before us. While good service is important, good food is mandatory. The best waiters and waitresses are completely dependent on the quality of the food. They make sure we have everything we need. They try to take away everything that might hinder our enjoyment. The convenience of the customer and not vice versa is their bottom line. They do their job and then let us enjoy our meals.

John was sent by God to serve others with the Light. He did not accept this calling to advance himself but to see those around him turn on to the Light. John could have assented to the opinion

that he was the Christ. He would have received even greater popularity and honor, thus enhancing his place for the moment.

But could you imagine sitting down in a restaurant where you are served in every way with one exception—the meal is never placed before you. We aren't there to have a quiet chat with the employees. We want to taste the cuisine. In order for those whom he served to enjoy the full meal, John had to exalt the Light while diminishing his own part in the serving. John was sent by God to serve others through seconding Jesus.

III. *Through seconding Jesus.* To second another is to assist, to support and/or to act as an aid. By high school my basketball days were nearly over. There were too many people who were taller, stronger and faster. I extended my career by learning to pass the ball to the better shooters. They scored plenty of points, the team won, the coach was happy, and I got to play. I had found my place on the team.

John knew his role on this team. He was not the star player. His job was to lift up the Light so that others would see the Light and not himself. The team would win only if the Light was lighting the lives of those whom John served.

John's role was crucial. God needed him to be sent as one who would prepare the way for the Light. The people needed John to tell them how they could see and follow the Light. Yet it was important that John never eclipse the Light. And so John was sent by God to serve others by seconding Jesus.—James M. Stinespring

SUNDAY: DECEMBER TWENTY-SECOND

SERVICE OF WORSHIP

Sermon: "What Child Is This?"

TEXT: Isa. 7:10–17; Matt. 1:18–25

Our Scripture for this Christmas Sunday is the story of the other nativity. There are two, you know; the one in Luke, that's the favorite one, and one in

Matthew, that's the other one. Luke features Mary in his story and Matthew features Joseph.

Matthew wants you to see that Jesus fulfills all the expectations of the world. So Matthew doesn't waste any time with the setting or with the characters, the details that make the story so beautiful. He leaves that up to Luke. He just moves directly to the point, and the point is to be found in the announcement of who this baby is. And who he is is revealed by his name. "You shall call his name Jesus, for he will save his people from their sins."

I. I suppose that the name you bear has significance, too, at least one of them. Most of us bear names that have family significance. We can sit down with our children or our grandchildren with the family photo album and point to great-uncles and to grandmothers and say, "You were named for him or for her."

a. Names carry tradition. And in the Bible this is especially so. In the Bible, names even reveal the person's destiny. "You shall call his name Jesus, and he will save his people from their sins." That's his destiny. Matthew wants you to see right off who this baby is. And who he is is revealed in his name. It's his destiny. "Jesus": the name means "God saves." Actually, the name "Joshua" means "God saves." Jesus is the Greek translation of the Hebrew name Joshua. Matthew wrote his gospel in Greek, and so we call him Jesus. But his daddy named him Joshua, which in Hebrew means "God saves."

b. You see, his name has a tradition. Jesus is named for somebody. Joshua was the one who led the Hebrews out of the desert into the Promised Land, as in "Joshua fought the battle of Jericho." His name reveals his destiny: He will save us. And it reveals how he will do it. He will do it by leading us to the promised life, like Joshua.

II. Now I don't know about you, but that helps me to understand what it means to say that Jesus saves us. People talk as if Jesus can't save somebody unless they are totally lost or unless they are in some terrible condition of degradation or misery, "sunk in sin."

a. You see, my problem is not what I have been that I have to get rid of, my problem is what I want to become and haven't attained. I didn't feel like a sinner; I felt like I was not who I could be. I call Jesus my Savior, not because he saved me from a terrible life, but because he has shown me a wonderful life, the kind of life that I want to live.

b. That's why the meaning of his name, Joshua, means so much to me. Because Joshua means "God saves" by leading you into a promised life. Joshua was a leader who led his people into a new life, a promised life. That's what it means to say, "Jesus saves you." It means he leads you into the new life, the life that God has created for you. The Hebrews called it the Promised Land. Moses, and then Joshua, led them into it. It's the life that we know is waiting for us to live. And Matthew wants us to see that Joshua, whom we call Jesus, has come to lead you into it.

c. You may have to renounce some things in order to follow him. He saves some people by forgiving their sins, that's true. But many more he saves simply because they recognized who he was and followed him. Every single disciple, all twelve of them, became a Christian that way. He didn't require confession of their past from them. He just required that they follow him into the future. They saw who he was and followed him. That was enough.

III. Christmas, for Matthew, is simply the announcement that the one you have been waiting for has come. He will lead you from whatever bondage you find yourself in. Immortality is a bondage, but so is fear. So is apathy. So is sorrow a bondage. He has come to lead you from whatever bondage you are in to the promised life.

a. I think that Christmas means so much to believers and nonbelievers alike because there is something in each of us that longs to know that there is a possibility for such a life, that there is something or someone who can release us from our bondage and lead us into that life that we know we are created for. So that at Christmas even the cynical and the hardened among us hope that maybe there really is a chance, maybe it's really true, this announcement, this incredible news that God has come to earth as one of us to lead us into the life He promised at the Creation.

b. "You shall call his name Jesus." The name means "God saves." That's his destiny, to save his people. And it reveals how we will do it, like Joshua, leading us into a promised life.—Mark Trotter

Illustrations

NAMES MAY MEAN SOMETHING.   Joseph Haroutunian was a beloved Presbyterian seminary professor who taught at the McCormick Seminary in Chicago for many years. Over the years I have heard wonderful stories told to me by Presbyterian friends who were taught by him. And John Killinger who taught with him told this story.

Haroutunian was an immigrant from Armenia to this country. When he arrived here his accent was very strong. Someone took him aside and said, "Look, Haroutunian, your accent is a problem, but you can do something about that. Your name, though, is something else. Nobody can spell Haroutunian, and that is going to be a handicap to you professionally in this country. So, why don't you change your name to Harwood or Harwell, something like that?" And Joe looked at the man for a moment and he asked, "What do they mean?" The man said, "What do what mean?" "Those names, Harwood and Harwell. What do they mean?" The man said, "Well, nothing. They're just easier to pronounce and to spell than Haroutunian." Then, Haroutunian said this: "Back in Armenia when my grandfather was baptized they named him Haroutun, which means 'Resurrection.' And when my father was born, they named him Haroutunian, which means 'son of Resurrection.' My name also means 'son of Resurrection.' I am Joseph Haroutunian and I will be a 'son of the Resurrection' all of my days."—Mark Trotter

VICTORY IN CHRIST.   To long to live in the new life is a preparation for communion. Jesus' words to the disciples that he would not drink of the fruit of the vine until he drank it new in his Father's kingdom were immediate words of high comfort, the tryst of a beloved for dark hours ahead. They were also words of joyous anticipation and promise. The kingdom was on its way! No one could stop it now! His death and Resurrection would only seal its victory.

We come to the Lord's Table in the joy of this victory. God has won. The resources of God's power are ours. Come, let us celebrate. The kingdom has come and we have been asked to live in it!

And Jesus Christ is here to drink of the cup new with us!—Lloyd John Oglivie

SERMON SUGGESTIONS

Topic: Foreshadowings
TEXT: 2 Sam. 7:1–11, 16
(1) The text is rightly understood, in the first place, as referring to an earthly dynasty of David. (2) The text is rightly understood, also, as having its ideal fulfillment in Jesus Christ and his kingdom embracing both earth and heaven.

Topic: God's Reversals
Text: Luke 1:47–55
(1) He chose a lowly maiden. (2) He is on the side of the weak and the poor. (3) He has helped his chosen people Israel far beyond and in ways different from Israel's expectations, yet faithful to his promises.

Worship Aids

CALL TO WORSHIP.   "I will sing of the mercies of the Lord forever: with my mouth will I make known thy faithfulness to all generations" (Ps. 89:1).

INVOCATION.   All that we hope for, O God, lies in your power and love. We trust that you are gracious, and we look to you for your forgiveness, for your guidance, and for your imparted strength to obey you. We thank you that Jesus has come to bring to us all your blessings. Today may we honor him and you by opening our hearts to everything that this service of worship may impart to us and through us to others.

OFFERTORY SENTENCE.   "When they were come into the house, they saw the young child with Mary his mother, and fell down, and worshiped him. And they presented unto him gifts; gold and frankincense, and myrrh" (Matt. 2:11).

OFFERTORY PRAYER. Our Lord Jesus Christ, whose birthday has become a season of benevolence and giving, bless these our gifts which we offer in thankfulness for your own self, God's unspeakably precious gift.

PRAYER. We wait upon you, O God, as those who wait for the morning. We wait in faith knowing that you are God who comes and anyone who waits upon you shall never be disappointed. Your coming to the lowliest, the neediest, the weakest is what this season affirms and calls us to celebrate. Your coming is such an advent that earth cannot contain the glory of it—the rapture of it—the wonder of it—but the heavens break forth into music and singing.

Something has happened that has never happened before, for almost every home has some symbol of your coming: a cradle, a wreath, a tree, bright lights. We praise you for your coming in the Meaning that enlightens us, in the Mystery that challenges us, in the Beauty that inspires us, in the Love that grasps us and does not let us go.

We praise you for your coming just now in the Word, music, song, fellowship of this time and place. Our hearts have been strangely warmed; our minds have been challenged to grasp new heights and depths of the meaning of your coming; our imaginations have been dared to let go of "that-is" to perceive the "not-yet."

O God of all comfort, we find ourselves mourning, but may we not mourn as those without hope, for the Dayspring from on high is come and the dawn of his advent shines more and more unto the perfect day. For those ill, and for those loved ones and friends who keep prayerful vigil in their behalf, we pray. Grant us the faith that begets the wisdom to pray for your mercy, where death is a blessing, releasing the Spirit from a diseased body. Bless those among us who are guests, that here they may experience the comradeship of your people, that together we may rejoice in the wonder of your love that so quickly removes any strangeness and baptizes into the communion of your Spirit.

We pray for peace, for we realize that we have neglected or ignored your call for justice for all peoples. We pray that somehow the meaning and power of love to reconcile may invade the minds and hearts of those who are so crazed with self-seeking power that they ruin that which they would rule and millions are left homeless and starving.

We pray for world leaders who agonize over a strategy that can bring sanity to troubled areas and for all who have left home and homeland on missions of mercy.

May we faithfully pray and wisely work for that day that all creation will echo back the angels' song of the first Christmas: "Glory to God in the highest and peace on earth to persons of good will."—John Thompson

LECTIONARY MESSAGE

Topic: God's Surprising Presence

TEXT: Luke 1:26–38

It's always a wonderful surprise to find something good in an unexpected place. The Bible is full of experiences like that. More often than not, the something good that is found in an unexpected place is none other than God!

Whatever it was that Mary was doing that day, she certainly did not expect to be confronted with a messenger from heaven. But suddenly, there he was—the angel Gabriel. It wasn't his presence that bothered her so much as what he said to her. According to Luke, it was something on the order of: "Congratulations! The Lord is very pleased with you." With that, Mary "was greatly troubled . . . and considered in her mind what sort of greeting that might be" (v. 29).

I suspect that Mary knew her own national history well enough to know that being the object of God's favor could be a rather dubious honor—at least, from the human point of view. In fact, as Scripture describes it, having God's favor is never a guarantee of smooth sailing through life. The truth is, most often it guarantees the exact opposite.

Noah was judged to be nothing more than a lunatic by his neighbors. They heckled and jeered him all the while he built and waterproofed that boat, and especially when he gathered his family and loaded all those animals. Moses found favor in God's sight and look where it got him. For forty years he led a group of complaining, grumbling people through the desert. Jeremiah, the prophet, was another one of God's favored. He was hated and rejected by his own people. In fact, he was despised so much that they tossed him into an abandoned well just to get him out of their sight. Apparently, Mary had good reason to be troubled at Gabriel's unexpected greeting.

Several lessons become clear in all of this.

I. Our lives are often reshaped by the unexpected intervention of God.

The Bible is quite literally the story of how God unexpectedly breaks into the lives of his people. Isn't that also the wonder of our Christian experience? Unexpectedly, sins are forgiven and guilt is removed. God comes suddenly, and whole new vistas are opened. Dreams are reshaped, lives are recreated, hope is renewed, faith is reinvigorated. New opportunities, new directions, and new goals are presented.

II. God uses ordinary people to do extraordinary things.

Almost exclusively in the Bible, God used ordinary people to do extraordinary jobs. For instance, Mary appears to be as ordinary a person as we can find anywhere in the Bible. In fact, the entire episode is extraordinary in its ordinariness.

You and I have this notion that when God speaks, his speaking is always accompanied by loud claps of thunder, rushing wind, and bright flashes of lightning.

We are always looking for him in the dramatic occurrences of life. But in Mary's encounter, there were no warnings. There were no bright lights or fireworks. The earth didn't tremble, shake, or open up underneath Mary's feet. Apparently, she wasn't even at worship. She was going about her everyday affairs when God came to her.

For us, that means that every day there's the possibility that we may be confronted by an angel who has an announcement directly from heaven to make to us—or maybe, God himself will appear. If it happens, of course it will be surprising and unexpected—just like it was for Mary. And what he says may seem impossible, or even a little crazy. But if it happens, it will likely occur in the midst of the most ordinary events of our life—while we're doing housework or homework, putting together some important deal or proposal, or at play with our friends.

I suspect that our world is just as full of heavenly announcements as was the biblical world. I suppose that God is just as talkative today as he was back then. There's just so much more to distract us today. Our eyes are not as keenly sensitive to his presence. Our hearing is not as finely tuned to his voice.

III. God never forces his will upon us.

God always *asks* for our cooperation. It's true that in God is concentrated all the power of the universe. His power is so great that we have a formal theological term for it. We say that God is "omnipotent"—meaning that there is no greater power in all the world—not combined, composite, nor even concentrated—that is equal to, or surpasses the power of God.

Yet God's all-powerfulness has certain limits, set by God, to be sure, but nevertheless real. When it comes to you and me, this all-powerful God never forces himself upon us. He always asks.

That element of the story is not seen until the last verse of the text. Up until that point, it almost seems that everything is already set and predetermined when Gabriel appears to Mary. "The Holy Spirit *will* come upon you . . . the power of the Most High *will* overshadow you" (v. 35). In the other Gospel that tells the details surrounding his birth, the angel announces to Joseph that Mary "*shall* conceive and bear a son, and you *shall* call his name Jesus." (Matt. 1:21). It all seems pretty definite and certain. It doesn't appear that Mary has much say at all in it.

But to interpret the story that way misses the whole point of the text. The point is: Mary didn't *have* to say "yes." All that God proposed and the angel announced were conditional upon Mary's response. Would she say "yes"—or, would she say, "no"? Would she cooperate in God's plan, or would she tell him to go find someone else? Her response was not coerced. It was purely, simply, and wonderfully voluntary: "Here I am, Lord. May it be done to me as you have said."

He calls us all, you know. He gives us each an opportunity to be a part of what he's up to in our world. I know that you and I haven't been called, as Mary was, to bring the Savior into the world. And yet, in another sense, that is precisely what God has called us to do. He asks us each to bring Christ into our own individual worlds, those personal, little universes in which we live and move and find our existence.

Like Mary, we can say either "yes" or "no." God won't *make* us do something that we don't want to do. He won't force us to bring Christ alive either within us or within our world. God is a God who chooses to ask first.—Gary C. Redding

SUNDAY: DECEMBER TWENTY-NINTH

SERVICE OF WORSHIP

Sermon: Old Simeon And Anna

TEXT: Luke 2:22–40

I. "What in the world are we going to do with those two old people? They are always here. They go through the motions and they participate in the service, and yet it never seems to be enough. It is like they keep waiting for something special to happen. What is wrong with them?

a. Ah, so you have met old Simeon and Anna. Nobody knows for sure how long either one of them has been here. But they are harmless. They won't bother you any. Although I will confess that sometimes it does get to be a little unnerving to have them wandering around mumbling that stuff about longing and hoping for the consolation of Israel all the time.

b. I used to resent them and the way they always were hanging around and sharing in the worship and then, as you suggest, kind of throwing a wet blanket on all of our successes. Just when we had one of the largest and best days in the Temple, there would be Simeon and Anna still with that look in their eyes and that longing in their hearts for that something more that you and I would never be able to give them.

c. You see that young family over there bringing that young boy here for the sacrament of dedication? If you were to ask them why they are bringing their child to the Temple, they would tell you in order that he might grow up according to the Law, that he might be shaped and nurtured according to the traditions of God. They might not say it that way, but that is why they come, and old Simeon and Anna are the best the system produces.

II. Old Simeon and Anna have lived all their lives waiting on the promise of God to bring about the redemption of his people. That one hope, that one vision, that one dream, has been the center of their entire lives. They have lived always awaiting, looking, longing for that moment when God moves in their lives.

a. Don't you know lawyers who are out there who once had a great passion for justice, for truth, for doing right, who over and over again discover that the law could not and did not give justice, truth, or the right. And slowly they gave up that passion for justice and decided to settle for the law, and now all they do is offer to be the best legal adviser around. They have settled for being legally correct. Doctors, who began with a great passion for helping and healing and giving life, and life more abundant, have discovered that all the science they know can really only give longevity to body functions, and so they have made that their passion and they keep people alive as long as possible without much regard to life. Teachers, who began as so excited about learning, curiosity, sharing, slowly realized that what they wanted to do couldn't be done in the context of where they teach, and so they settle for presenting the information and keeping discipline, and even that is not easy.

b. The most remarkable thing about them is that they have been able to participate in the Temple, to be nurtured in the Torah, to be fed by the traditions and the prophets, to be immersed in the benefits of all that we as priests are able to do and yet still to know that nothing we have been able to do was enough to satisfy. You said it well. Nothing we ever do satisfies them, for nothing we do is God's act to bring in his kingdom. All we are ever doing is preparing, bearing witness to, pointing in that direction.

III. Old Simeon and Anna are the best our religion can produce because they have not rejected and thrown away the ritual, the Temple, the Torah because it could not give them what they wanted, and they have compromised and agreed to settle for only what the system could offer. They have found that worship and the Temple were able to keep alive and burning in them the deep flame of expectancy; the Law did not fulfill that hope, but it did keep that flame alive, and they refuse to accept and be contented with any second best. They would not abandon the hope for the best to be satisfied with something less.

a. All of which makes their reaction to that baby seem so strange and mysterious. They start singing and praying and shouting as if they had seen what they were waiting for. A child, a gift of God to that family, and they suddenly have a contentment that they had never found before. Both of them act now like they could die tonight because they have finally seen what they were waiting for. They don't seem preoccupied with wanting to be here to see all the wonderful things that would happen.

b. And it is strange how as they saw that child, they realize for the first time that if God comes to bring his redemp- tion, to bring the consolation of Israel, it will have to be the consolation of the Gentiles as well, that if God moves in history to save the Jews, salvation will have to involve the whole world. The one who comes as God to redeem will be making redemption possible for all who desire redemption so that old Simeon and Anna begin talking radical changes in their old expectations and hopes from the moment they see this child.

IV. Funny how the moment they see the child it suddenly dawns on them that wherever the light comes it will have a divisive effect. The act of God's grace has a way of dividing those who are ready for that grace from those who do not want it and think they do not need it. The act of God's love is an intrusive love that comes in this child and is either welcomed or resented. At the moment when old Simeon and Anna are singing and rejoicing, they immediately start talking about the pain, the suffering, the burden of sacrifice the child will have and his followers will have as they offer goodness and mercy in a world that so often prefers its darkness.

Funny, one kind of thought that old Simeon and Anna were so set in their ways that they were going to die looking and longing for the Messiah; now they are acting like teenagers and claim they have seen what they have been waiting for in a baby, and that one glimpse at that baby filled their understanding of the grace of God with a universal note it seldom had before, and it put a tear of pain and sorrow in that Messiah that most of us had never considered.

Ah, it is time for the service, let us do what we know while we wait to see what happens.—Rick Brand

Illustrations

LETTING GOD WORK. As an institution, the Temple is as dubious as the Church. But an Israel that does not live in the past and put its faith in what has gone before, being open instead to God's new and astonishing act, will see this act as the fulfillment of what has gone before; it therefore begins appropriately in the

Temple (1:8–9, 2:22, 27, 37). The two prophet figures, like the parents of Jesus, represent a good but "unfulfilled" life. Such a life does not give up its yearning in resignation or heal it with some "religious" patent medicine but holds fast to the experience of God's grace, thereby truly hungering for God's presence to be realized and looking for it in the future.

Its coming, however, is totally different from what was expected. Anna and Simeon, therefore, have a sense of the sword of judgment without which God's good coming is impossible. Only those who allow themselves to be delivered from all perversion and extenuation know the meaning of grace and peace. That is the "consolation" of Israel. Here all that Israel had learned through the centuries from experiencing the word of its God becomes visible as a ministry to the nations, a ministry that gives Israel, too, its meaning and identity as "light to the nations" (Isa. 49:6). Simeon shows that peace can also consist in retreating to the rank and file and letting God work.—Eduard Schweizer

THE QUIET BELIEVERS. There was no Jew who did not regard his own nation as the chosen people. But the Jews saw quite clearly that by human means their nation could never attain to the supreme world greatness they believed their destiny involved. By far the greater number of them believed that because the Jews were the chosen people, they were bound someday to become masters of the world and lords of all the nation. To bring in that day some believed that some great, celestial champion would descend upon the earth; some believed that there would arise another king of David's line and that all the old glories would revive; some believed that God Himself would break directly into history by supernatural means. But in contrast to all that there were some few people who were known as *The Quiet in the Land*. They had no dreams of violence and of power and of armies with banners; they believed in a life of constant prayer and quiet watchfulness until God should come. All their lives they waited quietly and patiently

upon God. Simeon was like that; in prayer, in worship, in humble and faithful expectation, he was waiting for the day when God would comfort his people.—William Barclay

SERMON SUGGESTIONS

Topic: Why Praise the Lord?

TEXT: Ps. 148 NRSV

(1) The Lord created all things. (2) The Lord bends all things to his ultimate purpose. (3) We can know that the Lord's purpose toward us is a purpose of love, seen most clearly in his Son, Jesus Christ (see John 1:14, 18).

Topic: What They Saw in Jesus

TEXT: Luke 2:22–40

(1) What Simeon saw: (a) salvation; (b) revelation and good news for the Gentiles; (c) an occasion for judgment, verse 34. (2) What Anna saw: (a) an occasion for praise; (b) an occasion for sharing good news.

Worship Aids

CALL TO WORSHIP. "Praise ye the Lord: for it is good to sing praises unto our God; for it is pleasant; and praise is comely" (Ps. 147:1).

INVOCATION. Merciful God, not for the Church or the good have you sent your Son, but for the least and the lost, not for the bountiful people, as if to ask their endorsement, but for the vulnerable, the poor, and the plain; and not with news that they have won the lottery, whereby now to view the common herd as if visitors at a zoo, but with the simple gifts of hope and encouragement, of being treated with respect, somebodies worth God's worry, somebodies worth stage center on a cross. Forgive us what gets our attention and who, and who and what so often do not. Teach us, in our handing on of faith, that *first class* is determined by sender and not recipient, and that God so loved the world that he sent faith, hope, and love first class, and that they shall therefore be handed on with the care, respect, and compassion they deserve, paid for by sender and all saints, that love's such prodigal labors not be lost.

OFFERTORY SENTENCE. "God is not unrighteous to forget your work and labor of love, which ye have showed toward his name, in that ye have ministered to the saints, and do minister" (Heb. 6:10).

OFFERTORY PRAYER. Creator God, make us willing givers who match desire with ability and compassion with generosity in giving for the kingdom that God gave a Son to create.—E. Lee Phillips

PRAYER. God of love, we thank you for the gift of children: their new way of seeing things; their openness; their willingness to say just how they feel. We thank you that children are the world's fresh start.

We thank you, Lord, for the wonderful way that children can move from work to play, for their gift of laughter, and for children's gift of trust that cannot be far from the kingdom.

God of love, we thank you for the child advocates and for teachers who teach with love and sympathy, and with great patience. God of the covenant, we thank you for the many members of this church who truly take to heart their vow to raise baptized children in the love and mercy of our Lord Jesus Christ, leading them to faith by instruction and by example.

We pray, O Lord, for family life where children may learn trust; that we may be better listeners; that kids not be asked to have adult emotions nor play adult roles, but that kids be allowed to be kids; and we pray that every child have a teacher, a mentor, in the faith.

We pray that our children know persons of other cultures, and that they judge no one by color or class. Show us how we can work for a better world for all children, a world where no child need starve, a world where no child shall bear the scars of some great wrong. Hasten the day when the child shall safely place her hand over the adder's den, and they shall not hurt or destroy on all your holy mountain, for as the waters fill the sea, so shall the land be filled with the knowledge of the Lord.

And as Mary cradled Jesus, and the angel watched over Joseph, and Joseph over Jesus, saving him from Herod, may you watch over all your children, and may each of us be some child's Mary, some child's watchful Joseph, some child's timely angel.—Peter Fribley

LECTIONARY MESSAGE

Topic: What the Lord Has Done!

TEXT: Gal. 4:4–7

Few passages of the Bible summarize the Christian gospel as briefly and as well as the passage under consideration. In four short verses Paul alludes to the biblical concepts of creation, a biblical philosophy of history, the importance of the manner of Jesus' birth, the concept of adoptionist redemption, the relationship between the Jewish concept of "the Law" and the Christian doctrine of salvation, the Christian emphasis on the presence of the Spirit in believers, and the response to God that must be made in the life of the believer.

One can only stand in awe that such complicated relationships have been presented in such a complete yet succinct manner. It makes the related Scripture passages even more significant that this is "What the Lord has done" (Isa. 61:10), and that his action can produce the joy, victory, and praise of the believer in such a full manner.

I. The authors of Hebrew Scriptures believed in and based the whole authority of their Scriptures on the God who was the Creator of all the world and of every creature. They stood in awe of the power of this Creator but equally acknowledged the interest the Creator had in the continuing needs of his creations.

II. The Creator God did not create and then leave these creatures to their own devices. He continued to have an interest in and a plan for his creatures. The phrase "in the fullness of time" emphasizes his continued interest in and care for them, even as he gave them the opportunity either to respond to him or to wander from him.

III. The fact that God sent his Son, born of a woman, further stresses the initiative of God in what he has done for his creation and in answer to the problems produced by his creatures within his creation. The One sent to resolve the problems that existed had both the qualities of those he came to "save" and was, at the same time, divinely qualified and sent to perform God's purpose for them.

IV. Paul's emphasis upon "adoption" stresses both the result of creation and the consequences of disobedience in the life of God's creation. Paul further emphasizes that it is the action of God that makes possible the relationship between God the Father and his "adopted" sons and daughters. The relationship established by the action of God could be understood and appreciated by those to whom Paul wrote because they had even more immediate examples of what the new relationship implied in the lives of some known personally to them.

V. For Paul's contemporaries the tension between keeping "the Law" and the Christian doctrine of salvation had even more importance in one's identity and the relationship with how one could be saved. Today the emphasis between the two is more on one's own attempts at earning salvation or in trusting in the grace of God for it.

VI. The presence of the Spirit of God in the life of the believer is both the assurance of salvation and the result of this salvation. Both are a continuing assurance of the reality of salvation. The presence of the Spirit of God is the evidence of one's relationship with God, just as certain familial characteristics are evidence of one's physical parentage.

VII. The cry of the son or daughter to the father is also both evidence of and the result of the relationship. The tragedy of the abandoned child gives human evidence of the importance of the love both needed and received in the salvation experience. It also gives evidence of the response to God that must be made in the life of the believer.—Arthur L. Walker

SECTION III.
Messages for Communion Services

SERMON SUGGESTIONS

Topic: "Lift Up Your Hearts"

You will recognize at once that our topic, "Lift Up Your Hearts," is a part of the ritual for the Sacrament of the Lord's Supper. It is more than ritual; it is a guide to spiritual power. It is a word that has meant much to me and, I am sure, to countless others. When we confront the thousand problems that make up our day, we find in these words a direction and a dynamic that enable us to cope. When life's burdens drag you down, "Lift Up Your Hearts!"

I do not know any word more needed in modern life than this word of hope. It is a word that points us to God in all the experiences of life. When the minister says, "Lift up your hearts," the people reply, "We lift them up unto the Lord." Here is a saving word, that gives victory even in troubles. Faith that looks up to God gives new perspective, and we see at the heart of every trouble a promise placed there by God. This is the reason we can grow on troubles and difficulties. When we lift up our hearts, we give God a chance to make our life a wonderful adventure rather than a daily drudgery. To see the God-lighted side of our troubles is to find promise and meaning that give us zest and the power of going on.

How you look at the experiences of life is much more important than the experiences themselves. The late Dr. Harry N. Holmes of Australia used to say, "Life

is what you make it and how you take it." Our experiences are the raw materials that we are to use to shape our life. If we look at the dark side of our experiences, and live in the shadows of our anxieties and negativism, we will indeed find life a dreary struggle. But God is perpetually calling us to lift up our hearts so that we can live in the light of his presence and his purpose rather than in the shadows of our doubts and ignorance.

The last two lines of the antiphon have their own powerful inspiration.

Let us give thanks unto the Lord;
It is meet and right so to do.

Believing Christians give thanks to God at all times. They praise God no matter what happens. They find a shining splendor even in darkest tragedy. Their religion is centered in the cross—once a symbol of suffering, humiliation, and death, now transformed by God's grace into a symbol of hope and salvation. "Think it not strange concerning the fiery trial which is to try you as though some strange thing happened to you. But rejoice, inasmuch as you are partakers of Christ's sufferings." So 1 Peter 4:12 speaks to our situation the word of life. In every tragedy we can be sure of God's participating presence if we lift up our hearts and give thanks unto the Lord.

Gilbert Chesterton once said, "It is not true that Christianity has been tried and found wanting. It is true that it has been found difficult and not tried." It is not

251

true that God fails us when we suffer; it is true that we fail to lift up our hearts and give thanks in time of trouble. To turn to God is to find hope and light and strength. What we actually do is worry about our troubles until anxiety magnifies them and we are overwhelmed. Mark Twain said, "In my life I have known many troubles, most of which never happened." How many of our troubles are imaginary! How we distress ourselves by worrying about things that never happen! If we lift up our hearts and give thanks, faith will dispel fear and we will be given power to face toward with courage.

But what about troubles that are real, not imaginary? Let us accept them as facts of our mortal life, but let us get up on the God-lighted side of them. When we look at tragedy through the eyes of faith, we discover glorious meanings that God has put there. Obstacles become opportunities; millstones become milestones; trouble is something to grow on; we can face the worst, and believe the best.

There are shadows in our life, but we do not have to sit among them. The negative person is half defeated before he begins to struggle against difficulties. The positive person sees God in the experience with him and praises God for the promise that all things are possible to him who believes. When we look to God, we know that we can do all things through Christ who strengthens us.

You can be sure of this: God knows what he is about, and if he tolerates trouble and tragedy, it is because he has a special promise of grace for you. Whenever you face a trouble, begin by thanking God for his love and goodness. What a way to live! When you lift up your hearts in praise, your spiritual life deepens, you have new compassion for others, all of your horizons become bright with hope!

So lift up your hearts, give thanks unto the Lord, and no matter what your shadowed experience, get on the God-lighted side of it, and make a fresh beginning of faith today!—Lowell M. Atkinson

Topic: Communion Meditation: Lent

To follow Jesus in Lent or in any other season is to live close to him—to identify with him. To be his disciples is to commit ourselves to his disciplines. His life, ministry, passion, which Lent is about, reveal that the highest discipline is the discipline of the Father's love.

In the Gospel account we read that when Jesus had set his face like flint to go to Jerusalem, his disciples accompanying him on the journey were arguing about the chief seats in the coming kingdom. How out of step they were with their Master! Overhearing their discussion, Jesus confronts them: "Are you able to drink of the cup of which I am about to drink and be baptized with the baptism with which I am to be baptized?"

The cup of which he is about to drink was the cup of suffering, which he prayed in the garden he might be spared: "Father, if it be possible, let this cup pass from me. . . ." The baptism with which he was to be baptized was to be so immersed in the "Father's love as to give to the uttermost."

Topic: Prayer of Consecration

For your gift of Word and Sacrament by which the Church lives and by which we are enlightened and nurtured and nourished, we give you thanks. Consecrate now the Bread and Cup of the Sacrament that they may be for us the means of grace that Christ intended. May we come in such faith that our participation in the life and spirit of Jesus may be as real as though we were eating of his body and drinking of his blood.

Topic: Prayer of Thanksgiving

We praise you, O Father, that in your house there *is* bread enough and to spare—that there is a grace at the very heart of life that is not only sufficient but *more* than sufficient—that in life's strife we need not be victims, but we can be *victors*. We thank you for wine for the journey and sustenance for the Way. In the most untoward of circumstances may we be graceful—full of grace—that there may be in us light and not darkness.

Where there are life-threatening circumstances, we pray for the courage that makes us ready for anything. In this pilgrimage of Lent may we realize that the cross is not on a green hill far away but confronts us on the turf where our life is set—it is the challenge of the discipline of love that comes to every disciple—to give to the uttermost. O God, may we follow, if even afar off. For your glory and the sake of all of those for whom we have responsibility, we pray.

And, now may the grace of our Lord Jesus Christ—the love of God, and the *communion* of the Holy Spirit be with us all.—John Thompson

Topic: Jesus, Center Stage

TEXT: Matt. 26:26–30

Several years ago there was a basketball game, nationally televised, when North Carolina was playing Virginia for the ACC championship. In the second half, as soon as UNC had a small lead, they went into their famous four corners. The team just passed it around and around the outside of the court, just looking to kill time. The Virginia fans screamed, "Boring, boring," until they were blue in the face, but it didn't make any difference. For almost fifteen minutes, North Carolina held the ball, not making any attempt to score. The TV stations had to break away for a commercial while play was still going on, and when they came back, nothing had happened! The very next season, there was a forty-five-second clock to prevent anything like that from ever happening again!

Too much repetition, and we get bored. Yet here we have a meal, if you call bread and grape juice a meal, that Christians have been doing virtually the same way for two thousand years. We all know the words by heart—this is my body, this is my blood—we all know the routine. Why do we do the same thing over and over?

I. To answer the question, we look back at the very first time the meal ever happened, before it became a ritual. Jesus, on the very night when Judas turned him over to the Temple authorities, on the night before he was executed, gathered his disciples together for a meal. It wasn't just any night, or any meal, either; it was Passover, perhaps the most important night of all for Jews. All over the world that night, Jews were gathering in homes to eat the same foods: a roasted lamb, bitter herbs, flat unleavened bread, and wine. In every Jewish home, the host was taking up a piece of the flat bread and saying, "This is the bread of haste, which our ancestors ate in Egypt," and passing it around.

Jesus, though, broke the ritual. He did something new. "This is my body," he said, passing around the bread. "This is my blood of the covenant which is shed for many for the forgiveness of sins," he said, commanding everyone to drink from the cup. What did he mean?

The Passover meal celebrated the Jews' coming out of Egypt. They were slaves in Egypt, but God rescued them. He told them, "I will be your God; now you must follow my laws." Jesus' meal was also a covenant meal. He was saying, "I will be your Lord; now you must follow my laws," and then he himself was the sacrifice that sealed the covenant. Every time we eat the supper, then, we remember that his death brought us forgiveness of sins. He died to seal our deal with God, so that we could be His people.

There's an old Lucille Ball sketch where Lucy took a job at a cake-decorating factory. She had to squirt icing out of a tube onto the top of the cake, put a cherry on the top, and put it in the box. But the belt bringing the cakes out to her moved just a little too fast for her to keep up. She gradually got a little more behind until finally she was trying to balance about seven cakes in her hands while she dealt with the new ones that kept coming out.

That's humanity. We broke God's laws, and we could never quite make up the ground we lost. We needed someone to stop the assembly line, to keep us from having to fall over and over again and again. Jesus did that: a new covenant, based on his own sacrifice, that forgave our sins and gave us a fresh start. So when we eat the supper, we are celebrating the newness of Christianity. Jesus gave us a new covenant, a whole new chance at life. The meal takes us back to our very beginnings, every time we do it, reminding us of what a new thing it was.

II. When Jesus started the ritual of the supper, he was doing something new. After two thousand years, though, the new has sort of worn off. He told us to do it this way: Take, eat, this is my body; drink it, all of you. Jesus knew he was starting something that would be repeated so long as there were Christians left on earth to celebrate it. What's the value in so much repetition? Why keep doing the same ritual over and over?

Think of this: Jesus taught his followers to practice the supper. They went out and started churches and taught it to them. Paul, beginning churches in Corinth and Macedonia, taught the traditions of the supper. In the centuries that followed, while Christianity was illegal, they continued to meet in homes at their own peril to celebrate with the bread and the wine. The Church spread from Greece to Italy and from Italy to France and Spain and to North Africa; "This is my body" and "This is my blood" was spoken in Greek and Latin and Coptic and Syriac and Ethiopic and Slavonic.

After the Church became officially legal, the Christian faith was carried all over the world, as missionaries went to England and to China and to India and to Japan. Down through the Middle Ages, priests spoke the words, sometimes not even knowing what they meant, but they still spoke them. Down to the time of the Reformation, when Luther and Calvin and the rest reinterpreted the supper, down to our own Baptist ancestors in England, who celebrated communion secretly in the woods because it was illegal to do it except in the Anglican churches, down to your own great-grandparents and grandparents and parents and now down to you—Do you see? That's the value of repetition. It ties us to the whole history of the Christian Church. It makes us realize that we are the next step in the chain of tradition. Just as we depended on them, so future generations depend on us to be faithful.

And through it all, through all the changes and mistakes the Church has made and will make, Jesus has been our Lord, and we have followed his command to eat this meal.

Repetition—ritual—helps us to remember the past, and that is important. But unless we have a future, ritual is sort of sad; sort of like the hamster running around and around the treadmill in his cage, never going anywhere except where he's already been. If the supper reminds us of our beginnings, and of our past down to the present, then it is interesting, but sad. But Jesus said that it was also a promised meal. We eat, not just to remember, but to think about the future. Jesus said in verse 29, "I tell you, I will not drink from now on from the fruit of the vine until that day when I drink it new, with you all, in my Father's kingdom."

Think about that promise for a minute. When Jesus said it, there were hard times still ahead. Judas would betray him. Peter and the rest would deny him and leave him to die all alone. Most of all, there was the cross, the cup of death that Jesus wished with all his heart to be spared. But he was full of hope. For the disciples sharing the meal, there were hard times. All of them would be persecuted and die for their faith; but they could be full of hope. For us, too, life is no bed of roses. We face struggles with sin. We get slapped around by life, knocked down by sickness; we are mistreated by others, we are misunderstood, we fail. Some days life looks like the story of Sisyphus, the man condemned to roll a stone up a hill only to have it roll back down every time, for eternity.

Not so, brothers and sisters! Every time we celebrate the supper, we remind ourselves that we are heading toward God's kingdom. We are not going around and around, not sliding up and down the same hill. We repeat the supper, but every repetition takes us one step closer to the day when God will bring in his rule of justice and freedom for every human being. We move closer to God's kingdom every time we share this meal together.

The supper is a ritual that we have been repeating for two thousand years. If we do it mindlessly, by the numbers, it is simply an old habit, and the world would be justified to shout "Boring, boring" at us. But if we think about what we are doing as we do it, the supper is a moment of sacred time. In fact, it is like a time machine: it takes us back to that fateful night, the moment when the new covenant was born, it takes us through all the moments of Christian history to our own day, and it takes us into the future to the moment when God's justice will reign supreme. Let us enter into this moment with reverence.—Richard B. Vinson

ILLUSTRATIONS FOR COMMUNION

THE CUP OF WONDER.   Archbishop William Temple said that without the experience of communion, the faith would become too vague. Too theoretical. Communion is the Word of God illustrated. It is visualized and directed to more than one of the senses in order that we might not merely hear the message of divine grace but also see and taste it. We eat and drink, which means we receive that by which we live. Just as wheat bread is the nourishment of the body, Christ is the bread of soul.—Lloyd John Oglivie

THE OVERFLOWING HEART.   Dr. Frank S. Mead had a practical and pointed message in his book, *Rebels with a Cause*. He tells how London awarded General William Booth the freedom of the city. In his acceptance speech, General Booth told about an experience during the Boer War when it became necessary to ration food. It was decided that their limited supplies would be doled out by the churches to the people. The Anglican priest cried out, "All who belong to my communion, follow me!" The Methodist said, "All Methodists, follow me!" The Baptist and Lutheran said the same. Finally, the Salvation Army general said, "All you chaps who belong to nobody, follow me!" Do somebodies care for each other? Do somebodies care for nobodies? What about us? How much do we really care about others? Eugene Debs once said: "Where there is a lower class, I am in it, while there is a criminal element I am of it; where there is a soul in prison, I am not free."—J. Alfred Smith, Sr.

DREAMS COME TRUE.   I was reading recently a letter written by Tagore, the great poet of India. He was writing to a young English clergyman who had just arrived in that country as a missionary. "Do not be forever just preaching your doctrines, but give yourself in kindly, sacrificial service to the people of this land. Preaching is not sacrifice. It may be a form of self-indulgence more dangerous than any luxury. Men often feel that they have been doing their duty, when they were merely talking about it. And the best preaching of all is to 'go about doing good,' as we are told your Master did." All this from a man who did not call himself a Christian—he was a Hindu. Yet how much it sounds like that saying of the Lord, "If ye know these things, happy are ye, if ye do them"—and only then. "Inasmuch as ye have done it unto the least of these, the hungry and the sick, the lonely and the imprisoned, ye have done it unto me."—Charles R. Brown

THE FIRE OF TRUTH.   Samuel Rutherford, a Presbyterian minister imprisoned several hundred years ago in Scotland, was placed in a dungeon underground with only a tiny window through which at night he looked up at the stars. He once wrote to a friend that one night Jesus came into his cell and every star shone like a ruby. What made the difference was not that Rutherford got out but that Jesus got in! Dietrich Bonhoeffer's body never got out of prison, but his spirit did. And he once wrote, in his *Letters from Prison,* "O freedom, long have we sought thee in discipline and in action and in suffering. Dying, we behold thee now, and see in the face of God."—Raymond Bryan Brown

SECTION IV.
Messages for Funeral Services

SERMON SUGGESTIONS

Topic: A Funeral Tribute to Jimmy Marius

We have not met here to extol the virtues of some great man, rather to remember a child who experienced neither the joys nor the griefs of becoming a man, although he lived among us for sixty-five years.[1] I have known Jimmy for twenty-one of those years. He knew that I was the "preacher," his pastor, yet he always called me "Uncle Sherwood."

---

[1]Richard Marius is director of the expository writing program at Harvard University. He writes the following about his brother, Jimmy, the subject of this sermon: "James Henri Marius was a Down's Syndrome child. My mother and father moved to a farm at a place called Dixie Lee Junction in east Tennessee in 1930 so he could grow up in the tranquility of what was then a remote neighborhood. In time my family began attending the Midway Baptist Church, which adjoined one of our fields, and Jimmy—as we called him—became a fixture there. He had only one desire, and that was to be loved; he was much loved by the family and by the community. He died on the night of December 23, 1991, and about three hundred people turned out for his funeral on the evening of December 26. As it happened, December 26 was my late father's birthday. My brother John and I commented to each other that it was in a way a good birthday present for Dad because our family and our community had fulfilled Dad's greatest wish, that Jimmy be loved and cared for as long as he lived."

Why? I have no idea, but I'm glad I never tried to correct him. I'm glad he felt that close to me.

Jimmy was different; *unique* would probably be a better word. I'm not sure he knew how unique he was. He seemed to accept himself as he was, apparently giving little heed to the opinions of others. There were times he seemed to think we were the "different ones" and considered us rather silly. Perhaps we may conclude that he belongs in the category of the "little ones" Christ spoke of. We may even consider him as being "one of the least of these." I'm not wise enough to know how much Jimmy understood about sin, repentance, faith, and salvation. But this is one thing I am sure of: Jimmy trusted the Lord Jesus Christ with all of his heart, mind, and spirit. Jesus had some harsh words for those who would reject one of these "little ones": "Better for him that a millstone were hanged about his neck, and that he were drowned in the depth of the sea."

Jimmy's needs were simple; it didn't take much to please him. Three things he wanted with him at all times. He took his Bible with him everywhere, even to bed. He received a new Bible every Christmas, and even though he could not read, the old one was just about worn out. The second thing he carried was a pencil, unsharpened. He preferred striped ones. One Christmas, Virginia and I looked all over town trying to find him some striped pencils, but we couldn't. The third thing was a fan. Even on the coldest

256

days you would see Jimmy sitting in church fanning himself. It may have seemed odd to others, but he seemed to get a lot of joy from it.

Jimmy loved the church and always knew when it was time to go to worship. He looked forward to "family night"; that was when everyone brought a covered dish and we ate supper together. One icy, snowy Sunday morning Henry was afraid to drive on the slick roads and told Jimmy church services had been canceled because of the dangerous road conditions. In a little while Jimmy heard the church bell ringing and was so distressed about missing church that Henry carried him piggyback up the hill, across the field, through the snow to the church.

Jimmy loved to sing. It did not bother him that he could not harmonize with others, neither did it bother those who sat near him. His favorite song must have been "At Calvary," the song that Ella sang so beautifully a moment ago. He requested it to be sung every time he had an opportunity.

Some may think Jimmy's life was unproductive. On the contrary he unconsciously taught us many things: to be more compassionate toward the hurting, more patient with the weak, more tolerant toward the slow, and more aware of the feelings and needs of those we look upon as being less fortunate than we. Perhaps you could add many other lessons to these I have mentioned.

We are sad because of Jimmy's death; yet we are comforted because we know that Jimmy is not "different" anymore. John, the beloved apostle, reminds us "it doth not yet appear what we shall be: but we know that, when he shall appear, we shall be like him: for we shall see him as he is" (1 John 3:2)

Little was required of Jimmy because he possessed little. He could not discuss the profound subjects of life, death, and eternity. But you can, and because you possess much, much is required of you. Out there in eternity you will stand before the same God Jimmy is with today.—E. M. Sherwood

Topic: "Music to God's Ear"

(A memorial tribute to Mrs. Miriam Small, organist and choir director)

Each Sunday, congregations gather the world over, and together they raise their voices in songs of praise. Some who sing do so slightly off-key, while other voices are matched only by the melodious sounds of God's angelic choir. And yet, in those moments when my imagination is most playful—I wonder what constitutes music to God's ears.

After all, it could be that to God's ears a few thousand voices off-key sounds as beautiful as the satin singing of the Vienna Boy's Choir on Christmas Eve! Perhaps God listens for something more than simple melody, or vocal harmony, or pitch. Maybe God's ear is more sensitive than ours to the faith beneath and behind the singing. Or, to put it another way: Maybe God's ear listens for harmony of the heart—and not merely the voice!

And I wonder if perhaps that isn't one reason behind the great appeal of the Psalms. They are more than lyric and lyre, you know. The Psalms are expressions of the human heart given to song. They represent the voice of the heart in love with God.

I suppose you could say that the Psalms were written as a song-book testimony to the battles and blessings of faith. And like all good love songs, they reflect both the delights and the disappointments of this all too human love affair with a benevolent God.

So of course, the Psalms disclose those delights and disappointments from a human point of view. In fact, the Psalms reflect the struggles of people very much like you and me. People who worship and seek to serve God. And yet, people who are not above an occasional lover's spat with the Lord! But above and beyond all that, the Psalms sing from the heart of faith. And faith is something we all share in common.

Because it is humanly impossible to have life without having faith! Without some degree of faith, none of us would venture into relationships—or even be able to maintain those into which we did blindly venture. In fact, without faith, we would most likely hide beneath the bedsheets and never set foot outside the front door!

Faith enables us to enter life's flow with some level of confidence. We need to have faith that if we open our eyes tomorrow—the sun will shine, air will be there to breathe, and the earth will continue to spin on its axis! This is the kind of faith we all have to a greater or lesser degree. But this is not the kind of faith that gave birth to the beauty of the Psalms.

Only faith in God could have given birth to the Psalms. Because only faith in God empowers the heart to rise above the sob of sadness, with a song of hope. Only faith in God enables the heart to sing, when sickness wraps its fingers around your life. And only faith in God can gift a voice with the courage to belt out a song of praise, when all others are silent in the face of a certain death and despair.

Faith in God enables us to see that life is so much more than the sum total of today's trials and tomorrow's heartaches. Faith opens our eyes to the wonder of God as revealed in the glory of his creation.

Sometimes we are caught speechless when white blankets the earth, or when reds and yellows and pinks paint the horizon at sunset. Only faith in God moves us to sing the doxology whenever such sights fill our eyes with color and our hearts with joy. And only faith in God empowers us to believe in the goodness of creation, even after hurricanes have ripped through our homes!

I would dare to say that faith gives voice to the music of the believing heart! So, while the rest of the world groans under the weight of discouragement, the voice of faith sings songs of hope in the promises of God. While other voices wail the mournful tune of death and decay, faith lifts up its voice with the triumphant cantata of resurrection and God's coming kingdom!

The Psalms sing from the heart of such faith. And the music of such faith is first born in the faithful life. That is to say—long before the Psalms were written on paper, they were etched deep into the pages of life. The words were lived before they became lyrics! And the faith with which the Psalmist sings was practiced in the real world before it was penned on paper and set to rhythm. That's why I have selected Psalm Ninety-two as a tribute to the memory of Miriam.

You see, I don't believe that you can separate the memory of Miriam's love for music from the memory of her love of God. Her music issued from her faith. It was nothing less than the harmony of her heart in union with the will of God for her life. That's what made Miriam special. She was first, and foremost, devoted to God and God's Church. And because of her devotion, her music had the quality of true dedication and triumphant faith.

The Psalmist expresses what might otherwise have been written by Miriam herself: "For you make me glad by your deeds, O LORD; I sing for joy at the works of your hands." And Miriam sang this song of praise with her life as well as her musical talents! More than anything else, I will always remember the joy with which this petite saint sang her songs of praise to God with her life and love. And as far as I can tell, her life was nothing less than a melody of tenderness and mercy and goodwill.

I remember a conversation in which I questioned Miriam's busy schedule. I asked, "What in the name of God prompts you to run all over hill and dale playing music?!" She gave me that impish smile she was so famous for, and said, "Umm! That's exactly it, you see. I do it in the name of God!" Now that's classic Miriam, wouldn't you say?

"The righteous shall flourish like a palm tree," wrote the Psalmist, "They shall bear fruit in old age, they shall stay fresh and green, proclaiming, 'The LORD . . . he is my Rock!' " They sound like the reflections of a senior saint, don't they? And they strike me as the words of a well-seasoned saint also. A saint weathered by time and trial and triumph. One who has known the pitfalls of temptation and the power of God's salvation.

To be sure, they sound human! They are words of one who has survived the fires of tragedy and poor health; someone who has stood—on more than one occasion—wiping the dirt of an open grave from his hands; someone who has fallen on hard times and lived to see his hopes renewed.

Someone, I would say, like Miriam. A person of faith and commitment and compassion, deepened by the desire to serve God. A soul absorbed in the will and ways of God. A sister in Christ who sang of his salvation through her service; and played the rhythm of his passion with her life. You know, you might have missed it. But there's a promise locked away in the words of this Psalm. A promise that has been copied and rearranged in a thousand different hymns throughout the ages. A promise that will last beyond the shadows of time and into eternity. A promise embraced by Miriam, and now, embracing her. The Psalmist writes: "The righteous will stay fresh and green."

That means we shall live, long after age has turned our tired bones to dust—we shall live. And one day God will breathe his Spirit over the earth, and those who have fallen asleep in Christ will be raised to eternal life. That is the only promise that lends itself to a song of praise! And I believe Miriam would want us to learn the lyrics, and to sing that song with a resounding voice.

More important, I think Miriam would encourage us to live lives harmonious to that hope. She would advocate that we live each day to the fullest—and to do so for the sake of Christ, and not our own gain. I believe she would invite us to teach this song of faith to others who know neither the melody nor the lyrics. And above all else, I believe Miriam would admonish us to invite them to join with us in this choir of faith we call the Church.

I believe so because that's the kind of person she was. Miriam lived her life with the song of faith seeping through every pore of her being. Everything she touched turned to music that was bright, and light, and beautiful. In fact, her life reflected a heart in harmony with God's love.

Which leads me to believe that Miriam's life was nothing less than music to God's ears. I imagine that whenever God turned his ear to Miriam, he heard a heart beating out the rhythm of righteousness and a soul wrapped in a song of praise to his name. I suppose you could say that Miriam Small was a living Psalm! A note of praise here, a short lament there, but always the underlying song of thanksgiving.

But until that day, I believe that we who would honor the memory of this woman must be willing to receive and then live some portion of the faith she cherished. And to do that we must do as she did—commit to Christ's ministry of compassion. Perhaps we pay her memory no greater honor than to live our lives in such a way that we too can be certain that our hearts are in harmony with God's will—and our lives are music to God's ears!—Albert J. D. Walsh

Topic: A Memorial Tribute to Dr. Lone Sisk

It is not given to many people to live a life so long and at the same time so productively as God in his providence gave to Lone Sisk. We mourn his passing, to be sure, but not as those who mourn a life interrupted in its infancy or at the threshold or apex of an active life. So we can think of this occasion as a celebration. Just a week ago I wrote to a friend whose mother died and said, "It is a paradox that when we are impoverished by the loss of a loved one we are also enriched in ways beyond explaining." God gives special grace to enable us to pass through the deep waters and the valley of the shadow of death. And this grace often comes in a new appreciation of the Scriptures, of the faith handed down to us, of half-forgotten conversations and encouraging words, and of the presence of friends who care. This grace comes also in recognition and gratitude for what someone has meant to others as well as to ourselves.

I knew Lone Sisk mainly through his life in the church with its many relationships, as deacon, Sunday school superintendent, and teacher. When I was his pastor here, I could always count on seeing him sitting to my left as I stood in the pulpit. Now that did not have any political implications, religious or otherwise; however, he was an independent thinker, had his own well-thought-out convictions, but, at the same time, appreciated his heritage of faith and truly "belonged." His answer to a skeptic was not to belittle or condemn him but to give him an option in the spirit of Jesus, who said, "Whoever chooses to do the will of God will know whether my teaching comes from him or is merely my own."

Teaching was a large part of Lone Sisk's life. From 1926 to 1993 he taught a Sunday school class. He taught for twenty-two years at Science Hill High School and for forty years at Milligan College until he became professor emeritus, which did not mean that his teaching was over at the college. He was frequently called back to the classroom. During that time he served as associate alumni director and continued to return to the campus until May of this year. He knew the alumni and kept up with them. One example of his personal touch was, according to Alfreda, just typical of him. When he learned that a friend and fellow church member became ill in Hawaii, Dr. Sisk called a physician there who was an alumnus of Milligan and who had been one of his students. He asked his former student not simply to offer to help, but to *do* something, which he did graciously and gratefully. We can easily understand why a scholarship fund was established in Dr. Sisk's name.

Lone Sisk had a heart that reached out widely, and that love was reciprocated. He was well known for addressing people who were special to him as "dear heart." And this expression redounded to him a hundredfold, and many thought of him as "dear heart." But his own family were at the center of his affections and his concern: Alfreda, Zenobia, Lone, Jr., and his grandchildren and great grandchildren, who were especially close to his heart, as was Mrs. Sisk, whom he had loved long since and lost a while. Just days ago he said to Alfreda and Zenobia, "I hear your mother stirring around here somewhere." This remark could be explained by his recent infirmities; however, I am sure that, in a sense, she was always stirring around him somewhere. Take it from me, he, too, will always be stirring around us somewhere. When I saw a play by Shakespeare a few years ago, one of the characters addressed another with the words dear heart, and I thought of Lone Sisk.

His life in itself has been a declaration of faith. To him, *this* life is the gift of God and of inestimable worth. He believed with Jesus and Paul and John in the life to come as the glorious fulfillment of God's purpose for us, but he believed that this life also has meaning. Many years ago, one of the members of his Sunday school class quoted him as saying, "Even if there were no life to come, to be a Christian would be worth every sacrifice, for the Christian life has its rewards even here and now." This reminded me of what another man said: "There are people who long for immortality who don't know what to do with a rainy afternoon." One of Dr. Sisk's special delights was his garden—that was one of God's gifts to him.

Whenever we ponder birth and life and death, we are unavoidably faced with the meaning of it all. Even in the daily comic strips we meet the anguished question. It is an age-old problem that troubled the biblical writers, including Job, the Psalmist, and the apostle Paul. They saw clearly that life is lived out in a welter of vexing questions, but for them God made the difference. The suffering of the innocent, the Crucifixion of the Son of God, and such like had an answer but no neat explanation, and the answer was and is in the love of God, a God who can be trusted even when his ways are past finding out, the God who opened his heart to all humankind conclusively in Jesus Christ, the suffering Savior whose Resurrection assures us of what God can do with even the last enemy of us all, to say nothing of the little or greater ills that beset us from day to day. This is why Lone Sisk and you and I can find in this life assurances that Jesus was right when he said, "I am come that they might have life, and have it more abundantly," and that the writer of the Epistle to the Hebrews was on target when he said of this Jesus, that he "for the joy that was set before him endured the cross, despising the shame, and is set down at the right hand of the throne of God."—James W. Cox

Topic: "Moving Day"

(A funeral sermon for one who died following a long illness)

Text: John 14:1–3

It's never easy to say good-bye. It's hardest to say good-bye on moving day. When we stand among the piled-up boxes of our lives, sadness wells within our hearts. The apartment or house we leave has become our home. Even worse is the pain of moving out-of-state, for we must bid farewell to dear friends.

For ———, moving day has come. We cry because we will miss him. We are sad for he is no longer with us, to share our lives, our laughter, our hopes.

While moving day has its sadness, there is reason for joy. It can be happy. As we load up the last box and head for the open road, a sense of excitement and anticipation grips us. We wonder: What will our new home be like? Will we enjoy the neighborhood? Will we really feel "at home"?

With certainty, we know moving day was happy for ———, because we know where he moved! John 14:2 speaks of our heavenly Father's house. In this house are many rooms. Right now, I imagine ——— is getting settled into his new home. We feel sorry for ourselves, but we must not feel sorry for him. ——— is happy in the presence of Jesus.

Did you know even Christ had a moving day? For three years, the twelve disciples set their vocations aside to follow Jesus. Now his earthly ministry is coming to a head. For the last time, Jesus speaks of his departure. Confused, Simon asks, "Lord, where are you going?" The Savior

replies, "Where I am going you cannot follow now, but you will follow later."

Jesus' "moving day" meant he was returning to his Father in heaven. His work on earth was complete. The disciples wanted to follow him right away, wherever he was going, but Jesus knew that was impossible. Simon and the others still had much to accomplish on earth. Their time had not yet come. The Lord's departure meant temporary separation, but he gave them a wonderful promise: Ultimately, he would be reunited with his followers. Jesus assured them, "You will follow later."

The word *disciple* means "follower." Simon and the others were faithful followers of Christ. They called him "Master," and it was more than just a title. In every way, they had forsaken all else to serve Jesus. Because they followed him on earth, he assured them they would one day follow him to heaven. By the fruit of his testimony, we believe ——— followed Jesus to heaven. When you respond with obedience to the grace of God, God's Word tells us a "room" is reserved for you in the heavenly Father's house. As sure as I stand here today, for each of us is coming a "moving day." Scripture gives us only glimpses of heaven. We would rather have a detailed photograph, but are only provided with a shadowy portrait. Despite this, one proposition is sure: John 14:3 tells us: "I will come back and take you to be with me that you also may be where I am."

Jesus moved away, but one day he will return for a visit. When he does, the bodies of the dead will be transformed. We will be given resurrection bodies. The apostle Paul calls it a "mystery." Even he could not fully understand the nature of our heavenly uniform. What he does say is that what is temporary will become indestructible. What is miserably weak will become incredibly strong. No cancer can harm our resurrection bodies. No disease or infirmity will impair us then. ——— leaves behind a body used up, but when we see him again he will be the ——— of strong frame we once knew.

Moving day, from a spiritual standpoint, means giving up what we cannot keep for what we cannot lose. Anyway you look at it, it is to our advantage. For the Christian, heaven becomes our wonderful home. With our resurrection bodies, we will live with Jesus forever. What a promise!

Before moving day came for ————, he gave us an admirable example of trust in God and love for life.—J. Gregory Crofford

ILLUSTRATIONS FOR FUNERAL SERVICES

THE GOOD FIGHT.   This is a great retrospect. *I have finished my course.* Life is made up of ends and of beginnings. Death is but the greatest crisis of many, and all crises are like Janus in the Roman pantheon, two-faced. The end of one crisis is the beginning of another. But with all the ebbs and flows of life there must be a unity, some grand unity that constitutes life's reality. For us that unity is, in Paul's phrase, *"For me to live in Christ,"* that is, Christ is my career.

The unity of our life is therefore objective, outside ourselves. It is not in the evolution of life but in its goal. When Wordsworth writes of life whose days are bound each to each by natural piety, he is not truly Christian. When a man is truly Christian each day is bound to Christ, is devoted to him, is lived in him. Life is not realizing a plan but fulfilling a mission. Thus a broken column in a churchyard, symbolizing a broken life, is an anachronism. There is no such thing as a broken life for the man of faith. All life is complete in Christ, and always complete; no

matter when the end comes, the course is finished.—P. T. Forsyth

THIS AND THE BEYOND.   I know nothing about what form life will take in the beyond, but I know that it will not be an unincarnate, abstract, impersonal world of ideas, of pure anonymous spirits of phantoms. I know that I shall retain my personal identity; and it is a fact here below, in personal fellowship, in the person-to-person relationship when it is true, that I find a foretaste of heaven.— Paul Tournier

DARING TO HOPE.   If we dare to hope not only for the living but also for the dead and those still unborn, if we hope not only for the human race but for the whole of nature as well, we will repent of all petty visions of the future that absolutize the interests of a particular group. With the apostle Paul we will express our solidarity in hope with all of the groaning creation that restlessly awaits God's coming redemption (Rom. 8:21–23).—Daniel L. Migliori

GOING HOME.   How rich this earth seems when we regard it—crowded with the loves of home! Yet I am now getting to go home—to leave this world of homes and go home. When I reach that home, shall I even then seek yet to go home? Even then, I believe, I shall seek a yet warmer, deeper, purer home in the deeper knowledge of God—in the truer love of my fellow men. Eternity will be—my heart and my faith tell me—a traveling homeward, but in jubilation and confidence and vision of the beloved.—George MacDonald

SECTION V.
Lenten and Easter Preaching

SERMON SUGGESTIONS

Topic: Gethsemane

TEXT: Matt. 26:30–46

Think of the picture of Jesus in the Garden of Gethsemane. You've seen the same picture somewhere, I'll bet. Jesus, kneeling down, leaning against a rock, praying his heart out, looking rather sad. It is a sad story, no doubt about that, but it is more than that. I want you to take a few minutes to think with me about what this story, this most intimate picture of Jesus, tells us about the man we call "Savior."

I. The picture is right about making him look sad, I think. Listen to verses 37–38: "And taking with him Peter and the two sons of Zebedee, he began to be sorrowful and troubled. Then he said to them, 'My soul is very sorrowful, even to death; remain here, and watch with me.' " Deeply grieved, he said, hurt, aching, almost overcome with anguish: Why, Lord? Are you afraid to die? Are you worried about the Crucifixion?

We shrink back from saying yes because we call him "Lord" and "Son of God," but Jesus was also a real-live human man; and it would be inhuman to expect that he could be facing execution in such a painful fashion and not worry about it.

He doesn't just worry, he prays. "My father, if it be possible, let this cup pass by me; nevertheless, not as I will, but as thou wilt" (v. 39). The cup was a symbol of his death, used in the Old Testament a lot as a symbol of God's anger or wrath poured out on the world. "If it be possible." Think of it. In that moment, Jesus was admitting that he was asking for God to do something, but he wasn't sure if God would do it. We get so used to the picture of Jesus doing miracles, healing first one and then another, that we think of him as Superman—able to leap tall buildings, stop bullets with his chest, etc.

The New Testament paints a different picture. Jesus did not know everything; for example, he knew that someday, God would stop history and send in the angels to clean this place up. "But of that day and hour no one knows, not the angels in heaven or even the Son, but only the Father." Jesus could not do everything; the New Testament speaks of him being unable to do miracles in a certain place because the people there had no faith. He got tired, tired enough to lie down in a boat in the middle of a storm and go to sleep. He cried over the death of his friend; he yelled at the disciples when they failed to understand him for the thirtieth time. He was a real human being.

The man we call "Savior" was a real man, and in the garden we see him at his most vulnerable, his most human moment. To me, that is vitally important. Jesus was not Superman. He had no tricks up his sleeve. He was not invulnerable to pain or worry or grief. That is important, because I know that when I pray to him about my pain or worry or grief, he understands.

263

In the picture, you can only see Jesus leaning against his rock; but in the story, there were others there. Peter, who had promised only minutes earlier, "Even if I must die with you, I will not deny you." James and John, the two brothers who wanted to be Jesus' right- and left-hand men in the kingdom, who had said they, too, would drink from the cup Jesus had to drink from. They were there with Jesus. Did they suffer with him? Were they offering him consolation, asking "What's wrong, Lord? What can we do to help?"

No, they were asleep. In the hour of his greatest need, they let him down. As the scene continues, it gets worse, because they all flee and leave him to face his trial and death all alone. If we add them into our mental picture, they'd be bad guys. Jesus, praying his heart out, and these guys taking a nap over on the side of the garden—uncaring, irresponsible would be how we'd paint them.

Once in "Peanuts," Snoopy was holding a helium balloon for someone. "Don't let go, whatever you do, Snoopy." But he went to sleep and opened his mouth to yawn, and the balloon floated off into the sky. Much later he woke up and realized what he had done. The final frame showed him with a pack on his back, walking down the railroad bed, thinking, "One mistake, and you pay for it the rest of your life!"

II. But that's not how this story turns out. Jesus knew they would let him down and he told them, "You will all fall away because of me tonight; but after I am raised up, I will go before you to Galilee" (v. 31–32). There was hope, even for these sorry disciples who can talk big but can't carry through. There was hope, because the man we call Savior is a compassionate, redeeming man. He would not cast them away forever. He would come to them, even though they left him to die by himself, and forgive them. You can give your heart to a man like that. That's a Savior for you.

One final prayer before Jesus left the garden. He went back to his stone and prayed a similar prayer, only a little different. "My Father, if this cannot pass unless I drink it, thy will be done." The way he said "if this cannot pass" in Greek really could be better translated "since this cannot pass." In other words, by the time he went back to prayer, he knew that he would have to die. He took one look at those sleeping disciples and realized that there was no other way. He could have spent fifty years teaching them and still not transform them. He would have to die to bring the power of the Resurrection into the world. So he prayed, not to know God's will, but to give himself over to God's will.

That is the key to the whole Jesus business right there, I think. God was in Christ, the Bible tells us. People could look at him and see the face of God. How? By the fact that he always gave himself over to God's will. God in Christ wasn't magic. It was the result of Jesus' cleaving closely to God's will, holding tightly to what he knew God wanted him to do. That is a Savior for you.

The picture may not capture what Jesus actually looked like. I doubt that he had a halo around his head, for example, and I don't think he had blond hair and blue eyes. But the image of Jesus praying to know God's will, offering forgiveness and understanding to disciples who weren't worthy of it, and then asking for God's help in going to die for that crew, that is an unforgettable portrait. Sad, yes; but also seeking, compassionate, obedient, relying on God's strength. That's the man we call Savior; that's a Savior we can give our hearts to.—Richard B. Vinson

Topic: Judas's Story

TEXT: Matt. 26:3–5, 14–16, 47–56; 27:3–10

Think of the name "Elizabeth": perhaps you think of dignity or intelligence, a queenly presence, like Elizabeth I of England. Think of the name "Sophia," and perhaps you think of someone a little more exotic, a little less dignified, more beautiful, like Sophia Loren. Think of the name "Judas," and try as hard as you might, the only connotation that comes up is "traitor." No parent, surely, would saddle a child with a name like Judas, knowing the story in the Bible.

I. He's a little bit of a mystery man. He

is introduced in the text as "Judas Iscariot." According to John 6:71, his father's name was Simon Iscariot. Iscariot can be read two ways. It can be a place name: Judas from Kerioth, which was a small town in the south of Palestine. It can also be a nickname: *sicarius* was the name of a small knife. Jews who hated Romans sometimes carried these knives under their clothing, looking for opportunities to stab soldiers in alleys and on dark roads. So which was it? Was it Judas the man from a little town in Judah, or Judas the knife, the hot-blooded revolutionary? A lot depends on how you answer that question.

Why did he do it? The simplest answer is money. He was greedy, and he wanted the thirty pieces of silver. According to John, Judas had been guilty of misappropriating funds already—he kept the pouch where people made contributions to Jesus' ministry and stole it now and then. Maybe money had something to do with it, but there must have been more. Thirty pieces is not a lot of money—not enough to retire to Bermuda and live the easy life. There must have been more to it.

Again, there are two ways to read the story. *If* Judas was "Judas the knife," then maybe he was disappointed that Jesus hadn't done more to start the revolution against the Romans. If we look at Judas this way, he saw Jesus as someone who could help in his plans to drive the Romans out of the holy land. Jesus attracted crowds, he was a very popular speaker; maybe Judas could turn him around to his point of view. Maybe he could persuade Jesus to speak out against Roman rule. When they came to Jerusalem, Jesus made it clear that he was not going to try to start a fight, but was willing to die. Judas was desperate. He had to do something; he thought, "Maybe if I set up a scene where it looks like he will be arrested, Jesus will finally act." For a minute, in the garden, it looked like it might come off; Peter drew his sword and struck one of the servants, but Jesus would have none of it. Horrified, Judas could only watch as the Temple guards led Jesus away.

So goes one reading. The other is just the opposite. *If* Judas was "Judas the man from the little Judean town of Kerioth," then he was the only one of the twelve who was not from Galilee. What Jesus had done in the Temple offended and frightened him, just as it did the chief priests. Why should Jesus disrupt the Temple? Why should he put his country in danger? Didn't Jesus know that the Romans liked nothing better than a pretext to crucify fifty or sixty Judean Jews? So Judas betrayed Jesus because he was afraid. He no longer agreed with the man he had called Master, and he saw him as dangerous.

Would someone really betray Jesus for these reasons? You bet your life they would: money, ambition, fear—people have been betraying Jesus for generations for just these reasons. Recently a pastor sold out his Christian principles for money and embezzled from his own church. The man or woman who cheats on his income tax, or who does something a little shady in her business, betrays Jesus for money. The man or woman who is so eager for success in this life that he leaves no time to raise his family or who arranges her life to please the really important people betrays Jesus for ambition. The man or woman who sees injustice but will not speak out because of what others would do or say, or who is careful never to carry Christianity too far, because people would think he/she is a fanatic, betrays Jesus for fear.

Yes, any way that we read the story, it makes all too much sense. Judas betrayed Jesus for reasons that we understand much too well. We shun the name Judas because it rings with the sound of "traitor," but all of us have felt the shame of something we should have avoided, but we didn't, because of money or ambition or fear. We don't think of ourselves as great villains—but we know that if our life story were to be written down, like Judas's story was, there would be lots of little betrayals to smear our memory just as certainly as his.

II. The end of the story gives us something to think about. Judas made good on his promise. When Jesus and the disciples went to the olive orchard on the hill just opposite Jerusalem, outside the city gates, the moment had come. Judas hurried to the Temple and led an armed detachment of Temple soldiers out to the little garden. It was dark, and they knew Jesus was in the company of others, so Judas had planned to isolate Jesus for the soldiers by greeting him in the usual way—a kiss on the cheek. He did it—Jesus said, "Friend, do what you have to do"—there was a brief skirmish, and then they led Jesus off to his interrogation.

The next morning, Judas saw the chief priests leading Jesus to Pilate's residence. He was shocked. He never expected them to put Jesus to death. He repented; he tried to return the money and call the whole thing off, but it was too late. "I made a mistake, Jesus was innocent," he cried, but the Temple authorities would not listen. He threw the money into the courtyard where only the priests could go, ran off, and hanged himself. What an ending—talk about compounding tragedy! It is clear that there is a lesson here that Matthew wants us to learn, but again, there are two ways to read it.

Maybe the lesson is, "Be sure that your sins will find you out." Maybe Judas thought he'd be able to pocket the money, buy a business in Jerusalem, and put this whole chapter of his life behind him. He'd been wrong about Jesus; he'd given up his job to follow him for three years, and now it was time to start over. But in the end, his conscience would not let him live. Jesus had predicted earlier that the one who handed him over would not have a happy end—better if that man had not been born.

That is most certainly true. The Scriptures tell us, over and over, that even though it may look like the wicked prosper, that is only a temporary illusion. The man who sells crack may drive a BMW this week, but it will catch up with him. The woman who drinks to excess, the child who cheats or lies—eventually, our sins catch up with us. If our guilty consciences do not drive us crazy, then our lack of conscience makes us into something less than human. We simply cannot disobey God with impunity. If we try, we kill ourselves, one way or another.

There is a story—I don't know if it is true or not—about how the Eskimos kill a wolf. They take a knife and coat the blade with sheep's blood, letting it freeze, and then stick it in the snow, blade pointing up into the air. The wolf smells the blood and begins to lick it. Eventually, though, the razor-sharp edge cuts the wolf's tongue, but the air is so cold it doesn't hurt. The wolf keeps on licking, unaware that it is his own blood he is tasting, until he dies. One way or another, people, if we continually disobey God, we kill ourselves.

But there is a second way to read the story. There is an ancient tradition in the Church that Judas died in the hopes of being forgiven. On this reading, he really repented and wanted to ask Jesus' forgiveness. But it was too late for that. Judas knew that unless Jesus forgave him, he would go to hell; but he figured that, Jesus being the kind of man he was, he probably was down in hell at that moment, preaching the love of God to the sinners, hanging around with the wrong crowd just as he did on earth. So Judas killed himself, thinking that was the only way he could meet Jesus to ask his pardon.

Can that be true? I don't know; I don't think Matthew thought of the story that way. But this much is true—if Judas really did repent, and if Jesus really was in hell that day, and if Judas asked for forgiveness, Jesus forgave him. The love of God, and the forgiveness of Jesus, are greater than any sin, are broad enough to cover any sinner. Otherwise, there's no hope for all of us, is there?

III. The greatest lesson to learn from all of this is simply that. We need not let our sins drive us crazy, our guilts make us take our own lives. So many people, like the preacher in *The Scarlet Letter*, believe that their secret sins are completely unforgivable. Nothing could be further from the truth. Jesus' arms are open. He offers complete, unconditional forgiveness to any who will take it, no matter what the cause. We'll never know if that's what Judas wanted; but we can know for ourselves. We can turn from our petty betrayals and accept the forgiveness of the man we betray.—Richard B. Vinson

Topic: The Cry

TEXT: Matt. 27:27–54

The first real religious question I ever remember having was over this strange, sad verse we read today: "My God, my God, why have you forsaken me?" I had been raised to believe that Jesus was God's Son. Why would God abandon him? Why, if Jesus knew that God wanted him to be crucified, would he have any second thoughts, even on the cross? The preachers used to read it and say, "God had turned his back on him." Why? What had Jesus done to deserve that? Even if Jesus were dying for the sins of the world, he had done nothing wrong; that would be something noble, something courageous. Surely God would not let him down in his hour of greatest need.

When I grew up, I learned that others had the same sort of questions I did. Only Mark and Matthew have the terrible cry in their Gospels. Luke has Jesus forgive his enemies from the cross, offer a thief the chance at Paradise, and say, "Into your hands I commit myself, Father." That sounded more like Jesus to me! John's Gospel is even more that way. In John, Jesus says "It is finished." No pain, no remorse, no quibbling. Just very businesslike—"I'm done with all I had to do, so it's time for me to go home."

Jesus' cry of pain from the cross doesn't even sound as brave and noble as some of the martyrs who died in his name. Stephen, the first to die in Acts, echoed Jesus: "Father, lay not this sin to their charge." The earliest written account of a martyr's death was the account of a man named Polycarp, who died in the colosseum at Ephesus in the middle of the second century. As he died, he said a lengthy prayer, blessing God for the privilege of dying for Jesus. "For this and everything I praise thee, I bless thee, I glorify thee, through the eternal and heavenly High Priest Jesus Christ, thy beloved Servant."

What I'm saying here is that Jesus' cry does not fit our idea of how a brave man should die, much less how we'd imagine the Son of God dying. What should we think about it?

I. First, I think we should face it square on for what it sounds like. Jesus is telling God that he feels abandoned. After what he'd been going through for the past few hours, that was understandable.

After the trial by Pilate, when he'd handed Jesus over to the soldiers, they took him back to their barracks to taunt him some. They put one of their own scarlet legionnaire's robes on him and made a crown out of a bush with long thorns so that the spines would look like rays coming out of the crown the emperor wore. Then they mocked him, calling him "King of the Jews." People are so cruel. From childhood, people taunt the weakest ones, making fun of the ones who can't play the games or the ones who can be intimidated. The soldiers laughed at Jesus because he was weak and they were strong, and it made them feel even stronger to laugh at him.

Then the crowds got into the act. Hanging from the cross, all Jesus could hear were the raucous voices of the inhabitants of Jerusalem, razzing him, telling him to take himself down from the cross if he thought he was so great. Isn't it interesting how easily fame turns sour? Look how the crowd that cheers Jesus into the city on Sunday can yell for his crucifixion on Friday. Jesus had been their hero, but now he was weak, beaten, dying, and they took out their frustration and disappointment on him.

Add up the pain Jesus had been through before the cross, which must have been considerable. Put in the agony of hanging from your wrists. Then factor in the psychological pain of hearing no friendly voice in the crowd, of having no friends or support. Jesus was hurting inside and outside, and in his pain and grief he called out to God, "Where are you? Why have you abandoned me?"

If we are honest, we can probably say that we have felt that way, too. We have felt put upon, hurt, forgotten; when things are bad, when times are hard, we have wondered where God was in all of this. Tragedy: Where was God when the fire swept through the downstairs part of the Brooklyn supper club, trapping all the people upstairs? Don't you think the families of those people are asking themselves that? Boredom: Once a man in a nursing home killed himself, leaving behind a note that simply said, "I'm so tired of all the buttoning and unbuttoning." Where is God when all you have all day long is four walls to stare at?

Thank God for Jesus' honesty. He felt alone, he felt forgotten, and he said so. It is no sin to wonder why bad things happen to you, or to wonder whether God might have done things a little differently. Jesus' cry of pain is a genuinely human cry in which he identifies himself with you and me. As the writer to the Hebrews said, "He was tested in every way just like we are."

II. But that cry of pain was also a cry of faith. In desperate moments, we may not be able to pray, "Lord, I know your will is best," or "Lord, I know everything is going to work out all right." In those moments, faith is simply saying "Lord, why?" and then waiting for an answer.

Long before Jesus said those words, someone else had written them down. Psalm Twenty-two came from the pen of a man who had known pain and sickness. "I am poured out like water, and all my bones are out of joint; my heart is like wax, it is melted within my breast; my strength is dried up like an old broken plate, and my tongue cleaves to my jaws." Not only that, but his neighbors pointed at him and said that God was punishing him for his sins with an illness. "All those who see me mock at me, they make mouths at me, they wag their heads; they say, 'He committed his cause to the Lord; let him deliver him.'" Like Jesus, the man who wrote Psalm Twenty-two knew what pain was, and he knew about being forgotten by everyone.

And, like Jesus, he asked God a question and waited for an answer. In the first verse of the Psalm, he said, "Why have you forsaken me?" but later, he said "I will tell of thy name to my brethren." Sooner or later, he knew, God would show him what he needed to know.

That's the key to Jesus' cry. It is a cry of pain, but it is directed to God. Jesus may have felt that God abandoned him, but deep down in his heart, he knew God was still listening to his cries of pain. God didn't turn his back on Jesus. He allowed him to go through the pain and the shame of the cross, but God was right there with him. And come Easter morning, God raised him from the dead.

Brothers and sisters, when we feel down, when we feel low, when we feel forgotten, it is time to turn to God and tell him so. He can take it! And he doesn't get scared off by people asking why. In our darkest moments, in our deepest depressions, we can ask, "Why have you forsaken me?" It will not take away our suffering, but we will suffer differently, because we will know that God is listening to our pain.—Richard B. Vinson

Topic: Whose Fault Was It?

Text: Matt. 27:1–2, 11–26

When the glass is lying on the floor and the milk puddle is slowly spreading toward the rug, it would seem like the logical thing to do would be to yell, "Somebody bring a towel quick!" But sometimes what first comes to my mind and out of my mouth is "Who did this? Whose fault is it?" Fixing blame is so much more satisfying than fixing situations. You can point your finger and say, "He did it, he can clean it up," and then you're off the hook.

Imagine today that we are a congressional panel empowered to investigate the causes of Jesus' Crucifixion. We know he died by being crucified; we know it happened while Pilate was the procurator of Judea. What we want to know is whose fault it was. Who is responsible? Who should take the blame for letting an innocent man die?

I. Pilate is responsible, shouts one member of the committee. He was the leader in charge, after all; if he had not given the order, Jesus would not have been crucified. All the Gospels say that. As a matter of fact, one of the few times Jesus was mentioned by early historians other than the Gospel writers was in a book by a Roman named Tacitus, who said, and I quote, that Jesus "was executed at the hand of the procurator Pontius Pilate in the reign of the emperor Tiberius." Shouldn't Pilate carry most of the blame?

Imagine Pilate testifying in his own defense. "What could I do?" he says. "Here were the Temple leaders, clamoring for his head. I told them he seemed innocent to me, but they insisted on his death. I asked the crowd to choose between Barabbas, a well-known thug, and Jesus Christ, the innocent man, and they chose the criminal. When it looked like there would be a riot, and people would be hurt, I decided to let them have their way. But I made them take responsibility. I washed my hands, and the people all said they would take the blame, if there was any, for his death. Blame the crowd, not me."

Matthew's account makes Pilate sound very neutral, doesn't it? On the one hand, he gave the people a choice; he didn't just say, "Kill him and be done with it." On the other hand, he didn't do much of anything to stop the process. He could have told the Temple leaders to go suck eggs; as a matter of fact, when Pilate wanted a water line built into his palace, he stole Temple money over the objections of the priests. He did stand up to them when it suited him, but Jesus wasn't worth a fight. Pilate was willing to say Jesus was innocent and trick the crowds into taking responsibility for sentencing Jesus to death, but he would not stand up for what he thought was an innocent man. The most we can say about Pilate is that he was neutral. He allowed Jesus to be killed and did little to stop it.

II. The crowds, though—they said, "Let his blood be on us and on our children." There—they clearly accept responsibility for Jesus' death. Let's blame the crowds in Jerusalem for having Jesus put to death. If they hadn't shouted Pilate down, if they hadn't chosen Barabbas over Jesus, then he might never have been crucified.

Imagine Silas, a resident of Jerusalem at that time, is here to testify in his own defense. He'd probably say, "Yes, we all shouted for Jesus to die and Barabbas to live, but that was because our leaders told us he was a dangerous man. I'd never heard of Jesus at all until I heard a speech by Caiaphas, the high priest that year. He told us about Jesus predicting the Temple would fall and turning over tables in the Temple. He told us that if Jesus kept this stuff up, the Romans would take drastic measures against us. It sounded right to me, and coming from a man like Caiaphas, it carried a lot of weight; so I yelled for Jesus to die. If you're going to blame someone, blame our leaders."

Silas, then, says he was guilty perhaps of being too gullible. He condemned a man because his leaders told him to. He accepted responsibility for Jesus' death because the Temple leaders told him it would be OK. But he didn't have to do that. Silas and all the others in the city could have said, "Maybe things are as you say, but I'd like to hear him for myself before I sentence a man to die." Silas and the crowds could have found out for themselves; they could have been more interested in truth than in going along with the crowd. They could have stopped the death of an innocent man by choosing Jesus over Barabbas when Pilate offered them the choice; but they didn't. They raised such a commotion that Pilate felt pressured to give up his principles and let him die. From ignorance, they influenced Pilate to do something he knew was wrong.

III. Maybe Pilate was weak, and the crowds were ignorant, but the chief priests, the leaders of the Temple, were moving forces behind the whole sorry mess. According to Matthew, even Pilate saw that: "He knew it was out of envy that they had delivered him up." What might Caiaphas say in his own defense?

"Envy? You think we were jealous of a rag-tail preacher, a medicine man from a hick town in Galilee? Hardly! My family has been in the leadership of the Temple for more generations than you can imagine. We have been at the center of power within the Jewish nation ever since we came back from Babylon. Envy had nothing to do with it; it was simply prudent politics. If Jesus had kept on creating disturbances, innocent people would have died. That wretch Pilate had killed Jews before, and he would not hesitate to do it again. So we knew it would be better to arrest the troublemaker ourselves, hand him over to Pilate, and resolve the situation quickly.

"Actually, you know, Jesus killed himself. If he had not done what he did during festival time, when the crowds made the Roman soldiers nervous; if he had not ridden into town on that donkey; if he had not wrecked the outer Temple court in full view of the soldiers; if he had not been so public in his debates and predictions, maybe we could have shown him to the county line and told him never to come back south again. But he wouldn't listen to reason. Yes, we handed him over to Pilate; but remember this: We never asked him to come to Jerusalem and do all the things he did. Jesus dug his own grave, if you ask me."

All the buck passing sounds about right, doesn't it? Who broke the glass and spilled the milk? Well, I did it, but it was because he bumped me. Who killed Jesus? Well, I did, but he made me do it. Pass the buck, refuse the responsibility, let somebody else take the blame. Who really did it? Maybe we ought to hear from the victim himself. Jesus, who was responsible for killing you? Who ought to take the blame?

IV. Frederick Buechner, one of my favorite authors, says something very interesting here. He says that when Pilate offered the crowd the choice between Barabbas and Jesus, and they chose Barabbas, the crowd was doing just what Jesus would have done had he been allowed to have anything to say about it. There is a real sense in which Jesus really is responsible for his own death. He said nothing to Pilate to try to talk him out of crucifying him. He said nothing to the crowd in his own defense. And as Caiaphas, the high priest, reminded us, Jesus did all the things he did in Jerusalem deliberately. Nobody made him, and he knew the risks. He died on purpose because he knew it was God's will for his life.

So who killed Jesus? Whose fault was it? All of them bear some blame, I think. Pilate could have stood tall for justice, but he slunk behind his hand washing. The crowds could have called for Jesus instead of Barabbas, but they followed their leaders like sheep. The leaders could have turned Jesus loose, but they were more interested in safety than in justice. As Buechner says, the fact that the crowd chose Barabbas, and that Pilate offered the choice, and that the priests had turned him over in the first place—all of that simply illustrates what the Bible means when it says that all of us people are sinful and we need salvation.

Who killed Jesus? Who let the Sixteenth Street Church be bombed in 1963, killing four little black girls just because they were black? Who lets thousands of people across the world die from hunger, just because they are not Americans? Who lets the homeless sleep on the streets? Who turn their heads from corruption in government, from the abuse of children, from illiteracy. Good people, like me, who are caught up in other things. Good people, like me, who are sinners nevertheless.

So when the crowd chose Barabbas, they were doing what we do, and what we might well have done had we been there, too. But then Jesus would have chosen for Barabbas to live, too, and to understand that is to understand why the Bible calls him Savior. He'd rather die than let even one thug perish in his place. That is a world-saving, all-encompassing love. If Jesus had his way, Pilate, Silas and the crowds, and even Caiaphas, would all be forgiven and loved into the presence of God. Who killed Jesus? They did, but he wanted to die for them anyway, and for you and me. That's why we can go out of here and offer forgiveness in his name to anyone and everyone. That's why the buck passing stops with Jesus, and ends in salvation.—Richard B. Vinson

Topic: Dynamite

It was his custom to read the papers every morning, and he did so this day. Only one fact was different this day. His brother had died, and he expected to find some notice of it in the paper. So, he was astonished to find there, on the front page of his Swedish newspaper, his own obituary. It was an unfortunate mistake and mix-up, of course. His brother had died, and the newspeople had simply gotten it wrong, thinking he had died, not his brother. So, Alfred Nobel, Swedish industrialist, sat that morning reading what the world was ready to say of *him* at his death.

The article was full of glowing praise. It described how Nobel had begun his career as a poor and struggling experimental chemist in Sweden and how he had worked long, hard years until his discovery of "dynamite." To us more than a century later who have seen the power of the split atom and the hydrogen bomb, it is hard to appreciate what Nobel's discovery meant to his time and world. Nobel's invention of dynamite was the creation of an explosive that was twenty times more powerful than any other available. That invention catapulted Nobel into fame, power, and wealth.

Dynamite revolutionized industries like mining and construction, and it radically altered the making of war. Not only did dynamite greatly enhance the removal of minerals from the earth and increase the capacity of road builders to move mountains, but also dynamite made the weapons of war far, far more deadly. It made for a quantum jump in destruction. If one army had dynamite then, to be secure, any potential opposing army had to have it also. As inventor of dynamite, Nobel was sought after by business magnates and munition makers. He was courted by kings and prime ministers of governments from around the world. Generals and ministers of war sought from him the explosive they had to have. Nobel merchandised dynamite around the globe, and the demand was without end. There in the obituary, Nobel saw the result. He was praised as rich, powerful, successful and called again and again: "the Dynamite King."

That phrase, the Dynamite King, distressed Nobel deeply. Reading those words as the world's measure of what his life meant, he felt that something had gone very, very wrong. This was not what he had hoped for, not what he wanted. If he had worked hard, overcome great obstacles, only in the end to be summed up that way, then his life had missed its mark, gone very wrong.

Of course, he enjoyed the praise. He enjoyed being seen as a person of wealth, power, and influence, but he did not like realizing that he had lived under an illusion thinking it true. He had dreamed he was doing something better and saw the dream for what it was: a folly and a fraud.

You see, when Alfred Nobel discovered this revolutionary explosive, he thought he could serve his own needs and the needs of humanity also. When he made dynamite and realized its power, he had thought he had discovered an end to war. He believed that he had invented something so powerful, so destructive, that, if every nation's military had it, then they would be afraid to go to war. Believing that if all armies had it that no one would dare use it, he sold dynamite to the world. He sold and sold and sold, becoming the world's Dynamite King. He thought he could trade in fear and greed and make a world with less fear and greed. Nobel read the printed obituary before him and realized that it was not true. Dynamite had made him wealthy but had not made the world any more safe. It was the reverse. He had multiplied the world's power to destroy to a terrible degree, and he knew that men would not hold back from killing with greater ferocity. Through the printed words of his own obituary, Nobel began to look at his life through the prism of eternity and see that he had been wrong, dreadfully wrong.

It is not easy to look squarely at one's own life. It is far easier to look at the lives of others and judge. It is easier to see the divided heart, the self-seeking, the folly, evil, and self-deception in others. When we look at ourselves, we are so ready to give ourselves good marks. We are ready to count our intentions for good as the good itself. We are ready to make our small virtues seem larger, make the wrong we do seem unimportant. It was as if this newspaper's mistake had come to Nobel just to help him stop hiding from the truth. It was as if Someone did not want him to waste his life.

From that day onward, Nobel's life turned around. He began to sell his worldwide interests in chemical and munitions factories. With the immense wealth Nobel had made from dynamite, Nobel began to create and fund a public, charitable trust that would outlast his life. This trust would be able each year to give awards to the people who had made the greatest contributions and advances in the arts, literature, and the sciences. Nobel established one prize above all, dear to his heart, to be given to the person who had done the most to advance the cause of peace, the Nobel Peace Prize.

Somewhere someone said once that you can't be born again. It is not possible to reenter your mother's womb. What is done is done, they say. You live this life as best you can, and, no doubt, it will be a mix of good and bad, faith and fiction, wisdom and foolishness. If you miss the point of living, you cannot go back and try again, they say.

But Someone else, speaking from a deeper wisdom, said we are born once and can be born again. We are born of the earth and of flesh and we can be born from above, born of the spirit and hope. And there is at the heart of life One who cares, who cares that, in the midst of the mess, we be given, like Nobel, a second chance.—Charles H. Simonson

Topic: Easter Meditation
". . . Where was a garden." There are four outstanding garden incidents in the Bible.

1. *The Garden of Transgression.* In the cool of the evening when God walked in the garden of Eden, Adam and Eve were afraid and hid from God. They were afraid, for disobedience had entered that garden.

2. *The Garden of Confronting Conscience.* When Ahab, the king, took Naboth's vineyard and went to take possession, he was in high spirits. His plan had succeeded—the vineyard was his. But there arose out of the vineyard the rug-ged form of the prophet Elijah, the conscience of the nation. "Hast thou found me, O mine enemy?" cried the abashed Ahab. Elijah was always spoiling his well-laid plans of evil. When you take the garden of evil you must take it with an outraged conscience that rises up and confronts you. That is the fly in the ointment.

3. *The Garden of the Divine Hesitation.* This is the Garden of Gethsemane, where the Divine One hesitates at the price of man's redemption. But if it is the garden of Hesitation, it is also the garden of Decision. "Arise, let us be going"—to meet the issue—the cross.

4. *The Garden of the Divine Overcoming.* This is the garden of the Empty Tomb, and the Risen Lord. You and I need walk no longer in the garden of Transgression, nor in the garden of the Confronting Conscience, for since our Master has gone through the garden of the Divine Hesitation to the garden of the Divine Overcoming, we too can walk in that garden with the risen Lord.—E. Stanley Jones

ILLUSTRATIONS FOR LENT AND EASTER

NARROW RELIGION. In northern Michigan there is a roadside church only a little bit bigger than a doghouse. Inside there is a small pulpit, a tiny table, and a pew wide enough for one person. According to people in the neighborhood, the church was built by a peculiar farmer who, fairly certain that the whole wide world was going to hell, was at the same time satisfied that he himself was saved. So he built a church just big enough for himself and Jesus to meet in prayer.—David G. Buttrick

NOBODY WANTS BARABBAS. In order to gain the real meaning in the Gospel story of the man Barabbas we must not accent the choice of Barabbas but the rejection of Jesus. The tragedy is deeper and more subtle than appears on the surface. In a real sense the people did not choose Barabbas. The man had put himself outside the community of Israel by his detestable deeds. That this man should have been restored in the affections of his people even after this day is inconceivable. But the man is freed! The people had determined to reject Jesus; and Barabbas was the alternative. The rejection was the decision. They didn't really say yes to Barabbas; but they did say no to Jesus. Barabbas was all that was left.—Joseph A. Sittler

DIVINE GRACE. The Crucifixion is not at all what it seems to be, a tragedy of life, another case of a good man unjustly accused, a miscarriage of human justice. Far from that, it is the true statement of divine judgment on all mankind. Yet more and at the same time it is a true statement of divine grace. God did not conquer sin and solve man's predicament by fighting evil with evil but by conquering evil with suffering love. Simply put, the evangelists wanted simply to say, this is not only a fact of history, this is the true sovereignty of God.—James A. Sanders

HE HAS PAID OUR DEBTS. And so at last God comes to us in Jesus Christ, the Savior of sinners, who sups with Zaccharus, the notorious tax gatherer, collaborationist, and traitor, and who is therefore dubbed the friend of publicans and sinners, and who at last goes his way to the cross in the knowledge that he must not shrink from the uttermost sacrifice in order to consummate God's coming to man. Behold the man!—the servant of God who suffers for our sakes and bears our sins and so effaces them that they can no longer place a barrier between God and man. He has paid your debts. He has overcome the distance that separated the holy God from you, the unholy and miserable sinner, so that now there is no more any wall of partition blocking our access to God. For you and in your room he has suffered the criminal's death, the accursed death that you should have suffered, so that you may realize this truth: "God so loved the world that he gave his only begotten Son, that whosoever believeth in him should not perish but have everlasting life."—Emil Brunner

A LIVING PRESENCE. The appearances of the risen Lord recorded in the Gospel are in one sense no more than sketches from an artist's notebook, no more than a novelist's jotting down of key episodes for his story. But they were also the way in which the early Christians reported the presence of the risen Lord in their midst. They were reporting a living presence that challenged their unbelief, and whenever you and I behold the wounds given by injustice, the living Christ wrestles with our souls asking that we believe in him. The early Christians were reporting a living presence that turned them from concern about their own welfare and called instead that they take up the shepherding of the flock of God. Wherever you and I confront human need, the living presence wrestles with us to create in us a larger charity. They reported a living presence that sat down with them to eat and drink, but it was on behalf of something more than the immediate fellowship of the moment; it was on behalf of paradise.—W. B. Blakemore

WHERE IS EMMAUS? They went to Emmaus. And where was Emmaus and why did they go there? It was no place in particular, really, and the only reason they went there was that it was some seven miles distant from a situation that had become unbearable.

Do you understand what I mean when I say that there is not one of us who has not gone to Emmaus with them? Emmaus can be a trip to the movies just for the sake of seeing a movie or a cocktail party just for the sake of cocktails. Emmaus may be buying a new suit or a new car or smoking more cigarettes than you really want, or reading a second-rate novel or even writing one. Emmaus may be going to church on Sunday. Emmaus is whatever we do or wherever we go to make ourselves forget that the world holds nothing sacred: that even the wisest and bravest and loveliest decay and die; that even the noblest ideas that men have had—ideas about love and freedom and justice—have always in time been twisted out of shape by selfish men for selfish ends. Emmaus is where we go, where these two went, to try to forget about Jesus and the great failure of his life.—Frederick Buechner

THE PRAYERS OF THE PEOPLE EASTER SUNDAY. Thank you for the Easter people: simple sorts in storefront churches, blue-haired ladies with strands of pearls, kids in jeans, small, struggling parishes in out-of-the-way places, faces whose life is a wordless prayer, and whose spoken prayers are no hothouse plants but as organic matter upon the fields.

Thank you for the Easter people: persons also in positions of privilege and power who use their good fortune for the common good.

Thank you for the Easter people: those with the gift to teach us how to lose with class, whose Easter radiance is real, elegant, even in the ruins of some demolished hope, radiance made complete in loss, like some fine, hand-rubbed wood of quiet, burnished beauty, true as candlelight.

Thank you for the Easter people: who, by who they are, and the long shadows they cast, and boundaries wisely drawn, "such a thing is not done in Israel," bless their children with limits, with cross-formed graces: compassion, kindness, humility, gentleness, thoughtfulness, forgiving one another even as God in Christ has forgiven us, bless the next generation with those who, like the Psalmist, love the law, know it to be a lamp unto their feet, quite simply know it their friend.

Thank you for the Easter people: who by word and deed, teach true courtesy, truly royal bearing and grace, and especially to those who are lower down the food chain in this so-called classless society.

Thank you for the Easter people: who, by virtue of an uncluttered life, have room for others, clearings, time and focused minds to care, time, like Mary, to ponder things, and when they speak, their words are not strands of sand but pearls.

Thank you for the Easter people: sorts of people so inwardly free of double-entry goodness that to be in their debt is to be rich, is to be blessed, is to be obligated only as the music maker is obligated to sound, the engraver to sight, only as wine to the grape, the rain, the soil, the light.

Thank you for the Easter people: by whatever name they name you, *their* names are written in the Lamb's book of life, the quiet in the land whose meat and drink it is to love and serve you, not with a sullen face, like Shakespeare's schoolboy, but because, like the sun, laughing, warming stones is who they are, their thing, the day's course they run, to all who know them their signature note, their thumb, guilty as God of goodness, guilty as Jesus' face of most becoming grace, the word become flesh, the quiet life of leaven the bread of life raised, *sursum corda,* "Lift up your hearts." "We lift them up unto the Lord."

Thank you for all that is Easter; Hear our prayer for all that is not.

You call us to be a colony of heaven: a chosen race, a royal priesthood, a dedicated nation, a people claimed by God for his own, to proclaim the triumph of him who has called you out of darkness into his marvelous light (1 Pet. 2:9 NEB). Sometimes the darkness seems brighter than the light. Like Noah, this old world has too long been at sea, and in its heart of hearts, yearns for shore, but night after night on the evening news, the dove returns with no olive branch across its face, no empowering word for all the miles it has to go before it sleeps.

And like the first holocaust, when Cain killed Abel, how high the fires, how large the armies of the night, how many the boots of trampling warriors, the garments rolled in blood, how monotonous the daily office of the opening up of graves, and of the drawing down of blinds.

Passover. The death of the first-born. Only one? Pharaoh was lucky. He should have it so good.

"So much evil and only one God."

Yet everywhere where the sun rises, everywhere where the grass is green and sleep refreshes, there is tenderness, first fruits of the resurrection of the dead, ten thousand who have not bowed the knee to the reigning isms, consumerism, capitalism, nationalism, individualism, narcissism, whatever, everywhere "up" people transfiguring lonely, "down" places, like flowers in a granite wall. Everywhere where the sun also rises, everywhere where the grass is green, the grace of the Lord Jesus Christ, the love of God, the ecology of the Holy Spirit.

Alleluia! Christ is risen!

The Lord is risen indeed! Alleluia!

—Peter Fribley

SECTION VI.
Messages for Advent and Christmas

SERMON SUGGESTIONS

Topic: God's Work in Progress

TEXT: Gal. 4:1–9

Possibly in someone's office or over a desk you have seen that sign that says, "Please be patient. God isn't finished with me yet." I like that sign because I can apply it to myself and feel that things are not hopeless after all. It is good theology, too. It recognizes that God's work is always going on. A Scripture reference can be put alongside that sign, the words of the apostle Paul when he said, "I am confident of this, that God who began a good work among you will bring it to completion by the day of Jesus Christ."

God began "a good work" in our lives; God may be depended upon to complete that work, to bring it to appropriate fruition in the way and time of God's choosing. We can say as a result that human lives are like delicate construction projects where another sign can be hung, one that says, "God's work in progress." Like many construction projects, some of that work advances rapidly and some of it slowly. Adjustments and modifications come along. There are times when nothing seems to be happening and other times of genuine achievement. Through it all, the description rings true, that this is God's work in progress. Our lives are being fashioned according to God's plan.

I. So it has been since the human story began. God's work has been in progress. The world's development has remained uneven and unpredictable because God

forever grants people freedom. The divine purpose, nevertheless, continues to be worked out. Clear evidence of that is borne in upon us at this season when we celebrate again the Savior's birth, he who came (as the New Testament declares) "in the fullness of time." When the right moment had come, God entered life at the human level in the infant Jesus. Jesus became a man among men, one in whom the fullness of God dwelt. He brought a new way of living and a new way of understanding who God is and what God is up to. Because of him, you and I can know peace with God; we can claim divine forgiveness and the possibility for another chance. Our lives as well as the life of the world, as Jesus revealed, are still God's dominant concern. God's work is in progress—in us, around us, everywhere.

We see this work with the eyes of faith. Enough contrary evidence always exists to deny or make doubtful the activity of God in the affairs of the world. But the eyes of faith see beyond the immediate and look at a larger picture. Martin Luther made this point when he spoke about the Christmas story. "There are three wonders here," said Luther; "one, that God should become a man; another, that a virgin should bear a child; and the third, that Mary believed. And the greatest of these is that Mary believed." Belief is critical!

II. Since that moment in the fullness of time when Christ came, God's work in the world has been seen in terms of sav-

276

ing love, a love that has touched individuals of every race and nation. This powerful force affirms the dignity of every soul, advocates the rights of every person, and is a tireless messenger of mercy to the lost and least, the forgotten and forlorn, as well as to the wise and mighty. The downtrodden are lifted by it, while the vain and lofty are brought low. This saving love draws people together in community and bids them live at peace. It is a balm for the hurting, a strength for the faltering, a joy for all. It is the action of God through Jesus Christ, from that first day until now; it is God's work in progress.

The birth of Jesus brought all of these things near. "Your redemption draws nigh," Jesus said to his followers. The apostle Paul quoted from the book of Deuteronomy to say, "The word is near you, on your lips and in your heart." There is an immediacy about the work of God, in other words; it is contemporary and accessible. Preacher Harold Nicely explains, "The meaning of these days is that the living Christ returns to us again and again, when in the providence of God the fullness of the time has come." This preacher adds, "The vitality of our faith is derived, not by what has been, but by what is yet to be." The divine effort continues; God's work is always in progress, it is always going on.

That is why we call the Christmas story Good News. Could there be any better news than this? Does it get any better than learning that our sins are forgiven, that our past does not have to destroy our future, that our broken spirits can be healed and made whole again? Can it get any better than realizing (as an old gospel song says) that "the heart of the Eternal is most wonderfully kind"? What better news is there than knowing that we do not have to hide from God but can ask instead, where is he who has been born our king? Because God ceaselessly acts to draw us into divine-human fellowship, we can live joyfully, affirmatively, and with Good News singing in our hearts.

III. We can go even further, anticipating that final completion of the divine plan where people of all backgrounds and tongues live peaceably together, where there is security throughout the land and none make others afraid. That ancient prophetic ideal is not meant to be forgotten in spite of its seeming unreality, the ideal envisioned by Isaiah when he proclaimed a new harmony throughout creation saying, "The wolf and the lamb shall feed together, the lion shall eat straw like the ox. . . . They shall not hurt or destroy on all my holy mountain, says the Lord." This reversal of enmity and strife, this goal of peace, brotherhood, and sisterhood, also is the work of God—and that work, as our eyes of faith disclose, ceases not nor is stilled. Our confidence that God is not finished with us and has not given up on us or on our world is a mighty source of hope. In the midst of climates of resignation and despair, this is encouragement, indeed. There may be reason for pessimism in the short term, but optimism is the answer overall. It is not an easy optimism, to be sure. The shadow of a cross fell across that manger in Bethlehem. The coming of God to dwell among us in human form was not universally received with gladness. Jesus was crucified. But death could not hold him; he broke its bonds and lives that death may die. So has hope been unleashed among us and become our portion. It is hope built on the continuing work of God—God who began a good work in us and will bring it to completion by the day of Jesus Christ.

Let us open our eyes to see God-with-us in the person of Jesus, God acting to save, restore, and renew our souls. That insight, that perception will make this season beautiful and blessed, becoming for us the fullness of time—the way these days of December ought to be.—John H. Townsend

Topic: Who Are You?

Text: Matt. 11:2–11

Who are you? What is your purpose in living? What is your mission in life? The question of identity plays a central role in each of our lives. How we respond to this question reveals our fundamental beliefs and commitments. Our text shows Jesus both confronting this question about himself from John the Baptist and also asking this question about John.

I. *John's question about Jesus (v. 2–3).* Imprisoned by Herod (cf. 14:3) in the fortress of Machaerus, east of the Dead Sea, John sends a message to Jesus, which reveals both his hope and fear. One may imagine the anxious uncertainty of John as he languishes in prison, questioning the meaning of his own mission and wondering whether he should hope in Jesus as the Messiah. Was Jesus the one coming after John who was more powerful than the Baptist (3:11) or was Jesus just another forerunner of the Messiah? If Jesus was the Messiah, then where was the baptism "with the Holy Spirit and fire"?

Matthew wants to make certain that his readers have no doubt about the answer to John's question. So, at the beginning of verse 2 he writes, "When John heard in prison what *the Christ (Messiah)* was doing . . ." thus giving the answer to the question John is going to ask in verse 3.

II. *Jesus' answer to John (v. 4–6).* Jesus indirectly answers John's question by pointing to his works and words that fulfill messianic prophecy (cf. Is. 35:5–6 and 61:1). Jesus, however, is not ready to proclaim publicly his messianic identity. In effect, Jesus is saying, "You can know who I am by observing the way in which I work in the world." This process of discovering someone's true identity by the pattern of his or her actions in the world is a good method to discern the authenticity of our own identity as disciples of Jesus (cf. 7:16).

Jesus' remark in verse 6 must be understood in the context of Jewish expectations for a political messiah, who would deliver the nation from the oppression of the Romans. People would be offended at Jesus because, although he did the works predicted of the Messiah, he did not fulfill their expectations for a nationalistic deliverer.

III. *Jesus' testimony about John (v. 7—11).* Jesus asks the crowd to think about why John was the object of their curiosity and interest. John was not a fickle preacher ("a reed shaken by the wind"—v. 7) or a flattering courtier "dressed in soft robes" (v. 8). John is not

only a prophet, but the forerunner of the Messiah, who was predicted in Malachi 3:1. Yet John lived before the fulfillment of the kingdom of heaven (the reign of God) in Jesus the Messiah. As John Broadus describes this situation, "John's ministry was the dawn of the messianic reign, whose light gradually increased throughout the ministry of Jesus."

We Christians, who profess to be members in "the kingdom of heaven" (v. 11), are challenged to discover our identity in Christ and live out that identity in the world as agents of God's kingdom. —Charles J. Scalise

Topic: The Miracles of Birth

Text: Matt. 1:18–25

"The Apostles' Creed" emerges from the early pages of Christian history and affirms: "I believe in God the Father Almighty, Maker of heaven and earth: And in Jesus Christ his only Son our Lord: Who was conceived by the Holy Ghost, born of the Virgin Mary." From the beginning of Christianity the miracles of the birth of Jesus were foundations to faith in Jesus Christ, God's only Son, our Lord. Thus, belief in the virgin birth of Jesus has been passed down through the centuries as a central affirmation of our faith. The miracles of birth in the narratives of Matthew and Luke cannot and should not be reduced to a "yes/no" question. When the miraculous birth of Jesus becomes a test of orthodoxy, most of what we deny or affirm is either beneath or beyond the scope of the gospel witness.

I. *Birth is a miracle.* Birthdays are worthy of celebration. Every birth is a miracle of God. If you have not been moved to worship by the birth of your child, you are not paying attention. The introduction of a new life through the agency of marital love is an act of God for Christian parents who are aware of the presence and involvement of God in their lives. Every child is loved of God and special, but the love and the sense of destiny is not just in the birth of the child. The miracle is worked through the parents, the family, and the community in which we grow. God completes the miracle of life in the providence of community. We are indeed workers together with God.

To the Jewish mind, every child was a direct gift from God. The miracle of birth is certainly natural, but in the sense that God has acted, every birth is miraculous. Biblical miracles are acts of God. Even when the acts of God transcend the ordinary, people do not always perceive the presence of God. Thus, a miracle is an act of God perceived as revelation by the eyes of faith. I have experienced miracles. They are not personal exceptions to the rules by which the rest of you live, but the perception of God at work in the ordinary processes of life. Elizabeth Barrett Browning is profound: "Earth's crammed with heaven, And every common bush afire with God; but only he who sees, takes off his shoes." The popular idea of miracle as a private act of divine intervention in the ordinary flow of life usually celebrates the powers of some healer, the magical effect of a place, or the favoritism of God. The violation of the biblical nature of miracle is the modern attempt to find ways to scratch the ego itch with an exceptional evidence of divine favoritism.

In biblical retrospect, some children in history seem destined to be pivotal in the divine plan of salvation. Thus, Ishmael is conceived after a revelation from an angel, Isaac is born through divine intervention in the biological clock of Abraham and Sarah, Samson is born through the revelation of an angel to a barren woman, and Samuel's birth was an answer to the prayers of his saintly mother Hannah.

II. *All of the miracles of Advent revolve around the central miracle—the person of Jesus.* The four Gospels are full of the miracles performed by Jesus. The birth narratives of Matthew and Luke and the prologue to John begin the good news of Jesus the Christ with the central miracle: Christ himself. All four Gospels focus on the person of Christ in the miracle of the Resurrection. Christ is the miracle, the special act of God in history. Christmas, "the Christ Mass," centers in one day, one event—the birth of Jesus, "Jahweh Saves." The traditional observance of Ad-

vent, "the coming," reflects on the larger context. Thus, the birth narratives reach out to the surrounding people, times, and places to the conception of the child, the introduction of the holy family, the conception and birth of John, the hope of Israel reaching back to the Covenant promises of God in the Old Testament, the political-historical setting, and special revelations to shepherds in the field, magi from the East, Simeon, and Anna. To celebrate the coming of Christ, to read the New Testament, is to be reminded that Christmas was not an isolated event. Jesus is surrounded by a cast of supporting characters, each essential to the drama and each reflecting on the whole purpose of God. To celebrate the miracles of Advent is to acknowledge the whole picture presented by Matthew and Luke. The miraculous conception of Jesus is central to the person of Christ in Matthew and Luke, yet Advent is not just about the virgin birth of Jesus to Mary. The whole event of the coming of Christ is an act of God surrounded by Old Testament prophecy, angelic visitations, the conception and birth of John in the tradition of Isaac, and, perhaps the greatest miracle of all, the cooperation of people like Mary and Joseph under circumstances beyond comprehension.

We owe a debt of gratitude to Matthew for introducing human emotions in the birth of the Savior. After tracing Jesus through Joseph to David, Matthew pulls back the curtain on the inner struggle of Joseph with the pregnancy of Mary. We meet Joseph when he has arrived at the strategy to divorce his betrothed quietly. He knows that she is pregnant and that he is not the father of her child. The public humiliation of Mary would not only mean her total disgrace but could lead to a public stoning. In the context of Jewish culture, ignoring the fact of her pregnancy and probable promiscuity was unthinkable. The miraculous conception declares that Jesus is Emmanuel, "God with us." At the same time and just as important, the adoptive fatherhood of Joseph declares that Jesus is the son of David. Matthew does not explain in terms of biology and genetics how Jesus can be Son of God through the Holy Spirit and Son of David through Joseph while maintaining the virginity of Mary.

The miracles surrounding the birth of Jesus are not about modern biology and genetics. They are miracles of the coming of God in Christ. Affirmation of the special circumstances of the birth of Jesus is an affirmation that Jesus is the Christ of God. It is an affirmation of the central miracle of the New Testament, the miracle of the person of Christ. "I believe . . . in Jesus Christ his only Son our Lord." The priorities are correct. Faith rests in Jesus Christ. The witness of the Gospels to the work of the Holy Spirit in conception and his birth to a virgin named Mary support the central affirmation of faith. They call us to faith in Jesus as Lord, not faith in any facts surrounding his birth. I believe in Jesus Christ. Do you?—Larry Dipboye

Topic: The Challenge of His Coming
TEXT: Judg. 13:8

"What shall we do unto the child that shall be born?" Historically, there have been three answers to the question.

I. Herod's answer: The answer of hostility—"Let him be destroyed!"

II. The Bethlehem innkeeper's answer: The answer of secular preoccupation—"There is a stable—they are welcome to it, if they care to use it, but that is the best we can do."

III. The answer of Simeon in the Temple: The answer of commitment—"What does it matter whether life be long or short? If it is to be a long day's strenuous march, what joy, O Christ, to have thy blessed companionship all the way! If it is to be a brief moment and a sudden call—"Lord, now lettest thou thy servant depart in peace, for mine eyes have seen thy salvation."—James S. Stewart

ILLUSTRATIONS FOR ADVENT AND CHRISTMAS

WHY CELEBRATE CHRISTMAS?   When I am asked why I, as a Christian, celebrate Christmas, I answer first and foremost, "Because here something happens to me,

therefore something can happen *in* me—but only if I pause and surrender to it."

I live in the name of the miracle that God is no silent universal principle but that he comes to me in the depths. I see that in the One who lies as a child in the manger and is like all the rest of us in every other way. I see there how he whom "heaven and earth could not contain" enters the world of little things—my little things. The world of homelessness and refugee routes; the world of lepers, mental cases, prodigal sons, and poor widows; the world of cheating, dying, and killing.

Once in the history of the world—and it *did* happen once—the incredible occurred and someone stepped forward with the claim that he was God's Son and the assertion that "the Father and I are one" (John 10:30), not proving this claim by supernatural behavior, by astounding people with his wisdom or by imparting knowledge of higher realms, but seeking verification in the depths to which he was willing to descend. A Son of God who defends his title by arguing that he is still brother to the poorest and the guilt laden, whose burden he takes upon himself! A record like that evokes wondering disbelief—or worship. There is no third alternative. I must worship. That's why I celebrate Christmas.—Helmut Thielicke

HOW GOD WILLED IT.   The true Godhead and the true humanity of Jesus Christ in their unity do not depend on the fact that Christ was conceived by the Holy Spirit and born of the Virgin Mary. All that we can say is that it pleased God to let the mystery be real and become manifest in this shape and form.—Karl Barth

THE NEW SPLENDOR.   When Holy Scripture tells us that there is a "new song" in the world now that God's salvation is proclaimed—and no longer the old song of love and death—we may also speak of a new shining of earth in all its pits of darkness. This is not the old splendor with its illusory comfort and secret shadows. It is not the deceptive rhythm of joy and sorrow, day and night, winter and spring, the alternations of which seem to bring us brief redemption. No, this is the new splendor of the fact that we have been loved and visited and dearly bought by a love that caused the Child to be born in our misery and to suffer our terrible death on the cross.

What can separate us from the love of God?

Christ is here!—Helmut Thielicke

GOD MADE REAL.   It is said of a boy who greatly admired his father, who was in Europe fighting in World War II, that one day he stood for a long time just gazing at his father's picture. As his mother came into the room, he said, "Mother, do you know what I wish could happen? I wish my father could step out of that picture frame and be real to me."

This is what God does for us in Christ: He steps out of the farawayness and the distance and becomes real in a Person.—Benjamin P. Browne

RECOVERING THE CENTER.   If I look at a fine piece of fabric through a magnifying glass, I find that it is perfectly clear around the center of the glass, but around the edges it tends to become distorted. But this does not mislead me into thinking that the fabric itself is confused at this point. I know that this is caused by an optical illusion and therefore by the way in which I am looking at it. And so it is with the miracle of knowledge that is bestowed upon me by the Christmas event: If I see the world through the medium of the Good News, then the center is clear and bright. There I see the miracle of the love that descends to the depths of life. On the periphery, however, beyond the Christmas light, confusion and distortion prevail. The ordered lines grow tangled, and the labyrinthine mysteries of life threaten to overwhelm us. Therefore our sight, which grows aberrant as it strays afield, must recover its perspective by returning to the thematic center. The extraordinary thing is that the mystery of life is illuminated not by a formula but rather by another mystery, namely, the News, which can only be believed and yet is hardly believable, that God has become man and that now I am no longer alone in the darkness.—Helmut Thielicke

TO GOD'S HEART.   The decisive element in the Christian confession of faith in Christ is stated in the simple and expressive words of Luther: "We find the heart and will of the Father in Christ." Therein lies his "unity of substance with the Father." The deed of Christ removes the veil and reveals the heart of God. Christ is "the effulgence of his glory and the very image of his substance" (Heb. 1:3). He is not identical with God, but he and the Father are "one" (John 10:30); one in will, in heart, in purpose, and in work. This reflection of God's heart does not mean merely that faith should find here a certain likeness to God and that the love of Christ should be like God's love. "The substance of the Son" is not only *like* the Father's, it is the same; and the love of Christ is to faith the love of God himself. Where Christ is, there is God; and where Christ is active, there God is active also. The self-sacrificing and self-giving love of Christ is the love of God himself, its struggle against evil is God's own struggle, and its victory is God's own victory. In the deed of Christ God realizes his own will and love.—Gustaf Aulén

FAITH TODAY.   G. K. Chesterton was once being criticized by an agnostic friend for maintaining his Christian faith in the modern world. The argument was depressingly familiar: "Surely you can't hold to that kind of belief in this contemporary scientific world?" To which Chesterton replied: "My good sir, far from disbelieving, I'm actually prancing with belief."—John N. Gladstone

SECTION VII.
Evangelism and World Missions

SERMON SUGGESTIONS

Topic: The Love of God

TEXT: Prov. 4:1–10; Luke 15:11–24

All of us have inherited something from the past. Today, we shall probe the essence of inheritance in the light of God's Word as we look at two biblical passages together: one from the book of Proverbs, and the other from Luke's Gospel, the biblical story everyone seems to know: "The Story of the Prodigal Son."

Numberless sermons have been written about the prodigal son, his elder brother, and the father. We do not know the names of the three, or where the story originally took place, but most likely in the life of Israel. Jesus heard it some time ago, and now he shared it with his listeners.

There he is, the father, presumably in the prime of his life, an accomplished man. He had two sons, a prosperous estate with a sizable staff, animals of the fields. Musical instruments were kept in the main house and were brought out when there was time for festive occasions.

The house was spacious with a porch, where he rested after a long day, watching the sunset and gazing toward the horizon. Everything was in order, and life went on as usual.

I. Until one day, the younger of the sons went to him with a request, asking that the share of the property due to him, be given to him now.

Yet, the father was not surprised. It did not escape his attention that the son

had gradually separated himself from the rest of the family. The son eagerly listened to the stories of sojourners who stopped by the house and enjoyed the father's hospitality. His imagination was nurtured by the unlimited freedom of unknown places.

But what of the third person in the story, the older brother? He too had thoughts about the father. He disagreed with the father's decision. Instead of giving a large part of the fortune of the family to the brother, everything should have been kept together, let the wealth grow, so ultimately he would inherit an even larger property later. As we recall from Luke's account, the father did not prevent the son from leaving. No questions asked, no tone of arguments. Yet this same father will keep the son on his mind each day. He will be waiting for him and never stop watching for him. Every step he takes in the wrong direction will give the father pain.

And the younger brother took full advantage of his "new freedom." Gathered all his possessions, and journeyed into the "far country," the land of his dreams, followed his rainbow. He sought to explore every unknown experience of life. He had lots of "new friends" because the money was flowing.

Then, one day, all his fortune was gone, he was alone, destitute in a famine-stricken land. Hungry and lonely. Finally, he lowered himself down to the animals, to the swine, which to the Jews was the ultimate mark of degradation.

II. How far he strayed from his father and drifted away from God! Yet, there, in the "far country," he came closer and closer to his father. And when he lost everything, when his life was going down the hill, he was even more tied to his father than before.

But what was the most important thing that he took with him when he left home? The answer is in Proverbs. The father in Luke's narrative does not speak to the son directly. But in the fourth chapter of Proverbs, a father's plea is this:

"Hear, O sons, a father's instructions, and be attentive, that you may gain insight; for I give you good precepts: do not forsake my teaching. When I was a son with *my* father, tender, the only one in the sight of my mother, he taught me, and said to me: Let your heart hold fast my words, keep my commandments and *live.*"

This is what the younger son in Luke's account learned at home, from his father and loving mother, from his teachers, and the community—that is what he carried with him, and that is what made him "to come to himself." He did nothing more but set out to return. And it was infinitely more difficult to return as a failure than when he left from home: full of pride, confidence, and anticipation.

III. And the father was waiting for him, hoping for his return. And then, one day, one moment, the silhouette of the son, barely visible, hardly recognizable, appeared on the expanded horizon.

The father was confident, and he alone, that the son carried *more* with him, in him, than worldly possessions when he left.

And during all that time, the father was certain that the son had those inner reserves, that he had not forgotten the lessons he received in his youth about God. "I have sinned against heaven. . . ." The teachings at home, what he learned from his father and loving mother, the examples at home, the guiding hand of God: these caused him to realize what he really left behind and gave him the inner strength "to come to himself." This new discovery, this obvious truth simply overwhelmed him and set him free.

And as he was getting close to the place of his birth he recognized that the father was waiting, approaching, coming toward him. And when they met no words were needed. Yet the son seemed to say:

"Father, I have lost everything in the far country. I have suffered much, and atoned for my sins. *But now,* I have a claim on your acceptance, on your love. Father, receive me back as one of your hired servants, just don't withhold your love."

IV. A few months ago I was asked to lead a delegation of American academicians in Europe. The tour covered three countries, and the delegation's itinerary included a visit to the great city St. Petersburg, in Russia. There, in the midst of political, social, economic and cultural problems, is an island of beauty, the Hermitage Museum.

And in touring that magnificent treasure house, the guide leads you into the Rembrandt room, which is filled with the paintings of the Dutch master. And there, on one canvas, is one of the most moving paintings, depicting our story. "The Return of the Prodigal Son." It is one of the last masterpieces of Rembrandt from 1664, painted 330 years ago.

There he is, the father, tall, erect, with a happy face, as he is adoring, loving, blessing his son. The son, facing the father, in rags, with torn sandals, with his head down, asking for forgiveness. No words are needed. The older brother is halfway in the shadows with amazement and surprise on his face.

That painting says volumes about human life, particularly in the twentieth century.

During the seventy years of "barbaric atheism," when most churches were closed to worshipers, when generations suffered hardship and persecution for personal piety, that painting was a witness to human goodness, and forgiveness and hope. When human words were silenced, the artist through his brush strokes proclaimed the very Word of God and declared so eloquently a radiance of hope, and a new beginning, sometime in the unknown. Every time a human being meditated in front of the painting, it said something unique to each individual. In the midst of despair it ennobled human lives. The canvas *radiated,* and through it God proclaimed his love—and he alone—to each silent spectator.

V. The central figure, the hero of the story, is the forgiving father. But the ultimate theme of this story is not the father and the two sons but our heavenly Father. The son is embraced by his father as a symbol of heavenly reward that awaits the sincere Christian penitent. The father, who is waiting for us, to whom we may return. The ultimate glory of this story is not the faithfulness of man *but the faithfulness of God.*

And this is the reason why the joyful sound of festivity rings out from this story. We must read and hear this narrative in many languages, and in many lands. We must stand before the canvas of the God-inspired master, so we all know that there is good *news,* to all the peoples.

The *ultimate secret* of this story is this: There is a homecoming for us all, because there is a home.—Laszlo Kovacs

Topic: The Drawing Power of the Cross

Text: John 12:32–33

The text for this sermon gives John's clue to what draws people to Jesus Christ, and it's a bit of a surprise. If the question "What draws people to Christ?" were asked of most Bible-study groups, the answers would mention different aspects of his life, his teachings, or his ministry. There is a good chance that no one would suggest "the cross." Yet John ties the drawing power of Christ directly to the manner of Christ's death.

I. *A new view of life: fulfillment through sacrifice.* Part of the attractiveness of the cross is that through it Christ presents a completely new view of life: fulfillment through sacrifice. The announcement that "the hour is come" (v. 23) must have excited the people and filled them with a vision of the golden age toward which the Old Testament prophets pointed. But, like us, they tended to tie their nationalistic and religious expectations together.

They must have been staggered at the very idea of glorification in terms of sacrifice. Yet Jesus' analogy of the grain of wheat is a reference to his own death (v. 23). Just as the grain of wheat had to "die" in order to increase, so Christ must die to fulfill his mission. He made it clear that those who selfishly grasped life would ultimately lose it, and that it was only by surrendering one's life to God and to others that it was multiplied. It may come as a surprise to people today that this concept was strange to those who heard Christ, but we need to remember that the Jews did not connect the passages in the prophets that dealt with the suffering servant to their messianic expectancy. Even the apostles were confused at the concept of fulfillment through suffering.

Yet in spite of all this, it is the invitation to "take up your cross and follow me" that makes the Christian religion most attractive. The call to sacrifice challenges the self-centered life that, even in the midst of our self-indulgence, we know is really empty. Those who work with people who try to find fulfillment in materialism know that what is found is a larger emptiness. There is something in "taking up a cross" that strikes a chord deep within our souls.

II. *Faith sees victory and not defeat.* The cross draws us because it is the way in which Christ moved beyond all the tensions of his ministry to triumph. We should not judge the disciples' despair at the cross, for we look at the cross through the perspective of the empty tomb, through the reality of Resurrection. Ordinary vision would stand at the foot of the cross and say, "This is the end." Only the eyes of faith could take in that scene and say, "This is the beginning." But it helps us all to understand our natural tendency to draw back from sacrifice when we see what this text reveals of Christ's own inner conflict as he faced the cross.

The Gospel of John omits the account of Christ in the Garden of Gethsemane but records its tension here. The Bible often deals more honestly with Christ's inner conflict than we deal with our own doubts and fears. Verses 27 and 28 tell of Christ's thoughts when his soul began to be troubled. They were considered as both natural and real. This fact ought to rescue us from the false picture of a good Christian as one whose life has no doubts, no reluctance, or no inner conflicts.

It was as Christ saw the cross as the eternal purpose of God, and not as a miscarriage of justice, that a different picture of the cross emerged. When Christ realized that "for this cause came I unto this hour," then the cross became a mighty act of God's love and revelation and sacrifice. It was in this context that the sense of triumph developed.

What had been the symbol of death became the sign of new life. What had looked like humanity's worst mistake became God's greatest act. What seemed like Satan's triumph became God's eternal victory. What had looked like a tiny and narrow sect of Judaism became a worldwide religion with a message of hope for every human being. We are drawn to the cross because we see in it God's overruling sovereignty in our lives and in the world. The cross has become for us a symbol of triumph.

III. *The place where we meet God.* First, the cross is attractive to us because God speaks to us through it. We sense in our inmost being that it was God who was there dying on the cross. Thus it becomes a place of revelation. We learn that at the core of the universe there is a God who is personal, moral, caring, and purposeful. The cross contends that we have not been abandoned in this vast universe.

It is also a place of sacrifice. The cross indicates that God takes our sins seriously. There is, even with all the different theories of atonement that our scholars have developed, a sense of mystery as to how this can be. Yet, in the midst of our inability to comprehend it all, we are comfortable with standing at the cross and saying with the early Church, "Christ died for my sins."

It is also a word of hope to all who suffer. The cross shows how things will finally conclude with the devil being judged. Thus, the cross is a constant reminder that there will come a day when love will overcome hate, truth will conquer the lie, and even life will destroy death.

Consequently, the cross draws us because in the depths of our being we sense that we were somehow involved. The Negro spiritual asks the question, "Were you there when they crucified my Lord?" and our hearts answer, "We were there." And as we stand at that place, we are laid bare with what amounts to a spiritual soul scan.

At the cross, all the things that we call life are exposed for the sham that they are, and we are freed to dream of real life. While there is something in us that likes to hold on to our illusions, there is still the deep desire to know what is real and valuable and eternal. That is why the cross draws us.

We are drawn to the cross because we see operating there a power that has the potential for breaking our cycles of failure and rescuing us. In our self-centeredness we have sought freedom apart from God and have found slavery instead. At the cross we glimpse the possibility of real freedom—spiritual freedom.

At the cross we see a love that has forgiveness written all over it. Although I have no training in the field of counseling, I have great admiration for those who do. Once, when I was having lunch with a psychologist friend, I asked if there was one thing he wished he could do for his clients that was not possible for him to do. To my surprise, he said without hesitating, "I wish I could say to them, 'Your sins are forgiven.' So many of the people whom I see could manage their problems so much easier if they could find forgiveness for their sins." At the cross people can stand and hear the words of forgiveness, and this continues to draw people to the cross.—Kenneth L. Chafin

Topic: Who Is on Trial Here?

TEXT: John 19:12–16

If there is one question that reverberates throughout John's story of the trial of Jesus, it is the question: Who is really on trial here? A court reporter would quickly say that it was Jesus, of course, who was on trial. He was the one being held by the police. He was the one who had to answer to the charges. He was the one accused and placed on the stand and interrogated. Jesus was the one on trial. Nothing could be plainer than that.

But listen to the way John tells the story, the way he uses irony, the way he depicts the ambiguities in the accusers of Jesus, the way he unfolds the court record, keeps switching our perspective in the courtroom until we are no longer sure who is actually on trial. The prosecutor's table begins to look more and more like it is really the prisoner's dock, that accused Jesus appears less and less like the defendant and more and more like the true judge.

For example, listen to the exchange between Jesus and Caiaphas, the religious district attorney. I picture Caiaphas leaning back on two legs of his chair. You know when people are sure of themselves, relaxed, comfortable . . . they sometimes lean back in their chairs. I can picture calm Caiaphas doing that, crossing his arms, smiling confidently, and asking, "So, Jesus tell us about your teaching." In other words, here is a piece of rope long enough to hang you. Wrap it around your own neck. Tell us about the heresies you proclaimed. Tell us about the laws you undermined. Tell us about the treason you breathed. Just a simple, little open-ended question. "Tell us about your teaching," he said, leaning back in his chair.

"Everything I said," replied Jesus, "I said out in the open. I taught in the synagogue. I taught in the Temple. Everybody heard what I said. My motivations were clear, but what about yours? Why do you ask me this question?" No doubt Caiaphas's chair thudded back to four legs. Who is on trial here?

Then they transferred the trial to the federal court, and there is confused and weary old Pilate, leafing through Jesus' folder, looking for the list of charges. He was probably muttering to himself that sometimes he would rather be a file clerk in Rome than deal one more day with these crazy Jews. "I apply for Iconium and what do they give me? Jerusalem." Finally he finds the paragraph he is looking for. "Are *you* the King of the Jews?"

"Is this your question," said Jesus, "or did someone else put you up to it? Is this someone else's idea or do *you* want to know?"

"Do *I* want to know? Look at me. Do I look Jewish to you? Do *I* want to know? . . . Do I *want* to know?" Who is on trial here?

Perhaps you know the legend that circulates in the art world about the inexpensive painting purchased in a secondhand shop. Cheap art, but it would at least add a little color to a drab wall. The new owner, before hanging it on the wall, decides to clean the painting, so out come the cotton balls and the solvent. But as the owner begins to clean, the surface paint itself dissolves, and underneath there is another painting. A professional art restorer is brought in, and as the surface paint is washed away there is gradually revealed the work of a master. So it is with the Gospel of John. It is impossible to read this story carefully without discovering that beneath the cheap theatrics and cosmetics of Jesus' trial there appears another picture. In this picture, it is not Jesus on trial, but Caiaphas. It is not Jesus on trial, but Pilate. It is not Jesus on trial, but the world . . . all of us. We discover that we are, all of us, on trial.

Ever seen one of those game shows on television? The contestant is standing there trembling with excitement. He has just won the luggage and a trip to Hawaii, and now the emcee wants to know if he will risk it all for the sailboat and the convertible. His brow wrinkles with uncertainty, and the audience begins to cheer, "Go for it! Go for it!" And we're with them. A new car, sailboat. Go for it! Go for it!

Jesus said, "My kingdom is not of this world. Do not labor for the food which perishes, but for the food which endures to eternal life."

"Shall I crucify your king?" asks the emcee.

"We have no king but Caesar," we say, eyeing the sailboat. "Go for it!"

When they found Mary Ann Cardell, she had been dead for several hours. Mary Ann was an elderly woman who lived alone in an Atlanta welfare hotel, and her only two comforts in life were a bottle and a pen. With the bottle she eased her pain; with the pen she wrote about her thoughts and feelings. Eventually the bottle became more demanding than the rent, and one day she was evicted from her room. She tried to find a place to spend the night, but there was alcohol on her breath, and no one would take her in. When they found her, her body was in a litter-filled field of weeds, cold and blue, and there was a note beside her. Mary Ann had written, "I have nowhere to go, and there is no one to understand. God is not dead. He is only sleeping, but sleeping very soundly."[1]

Jesus said, "This I command you, to love one another."

"Shall I crucify your king?" we are asked again.

"We have no king but Caesar," we reply, and all of the Mary Ann Cardells are left once more to believe that God sleeps through their cold nights.

When we stand at the foot of the cross, we look at the condemned man, and then we look inside ourselves, and we know who is truly worthy of being condemned. We hear his voice saying, "Let not your hearts be troubled. You believe in God, believe also in me." But our troubled hearts let us know who is really on trial here.

So, there we stand in the courtroom, and the verdict rings out, "Guilty!" There is no escaping this judgment, and we have now only one hope. It is this: The Jesus whom we crucified is now the judge of all time, and our only hope is in the mercy of this judge. "Who is to condemn?" asks Paul. "It is Christ Jesus, who died, yes, who was raised from the dead, who is at the right hand of God, who indeed intercedes for us ... " (Rom. 8:33).—Thomas G. Long

ILLUSTRATIONS OF EVANGELISM AND WORLD MISSIONS

THE GOD OF OUR SALVATION. He saved me yesterday. That involves all that my crimson sin had come to mean. He washed me from the guilt, and saved me from the power and dominion of sin.

He saves me today. That involves all that temptation, and faltering, and stumbling can mean. It can be spoken in all the meaning of the infinite tenderness of the infinite Savior, who shielded from blame the poor sinful woman who wanted a chance at a new life, as well as in the offered meaning of the infinite promise to help us all and each.

He will save tomorrow. That involves all that can be run into the meaning of hell and heaven in the destiny of the human soul.—Merton S. Rice

THE TIDE IS IN. Have you noticed Southampton water when the tide is out? I am not thinking now of the unsightliness of the view so much as of what happens to the boats and little vessels along its shores. When the tide is out, there they lie on their sides in the mud and slime, the very pictures of weakness and helplessness! But when the tide sweeps in, those same boats are tugging at their anchors and dancing on the waves, the very pictures of life and restrained energy. It is all the difference between life and death, between helplessness and power! And that is what I have to say to you men and women: The tide is in! What excuse have we for weakness, failure, despair? None whatever! For of his fullness we may all receive. And, strengthened by his Spirit in our inward man, we shall be able to stand in the evil day, and, having done all, to stand.—J. D. Jones

"WANTED, A VERDICT!" The more I live, the more I study life; the more I see its aimless, goalless driftings, the more I counsel a definite deliberateness in the

[1]As recorded by Ed Loring in *Hospitality* 3, no. 5:3, the newsletter of the Open Door Community, Atlanta, Georgia.

determination of a Christian life. Yes, I would even go as far as to say that I would have men break up their indecision by a deliberate action that is striking and dramatic. I do not mean a stagy spectacle, with an applauding audience looking on, but a dramatic moment in secret, when a man smashes up his moral hesitancies and indecision, and, laying a firm hand upon the neglected helm of his boat, shall say, "Now! henceforth for me to live is Christ!" "Choose you this day whom ye will serve; . . . as for me and my house, we will serve the Lord."—John H. Jowett

REAL LIFE IN GIVING.   In one of my classes, a student said in his sermon, "If we preached the cross, it would empty our churches." I'm inclined to think that the opposite might be true. It is the loss of the call to sacrifice that lessens the attractiveness of the Church. This is why so many young people are so vulnerable to the religious sects that prey upon their sense of guilt at having so much and giving so little. They have been provided with everything by churches that loved them, but which were not wise enough to see their need to be told that real life would come not from getting everything but from giving all.—Kenneth L. Chafin

THE DEAD MAN.   Did I not hear one say, who had reveled forty years in sin, and who had become united with the Lord, that that forty-year-old man was dead, "crucified with Christ," and if any accusing day should shake a threatening finger at him, he would laugh in triumph, the finger was pointed at the dead, for that particular man "was crucified, dead and buried, and his life was hid with Christ in God"?—John H. Jowett

SECTION VIII.
Preaching from Amos

BY JOHN J. OWENS

When one seeks to interpret any Scripture, it is important to examine its content and where it fits into the total context of the Bible. For instance in the Old Testament, there are five books of the Torah (law), five books of the Psalms, five Writings, and five Scrolls.

As we look at the book of Amos, we note that it is among the prophets. There are five books of Prophets. These are: (1) the Earlier Prophets; (2) Isaiah; (3) Jeremiah; (4) Ezekiel; and (5) the Book of the Twelve. Amos is one segment of the Book of the Twelve. It is tied to all of the other "minor prophets." We class them as minor only because they are shorter. Amos is tied to the preceding Joel by the presence of several ideas that are found in both books. Also, Amos is stitched to the book of Obadiah by the same device. This phenomenon has been outlined clearly and at length by Professor James Nogalski in his Ph.D. dissertation in the University of Zurich recently. These concepts are noted as stitch words that can be found in the individual shorter prophets.

The "stitch words" of Joel, which are also in Amos, are important. *Tyre* (Joel 3:4; Amos 1:9, 10); *Philistia* (Joel 3:4; Amos 1:6–11); *Edom* (Joel 3:19; Amos 1:6, 9, 11); *Zion* (Joel 3:17, 21; Amos 1:2); *Jerusalem* (Joel 3:16, 17, 20; Amos 1:2); and *And the Lord roars from Zion, and utters his voice from Jerusalem* (Joel 3:16; Amos 1:2).

The ideas that occur at the end of Amos and also at the beginning of Oba-diah are: *Though . . . from there* (or thence) (Amos 9:2, 3, 4; Obadiah 1:4); *Edom . . . the nations* (Amos 9:12; Obadiah 1:11, 2, 4). *I will bring them down* (Amos 9:2; Obadiah 1:4); *in* (on) *that day* (Amos 9:11; Obadiah 1:8); *the mountains* (Mount Esau) (Amos 9:13; Obadiah 1:8–9).

Amos is the third segment of the Book of the Twelve. The key verse is in 5:24: *But let justice roll down like waters, and righteousness like an ever-flowing 'stream.* The word *justice* is "mishpat," which is the basic concept of judgment. Judgment becomes justice only when it is the judgment that God would make. The word *righteousness* ("tsedekah") has the basic concept of straightness. When the two terms *justice* and *righteousness* are used by an author in parallel they form a compounded relationship of judgment and straightness.

One should consult some solid books on Amos, such as *Amos* in the Old Testament Library series written by James Luther Mays (Westminster); *The Book of Amos* of the Shield Bible Study Outlines by Page H. Kelley (Baker) and *Amos and His Message,* by Roy Lee Honeycutt (Broadman).

One should expect each segment to have an introduction, a body, and a conclusion. In Amos, chapters 1 and 2 form the introduction; chapters 3 through 9:6 are the body of Amos; chapter 9:7–15 form the conclusion.

This format of the Hebrew mind will be incorporated in each prophet. My Old Testament professor used to say that

289

each writer would use the same basic outline, that is, he would tell you what he was going to tell you; then he would tell you; then he would tell you what he said he was going to tell you, thus forming the three-point outline of each segment of the Old Testament Scripture.

Topic: Thus Saith the Lord

Text: Amos 1:3, 6, 9, 11, 12; 2:1, 4, 6

It makes a huge difference who says anything. When our parents spoke, we were wise to listen and pay close attention. So when Yahweh, the Covenant Savior and the Loving Lord, speaks, it behooves us to listen. Such an authority! These quotations from him are not idle remarks but should be noted as important, almost commanded, thoughts. Hearken, this is Yahweh speaking!

Topic: Yahweh Roars

Text: Amos 1:2

In those days, when anyone could hear the roar of a lion, he knew instinctively that the fierce animal was near enough to be able to do anything he wished. Furthermore, a lion would let out such an outcry immediately prior to leaping on his prey and tearing them to pieces. So when there was a roar, there would be an immediate response. The roar was a warning that something imminently was occurring. It was a warning—not a watch!

A few days ago, the weather forecasters warned of an approaching tornado. We knew that something was imminent, and we went immediately to a safe place. This statement in Amos 1:2 is a first warning and should evoke an immediate response. We should heed such a word from the prophet of Yahweh.

Topic: We Have Sinned

Text: Amos 1:3, 6, 9, 11, 13; 2:1, 4, 6

In Wisdom literature the use of successive numbers is a statement of more than a fact. We have sinned and come short of the glory of God. Each group mentioned has been guilty of successive sins. Not only a sin against God, but indeed sins against fellow beings.

Topic: Selling the Righteous

Text: Amos 2:6; 8:6

The righteous are not supposed to be treated as things (chattel). The Torah was replete with exhortations to exalt the righteous. Righteousness should have been rewarded. But evidently Israel was guilty of treating the righteous as disposable instead of something to be protected.

Selling for silver was doing the deed in a legal fashion. Selling the needy for a pair of shoes would have been seen as doing something improper in a proper fashion, that is, doing an illegal deed in a legal fashion. Seeing something as legal is not synonymous with righteousness! Of all things—a people who were supposed to be righteous being viewed on the lawful stratum was unthinkable. When a person stoops or lowers himself to the level of the law, he casts a spell of gloom on any righteousness involved.

Topic: An Appointment

Text: Amos 3:2

When God says that a family has been recognized, it is a distinct honor. God had singled out Judah/Israel as unique—his special people. They were unique, for God had selected them out of all his choices. They were God's chosen people with great responsibilities. They had been given many privileges, so they had much to live up to. If they did not live up to these responsibilities, they would be judged concomitantly in accord with the privileges. Amos reminds God's people that it is no accident that they had been chosen. God knew what he was doing when he selected them. They had great possibility and thus they had great responsibility. Two cannot accidentally fall into step. There was an agreement between God and his people. Thus the cause and effect was a reality.

Topic: Put Your Ears On!

Text: Amos 3:1; 4:1; 5:1; 8:4

One of the greatest needs of all time is the need to listen. People of all ages need to have a good listener. The elder generation needs to have some one person who will take the time to "hear" them. Many elderly persons repeat the same stories because they feel that no one is listening to them. One of the greatest gifts that can be given to another person is the gift of an open ear.

A fundamental element of Old Testament religion is found in Deuteronomy 4:1 and 5:1. In Deuteronomy 6:4 we read the *Shema*, which is "Hear, O Israel." Repeatedly we are admonished to listen or hear. Could this be why we have two ears and only one mouth? Actually, most of us use our mouth more readily than we use our ears. But it is essential for us to listen.

Repeatedly Amos exhorts his readers to "hear" or "listen." Such was a need in that day, and such is a need in our day. People need to hear. There is no question as to our having our say or putting in our two cents' worth. But seldom do we acknowledge the quality of a person by recognizing that they have been good listeners.

Topic: Seek the Lord

Text: Amos 5:4, 6

Our modern generation puts so much emphasis upon man and the common good. But we need to be brought down to earth in realizing that man is not the center of the universe. Most of the time, each of us centers our thoughts on our selfish welfare. For instance, how often do we ask where God is when we are suffering or are in pain? How often do we ask where God is when we have pleasure or gain? We put so much emphasis on our own desires and wants and pleasure to the exclusion of the will of God. We spend so much time, thought, and energy on ourselves that we seldom have time to think about God's will. When God created this world, he did *not* command all things into existence. There was no divine fiat. There was a *divine wish* that all things come into existence. Likewise, we should not do things because God commands them. We should do certain things because we want to please God. Life should be seen as a privilege and not as an ordeal. We select our activities to please another instead of pleasing our-

selves. If we really want to live, Amos tells us to seek the will of another. In this case, it is God that should be the center of everything. If God is pleased, that should take precedence over our own desire.

Topic: Let Justice Roll

Text: Amos 5:24

This is the key verse to the book of Amos. It should be the key to our own existence. Justice is important in court and also in all areas of life. There is no word in the Old Testament for right decisions at the court of law. The word *justice* is the word *judgment*. When the biblical context calls for the right judgment at law, it is God's law that is concerned. When our decision is the right one—that is, it is the decision that God would make if he were on earth—it becomes justice. Just because a certain official or group of officials make a decision, it is not necessarily justice. Only when it is the right decision—that is, the decision God would make if he were here in person—does judgment become justice.

Our disordered world needs justice. Why should we have prosperity when the rest of the world struggles and suffers? Let justice be a way of life everywhere.

"Roll" is unstoppable. When we hear that such a person is "on a roll" we assume that she/he cannot be stopped. When water is "rolling," there is a dam in the world that can temporarily stop it. Such might cause a temporary slowing of a stream of water. But water keeps on coming and will rise above the dam. It will roll over the top of it and continue to flow into the waiting fields below.

"Justice" and "righteousness" are parallels. They are two sides of the same coin. They are not supplementary but rather are complementary. The author is expressing a single idea, or rather two terms to express a single thought. Righteousness is doing what God would do if he were here in person. Our responsibility is to live so close to him that we automatically do the *right* thing because it is what he would do.

Topic: What Are You Looking At?

Text: Amos 7:7; 8:1

"Amos, what do you see?" is an important concept. We only see what we are looking at! Which way are we looking? Upon whom are we fixing our gaze? One of the earlier translations of *prophet* was "seer," so the author may be asking Amos, what kind of a prophet are you going to be? There are many "reverends" who are not worthy of being addressed as deserving reverence. The persons who are designated as religious leaders do not deserve such recognition by virtue of themselves. It is only when a person takes his authority from God rather than from his position or person that he really can lay claim to reverence or even respect. There is a great difference between living up to the authority God gives us and living a boastful existence because of who we are. Amos, What are you looking at? Christian, To whom are you looking for your position or authority?

Topic: The Lord Showed Me
TEXT: Amos 7:1; 8:1 (see also 7:4, 7)

Our God is a revealing God. He showed Amos many things. In our day, the same God is trying to reveal many things to us, if only we will listen. Closely related to this concept is the idea that Amos saw. Likewise, he will cause us to see.

Topic: Start Where You Are
TEXT: Amos 7:14

We know very little about the prophet Amos. Most of our information is found in Amos 7:14–15. This biographical section tells us that God found Amos working and intervened in his existence. This experience changed Amos's outlook and activity. It put him to work in his community and in his world. When Amos opened his eyes, he saw his world as being in need of some enlightening ideas and actions.

Topic: Hope for the Future
TEXT: Amos 9:11

Throughout God's Word we find references to the future. We are involved with our present and also with the future. What we do impinges upon the world in the days to come. What we do today will have its effect upon what happens in the future. The prophet lifts our eyes from the present to the fact that God has a long look backward and also toward the future.

Topic: Restore the Fortunes
TEXT: Amos 9:14

This term is often used to emphasize that Judah and Israel will be restored (Jeremiah 29:14; 30:3, 18; 31:23; 32:44; 33:7, 26; Ezekiel 16:53; 39:25). The term appears once in Hosea (6:11), once in Joel (4:1) and once in Zephaniah (3:20). It is a Jeremianic term (at least eleven times) and is found three times in Ezekiel. This same promise is made to Judah, Egypt, Moab, Ammon, and Elam. This is our Father's world. It is our responsibility to help take care of it. But in the final end, God will take care of all of us.

SECTION IX.
Preaching from Great New Testament Texts

BY DAVID S. DOCKERY

Topic: God's Grace

TEXT: Rom. 3:21–26

This passage was strategic for the concerns of the reformers over 450 years ago. We will all agree that our generation brings different questions to the Bible today than those brought by the great reformers, Luther and Calvin. There is a need always to apply and contextualize the biblical text, but we must never allow our concern to be relevant to drown the voice of the apostles. Contemporary concerns have shifted the focus of the gospel toward the needs of men and women, which is both appropriate and disconcerting. The centrality of the gospel and the message of grace found in this passage reminds us of the priority of the gospel and the message of justification by faith. Martin Luther said that if Romans is a little New Testament, then Romans 3:21–26 is a little Romans. He maintained that one had to understand these verses correctly in order to comprehend the gospel. While that might be an overstatement, it is indicative of the significance of this great passage. These verses present us with words like *righteousness, justification, sacrifice, atonement,* and *redemption*—all filled with theological content.

Because of the quantity and quality of these thought-filled terms, our tendencies and those of our congregations are to ignore them. But it is good to focus on the theocentric gospel of grace.

I. Paul maintained that the gospel is apart from the law. With him, we must recognize that the righteousness that God gives to us is apart from law, but nevertheless it has been testified in the Law. In the Law and the Prophets we see over and over the picture of men and women sinning and God pronouncing judgment. This is followed by a sacrifice for sins and a granting of pardon or release. Constantly this picture is presented: sin, judgment, sacrifice, and release. In a way similar to Pavlov in his famous experiment, God, in the Old Testament, by conditioned response was teaching us that sin brings judgment and demands sacrifice; likewise, sacrifice, offered in faith, brings release.

II. The apostles stressed that righteousness comes from God and this righteousness is a God-type righteousness. Our problem is not only that we don't have enough righteousness, but that we have the wrong kind. What is needed is a divine righteousness, that can only be given by God.

Recently, it was reported that the world Monopoly championship was won by an eleven-year-old boy. He collected all sorts of money, bought real estate, houses, and hotels on the significant places on the game board like Boardwalk and Park Place. Imagine that that young man took those winnings and attempted to trade them for "real" estate. He would not have been able to do so; not because he did not have enough money in real estate but because he had the wrong kind. So it is with us. We have the wrong quality of righteousness. We have a human righteousness that falls short of the quality of a God-type righteousness.

III. The strategic third affirmation of this passage is that the gospel is for sinners. All have sinned and fall short of the glory of God. In the previous chapters, Paul has maintained that the unbelievers who have rejected natural revelation are sinners. As a result of rejecting natural revelation, they stand under the judgment of God. Then he stressed that moral persons—even those who do moral deeds in the sight of society—are sinners because they have rejected the revelation of conscience. Paul contends that even the most religious person, the one who teaches the oracles of God but does not practice them, stands under the judgment of God. So the Reformation proclamation following Paul is that all (pagan, moral, or religious people) fall short of the glory of God; everyone is in desperate need of the gospel. The message of Romans is that we must understand the bad news before we see the need for the good news.

IV. The good news is that this justifying gospel is given freely by God's grace to undeserving sinners. What does it mean to be justified? Justification is more than being pardoned; it means that we are clothed within the righteousness of Jesus Christ and that justification comes to us freely. It is nothing that we can do for ourselves but is a declaration from God that we stand righteous and acceptable before him. How does this come about? It comes freely to us, but it is costly to God. That is what grace is—God's unmerited riches at Christ's great expense. It cost Jesus Christ his life and says that we are redeemed through the cross. Christ purchased us out from our sin with his own life, a price so high that we can never be reclaimed by sin again. Christ has provided redemption so that we might come to God.

The apostle also stressed that Jesus' death satisfied all the righteous and holy demands of God. God the Father gave God the Son as a sacrifice of atonement, a satisfaction for the holiness of God. While Martin Luther stressed the idea of redemption, John Calvin emphasized the concept of atonement, yet each agreed on the importance of both things. Their point, commonly misunderstood today, was that only God could provide that sacrifice. It is not some idea of satisfying an angry pagan deity; rather, this sacrifice is motivated from the infinite love of God who sends himself to take the penalty for the sins of humankind. By this means, justice has been done, all that will ever be pardoned or judged and punished in the person of God the Son, and it is on this basis that pardon is now offered to us offenders.

V. The final point of this important message is that God purposefully demonstrated his justice as well as his grace in providing this free gift of salvation. In this way God can accept sinners and declare them to be righteous. Thus, he can be both just and the justifier.

He can be just in himself because of the satisfaction of his holiness. He can be justifier because of what the Lord Jesus has done for us. At the cross of Jesus, God's love and justice come together and are purposefully demonstrated. God is a just God who must punish sins; yet, he is a gracious God who wants to forgive our sins. At the cross, God's righteousness and his mercy kissed; his retributive justice and his redeeming grace are simultaneously manifested.

The message of justification by faith is that all are sinners and must trust in what Jesus has done on the cross of Calvary. By trusting in his death, burial, Resurrection, and exhortation, we come to know that God accepts us. This need of acceptance and belonging is as pressing today as it was in the first century or the sixteenth. This reminder of God's justifying grace can be a relevant, yet God-centered word to our hurting world in need of divine forgiveness, divine righteousness, and divine acceptance.

Topic: Power of the Gospel

TEXT: Rom. 1:16–17

The theme of Paul's grand Epistle to the Romans is summarized in these two significant verses. Here we see the gospel as a revelation of the righteousness of

God. "The righteous will live by faith" is without question near the soul of Pauline theology; indeed as C. K. Barrett notes it is not wrong to see in these verses "a summary of Paul's theology as a whole."

The worthy reputation of this important theme is well attested in both the Jewish and Christian literature. That it was of special importance in Jewish circles can be seen in the famous remark of Rabbi Simlai (ca. A.D. 250) recorded in the Talmud in Makkot 23B, "Moses gave Israel 613 commandments, David reduced them to 10, Isaiah to 2, but Habbakuk to 1: 'The righteous shall live by his faith.' " The importance of this theme for the primitive Church is attested not only by its usage in Romans 1 but also in Galatians 3:11 and Hebrews 10:38. Historically, the primacy of this theme continued to increase. The preeminent illustration of this phenomenon was the text's catalytic effect in leading to the Reformation. It has been correctly observed that Habbakuk's great texts, with his son Paul's comments and additions, became the banner of the Protestant Reformation in the hands of Habbakuk's grandson, Martin Luther. Let us now look more carefully at these verses and briefly note their theological implications for the doctrine of "justification by faith."

I. The negative manner in which Paul expresses himself in verse 16 is not to be understood as an example of understatement implying that he is proud of the gospel, but rather as a sober reflection of the reality that the gospel is something of which Christians will, while still in this world, continually be tempted to be ashamed (see Mark 8:38; Luke 9:26; 2 Tim. 1:8). This is the case not only because of the paradoxical nature of the gospel itself, which appears as weakness and foolishness to those in the world, it is also because of the world's continuing hostility to the revelation of God. Paul is not ashamed of this gospel; it is a gospel in which he believes and proclaims. This we know, but we must ask, "What is this gospel?"

II. The gospel is the almighty power of God directed toward the salvation of women and men. It is on account of

Paul's understanding the gospel that he does not yield to the temptation to be ashamed of the gospel but rather lives to proclaim it. His divine commission has created a sense of compelling urgency that made him cry out, "Woe to me if I do not preach the gospel" (1 Cor. 9:16). The gospel that Paul received and proclaimed is summarized in 1 Cor. 15:3–4: "Christ died for our sins according to the scriptures, he was buried, he was raised on the third day according to the scriptures."

For Paul the gospel meant that eternal issues were at stake. Those whose minds were blinded and did not believe and obey the gospel were perishing (2 Cor. 4:3) and will ultimately fall under divine wrath (2 Thess. 1:9). On the other hand, to those who believed, the gospel effectively becomes the power of God for salvation.

III. The gospel is to be believed and proclaimed and is for everyone. This gospel is a revealing of the righteousness of God. The present tense used by the apostle indicates that Paul thought of revelation coming through the ongoing preaching of the gospel message. In the preaching, God is revealing his righteousness. Righteousness denotes the righteous status that is given by God to believers, thus indicating God's action of justifying them by grace through faith.

The background of Paul's concept of righteousness was the Jewish conviction that a day of judgment was coming in which God would condemn and punish all who were guilty of breaking his laws. Paul affirmed that Christ himself would judge the world in righteousness, in the day of wrath, and revelation of the righteous judgment of God (see Rom. 2:16; also Acts 17:31). Against this background, amplified in Romans 1:18–3:20, Paul proclaims that sinners can be justified by grace through faith in Christ.

Based on the Old Testament's background of righteousness, justification is an eschatological declaration that believers stand righteous before a holy God. Much more than the popular interpretation, "just-as-if-I'd-never sinned," which is only a pronouncement of innocence, the meaning of justification has two sides. On the one hand, it means pardon, remission, and nonimputation of all sins, reconciliation to God, and the end of enmity and wrath. On the other hand, it means the bestowal of a righteous person's status and a title to all the blessings promised for the just, which includes not only the gift of righteousness, as marvelous as that is, but also adoption into God's family (see Rom. 8:14–17), the inheritance of the gift of God's Spirit (see Eph. 1:13), and the promise of eternal life, bringing God's future reality into the present. When the gospel reveals a righteousness of God, it declares that all who believe are justified receiving permanent reinstatement to favor and privilege, as well as complete forgiveness of all sins.

This marvelous gift of justification comes to us by faith. Very important for us is to see that the apostle does not utilize faith in his explanation of justification as the grounds of justification, which would make faith a meritorious work and the gospel merely another version of justification by works, a teaching which for Paul and his children, the reformers, was irreconcilable with grace and spiritually ruinous. Paul says that believers are justified through faith and by faith, but never on account of faith. Faith, then, is not itself our justifying righteousness, but rather it is the outstretched empty hand that receives righteousness by receiving Christ. Paul's concept of justification is a complete and total work of God, and we can do nothing to earn this gift of righteousness.

IV. What do the ideas of faith and righteousness mean for the proclamation of the contemporary Church and the lives of believers? The Church must proclaim that God is the giver of salvation, the gift of righteousness, and this gift is for all who will receive it by faith. The Church must also properly conceive a faith as ongoing commitment to Jesus Christ. The Church's proclamation cannot and must not separate faith from faithfulness, although these ideas need to be distinguished as justification is from sanctification. Paul would be disturbed to discover that in much contemporary preaching faith is improperly separated from faithful works and assurance is grounded in a decision rather than in the atoning and justifying work of Jesus Christ.

Finally, what does the gift of righteousness mean for contemporary Christians? It means our lives can be changed as we respond to God's acceptance. When we feel depressed, despairing, discouraged, or defeated, we must remind ourselves that God has reconciled us, accepted us, and given us value and significance in his sight, not on our own merits, but because of the work of Jesus Christ for us. Nothing can be added to this gift of righteousness revealed in the gospel to everyone who believes. With Paul, we joyfully and unashamedly believe and proclaim this gospel.

Topic: Unity of the Church
Text: Eph. 4:1–6

I grew up in the age of television. Like many in the TV generation, many of my interests were shaped by the shows and advertisements of that time period. My father was a tire dealer, so tire advertisements were of particular interest in our home. The "blimp," "the tigerpaw," the tire that "gripped the road," and a "721 radial" were ads that caught my attention. The "721" featured the new technology of the time for radial tires. It developed its name from the layers within the tire: seven wrapped around one. In Ephesians 4:1–6, Paul introduces us not to a "721" but to a "731." The reader of these verses is struck by the apostle's repetition of the word *one*, which occurs seven times. Further observation reveals the seven *ones* are grounded in the "three" members of the Trinity (one Spirit, verse 4; one Lord, verse 5; and one God and Father of us all, verse 6). Let us turn to examine the relationship of Paul's "731" to the unity of the Church and our corporate Christian experience.

I. In the first half of Ephesians, Paul has brilliantly disclosed the eternal purpose of God as it is worked out in history. The apostle indicates God is creating something entirely new, not just a new life for individuals, but a new corporate humanity: the Church. This magnificent vision portrays the reconciliation of an alienated and fractured humanity. The reconciled new humanity has new standards. Paul urges his readers to "live a life worthy of their calling" (v. 1). The exhortation serves as a major transition in the letter as it moves from the Church's credenda to the Church's agenda. Paul insists their earthly behavior should be worthy of their divine calling.

He presents four specific virtues that produce and exemplify a life worthy of the Christian calling. All of these virtues are modeled after the life of Jesus Christ. The Church is told to demonstrate humility, gentleness, patience, and forbearance. These four characteristics are to be grounded in "love." In Ephesians 3:17, he prays for believers to be "rooted and established in love." If the Church is to demonstrate unity before a watching world, love as the embracing virtue and the crown and sum of all virtues must characterize God's people (John 13:34–35). Love focuses on the good of the believing community and concentrates on the welfare of others. Genuine unity among the people of God will take place only when these Christian virtues characterize our lives individually and corporately.

II. The apostle now urges the Church to make every effort to keep the unity of the Spirit through the bond of peace. The unity spoken of here is the unity of heart that the Spirit of God energizes in a community of believers and is made visible to an observing world. The relationship between verses 2 and 3 in this passage is clear. When the virtues described in verse 2 are cultivated and practiced, the unity of the Spirit is displayed and preserved (see Phil. 2:1–8; Col. 3:14). Paul's stirring challenge in verse 3 often falls on deaf ears. God is the author of peace, and the stirring up of dissension among his people is detestable to him. From this admonition to unity, Paul moves to the basis of this unity in verses 4 through 6.

III. Verses 4 through 6 point to the seven "ones" that constitute the foundation on which the Trinitarian God effects a true oneness in the Church. The unity of the Church is seen from the vantage point of the work of the one Spirit (creating one body), the one Lord Jesus Christ (creating one hope, faith, and baptism), and the one God the Father (bringing about the one people of God).

There is one body because there is one Spirit. The one body refers to the Church, the one body of Christ, and is comprised of Jew and Gentile, free and slave, and male and female (see Gal. 3:28; 1 Cor. 12:13). Cohesion of the body comes from the Holy Spirit who indwells, seals, and energizes the members of the body.

Second, there is "one hope," "one faith," and "one baptism" because there is only one Lord. It is Jesus Christ in whom we have believed, Jesus Christ into whom we have been baptized, and Jesus Christ for whose coming we wait with expectant hope. The "one hope" of our calling is the hope of sharing the glory of Christ. This one hope is set before all believers, and there is no distinction between them. There are no favored elite members within the believing community for whom better things are reserved from the rank and file grassroots people.

"One faith" may denote the act of believing, or it may refer to the substance of one's belief. It is true in both senses. There can be no Christian unity until there is a common commitment to Christian doctrine. But the emphasis of the passage is the shared experience of faith in Christ and the same access to him.

"One baptism" pictures the divine seal on the one faith in the one Lord. Baptism is the outward and visible sign in water by which those who believe the gospel, repent of their sins, and acknowledge Jesus as Lord are publicly incorporated in the body of Christ. The reference is not to a mode of baptism, nor is it an attempt to distinguish "Spirit baptism" from "water baptism." That is not the apostle's intention. The point here is that Jewish and Gentile believers alike who acknowledge Jesus as the "one Lord" share a common faith in him and are initiated into Jesus

Christ and his Church in the waters of baptism (see Gal. 3:27).

The last emphasis of this passage concerning this new humanity is that the one Christian family belongs to the "one God and Father of all, who is over all and through all, and in all." The previous chapters of Ephesians serve to help us understand that the "all" for whom God is Father are the people of God, his redeemed children. We can confess by way of conclusion that Christian unity is imperative because there is only one Christian faith, hope, and baptism, and one Christian body. This confession rests on the truth that there is one God: Father, Son, and Holy Spirit.

IV. The infighting discord that so often characterizes our churches indicates how far we fall short of God's expectations. A genuine commitment to the gospel helps us realize the high priority that the call for unity among God's people takes in the Scriptures (see Ps. 133:1; John 17; 1 Cor. 12:4–6). We must confess our sins of discord and ask God to bring renewal and unity among his people.

If the Church is truly to be the people of God, it must visibly exhibit an attitude of unity. God's own oneness defines the Church's oneness. As God is one in three, so the Church is made up of different parts with a variety of expressions; yet, the body functions as a unity. The Church attests to the oneness of God (one in three) as it manifests its unity in variety. Let us affirm the Church's visible unity in truth is God's purpose for his people. Let us pray and work for renewal and unity in our worship, witness, and fellowship.

Topic: A Joyful Salvation

TEXT: 1 Pet. 1:3–9

It often seems as if God is very distant in the midst of our suffering. We often ask how these things can happen. At times we feel hopeless and helpless and think that God does not care. But Peter in these verses calls for us to recognize that God does care and has provided salvation for us so that we may be joyful even in the midst of difficult days.

I. The apostle Peter knows what his readers are facing. He knows that they are being challenged. They are being oppressed, and he writes to give them confidence and assurance of God's mercy in their lives. The readers of this epistle, both ancient and present, need to know that even though they are facing some difficult times in which it appears that God is distant and, perhaps, even silent, he has been and still is merciful. Thus, Peter begins with this beautiful benediction of praise to God the Father of our Lord Jesus Christ. God is the source of mercy that is shown to those who are hurting. The first evidence that God is a merciful and a loving God is that he has brought us to the point of being born anew. We have experienced the new birth.

Peter reminds us of God's mercy and new life. Jesus Christ has come to give us a new heart, to turn our life around, to set us free from sin and to give us a new start. This new birth has been given by God through his Spirit, through his Word, and has brought about a living hope in our lives through the Resurrection of Jesus Christ.

There is hope in the midst of suffering because of the resurrection, therefore it is a living hope. We have received a new birth and have received a living hope that makes it possible for us to endure and continue in the sufferings we face day to day. But Peter adds to this wonderful news about our joyful salvation even another important layer. Not only have we received a new birth and a new hope, but we have received an inheritance.

II. An inheritance is not so much a promise of something in the future as it is a secure possession. In the Old Testament this inheritance had to do with the gift of the Promised Land to the people of Israel. Here in 1 Peter the inheritance is not a land, but it is the Lord himself. Believers have been given a special relationship with the Lord that is theirs now even in the midst of difficult suffering. So by the grace and mercy of God we have been given an inheritance that is the Lord himself, and regardless of what comes into our life that inheritance cannot be taken away.

Peter describes our inheritance as something that can never perish, spoil, or fade. In the Greek text, it is almost poetic and rhythmic. Peter writes it is *atharton, amaronton,* and *amionton.* You don't have to know the Greek language to hear the poetic expressions evident in this phrase indicating that this joyful salvation in the Lord will never fade and cannot spoil. That is the reason that Jesus in Matthew 6 told us to lay up our treasures not on earth but in heaven, for there they will not be taken away. There will be no thieves; there will be no moths to come in and eat them; nothing can destroy them because our inheritance is kept for us in heaven.

This joyful salvation in the Lord is secure because a fort has been built around it. Peter says that nothing can touch this inheritance; because it is so secure, it cannot be taken away. We can imagine being in such a difficult situation that we would think that the inheritance of God could be stripped away, but Peter reminds us that God has not abandoned and will not abandon us in those situations. He may appear silent or distant, but his inheritance cannot spoil, it cannot fade, it cannot perish. It is kept in heaven and is shielded and protected. Thus, he describes our true spiritual situation in order to give us comfort, peace, and hope to enable us to persevere in the faith.

III. Peter describes this beautiful picture of security, but in verse 6 he makes a very sharp and quick turn. He moves from ecstasy to agony. He says this salvation that you have received is something in which you greatly rejoice, though now for a little while there is grief. You can almost hear them begin to wonder aloud. You can hear them say all these things are true that you are describing about these wonderful heavenly truths, but we don't feel these things to be true because we are not experiencing them. Peter responds, "These things are true about the mercy of God and about your joyful salvation and it is this and this alone that will substantiate you and uphold you during these difficult times." Peter did not turn philosopher and try to explain

their suffering. Instead, he turned pastoral in order to deal with their suffering.

IV. When the question is asked, Where is God?, in the midst of our difficulties, Peter answers with four helpful responses. The first one is found in verse 6: Hope in Christ points us beyond our trials. Our troubles last for only a little while. Our hope in Christ is forever. Peter invites his readers to take a step back from the difficulty of their suffering to see life from God's perspective, from the standpoint of eternity. Viewing life from an eternal perspective will help us recognize that the trials we are facing last only for a little while; therefore, the hope we have in the future points us beyond our present difficulties. Our hope in Christ allows us to go on and gives us endurance and energy for tasks.

Secondly, Peter says that these difficulties actually strengthen us (see v. 7). He says that hope and joy are actually strengthened through the sufferings we endure. Going through the trials and going through the situation do not take away your strength but actually strengthen you. It does not take away your faith, it actually adds to your faith. Peter says these difficult times shape us and refine us. They burn away our impurities. They burn away our self-confidence, which can be replaced with authentic faith that is of greater worth than gold.

The third positive value we can learn in the midst of suffering is the truth that a just end to suffering will come when Jesus returns. By placing our hope on him, we will recognize that he will bring us the reward of blessing. Peter says we will know our faith, which has been proved genuine through the fire, may now result in praise, glory, and honor when Jesus Christ is revealed.

The fourth thing that Peter says about our joyful salvation during difficult times is found in verse 9. The apostle notes that we will receive the goal of our faith, which is the salvation of our souls. When we take a step back and see our situation, our difficulties, and our trails from this perspective, the whole nature of suffering is changed. We realize that somehow our anguish can bring honor and glory to Jesus Christ.

V. Because of what is going on in your life at this time, God might seem distant to you, but Peter says to you, you are now filled with a glorious joy. Hope seems distant. Joy seems to have dissipated. The words from Peter can revive you and renew you. They can encourage you. You are filled now with an inexpressible and glorious joy.

How does that happen? It comes through faith and hope of knowing Jesus Christ. The salvation of our souls in the last day is the goal of our faith. We wait for this salvation, and it encourages us and enables us to persevere. Yet, we are already somehow experiencing this joyful salvation. This tension between the "now" and "yet to come" is at the heart of the entire New Testament message. Because Jesus has already come in the flesh, the Holy Spirit has already been given, the kingdom has been inaugurated. But yet, Jesus is still coming again. The fullness of the kingdom is not yet. Our faith is still future in some sense. And it is this future element that drives us and shapes us in the present.

Sometimes in modern-day Christianity, we cannot continue through trials and difficulties because we have lost sight of this future aspect of the faith. We have lost this future dimension. We have grown so used to our present situation, to hearing that Christ is going to come, but we really do not believe it to be true. We don't live with that kind of expectation of the revelation of Christ. We say we believe the future hope. But if we really did, it would mold us and shape us and direct us and enable us through difficulties so that we could live in the present as though we are living in the future. This is not something that takes place only in our imagination, but is a genuine hope, a certainty, an assurance, a trust in God who has worked in the past and who will work in the future. We can know the joy of our salvation in the present because God has raised Jesus from the dead and given us a living hope, he has given us a secure inheritance, and he gives us now strength and courage to face the challenges in our life this day and days to come.

Topic: The Righteousness of God's People

TEXT: Matt. 5:17–20

Jesus begins his instructions on life under God's reign with a key statement about his relationship to the Law and the prophets. He cautions his listeners not to presume that he came to do away with the Law or the prophets. But Jesus assures his listeners beforehand that he does not abolish or invalidate the Law, since it faithfully expresses God's will. What Jesus does and teaches complies with the Law and the prophets; but furthermore, he completes them as he explains righteousness for kingdom citizens.

I. Jesus fulfills the Law and the prophets in three ways: by living in perfect obedience to them, by recapturing their divine purpose, and by completing their promises. He embodies God's demand that his people be a holy people. For this reason, the disciples are to listen to him and not to the other voices that claim to have authority on high. Jesus faithfully kept the Law. He submitted to John's baptism in order to "fulfill all righteousness" (Matt. 3:15). In the temptation, Jesus faced down the enemy that haunts all of us. Satan tried to preempt the Spirit and direct Jesus' life. Satan vied with God's will with lying words that sounded religious, but Jesus successfully countered each temptation with God's Word. He resisted the word of pride and special privilege. He combated the word of selfish ambition. The devil claimed that the world was his to do with it as he pleased, and he offered it all to Jesus on easy terms. He would give it to him. No need to follow the hard road of obedience that would lead from Gethsemane to Golgotha. Jesus banished Satan by his uncompromising obedience to God. The Gospel story shows that Jesus was perfectly obedient to God's will each step of the way. By contrast, the rival Jewish teachers are shown in Matthew's Gospel to be corrupt. Because of their wickedness, they are quite unreliable as guides to the true meaning of God's Law. Jesus calls them sons of snakes who draw from an evil treasure and who could not give voice to anything good (see Matt. 12:33–37). They are hypocrites who wish to bask in the admiration of others (see Matt. 23:5). Like whitewashed tombs, their outer appearance masks the stench and decay within (see Matt. 23:27–28). They are blind guides who will lead everyone who follows them astray. Who is it that one should heed, those false teachers who put on a show of piety or the one who sincerely performs what God requires in the Law?

II. Jesus was not only the perfect expression of what God intended in the Law, he gave perfect expression to what God's Law required. He reclaimed the original intention of the Law and the prophets. In setting forth God's intention in the Law, Jesus did not set aside the Law.

When Jesus presented what we call "the Golden Rule," he stressed that "this sums up the Law and the Prophets" (Matt. 7:12). What he taught is not contrary to the Law and the prophets; it was what they were all about in the first place. They still needed to be obeyed then and they need to be obeyed today—but as interpreted and even intensified by Jesus.

The purpose of the Law was to lead one to God and to point the way to a Godly life. But the rival teachers had littered the pathway with human barriers that distracted people from what was vital. Some of their rules even hampered obedience rather than encouraging it. Jesus blamed these teachers for misleading the people. Jesus also accused the teachers of saddling the people with heavy burdens that had nothing to do with God's purposes. The heap of regulations regarding such things as ritual purity and the proper observance of the Sabbath bewildered most people. Worse, it missed the whole point. Jesus indicted the scribes and the Pharisees for "majoring on the minors while minoring on the majors."

Jesus' teaching redirected the way the Scriptures were to be heard. He ascended the mountain as a new Moses who defines the Law in a new way. The distinctive characteristic of Jesus' interpretation of the Law was his insistence that the Laws of God and the love of neighbor be foremost. When Jesus is asked later in Matthew's Gospel, "Which is the greatest commandment in the Law?" his answer is, "To love the Lord your God with all your heart, soul, and mind." He then mentions a second, "To love your neighbor as yourself." He explains that the whole Law and the prophets hang on these two commandments (see Matt. 22:33–40). Jesus' teaching restores them to the supreme importance as the sum and substance of Law and the prophets.

III. Jesus fulfilled the Law and the prophets in a third and even more significant way. The words "I have come" expressed awareness that he had a special status and that he had come with a special mission.

His statement affirmed that the Scriptures witnessed to him. Their complete veracity is therefore confirmed by his arrival. His long-awaited arrival fulfilled the promise of the Scriptures.

Christ is the fulfillment of the Law and the prophets; but as the Son of God, he now has the same status as the Law and the prophets. Indeed, he has a greater place because the Law and the prophets point to him. It should be clear from these verses that Jesus' words represent the ultimate expression of God's will. He truly fulfills both the Law and the prophets in every way.

IV. Jesus must have startled his listeners when he went on to announce, "Unless your righteousness exceeds that of the Scribes and Pharisees, you will not enter the kingdom of heaven." No one would ever question that the righteousness of those who wanted to enter into the kingdom of heaven must exceed that of the tax collector or the heathen. But Jesus insisted that the disciples' righteousness must also exceed that of the proverbial righteous. Although Jesus assails the righteousness of the scribes and Pharisees as hypocrisy, most people in his day regarded them as exceptionally devout. Few others went to such extremes to be pious. Yet, God insisted on something greater.

The concern for a greater righteousness captures the main theme of Jesus' message: What are you doing that is more than others? The "more" that Jesus requires has as much to do with quantity as with quality. It makes clear that the righteousness Jesus has in mind in the Sermon on the Mount has to do with conduct. It is conduct that flows out of a life that has been inwardly transformed by Jesus himself. Obedience cannot come only from external motivation but must come from internal transmission. It is this antithesis on which the teachings of Jesus rests. Jesus does not offer his statements as something optional for extra credit in this life. They are the basic requirements of righteousness. They are examples of how Jesus interpreted the Law and the prophets to reveal the will of God. Love is the controlling principle and the central interpretive aspect to truly understanding the intention of the Law and the prophets. Our everyday relations with others, then, are to be governed supremely by love to reveal God's righteousness.

Topic: Spiritual Transformation

TEXT: Eph. 2:7–10

One of the most common mistakes in our time is to think of evangelism more in terms of a method than a message. Such is sometimes the case with revivalists or evangelists who have suggested that evangelism can only take place when the "right words" are uttered or when the "right prayer" is prayed by the professing respondent. What has been lost, or at least misplaced, is the recognition that accompanying genuine evangelism must be a firm theological foundation. Evangelism is the proclamation of the good news in words, as well as the manifestation of this good news in deeds, with the purpose of bringing about spiritual transformation among men and women. The focus of these key verses in the second chapter of the letter to the Ephesians is the message of the good news of the gospel and the reconciliation that has been accomplished by Jesus Christ.

I. This section contrasts the old way of life with the new life manifested in God's gracious acceptance of sinners. Formerly we were dead, we were enslaved, we were objects of wrath, we walked among the disobedient, and we lived under Satan's dominion. But now we are alive, enthroned, objects of grace, and we have fellowship and union with Christ. Paul describes the work of reconciliation with four key terms in verses 7 through 10. These are: "kindness," "grace," "faith," and "salvation." The emphasis is found in verse 8 in the most important phrase, "by grace through faith." The work of salvation is for God's glory, and it is not the accomplishment of human works. The whole process of salvation is not our achievement, but is an act of God's goodness. The emphasis is always on the object of faith who is Christ himself, not the amount of faith offered by the believing person.

Salvation is not a result of anything that we have, anything we have done, or anything that we can do. Any kind of human self-effort is comprehensively ruled out by the expression "not by works so that no one can boast." It is to prevent the slightest self-congratulations or boasting. This salvation is not a complete unmerited favor of God. We cannot understand grace as God's part and faith as our part, for all of it is a gift from God.

II. This discussion leads to the importance of a further understanding of the meaning of faith. The Bible maintains that faith is the means by which we receive an appropriate salvation. Faith includes a full commitment of the whole person to the Lord Jesus, a commitment that involves knowledge, trust, and obedience. Faith is not merely an intellectual assent or an emotional response but a complete inward spiritual transformation confirmed to us by the Holy Spirit. Faith is altogether brought about by God, and it is altogether the human response bringing about complete submission to God and full liberation from the snare of sin. The object of faith is not so much the teaching about Christ, but Christ himself.

Though faith is more than doctrinal assent, it must include adherence to doctrine. In our belief in and commitment to Jesus Christ, we acknowledge him as Savior from sin and Lord of our lives, even Lord of creation (see Rom. 10:9). True spiritual transformation and conversion definitely involves a personal belief in Jesus Christ as the God-man and in his work as Savior. We must remember, however, that it is possible to have an orthodox understanding of Christ without a living faith in him. The apostle Paul's understanding of "by grace through faith" can be understood in no other terms.

III. The work of our salvation is a display of divine handiwork (see v. 10). Paul never intended verses 8 and 9 to be read apart from verse 10. We were dead; now we are his workmanship, his work of art. This is the display to the watching world and an evidence of grace. Works are fruit of salvation, not the cause of salvation. Now that we are united with Christ, we are to be like him—for he went about doing good.

The good works are not incidental to God's plan. They are a part of God's plan and are in sharp contrast to the "walking about in the ways of this world" and "following the ruler of this world," which we formerly did according to Paul's words in Ephesians 2:2. Our good works are demonstrated in gratitude, character, and actions. Grace does not encourage sinful living but living in freedom and in righteousness.

IV. This marvelous salvation has been accomplished by what Paul describes in Ephesians 1:7 as the redemptive work of Christ. The idea of redemption is vitally related to the themes of liberation, deliverance, and ransom. Paul understood there was a struggle between the kingdom of God and the hostile powers enslaving humankind. Redemption is the idea of bringing sinners out of such a hostile bondage into authentic freedom (see Col. 2:15). As redeemer, Jesus breaks the power of sin and creates a new and obedient heart by delivering us from the power of sin, guilt, death, and Satan, bringing about a people who have been brought with a price (see 1 Pet. 1:18).

God made our salvation possible. He has created us and recreated us. We were created out of nothing; we have been liberated out of bondage and resurrected out of death. We are now persons who have been forgiven, released from sin, and spiritually transformed.

SECTION X.
Children's Sermons and Stories

January 7: The Legend of the Glowworm

There is a lovely legend concerning the glowworm. This tiny creature—so the legend goes—was present at the first Christmas. It saw the star in the sky. It saw the shepherds who came to the manger to adore the Christ Child. It saw the magi who came from afar with their magnificent gifts. The glowworm wondered if it too might go to the manger and bring to the baby Jesus a little gift.

At that time the glowworm was a very ordinary insect. Yet it felt the thrill and the glory of the holy birth. So it uncovered a seed of grain that it had stored away against a bad day. This was its one treasure. The little creature would give it to the Christ Child.

Laboriously the glowworm made its way, pushing, pulling, and dragging the seed of grain for the Christ Child. At last the glowworm arrived at the manger where the Holy Child was lying. Mary and Joseph stood nearby. The glowworm was so small that the human eye could hardly see it. But the baby Jesus saw it! As the glowworm made one supreme effort and pushed its treasure into his infant hand, a loving smile appeared on the baby's face. A tiny hand reached out—or so it seemed—and touched the glowworm. Immediately the tiny creature began to glow, its whole being lighted with happiness in response to the Christ Child's love. It has been glowing ever since, the legend affirms, a perpetual witness to the glory of the touch of Christ.

This is only a legend, of course, but it portrays a mighty truth. Anyone who brings his gift of love to Christ will feel the blessing of his touch! This is the Christmas blessing that God intends for all—the glory of the radiant life. Christ can set our lives aglow with peace and joy within!—Lowell M. Atkinson

January 14: Jesus Listened at Church

Text: Luke 2:46

Object: Headphones

These are headphones. When these are plugged into a radio or tape player, the music, entertainment, or instruction can be heard clearly. Headphones are very useful because they help us not to miss important information.

When Jesus was about twelve years old, he went to the city of Jerusalem. The trip took several days of walking. His family traveled with a group of friends from the village of Nazareth. After the religious services in Jerusalem were over, the group began the long walk back to their homes. While they were going, it was discovered that Jesus was missing. When his worried parents finally located Jesus, he was in the Temple. Listen to this verse that describes what Jesus was doing.

The verse says that Jesus was listening to the teachers. Listening is very important. God wants us to listen to him. A place we are to hear God speak to us is in church. God speaks to us through Sunday school lessons, songs, and sermons.

A long time ago God wanted to speak an extra special message to a boy named Samuel. Each time God spoke to Samuel, the little boy ran to his master. Samuel thought that the older man he served was calling him. Finally, the third time God called to Samuel, he did not run to his master. Instead he said, "Speak, Lord, for your servant is listening." Then the Lord was able to get his message to Samuel.

When we come to church, it is easy to leave without hearing from God. Sometimes we talk to others, think about other things, or draw through the whole service. If we will come into church and expect to hear from God, we will be able to hear from him.

The Lord wants to speak to us. We don't need headphones, we only need the right attitude. Today, let's say what Samuel said to God: "Speak, Lord, for your servant is listening." When we listen, God always has an important message for us.—Ken Cox

January 21: What Missionaries Ask for Most

TEXT: Eph. 6:19

Object: Prayer guide or prayer request slip

Foreign missionaries serve in another country. The country may be overseas, and the missionaries may have to learn another language to communicate with the people who live there. Some missionaries serve in the United States. These home missionaries may work in a large city like Chicago, feeding people who are homeless. Being a missionary is very challenging. Missionaries carry the message of Jesus Christ to those who have not heard of the Lord.

There are a lot of things that missionaries need to do their work. To be a missionary in Africa, special vehicles must be bought to drive over the bumpy roads. In Chicago a computer may be necessary to keep track of the people who are helped. In some places churches have to be built. In almost all areas Bibles have to be purchased. With all of these things being needed, there is one thing that a missionary needs most of all. It's something that I have noticed that they ask for the most. It's prayer.

This is a prayer guide, for our missionaries have listed what they want us to pray about. The apostle Paul was a missionary, too. Listen to this verse from one of his letters: (read Eph. 6:14).

We help missionaries with our donations of money. But remember the thing that they ask for most is prayer. We support our missionaries with our dedication to praying for them.—Ken Cox

January 28: Stay in Touch with God

TEXT: 1 Thess. 5:17

Object: Poster with Morse code "S.O.S." and a buzzer or beeper

One of the earliest forms of electronic communication was by telegraph using the Morse code. This form of communication was used before the telephone was invented. This poster has a code message. These dots and dashes were transmitted over telegraph lines because there was no way for people to send their voices over long distances of wire like today. This is what it sounded like. (Demonstrate buzzer/beeper.) For every letter in the alphabet there was a code, and each word had to be spelled out to send a message.

During the Civil War one of the first things that the opposing sides tried to do was destroy the telegraph lines that carried the Morse code signals. If communication lines were destroyed, the enemy could be easily defeated because they couldn't work together.

God tells us that communication with him is very important. Communication with God is called prayer. God doesn't need a code, wires, a transmitter, or even a telephone. God can hear us wherever we are and whenever we start talking to him. We are always to talk with God; he loves us and prayer gives us strength.

Whenever you have a need in your life, talk to God about it by praying. Talk to him like you would a very close friend. God likes for you to stay in touch with him through prayer. Don't ever have your lines of communication cut off from God by failing to pray.—Ken Cox

February 4: Some Rules for Fishing

Text: Luke 5:1–11: Master, we have worked all night long but have caught nothing. Yet if you say so, I will let down the nets (v. 5).

Object: A fishing pole (or something to do with fishing)

Good morning, boys and girls. How many of you have ever gone fishing with someone? (Let them answer.) I brought a fishing pole with me. One thing about fishing is that you have to be very patient. That means that you have to be prepared to wait for the fish to bite. I want to tell you the story about a girl your age and her father, who went fishing. The girl had never gone fishing before. The two went out on a quiet stream in a boat. The girl's father showed the girl the fishing pole and how to cast it. Then the two began to fish. Their poles were in the water for the longest time before anything happened. The girl asked her father, "Why aren't we catching anything?" The girl was losing her patience. She wanted to give up. Just as she was ready to say, "Let's stop and go home," her father said, "Let's move to another spot and try it again." The girl answered, "But, Dad, we've fished all day and haven't caught a thing. But if you say so, I'll try it again." Right after they moved, they began to catch more fish than they knew what to do with. They became excited as they caught all those fish.

A story similar to this happened to Jesus and Peter. Peter was a fisherman who had fished all night and hadn't caught one fish. Peter lost his patience with fishing. Then Jesus came along and told Peter to try fishing in another spot. Peter replied, "Anything you say, Lord." Peter began to fish where Jesus suggested and began to catch more fish than he knew what to do with.

Jesus told Peter that from then on Peter would be catching people instead of fish. Peter immediately became one of Jesus' disciples. The next time you lose your patience, remember Jesus and Peter. Peter lost his patience. Jesus told Peter to try one more time. Peter followed Jesus' advice and caught more than he knew what to do with.—Children's Sermon Service Plus!

February 11: Threading God's Needle

Text: Mark 10:17–31: It is easier for a camel to go through the eye of a needle than for someone who is rich to enter the kingdom of God (v. 25).

Object: Needle and thread

Good morning, boys and girls. This morning I brought a needle and thread with me. How many of you know how to thread a needle? (Let them answer.) It can be rather difficult to thread a needle if you haven't done it before. This needle and thread reminds me of this morning's lesson. In the lesson Jesus tells his disciples that it is more difficult for a camel to go through the eye of a needle than it is for a rich person to enter God's kingdom.

I want to tell you a story that may help explain what Jesus meant by this story. Once there was a little boy about your age. The boy was carrying many things with him. He had on a big heavy coat. He was carrying a big suitcase. He had a backpack on his back. He was also wearing a large hat. He even had roller skates on his feet. He probably looked pretty funny with all those things on, don't you think? (Let them answer.) He had all these things with him as he was walking up to his house. He wanted to go into the house, but there was something wrong with the door. It wouldn't open all the way. Since the door wouldn't open very far, the boy couldn't get through the doorway. So, he took off his backpack, his hat, his roller skates, and put down his suitcase. Then he was able to squeeze through the door.

The boy was a little like the camel trying to get through the eye of the needle. (Hold up the needle.) Here's what I want you to remember this week. Jesus wants all of us to be in his kingdom. Some people think that the way to get in is to be rich. Others think the way in is to know all of God's laws. Others think it is by doing things better than others.

Jesus wants you to get rid of all those

ideas. Get rid of those ideas, just like the boy did when he took off his hat, coat, suitcase, and backpack. When he took them off, he was able to enter his house. The same is true in entering God's kingdom. You enter God's kingdom as a gift from God. You receive the gift when you become a follower of Jesus. It's that simple. You don't need money or other things. You only need to trust Jesus. That's the way to get into God's kingdom.—Children's Sermon Service Plus!

February 18: The Secret

When George Muller was in his eighties, he was asked to speak to a group of seminary students. As the old man finished his address, one of the students raised his hand and said, "Mr. Muller, some of us would like to ask you a question." "Yes?" said Muller as he strained to listen. The young man asked, "What is your secret?" Muller pulled his chair back and began to bend his old, cold limbs to the floor, kneeling in prayer. "This is the secret," replied Muller. One of his biographers wrote that when Muller died, someone discovered two ridges or grooves cut into the wooden floor at his bedside. Muller literally had worn two depressions in the wooden floor as he knelt and prayed beside his bed.[1]—Keith Bradsher

February 25: Flashing Red Lights

One of the things you have to learn as you move around our community is the meaning of red and green lights. So, let me test you and make sure you know what to do. When you see a red light, what does that mean? And a green light? Right! Now, I hope this has not happened to you, but if you are in the car with your parents, and you see a flashing red light on top of a police car behind you, what does that mean? And if the police officer was flashing the red light for your car to stop, what a terrible feeling

your parents had as that police officer walked toward your car. Whoever was driving probably said, "Oh, no! What did I do wrong now?"

It is very hard for all of us to admit that we did something wrong; but that is the only way to set things right. When we do that, then we can take the next step, which is what we call "repentance." Now, the name of this action is not important. What is important is what happens to you when you do it. Some people blame someone else, or the conditions around them, or they just say, "I'm sorry." But that is not enough. Having admitted to going in the wrong direction, the next step is to try and find the right way. When you are moving in a new direction, then you will begin to understand the meaning of repentance as the way to new life with God. So, whenever you see a flashing red light on a police car, think about this: Having someone tell you about what you did wrong is the first step in finding the way to what is right. —Kenneth Mortonson

March 3: Starting with a Clean Slate

TEXT: Phil. 3:13–14

Object: A small chalkboard

I have written an arithmetic equation on this little chalkboard. Can you see the error? Two plus two does not equal five, does it? Let's erase the wrong answer and put four. Let's write a four in place of the five.

Erasing the error we made was easy on this chalkboard. The Lord allows us to do this with our lives whenever we are able to wipe the slate clean and make a fresh start. Listen to these verses.

A man by the name of Paul wrote this passage. Paul made some very serious mistakes in his life. At one point, Paul tried to hurt members of the Church. Paul put some of the disciples of Jesus in jail and made others miserable by persecuting them. God changed Paul's belief about Jesus one day as he was traveling to a city named Damascus. God sent out a blinding light and a voice to help Paul know the truth about Jesus. After that, Paul changed and worked for the Church instead of against it. Paul felt

---

[1] Harold J. Sala, *Guidelines for Living* (Grand Rapids, MI: Baker Book House, 1982), 97–98.

very bad about his earlier days when he made people in the Church suffer. Paul couldn't change his mistakes, but he learned a valuable lesson in life from God's grace. Paul learned that God doesn't want us to dwell upon our errors but to look to the future and the positive things we can do for him.

We can't go back and change the things that we have done that are wrong. God wants us to know we can wipe our slates clean with him and think about the days to come. As we live for Jesus day by day, we can please the Lord by our obedience to him. It's great to know that the Lord forgives us for our mistakes and wants us to look forward to good things we can do with our lives. Truly, God loves us and wants the best for us.—Ken Cox

March 10: Jacob's Special Day

TEXT: Gen. 28:15, 18

Object: A birthday card

An important day in everyone's life is their birthday. This is a birthday card, and it's a way of saying, "Remember your special day."

God makes special days for us too. The Lord does this for us by letting us know his presence and power in a personal way.

A man named Jacob lived long ago. He was the grandson of Abraham. Jacob had to leave home because he had tricked his brother, Esau. Esau was very strong and temperamental. Jacob was convinced that Esau was going to harm him. So Jacob left home and began a long journey to a place where he would feel safe. On the first night of his trip he slept under the stars and used a rock as a pillow. During the night, God caused Jacob to have a dream. In the dream, Jacob saw a ladder coming out of heaven and angels were going up and down the ladder. This dream helped Jacob understand that God would always be with him and protect him. It was God's unique way of communicating with Jacob. Listen to these verses.

This dream of the ladder became a special time for Jacob. To remember the place of his dream, Jacob set up the stone that he had used as a pillow as a marker and called the place "Bethel." Whenever Jacob felt lonely, he remembered that special day. Years later when Jacob returned home, he saw the special stone. The place and the promise of God's presence always had a significant meaning to him.

God has special days for us too. The Lord wants to reveal himself to us in these memorable and personal ways so we will trust in him. Such days include the time when we ask Jesus to be our Savior. Other memorable events include when an important prayer is answered. The Lord may not use the dream of a ladder for us. He may use an encouraging word from the Bible. He may use a church member to show the kindness of God's love to us.

It's great to know that we can have special days with Jesus. Remembering those times will give us confidence for all the challenges of life.—Ken Cox

March 17: Living with Doubts

Object: A large coffee can with several holes punched into it. Use water at your own discretion.

I am sure you know what will happen if I pour some water into this can that has several holes in it. The water will flow out until it gets to the lowest hole. If you want the can to hold more water, you will have to plug the holes. But what if you cannot plug the hole and yet you really want more water in the can? There is one other way to keep this container nearly full, even though some of the water runs out. What you have to do is put in more water than what is flowing out.

No one here is a perfect person. When it comes to the Christian faith, we all have things that we cannot fully understand. We call them doubts, or mysteries, or just things we have trouble figuring out. They are the holes in what we believe. But we want as much faith as we can get just as we might want to increase the amount of water in this can. So, what we need is to do as much as we can to add to our understanding of what we believe. We need to increase our exposure to the things of our faith. We do this by studying the Bible and coming to church each Sunday, and by praying to God every day. We do it by putting our faith to work in the way we live. We do it by following the Good Shepherd. Remembering what King David said, in the Twenty-third Psalm, "The Lord is my shepherd, I shall not want." With him, our cup overflows.—Kenneth Mortonson

March 24: God Has Plans for You

TEXT: John 1:14

Object: Blueprints, schematic drawings, etc.

These are some pretty complicated drawings. These plans were drawn by an architect. The architect had an idea about how a new building should look, and he brings that notion into reality by these plans. All these lines and numbers mean something special to carpenters, electricians, and masons. When skilled workers follow these drawings, the building conceived by the architect will be the end product.

God has some plans for our world that are like these blueprints. God designed what the earth would be like before it was created. He planned each one of us too. We were created by the Lord and he has a purpose for our lives.

One very important part of God's plan for our world was to send Jesus, his son, into the world. Listen to this verse.

One reason that Jesus was sent into the world was because God wanted to be with us. Jesus was God in the flesh. A story I know can explain why God came to be with us.

A little boy was very scared one night as he lay in his bed. A storm had come into town, and the sight and sound of the wind, rain, thunder, and lightning were frightening to him. The boy called for his mother to come and be with him. After staying with her son for a little while, the mother got up to go. The little boy was still scared and started crying. His mom assured him that God was with him and he didn't need to be afraid. The boy replied, "But I need someone with skin on." I think we know how the little boy felt. When we're afraid, it's good to

have someone with us we can see and hold on to.

When God came into the world through Jesus, that's exactly what God did. God was not content to be known only as a spirit. God wanted to be up close and personal. He wanted to be seen, felt, and experienced. That's why God sent His son, Jesus.

According to God's plan, we are to believe in Jesus, trusting him as our Savior. Also, God's plan for the world includes Jesus' return to earth. One day Jesus will come back for all those that believe in him. God has a perfect plan for the world. He also has a wonderful plan for your life.—Ken Cox

April 7: Jesus Loves Me (Easter)

TEXT: Luke 23:34a

Object: A cross

While he was being crucified, Jesus said a prayer that expressed his desire for the people who were responsible for putting him on the cross. Listen to this verse.

The Bible tells us that all of us have done wrong things, just like the people that crucified Jesus. God's word also says that we may receive forgiveness for any sin, no matter what those sins might be, if we will just confess those sins to the Lord.

When we admit that we have done wrong and receive forgiveness, we always feel very good. Let me tell you a story about a young girl named Betty. One night after supper, while Betty was helping wash the dishes, her soapy hands slipped on a blue serving dish and it fell and broke on the floor. The dish was a favorite of her mother's and had been handed down from Betty's grandmother. Betty knew that the dish could not be replaced, and she was afraid to admit what she had done. So Betty gathered up the pieces of glass, put them in a box, and hid the box in the garage. A week later, Betty heard her mother looking for the serving dish. Her mother said, "Where is the blue serving dish; Betty, have you seen the blue serving dish?"

Betty said, "No. I haven't seen it." Betty felt bad about what she had done. She also felt terrible about not telling the truth to her mom. Betty kept her dark secret for several days. Finally, Betty went to the garage and brought the box with the parts of the broken dish to her mother, telling her the full story of what had happened. Betty was ready to get punished. She was tired of her conscience hurting her.

When Betty's mother saw the broken dish, she was really upset. But she was more unhappy when she saw the tears on Betty's face. Betty's mother knew how scared Betty must have been to hide the broken dish. Betty's mom didn't punish Betty. She hugged her, forgave her, and told her not to worry anymore.

That's what Jesus did by saying that special prayer on the cross. He asked for us to be forgiven, no matter what we had done.

At Easter we remember that if we come to Jesus and say we're sorry for the things we have done that are wrong, he will always forgive us. And when we're forgiven, we're always very happy.—Ken Cox

April 14: Christians Love One Another

TEXT: John 13:34–35

Object: A team jersey

On the playing field a jersey is very important. If it weren't for the distinctive colors of the jerseys, the fans couldn't tell the teams apart, nor could the officials or players. The jerseys help set the teams apart.

On the field of life, people don't recognize Christians because of a team jersey. They don't recognize Christians by the clothes they wear, the cars they drive, or even where they live. Jesus said Christians would be known by their love for one another. Love is a very important aspect of a Christian's life. Listen to this verse.

Love for others is shown in many ways. Let's talk about two of them. First, love puts others first. Since we are followers of Jesus, we consider others as being more important than ourselves and we seek their well-being. Second, love forgives. If someone has done something wrong to us, whether they know it or not we always forgive them.

This week, let's love one another so the people in the world can know that we are disciples of Jesus.—Ken Cox

April 21: God Is Light

TEXT: 1 John 1:5

Object: A night-light

Good morning, boys and girls. Are any of you afraid of the dark? (Let them answer.) I think just about everyone in this church was afraid of the dark at one time. How many of you have a night-light to help you sleep at night? (Let them answer and show the night-light.)

I want to tell you about a little girl about your age who was afraid of the dark. When she went to bed at night, she would cry, "Please turn on the light, I'm afraid." Then someone would come to her room and turn on a lamp, or her closet light or the hall light. Has that ever happened to any of you? (Let them answer.)

Her parents wanted to help her get to sleep. So, they bought a night-light, like this one. They put it in her room. She was able to turn it on herself at night. Her night-light had a warm glow to it that really made her feel safe. Whenever she went to bed from then on, she had no problem getting to sleep because she felt safe with her night-light.

This night-light makes me think of God. In this morning's lesson the Bible says that God is light and in him there is no darkness at all. The Bible says that when we walk in the light we are walking like other Christians. When I think of God being like this night-light, I think of God spreading a light over a world of darkness. So, tonight when you go to bed, remember to turn on your night-light. If you don't have one, someone probably turns on a lamp or a hall light for you. Remember that God is like a night-light. In God there is no darkness at all.—Children's Sermon Service Plus!

April 28: The Door

This morning, as always, I came into the sanctuary by way of a door. You also came into the church through a doorway. A door is a very interesting thing. I remember learning a little song in Sunday school, a long time ago, that began:

> One door and only one and yet its sides are two.
> Inside and outside, on which side are you?

The door is a symbol for making a decision. You may choose to stay on one side; or you may decide to open the door and go through it to the other side. But you cannot be on both sides at the same time.

We find this happening to us every day. We have to make a decision about where we want to be. For example, when the hour comes for the time of worship on Sunday morning and you have not passed through a door into a place of worship, then you have decided not to be in church that day; which means you decided to do something else.

Jesus referred to himself as a door. In John 10:9, we hear him say, "I am the door; if anyone enters by me, he will be saved, and will go in and out and find pasture." He used that illustration as he was talking about being the Good Shepherd. What he meant was that he was the way through which we can find what we really need for the living of life. But we have to decide to spend time with him if we are to learn from him.

> One door and only one and yet its sides are two.
> Inside and outside, on which side are you?

> —Kenneth Mortonson

May 5: Prayer

This morning I want to talk to you about something we do together each Sunday and that I assume you have done at home. We call it "prayer." You may use prayers in your family when you sit down to have a meal; or when you are getting ready to go to sleep. Those are special times for prayers, but I hope you know that you can pray anytime, anywhere.

Long ago, people used altars and smoke and fire to help them when they prayed. For example, a person might write a prayer on a piece of paper and then set the paper on fire on an altar, and as the smoke rose the one praying felt that what was desired in prayer was being carried to the gods in the heavens.

Today, however, because of Jesus, we believe that we do not need such things to help us pray. All we have to do is to talk to God as we would talk to a friend or to our parents. You see, when Jesus taught his disciples to pray, he told them to begin by saying, "Our Father, who art in heaven . . . "

Prayer is very important to your life as a Christian, for it is one way that you can bring God into your life, just as you let a friend be a part of your life when you talk to that person. Remember, God is everywhere, so to talk to him all you need to do is to think the thoughts that you want to share with him and they shall be shared. I hope you boys and girls will take time, every day, to let your thoughts go to God in prayer.—Kenneth Mortonson

May 12: God's Love Letter

Text: 1 John 4:8

Boys and girls, do you like to get letters? Would you like to tell me someone who has written you a letter? (Let them respond.) Isn't it exciting to open the mailbox and find a letter with your name on it? It's fun to see whose name is on the letter and to open the letter and read it. Sometimes we find a gift of money inside.

Have you ever written a love letter? Have you ever gotten a love letter? Guess what! Each one of you has gotten a love letter from God. (Hold up the Bible.) This is God's love letter to all of us. It is written to you and to me just as much as if it had "Dear Billy" or "Dear Sally" on it and signed: All my love, *God*.

In this wonderful letter, God tells us that he loves us. He loves us so much that he gave his Son Jesus to save us from our sins. He loves us so much he tells us what to do to be happy, how to obey and please him, and how to get to heaven.

How are you going to find out what God has said in his love letter? (Let them respond.) Of course, you must read it just like you would read a letter from Grandmother and Granddaddy to see what they said. If you can't read, maybe you can get your mother or daddy or brother or sister or maybe your Sunday school teacher to read the Bible to you. Today as we close our time together, let's read our Bible verse for today. (Read, "God is love." Have the children repeat it together.) Now, let's thank God for this wonderful love letter he has written us.

Prayer: Thank you, God, for the Bible. Thank you for loving us, and thank you for telling us in the Bible about your love.—Jeffrey Scott and Bill Chitwood

May 19: Keeping Things Alive

People who know their Bible stories will like this pleasant little story about Zacchaeus, the small, insignificant-looking tax collector who climbed into a tree so that he could see Jesus one day when he was passing. As a result of that experience Jesus befriended this despised man, restored his self-respect, and saved his soul.

The story has it that when Zacchaeus was an old man he still dwelt in Jericho, humble and pious. Every morning at sunrise he went out into the fields for a walk and came back with a calm and happy mind, no matter in what mood he went forth. After that, he was ready to begin his day's work with strength and courage.

His wife wondered where he went on those walks, but he never spoke to her of the matter. So, being curious, as most women are, she followed him one morning.

He went straight to the tree from which he had first seen Jesus on that immortal morning when he found a new friend and found his own soul. Taking a large urn to a nearby spring, he filled it with water, carried it to the tree, and poured it around the roots, which were getting dry in that hot climate. He pulled up all the weeds around the tree. Then he looked up among the branches where he had sat that day when he first saw the Lord; and a new light of peace and contentment came into his old eyes. He

turned away with a smile of gratitude and went back to his work.

Zacchaeus knew in his soul that he wanted to keep the spirit of that unusual experience alive, and to do so he tried to keep the tree alive. How true that necessity is in everyday life!—William L. Stidger

May 26: John the Baptist Was Brave

TEXT: Matt. 11:7–9

Object: A medal

This is a medal that was awarded to one of our members for bravery during World War II. A medal is something to be especially proud of. Because of the bravery of soldiers that served in the armed forces, we can enjoy freedom today.

The life of John the Baptist is presented in the Bible. He had a very special life. His mother was told about his coming birth so he could be brought up in a special way. He preached in the desert, and even though the conditions were horrible in the wilderness, thousands of people came to hear him preach the word of God. Another very important aspect of his life was bravery. Listen to this verse.

John the Baptist demonstrated a special kind of bravery. Some may think that a movie character like Rambo or the action personalities portrayed by Arnold Schwarzenegger are brave. Others may think that Troy Aikman, the Dallas Cowboy quarterback, is brave. In some ways these movie and real personalities are brave. However, real bravery is defined in the Bible as boldly living for the Lord and proclaiming the message of God in a loving, positive, and helpful way. We do this by what we say and do. John the Baptist demonstrated that kind of bravery. John the Baptist refused to copy the wrong attitudes and actions of his time. By the way he lived and by what he said, he stood as a hero for God. John the Baptist finally gave his life for refusing to give in to what was wrong. That is one reason why we know about him today.

We need to be brave for the Lord too. We demonstrate our bravery by being a friend to someone who may be bullied at school. We can be a hero by refusing to take drugs or be friends with those who steal and say curse words. We also prove our strength by always telling the truth and being honest. In addition to all this we show that we are heroes by telling our friends about the love of Jesus. Jesus' love and truth is the good news that we have the opportunity of sharing with the world.—Ken Cox

June 2: As You Will, Sir!

Traveling in China, I picked up many a wise parable or legend universal in its application to life as we live it today. One of those stories was about a would-be cynic who tried to outwit a wise old sage of China.

The cynic came to the sage with a tiny bird in his palm and cried, "What have I in my hand, O sage?"

The sage replied, "A bird, sir!"

Then the cynic, proposing to trap the sage, held the tiny, helpless bird in his hand and said, "Dead or alive, O sage?" intending to crush the bird in his brutal palm if the sage replied "alive" or to loosen the bird from his hand and let it fly away triumphantly into the blue skies if the sage answered "dead."

But the old sage replied, "As you will, sir!"

So it is in human life. Life may be just about what we will it to be. Life may either be crushed to death in the brutal palm of selfishness, deceit, anger, malice, and hate, or it may be permitted to fly into higher realms of light and love. "As you will, sir!"—William L. Stidger

June 9: The Devil's Question

TEXT: Gen. 3:1b
Object: A baseball

If a baseball is gripped just right and twisted when it is thrown, the ball curves away from the batter. I have heard that some batters never learn to hit a curve ball. A good curve ball is hard to spot, and the ball moves just out of reach when it crosses the plate.

When Adam and Eve were in the Garden of Eden, Satan deceived them with a question that was like a curve ball. The devil puts a spin on the things he says. It is hard to detect his fabrications, and many are tricked by his lies.

The Garden of Eden was a perfect place. There was no sickness, sin, or heartache. There was meaningful work for Adam and Eve, and there was no want. God did set some specific rules that limited what Adam and Eve could do. Adam and Even could eat the fruit from any tree in the garden except for the tree of the knowledge of good and evil. God told Adam and Eve not to eat from that one tree.

Listen to what Satan said to Eve about the rules in the garden. (Read verse.) The devil questioned what Eve knew for certain and caused some doubt in her mind. Because she had some doubt, by the "curve ball" thrown by the devil, Eve broke the one rule set by the Lord. Adam broke the rule too. Thus they were put out of the garden, and sin has been a problem in the human race ever since.

Satan is still throwing curves. He uses doubt and disbelief to cause us to disobey God. We learn the truth that is in God's word in Sunday School and church. Once we have learned the truth, we need to hold on to it and not be swayed from what we know is right. Remember, God never changes, and everything he has said will come true.—Ken Cox

June 16: People Around Us

Our kids love Winnie the Pooh and the host of characters who are Pooh's friends. One of Pooh's friends is an old gray donkey named Eeyore. Eeyore is fond of saying, "Thanks for noticing me." The otherwise overlooked and lonely Eeyore is always happy when someone pays particular attention to him.

Many people who come to our churches every Sunday are like Eeyore. A friendly smile and a warm handshake may be the most intimate interaction they have during the week. These people are sometimes visitors and sometimes our members. Eeyores may be people who have had a hard week or who just feel a little down. They may be young people, small children, or the elderly. They are people who need someone to call their name and notice them as individuals. They need to be more than a face in the crowd. Let's face it—we all are a little like Eeyore. We like to be noticed by others.

Eeyores, they are with us every Sunday and around us everyday. Have you noticed one lately?—Stephen D. Cloud

June 23: Don't Fear, Only Believe

TEXT: Mark 5:21–43

Object: A hiking stick

Good morning, boys and girls. I brought a hiking stick with me this morning. Sometimes when people take hikes in mountains or hills, they walk with a stick like this. It helps them as they walk up a hill. I want to tell you a story about a father and his daughter who took a hike in the hills. It was in a place where very few people live. Their hike was along a path on a very steep hill. The father and daughter began their hike. Somewhere along the way the daughter tripped and fell off the path into a crevice in the rocks. That's a spot like a cave only very difficult to get into if you are big like her father. Her father couldn't reach his daughter. He told her that he would run for help to get her out. He ran down the path for help. He found a house where two people lived. He told them, "My daughter is in danger. Please come quick to help!" One of the people in the house said, "I'm sorry, there's nothing we can do to help." But the father didn't give up. "Please come help!" he cried. Then the other person in the house said, "Don't fear. I know the spot on the hill. I'll come along with you." The father and the helper raced back to the girl. The father was amazed to find that the man who agreed to help could reach down into the crevice and pull the girl out! The girl was safe thanks to the man who agreed to help.

This story is similar to something that happened to Jesus. A father came to Jesus. The father's daughter was sick. The father wanted Jesus to help the girl. Jesus said, "Don't fear, only believe." Jesus went to the sick girl and made her well.

This week remember that Jesus is like the man who helped the girl climb to safety. Jesus cares about people in trouble. Jesus is our friend when we need help.—Children's Sermon Service Plus!

June 30: The Lord Is My Shepherd

TEXT: Ps. 23:1–2

Object: A shepherd's staff, picture of sheep or slingshot.

A favorite Psalm of many believers is the Twenty-Third Psalm. It is a Psalm about sheep and shepherd. Listen to these verses.

In our country sheep may be put in a fenced area and left alone for hours at a time. In the land where Jesus was born and lived, the shepherd had to always be with the sheep. The shepherd had to herd the sheep around the countryside to find enough grass for the sheep to eat. Water was hard to find, and the sheep had to be moved from place to place to quench their thirst too. At night since the sheep weren't put in a fenced area, the shepherd had to spend the night with the sheep. Today in the land of Israel whenever sheep are seen, a shepherd will be close by taking care of them.

The Twenty-Third Psalm was written under the inspiration of God by a shepherd named David. David was famous for his slingshot. He had used his sling to chase away bears and lions from his sheep. As David's faith grew, he realized that God took care of him like the sheep he was responsible for. He began to say, "The Lord is my shepherd," meaning that the Lord was with him all the time watching over him and seeing to his needs.

This Psalm is a favorite in our day because we can say, "The Lord is my shepherd," too. God is always with us. He protects and cares for us just like a loving shepherd takes care of his sheep.—Ken Cox

July 7: The Lord Is with Us in the Valley

TEXT: Ps. 23:4a

Object: Medicine bottle, pills, etc.

In this bottle are pills to take when a person is sick. Being sick and other difficult times are called "valley" experiences. When good or uplifting things happen, we call them "mountaintop" experiences. Thus when things are sad in our lives we say we are in the valley and when we are happy, we describe those days as being on the mountaintop.

This Psalm is called the shepherd's Psalm. The verses describe how a shepherd takes care of his sheep. When summer comes the shepherd must take his sheep from the low, hot areas where there is little grass and water to the cooler mountain pastures. To get to these better feeding areas, the sheep have to be led through the valley passes up to the mountaintop. These valleys are frightening. There are places that are dark and scary because the sun is blocked out by the mountain. There is also a feeling of being trapped by the high walls of the canyons. The sheep aren't scared, because they can always see the shepherd there with them. The followers of Jesus love these verses because we are the Lord's sheep and he is our shepherd.

When we have a difficult time in life, or we are afraid or feel lonely, we can know that the Lord is always with us. No shepherd would ever leave his sheep to make it through the valley alone. In the same way, the Lord doesn't expect us to make it through difficult times by ourselves. God comes to us and helps us.

We must not forget that there are good things in the valley. For sheep there is good grass and abundant water because water flows through the valley after it rains. Even though we may experience tough times, the Lord Jesus uses those difficulties to prepare us to help others. Since we have been in difficult days, we understand how others feel they have problems. These valley experiences also make us strong in character. Like exercise builds our muscles, so hardships make us stronger. We become better people by depending upon the Lord's help in difficult days.

The final mountaintop experience will be living in heaven with Jesus. We can feel like we are on a mountaintop now when we believe that the Lord is our shepherd! — Ken Cox

July 14: What Are You Leaving Behind?

TEXT: Acts 9:39

Object: A drawing of some footprints, fingerprints, etc.

Footprints like these were left behind by someone who walked by. Wherever we go we leave something behind. Detectives can find fingerprints on doorknobs and on furniture when one of us has been in a room. Investigators can find a strand of hair and prove that it is ours. So, wherever we go we leave something behind.

The Bible teaches that what we leave behind is very important. Jesus wants his disciples to leave behind deeds that glorify him. To glorify Jesus means to make others think more highly of him because of his disciples' words or actions.

A woman by the name of Dorcas left behind some things that glorified Jesus. We learn about her life in the New Testament book of Acts. When Dorcas died, her friends missed her so much that they sent for the apostle Peter. Listen to this verse.

Did you hear what the saddened friends of Dorcas did? They showed the robes and clothing that Dorcas had made to Peter. These items were evidence of the love that Dorcas had shown to others while she lived. The things that Dorcas had made were her fingerprints or footprints. Her handiwork was a testimony of a very good life. This was such a special case that Dorcas was brought back to life and continued to live for Jesus.

We ought to follow the example set by Dorcas. We should leave traces of our kindness and thoughtfulness wherever we go. Hopefully, when people hear our name, they will think about our good deeds. More important, they will think about how good Jesus must be for us to be his followers. That way we will be glorifying Jesus by our actions.

Jesus left behind a testimony of his generosity and love. Every time we see the cross we are reminded of that. Let's live our lives to leave behind footprints of our love too. — Ken Cox

July 21: Changing Nature

Object: Cut two flowers from the weed known as Queen Anne's lace. Place one cut stem in water colored with red food dye.

This morning I would like you to look at something that we can see everywhere at this time of the year. Does anyone know what this flower is called? (Queen Anne's lace.) Notice how nice and white it is. Now, let me show you a different Queen Anne's lace. This one is colored red. Let me tell you how I did this. After I cut off the flower and took it home, I placed it in a glass of water that I colored by adding red food dye. Then I just waited, and in a day or so, the flower changed colors.

The lesson from this is simple. The conditions under which we live have an effect upon us. If the people in your house are always fighting with one another, that will make you feel unhappy inside and it will show in the way you look and act. The things you watch on television can affect how you feel about what is important in life and that can affect what you do. The type of friends you have can also affect the way you behave. We all need to be careful about the conditions that surround us as we live each day, for they can influence how we feel inside. And how we feel inside can change how we act toward other people. Now, I hope your time in church will help you to know that you are loved by God and by the members of your church family. Knowing that, I hope it will make you happy and that you will be more loving to others.—Kenneth Mortonson

July 28: Like a Fish Out of Water

TEXT: Jonah 2

What I brought to show you is too big to hide in any bag. So it is right out in front of you this morning. What is it? . . . That's right, this is a fish net, and you are also right, it is a big net. That seems appropriate because we have been reading about a "big fish." Now I want to ask how you would feel if you were a fish picked up in this net and lifted out of the water? Yes, I think you would feel bad. Several of you said "afraid" because if you were out of the water too long and you were a fish, you would die. That's a scary thing being lifted out of everything you are used to and that fills you with life.

But watch what I am doing with the net and think about a person who cares for the fish, lifting it out of the water. As I am moving the net from one side to the other, the fish might "think" it is going to die but really the caretaker is saving the fish. Trout, for instance, have to be in cold and clear water. So moving the fish into a better place may feel like danger or death to the fish, but it is really safety and life. Just as Jonah thought he was given up for dead, God loved him and would not let him go. God used the belly of the big fish to save him. That's a good thing to remember. Sometimes you will go through a difficult move to a new place or there will be big changes in your family. That's a time to remember that although you feel like fish out of water, God has you in a big net of his love and care. God's love will not let you go, and that's worth remembering.—Gary D. Stratman

August 4: Love One Another

TEXT: Matt. 22:39

There is a story in the Bible about a man who went on a journey. While he was traveling, he saw someone hurt lying at the side of the road. This man stopped to help the one who had been hurt. The man took the wounded fellow to a place where the hurt man could get better. The kind man helped make sure the wounded man was okay before he left. He took good care of the man who had been hurt. He helped someone he did not even know! He made sure the hurt man had plenty to eat and a place to stay. He even made sure that someone would take care of the man who was hurt.

You know, the Bible tells us to love each other. In this story, a kind man took care of someone he did not know. He showed the hurt man love by helping him get better. We need to be kind to everyone, but sometimes it's very hard to be kind to the people who are closest to us like our parents or our brothers and sisters. It is hard to be nice to them because we are with them all of the time. They see us when we are grumpy and tired. Sometimes they bother our toys or make us do things we do not want to do. But that does not mean that we should be mean to them. Jesus wants us to be nice to them just like he wants us to love everyone else.

Try today to show your parents or your brothers and sisters that you love them by not being grumpy with them or by doing something extra special for them. That's what Jesus would want to do.—Lou Ellen Rich

August 11: Jesus and Children

This morning, I'm not going to talk just to the children. Instead, I want to talk about being a child in our church. To make it easier for us to see them, I would like all the children who are under the age of ten to raise both hands high above your head.

These are the children; but they are not the only children who are here today. In the Bible, the word "children" has two meanings. There is the obvious meaning, as we have just seen, as it refers to a person's age. The second meaning is to use the word to refer to any person who is still in need of maturing in his or her understanding and use of what Jesus taught. We tend to forget about these children, who were also of great concern to Jesus. Even after his Resurrection, Jesus called his disciples "children" (John 21:5).

Maturity in the faith is not measured in chronological terms. When we see an adult responding to a situation in a way that shows a lack of understanding of what the Christian faith is all about, do not say, "I doubt" or "He's not a Christian"; rather, see the actions as a sign that that person still has a lot to learn and be willing to share what you think and to help make that time a learning opportunity—just as you might do with a child who is young in years. In the Church, upbuilding the body of believers in love is everyone's responsibility (Eph. 4:15, 16). —Kenneth Mortonson

August 18: Pests

This morning I want to share an interesting word with you. The word is *"pests!"* Who can tell me what that word means? At this time of the year, when the windows to our sanctuary are open, we often have flies or other bugs come in. Then, when I am leading our worship service, a little fly may come and buzz around my ear or even land on my nose. If that happens, I will try to chase the fly away, but it may come back again and again to bother me, and that is why we call it a pest.

Now, there are times when a person may be a pest. Whenever someone continues to do things that annoy us, especially after we have asked them to stop, that person is being a pest. And sometimes, we become a pest to someone else. This may happen without our knowing it! For example, when people talk at a movie when they are supposed to be quiet, that is being a pest. When they tap their feet on the floor when someone is trying to concentrate on something, that is being a pest. When they talk in the worship service when people are trying to listen to the minister, that is being a pest.

Now, if we are concerned about other people, as we should be as Christians, then we will not want to pester them; that is, we will not want to be a pest to them. So, I hope you will remember that we all need to be aware of what annoys other people, especially those whom we love, and then not do it when they are near.— Kenneth Mortonson

August 25: Pruning Helps a Christian Grow

Text: John 15:2
Object: A potted plant
This is a plant I have had for some time. I noticed that it wasn't growing, so I tried something to help it grow. I trimmed off some of the old dead branches and leaves, and soon, some new leaves started appearing. These new leaves could grow only after this "pruning" had been done. Old dead branches and leaves, though they are not growing, draw moisture and nutrients out of the

soil that could be going to new branches and leaves. If old branches are not taken away, new leaves or branches are slow to develop.

A similar thing must be done for Christians. Listen to this verse. The Lord says our lives are like branches growing out of him that should be producing good works. These good works are called fruit. Jesus is very concerned about how fruitful we are for him. The Lord requires that some pruning go on in our lives so we can be as fruitful as possible.

Our lives are just like this plant that requires moisture and nutrients. With only a limited amount of moisture and nutrients to go around, we must be careful not to waste those things that help us grow strong. If we watch the wrong kind of television programs, or spend time with boys and girls who are always misbehaving and doing bad things, we will waste our time and talents. To help our lives become what they should be, we have to prune away the wrong things and allow the right things to remain.

Some of the things that we should do are actively develop our truthfulness and honesty. We should be kind to others, always treating them as we would like to be treated. We must be very careful how we talk and act. We should read our Bibles. We should also pray. We should also look to serve Jesus by telling others his truth. When we do, we become like a flourishing plant in God's kingdom, and that pleases him.—Ken Cox

September 1: Helping Hands

TEXT: Rom. 13:10

Good morning, boys and girls. I would like everyone to do a favor for me. I would like everyone to look at your hands, please. Look all over them. Look at your fingers. Wiggle them around. Hands are very useful things. We can do a lot of different things with our hands. We can use our hands to wave at our friends. We can shake hands with people and make them feel welcome. With our hands we can help our family around the house by doing chores and helping out whenever we can. Our hands can also clap together to tell someone she/he has done a good job. We can use our hands to build wonderful things. Our hands can do some wonderful things to show people that we love them.

Our hands can also do some bad things, can't they? We can use them to hit someone and hurt them. We can use them to break things. Our hands can do some very bad things.

We need to remember that we need to use our hands to show people we love them and care for them. In Romans 13:10 there is verse that says, "Love does no harm to its neighbor." God does not want us to hurt each other. Remember this week to try to use your hands to help someone and show to them that God loves them.—Lou Ellen Rich

September 8: Why Do We Want to Learn?

Object: One large jar and two smaller jars. In one small jar, using food coloring, place yellow water. In the other small jar, place blue water.

How many of you boys and girls are going or hope to go to school? Why do people go to school? Learning new things is very important to everybody, even for adults. We never outgrow our need to learn. The reason for this is that the new things we learn change us; and the more we know, the more we can do.

Let me illustrate what I mean. When people are born, they don't know very much. But as they grow and learn, new things are added to their life. (Pour the blue water into the large jar.) Then, as they grow older, they learn different things, as represented by this yellow water. Now, do you know what will happen when I add the yellow water to the blue water? If you have been to school you probably know that yellow and blue make green. Green is the color of things that are growing. It tells us that life is present and active in many plants. It is a good color to remind us that we all need to keep on learning and growing. We all need to be adding new things to our store of knowledge. As we do so, year after year, life will change and be better. That is why we should never stop learning new things.—Kenneth Mortonson

September 15: We Get Back What We Give Out

TEXT: Gal. 6:7

Object: A boomerang

This is a boomerang. It is an Australian hunting weapon that has a unique characteristic; when you throw it out, it comes back to you.

God's word tells us that all of our deeds are like boomerangs. Listen to this verse. God is instructing us that our deeds are like crops. If we plant a corn seed in the ground, a tomato plant is not going to grow. If we want a tomato plant, we must plant tomato seeds. Furthermore, seeds yield a tremendous return. If one corn seed is planted, numerous ears of corn will grow from the resulting stock and thousands of kernels will be produced. Applied to deeds, this means that one action on our part gives rise to numerous other actions. That is, if we call someone "stupid," that person is likely to call us "stupid" in return and insult someone else with the same awful remark. But if we encourage someone and help them up when they are down, our kindness will be multiplied through that person's actions to others and somehow return to us.

The Lord wants us to know that there is a law of results that is applied to all of our behavior. The law of gravity cannot be broken; whatever goes up must come down. It is the same with sowing and reaping our actions. If we are selfish in our behavior, we will receive nothing from others. On the other hand, if we are generous and giving, we will discover a life that is full and rewarding. The verse says, "Don't be deceived." In other words, don't think you can be mean and get kindness back. Don't think you can lie and get told the truth in return. Some people have a tendency to think that this law applies to everyone else but them.

Our deeds and actions are just like this boomerang; they come back to us. So, what kind of deeds are you going to do? That's right, the kind of deeds that we want to come back to us. — Ken Cox

September 22: Doing Small Things for Jesus

TEXT: Matt. 10:42

Object: A cup and pitcher of water

When we see a big problem, we might be overwhelmed. For instance, we may see a news report on television about a food shortage in Africa where thousands of people are hungry. We feel a desire to help, but since we only have two dollars from our allowance that we can send in, we may end up doing nothing. This happens because we begin to think about the enormous problem and say, "What good will two dollars do?" News reports about the problem just frustrate us.

Some problems in life are like that. The difficulty seems so big that we don't feel like the Lord can use us to help. But the Lord does plan to use us. God wants to take the little we can do and multiply it to make a positive difference in the world. Jesus wants us to do what we can because our deeds are the beginning of the solution.

One day long ago, thousands of people were gathered to hear Jesus preach. At lunch time they all became hungry, and there wasn't enough food to feed all those folks. One little boy gave his small lunch to Jesus, but all he had was five loaves of bread and two small fish. Jesus took that small amount, multiplied it by a miracle of his grace, and everyone received plenty to eat. Little became much when it was placed in Jesus' hands.

We can all do something, no matter how small. That is all God wants us to do. Listen to this verse. Even if we pour a glass of water for someone that is thirsty, that is something that God can bless. (Pour the small cup full of water from the pitcher.)

Therefore, let's not worry about solving all the world's problems at once. Let's do what we can, being faithful with our abilities, and Jesus will take care of the rest. By the way, if five thousand boys and girls sent in two dollars each to feed the hungry, that ten thousand dollars would feed a lot of people. When we all do what we can, great problems can be solved. — Ken Cox

September 29: Standing on Two Feet

This morning, I would like each one of you to stand up. Now, stand on just one foot, and as soon as you lose your balance and have to touch the floor with the other foot, sit down.

Some people find that they can stand on one foot for a long time, but such people usually have to concentrate on what they are doing to maintain their balance. Now, everybody stand on two feet again. Which way is easier? It is much easier for us to stand or move about when we use both feet. Our feet give us a special stability in life when we use them properly.

This is also true in regard to the things we learn in life. All of you are, or will be, expected to go to school during the week. There are basic things that you must learn to be able to function properly in life as you grow up. But that education is just part of what you need. It is like standing on one foot.

In the church, we believe that in order to be a complete person you also need to learn the things that are offered to you on Sunday in the church school program. This is like the second foot that enables you to stand or move about through life. So, I hope you will remember how important it is to get a complete education. Your Sunday education is just as important as your weekday education. I hope you will pay attention both here and at school so that you can learn all the important things you need to know in life.—Kenneth Mortonson

October 6: What Makes Us Strong

A traveler in Italy watched as a lumberman occasionally jabbed his sharp hook into a log, separating it from the others floating down a mountain stream. When asked why he did this, the worker replied, "These may all look alike to you, but a few of them are quite different. The ones I let pass are from trees that grew in a valley where they were always protected from the storms. Their grain is coarse. The ones I have hooked and kept apart came from high on the mountains. From the time they were small they were beaten by strong winds. This toughens the trees and gives them a fine grain.

We save them for choice work. They are too good to make into plain lumber."
—Wayne Rouse

October 13: A Prayer You Can See

A poor man was injured one day trying to repair the roof of his modest home. He would be out of work for quite a while. With a large family and meager savings, the future looked grave. His church family met at the church to pray for him. Fervent prayers went up for God to provide for the family. Right in the middle of one particularly pious prayer came a rapping at the door. Someone got up, walked quietly to the door, opened it, and saw a young farm boy. The lad whispered, "Dad couldn't come to the meeting tonight, so he sent his prayers in a wagon." Down at the curb was a buckboard full of potatoes, beans, canned goods, and fruit.[1]—Cecil Taylor

October 20: Thoughts

The Scriptures teach that we become like the things we habitually think about. In the face of this truth, how can we hope for much spirituality in this day when conversations, radio, television, videos, movies, magazines, and books keep before our minds so much that is the very antithesis to a spiritual attitude?

Paul gave an effective recipe for our thought life: "Whatsoever things are true, whatsoever things are honest, whatsoever things are just, whatsoever things are pure, . . . think on these things" (Phil 4:8). Thoughts of these things will block the entry of evil thoughts or push them out if they have found entry.

Through Bible reading, prayer, godly conversations, holy meditation, clean reading and viewing materials, and spiritual songs and music we can enjoy moment-by-moment fellowship with our Lord.

As Spurgeon once admonished, we need to "wear Christ on our eyeballs."

[1]John Allan Lavender, *Why Prayers Are Unanswered* (Valley Forge: Judson Press, 1967), 53.

We also need to ask him to stand guard over our eye-gate and ear-gate.—L. D. Kennedy

October 27: God Is With Us

TEXT: Ps. 46

More than five hundred years ago a man was born who did many wonderful things to help people to learn how to worship God better. His name was Martin Luther. Today, the church he started is named for him. In many parts of the world there are Lutheran churches. One special thing that he did was to help people, all the people, in the churches to learn how to sing together, telling God in song how much they love him and trust in him. He wrote thirty-seven hymns to be sung in church. There is one special hymn that he wrote that people in all Christian churches like to sing. It is "A Mighty Fortress Is Our God." He got his ideas for the song from one of the Psalms, which says some wonderful things about God. It tells us that God is a hiding place for us when things go wrong, that God is strong when we are weak, that God will help us in times of trouble. The times were very bad when Martin Luther wrote his hymn saying the same things that Psalm Forty-six said, but people were encouraged and made strong in the Lord when they sang the wonderful song together. Is there a favorite song you like to sing from our hymnbook that helps you to tell God how much you love him or that tells you how much God loves you?—James W. Cox

November 3: Caring for Creation

TEXT: Gen. 1

Object: Pictures of animals and plants in the order of creation

Boys and girls, did you know that every living creature on the earth is very important? God created the sun and the moon, the ocean and the land. He made the fruits and vegetables, trees and plants. When he got finished making these things he said, "This is good." Then God made all the different fish in the sea, the whales, the shrimp, the sharks. Everything! Then, he made all the birds. When he finished, you know what he said? "This is good!"

After God filled up the ocean with life, God made all the land animals. He made all the mice and the elephants. He made all the cows and all the chickens. He made all the bugs and all the rhinoceroses. God made all those things, and you know what he said? "This is good!"

Finally, God made people. God made Adam and Eve. He made them and told them to take care of the earth and all of the creatures and plants that God made. After God had finished creating everything, you know what he said? "This is *very* good!"

We need to remember that God made everything and God cares for everything. God wanted for us to take care of what he made. So remember to thank God for making the world and show that you appreciate it by picking up trash outside and caring for things that can't take care of themselves.—Lou Ellen Rich

November 10: The Silent Language

Object: A small pane of glass

What do you see in my hand? Your first answer might be simply "a piece of glass." But look again and think about how you might use this piece of glass. What do you see? If you were a homeowner you might see a pane of glass for a broken window. If you have fish in the house this might be a cover for a fishbowl, to keep the goldfish in and the cat out. If you like the garden you might see this as a protection for a tabletop upon which a flowerpot might be placed. If you were an artist, this could be a surface upon which to mix some colors if you were painting with oil paint. This piece of glass is a very simple object, and yet it can have different meanings to just as many different people.

I find that very interesting. We can learn something about a person just by seeing how they make use of what is around them. And how we use the things that we have tells other people something about us.

Now, as Christians, we want people to see that we are followers of Jesus, and that means using what we have in a proper way. We come to church to try to see things in a new way; to see things as God sees them. And the closer we come to seeing life as God wants us to see it, the closer we come to finding true life. So, keep your eyes and ears and heart and mind open here. What you find in church may surprise you; and it may help you to see life in a different way.— Kenneth Mortonson

November 17: The Selflessness of Prayer

TEXT: 1 Tim. 2:1

Object: Praying hands

These praying hands should look familiar to us. These hands have been reproduced in numerous paintings, sculptures, or in ceramics like this. They are symbolic of the love and giving attitude that is demonstrated by prayer.

This ceramic duplication has an interesting story behind it. Long ago, a young man named Albrecht Dürer left home to study with a famous artist. Albrecht had wanted to be an artist since childhood. In the town where he moved to study he had to locate a roommate because he was poor. The roommate and Albrecht had to make an agreement, since they didn't have enough money for both of them to go to school. Albrecht's roommate suggested that Albrecht go to school while he worked. Then after graduation when Albrecht was earning enough money, the roommate would take his turn at school.

Finally the day came when Albrecht was trained and sold a wood carving. There was now enough money for Albrecht's friend to go to school. But the roommate had worked so hard with his hands that he could no longer paint with skill. His ability to paint was forever gone.

One day Albrecht came home and heard his roommate praying. Albrecht captured his praying hands in a wood sculpture as a testimony of giving and love.

One of the finest things we can do for somebody is to pray for them. Listen to this verse. Let's remember the lesson of the praying hands and give of ourselves through prayer to someone today.— Ken Cox

November 24: Say Thank You

TEXT: Luke 17:12–19

Jesus tells us a story about ten people who were very sick and could not get better. One day, these ten people went to see Jesus because they knew that he could do a miracle and heal them. When they saw Jesus, they called out to him and asked Jesus to heal them, and Jesus did. They were so excited! Their sickness was gone, and they did not have to worry about it anymore. Jesus did a wonderful thing for them. But do you know what happened? They forgot to do something very important. They forgot to say thank you. Only one person ran to Jesus and said thank you.

Sometimes, we forget to say thank you, don't we? We have people do things for us every day. Our teachers help us, our family helps us, our friends help us. So many people help us every day that it is easy to forget to say thank you. Sometimes, we are even like the people in the story, and we forget to tell Jesus thank you for the things he does for us. So remember, even though we have a lot of people doing things for us and we sometimes forget, it is always very important for us to say thank you.— Lou Ellen Rich

December 1: Salvation

In his book *In the Eye of the Storm,* Max Lucado tells of a young boy who went into a pet shop to look for a puppy. The owner showed the boy a litter of puppies in a box at the back of the store. The boy examined each one. After a couple of minutes he went back to the owner and said, "I've picked one out. How much will it cost?" The owner gave him the price, and the boy promised to return in a few days with the money. The owner said, "Don't take too long. Puppies like these sell quickly."

The boy replied, "I'm not worried. Mine still will be here." He went to work, washing windows and cleaning yards. He worked hard and saved his money. When he had enough, he returned to the store.

He went up to the counter and presented the store owner with a wad of bills. The owner patiently counted out the money and told the boy, "All right, you can go get your puppy." The boy reached in and pulled a skinny little dog with a limp leg and started to leave.

The owner called out to him and said, "Don't take that puppy. He's crippled. He can't play. He'll never run with you. He can't fetch. Get one of the healthy pups."

The boy turned around and said, "No thank you, sir. This is exactly the kind of dog I've been looking for."

As the boy turned to leave, the owner started to speak again but remained silent. Suddenly, he understood what the boy was doing. Extending out from the bottom of the boy's pants was a brace for his leg.

The boy knew how the puppy felt and rescued it. Jesus knows how we feel. He became one of us and rescued us from our sin and lostness.[1]—David Charlton

December 8: The Bible—Word of God

Jim Harvey of the Baptist Sunday School Board shared the following true story from the files of the American Bible Society.

A missionary was standing on the street of a city in Africa with a small New Testament in his hand. An African man approached him and asked if he could have the little book. The missionary was not reluctant to part with the testament, but he was curious as to why the man wanted it.

"Its pages are the perfect size for rolling cigarettes," the man confessed.

The missionary was impressed with the honesty of the African and decided to extend a challenge.

"I will give you this book if you will promise to read every word on each page before you roll a cigarette with it," said the missionary.

The African accepted the challenge and was given the New Testament. About fifteen years later the missionary went to a revival being preached by an African evangelist. When the black evangelist saw the white man, he approached him and said:

"You don't remember me, do you?"

"No," said the missionary. "Have we met before?"

"Yes, fifteen years ago you gave me a New Testament and made me promise to read every word on the page before I rolled a cigarette with it. It took me from Matthew's Gospel until the third chapter of John before I quit smoking the Word and started preaching it. That New Testament is the reason I'm here to preach the Word tonight!"[1]

Why preach the Word of God? Because "the Word of God is living and powerful, and sharper than any two-edged sword, piercing even to the division of soul and spirit, and of the joint and marrow, and is a discerner of the thoughts and intents of the heart" (Heb. 4:12 NKJV).[2]—Steve McKown

December 15: Don't Forget

In an issue of the cartoon strip "The Family Circus," young Billy sees many of the signs common to Christmas. One child shouts out, "Don't forget Christmas candy." Another says, "Don't forget the wrapping paper." Everywhere Billy turns, he finds more of the same: "Don't forget the Christmas lights." "Don't forget to visit Santa." "Don't forget the last-minute Christmas gifts."

The final panel of the comic strip shows Billy drawing a picture. The scene is the stable with Mary and Joseph standing beside the baby Jesus. Above the scene Billy wrote, "Don't forget."

If we are not careful, we get caught up in the hustle and bustle of Christmas and forget what we are celebrating.—David Charlton

[1] American Bible Society quote.
[2] From the *New King James Version*. Copyright 1979, 1980, 1982, Thomas Nelson, Inc., Publishers.

[1] Max Lucado, *In the Eye of the Storm* (Dallas: Word Publishing, 1991), 48–49.

December 22: The Voice of John the Baptist

TEXT: Matt. 3:1, 5

Object: A stadium seat

This is a special seat to sit on at a ball-park. Bleachers are hard and uncomfortable. This special cushion makes being in the stadium more pleasant. People like to be comfortable when attending a ball game or coming to church. However, when an event is worthwhile, people are willing to be uncomfortable.

John the Baptist was a very special man we read about in the Bible. His mother was told about his special birth so he could be brought up properly by his parents. His preaching was special too. Listen to this verse.

Whenever people went to hear John the Baptist preach, they had to walk for miles in the barren desert. There were no cars to ride in. There were no concession stands and no air conditioners. Thousands of people endured heat, thirst, and hunger to hear John the Baptist preach. The people did this because they felt it was worth it.

John preached so Jesus would be able to make a positive difference in people's lives. There were some barriers in the way that had to be removed before Jesus could enter their lives. John said, "Prepare the way for the Lord." This is the same as clearing a road. If a big rock falls onto a road, the rock must be removed so that cars can pass through on the highway. That's what John the Baptist was saying. He was urging those who listened to clear the rocks off the road to their hearts, making the way clear for the Lord to come in.

Just think about it. People walked through the desert for miles to hear John the Baptist preach. Hearing him was worth the trouble because Jesus could become a blessing to them. Hearing the word of the Lord is still worth it. When we come to church, we must pay close attention to what God says to us through our Sunday school teachers and pastor. God wants to have a clear passage into our hearts. We must hear the message and remove anything that hinders the Lord from coming into our lives.—Ken Cox

December 29: The Wise Man Who Brought His Best

TEXT: Matt. 2:11

Object: A nativity scene wise man

This is one of the magi from a nativity scene. Christmas is a time when we sing about wise men bringing their gifts to the baby Jesus. Did you know that the Bible doesn't indicate that there were three wise men? We have concluded there were three men because they brought three gifts: gold, frankincense, and myrrh.

Assuming that each wise man brought one gift, we are going to consider the wise man that brought gold. This gift stands for bringing the very best to Jesus. There are several indicators that the wise man gave his best to the Lord.

First, he took a long trip to find Jesus. When we are willing to use our time for Jesus, we reveal a willingness to give of the most precious of our resources.

Second, the wise man was willing to stop what he was doing to search for Jesus. It is possible to become so busy with our projects that we don't want to be bothered by the Lord's plans. If we are called to come home when we are playing with our friends, we may want to keep playing and act like we didn't hear Mom or Dad calling. This requires that parent to call over and over again, or even come and get us. When God calls we may be tempted to act like we don't hear him either. When we obey the Lord's instructions, like being kind to our neighbor, we reveal that Jesus is very important to us.

Third, the wise man did not keep his wealth but shared it with Jesus. In the days when Jesus was born, the wise man wouldn't have carried paper money or had a bank account. All his wealth would have been possessed in the precious metal, gold. We should give from our allowance funds to help those that are in need. When we share our money, we honor Jesus just like the wise man who brought his gold on the first Christmas.

God deserves our best because he gave his only son Jesus for us. I saw a sign painted on a building once that read, "Wise Men Still Seek Him." As we seek Jesus, let's always bring him our best.—Ken Cox

SECTION XI.
A Little Treasury of Sermon Illustrations

LOSING HEROES.   Some time ago a father sat across a restaurant table from me and unfolded the story of his youngest son. The boy was the last of several children and had been born into a home and community with every possible advantage. But he had dropped out of school at the eighth-grade level with an IQ in the 140s. He was just sitting around the house, his father said; he was incapable of making it out there in the world. I wanted to know why. And the father replied, "You see, he had three heroes. You may guess who they were: John Kennedy, Martin Luther King, and Robert Kennedy." The man held back a sob, but there were tears running down his face as he said, "It is a terrible thing when the young lose their heroes."— Roger Lovette

SOURCES OF PREJUDICE.   Whence come these prejudices of ours? It would seem at times that they derive from thin air. As was said by one of its victims, "Prejudice, like the spider, makes everywhere its home and lives where there seems nothing to live on."—Ralph W. Sockman

THE GOSPEL FOR ALL.   A young student drifted into the office some months ago and complained that he served four different congregations. "I perceive you're a Methodist," we remarked. No, it turned out the young man's four congregations were all wrapped up in one. There were the 1950s Christians who couldn't understand why the Church wasn't expanding;

they wanted more members and bigger buildings. Then there were the 1960s Christians who kept talking about "getting involved." They were followed by the 1970s Christians, many of whom were still keeping faith-journey diaries. Mostly, he was stuck with 1980s Christians who, filled with nostalgia, wanted to turn back to old-time religion. "You see," he said plaintively, "I have four congregations!" He is not alone. Here we are in the 1990s, and churches are still haunted by cultural styles from the past. But then, we never preach Christian faith to empty heads; the gospel addresses all sorts of well-formed culture faiths in any congregation.—David G. Buttrick

THE SACRIFICE OF GOD.   I read the following account of the parting of a minister and his son at the landing stage in Boston in the United States. The son was going to be a missionary doctor in Turkey, and the father had come to the wharf to say good-bye to him. When the *Romanic,* which was the ship in which the son was sailing, began to move, the father, his face wet with tears, bared his white head, and lifting his hand high above the throng, cried, "Good-bye, my boy; 1 Corinthians 16:13, 14." A hush fell upon the group as once again the father, lifting himself to his full height, shouted, "Stanley, 1 Corinthians 16:13, 14: 'Quit you like men, be strong.' Make it your motto for life. God bless you, my boy." And the crowd in solemn awe watched what they knew was a great sacrifice. Afterwards the white-haired old minister, who had just given his son for love of God and men, said to one at his side as they walked away together, "Now I know what Moody meant. I heard him say once that before he was a father he preached much about the sacrifice of the Son; but after he became a father he learned to preach above all the sacrifice of the Father. Now I know what he meant."—J. D. Jones

PATHS TO GOD. Theology and spirituality are two paths by which men seek God. On first glance, they look like very different paths, but finally they converge. Spirituality proceeds by way of prayer, worship, discipline. By these means, men have transcended themselves, their personal being has been enhanced, and they have known communion with God. Theology, on the other hand, proceeds by way of intellectual inquiry. It accepts the rigor of a commitment to intellectual honesty. Yet those who pursue the way of theology find that this too is a discipline drawing them beyond themselves. They are drawn to a Truth that is no dead truth to be locked up in propositions or stored away in a book, but a living Truth, self-communicating and itself the source of all truth. A dynamic theology does not cease to be a scientific discipline because it is inspired by the passion of an intellectual love. It cannot rest content with a knowledge *about* God, and it positively abhors a chattering about God. Knowledge of God, like knowledge of our friends, must finally be a knowledge based on communing. The knowledge of God merges with the love of God.—John Macquarrie

MAGNANIMITY. In the early days of the Southern Confederacy, General Robert E. Lee was severely criticized by General Whiting. It might have been expected that Lee would wait for a time when he could get even with Whiting. A day came when President Jefferson Davis asked General Lee to come for consultation. Davis wanted to know what Lee thought of General Whiting. Without hesitation Lee commended Whiting in high terms and called him one of the ablest men in the Confederate army. An officer present motioned Lee aside to suggest that he must not know what unkind things Whiting had been saying about him. Lee answered: "I understood that the president desired to know my opinion of Whiting, not Whiting's opinion of me."—Ralph W. Sockman

RESURRECTION. There is the story of an Austrian empress who was a great atheist. She arranged that when she died, a granite tomb should be erected for her body, and on it was to be inscribed, "Sealed for all eternity." In this way she sought to give the lie to him who said: "There shall be a resurrection, . . . both of the just and unjust." We would have answered the challenge with dynamite, and blown her tomb to pieces. God caused the seed of a tree to lodge in a tiny crevice between the great stones. Year after year it grew, and at last it completely destroyed the tomb.—W. W. Weeks

OTHER WORLDS. I would like to see a strong attempt made to detect signals from space that might indicate the presence of another working civilization. Surely any civilization that can send out signals we can receive is at least as advanced as we are. Very likely, it has far surpassed us. Such signals would at once give us an all-important message, even if we understood absolutely nothing of what was being said. The message would be, "We have a technology more advanced than yours and we have managed to survive. Take heart! You can do so, too." It is encouragement we badly need.—Isaac Asimov

COUNT YOUR BLESSINGS. Even in the shadow of his cross Jesus gave thanks. A tragedy was transfigured into a sacrament, hallowing all the ages. Truly, it is not what happens to us but what we do with it that counts.

Just a loaf of bread, made of wheat grown in any field, ground in any mill, baked in any oven—yet it became the bread of God, feeding millions of hungry human souls. "A *Te Deum* of the commonplace," John Oxenham called it, turning an hour of parting into a celebration of immortality.—Joseph Fort Newton

TRUE LOVE.   In Charles Dickens's novel *A Tale of Two Cities,* the climax came when a family was in deep trouble. The husband was about to be executed during the Reign of Terror in Paris, and the man who loved the hero's wife had the strange gift of being virtually identical in appearance to the condemned man. Had the hero died, perhaps this character would have had the opportunity to court the dead man's wife. Instead, he substituted himself for the hero, through trickery, thus becoming the hero himself. He went to the guillotine and died in place of the other with the words, "It is a far, far better thing that I do, than I have ever done." In this bit of fiction one sees the sort of love that is not self-interested but is self-giving, knowing that nothing will ever come back in return.—Harry L. Poe

KINDNESS: THE NEGLECTED VIRTUE.   Ed Goldfader owns and operates Tracers Company of America, Inc., a New York agency that specializes in finding lost persons. He says more wives than ever are running away, not because they have found new lovers but because they are bored and feel that there must be more to life than playing handmaiden to unappreciative husbands. A clue as to why the women feel unappreciated lies in this bit of information Goldfader supplied recently: When a man comes to Tracers for help in finding his wife, the agency asks questions about his wife's personal history and personal appearance. Often he is unable to remember the color of her eyes![1]—Alan Loy McGinnis

THE CHURCH AT FAULT.   "He cannot have God for his Father who does not have the Church for his Mother," declared Cyprian. No salvation outside the Church—"*Extra ecclesiam nulla salus*"—has been the slogan through which the Church attempted to counter those who attacked it. Vatican I (1869–70) responded to modernist detractors of the Church by restating what the Church had always claimed: "Outside the church no one can be saved . . . . Who is not in this ark will perish in the flood."

Anyone with an even casual acquaintance with the average church may find the slogan "No salvation outside the Church" to be a patent absurdity. We all know wonderful people outside the Church—people even better than many within. For most of us, the Church is an embarrassment. In Christian apologetics, the Church is treated as something that must be explained or excused, a necessary evil at best, a hindrance to the advancement of the gospel at worst. I have heard television evangelists fulminate against the evils of "Churchianity" as opposed to "Christianity." And who can blame them? How far can one get urging people to come to Jesus with nothing better to commend this Savior than his would-be disciples in today's Church?—William H. Willimon

CHRIST LIFTED UP.   Our separate churches, their beloved and hallowed traditions of devotion and practice, are the visible means by which we have known Christ, been nourished in him, been united in him. There is, there ought to be, nothing on earth more precious to us. And yet it is these same traditions in their separateness, in their mutual exclusiveness, in their excessive hallowing of separate traditions, and in their corporate pride—it is these in their separateness that hide from the world the all-sufficiency of the cross. "I, when I am lifted up from the earth, will draw all men to myself."—J. E. Lesslie Newbigin

CHRISTIAN HEROISM.   There is an Indian saying that "the perfume of holiness travels even against the wind." Is it not true? When a really heroic Christian life, a life after the pattern of New Testament Christianity, makes its rare appearance

[1]Gail Sheehy, *Passages* (New York: Dutton, 1976), 264.

among us, the fame of it still runs through all the land, and the perfume of it really does travel against all the winds of contemporary indifference and unbelief. Who shall I venture to mention as examples within our own generation—an Albert Schweitzer, an Edward Wilson, a Bonhoeffer, a Bishop Berggrav, a Martin Niemoeller, a Hugh Lister, a William Temple? Such men as these stand out hardly less clearly against the background of the modern West than they would have done against the background of ancient paganism.—John Baillie

THE RELIGION OF MATURITY. We may then say that the mature religious sentiment is ordinarily fashioned in the workshop of doubt. Though it has known intimately "the dark night of the soul," it has decided that theoretical skepticism is not incompatible with practical absolutism. While it knows all the grounds for skepticism, it serenely affirms its wager. In so doing, it finds that the successive acts of commitment, with their beneficent consequences, slowly strengthen the faith and cause the moments of doubt gradually to disappear.—Gordon W. Allport

ALL THINGS NEW? A great preacher used to tell the story about an old Indian army officer who was a clever public speaker. He would delight his audiences with stirring tales, vividly describing his skirmishes, sieges, and hairbreadth escapes. As he worked upon the imagination and feelings of his listeners, he would suddenly stop and, after a dramatic pause, would continue: "I expect to see something much more wonderful than all that I have seen already." He was well over seventy years of age, and it was obvious that his audience received his charged announcement with skepticism. But in seconds it was gone when he continued, "I mean, in the first five minutes after death!"—Elam Davies

KNOWING, BELIEVING, AND DOING. We are united to Christ, not by the doctrine of his nature and work, needful as that is, but by trusting in him as that which the doctrine declares him to be—Redeemer, Friend, Sacrifice, Divine Lover of our souls. Let us always remember that it is not the amount of religious knowledge that I have got, but the amount that I use, that determines my religious position and character.—Alexander Maclaren

CONTEMPLATION. I once knew a mother who gave her son twenty minutes of love each day and singled out the child for that purpose. Now there is nothing to be sneered at in a third of an hour of anyone's tender loving care, least of all a mother's. But the thing that is incongruous to us and that makes us snort at such a regimen is that there is on our part an assumption that this tender loving care is standard equipment on the part of a mother in relation to her son. If this standard is too high, there is still a revolt in us that it should be so contrived and so self-consciously doled out at a given time in a given place. There would be far less uneasiness about the matter if each time the son appeared or when the mother's time permitted it, she turned to him with a loving attitude. This comes very close to what I want to say about the common use of contemplation. It can take place anywhere, at any time, in any circumstance, and its naturalness is the neglected factor.—Douglas V. Steere

CHRISTIAN UNITY AND CONVICTION. Our denominations do not come to the goal of Church unity in forgetfulness of their high experience, but they do trail clouds of glory. The glint of valid glory will find a place in God's rainbow of color. There is no blessing in that sorry goal, a "church of the least common denominator." An old equation is true in the world of Church life as it is in the world of arithmetic: "Zero plus zero equals zero." Churches that have reduced their convictions to zero, when added together, no matter how many of them, will still add to zero. A "glorious church" will include many "clouds of glory."—Halford E. Luccock

THE COMMUNITY OF THE HOLY SPIRIT. There is an old Indian Buddhist story, which I believe has often been told in Christian pulpits, about a wise king who undertook to teach a young man the secret of spiritual freedom. This was how he did it. The young man was to be given a jar filled with oil to the very brim, and he was to carry it through the street of the town, where a fair was going on, without spilling a drop. An executioner, with drawn sword, was ordered to walk behind him, and upon the first drop of oil being spilt, was to strike off the young man's head. The young fellow agreed, did what he was told, and carried the jar safely back to the king without having lost a drop. The king asked him: "As you walked through the town, whom and what did you see?" "Sir," said the young man, "I kept my eyes fixed on the vessel of oil, and saw and heard nothing else." And then the king told him that such was the secret of spiritual freedom: to be so intent on keeping one's own soul that one was blind to the affairs of one's fellows.

It is a good story. But that is a Buddhist parable of spiritual freedom. And now, for contrast, take the Christian picture. It comes just after the story of Pentecost, and the people of whom it speaks are the people who had had that deep personal experience of the Holy Spirit of God searching out the depths of their individual souls. But this is how it showed to the world: "And all those who believed had all things in common, and they sold their possessions and goods, and distributed them to all, as anybody had need.—D. M. Baillie

THE LIFE OF THE CHURCH.   The Church would surely die if its life were suspended upon anything peculiar to the twentieth century. If we base the life and health of the Church only on some specifically modern development, on any manifestation not first found in the apostolic era, the gates of hell will surely prevail against it. The Church of Christ is a supernatural creation. Its life is rooted neither in the present nor even in the past; rather, its life flows from the eternal order. The Church is a supernatural creation whose existence is nei-

ther spontaneously generated nor self-perpetuated.—Carl F. H. Henry

GOD'S CARE.   There is significance in the remark that Galileo made when he was accused of moving God too far out of the universe so that men grew discouraged and felt forsaken. "The sun," he said, "which has all those planets revolving about it and dependent on it for their orderly functions can ripen a bunch of grapes as if it had nothing else in the world to do." God is able to tend your soul as if he had nothing else in the world to do.—Samuel H. Miller

THE EXPERIENCE OF FAITH.   The story of Edwin Muir illustrates a change toward a faith in God that was both purifying and undeniable. It shows the response of change. Faith as deep-seated trust is shown in his testimony recorded in his autobiography. The impact of others in developing faith is also seen. The pressure from his mother, combined with the feelings of rejection by her because of his original unwillingness to experience conversion, prompted the boy's first step. "I felt alone in the hours," he wrote. "I felt impelled towards the only act which would make me one with my family again; for my father and mother and sister were saved, and I was outside, separated from them by an invisible world." After some time his change at fourteen was recapitulated at twenty-one with a conversion to socialism. Often after a faith experience individuals feel responsible for their relationships in the world. They notice new concerns, new commitments, and new energy to focus their lives. Often these changes toward God are triggered by others.—V. Bailey Gillespie

GOD DESCRIBED.   When Jesus used the word "father" to describe God, he pictured a person of authority. This may contrast with the idea of a father held by many people today. In Bible days, the father figure meant strength and authority as well as loving concern. In our prayer life, we find new confidence if we remember this—that our God is the Father in heaven whose power will make his purposes of love prevail. No matter what happens, we can trust him, for he is strong. With his strong help, we can win through all the difficult experiences and vicissitudes of this our challenging and changeful life. Because of his goodness, love, and strength, we put our total trust in him, and in his will, we find our peace.—Lowell M. Atkinson

THANKSGIVING.   When we first meet J. B. and his family in Archibald MacLeish's play by that name, they are gathered about the dining room table. With great hilarity they attack the turkey and eat the food of a Thanksgiving dinner. Sarah, J. B.'s wife, enters into the joy of the occasion, and yet she is troubled by what is happening with her family. She wonders if the children and J. B. really know what day it is. J. B. assures her that they do, and when she asks the children what day it is, they cry out with laughter: turkey day, cranberry day, stuffing day. But then Sarah breaks in: "Job, I'm serious. Answer your father's question, Jonathan. Tell him what day it is." "Thanksgiving." Sarah presses: "What day is that?" "Thanksgiving Day." And one of the children puts in: "The day we give thanks to God." And another one adds: "For his goodness." Then Sarah asks: "And did you, David, did you, Mary? Has any one of you thanked God? Really thanked him? Thanked him for everything?"—Harry Baker Adams

UNDERSTANDING WHAT DEATH IS.   Children as young as three know when they have a fatal illness or are near death. Separation from parents by death becomes a growing realization for young children even when no one tells them. Spiritual development is often accelerated in dying children, who may display a wisdom beyond their years. Sarah was dying of leukemia. Tears flowed from her mother's eyes as she cradled the toddler in her arms. Sarah reached up and patted her mother on the cheek, saying, "It's okay, Mommy. God will take care of me." Three-year-old Tina, in the terminal stage of cystic fibrosis, seemed especially anxious when she was readmitted to the hospital after a brief time at home. Her mother tried to reassure her that she would be coming home again soon, but Tina responded, "No, tonight I'm going to heaven with Jesus." She died that evening.—Judith Allen Shelly et al.

HOW TO DIE.   A few years ago the bishop of Atlanta was preaching a mission in a parish in his diocese, and on the closing night he was talking of the life everlasting. After he had affirmed his faith in the reality of the life to come, his expression changed markedly. His wife noticed it instantly. He searched for her eyes in the congregation and, finding them, said firmly, "Death is like going through an open door. We shed one garment and put on another. It is not hard to die. . . ." He ended his sermon quickly; he was taken to the hospital and died.

Since a man must die, that was a wonderful way to do it. He knew he was dying and faced it courageously—and meaningfully. The hope of that kind of death lies behind the familiar prayer, "From sudden death, Good Lord, deliver us." "From sudden death, Good Lord, deliver us" is quite the reverse of the modern notion. How often we hear, "Isn't it nice that he passed so quickly?" "Isn't it wonderful that he never knew he was dying?"—James A. Pike

USELESSNESS.   I read about a boy whose father's will provided that he was to receive two thousand dollars per year as long as he was in college. The boy continued in college for forty-six years, and when he died he had eleven degrees, but his education was not good because he never used it. And there are people who have spent a lifetime reading their Bibles, praying and going to church, but they never actually used their religion.—Charles L. Allen

RECOVERY.   There was an extensive search for a lost six-year-old boy in the San Bernardino Mountains in June 1969. After five days he was found, just barely alive, by two teenaged searchers. The father, overjoyed with the news that his son was found and alive, had a taste of the heavenly Father's joy in the salvation of one lost soul. The joy of discovery belongs to the Father as well as the lost.—Richard Andersen

TRANSCENDENT VALUES. "Prayer does not stop bullets," was the refrain of many veterans; "They perforate both devout and infidel." "Religion has no survival value for me." A faith centered in self-advantage is bound to break up. To endure at all it must envisage a universe that extends beyond personal whim and is anchored in values that transcend the immediate interest of the individual as interpreted by himself.—Gordon W. Allport

HOW TO LIVE IN PEACE. A young man, about to embark with his family to the mission field, told of the struggle that preceded his decision to be a missionary. He was miserably unhappy in his pastorate and he had no peace of mind, for he was convinced that God had chosen one field of work for him and he had chosen another. At home one morning he hurried to help his daughter, who was crying as though her heart would break. Pointing to a little fish that had jumped out of the aquarium and was dying on the floor, the child exclaimed, "Daddy, he is where he doesn't belong, isn't he?"

That did it! The father saw in the fish's predicament and his daughter's words the position in which he found himself. Then and there, he determined to go where he knew God was leading him.

Now on the threshold of a new spiritual adventure, he said, "I have peace in my heart tonight because I am going to be where God wants me to be, and I shall be doing what God wants me to do."—Theodore F. Adams

A WORRY TABLE. Some of us would do well to emulate the woman who realized that her fears were ruining her life, so she made for herself a "worry table." In tabulating her worries she discovered that 40 percent will never happen; 30 percent were all about decisions that cannot be altered; 12 percent were about others' criticisms of me, most untrue; 10 percent were about my health, which gets worse as I worry; 8 percent were legitimate since life has some real problems to meet."—Thomas Kepler

JESUS CHRIST IS LORD. Dr. Lynn Harold Hough has pointed out that it makes a mighty difference to every disciple whether he thinks of Jesus as "man's highest upreach toward God, or God's farthest downreach toward man." Is the Son of Man just a mighty man climbing up to God; or is he the eternal God reaching down to man? And the history of the Church furnishes the crowning answer: *Jesus Christ is Lord.*—Ralph S. Cushman

DESPAIR REPUDIATED. Back in 1886 the United States commissioner of labor said that progress had come to pretty much of a standstill. We'd have to content ourselves with what we had already. And in that year Thomas Edison was thirty-nine, Henry Ford was twenty-three, Charles Steinmetz was twenty-one, Orville Wright was fifteen, Madame Curie was nineteen, Robert Millikan was eighteen, Marconi twelve, Einstein seven—and the Compton brothers hadn't been born.—Paul Scherer

THIS IS THE ANSWER. A husband and wife were discussing before their young daughter a grave problem in the home. Apparently they could find no answer and said so. The little girl was studying arithmetic and was intrigued greatly with the fact that she could find the answers to the problems in the back of the book. As the discussion wore on with no conclusion reached, she said, "Daddy, why don't you look in the back of the book?"

It is Halford Luccock who suggests that we turn to the Book, the last page of the last book, and read *the* answer: "He which testifieth these things saith, Surely I come quickly. . . . Even so, come, Lord Jesus."—Henry Irving Rasmus

ACKNOWLEDGMENTS

Acknowledgment and gratitude are hereby expressed to the following for kind permission to reprint material from the books and periodicals listed below.

SUNDAY SCHOOL BOARD OF THE SOUTHERN BAPTIST CONVENTION: Each of the following is used by permission. Excerpt from James Porch in *Proclaim*, April-June 1991, p. 37, © 1991, The Sunday School Board of the Southern Baptist Convention; Excerpt from M. John Lepper in *Proclaim*, April-June 1988, pp. 12–14, © 1988, The Sunday School Board of the Southern Baptist Convention; Excerpt from Mark Sutton in *Proclaim*, October-December 1994, p. 30, © 1994, The Sunday School Board of the Southern Baptist Convention; Excerpt from Wayne Rouse in *Proclaim*, July-September 1994, p. 21, © 1994, The Sunday School Board of the Southern Baptist Convention; Excerpt from William Richard Ezell in *Proclaim*, January-March 1995, pp. 24–25, © 1994, The Sunday School Board of the Southern Baptist Convention; Excerpt from Keith Bradsher in *Proclaim*, April-June, 1994, p. 29, © 1994, The Sunday School Board of the Southern Baptist Convention; Excerpt from Jeffery Scott and Bill Chitwood in *Proclaim*, January-March, 1995, p. 27, © 1994, The Sunday School Board of the Southern Baptist Convention; Excerpt from Stephen D. Cloud in *Proclaim*, January-March 1992, p. 27, © 1991, The Sunday School Board of the Southern Baptist Convention; Excerpt from Wayne Rouse in *Proclaim*, April-June, 1994, p. 30, © 1994, The Sunday School Board of the Southern Baptist Convention; Excerpt from Cecil Taylor in *Proclaim*, April-June, 1991, p. 33, © 1991, The Sunday School Board of the Southern Baptist Convention; Excerpt from L. D. Kennedy in *Proclaim*, April-June, 1991, p. 35, © 1991, The Sunday School Board of the Southern Baptist Convention; Excerpt from David Charlton in *Proclaim*, January-March, 1995, p. 32, © 1994, The Sunday School Board of the Southern Baptist Convention; Excerpt from Steve McKown in *Proclaim*, April-June, 1994, p. 27, © 1994, The Sunday School Board of the Southern Baptist Convention; Excerpt from David Charlton in *Proclaim*, January-March, 1995, p. 28, © 1994, The Sunday School Board of the Southern Baptist Convention.

Broadman Press: Each of the following is used by permission. Excerpts from Hugh Litchfield, *Sermons on Those Other Special Days*, pp. 19–27, © 1990, Broadman Press; Excerpts from Chester Swor, *The Best of Chester Swor*, pp. 43–57, © 1981, Broadman Press; Excerpts from Jerry Hayner, *Yes, God Can*, pp. 64–77, © 1985, Broadman Press; Excerpts from Nolan P. Howington, *A Royal Priesthood*, pp. 67–75, © 1986, Broadman Press; Excerpts from Chevis F. Horne, *Preaching the Great Themes of the Bible*, pp. 145–55, © 1986, Broadman Press; Excerpts from Hugh Litchfield, *Preaching the Christmas Story*, pp. 73–78, © 1984, Broadman Press.

INDEX OF CONTRIBUTORS

SERMON TITLE INDEX

(Children's stories and sermons are identified as **cs**; *sermon suggestions as* **ss***)*

SCRIPTURAL INDEX

INDEX OF PRAYERS

INDEX OF MATERIALS USEFUL AS CHILDREN'S STORIES AND SERMONS NOT INCLUDED IN SECTION X

INDEX OF MATERIALS USEFUL FOR SMALL GROUPS

TOPICAL INDEX